NURSING CARE OF
THE ADDICTED CLIENT

KAREN M. ALLEN, PHD, RN, CARN

Assistant Professor
Department of Psychiatry, Community Health and
Adult Primary Care
Community Addictions Nursing
University of Maryland at Baltimore School of Nursing
Baltimore, Maryland

WITH 21 CONTRIBUTORS

Lippincott
Philadelphia • New York

Acquisitions Editor: Margaret Belcher
Sponsoring Editor: Emily Cotlier
Production Editor: Virginia Barishek
Production Manager: Janet Greenwood
Production Service: Berliner, Inc.
Cover Designer: Lou Fuiano
Indexer: David Prout
Printer/Binder: RR Donnelley & Sons Company/Crawfordsville

Library of Congress Cataloging-in-Publication Data

Nursing care of the addicted client / Karen M. Allen : with 21
   contributors.
       p.   cm.
   Includes bibliographical references and index.
   ISBN 0-397-55204-1
   1. Substance abuse—Nursing.   I. Allen, Karen M.
   [DNLM: 1. Substance Use Disorders—nursing. 2. Behavior,
Addictive—nursing.   WY 160 N97425 1996]
RC564.N875 1996
610.73'68—dc20
DNLM/DLC
for Library of Congress   95-50020
                                                                      CIP

The material contained in this volume was submitted as previously unpublished material, except in the instances in which credit has been given to the source from which some of the illustrative material was derived.

Any procedure or practice described in this book should be applied by the health-care practitioner under appropriate supervision in accordance with professional standards of care used with regard to the unique circumstances that apply in each practice situation. Care has been taken to confirm the accuracy of information presented and to describe generally accepted practices. However, the authors, editors, and publisher cannot accept any responsibility for errors or omissions or for any consequences from application of the information in this book and make no warranty, express or implied, with respect to the contents of the book.

The authors and publisher have exerted every effort to ensure that drug selection and dosage set forth in this text are in accordance with current recommendations and practice at the time of publication. However, in view of ongoing research, changes in government regulations, and the constant flow of information relating to drug therapy and drug reactions, the reader is urged to check the package insert for each drug for any change in indications and dosage and for added warnings and precautions. This is particularly important when the recommended agent is a new or infrequently employed drug.

Materials appearing in this book prepared by individuals as part of their official duties as U.S. Government employees are not covered by the above-mentioned copyright.

9   8   7   6   5   4   3   2   1

To my husband, Clifford L. Allen.
His love and support helped to make this book possible.

CONTRIBUTORS

KAREN M. ALLEN, PHD, RN, CARN
Assistant Professor
Department of Psychiatry, Community Health
   and Adult Primary Care
Community Addictions Nursing
University of Maryland at Baltimore School of
   Nursing
Baltimore, Maryland

CAROLYN BUPPERT, JD, RN, CRNP
Clinical Assistant Professor
Department of Psychiatry, Community Health
   and Adult Primary Care
University of Maryland at Baltimore School
   of Nursing
Baltimore, Maryland

KATHLEEN A. S. CANELLA, PHD, MS, MN, RN, CS
Clinical Specialist
Pulmonary and Critical Medicine Section
Veterans Administration Medical Center
Atlanta, Georgia

SHIRLEY D. COLETTI
President, Operation PAR, Inc.
Comprehensive Substance Abuse Treatment,
   Prevention and Training for Women
   and Children
Clearwater, Florida

MARGARET COMPTON, PHD, RN
Research Scientist
Los Angeles Addiction Treatment Research Center
Los Angeles, California

PAMELA L. DONALDSON, RNC, MS, ARNP, CARN
Clinical Researcher/Nurse Practitioner
Operation PAR, Inc.
Comprehensive Substance Abuse Treatment,
   Prevention and Training for Women
   and Children
Clearwater, Florida

MARY ANN EELLS, EDD, RN, CS
Associate Professor and
Director, Community Addictions Nursing
University of Maryland at Baltimore School
   of Nursing
Baltimore, Maryland

ELAINE FEENEY, BSN, RNC
Research Assistant
Community Addictions Nursing
University of Maryland at Baltimore School
   of Nursing
Baltimore, Maryland

JANICE COOKE FEIGENBAUM, PHD, RN
Professor and Coordinator
Community Addictions Nursing Program
D'Youville College
Buffalo, New York

LAINA M. GERACE, PHD, RN
Associate Professor and Director
Rockford Regional Programs
College of Nursing
University of Illinois at Chicago
Rockford, Illinois

SUSAN E. HETHERINGTON, DrPH, CNM, CS-P
Professor
Department of Psychiatry, Community Health
   and Adult Primary Care
University of Maryland at Baltimore School
   of Nursing
Baltimore, Maryland

FAITH HAWLEY HOWARTH, BSN, EDM, RN, CMC
President
Human Service Management Associates
Annapolis, Maryland

LOTTY INSELBERG, PHD, RN, CARN
Program Coordinator & Clinical Specialist
Hillside Hospital
Division of Long Island Jewish Hospital
Long Island, New York

SANDRA JAFFE-JOHNSON, EDD, RN, CS, NPP,
   NCAC-II, CARN
President
Snug Harbor Counseling Associates, Inc.
Adjunct Clinical Professor
State University of New York at Stony Brook
   School of Nursing
Stony Brook, New York

KEM LOUIE, PHD, RN, CS, FAAN
Associate Professor and Chairperson, Graduate
   Nursing Programs
Department of Nursing
College of Mount Saint Vincent
Bronx, New York

ANN B. MECH, JD, RN
Coordinator, Legal and Contractual Services
Assistant Professor
Department of Education, Administration,
   Health Policy, and Informatics
University of Maryland at Baltimore School
   of Nursing
Baltimore, Maryland

KEITH PLOWDEN, MS, RN, CCRN
Assistant Chief Nurse Trainee
Veterans Administration Medical Center
Atlanta, Georgia

CHRISTINE SAVAGE, MS, RN, CARN
Director of Private Care Services
Lancaster Visiting Nurses Association
Lancaster, Pennsylvania

PATRICIA A. STATEN, MSA, RN
Associate Director
Department of Performance, Measure, &
   Interpretation
Joint Committee on the Accreditation of
   Healthcare Organizations
Bethesda, Maryland

JUDITH SUTHERLAND, PHD, RN, CS, LCDC
Associate Professor
Abilene Intercollegiate School of Nursing
Abilene, Texas

MARILYN VRANAS, MSN, RN, CS, CARN
Public Health Advisor
Center for Substance Abuse Treatment
Substance Abuse and Mental Health Services
   Administration
US Department of Health and Human Services
Bethesda, Maryland

BETTYE J. BEATTY WILSON, EDM, RN, CS, CNA
Nurse Manager
Substance Abuse Section
Veterans Administration Medical Center
Atlanta, Georgia

FOREWORD

Access, quality, and cost are the linchpins for all health care services. As the fundamental transformations rapidly take place in health care delivery, nurses and, in fact, all practitioners must be prepared to function optimally in the new integrated delivery networks and sites. Population-based care delivery systems, cost constraints, interdisciplinary teamwork, practice accountability, primary care, prevention, and clinical effectiveness through research and outcomes are the current and future lexicon. To be successful, each and every nurse must master these.

It is a fact that nurses in all areas of practice and across the life span come in contact daily with addiction problems. It is also a fact that the educational components of nursing programs are not where many experts want them to be with content for identifying and intervening in this area.

Nursing leaders have undertaken a serious study of the educational needs for the nurse of the 1990s to transition into the workforce of the 21st century. Flexibility, versatility, and a combination of communication and business skills to complement clinical and direct care expertise will be critical. Economics, finance, and occupational and environmental health will be basic content. Successful nurses will be the creative, active learners, with acceptance and application of latest technology, and an understanding of and sensitivity to cultural diversity. Telehealth, cost/benefit analysis, and data retrieval/use/storage are more than concepts for the future. These are the essentials of all practice delivery. To be effective, the nurse must have skills in critical thinking, communication, organizational management, and economics.

Nursing Care of the Addicted Client is now available to provide the nurse with the most helpful map for delivery of quality, safe care. This book, with specific attention to the continuum of information about care for addicted clients, from fundamental information through interventions and research, gives the breadth of perspective needed by nurses. Presentation of materials related to Standards of Care for Addicted Clients demonstrates the attention of nurses to accountability to the public. The importance of showing the linkage of nursing interventions to client outcomes is critical to move addictions nurses forward as qualified cost-effectiveness practitioners.

Discussion of collegiality and collaborative practice is of crucial importance. Without this focus, nurses will continue to attempt to remove barriers in order to penetrate new configurations of delivery systems in isolation. While adding to professional disillusionment and frustration, clients' access to care is also greatly reduced by the absence of qualified nurse clinicians.

As nurses move out of institutions and from direct oversight of organizational supervision to the client in community and home settings, the broadest aspects of addictions issues should be part of their background. Current, concise content that stimulates the learner to seek more development is needed.

Karen Allen and distinguished colleagues have provided the profession with a timely and substantial text to establish the care of addicted clients as central to the practice of all nurses. It is through sharing that the profession is strengthened to advance quality practice. *Nursing Care of the Addicted Client* is an example of another major step forward in this aspect of nursing care.

SARAH STANLEY, MS, RN, CS
Director
Department of Nursing Practice
American Nurses Association

PREFACE

Today, it is inevitable that nurses find themselves providing care for clients addicted to alcohol and other drugs. The addicted person is sure to be encountered, regardless of the clinical setting or nursing specialty. More and more, nursing education programs and health care organizations recognize the need for knowledge specific to this problem. This book seeks to fill that need by providing the information most sought by nurses who need to give competent care to addicted clients.

Nursing Care of the Addicted Client is a comprehensive textbook and clinical resource for heath care professionals at all levels of expertise in the area of addiction, from the novice to the expert. It is organized into four sections, which cover historical and foundational information, highlights of care related to specific clinical settings, the major components of care for addicted clients, and issues that seriously impact the care provided to these clients. Assessment tools, a special feature of the text, are presented throughout various chapters and are identified with a checkmark.

Section I, Foundations for Nursing the Addicted Client, presents definitions of addictions, information about the main categories of addicting drugs and their mechanisms of action, the process of addiction, and theories of addiction. Also presented in this section are "Standards of Care" used nationally with addicted clients as outlined by the Joint Commission on the Accreditation of Healthcare Organizations. "Standards of Nursing Practice" for addicted clients, published by the American Nurses Association and National Nurses Society on Addictions, are interspersed throughout the text and addressed in the context of relevant care components and issues.

Section II, Recognizing Addictions in Nursing Practice, provides an in-depth examination of the extent of addiction and opportunities to provide care in the specialties of Maternal Child Health and Psychiatry. The section introduction discusses the importance of recognizing addiction in all practice settings; however, these two practice areas were chosen for discussion because of the attention that addicted mothers and babies as well as dual-diagnosis is receiving at the state and federal levels.

Section III, Nursing Care of Addicted Clients, addresses the range of services and the continuum of care necessary for addicted clients in all clinical settings. Contributors have combined years of experience, cutting edge information obtained at the federal level, and extensive research to present chapters on "Prevention," "Screening and Detection," "Assessment and Diagnosis," "Detoxification," "Interventions and Treatment," "Sobriety-Focused Care" (Relapse Prevention), and "Evaluating the Effectiveness of Nursing Care."

Section IV, Issues Impacting Care of Addicted Clients, presents many "firsts." It addresses major issues that every nurse encounters when caring for addicted clients, but that are rarely explored in texts addressing nursing care of addicted clients. These chapters provide knowledge and skills that 1) aid nurses in handling these unique issues; 2) protect and support the nurse when caring for the addicted client; and 3) develop the requisite professional nursing resources necessary for providing nursing care for addicted clients.

Because addiction is an equal opportunity disease, nurses must understand cultural diversity considerations relevant to caring for addicted clients. Chapter 13, "Cultural Competence," provides background information on major ethnic groups and strategies on how to become more culturally sensitive and competent when addressing the problem of addiction with every individual. The focus is on how to approach and effectively communicate with these clients.

A first for any addictions nursing text is Chapter 14, "Ethical Issues in the Care of Addicted Clients." It provides an understanding of ethics and how it relates to the problem of addictions. Some models of solutions are presented for common dilemmas and situations associated with the care of addicted clents.

Chapter 15, "Legal Issues in the Care of Addicted Clients," another chapter unique to this text, provides essential and important legal content. It outlines in practical terms the legal issues that exist when providing care for addicted clients and some recommendations for their management. The focus is on malpractice, privileged communication, patient right to privacy, and drug testing in the workplace.

Another first is Chapter 16, "Intimate Behavior of Clients, Nurses, and Family Members During Treatment and Recovery." Intimacy issues among health care providers and clients, between clients, and in client and significant other relationships have a great impact on care of the addicted client. The chapter details the importance of boundaries and keeping intimacy in proper perspective, and provides case studies describing a range of addictions-impacted intimacy issues.

Chapter 17, "Attrition," is the first chapter of its kind in any addictions nursing text. This chapter addresses the important problem of keeping clients engaged in receiving care for their addictions problems. A framework for understanding attrition is provided, followed by practical procedures for preventing attrition and interrupting a client in the process of dropping out.

The current health care environment calls for collaborative practice—working in conjunction with other health care professionals—in caring for all clients. Collaborative practice is especially valuable in caring for the addicted client. Chapter 18, "Interdisciplinary Collegiality," includes current derfinitions and necesssary components of collaborative practice. For the first time in any addictions nursing text, this chapter presents application of this concept to provide clear examples of the potential, operational steps, and the results of collaborative practice with addicted clients. The critical pathway for alcohol detoxification found in Chapter 9, "Detoxification," provides an example of operationalizing collaborative practice.

Finally, Chapter 19, "Research in Addictions Nursing," presents another first of its kind chapter. It combines information on how inquiry is related to care of addicted clients, along with an inside look at one of the the foremost drug addiction research organizations in the country—The National Institute on Drug Abuse. It shares key points on how to write research proposals and secure funding.

According to a recent Gallup poll, drug abuse was selected by American voters as the fourth major concern that they had about the country overall, following crime, unemployment, and health care. This concern probably includes the effects of alcohol and other drug addictions on family, work, community, economics, and, most of all, health.

The nursing profession has traditionally worked to make its practice responsive to the health needs and concerns of society. To recognize the importance of improving the level of nursing care for addicted clients in all practice areas, and then to use resources such as this text to begin to develop competence, continues this trend.

Karen M. Allen, PhD, RN, CARN

ACKNOWLEDGMENTS

First, I thank God—the greatest contributor overall—for the success of this book. Next, I want to acknowledge and thank each author for his/her commitment to care of the addicted client, as exhibited by the excellent chapters contained in this text. Special thanks is extended to Jean Craft Comolli for assistance in some of the information provided in the chapter on sobriety-focused care.

I would also like to express my appreciation to the many addicted clients whom I have nursed, for allowing me to participate in their recovery process. In addition, I offer them my admiration for providing examples to nurses everywhere that there are two sides to addiction.

CONTENTS

I

FOUNDATIONS FOR NURSING THE ADDICTED CLIENT

 ## INTRODUCTION: ALCOHOL, TOBACCO, OTHER DRUGS, AND SOCIETY

During the early 20th century, nurses were able to verbalize a choice about caring for someone addicted to alcohol and other drugs. Increasingly, research is highlighting a variety of illnesses and a range of symptomatology related to alcohol and other drug addictions. It is evident that a growing number of clients cared for by nurses in all settings might have an addiction to nicotine, caffeine, alcohol, prescription drugs, over-the-counter drugs, or street drugs; these addictions are the number one health problem in this country. As the 21st century approaches, nurses need to become competent in providing care to the "whole" client by learning the major components of addictions nursing practice: prevention, screening, detoxification, assessment, interventions and treatment, and evaluation.

What is addictions nursing? Previously, it was believed to be the specific care of clients addicted to alcohol and other drugs in an addictions-specific treatment setting (inpatient or outpatient). Currently, it is viewed as care given by any nurse, from any specialty, in any setting to a client experiencing alcohol and other drug addiction.

Anderson (1990) noted "...it is ironic that those [nurses] least specialized in addictions have the most difficult task: identifying the addiction hidden beneath the primary admitting diagnosis." Cutezo and Dellasega (1992) posited that knowledgeable and alert nurses are the most likely professionals to look beyond the obvious medical condition and identify a hidden addiction problem.

Some estimates indicate that half of all hospital beds are filled with clients who have health problems related to alcohol and other drug addictions (Jack, 1993). These include heart disease, cancer, HIV/AIDS, respiratory distress, and trauma.

In addition, Tweed and Plumlee (1995) state that alcohol and other drug addictions adversely affect the emotional and physical health and well-being of family members, who then become users of the health care system along with the addict. For example, among children of alcoholics, there is 1) a 62% greater hospital use rate; 2) a 24% increase in hospital admissions; 3) a 29% longer average stay in the hospital; and 4) a 36% increase in average hospital costs (Center for Substance Abuse Prevention, 1994). It is likely that a similar pattern exists for the children of persons addicted to illicit drugs.

The following timelines provide an overview of the struggle to address the consequences of addiction to alcohol, tobacco, and other drugs experienced by society in the United States.

I. AMERICA'S STRUGGLE WITH ALCOHOL, TOBACCO, AND OTHER DRUGS

1492
- Native Americans cultivate and use tobacco in various forms

1600
- Tobacco becomes an important cash crop for North Carolina
- New England institutes the "Triangular Trade"—manufacturing rum to barter for slave trade in Africa, and trading slaves in West Indies for molasses to make more rum in New England

1800
- Prevalence of alcoholism so high and disruptive effects so bad, both Presidents Washington and Jefferson suggest people drink beer and wine rather than hard liquor
- Legal to smoke opium and cocaine

1807
- Congress prohibits importation of slaves, so whiskey production with corn and rye begins

1864
- Federal tax imposed on cigarettes to help finance Civil War

1874
- Women's Christian Temperance Union formed and alcohol consumption decreased

1890
- Cigarette machines perfected to allow production in greater volume

1900
- Patent medicines, tonics, and elixirs include liberal amounts of opium, cocaine, and alcohol
- Amphetamine dependence managed medically

1914
- An estimated 200,000 American opiate addicts existed—roughly 1 in 400 citizens
- Harrison Narcotics Act instituted—all dealers in narcotics must register with the Internal Revenue Service (IRS) (physicians, dentists, veterinarians)

1919
- Prohibition of manufacture, transportation, and sale of alcohol

1922
- Jones-Miller Act instituted—imports of narcotics limited to crude opium and coca leaves for medical purposes

1924
- Heroin Act instituted—illegal to manufacture or process heroin for any purpose other than government controlled research

1928
- More than one-third of all prisoners in the United States serving sentences for drug-related offenses; nearly one-half were convicted for use of mescaline and marijuana (classified as narcotics at that time)

1929
- Federal government authorized establishment of two narcotics treatment programs: Lexington, Kentucky—opened in 1935; Fort Worth, Texas—opened in 1938

1933
- Prohibition repealed

1937
- Marijuana Tax Act—tax levied on all transactions connected with marijuana

1939
- Alcoholics Anonymous founded

1942
- Opium Poppy Control Act—law passed to license growth of poppies in United States for use in medicine

1950
- Filter cigarettes promoted

1951
- The Boggs Amendment—amendment to the Harrison Act establishing a minimum mandatory sentences for all narcotic and marijuana offenses

1952	• E.M. Jellinek develops the "Disease Theory" of alcoholism
1954	• The American Medical Association declares alcoholism to be a disease
	• First article published linking smoking to cancer
1960	• Low-tar cigarettes introduced
1962	• U.S. Supreme Court rules that labeling drug dependence and alcoholism as a crime is unconstitutional; and declares that they should be regarded as diseases
1963	• Cigarette consumption peaks at 4,345 cigarettes per person (ages 18 and older)
1964	• Surgeon General's report linking cigarette smoke to health problems
	• World Health Organization announces an official definition of addiction
1965	• Barbiturate and amphetamine use restricted by federal law
	• Modern treatment modalities for alcoholism and drug dependence emerge (methadone maintenance, therapeutic communities, outpatient care, etc.)
1966	• Narcotic Addict Rehabilitation Act—allows treatment as an alternative to jail
1970	• Use of a variety of illicit drugs among the general population increases
	• Comprehensive Drug Abuse Prevention and Control Act—replaces or updates all other laws concerning narcotics and dangerous drugs
1971	• Ban on broadcast media advertisements for cigarettes
1972	• FDA released methadone for use in treating opiate addiction
	• Drug Abuse Office and Treatment Act—establishes $1.1 billion over 3 years to combat drug abuse and start treatment programs
1973	• President Nixon declares war on drugs
	• Federal agencies—National Institute on Mental Health, National Institute on Alcohol Abuse and Alcoholism, and National Institute on Drug Abuse—consolidated under one organization known as Alcohol, Drug Abuse and Mental Health Administration (ADAMHA)—set up for research in alcohol and other drug problems
1980	• M.A.D.D. (Mothers Against Drunk Driving) founded
	• Smokeless and perfumed cigarettes introduced
1981	• Mandatory military drug testing instituted
	• S.A.D.D. (Students Against Drunk Driving) founded
1984	• Crime Control Act—increases federal penalties for drug offenses
	• National Minimum Drinking Ages Act instituted
1986	• Controlled Substances Analogue Enforcement Act—sets up controls for the enforcement of "designer drugs"
	• Establishes the Office for Substance Abuse Prevention in ADAMHA
1987	• All states have complied with minimal drinking age requirements—including military bases
1989	• President Bush declares war on drugs
1990	• Office of National Drug Control Policy established to oversee all federal policies regarding research about and control of drugs of abuse
1992	• Reorganization of the Alcohol, Drug Abuse, and Mental Health Administration (which housed the Offices of Substance Abuse Prevention and Treatment, and the National Institute of Alcohol Abuse and Alcoholism and Drug Abuse) to become the Substance Abuse and Mental Health Services Administration, which incorporates three Centers: Center for Substance Abuse Treatment, Center for Substance Abuse Prevention, and Center for Mental Health Services; the Institute for Alcohol Abuse and Alcoholism and Drug Abuse become a part of the National Institutes of Health
1994	• President Clinton signs the "CRIME BILL," which calls for life imprisonment after three drug offenses
1995	• Food and Drug Administration (FDA) releases naltrexone (Trexan) for use in treating alcoholism

II. NURSING'S RESPONSE TO THE STRUGGLE

1950
- American Nurses Association (ANA) encourages the use of films on alcoholism in schools of nursing

1971
- The National Institute on Alcohol Abuse and Alcoholism (NIAAA) and The National Institute on Drug Abuse (NIDA) begin federal initiatives to make funds available to establish educational programs on alcoholism for nurses
- ANA reports a 1-year $40,000 grant to develop curriculum guidelines on drug abuse education programs for nurses

1974
- First graduate nursing program with a specialty track in alcoholism developed at the University of Washington School of Nursing

1975
- First specialty organization in addictions nursing formed: National Nurses Society on Alcoholism (later changed to Addictions) (NNSA)

1978
- Second specialty organization in addictions nursing formed: Drug and Alcohol Nurses Association (DANA)

1987
- Third specialty organization in addictions nursing formed: National Consortium of Chemical Dependency Nurses (NCCDN)
- Initial scope of practice statement reflecting the range and roles for nurses caring for addicted clients developed jointly by ANA, DANA, and NNSA

1988
- First standards of practice for care of addicted clients developed jointly by ANA and NNSA
- Select schools of nursing accept grants from NIDA, NIAAA, and Office of Substance Abuse Prevention (OSAP) to identify models for curricular change and develop learning strategies that could readily be incorporated into nursing education

1990
- ANA House of Delegates passes a resolution to convene an ANA Task Force on Drug and Alcohol Abuse

1991
- ANA develops a position paper that calls for: substance abuse education in every nursing curriculum and for every setting where nurses are employed; more substance abuse items on state board examinations; mandatory substance abuse courses in states that require continuing education for relicensure; and an increased number of substance abuse specialty tracks in graduate nursing programs

1992
- American Association of Colleges of Nurses (AACN) forms a Substance Abuse Task Force to develop a policy statement to address the problem of addiction in the nursing education community

1993
- AACN develop position statement on the need for content on addictions being included in undergraduate and graduate nursing curriculums

1994
- The nursing profession is invited to participate in developing the strategic goals and mission of NIDA
- A nurse is appointed to serve as part of the NIAAA National Advisory Council
- First nurse appointed to serve on the National Advisory Committee for the U.S. Department of Health and Human Services Substance Abuse and Mental Health Service Administration's Center for Substance Abuse Treatment

1995
- Nursing profession invited to NIDA's National Advisory Council Meeting to provide input from nursing's perspective
- NIDA provides special training in research proposal development specifically for nurse researchers in the addictions field
- A nurse serves as "Senior Drug Policy Advisor" to the U.S. Secretary of Health and Human Services

Although the nursing profession's response in this country does not parallel the amount of time the problem has been in existence, it demonstrates a commitment to being a part of the solution. Professional nursing organizations are advocating for the education of the largest group of health care providers to foster care for clients who are addicted or experiencing the consequences of someone else's addiction.

BIBLIOGRAPHY

Anderson, A. (1990). The postoperative client in withdrawal on a general medical-surgical unit. In L. Jack (Ed.) *Nursing care planning with the addicted client, Vol. II.* (pp. 147–165). Skokie, IL: Midwest Educational Associates.

Center for Substance Abuse Prevention. (1994). *Invest in prevention: Prevention works in health care delivery systems. Pre-session materials.* Rockville, MD: Center for Substance Abuse Prevention.

Cutezo, E., & Dellasega, C. (1992). Substance abuse in the homebound elderly. *Home Healthcare Nurse, 10,* 19–23.

Jack, L. (Spring, 1993). Addictions. *Graduate Nurse,* 26–29.

National Nurses Society on Addictions. (1990). *The core curriculum of addictions nursing.* Skokie, Illinois: Midwest Education Association, Inc.

Institute for Health Policy. (1993). *Substance abuse: The nation's number one health problem: Key indicators for policy.* New Brunswick, New Jersey: The Robert Wood Johnson Foundation.

Tweed, S., & Plumlee, A. (1995). Substance abuse in families, children, and adolescents. In E.J. Sullivan (Ed.) *Nursing Care of clients with substance abuse* (pp. 234–269). St. Louis, MO: Mosby-Year Book.

Witters, W., Venturelli, P., & Hanson, G. (1992). *Drugs and society* (3rd ed.). Boston: Jones & Bartlett.

Alcohol, Tobacco, and Other Drug Addictions: Definitions, Categories, and Characteristics

Karen M. Allen, PhD, RN, CARN

DEFINITIONS

Alcohol, Tobacco, and Other Drug Use, Abuse, and Dependence

When discussing alcohol and other drug addiction, various terms are applied interchangeably. Some researchers prefer to use the words "substance" use, abuse, and dependence, whereas others like the term "chemical" use, abuse, and dependence. Still, others use the word "addiction" when addressing the problem of dependence to alcohol or other drugs. The Center for Substance Abuse Prevention recently decided to include tobacco in discussions related to alcohol and other drugs so that their current phraseology is "alcohol, tobacco, and other drugs."

With so much variation, not only are experts, practitioners, and researchers in the field confused, those who do not interact consistently with clients or issues related to this area experience much difficulty in trying to grasp the concepts as well. Hence, in this section definitions for alcohol, tobacco, and other drug (ATOD) use, abuse, dependence, and addiction will be provided. The "other drugs" category includes: nicotine, caffeine, marijuana, cocaine, central nervous system (CNS) depressants and stimulants, hallucinogens, opiates, over-the-counter drugs, prescription drugs, and inhalants.

Definitions for ATOD use, abuse, and dependence will be based on that found in the Alcohol and Other Drug Thesaurus (National Institute on Alcohol Abuse and Alcoholism [NIAAA] and Center for Substance Abuse Prevention [CSAP], 1993). ATOD *use* is defined as self-administration of a psychoactive substance. ATOD *abuse* is defined as the use of a psychoactive substance for a purpose not consistent with legal or medical guidelines, as in the nonmedical use of prescription medications. ATOD *dependence* is defined as the need for repeated doses of alcohol, tobacco, or other drugs to feel good or to avoid feeling bad. Dependence is a "cluster of cognitive, behavioral, and physiological symptoms that indicate a person has impaired control of psychoactive substance use, and continues use of the substance despite adverse consequences." Dependence refers to both physical and psychological elements. Psychological or psychic dependence refers to the experience of impaired control over drinking and drug use; physiological or physical dependence refers to tolerance and withdrawal symptoms (NIAAA & CSAP, 1993).

Substance Abuse and Dependence

The American Psychiatric Association's *Diagnostic and Statistical Manual of Mental Disorders, Fourth Edition* (DSM-IV) uses the terms "substance abuse" and "substance dependence" (American Psychiatric Association [APA], 1994). According to the DSM-IV, *substance abuse* is defined as a maladaptive pattern of substance use manifested by recurrent and significant adverse consequences related to the repeated use of substances. There may be repeated failure to fulfill major role obligations, repeated use in situations in which it is physically hazardous, multiple legal problems, and recurrent social and interpersonal problems. *Substance dependence* is a cluster of cognitive, behavioral, and physiological symptoms indicating that the individual continues to use of the substance despite significant substance-related problems. There is a pattern of repeated self-administration that usually results in tolerance, withdrawal, and compulsive drug-taking behavior. The DSM-IV posits that a diagnosis of substance dependence can be applied to every class of substance except caffeine (APA, 1994).

Addiction

The word "addiction" is derived from the Latin verb *addicere*, which refers to the process of binding to things. Today, the word largely refers to a chronic adherence to drugs and includes physical and/or psychological dependence (Hanson & Venturelli, 1995). Addiction implies compulsive use, impaired control over using the substance, preoccupation with obtaining and using the drug, and continued use despite adverse consequences (Morse & Flavin, 1992).

The terms substance abuse, substance dependence, and addiction are frequently used interchangeably, mostly because definitions are similar. At the federal level, major research institutes are labeled: alcohol abuse and alcoholism, and drug abuse. In the past, service organizations at the federal level used the terms "alcohol and drug abuse," but currently they use "substance abuse." Many professional organizations in the field use different terminology (i.e., National Nurses Society on Addictions, Drug and Alcohol Nurses Association, National Consortium of Chemical Dependency Nurses). Professional journals use a different terminology (i.e., *Perspectives on Addictions Nursing, Addictions Nursing Network, Journal of Substance Abuse Treatment, International Journal of the Addictions, American Journal of Drug and Alcohol Abuse, Addictive Behaviors*).

Persons involved in direct or indirect prevention, care, education related to, or research of addicted clients, have preferences about which terms they use, therefore, the reader will see use of both terms—addiction and substance abuse—throughout this text. The definitions of terms are similar and they both refer to problem use and chronic adherence to ATOD, thus, using both terms will not interfere with understanding the knowledge discussed.

However, addiction is the chosen term to be used primarily with this text. This choice was made because substance use, abuse, and dependence are all part of a total process known as "The Process of Addiction" (Substance Abuse and Mental Health Services Administration [SAMHSA] Center for Substance Abuse Treatment [CSAT], 1994).

The Process of Addiction

The process of addiction involves four stages: 1) experimental and social use of ATOD; 2) problem use/abuse; 3) dependency/ addiction; and 4) recovery/relapse. On the basis of information from Doweiko (1990) and the Institute of Medicine (1990) CSAT (1994) diagramed the process of addiction as shown in Figure 1-1. The shaded areas show how ATOD addiction escalates from no use to certain levels of use in the various stages.

Based on information obtained from Beschner (1986), Institute of Medicine (1990), Jaynes and Rugg (1988), MacDonald (1989), and Nowinski (1990), CSAT (1994) outlined specific aspects of each stage in the addictive process. As can be seen in Boxes 1.1–1.3, for each stage, the frequency of use, source of ATOD, reasons for use, effects and behavioral indicators, differ. As the change from stage to stage is seen (based on escalation of ATOD use), the deterioration associated with the addictive process is clearly evident.

The diagram in Figure 1-1 shows at what point prevention and intervention/treatment programs should be implemented as the problem escalates along the process of addiction continuum. From the beginning to the end of this continuum, opportunities exist for nurses to address addiction among clients seen in their particular areas of practice, regardless of whether the nurses' work takes place mostly in inpatient or outpatient sites.

Within the period of abstinence and experimental and social use, primary prevention should take place. During this time, education, information, alternatives, and personal and social growth should be emphasized. During the stages of problem use/abuse, "interventions" should take place. At this point, screening and detection, assessment, early diagnosis, crisis intervention and monitoring, and referral are important. During the stages of dependency/ addiction and recovery/relapse, detoxification, treatment (inpatient and/or outpatient), and maintenance should be the focus.

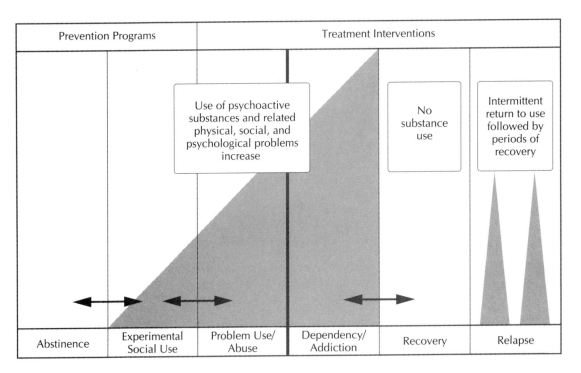

Figure 1-1. The process of addiction.

BOX 1-1. Stage 1: Experimental and Social Use of ATOD

FREQUENCY OF USE

Occasional, perhaps a few times monthly. Usually on weekends when at parties or with friends. May use when alone.

SOURCES

Friends/peers primarily. Youth may use parents' alcohol.

REASONS FOR USE

- To satisfy curiosity
- To acquiesce to peer pressure
- To obtain social acceptance
- To defy parental limits
- To take a risk or seek a thrill
- To appear grown up
- To relieve boredom
- To produce pleasurable feelings
- To diminish inhibitions in social situations

EFFECTS

At this stage the person will experience euphoria and return to a normal state after using. A small amount may cause intoxication. Feelings sought include:

- Fun, excitement
- Thrill
- Belonging
- Control

BEHAVIORAL INDICATORS

- Little noticeable change
- Some may lie about use or whereabouts
- Some may experience moderate hangovers; occasionally, there is evidence of use, such as a beer can or marijuana joint

AN OVERVIEW OF CURRENT DRUG USE

An incredible amount of money is spent each year for chemicals that alter consciousness, awareness, or mood. The average household owns about 35 drugs (one of five being prescription and the other four over-the-counter). Of the many prescriptions written by physicians, approximately one-fourth modify moods and behaviors in one way or another (Hanson & Venturelli, 1995).

In summarizing results from the 1994 National Household Survey on Drug Abuse (SAMHSA, 1995) the following trend remains:

BOX 1-2. Stage 2: Problem Use/Abuse

FREQUENCY OF USE

Regular, may use several times per week. May begin using during the day. May be using alone rather than with friends.

SOURCES

Friends; begins buying enough to be prepared. May sell drugs to keep a supply for personal use. May begin stealing to have money to buy drugs/alcohol.

REASONS FOR USE

- To manipulate emotions; to experience the pleasure the substances produce; to cope with stress and uncomfortable feelings such as pain, guilt, anxiety, and sadness; and to overcome feelings of inadequacy
- Persons who progress to this stage of drug/alcohol involvement often experience depression or other uncomfortable feelings when not using. Substances are used to stay high or at least maintain normal feelings

EFFECTS

- Euphoria is the desired feeling; may return to a normal state following use or may experience pain, depression, and general discomfort. However, intoxication begins to occur regularly
- Feelings sought include:
  — Pleasure
  — Relief from negative feelings, such as boredom and anxiety
  — Stress reduction
- May begin to feel some guilt, fear, and shame
- May have suicidal ideations/attempts. Tries to control use, but is unsuccessful. Feels shame and guilt. More of a substance is needed to produce the same effect

BEHAVIORAL INDICATORS

- School or work performance and attendance may decline
- Mood swings
- Changes in personality
- Lying and conning
- Change in friendships—will have drug-using friends
- Decrease in extracurricular activities
- Begins adopting drug culture appearance (clothing, grooming, hairstyles, jewelry)
- Conflict with family members may be exacerbated
- Behavior may be more rebellious
- All interest is focused on procuring and using drugs/alcohol

BOX 1-3. Stage 3: Dependency/Addiction

FREQUENCY OF USE

Daily use, continuous

SOURCES

- Will use any means necessary to obtain and secure needed drugs/alcohol
- Will take serious risks
- Will often engage in criminal behavior such as shoplifting and burglary

REASONS FOR USE

- Drugs/alcohol are needed to avoid pain and depression
- Many wish to escape the realities of daily living
- Use is out of control

EFFECTS

- Person's normal state is pain or discomfort
- Drugs/alcohol help them feel normal; when the effects wear off, they again feel pain
- They are unlikely to experience euphoria at this stage
- They may experience suicidal thoughts or attempts
- They often feel guilt, shame, and remorse
- They may experience blackouts
- They may experience changing emotions, such as depression, aggression, irritation, and apathy

BEHAVIORAL INDICATORS

- Physical deterioration includes weight loss, health problems
- Appearance is poor
- May experience memory loss, flashbacks, paranoia, volatile mood swings, and other mental problems
- Likely to drop out or to be expelled from school or lose jobs
- May be absent from home much of the time
- Possible overdoses
- Lack of concern about being caught—focused only on procuring and using drugs/alcohol

- Alcohol is by far the most widely used drug.
- Tobacco is the second most widely used drug.
- Marijuana is the most commonly used illicit drug.
- Nonmedical use of psychotherapeutic (prescription) drugs and cocaine are the most used illicit drugs, after marijuana.
- Use of the other illicit drugs (heroin, crack, hallucinogens, and inhalants) is so small that the percentage remains in the single digits.

ATOD are simply compounds that cause or produce certain effects in individuals. Whether the use of a drug is good or bad becomes a matter of opinion when it is viewed culturally, socially, economically, politically, and religiously. Without culture and society drugs are neither good nor bad. Society has labeled alcohol and tobacco as "social drugs," prescription medication as "ethical drugs," day-to-day health and sleep aids as "over-the-counter drugs," and view them all as "legal drugs," while use of marijuana, cocaine, crack, heroin, hallucinogens, and inhalants is viewed as illegal (Hanson & Venturelli, 1995).

Many people connect the use of drugs labeled as illegal by society with persons from poor and disadvantaged lifestyles. However, according to the 1993 National Institute on Drug Abuse Research on Drugs and the Workplace, 70% of current users of illicit drugs are employed. Twelve percent are students, 5% are homemakers, 2% retired, 2% other, and only 10% are unemployed. That just covers the illicit drug use. Although some people do not use alcohol and tobacco, most do.

It can be said that alcohol, tobacco, and other drugs have always been a part of this society and will continue to be. Unfortunately, there are major economic, social, and health consequences resulting from the addictive process that occurs among some individuals. Therefore, it is important for health care providers to have knowledge related to the various categories of drugs liable for abuse and addiction along with their mechanism of action, and what are the desired effects and health consequences. The following section highlights this information.

CATEGORIES AND CHARACTERISTICS OF ADDICTING DRUGS

Central Nervous System Stimulants

NATURE AND PHYSIOLOGICAL MECHANISM OF ACTION

All of the major stimulants cause increased alertness, excitation, and euphoria; thus, these drugs are referred to as "uppers" (Table 1-1). The major stimulants are classified as either Schedule I (designer amphetamines) or Schedule II (amphetamine and cocaine) controlled substances because of their abuse potential (Hanson & Venturelli, 1995, p. 260).

COCAINE is taken from the leaves of the coca plant, *Erythroxylon coca*, and has three main pharmacologic actions: 1) a local anesthetic; 2) a peripheral nervous system stimulant; and 3) a potent brain and brainstem (CNS) stimulant.

Cocaine hydrochloride powder is the form of cocaine most commonly used in the United States. In description, it is a white crystalline substance sold as an illicit drug in grams. The price ranges from $75 to $100 per gram, and may be purchased in large amounts or by the ounce. An ounce is around 28 grams, a "quarter" of an ounce is around 7 grams, and an "eighth" of an ounce is about 3.5 grams.

Cocaine chemically alters brain function and, as a result, induces feelings of stimulation and euphoria. It stimulates selective areas of the brain by releasing specific chemical messengers—dopamine and norepinephrine—from nerve cells. In addition, it interferes with the reabsorption of these chemical messengers (otherwise known as neurotransmitters) into the nerve cells, which results in an accumulation of them at the nerve endings that leads to increased firing of the nerve and increase in their effects. This is the "rush" felt by the user. Using cocaine on a chronic basis eventually leads to depletion of dopamine as well as other neurotransmitters, which drives the compulsive use and addiction of cocaine.

Cocaine can be taken by mouth, snorted through the nose, injected in the veins, or smoked. The way a person administers it impacts on the effect that it has.

Taking cocaine by mouth involves chewing the coca leaf for a long period of time; however, that is not a common practice in the United States. Taking cocaine orally has the least

TABLE 1-1 Central Nervous System Stimulants

Drug	The Desired Effects	Health Consequences
Cocaine	Elevated mood, enhanced sexual stimulation	Hypertension, increased alertness, local anesthesia, heart and respiratory rates, cardiac arrest, cerebral vascular accident, paranoia, hallucinations, seizures, death, toxic effects to fetus
Amphetamines (benzedrine, uppers, bennies, ecstasy, ice, crack, MDA)	Euphoria, relief of fatigue, increase in alertness, loss of appetite	Increased heart and respiratory rates, irregular heartbeat, physical collapse, high fever, cardiovascular accident and cardiac arrest, psychosis
Nicotine (cigarettes, snuff, chewing tobacco, pipes, cigars)	Relaxation, relief of compliance with social custom; appetite control, increase in energy	Increased illness and absence from work; chronic obstructive lung diseases—emphysema & bronchitis associated with shortness of breath, cough, and excessive phlegm, coronary heart disease, cancer of mouth and lungs, interaction of tobacco smoke with medications leading to decreased effectiveness
Caffeine (coffee, teas, colas, and other soft drinks, chocolate)	Relaxation, compliance with social custom, increased awakeness, increased alertness, and a diminished sense of fatigue. Often used to block drowsiness and facilitate mental activity	Muscle twitching, rambling thoughts and speech, heart arrhythmias, motor agitation, ringing in the ears, flashes of light, stomach complaints, breast cysts, and spontaneous fetal loss

potent impact on the user because most of it is destroyed in the stomach or liver before it reaches the brain, and the onset of its effects is slower with a milder, more sustained stimulation.

When snorting cocaine, the user inhales cocaine hydrochloride powder into their nostrils. It is readily absorbed into the bloodstream through the nasal mucosa. Deposits form on the lining of the nasal passages while the drug passes through the mucosal tissues into the bloodstream. Snorting is a choice of administration over oral because it provides strong stimulation of the CNS in a matter of minutes. However, it only lasts for 30 to 40 minutes before it begins to subside. Hence, snorting provides effects that occur faster, are more intense, and with more of the drug getting to the brain quicker than taking it orally. However, it lasts a shorter time and its side effects are more severe because the concentration of cocaine in the body is higher.

The side effect most often voiced by snorters of cocaine is intense depression—described by some as a "crash." According to Goldstein (1995) the intensity of the depression correlates with the intensity of the euphoria.

Administering cocaine by injection 1) allows large amounts of cocaine to be very rapidly introduced into the body; 2) causes severe side effects and dependence; 3) provides a high experienced within seconds after injection; 4) has an intense, but short-lived "high" (within 15 to 20 minutes the user has dysphoria and is heading for a crash); and 5) promotes readministration every 10 to 30 minutes to avoid the crash (which is known as binges or "runs" that can last from 4 to 24 hours).

Cocaine powder is not smokable because the active drug decomposes at the temperatures achieved by a match or cigarette lighter. However, freebasing is the method developed to transform the powder into a smokable form. As it is smoked the drug passes through the lining of the lungs into the blood vessels, which carry it directly to the brain. Smoking generates an instant and extremely intense euphoria, rush, or high. The downside is a much more severe depression. "Crack," the name for the smokable form of cocaine, provides a high that lasts only 3 to 5 minutes and the resulting depression lasts from 10 to 40 minutes.

Cocaine can be detected in urine and blood. However, because it is rapidly metabolized, reliable detection is dependent on use of the enzyme immunoassay or radioimmunoassay laboratory procedures. Accurate results can be obtained for up to 48 to 72 hours following last use.

AMPHETAMINES are synthetics that are similar to natural neurotransmitters such as norepinephrine (noradrenalin), dopamine, and the stress hormone epinephrine (adrenalin). They can be taken orally, intravenously, or by smoking, with the intensity and duration of effects varying according to the mode of administration. The "speed freak" uses chronic, high doses intravenously; however, smoking "ice" causes an effect just as potent but more prolonged than the intravenous dose (Witters, Venturelli, & Hanson, 1992).

Within approximately 30 minutes of taking it by mouth, or 5 minutes of taking it by injection, amphetamines begin to exert effects. They begin almost instantly after intravenous administration and are extremely intense.

Amphetamines cause an arousal or activating response that is similar to the normal reaction to emergency situations or crises. In addition, it causes alertness so that the person becomes aroused, hypersensitive to stimuli, and feels "turned on" (which can occur without external sensory input). Also, amphetamines have potent effects on dopamine in the reward center of the brain, which causes the sudden feeling of intense pleasure that occurs when amphetamine is taken intravenously (Hanson & Venturelli, 1995, p. 262).

Amphetamines increase the activity of norepinephrine, dopamine, and epinephrine in nerve cells of the brain as well as the sympathetic nervous system. They 1) cause the release of the above mentioned neurotransmitters, sending a message to the next neuron much like the normal process of nerve message transmission; 2) cause prolonged effects of these neurotransmitters at the nerve cell receptor sites by blocking the enzyme that metabolizes them (monoamine oxidase); and 3) block the reuptake of these neurotransmitters, which enhances their own effects as well as those resulting from normal stimulation; as a result, the effect on other neurons lasts longer.

Urine and blood assays for amphetamines are available and will remain positive for 2 days after the last dose.

NICOTINE Although approximately 4000 chemicals are found in tobacco, nicotine is believed to be the substance that causes dependence. The smoker who inhales gets about 90% of the nicotine in the bloodstream, compared to 20 to 50% gotten by the smoker who first takes it in their mouth and then exhales. The blood carries nicotine to the heart, which distributes the substance rapidly throughout the body. Nicotine inhaled from tobacco smoke reaches the brain in 7 seconds. Other methods for nicotine administration include smokeless tobacco (chewing tobacco and snuff). Both are comprised of tobacco leaves that are shredded and twisted into strands and then either chewed or placed in the cheek between the lower lip and gum. Research has shown that taking one pinch of snuff has effects equivalent to those of smoking three or four cigarettes. Tobacco-chewing snuff dipping involves the absorption of nicotine through the mucous lining of the mouth (Hanson & Venturelli, 1995, pp. 304–305).

Nicotine produces an intense effect on the CNS, and inhalation of tobacco smoke as well as mouth absorption of smokeless tobacco is akin to an intravenous injection of nicotine. Cigarette tobacco contains between 1.5 and 3% of nicotine, with each cigarette containing between 29 to 30 milligrams of the drug. A cigar contains between 15 and 40 milligrams of nicotine. Although tolerance to nicotine builds up rapidly, the fatal dose for adults is 60 milligrams. Nicotine has a biological half-life of approximately 20 to 30 minutes and is mostly metabolized in the liver, producing inactive compounds that are removed through the kidneys. The rapid metabolism and clearance of nicotine allows frequent and repeated use, which is encouraged by the rapid onset of withdrawal symptoms (Witters, Venturelli, & Hanson, 1992). Nicotine distributes quickly and widely, concentrating in the brain at up to five times the blood level, and at the sympathetic ganglia, adrenal medulla, parotid glands, stomach, thyroid, pancreas, and kidneys (Hanson & Venturelli, 1995, pp. 304–305).

Nicotine first stimulates and then depresses the nervous system. It acts to shift brain waves into an arousal pattern. Yet, most smokers claim that it helps them to relax and relieves tension. Nicotine does its work by speeding up and intensifying the flow of glutamate, a neurotransmitter that is a key signal carrier within the brain. This faster flow is akin to turning up the volume on a radio. There appears to be specific nicotinic receptors in the brain that respond to nicotine.

Nicotine stimulates cholinergic receptors first, but is not removed from the receptors rapidly; therefore, the next effect is depression, caused by blocked nerve activity. It increases the respiration rate at low dose levels because it stimulates the receptors in the carotid artery (in the neck) that monitor the brain's need for oxygen. It stimulates the cardiovascular system by releasing epinephrine, causing increases in coronary blood flow, heart rate, and blood pressure. The effect is to increase the oxygen requirements of the heart muscle, but not the oxygen supply. Nicotine and perhaps other substances in tobacco smoke tend to inhibit hunger contractions in the stomach for up to 1 hour. At the same time, it causes a slight increase in blood sugar and deadens the taste buds, which may be the reason for decreased feelings of hunger in so many smokers. In addition, nicotine crosses the placenta, thereby contributing to fetal injury, premature birth, and low birth weight (Brunton, 1991; Hanson & Venturelli, 1995).

CAFFEINE   belongs to a group of drugs that have similar chemical structures and are known as xanthines. Abuse of xanthines is not viewed as a major health problem because serious dysfunction due to dependence is infrequent. However, it is the world's most frequently used stimulant and frequent use of high doses causes psychological as well as physical problems called caffeinism—a condition where the person must substantially increase consumption of caffeine to regain the CNS stimulatory action (Witters, Venturelli, & Hanson, 1992).

Caffeine causes limited dependence, which is relatively minor compared to other stimulants. The degree of physical dependence is highly variable but related to dose. Usually consuming two to three cups of coffee per day is viewed as being relatively safe; but add more cups, along with soft drinks with meals and the amount of caffeine consumed easily rises (Witters, Venturelli, & Hanson, 1992).

Caffeine is eventually absorbed entirely from the gastrointestinal tract after oral consumption. In most users 90% of the drug reaches the bloodstream within 20 minutes, and is distributed quickly into the brain and throughout the body. However, the rate of absorption from the stomach and intestines differs from person to person. Xanthines usually cause minor vasodilation in most of the body. However, the cerebral blood vessels are vasoconstricted by the action of caffeine (Hanson & Venturelli, 1995).

Although the consumption of beverages is by far the most common source of xanthines, a number of popular over-the-counter products contain significant quantities of caffeine.

For example, analgesic products (i.e., Anacin, Excedrin) contain 30 mg of caffeine per tablet and picker-uppers like No-doz, Caffedrine, and Vivarin contain 100 to 200 mg of caffeine per tablet (Witters, Venturelli, & Hanson, 1992).

Central Nervous System Depressants

NATURE AND PHYSIOLOGICAL MECHANISM OF ACTION

The effects of CNS depressants tend to be dose dependent. All CNS depressants are not "created equal." Some have wider margins of safety, while others have a greater potential for nonmedical abuse (Table 1-2).

ALCOHOL contains the psychoactive substance ethanol that is found in beer, wine, liqueurs or cordials, and distilled spirits. In addition, it contains a variety of other chemical constituents such as grains, grapes, other fruit, and congeners, which are produced during fermentation, distillation, or storage. Alcohol has direct contact with the mouth, esophagus, stomach, and intestine, acting as an irritant and an anesthetic. It influences almost every organ system in the body after entering the bloodstream (Hanson & Venturelli, 1995, p. 179).

Alcohol is quickly and efficiently absorbed from the gastrointestinal tract and requires no digestion. The rate of absorption depends on the concentration of alcohol, as well as the presence or absence of food in the stomach, or if the liquid is carbonated. Alcohol that is diluted is absorbed more slowly unless it is diluted with carbonation or if it is effervescent itself. Then it will pass more rapidly into the small bowel and be absorbed even faster than in the stomach. Eating foods that contain fat and/or protein before or while drinking alcohol will help to delay its absorption (Substance Abuse and Mental Health Services Administration's Center for Substance Abuse Treatment, [CSAT], 1993).

The effects of alcohol on the human body depend on the amount of alcohol in the blood or blood alcohol concentration (BAC). Because the brain has a large blood supply, its activity is quickly affected by a high alcohol concentration in the blood (Hanson & Venturelli, 1995, p. 179). Effects of alcohol are noticed approximately 10 minutes after drinking and they peak at approximately 40 to 60 minutes after drinking. Alcohol remains in the bloodstream until it is metabolized by the liver; therefore, if someone drinks faster than the alcohol is metabolized the blood concentration of alcohol will increase, and this is recognized as a "blood alcohol level."

Blood alcohol levels are expressed as grams of alcohol per 100 milliliters of blood. A level of 0.05% usually produces a "high" feeling; at a level of 0.20% a person is clearly "intoxicated"; a level of 0.30% often leads to stuporousness; and blood levels of 0.40% and higher is associated with coma and death. Blood levels are assessed by direct examination of blood, or examination of saliva and breath with a "breathylizer."

Alcohol acts on the type A gamma-aminobutyric acid (GABA) receptor, which is the site of action of all sedative/anesthetic drugs. However, the action of alcohol at this site differs from that of the benzodiazepines or barbiturates in that it is less effective at potentiating receptor function and acts only on select subtypes of the receptor. Alcohol depresses the CNS activity at all doses by stimulating GABA—the major inhibitory neurotransmitter in the brain. At low-to-moderate doses, disinhibition often occurs, resulting from depression of inhibitory centers in the brain (U.S. Department of Health and Human Services, 1994).

Alcohol ingestion produces increases in dopamine levels in the nucleus accumbens and other reward centers. In addition, neuronal activity is increased just after alcohol consumption in areas of the brain that are rich in dopamine, contributing to the craving that goes in hand with addiction (U.S. Department of Health and Human Services, 1994).

TABLE 1-2 Central Nervous System Depressants

Drug	The Desired Effects	Health Consequences
Alcohol	Relaxation, euphoria, disinhibition, sedation, compliance with social custom, decreased tension and anxiety	Death from overdose alone or in combination with other CNS depressants, illnesses resulting from damage caused by chronic exposure of tissues in every organ and system of the body due to toxic effects, irreversible brain damage and resultant cognitive difficulties, fetal alcohol syndrome, trauma and accidents
Barbiturates (Amytal, butabarbital sodium, pentobarbital sodium [Nembutal], secobarbital [Seconal], Tuinal)	Decreased inhibition, sedation, mental relaxation, sociability, decreased tension and anxiety	Respiratory depression, coma and seizures, death from respiratory failure
Nonbarbiturates (chloral hydrate, Doriden, Equanil, Miltown)	Decreased inhibition, sedation, increased sociability, decreased tension and anxiety, induced sleep	Respiratory depression, coma and seizures, death from respiratory failure
Benzo diazepines (Valium, Librium, Ativan, Xanax, Serax)	Relief of anxiety, inducement of sleep, relaxation, euphoria, to slow down effects of other drugs, disinhibition, rush, muscle relaxation, treatment of convulsions, treat withdrawal symptoms	Skin rashes, lethargy, impaired mental and physical activities, diminished libido, irregularities in menstrual cycle, blood cell abnormalities
Narcotics (morphine sulfate, Percodan, Dilaudid, Demerol, Dolophine, Darvon, Talwin, Stadol, heroin, codeine)	Euphoria, a thrill similar to orgasm, a diminished response to pain, drowsiness, decreased anxiety and fear	Respiratory failure, coma, death, trauma and accidents during drug-seeking behavior, AIDS and hepatitis, localized and systemic infections, convulsions

BARBITURATES are defined as "barbituric acid" derivatives used in medicine as sedatives and hypnotics. The precise mechanism of action for barbiturates is unclear. It is believed that they interfere with activity in the reticular activating system, the limbic system, and the motor cortex; however, they do not interfere at a specific receptor site. It is more likely that they have a general effect on the activity of certain neurons due to effects on calcium and chloride, and these changes in calcium and chloride seem to enhance the activity of the inhibitory transmitter GABA (Hanson & Venturelli, 1995).

Barbiturates are classified as long-acting (12 to 24 hours [such as phenobarbital]); intermediate acting (8 to 10 hours [such as amobarbital]); short-acting (4 to 8 hours [such as pentobarbital]); and ultrashort acting (3 to 4 hours [such as thiopental]). They are rapidly absorbed by mouth or injection just under the skin, after which they are either detoxified in the liver or excreted unchanged in the urine. Barbiturate do not leave the body after the effects are gone because they can be stored in the fatty tissues. Those barbiturates that are faster in action, act for a shorter length of time, cause more sleepiness, and are stored in the fat easier (CSAT, 1993).

The more lipid soluble the barbiturate, the more easily it enters the brain, the faster it will act, and the more potent it will be as a depressant. This is because the brain matter that contains nerves has a high fat content; thus, the rapidly acting barbiturates are quickly taken up by the gray matter and sleep is induced within minutes. Furthermore, it can clearly be seen that with such high fat solubility of barbiturates, this increases the duration of its effects (CSAT, 1993).

BENZODIAZEPINES are by far the most frequently prescribed CNS depressants for anxiety and sleep. After being taken orally, they are all readily and rapidly absorbed from the stomach. They can all be stored in the fatty tissues to different degrees, but they tend to be widely distributed into other body tissues (CSAT, 1993).

In contrast to barbiturate-type drugs—which cause general depression of most neuronal activity—benzodiazepines act on specific neurons that have receptors for the neurotransmitter GABA. GABA is a very important inhibitory transmitter in various brain regions including the limbic system, the reticular activating system, and the motor cortex. In the presence of benzodiazepines, the inhibitory effects of GABA are increased. Depression of activity in these brain regions may account for the ability of benzodiazepines to alter mood (a limbic function); cause drowsiness (a reticular-activating system function); and relax muscles (a cortical function) (Hanson & Venturelli, 1995, p. 158).

Blood and urine tests can be used to detect the presence of benzodiazepines in the body.

NARCOTICS can be taken by mouth in pill form, inhaled through the nose or "snorting" powder, injected intramuscularly or under the skin (skin popping), smoked, or injected intravenously; producing a high that last from 4 to 12 hours. All narcotics have a specific affinity to bind with specific nerve structures in the brain, and the effectiveness of each drug depends mostly on how well it binds with these nerve structures (CSAT, 1993).

Taken orally, opiates are readily absorbed from the gastrointestinal tract. Taken by inhalation, the effects of the drug is felt in about 30 minutes. Injecting it under the skin results in experiencing opiate effects in 15 minutes. And injecting it intravenously produces a very intense effect almost immediately.

Heroin is broken down into morphine in the liver, with 90% excreted from the body within 24 hours of taking it. However, with methadone—which is taken orally—the effects are felt within 30 minutes and peak blood levels reached in 4 to 6 hours. Its excretion takes place slowly.

The opiate receptors are the site of action of the endorphin peptide transmitters. They are found throughout the brain, spinal cord, autonomic nervous system, and intestines, and are associated with important functions. The opiate receptors are also present in high concentration within the limbic system of the brain. Due to the role of the limbic system in drug addiction, this is likely the site of action related to the abuse potential of narcotics (Hanson & Venturelli, 1995).

Stimulation of these receptors by narcotics causes release of the transmitter dopamine in limbic brain regions. This effect contributes to the rewarding actions of these drugs, and this leads to dependence and abuse (Hanson & Venturelli, 1995).

Hallucinogens

NATURE AND PHYSIOLOGICAL MECHANISM OF ACTION

Hallucinogens are otherwise known as psychedelics—substances that expand or heighten perception and consciousness. Typical users experience several stages of sensory experiences; they can go through all stages during a single "trip" or more likely, they will only pass through some. These stages include: 1) heightened, exaggerated senses; 2) loss of control; 3) self-reflection; and 4) loss of identity (a sense of cosmic merging). Three major types of hallucinogens exist: 1) the traditional psychedelics (LSD, mescaline); 2) those with amphetamine-like molecular structures and that also possess some stimulant action [DOM (dimethoxymethylamphetamine), MDA (methylenendioxyamphetamine), MDMA (methylenedioxymethamphetamine)]; and 3) anticholinergic drugs, which block muscarinic receptors (a receptor type activated by acetylcholine, which is usually inhibitory). Almost all drugs that antagonize the muscarinic receptors cause hallucinations (Witters, Venturelli, & Hanson, 1992).

The hallucinogens probably exert their effects by modifying neurotransmitter pathways in the brain. Some (psilocybin and LSD) have chemical structures similar to the natural brain neurotransmitter serotonin. Others (mescaline and synthetically made STP, another dimethoxymethylamphetamine) are also similar to neurotransmitters (CSAT, 1993)(Table 1-3).

LSD is the most potent hallucinogen. It is colorless, odorless, and tasteless, and can be purchased in tablets, capsules, and occasionally a liquid. It is taken orally, sometimes injected, and added to absorbent paper. It is effective orally in minute doses (30 to 50 micrograms per dose) and is readily absorbed and diffused into all tissues.

TABLE 1-3 Hallucinogens

Drug	The Desired Effects	Health Consequences
LSD, PCP, STP, MDA, MDMA, DOM, mescaline, psilocybin	Altered perceptions, heightened awareness, sense of religious insight, increased sexual pleasure	Violence and self-inflicted injuries, memory loss and illusions, speech difficulty, convulsions, coma, ruptured blood vessels in the brain, cardiac and respiratory failure, psychotic episodes, flashbacks
Cannabis hashish, THC	Compliance with social custom, sense of well-being, relaxation, altered perceptions, euphoria, increased appetite, relief of nausea and vomiting, heightened sensory awareness, enhanced sociability	Marijuana: dry mouth, sore throat, increased heart rate, orthostatic hypotension, bronchitis, immunosuppression, reduction in testosterone and sperm count, disrupts menstrual periods and ovulation, anxiety and extreme self-consciousness, paranoia and panic, impaired judgment, decreased REM sleep, impaired ability to carry out goal-directed tasks, apathy, or social withdrawal decreased concentration, hallucinations and delusions

Within the brain, LSD is particularly concentrated in the hypothalamus, the limbic system, and the auditory and visual reflex areas. Electrodes placed in the limbic system show an "electrical storm" or massive increase in neural activity. About half of the substance is cleared from the body within 3 hours, and more than 90% is excreted within 24 hours. Because there are no withdrawal symptoms, a person does not become physically dependent; however, some psychological dependence can occur (Hanson & Venturelli, 1995).

MESCALINE is one of approximately 30 psychoactive chemicals that have been isolated from the peyote cactus, and used for centuries in the Americas. Within 30 to 120 minutes after ingestion, mescaline reaches a maximum concentration in the brain and may persist for up to 9 or 10 hours. Hallucinations may last up to 2 hours and are usually affected by the dose level. About half the dose is excreted unchanged after 6 hours and can be recovered in the urine for reuse. A slow tolerance builds up after repeated use, and there is cross-tolerance to LSD. As with LSD, mescaline intoxication can be alleviated or stopped by taking a dose of Thorazine, and to a lesser extent, Valium (Hanson & Venturelli, 1995).

PHENYLETHYLAMINE HALLUCINOGENS (DOM, MDA, MDMA) are chemically related to amphetamines. They have varying degrees of hallucinogenic and CNS stimulant effects, which are likely related to their ability to release serotonin and dopamine, respectively. Consequently, those that predominantly release serotonin are dominated by their hallucinogenic action and are LSD-like; whereas those more inclined to release dopamine are dominated by their stimulant effects and are cocaine-like (Hanson & Venturelli, 1995).

CANNABIS (MARIJUANA) is obtained from the hemp plant (*Cannabis sativa*). This plant contains over 400 different chemicals, but its psychoactive properties are related to the content of THC (delta-9-tetrahydrocannabinol) and other forms of cannabis found in the plant. A resinous exudate called hashish—derived from the top of female plants—contains the greatest concentration of active material.

When marijuana smoke is inhaled into the lungs, THC is readily distributed from the bloodstream into tissues throughout the body. THC and its metabolites are broken down by the liver and may be detected in the urine within an hour after the drug has been smoked. It is important to note that metabolites may be stored in the fatty tissues of heavy users causing a urine assay to show as positive for as long as 30 days after last use. Thus, interpretation of results need to be done in conjunction with a history unless more sophisticated testing is done to ascertain a change in level of THC.

In smokers, lung absorption and transport of THC to the brain are rapid; THC reaches the brain within as little as 14 seconds after inhalation. Marijuana is metabolized more efficiently through smoking than intravenous injection or oral ingestion. It is possible that THC alters several receptor or transmitter systems in the brain, which would account for its diverse and somewhat unpredictable effects (Hanson & Venturelli, 1995, p. 373).

According to the National Institute on Drug Abuse (1994), researchers have discovered anandamide (a natural compound in the body that binds to the brain's cannabinoid receptor). They also discovered a second cannabinoid ligand—2-Ara-G1—in the spleen. Hence, the body has at least two cannabinoid-binding compounds, one in the brain and one in the body or periphery. At the moment we do not know their specific role; however, they do influence the CNS and impact on emotions.

Inhalants

NATURE AND PHYSIOLOGICAL MECHANISM OF ACTION

Inhalants are gases that can be introduced into the body through the pulmonary (lungs) route. This category of drugs includes an array of different compounds and can be classified

TABLE 1-4 Inhalants

Drug	The Desired Effects	Health Consequences
Acetone, benzene, amyl and butyl nitrate, nitrous oxide, gasoline, toluene	Disorientation, increased euphoria	Mouth ulcers, gastrointestinal problems, anorexia, confusion, headache, ataxia, convulsions, death from asphyxiation, permanent brain damage, memory interference, damage to airways, lungs, kidneys and liver, nose bleeds

into three major groups: volatile solvents, anesthetics, and nitrites (Swan, 1993). Most of the inhalants can cause hallucinations as well as create intoxicating and euphorogenic effects. Volatile solvents include glue, paint thinner, aerosols, liquid paper correction fluid, nail polish remover, felt-tip marking pens, lighter and cleaning fluids, and gasoline. They are not regulated like other abusable drugs and therefore, are easily obtained by adolescents and children. The anesthetic most frequently used is nitrous oxide (laughing gas) (Table 1-4).

Inhalation is accomplished in a variety of ways. It may be poured or sprayed into a plastic bag and inhaled from the bag; liquid can be soaked into rags and placed over the mouth and nose; or inhaled directly from the bottle. Once the chemical is inhaled, it is rapidly absorbed into the lungs and begins to effect the CNS within seconds. As a result, the mental state is altered for 5 to 15 minutes. Tolerance often develops in chronic users, but withdrawal symptoms are rare (CSAT, 1993).

Anabolic Steroids

NATURE AND PHYSIOLOGICAL MECHANISM OF ACTION

Anabolic steroids are synthetic derivatives of the male hormone testosterone. The full name is "androgenic (promoting masculine characteristics) anabolic (building) steroids" (the class of drugs). These derivatives of testosterone promote the growth of skeletal muscle and increase lean body mass (NIDA, 1993).

Anabolic steroids were first abused nonmedically by elite athletes seeking to improve performance. Today, athletes and nonathletes use steroids to enhance performance, and also to improve physical appearance (NIDA, 1993) (Table 1-5).

TABLE 1-5 Anabolic Steroids

Drug	The Desired Effects	Health Consequences
Clostebol, dehydrochlor-methyltestosterone, fluoxymesterone, mesterolone, methenlone, nandrolone, testosterone, and related compounds	Maintenance of or improvement of athletic performance, increased muscle size and strength, increased aggressiveness	Liver damage and liver cancer, endocrine abnormalities (such as decreased plasma testosterone, decreased luteinizing hormone, and atrophy of testes), decreased libido, acne, water and salt retention, stunting of bone growth in children, impotence, mood swings with paranoia, violent behavior

Steroids are taken orally or injected and used typically in cycles of weeks or months—rather than continuously—in patterns called cycling. Cycling involves taking multiple doses of steroids over a specified period of time, stopping for a period of time and starting again. In addition, several different types of steroids may be combined to maximize effectiveness and minimize negative side effects, a process known as stacking (NIDA, 1993).

Side effects found to occur with heavy steroid use include: steroid craving, fatigue, depression, restlessness, loss of appetite, insomnia, diminished sex drive, headaches (all referred to as withdrawal), and unusual expression of aggression and rage (Hanson & Venturelli, 1995).

Over-the-counter (OTC) Drugs

The most frequently used categories of OTCs in descending order are: pain relievers (internal), vitamins, skin products, antacids, laxatives, eye medications, external pain relievers, cold remedies, antihistamines, and cough suppressants (Pharmacy Times, 1990). Over $12 billion is spent each year in the United States on drug products that are purchased over the counter; and this market is projected to reach $28 billion by the year 2010 (Covington, 1993; Laskoski, 1992 [as cited in Hanson & Venturelli, 1995]).

Approximately 40% of Americans use at least one OTC medication within a 2-day period, and an estimated three of four individuals routinely self-medicate with these drug products (Covington, 1993). Excessive use of some OTC medications can cause physical dependence, tolerance, and withdrawal (signs of addiction). This is probably due to their ingredients.

A number of OTC analgesics contain caffeine (which according to Sawynok and Yaksh [1993] relieves some types of pain), alcohol, and antihistamines (which are CNS depressants that can cause sedation and an antianxiety action and act like stimulants). Even frequent use of antacids can be habit forming. In addition, OTC drugs can interact with prescription drugs in a dangerous and sometimes even lethal manner (Hanson & Venturelli, 1995).

COMMON DRUG INTERACTIONS

The effect of one drug may be altered quite a bit if another drug is present in the body at the same time. This is referred to as drug interaction. Many drugs influence the actions and effects of other drugs and medical problems often arise. Also, drug interactions are frequently misdiagnosed as symptoms of an illness and results in inappropriate medical care being provided.

Depending on the effect on the body, drug interaction may be categorized into three types: additive, antagonistic (inhibitory), and potentiative (synergistic). Additive interactions are the combined effects of drugs taken concurrently. Antagonistic interactions occur when one drug cancels or blocks the effect of another. Potentiation occurs when the effect of a drug is enhanced due to the presence of another drug, which may increase the duration and/or potency of the effects of the first drug (Hanson & Venturelli, 1995). The following are common interactions among abusing and addicting drugs as outlined by Hanson and Venturelli (1995, p. 109) (Table 1-6).

Drug interaction is a major problem in drug abusing populations. Most addicted persons are multiple drug users (polydrug abusers), with little concern for the dangerous interactions that could occur. It is common for them to combine multiple CNS depressants to enhance their effects or a depressant with a stimulant to titrate a CNS effect (to determine

TABLE 1-6 Common Drug Interactions

Drug	Combined With	Interaction
Sedatives (Valium, Halcion)	Alcohol, barbiturates	Increase sedation
Stimulants (amphetamines, cocaine)	Insulin Antidepressants	Decrease insulin effect Cause hypertension
Narcotics (heroin, morphine)	Barbiturates, Valium Anticoagulants Antidepressants Amphetamines	Increase sedation Increase bleeding Cause sedation Increase euphoria
Tobacco (nicotine)	Blood pressure medication, amphetamines, cocaine	Elevate blood pressure Increase cardiovascular effects
Alcohol	Cocaine	Produce cocaethylene, which enhances euphoria and toxicity

the smallest amount that can be taken to achieve the desired high). Also it is common for them to experiment with a combination of stimulants, depressants, and hallucinogens to see what happens. The effects of such haphazard drug mixing are impossible to predict, difficult to treat in emergency situations, complex for detoxification and safe withdrawal, and frequently fatal (Hanson & Venturelli, 1995, p. 110).

CONCLUSION

There are specific effects one looks for when taking a medication or drug. Some are for modifying the nervous system and states of consciousness and others are not. Whether taking a drug for medical reasons, social reasons, recreational reasons, or experimental reasons, no one sets out to become addicted. Yet, addiction remains a major problem in this society. It is a chronic, progressive, relapsing disorder that affects all of us one way or another. At present, according to CSAT (1994) estimates of the number of persons addicted range from 6.5 to 37.5 million.

For some people ATOD use has progressed to addiction, and major consequences ensue for individuals, families, and society. Addicted persons usually experience increasingly debilitating or dysfunctional physical, social, financial, and emotional effects. Because of this devastation a search for the cause or causes of addiction continues. With a clear perspective on theories and causes related to addiction, one can plan more appropriate and effective prevention, intervention, and treatment, and relapse prevention strategies.

REFERENCES

American Psychiatric Association. (1994). *Diagnostic and statistical manual of mental disorders* (4th ed.). Washington, D.C.: American Psychiatric Association.

Beschner, G. (1986). Understanding teenage drug use. In G. Beschner & A.S. Friedman (Eds.) *Teen drug use*. Lexington, MA: D.C. Heath Company.

Brunton, S. (1991). *Nicotine addiction and smoking cessation*. New York: Medical Information Services.

Covington, T. (February, 1993). Trends in self care: The Rx to OTC switch movement. *Drug Newsletter, 12*, 15–16.

Doweiko, H. (1990). *Concepts of chemical dependency*. Pacific Grove, CA: Brooks/Cole Publishing Company.

Goldstein, F. (1995). Pharmacological aspects of substance abuse. In A.R. Genaro (Ed.) *Remington's pharmaceutical sciences* (19th ed.). Easton, PA: Mack.

Hanson, G., & Venturelli, P. (1995). *Drugs and society* (4th ed.). Boston, MA: Jones and Bartlett Publishers.

Institute of Medicine. (1990). *Treating drug problems* (Vol. 1). Washington, D.C.: National Academy Press.

Jaynes, J., & Rugg, C. (1988). *Adolescents, alcohol and drugs*. Springfield, IL: Charles Thomas, Publisher.

Laskoski, G. (December, 1992). Rx to OTC. *American Druggist*, 47–50.

MacDonald, D. (1989). *Drugs, drinking and adolescents*. Chicago, IL: Year Book Medical Publishers.

Morse, R., & Flavin, D. (1992). The definition of alcoholism. *Journal of the American Medical Association, 268(8)*, 1012–1014.

National Institute on Alcohol Abuse and Alcoholism, Center for Substance Abuse Prevention. (1993). *The alcohol and other drug thesaurus: A guide to concepts and terminology in substance abuse and addiction*. Washington, D.C.: Department of Health and Human Services.

National Institute on Drug Abuse. (1990b, 1993). Research on drugs and the workplace. *Capsules (CAPS) 24*. Rockville, MD: National Institutes of Health.

National Institute on Drug Abuse. (Sept/Oct, 1994). NIDA reflects on 20 years of neuroscience research. *NIDA NOTES*, Special Section. Rockville, MD: National Institutes of Health.

Nowinski, J. (1990). *Substance abuse in adolescents and young adults: a guide to treatment*. New York: W.W. Norton & Company.

Pharmacy Times. (March, 1990). Top 200 drugs of 1992.

Sawynok, J., & Yaksh, T. (1993). Caffeine as an analgesic adjuvant: A review of pharmacology and mechanisms of action. *Pharmacology Review, 45*, 43–85.

Secretary of U.S. Department of Health and Human Services. (1994). *Eighth Special Report to the U.S. Congress on Alcohol and Health*. NIH Publication No. 94-3699. Bethesda, MD: U.S. Department of Health and Human Services.

Substance Abuse and Mental Health Services Administration, Center for Substance Abuse Treatment (CSAT). (1994). *Treatment for alcohol and other drug abuse: Opportunities for coordination*. (Technical assistance publication series #11). DHHS Publication No. (SMA) 94-2075. Rockville, MD: Substance Abuse and Mental Health Services Administration.

Substance Abuse and Mental Health Services Administration, CSAT. (1993). *Guidelines for the treatment of alcohol and other drug abusing adolescents*. (Treatment improvement protocol series). DHHS Publication No. (SMA) 93-2010. Rockville, MD: Substance Abuse and Mental Health Services Administration.

Substance Abuse and Mental Health Services Administration (SAMHSA). (1995). *National household survey on drug abuse: Population estimates 1994*. DHHS Publication No. (SMA) 95-3063, SAMHSA.

Swan, N. (July/August, 1993). Inhalant abuse and its dangers are nothing to sniff at. *NIDA NOTES*, 15.

Witters, W., Venturelli, P., & Hanson, G. (1992). *Drugs and society* (3rd ed.). Boston: Jones and Bartlett Publishers.

Theoretical Perspectives for Addictions Nursing Practice

Karen M. Allen, PhD, RN, CARN

INTRODUCTION

Theories, models, and conceptual frameworks serve to order the experienced world (Dubin, 1978). They are identical in structure; composed of sets of relationship statements that can describe, explain, and/or predict phenomenon; and exist on a continuum ranging from micro to grand. Micro theories are the least complex. They contain the least complex concepts and refer to specific, easily defined phenomena. They are narrow in scope because they attempt to explain a small aspect of reality and are primarily composed of concepts based on "association," or concepts that can be listed, or counted off. Grand theories are the most complex and broadest in scope. They attempt to explain broad areas within a discipline, are composed of summative concepts, and incorporate numerous narrower range theories. When theories, models, or conceptual frameworks are used to guide nursing research, education, and practice, they result in a purpose for nursing practice and rationales for interventions (Marriner-Tomey, 1994). Although theory is used in nursing research and education, unfortunately it is not done so consistently in nursing practice.

Over a decade ago, Walker and Avant (1983) recommended that future direction in nursing include a focus on using conceptual frameworks to structure nursing practice and interventions. Today, nursing scholars and practitioners are still advocating for increased attention to the relationship between theory and practice. Identified priorities include: 1) continued development and/or application of theory to relevant areas of nursing practice, and 2) increased use of existing theories in clinical decision making (Bishop, 1994a). An area of health care in which there exists a deficit of nursing practice and interventions guided by theory or conceptual frameworks is that of addictions.

The first standard of practice for nurses providing care to addicted clients—developed jointly by the American Nurses Association and the National Nurses Society on Addictions (1988)—stresses the importance of using appropriate knowledge of theory related to addictions from nursing and from other disciplines to guide that care. Naegle (1995) points out that no overall theory has emerged to guide nursing care of individuals, families, and communities experiencing addiction problems. Nevertheless, as long as nurses become knowledgeable about and use theory from other disciplines to: 1) explain and describe the multidimensional nature of abuse and addiction, and 2) provide a framework from which practice approaches congruent with a nursing paradigm can be delineated, theory is being used in accurate and appropriate ways to guide nursing practice. Some nurses have begun to develop practice approaches congruent within nursing paradigms with certain addicted populations. These practice approaches are also congruent with explanations and descriptions of the multidimensional nature of addiction.

Therefore, the purpose of this chapter is to discuss theories of addiction to guide the practitioner providing health care to addicted clients. These theories are important to know because the way in which causes of addiction are understood helps determine the focus for prevention, screening, assessment, and interventions/treatment of substance abuse/addictive disorders.

In addition, the practice of nursing is defined as "treating the actual and potential responses to illnesses and diseases." Hence, this chapter presents the two current nursing theories developed for practice with addicted clients, aimed at treating and managing clients' actual and perceived biological, psychological, and social responses to this problem.

THE CLASSIC THEORY OF ADDICTION

For centuries the world has been experiencing the phenomenon of addictions to alcohol, tobacco, and other drugs. However, because of the difficulty in describing, explaining, or predicting these addictions, providing appropriate and successful primary and secondary prevention as well as treatment, has been hampered.

In 1946, E.M. Jellinek analyzed data from a questionnaire developed by, and administered to, members of Alcoholics Anonymous (A.A.). His analysis led him to conclude that "the probability of becoming alcoholic was smaller or greater based on: 1) the assets and liabilities of the total heredity of the person; 2) the conditioning of the person's responses at an early age; 3) educational assets; 4) social experiences in general and educational and marital experiences in particular; and 5) the pattern of living in the person's cultural group" (pp. 70–71). These conclusions led to Jellinek's contention that the etiology or cause of this alcoholism had a biopsychosocial basis.

However, in 1960 when Jellinek presented his conceptual framework for alcoholism known as "The Disease Concept of Alcoholism," it reflected the prevailing scientific view that cause is unidimensional. Jellinek posited that alcoholism was a primary medical disease that was chronic and progressive as the person experienced the "loss of control" phenomenon, as well as 40 other symptoms that progressed sequentially through four phases.

These phases were described as follows: 1) the prealcoholic phase; 2) the prodromal phase, otherwise described as early alcoholism; 3) the crucial phase or frank addiction; and 4) the chronic phase where chronic illness is present. The phases were later collapsed into three and identified as: 1) the early stage, distinguished by the presence of blackouts; 2) the middle stage, distinguished by a loss of control and change in tolerance; and 3) the late stage, distinguished by the presence of withdrawal.

For more than 30 years Jellinek's disease concept has been the cornerstone theory used by most in the discipline of addictions to guide prevention, research, and the practice of treating addicted clients, and therefore, is viewed as the classic theory. It is has become the classic theoretical approach because many persons experiencing this problem exhibited the symptoms and course of illness outlined by the theory. However, several critiques of the disease concept of addictions for alcohol and other drugs have emerged, mostly due to: 1) the lack of success in providing care or treatment for addictions by addressing just the physical perspective based on this theory; and 2) the development of new knowledge, as is expected in science.

Progress in science occurs when researchers logically and dispassionately review the status of a field of inquiry, pose precisely delimited questions, and use scientific methods to answer them (Moos, 1994). This is otherwise known as a paradigm shift. Keck (1994) explains that the word "paradigm" stems from the 1960s work of philosopher Thomas Kuhn, and is used to denote the prevailing network of science, philosophy, and theory accepted by a community of individuals comprising a certain discipline. This prevailing network of information then directs the research, education, and practice of that discipline. And as stated by Donovan (1988) without a conceptual framework, unitary set of rules, or standards of practice provided by a paradigm, it is difficult to agree on the important parameters of addictive behaviors.

Reviewing the status of the addictions field, and trying to find parameters of addictive behavior to agree on—supported by the existing "disease concept" theory—resulted in the emergence of many other micro and grand theories. These theories are based on a unicausal perspective and arise from the biological, psychological, and sociocultural arenas. Outlined below are some of these theories as discussed in The Alcohol and Other Drug Thesaurus (National Institute on Alcohol Abuse and Alcoholism & Center for Substance Abuse Prevention, 1993).

OTHER THEORIES OF ADDICTION

Biological Alcohol or Other Drug Use Disorder Theories

DISEASE THEORY

The belief that alcoholism is a condition of primary biological causation and predictable natural history, conforming to accepted definitions of a disease (Jellinek, 1946, 1960; Vaillant, 1983).

NEUROBIOLOGICAL THEORY

Research conducted by Wise (1980, 1987), Wise and Bozarth (1987), McBride, Murphy, Gatto, Levy, Lumeng, and Li (1991), Blum and Payne (1991), Kilty, Lorang, and Amara (1991), and others support the view that neuroadaptive processes play an important role in the etiology of alcohol or other drug use disorders. Pickens, Svikis, McGue, Lykken, Hesten, and Clayton (1991) and Phillips and Dudek (1991) are examples of researchers working to validate that genetic predetermination also plays a large role in this theory.

GENETIC THEORY

The belief that alcohol or other drug use disorders may be hereditary and not acquired has been empirically proven since the 1960s with the research of Kaij (1960), Goodwin, Schulsinger, Hermansen, Guze, and Winokur (1973), Cloninger, Bohman, and Sigvardsson (1981), Hrubec and Omenn (1981), Kaprio, Koskenvuo, Langinvainio, Romanov, Sarna, and Rose (1987), Pickens, Svikis, McGue, Lykken, Hesten, and Clayton (1991), and McGue, Pickens, and Svikis (1992).

Psychological Alcohol or Other Drug Use Disorder Theories

PERSONALITY THEORY

This theory encompasses the study of personality vis-à-vis alcohol or other drug use disorders and relates the patients' personalities to the development and maintenance of their disorder. Research conducted by Sher (1987), Newlin and Thomson (1990), and Sher, Walitzer, Wood, and Brent (1991) document the existence of what is known as "behavioral undercontrol"—a measure or personality that includes traits like hyperactivity, sensation-seeking, antisocial behavior, and impulsivity.

SELF-AWARENESS THEORY

This theory attempts to understand the causes and effects of alcohol or other drug use in terms of alcohol or other drug pharmacologic action. It is thought that the pharmacologic action affects the cognitive processes—specifically the self-aware state—rather than the physiologic processes (particularly the stress response). Alcohol or other drug use decreases self-awareness, which in turn has behavioral consequences opposite those associated with increased self-awareness, thus decreasing appropriate behaviors.

PSYCHOANALYTIC THEORY

This theory follows Freud and his ideas regarding the components of the self and their functioning during the four stages of psychosexual development. The etiology of alcohol or other drug disorders develops from three main sources of maladaptive behavior: 1) seeking sensual satisfaction (this includes escaping pain or anxiety); 2) conflict among the components of the self (the id, superego, and ego); and 3) fixation in the infantile past. Research attempting to support this theoretical hypothesis for cause has failed (Cutter, Key, Rothstein, & Jones, 1973).

SOCIAL LEARNING THEORY

This theory—also known as the "cognitive social learning theory"—posits that personal factors, environment, and behavior are interlocking determinants. The principles of learning, cognition, and reinforcement are important in this theoretical viewpoint. This theory examines the individual's social learning history; his/her cognitive set, such as expectations or beliefs about the effects of alcohol or other drugs; and the physical and social setting in which usage occurs. Research conducted by Becker (1966), Kandel and Andrews (1987), and Barnes (1990) provide support for this theory.

CONDITIONING THEORY

This theory involves the relevance and implications of classic conditioning with respect to preferences and aversions to alcohol or other drugs, alcohol or other drug tolerance, alcohol or other drug urges or cravings, and the role of classic conditioning in alcohol or other drug withdrawal. Researchers such as Conger (1956) and Mello (1980) have contributed results in support of this theory.

EXPECTANCY THEORY

This theory stresses the importance of cognitive factors in the initiation and maintenance of alcohol or other drug use behaviors. Expectancy refers to the anticipation of a systematic relationship between events or objects in a specific upcoming situation. Several studies have been conducted to provide empirical support for this theory: Miller, Smith, and Goldman (1990), Stacy, Widaman, and Marlatt (1990), and Sher, Walitzer, Wood, and Brent (1991).

TENSION REDUCTION THEORY

Among others, research by Cappell and Greeley (1987) provided support for this theory. The tension reduction theory is based on behavioral learning principles and contains two hypotheses: 1) that alcohol or other drugs reduce tension and 2) that individuals use alcohol or other drugs for their tension-reducing properties. Tension reduction theory is a component of other etiological models such as stress response dampening.

Sociocultural Alcohol or Other Drug Use Disorder Theories

SYSTEMS THEORY

The main premise of this theory is that behavior is determined and maintained by the ongoing dynamics and demand of the key interpersonal systems within which the individual interacts. The theory views people primarily as social beings rather than as a reflection of personality and psychological variables. Research by Barnes (1990), Bennett and Wolin (1990), Chassin, Rogosch, and Barrera (1991), and Kumpfer and Turner (1990–1991) has provided empirical support for this theory.

AVAILABILITY THEORY

This theory maintains that the greater the availability of alcohol or other drugs in society, the greater the prevalence and severity of alcohol or other drug-related problems in society.

ANTHROPOLOGICAL THEORY

Based on research conducted by Room, Greenfield, and Weisner (in press) and Ringwalt and Palmer (1990), this theory emphasizes the beliefs, attitudes, norms, and values that a population holds with respect to alcohol or other drugs, and the ways in which they shape behavior, which in turn affects the individual. Often this theory is viewed as culturally focused.

ECONOMIC THEORY

This theory emphasizes the investigation of the social costs of excessive alcohol or other drug use, and the economic dimensions of government policies aimed at changing consumption habits. Economic models have been developed to investigate the factors that influence alcohol or other drug consumption and how alcohol or other drug-related problems are linked to consumption levels. Two key elements of economic models are the modeling of alcohol or other drug consumption and the linking of alcohol or other drug consumption with alcohol or other drug abuse and dependence.

These researchers believe that a major economic perspective that needs to be considered in cause of addiction is the economic culture of selling drugs. Selling drugs has become a viable option of employment for those who are underemployed or unemployed, as well as those who move in the top circles of persons of higher socioeconomic status. Participating in the vending of drugs sometimes leads to use, abuse, and addiction.

This theory posits that certain drugs—whether licit or illicit—serve as "gateways" or open the way to the use of another drug, usually one viewed as more problematic. Many studies, particularly among adolescents, have found that alcohol use is the first stage. The term "stage" in drug use refers to the sequence of use of, and addiction to, a class of increasingly addictive drugs, from alcohol to tobacco to marijuana to pills to hard drugs.

CONTEMPORARY THEORIES OF ADDICTION

Recently, scientists comprising the addictions discipline have begun movement away from viewing addictions as having a unidimensional cause, toward an integrative and multidimensional perspective. According to the U.S. Department of Health and Human Services Substance Abuse and Mental Health Services Administration (SAMHSA) (1994), "as an understanding of addiction has evolved and knowledge has been gained through research, the complexity of the causes for and persistence of substance abuse/addictions has been compounded. It now appears as if a constellation of factors can be correlated with initiation and continuation of substance abuse and addiction. No single explanation appears adequate, particularly since there are wide variances in precipitating factors and motivations for continued use" (p. 26).

Other movement in science has been away from the view that one needs to look for a "cause" in a theory to explain a certain phenomenon. Bishop (1994b) cites several researchers who have presented analyses challenging the "positivist" position of discovering truth as a determination for cause, thus offering the basis for a new perspective of science or theory. According to Bell and Khantzian (1991) current scientific thinking tends toward viewing theories as inventions or pictures to help organize thinking and clarify vision. There is less concern now with discovering what "really is" and more interest in defining and creating "perspectives" or "visions" of reality. They further state that modern theories are understood as created "points of view" or "conceptual lenses" that momentarily bring into focus something one wants to look at.

An effective way to accomplish this is to approach it from a grand theoretical perspective. A few grand theories that 1) create a perspective or vision of the reality of addiction and help to organize and clarify what that reality is; and 2) can be used to guide prevention, research, and practice with addicted persons, are discussed next.

The Public Health Theoretical Perspective on Addictions

In the mid-1960s Leavell and Clark (1965) identified three levels of prevention—primary, secondary, and tertiary—and postulated "The Public Health Model" of disease. According to this model, to address a disease or condition, you must understand its natural life history including how host, agent, and environment interact to produce that disease or condition.

Experts in the field of addictions have taken that model and used it to create a perspective or vision of reality about addictions. The public health perspective of addiction stresses that biological, psychological, pharmacologic, and social factors constantly interact and influence the problem of addiction in any person or group of people. Drug addiction is conceptualized as:

HOST + AGENT + ENVIRONMENT = ADDICTION

The host is a person or cluster of people grouped by ethnicity, age, sex, race, vocation, geographical location, and their drug use, abuse, or dependence. In addition, consideration of relevant biological, physiological, and psychological aspects must also be included. The agent is the substance of abuse. Any adulterants and contaminants that are present in the drug, along with the pharmacologic characteristics of the drug itself must be considered. The environment consists of the meanings, values, and norms assigned to a drug by its culture, community, and society; as well as all the elements in which the problem and resources exist (Levin, 1986; Westermeyer, 1987).

The public health theoretical perspective is used as a basis for primary and secondary prevention, as well as treatment of alcohol and other drug problems, by many community groups as well as federal agencies. According to SAMHSA's Center for Substance Abuse Prevention (formerly the Office of Substance Abuse Prevention) (1992), experience has shown that the most effective prevention efforts are approaches that include multiple components directed at multiple organizational levels and multiple target groups within the community. By basing prevention interventions from the public health theoretical perspective aimed at the host, the agent (drug), and the environment, you use multiple components and focus on multiple targets. As a result, large numbers of individuals are reached in a cost-efficient way that can be easily replicated.

When treating addicted persons guided by the public health theory, the health care provider considers 1) the person and all of his or her biological and psychological vulnerability; 2) the addicting power of the substance or process with which the person is involved; and 3) the cultural aspects that impact on the problem. In addition, the current environment (community) in which the person lives, works, and exists, and the support or interference it provides for recovery is acknowledged. Then, based on resulting data, an effective plan of care for addictions would include interventions in all three dimensions. If any dimension is disregarded, treatment goals probably will not be attained.

Biopsychosocial Theoretical Perspectives on Addictions

A recent trend has been to create realistic visions of addictions by conceptually organizing the development of it within a "biopsychosocial" framework. Gorski (1994), a well-known expert in the addictions field defines "biopsychosocial" as bio—being short for biological, which refers to the brain chemistry problems that underlie addictions; psycho—meaning psychological, which refers to the deeply entrenched habits of perceiving, thinking, feeling, and acting that are related to addictions; and social—which expands the concept to society and refers to the problems that develop in work, and social and intimate relationships as a result of the addiction.

This definition coincides with the one from the SAMHSA Center for Substance Abuse Treatment (1994) that views bio as biological, psycho as psychological, and social as societal. Biological causes of addiction include hereditary predisposition and altered brain chemistry. Psychological causes of addiction point to substance abuse and addiction being initiated and continued because individuals experience emotional and psychological problems. Social means that alcohol and other drug use often begins in social situations, and it is through social interactions that substance use is learned and reinforced. Also, addiction is frequently correlated with various social problems such as unemployment, poverty, racism, and family dysfunction.

The biopsychosocial model has emerged to provide a broader, more holistic perspective of substance abuse/addictions and its prevention, treatment, and research. It is the model that is most widely endorsed because it can most adequately explain the intricate nature of addiction. This model incorporates elements of all the other more narrowly focused models previously discussed.

Kumpfer, Trunnell, and Whiteside (1990) proposed a biopsychosocial "Vulnerability Model" as one potential theoretical framework to use in organizing etiological factors that contribute to addiction. The model includes cluster factors of biological variables and cluster factors of psychosocial environmental variables. Biological variables include genetic inheritance, in utero damage, and temperament or other physiological differences; and psychosocial environmental variables include the family, community and/or school, and peer or social pressure.

The biopsychosocial vulnerability framework views these variables as temporally ordered in its interactions that lead to addictions. It posits that first, existing genetic factors followed by any "in utero" or later physiological damage that may occur after birth in the child's life, cause a person to become vulnerable to being addicted. Then, when a number of these biological factors converge and interact with nonsupportive and negative environmental conditions existing within the family (which has the greatest impact on the person), followed by the community or school (with the next greatest impact), and finally the peer or social variables, addictions can emerge.

The thrust of the biopsychosocial vulnerability framework is that considerable interaction exists between and within the biological and psychosocial factors. And just as much emphasis is placed on environmental factors as is placed on biological factors in contributing to the development of an addiction. According to Kumpfer et al. (1990), the major mandate of this biopsychosocial framework is that the health care provider understand the person in relation to his or her total biopsychosocial environment, whether the goal is prevention, treatment, or research.

The only element missing from the model by Kumpfer et al. is psychiatric illness. Although psychosocial aspects are allowed for in the model, when explaining which elements are subsumed under "biopsychosocial," psychiatric illnesses were not mentioned. Psychiatric illnesses contribute a great deal to substance abuse and addictions disorders for some people. Dual diagnosis is a major issue for concern in both the psychiatric and addictions arenas.

According to Kumpfer (personal communication, 1995), they did not stress psychiatric illness at that time. However, the model would be equally useful in examining the precursors of psychiatric disorders that serve as significant comorbid predictors of substance abuse. Therefore, if one decided to use the Kumpfer et al. (1990) model as a biopsychosocial perspective for guiding prevention, intervention, treatment, and research related to addictions, psychiatric illness would need to be added for assessment and consideration.

Chatlos and Jaffe (1994) describe a biopsychosocial framework developed specifically for use with adolescents as well as adults that allows for inclusion of dual diagnoses and can be used to guide prevention, interventions and treatment, and research of addictions. As can be seen in Figure 2-1, the framework focuses on three factors derived from research on the antecedents, concomitant, and maintenance factors of addiction, and mental disorders:

$$PREDISPOSITION + DRUG\ USE/EVENT + ENABLING\ SYSTEM =$$
$$ADDICTION$$

According to Chatlos and Jaffe, *predisposition* represents genetic, constitutional (biological and biochemical), psychological and sociocultural issues. *Drug use/event* is separated into initiation and progression. Major factors impacting on initiation include: availability, peer influence, and perceived risk of harmfulness. Progression for adolescents occurs in four stages:

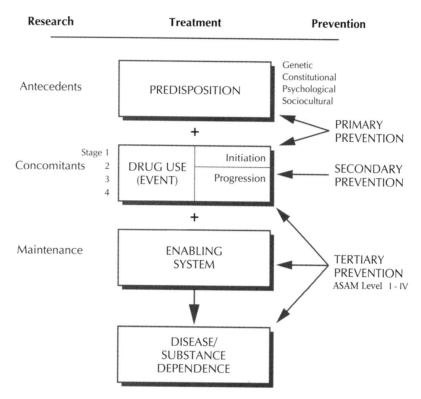

Figure 2-1. Developmental biopsychosocial disease model. (Source: Chatlos, C., & Jaffe, S. [1994]. A developmental biopsychosocial model of adolescent addiction. In N. S. Miller [Ed.], *Principles of addiction medicine* [Chpt. 1]. Chevy Chase, MD: American Society of Addiction Medicine, Inc. Reprinted with permission.)

1) experimental use; 2) regular use; 3) daily preoccupation; and 4) harmful dependency. According to SAMHSA (1994), progression in adults occurs in three stages: 1) experimental and social use; 2) abuse; and 3) dependency/addiction. *Enabling system* includes: the family, peer social network, school, job, and community, which contribute to the maintenance of the substance abuse/addiction.

Chatlos and Earl (1994) discuss how mental disorders can be viewed from a framework of "predisposition + event + enabling system." Most mental disorders have a known predisposition that can be divided into genetic, constitutional, psychological, and sociocultural factors similar to addiction. Instead of drug use, a precipitating or initiating *event* occurs that may be a biological event (such as puberty) or a psychosocial event (such as loss or traumatic incident). There is a describable progression that occurs within an enabling system of family, peers, school, job, and community. This developmental approach has been useful with affective disorders, eating disorders, conduct disorders and delinquency, personality disorders, anxiety disorders, attention deficit disorders, sexual disorders, and post-traumatic stress disorders.

In addition, as can be seen in Figure 2-2, this biopsychosocial model allows for a relationship that can exist with the presence of two diagnoses—addiction and psychiatric disorders—with a bidirectional interaction of two or more disorders that can occur at any level

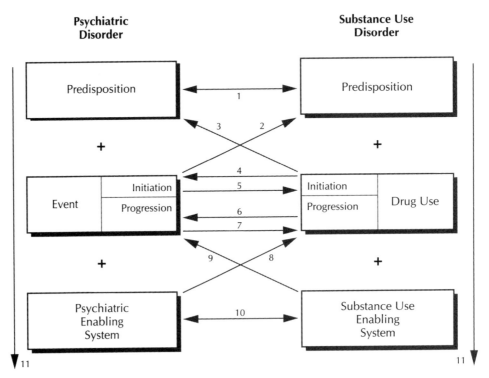

Figure 2-2. Relationships between two disorders using development model. (Source: Chatlos, C. [1993, Summer]. Integrating research, prevention and treatment: A developmental approach. *NAPPA Bulletin,* 1[3], 1–6. Reprinted with permission.)

such as antecedent, concomitant or maintenance. Using this model, Chatlos and Earl show that 1) risk factors may interact or overlap for the two disorders; 2) axis I or II psychopathology may serve as a risk factor for addictive disorders; 3) addictive disorders may serve as a risk factor for psychopathology; 4) psychiatric symptoms may develop as a result of acute intoxication and initiate the onset of a psychiatric disorder; 5) a psychiatric disorder may lead to initiation or acute intoxication as an attempt to self medicate; 6) some psychiatric disorders emerge as a consequence of use and persist into the period of remission (this may be related to withdrawal or chronic use systems); 7) psychopathology may modify the course of addictive disorder in terms of rapidity of course, response to treatment, symptom picture, and long-term outcome; 8) maintenance aspects (personal and social) of psychiatric disorders may lead to continued progression, consolidation, or relapse of addiction disorders (personal and family aspects of chronic schizophrenia or impulse disorder such as pathological gambling or intermittent explosive disorder; 9) vice versa; 10) members or aspects of one enabling system interact with another (depressive family system fostering continued hopelessness of substance-using family system, violence of alcoholic family system consolidating continued manipulation of an antisocial disorder system, community system of drug dealing for economics promoting continued interactions with drugs during recovery, etc.); and 11) some psychopathological conditions and addictive disorders are independent and not specifically related.

The model of Chatlos and Earl extends the traditional "Public Health Model" of agent—host—environment into a developmental continuum (see Figure 2-3). Whether doing primary and secondary prevention, interventions and treatment, or research, activities must be comprehensive and all encompassing, starting with the host, building on that with the agent, and going on further to address the environment. Or as described in the models of Kumpfer et al. and Chatlos and Earl: address biological and hereditary predisposition factors, add to that drug use/event and psychological factors, and in addition address the enabling systems of society and community environments.

As can be seen in Figure 2-1, using Chatlos and Earl's biopsychosocial model of substance dependence/addiction model as a guide, primary prevention would focus on predisposition (the antecedents to addiction or psychiatric events—specifics related to the host) and initiation factors. Secondary prevention—screening and detection—would focus on the progression of the disease (specifics related to co-occurring activities such as the drug use and/or any psychiatric events). Tertiary prevention—interventions and/or treatment—would focus on the progression of the disease and the enabling system (specific factors of the environment that contribute to addiction or recovery).

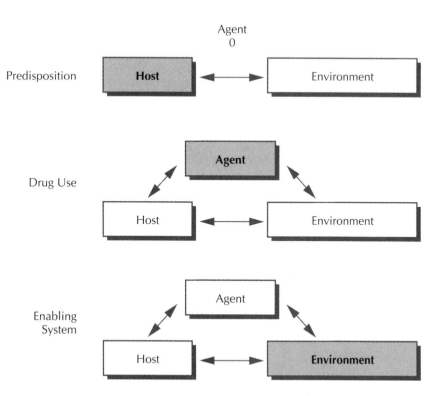

Figure 2-3. Developmental model and public health model. (Source: Chatlos, C. [1993, Summer]. Integrating research, prevention and treatment: A developmental approach. *NAPPA Bulletin,* 1[3], 1–6. Reprinted with permission.)

NURSING MODELS FOR GUIDING CARE OF ADDICTED CLIENTS

Although the focus of nursing care is to treat actual or potential responses to diseases and illnesses it is important that nurses use a model for practice that allows them to treat or address responses that emerge from the biological, psychological, and social realms of the addict's life. The first model to be presented is the "LIGHT model" for use in guiding care of the addicted client, which was developed by Anderson and Smereck (1989). This theory of practice is based on a combination of Martha Roger's theory that views illness as a result of interactions in the human–environmental energy fields, and Aristotle's view of well-being, in that the nurse "knowingly participates" with the client to improve his or her well-being to an optimal level—whatever that is for the individual. This is exhibited by "personalized care and personalized action," a joint endeavor of the nurse and the client in the continuous process of innovative change for the client (Anderson & Smereck, 1989).

Both general and advanced practice nurses can use this model by developing an understanding of the client's point of view with respect to each step in the nursing process (i.e., assessment, development of a focal concern list, goal development, intervention, and evaluation). Then she or he helps the clients to plan and take action on their own behalf to remedy their self-identified focal concern. The LIGHT model has two tracks: 1) the "Personalized Care Track" where all actions are taken by the nurse; and 2) the "Personalized Action Track" where all actions are taken by the client. Both tracks are described by the acronym LIGHT. Nurses practicing the model are admonished to practice Personalized Care:

L   ove the client
I   ntend to help
G   ive care gently
H   elp the client improve his or her well-being
T   each the Personalized Action Process to the client;

and this will actively assist clients to practice Personalized Action:

L   ove themselves
I   dentify a focal concern
G   ive themselves a goal
H   ave confidence
T   ake action.

This model was developed to involve clients in their own recovery process. It posits that clients must learn to love self and have the confidence to increase their sense of well-being. A goal is to eliminate negative emotional states that served as motivations for drug use. The clients are assisted to identify areas of concern related to health, drug use, and other life spheres, and to identify options for addressing their concerns. From these options clients are asked to develop a plan and to take action. Nurses individualize the interventions, building on the talents and aspirations of the client. The result is that the well-being of clients is enhanced when clients themselves take action to remedy their focal concerns and build on their talents in the pursuit of excellence (Anderson, Smereck, & Braunstein, 1993).

Utilizing research to test the effectiveness of using this model to guide care provided to over 2000 addicted clients in emergency rooms in three large cities, the authors found the following outstanding results: 1) there was a significant reduction in frequency of intravenous drug use (heroin and cocaine); and 2) a significant increase in well-being. Because addictions is a biopsychosocial disease, the LIGHT model can be applied to address any focal concerns coming from clients in any of the three realms. It is important that health care providers, such as nurses, familiarize themselves with this model regardless of their clinical practice area to consider its appropriateness to help guide prevention, assessment, and whatever interventions/treatment they feel necessary.

Chenitz (1989) used grounded theory methodology to study nursing interventions in a methadone maintenance clinic. Participant-observation as a clinic staff nurse during 4 months was the principal method of data collection. From this work a substantive theory called "managing vulnerability" was developed to describe nursing treatment of heroin addicts during methadone maintenance. Just like the LIGHT model, managing vulnerability is based on a parallel process between the nurse and the client. There are three stages: 1) learning to be vulnerable; 2) living with vulnerability; and 3) beyond vulnerability. Conditions required for the effective use of this theoretical guide to care include: 1) the dispensing (giving) of medication; 2) the nurse having an attitude of unconditional friendliness or nonjudgmental approach (described as being therapeutic neutrality); and 3) effective communication among staff and the existence of clear clinic or program policy, and support for nursing staff when enforcing the policy.

While the nurse engages in his or her stages, the client is also engaging in his or hers. In stage one, the nurse is working to decrease the client's sense of vulnerability by explaining intervention or treatment rules, equalizing control over interactions with the client, checking the client's agenda, establishing a medication (intervention) dose, and setting limits on behavior. At the same time, the client will be developing a style to decrease the sense of vulnerability by learning the rules, testing the rules, and testing the nurse in developing mutual trust. In stage two of the process, the nurse begins to stabilize the client by teaching how to live with vulnerability: monitoring and intervening on problems as well as limit setting on behavior. At the same time, the client is providing information regarding identified problems and establishing self as a part of the clinic. Finally, at the third stage, the nurse is teaching problem solving, goal development, and goal achievement. This can include things such as detoxifying or maintaining; teaching the client how to work through crises, create small goals, improve self-care, achieve goals and evaluate goals. Concomitantly, the client learns how to problem solve, learn to live through crises, and how to get and achieve goals (Chenitz, 1989).

To date, the theory of "managing vulnerability" has not been tested empirically with another group of methadone maintenance clients or other addicts for determination of effectiveness as an overall approach. However, its applicability is highly possible with use of other heroin addicts receiving methadone, or other addicts being dispensed other medications or treatment interventions. The dispensing of medications provides the opening opportunity for the nurse to proceed through the phases.

As shown above, addictions nurse researchers are beginning to formulate conceptualizations and organize knowledge related to caring for addicted clients. These theories are being developed for use in all clinical settings where addicted clients are seen, rather than settings specific to addictions treatment.

CONCLUSION

It is clear that a considerable degree of change has taken place during the past decade regarding theoretical aspects of addiction. Addiction is now seen as having multiple causes and being based on interactions that take place in the biological, psychological, and social arenas of life. Therefore, a comprehensive and integrated approach must be taken when health care providers participate in primary and secondary prevention, treatment, and research.

A survey conducted by the U.S. Department of Health and Human Services (1994), revealed that 1.9 million registered nurses (the largest health care provider group in the country), work in various settings. Two of three nurses work in hospitals in the following areas: 449,000 in general medical–surgical units; 203,000 in intensive care units; 128,000 in operating recovery rooms; 76,000 in emergency rooms; 70,000 in stepdown from intensive care units; 63,000 in labor and delivery; and 62,000 in outpatient units.

Other settings where registered nurses work include: 180,000 in community/public health; 144,000 in physicians offices/ambulatory care facilities; 129,000 in nursing homes; 51,000 in school health; 36,500 in nursing education; 20,000 in insurance companies/managed care; and 19,000 in occupational health. In addition to the settings, nurses have varying functions along the continuum of prevention, treatment, and research, on both the general and advanced practice level.

Nurses used to be able to choose whether or not to work in a setting that involved caring for substance abusing/addicted clients. However, that is no longer possible. As will be discussed in the next section, regardless of area of practice or specialty, all nurses encounter substance abusing/addicted clients, and most often they are the first person the client sees for care. Therefore, it is imperative that all nurses have the required knowledge base necessary to care for these clients, which begins by understanding what it is that they see; and applying theoretical models from nursing as well as other disciplines to guide care provided. Viewing substance abuse/addictions from the biopsychosocial theoretical perspective allows the opportunity to understand and provides a framework for developing practice approaches for prevention, screening, assessment and diagnosis, intervention/treatment, and research; and addressing actual or potential responses resulting from addiction.

REFERENCES

American Nurses Association, Drug and Alcohol Nurses Association and the National Nurses Society on Addictions. (1988). *Standards of addictions nursing practice with selected diagnoses and criteria.* Kansas City: American Nurses Association.

Anderson, M., & Smereck, G. (1989). Personalized nursing LIGHT model. *Nursing Science Quarterly, 2* (3), 120–130.

Anderson, M., Smereck, G., & Braunstein, M. (1993). LIGHT model: An effective intervention model to change high-risk AIDS behaviors among hard-to-reach urban drug users. *American Journal of Drug and Alcohol Abuse, 19* (3), 309–325.

Barnes, G. (1990). Impact of the family on adolescent drinking patterns. In R. Collins, K. Leonard, and J. Searles (Eds.), *Alcohol and the family: Research and clinical perspectives.* New York: Guilford Press.

Becker, H. (1966). *Outsiders: Studies in the sociology of deviance.* New York: The Free Press.

Bell, C.M., & Khantzian, E.J. (1991). Contemporary psychodynamic perspectives and the disease concept of addiction: Complimentary or competing models? *Psychiatric Annals, 21,* 273–281.

Bennett, L., & Wolin, S. (1990). Family culture and alcoholism transmission. In R. Collins, K. Leonard, & J. Searles (Eds.), *Alcohol and the family: Research and clinical perspectives.* New York: Guilford Press.

Bishop, S.M. (1994a). Theory development process. In A. Marriner-Tomey (Ed.), *Nursing theorists and their work* (3rd ed., pp. 45–57). St. Louis: Mosby.

Bishop, S.M. (1994b). History and philosophy of science. In A. Marriner-Tomey (Ed.), *Nursing theorists and their work* (3rd ed., pp. 27–36). St. Louis: Mosby.

Blum, K., & Payne, J. (1991). *The addicted brain.* New York: The Free Press.

Cappell, H., & Greeley, J. (1987). Alcohol and tension reduction: An update on research and theory. In H. Blane & K. Leonard (Eds.), *Psychological theories of drinking and alcoholism.* New York: Guilford Press.

Chassin, L., Rogosch, F., & Barrera, M. (1991). Substance use and symptomatology among adolescent children of alcoholics. *Journal of Abnormal Psychology, 100*(4), 449–463.

Chatlos, C. (1993, Summer). Integrating research, prevention and treatment: A developmental approach. *NAPPA Bulletin, 1* (3), 1–6.

Chatlos, C., & Earl, D. (1994). Adolescent dual diagnosis. In N.S. Miller (Ed.), *Principles of addiction medicine* (Chpt. 3). Chevy Chase, MD: American Society of Addiction Medicine, Inc.

Chatlos, C., & Jaffe, S. (1994). A developmental biopsychosocial model of adolescent addiction. In N. S. Miller (Ed.), *Principles of addiction medicine* (Chpt. 1). Chevy Chase, MD: American Society of Addiction Medicine, Inc.

Chenitz, C. (Winter, 1989). Managing vulnerability: Nursing treatment for heroin addicts. *Image: Journal of Nursing Scholarship, 21*(4), 210–214.

Cloninger, C., Bohman, M., & Sigvardsson, S. (1981). Inheritance of alcohol abuse: Cross-fostering analysis of adopted men. *Archives of General Psychiatry, 38*(8), 861–868.

Conger, J. (1956). Alcoholism: Theory, problem and challenge. II. Reinforcement theory and the dynamics of alcoholism. *Quarterly Journal of Studies on Alcohol, 17*, 296–305.

Cutter, H., Key, J., Rothstein, E., & Jones, W. (1973). Alcohol, power and inhibition. *Quarterly Journal of Studies on Alcohol, 34*(2), 381–389.

Donovan, D.M. (1988). Assessment of addictive behaviors: Implications of an emerging biopsychosocial model. In D.M. Donovan & G.A. Marlatt (Eds.), *Assessment of addictive behaviors* (pp. 3–48). New York: The Guilford Press.

Dubin, R. (1978). *Theory building.* New York: The Free Press.

Goodwin, D., Schulsinger, F., Hermansen, L., Guze, S., & Winokur, G. (1973). Alcohol problems in adoptees raised apart from alcoholic biological parents. *Archives of General Psychiatry, 28*(2), 238–243.

Gorski, T.T. (1994, March/April). A suggestion for conceptualizing dual diagnosis: A systematic analysis to help cut through the confusion and mismanagement. *Behavioral Health Management,* 50–53.

Hrubec, Z., & Omenn, G. (1981). Evidence of genetic predisposition to alcoholic cirrhosis and psychosis: Twin concordances for alcoholism and its biological end points by zygosity among male veterans. *Alcohol Clinical and Experimental Research, 5*(2), 207–215.

Jellinek, E.M. (1946). Phases in the drinking history of alcoholics: An analysis of a survey conducted by the official organ of Alcoholics Anonymous. *Quarterly Journal of Studies on Alcohol, 7*, 1–88.

Jellinek, E.M. (1960). *The disease concept of alcoholism.* New Haven, CT: Hillhouse Press.

Kaij, L. (1960). *Alcoholism in twins: Studies on the etiology and sequelae of abuse of alcohol.* Stockholm: Almqvist and Wiksell Publishers.

Kandel, D., & Andrews, K. (1987). Processes of adolescent socialization by parents and peers. *International Journal of the Addictions, 22*(4), 319–342.

Kaprio, J., Koskenvuo, M., Langinvainio, H., Romanov, K., Sarna, S., and Rose, R. (1987). Genetic influences on use and abuse of alcohol: A study of 5,638 adult Finnish twin brothers. *Alcohol Clinical and Experimental Research, 11*(4), 349–356.

Keck, J. (1994). Terminology of theory development. In A. Marriner-Tomey (Ed.), *Nursing theorists and their work* (3rd ed., pp. 17–26). St. Louis: Mosby.

Kilty, J., Lorang, D., & Amara, S. (1991). Cloning and expression of a cocaine-sensitive rat dopamine transporter. *Science, 254*(5031), 578–579.

Kumpfer, K.L., Trunnell, E.P., & Whiteside, H.O. (1990). The biopsychosocial model: Application to the addictions field. In R.C. Eng (Ed.), *Controversies in the addictions field: Vol. 1.* Dubuque, Iowa: Kendall/Hunt Publishing Company.

Kumpfer, K., & Turner, C. (1990-1991). The social ecology model of adolescent substance abuse: Implications for prevention. *The International Journal of the Addictions, 25*(4a), 435–363.

Leavell, H.R., & Clark, E.G. (1965). *Preventive medicine for the doctor in your community.* New York: McGraw-Hill.

Levin, J. (1986). *Drugs and society: A biological and public health perspective.* Unpublished manuscript.

Marriner-Tomey, A. (1994). Introduction to analysis of nursing theories. In A. Marriner-Tomey (Ed.), *Nursing theorists and their work* (3rd ed., pp. 3–16). St. Louis: Mosby.

McBride, W., Murphy, J., Gatto, G., Levy, A., Lumeng, L., & Li, T. (1991). Serotonin and dopamine systems regulating alcohol intake. In H. Kalant, J. Khanna, & Y. Israel (Eds.), *Advances in biomedical alcohol research: Proceedings of the 5th ISBRA/RSA Congress, Toronto, June 17–22.* Oxford, England: Pergamon Press.

McGue, M., Pickens, R., & Svikis, D. (1992). Sex and age effects on the inheritance of alcohol problems: A twin study. *Journal of Abnormal Psychology, 101*(1), 3–17.

Mello, K. (1980). *Stimulus self-administration: Some implications for the prediction of drug abuse liability.* Proceedings of the Conference on Prediction of Abuse Liability of Stimulant and Depressant Drugs. Committee on Problems of Drug Dependence, National Academy of Sciences, National Research Council, Washington, D.C.

Miller, P., Smith, G., & Goldman, M. (1990). Emergence of alcohol expectancies in childhood: A possible critical period. *Journal of Studies on Alcohol, 51*(4), 343–349.

Moos, R. (1994). Why do some people recover from alcohol dependence, whereas others continue to drink and become worse over time. *Addiction, 89*, 31–34.

Naegle, M. (1995). Education, research and theory development. In E. J. Sullivan (Ed.), *Nursing care of clients with substance abuse.* St. Louis: Mosby.

National Institute on Alcohol Abuse and Alcoholism & Center for Substance Abuse Prevention. (1993). *The alcohol and other drug thesaurus: A guide to concepts and terminology in substance abuse and addiction.* Washington, D.C.: CSR, Inc.

Newlin, D., & Thomson, J. (1990). Alcohol challenge with sons of alcoholics: A critical review and analysis. *Psychological Bulletin, 108*(3), 383–402.

Pickens, R., Svikis, D., McGue, M., Lykken, D., Hesten,L., & Clayton, P. (1991). Heterogeneity in the inheritance of alcoholism. *Archives of General Psychiatry, 48*(1), 19–28.

Phillips, T., & Dudek, B. (1991). Locomotor activity responses to ethanol in selectively bred long- and short-sleep mice; two in-bred mouse strains, and their F1 hybrids. *Alcohol Clinical and Experimental Research, 15*(2), 255–261.

Ringwalt, C., & Palmer, J. (1990). Differences between white and black youth who drink heavily. *Addictive Behavior, 15*, 455–460.

Room, R., Greenfield, T., & Weisner, C. (in press). People who might have liked you to drink less: Changing responses to drinking by U.S. family members and friends, 1979–1990. *Contemporary Drug Problems.*

Sher, K. (1987). Stress response dampening. In H. Blane & K. Leonard (Eds.), *Psychological theories of drinking and alcoholism.* New York: Guilford Press.

Sher, K., Walitzer, K., Wood, P., & Brent, E. (1991). Characteristics of children of alcoholics: Putative risk factors, substance use and abuse, and psychopathology. *Journal of Abnormal Psychology, 100*(4), 427–448.

Stacy, A., Widaman, K., & Marlatt, G. (1990). Expectancy models of alcohol use. *Journal of Personal and Social Psychology, 58*(5), 918–928.

Substance Abuse and Mental Health Services Administration (Center for Substance Abuse Treatment). (1994). Causes of addiction and modalities for treatment. In *Treatment for alcohol and other drug abuse: Opportunities for coordination.* DHHS Publication No. (SMA) 94-2075. Rockville, MD: Substance Abuse and Mental Health Services Administration.

U.S. Department of Health and Human Services. (1992). *Cultural competence for evaluators: A guide for alcohol and other drug abuse prevention practitioners working with ethnic/racial communities.* DHHS Publication No. (ADM) 92-1884. Rockville, MD: Office for Substance Abuse Prevention.

U.S. Department of Health and Human Services. (1994). *The registered nurse population: Findings from the national sample survey of registered nurses, March 1992.* Washington, D.C.: U.S. Government Printing Office.

Vaillant, G. (1983). *The Natural history of alcoholism.* Cambridge, MA: Harvard Press.

Walker, L., & Avant, K. (1983). *Strategies for theory construction in nursing.* Norwalk, CT: Appleton-Century-Crofts.

Westermeyer, J. (1987). Cultural patterns of drug and alcohol use: An analysis of host and agent in the cultural environment. *Bulletin on Narcotics, 38*(2), 11–27.

Wise, R. (1980). Action of drugs of abuse on brain reward systems. *Pharmacol Biochem Behav, 13*(Suppl. 1), 213–223.

Wise, R. (1987). The role of reward pathways in the development of drug dependence. *Pharmacological Therapy, 35*(1–2), 227–263.

Wise, R., & Bozarth, M. (1987). A psychomotor stimulant theory of addiction. *Psychological Review 94*(4), 469–492.

Standards of Care for Services to Addicted Clients

Patricia A. Staten, MSA, RN

INTRODUCTION

In the beginning, there was someone who needed care to heal. Then, there were clinicians, hospitals, health care systems, and now, health care organizations. The first organized attempt at providing care to help people heal from addiction was when the federal government established narcotic treatment programs in the 1930s. These programs were for addicts who were in prison and they were intended to be more of a prison than a treatment center. Needless to say, quality was not high on the priority list.

Because the addicted clientele was viewed negatively and judgmentally by both the medical community and society, the quality was still not an expectation, although more programs were developed. However, over the years with increased education and recognition of the fact that addiction crosses all socioeconomic levels, quality in treating addicted clients has become a societal imperative.

Many consumers, hospitals, health care systems, and organizations are demanding the presence of and providing for evaluation of quality care. An organization developed and committed to this goal is the Joint Commission on Accreditation of Healthcare Organizations (JCAHO). The purpose of this chapter is to discuss this organization's involvement with hospitals, individual practices, health management organizations (HMOs), preferred provider organizations (PPOs), and others in ensuring quality treatment for addicted clients.

The Joint Commission on Accreditation of Healthcare Organizations exists to improve the quality of health care provided to the public. For more than four decades the Joint Commission—working with health care professionals and the public—has developed state-of-the-art standards and evaluated compliance of health care organizations with those standards.

In 1987, the Joint Commission launched its "Agenda for Change." Its broad objective was to create a more meaningful accreditation process. The three major initiatives involved were reformulating the Joint Commission standards, redesigning the survey process, and developing a national data base of performance measures.

RECASTING THE STANDARDS

The new Joint Commission standards focus on the performance of those activities that are most important to patient outcomes. This transition from capability-focused standards—addressing polices and procedures, equipment, staffing—to performance-focused standards emphasizes both outcomes and the performance of processes used to achieve them.

Areas addressed by the new standards include patient care functions (e.g., patient assessment, patient education, continuum of care) and organizational functions (e.g., leadership, human resources management, information management). These new standards are intended to make the accreditation process a more powerful catalyst for continuous improvement. To this end, the standards are flexible enough to provide each organization with the opportunity to be innovative in making those improvements within the context of its patients' needs and the organization's resources.

The reformulation of standards was partially introduced for hospitals in the 1994 *Accreditation Manual for Hospitals (AMH)*. Since that time it has been completed for hospitals, home care, mental health, substance abuse/addictions, and mental retardation/developmental disabilities organizations for use in surveys conducted after January 1, 1995. In 1996, the standards for ambulatory, long-term care organizations, and pathology and clinical laboratories will be similarly revised.

A SURVEY PROCESS EMPHASIZING PERFORMANCE OF PROCESSES

Patient outcomes and patient satisfaction are the result not only of what nurses and other health professionals do, but also, how well they do it as a team. This underscores the importance of working as collegial interdisciplinary teams. This is also the result of the health care organization's systems and processes (such as how it manages clinical information).

For this reason, the redesigned survey process, implemented in hospitals in January 1994, together with the new standards, focuses more on the performance of important patient care and organizational functions throughout the organization, and less on the department/service structure or individual clinical disciplines. Surveyors spend time in patient care areas talking with both staff and patients to determine how well the organization performs the patient care and organizational functions.

Rather than conducting three different discipline-specific surveys, the three members of the typical hospital survey team (physician, nurse, and administrator) each survey the performance of all the important functions throughout the organization. Then they integrate their findings to provide a balanced evaluation of how well the organization as a whole performs in providing patient care.

This new process increases contact between the surveyors and the staff throughout the organization to enhance the educational and consultative value of the survey—an enhancement widely attested to by those who have experienced a hospital survey since January 1994. It is important to note that the process has been improved based on what organizations have said that they wanted changed to make the survey experience better and more helpful in improving their performance.

THE IMSYSTEM: IMPROVING PATIENT OUTCOMES

The evaluation of alcohol and other drug interventions and treatment programs is vital. Accountability is a critical area of substance abuse/addictions treatment. Both the health care providers and the clients must be held accountable for how they conduct themselves and the results of their efforts. Program evaluation helps determine whether a particular agency is performing the intended services, and how effective it is in achieving goals. To evaluate the programs, outcomes are examined to measure their performance—to determine whether interventions and treatment services are provided as they say, and if they are consistent with currently acceptable addiction services standards (SAMHSA, 1994). Ultimately, program evaluation improves client outcomes; and the Joint Commission's purpose for existence is to provide mechanisms in support of improved client outcomes. Therefore, health care providers can benefit from having their programs in line with JCAHO standards.

In 1987, The Joint Commission began developing performance measures (indicators), including outcomes measures. It became evident that using *both* standards and performance measures would provide a more useful evaluation of an organization than by using either one alone. While outcome measures (when appropriately risk adjusted) show what an organization *has* accomplished, compliance with up-to-date standards increases the likelihood that good outcomes will continue to be achieved in the *future* and even improved.

The Indicator Measurement System (IMSystem) is a reference data base of performance measures designed by the Joint Commission to measure organizational performance using *nationally* uniform measures.

Initiated in 1994 for hospitals, the IMSystem will eventually include performance measures for all types of provider organizations. Implemented 1995, the IMSystem for hospitals includes 25 indicators implemented in 1994 (five for obstetrical care, five for perioperative care) and 15 new indicators for cardiovascular, oncology, and trauma care. Testing of medication use and infection control indicators have been completed, and indicators focused on home infusion therapy, care of depressive disorders, and health care network performance are under development.

The IMSystem was developed as part of a modern and credible accreditation process that incorporates patient outcomes and other performance data, as well as measures of standards compliance. Therefore, although current participation in the IMSystem is voluntary, it will eventually become an integral part of the accreditation process, probably between 1997 and 1998.

OTHER KEY INITIATIVES

Together with the aforementioned, 1994 signaled the rollout of two other important Joint Commission initiatives: public disclosure and network accreditation.

Public Disclosure

Increasingly, consumers and payors of health care are demanding useful, accurate, and current performance information about health care organizations, and the need for useful data will only increase. In 1994, in response to these needs, the Joint Commission began an initiative to make specific information available to the public about the performance of individual organizations seeking accreditation.

These performance reports provide accurate and reliable information about accredited hospitals, home care agencies, long-term care organizations, mental health, substance abuse/addictions, and mental retardation/developmental disabilities facilities, ambulatory care centers, and health care networks. This organization-specific information will be released only for those organizations surveyed after January 1, 1994.

Network Accreditation

Emerging health care networks, made up of integrated components such as hospitals, mental health organizations, nursing homes, and practitioner offices, are poised to play a key role in the American health care system of the future. The Joint Commission's new "Health Care Network Accreditation Program" is designed to help networks improve care, demonstrate their commitment to quality, and control costs.

All networks and health plans including HMOs, PPOs, physician health organizations (PHOs), individual practice associations (IPAs), and vertically integrated networks, which offer integrated services (whether comprehensive or specialty, such as mental health) to a defined population, are eligible for accreditation. Standards for networks focus on key functions such as: 1) preventive care; 2) the continuum of care; 3) the credentialing of health care practitioners; 4) the rights of members; 5) the procedures in place for measuring and improving the quality of care provided by the network to its member; and 6) education and communication, network leadership, and management of information.

Network surveys focus on the network's effectiveness in meeting these standards; the coordination and integration of services across components; the performance of components; and the network's relationship to practitioner offices. This focus is in line with the position of the U.S. Substance Abuse and Mental Health Services Administration (SAMHSA) Center for Substance Abuse Treatment (CSAT) (1993), which because of the chronic, relapsing nature of alcohol, other drug and mental health disorders, often a lifetime of interventions is necessary. Therefore, continuity of care and coordination of services for these clients are essential. The Joint Commission standards for networks would assure that CSAT's standard of coordination—the degree to which collaboration and exchange exists among an aggregate of service providers, so that services for addicted clients is delivered in a meaningful, appropriate sequence—takes place.

THE JOINT COMMISSION'S COMMITMENT TO QUALITY

Accreditation began in 1912 as an attempt by physicians to set standards that they believed would improve care. The structure and function of the Joint Commission continues to be based on the assumption that health care professionals have both the desire and professional obligation to provide high quality care to their patients.

The Joint Commission's five major initiatives—performance-based standards, new survey process, IMSystem, public disclosure, and health care network accreditation—all shift the emphasis of the accredited health care organizations' approach to quality management from traditional quality assurance to the continuous improvement of performance. This has meant a shift away from a problem-oriented, individual-blaming approach to one that encompasses the core principles of continuous quality improvement.

Most of us would agree that the vast majority of health care professionals are dedicated to providing quality care—and to improving its quality. However, most individual-focused quality assurance (QA) methods have been inefficient (often requiring hours of chart review by QA professionals) and relatively ineffective (yielding little information that really helped improve care for most patients).

The Joint Commission and others now recognize that most improvements in patient outcomes will result from increasing the effectiveness and efficiency of the performance of important clinical and organizational functions and processes. Organizations must turn their attention to those functions that are complex, interdependent, and involve the coordination and collaboration of many health care professionals and other staff throughout the organization.

STANDARDS OF CARE FOR SERVICES TO ADDICTED CLIENTS

Previously, the 1993 *Mental Health Manual (MHM)*[1] included a chapter titled "Alcoholism and Other Drug-Dependence Services." In the 1995 *MHM* these standards have been folded into two sections: patient-focused functions (Assessment of Patients; Patient Rights and Organizational Ethics; Care of Patients; and Continuum of Care) and organizational functions (Management of Human Resources).

Standards Related to Care of Client

One of the most important skills that is needed by a nurse or any other health care professional caring for an addicted client is the ability to assess accurately the client's state of being on physical, mental and spiritual levels.

When the patient enters the setting or service, information is gathered to identify the reason or reasons that brought the person into the organization. The information gathered at the first patient contact can indicate the need for more data regarding the patient's physical, psychological (including cognitive and communicative skills or development), or social status. The need for such further assessment is determined, at least, by the treatment the individual is seeking, his or her condition, and his or her consent to treatment.

Joint Commission's 1995 *Accreditation Manual for Hospitals (AMH)*[2] and *Accreditation Manual for Mental Health, Chemical Dependency, and Mental Retardation/Developmental Disabilities Services (MHM)* section entitled, "Assessment of Patients," provides expectations for a proper assessment. The care provided to any patient results from a determination of that patient's needs. This determination is based on a timely and accurate assessment of the patient's relevant physical, psychological, and social status. To determine the proper type of care a patient should receive, the following processes must be performed:

1. Data must be collected to assess the patient's needs.
2. These data must be analyzed to create the information necessary to decide the approach to meet care needs.
3. Decisions must be made regarding patient care based on analysis of information.
4. An initial screening process may be done at the point of admission as part of the overall assessment process.

Each individual can be screened for any mental and/or physical health problems that indicate the need for supervision or intervention. This screening then serves as the basis for the initial treatment plan.

The care provided to each individual is based on a determination of the individual's needs. This determination is based on an assessment of the individual's relevant physical and psychological needs and social functioning, as appropriate to the setting and circumstances. The assessment includes the collection and analysis of data about the individual to determine the need for any additional data, his or her care needs, and the care to be provided.

Under "Additional Requirements for Specific Patient Populations," PE.1.18 states, "The assessment and/or reassessment of patients receiving treatment for alcoholism or other drug dependencies specifically includes:

PE.1.18.1.   a history of the use of alcohol and other drugs, including age of onset, duration, patterns, and consequences of use;

PE.1.18.2.   the history of physical problems associated with dependence;

PE.1.18.3.   use of alcohol and other drugs by family members;

PE.1.18.4.   the spiritual orientation of the patient;

PE.1.18.5.   types of previous treatment and responses to that treatment;

PE.1.18.6.   any history of physical abuse; and the patient's sexual history, including sexual abuse (either as the abuser or the abused) and orientation."

Some areas of assessment are unique to those patients receiving treatment for alcohol and other drug dependencies. These same areas are appropriate for review in the reassessment process. Although the setting may vary (e.g., inpatient, outpatient, community health center, private practitioner office, HMO), the scope of assessment depends on the consistent inclusion of the areas addressed in PE.1.18.1. through PE.1.18.6.

This ongoing review process throughout the patient's contact with the organization is triggered at key decision points as well as at intervals between assessments. It is defined in hospital policy for both inpatient and outpatient populations served by the organization. Reassessment of the patient receiving treatment for alcoholism or other drug dependence considers the impact of life changes on the patient's treatment.

In addition to the assessment information documented in the patient's medical record by medical personnel, there may be numerous other discipline-specific assessments performed for each individual. The data gathered, the analyses of these data, and the subsequent integration of information about the individual are consolidated to facilitate identifying and prioritizing the individual's needs and determining the course of his or her care and considered treatment.

Standards Related to Health Care Provider Competence

In the "Management of Human Resource" chapter, specific standards reference the competency of the caregivers. The essential processes required to carry out this function include:

1. Planning by the organization's leaders that defines the qualifications, competencies, and staffing needed to carry out the mission of the organization
2. Providing competent staff members either through traditional employer–employee arrangements or the negotiation of contractual arrangements with other entities
3. Developing and implementing processes designed to ensure that the competence of all staff members are assessed, maintained, and improved, and demonstrated throughout their association with the organization
4. Providing a work environment that promotes self-development and learning

An overview of the specific focus of the standards follows:

HR.2   Processes are designed to ensure that competence of all staff members is assessed, maintained, demonstrated, and improved on a continuing basis.
    HR.2.1 The organization has established methods and practices that encourage self-development and learning for all staff.
HR.3   The organization assesses each individual's ability to achieve job expectations as stated in their job description.

HR.4   The organization has established policies and mechanisms that address any request by a staff member not to participate in an aspect of patient care, including treatment. These policies and mechanisms address:

HR.4.1   Which specific aspects of patient care or treatment are included in those situations where there is perceived conflict with the staff member's cultural values or religious beliefs; and

HR.4.2   How the organization will ensure that a patient's care, including treatment, will not be negatively affected if the request is granted.

Meeting patient care needs is an organization's priority. Therefore, the impact of a caregiver's personal cultural values, ethics, and beliefs on the care provided must be understood so the organization can establish mechanisms designed to ensure that an individual staff member's refusal to participate in an aspect of care will not negatively affect the patient's care and that there is an alternative method or methods of care delivery in such a situation.

It is critical to the success of any patient's treatment plan that nurses and other staff members do not judge a patient's beliefs or lifestyle, or impose their personal values on that patient. Addicted clients may have related problems (e.g., being HIV positive, homelessness, indigent) and if a nurse or staff member finds that his or her personal beliefs or values are in direct conflict with that client, then it is in the patient's best interest to reassign the nurse or staff member whenever possible.

HR.5.1–   Those responsible for developing treatment planning services have been
HR.5.1.1.   determined to be competent by reason of education, training, experience, and performance as demonstrated through quality measurement and improvement activities. It is essential that those responsible for developing the summary and treatment plan have demonstrated competence in obtaining and interpreting information pertaining to dependence including the ability to:

1. Obtain information about and assess:
   a. The relationship of the physical status of the patient to the dependence
   b. The relationship of the psychiatric/psychological status of the patient to the dependence
   c. The nature of the patient's emotional compulsion to use alcohol and/or other drugs
   d. The intensity of the patient's mental preoccupation with using alcohol and/or other drugs
2. Interpret information pertaining to an individual's use of alcohol and/or other drugs and develop a summary based on an established and recognized diagnostic system
3. Develop treatment plans based on the problems and needs of the patients.

In addition, these persons should have:

HR.5.1.2.   Knowledge of the natural history of alcohol and other drug dependence
HR.5.1.3.   Understanding of the biological and sociocultural dimensions influencing the dependence
HR.5.1.4.   General understanding of the range of treatment needed by alcohol and other drug-dependent clients
HR.5.1.5.   Knowledge of available treatment resources and their appropriate use

The performance of any staff member is the result of that person's competence and the nature of the work setting. In addition to assessing staff competence, the organization is responsible for creating a work environment that helps staff discover what they need to learn and assists them, as appropriate, in acquiring new knowledge and skills. Regular feedback from staff helps the organization manage its effort to create this kind of work environment.

HOW THESE STANDARDS RELATE TO CARE PROVIDED BY NURSES INTERVENING WITH ADDICTED PERSONS IN ALL SETTINGS

An addicted client can enter the health care arena at many different points and for many different reasons, requiring consistent, competent care and timely assessment of his or her needs. Therefore, it is important for nurses and other health care professionals throughout health care organizations, systems, or networks, to understand what is essential, as well as the acceptable standard of care for an addicted client.

Care decisions are based on individual needs identified through analyzing assessment data. Whether or not appropriate professional interventions are performed on an addicted client, provides data about the health care provider's: 1) demonstrated knowledge of the natural history of alcoholism and substance abuse and associated disorders; 2) ability to interpret information in terms of the addictive process; and 3) a degree of responsibility to the substance abusing/addicted client as reflected in the treatment design.

On a different but related note, lengths of stay in most treatment settings have decreased so much that it is virtually impossible to address an addicted client's problems at one sitting, during one short stay, or within one level. Care must be ongoing. Tapping into outside resources such as family-help and self-help groups and referrals to other types of care delivery along a continuum must be explored and begun immediately.

A new chapter in the 1995 *AMH*,[3] entitled, "Continuum of Care," and the *MHM*, entitled "Continuum" demands a health care organization's leaders to consider the needs of the populations served, available resources, strategies, and settings for delivery of services when making care available to those who need it. It is also necessary to provide the care in a continuous manner and use care settings appropriate to patient needs.

The Joint Commission, along with countless health care organizations, has embraced the concept of a continuum of care matching the patient's needs with the appropriate level and type of medical, health, or social service. For addicted clients who, as a defined patient population, have a high percentage of return visits when treated only on an inpatient setting, there is a much greater potential for success when using a wide range of services appropriately tailored to their continuing needs.

Organizations must look keenly at their patient population and collect valid data to determine what types of services should be provided throughout the continuum. The ultimate question to be asked is, "Will these services meet the needs of both the patient and our organization?"

CONCLUSION

Working with addicted clients is a complex process that demands a breadth of skills for all health care providers. And it is essential that all health care providers be competent in addressing the biopsychosocial components of a client's addictive process within acceptable guidelines and standards.

The acceptable standard of care delivered to addicted clients as outlined by the U.S. Center for Substance Abuse Treatment includes among other items: preventive care, assessment, interventions, liaison (coordination) of services, and appropriately trained and qualified staff (SAMHSA, 1994). The acceptable standard of care for addicted clients as outlined by the Joint Commission is inclusive of these activities as well.

The Joint Commission can provide: 1) standards and guidelines for caring for addicted clients that are in sync with those of the U.S. Center for Substance Abuse Treatment; 2) measures for evaluation of performance as well as outcome indicators—according to standards for care of addicted clients; 3) reports to consumers, payors, and policymakers that substantiate the effectiveness of interventions and treatment of organizations, systems, and agencies intervening with and treating these clients; and 4) leverage among network providers for ensuring that addicted clients receive comprehensive, nonfragmented care. However, overall, it provides to anyone of us who might become addicted or have significant others who are addicted, the assurance that quality of care is possible as well as expected when taking the step to seek help.

ENDNOTES

[1]These standards are quoted from the Joint Commission's *Accreditation Manual for Mental Health, Chemical Dependency, and Mental Retardation/Developmental Disabilities Services (MHM); Vol. I. Standards,* 1995 edition, and are presented with the permission of the Joint Commission. The companion document, *HHM; Vol. II. Scoring Guidelines,* provides additional information about these standards, the underlying principles and intent of these standards, examples of how to comply with the standards, and scoring scales to be used in organizational self-assessment activities.

[2]These standards were quoted from the Joint Commission's *Accreditation Manual for Hospitals (AMH); Vol. I. Standards,* 1995 edition, and are presented with the permission of the Joint Commission. The companion document, *AMH; Vol. II. Scoring Guidelines,* provides additional information about these standards, the underlying principles and intent of the standards, example of how to comply with the standards, and scoring scales to be used in organizational self-assessment activities.

[3]These standards were quoted from the Joint Commission's *Accreditation Manual for Mental Health, Chemical Dependency and Mental Retardation/Developmental Disabilities Services (MHM); Vol. I. Standards,* 1995 edition, and are presented with the permission of the Joint Commission. The companion document, *AMH; Vol. II. Scoring Guidelines,* provides additional information about these standards, and scoring scales to be used in organizational self-assessment activities.

REFERENCES

Joint Commission on Accreditation of Healthcare Organizations. (1995). *Accreditation Manual for Hospitals (AMH); Vol. I. Standards.* Oakbrook Terrace, IL: Joint Commission on Accreditation of Healthcare Organizations.

Joint Commission on Accreditation of Healthcare Organizations. (1995). *Accreditation Manual for Hospitals (AMH); Vol. II. Standards.* Oakbrook Terrace, IL: Joint Commission on Accreditation of Healthcare Organizations.

Joint Commission on Accreditation of Healthcare Organizations. (1993). *Mental Health Manual for Mental Health, Chemical Dependency, and Mental Retardation/Developmental Disabilities Services.* Oakbrook Terrace, IL: Joint Commission on Accreditation of Healthcare Organizations.

Joint Commission on Accreditation of Healthcare Organizations. (1993). *Mental Health Accreditation Manual (MHM), Vol. II Standards.* Oakbrook Terrace, IL: Joint Commission on Accreditation of Healthcare Organizations.

Joint Commission on Accreditation of Healthcare Organizations. (1992). *Patient Records in Addiction Treatment.* Oakbrook Terrace, IL: Joint Commission on Accreditation of Healthcare Organizations.

Substance Abuse and Mental Health Services Administration (Center for Substance Abuse Treatment). (1993). *Coordination of alcohol, drug abuse, and mental health services.* DHHS Publication No. (SMA) 93-1742. Rockville, MD: Substance Abuse and Mental Health Services Administration.

Substance Abuse and Mental Health Services Administration (Center for Substance Abuse Treatment). (1994). *Treatment for alcohol and other drug abuse: Opportunities for coordination.* DHHS Publication No. (SMA) 94-2075. Rockville, MD: Substance Abuse and Mental Health Services Administration.

RECOGNIZING ADDICTIONS IN NURSING PRACTICE

INTRODUCTION: RESPONDING TO OPPORTUNITIES

In ambulatory care settings, it is estimated that at least 20% of persons seen have alcohol and other drug problems (Searight, 1992). According to Barnes (1995), addicted clients seen in a primary care setting include: 1) clients whose addiction problems have not yet been identified; 2) those clients whose drug and alcohol problems do not require specialized addictions care; 3) clients who have significant problems with addiction but are unwilling to seek specialized addictions treatment; and 4) addicted clients whose other medical problems—whether an acute illness or chronic condition—seem more pressing.

Opportunities in the community in which alcohol and other drug addiction exist and can be easily recognized by nurses include: 1) schools; 2) workplace settings; 3) parishes (or church settings); 4) public health departments/community health centers; 5) community mental health centers; 6) correctional settings (detention, jails, prisons); 7) health care involving the homeless; 8) domestic violence shelters or settings; 9) rural health care; and 10) wellness centers. Many opportunities exist and arise in the general medical and community health settings that require the use of knowledge and skills specific to working with addicted clients.

Health care practitioners in these areas often fail to recognize, assess, and intervene appropriately with alcohol and other drug-addicted clients. This may be due to a variety of reasons, including uncertainty about what to do if and when they do identify someone; feelings of helplessness regarding how to help the person change their lifestyle; a belief that interventions or treatment is futile; having negative attitudes about addicted persons; a misconception that the person has to be motivated for treatment before intervention is effective; inability to address denial, manipulation, hostility, and drug-seeking behavior; and nursing's response or lack of response to the existing problem, in education and practice.

It is not necessary to present extensive statistics to substantiate that alcohol and other drug addictions are prevalent in all arenas within which nurses practice today. The magnitude of this health problem is evident. The important issues are whether or not the profession 1) realizes the opportunities that exist in providing care for these clients, and 2) is responding as necessary, by educating nurses on this important health problem. Although some schools of nursing have begun including addictions content in their curriculum, it must be a requirement at *all* schools of nursing in order to meet the challenge of dealing with alcohol and other drug addiction problems, and thereby effectively treat a prominent health care need of the 21st century.

Hospital emergency rooms and trauma settings are being flooded with opportunities to care for addicted clients. In addition, medical units have a large number of clients for whom they provide care with illnesses resulting from or as a complication of the addiction. With care moving into the community, the same situation exists there for the health care provider. The groups of clients that seem to be the most vulnerable to addiction and its consequences are addicted pregnant women and children and clients with dual problems of psychiatric and alcohol and other drug addiction problems.

When addiction complicates the situations of pregnancy and mental illness, the results have ramifications for society at large. Therefore, much support is provided for these persons, evidenced by the fact that financing continues to pour into states from the federal government for provision of services to pregnant addicted women; and private payors of coverage for health care continue to readily pay for care provided to clients with psychiatric illnesses. As a result, many opportunities exist for nurses to assist these clients with their problem.

The following section provides an in-depth look at the magnitude of the problem, opportunities, and components of care for pregnant addicted women as well as the dual diagnosed person faced with a mental illness and an addiction.

REFERENCES

Barnes, H. (1995). Listening for stories: Addiction psychotherapy, and primary care. *Substance Abuse, 16*(1), 31–38.

Searight, H. (1992). Screening for alcohol abuse in primary care: Current and research needs. *Family Practice Research Journal, 12*, 193–204.

Maternal–Child Nursing

Shirley D. Coletti
Pamela L. Donaldson*, RNC, MS, ARNP, CARN

INTRODUCTION

Maternal–child nursing has drastically changed over the years. Health care economics as well as demographic trends, technology, and women's preferences have had an impact on what responsibilities nurses in general, and advanced practice nurses in particular, are asked to assume. Challenges in maternal–child nursing include populations with special needs such as pregnant women, infants and children, adolescents, and HIV-infected mothers and children. When these families are afflicted by the effects of perinatal addictions, the results are often tragic. In recent years families affected by the complex issue of perinatal substance abuse have received varying degrees of society's attention, primarily due to actual and projected costs to society. This chapter will 1) explore opportunities for maternal–child nurses of the 21st century to assist those affected by perinatal addictions; 2) discuss the magnitude of perinatal addictions; and 3) discuss nursing's response to the problem of perinatal addictions.

OPPORTUNITIES FOR MATERNAL–CHILD NURSING WITH ADDICTED CLIENTS

Demographic Trends and Age Distribution

Klerman (1994) predicts major changes in maternal–child health care in response to demographic trends, pressures to reduce health care costs, and improve access, biomedical research, and women's preferences. By the year 2007, births in the United States should exceed 4 million and continue to increase to 5 million by 2050 (U.S. Bureau of the Census, 1992).

There are no current projections regarding future substance-exposed births. Recent estimates appear to range from 0.4% to 27% with an overall prevalence of 11.9% (Chasnoff, 1989; Gomby & Shiono, 1991). While the type of drug use may vary, there is little doubt that perinatal addictions will continue to be a problem into the next century.

The childbearing age of women greatly affects the birth rate as well. In recent years, partly due to personal preference and medical technology, women have delayed the start of their

---

*Daughter of Shirley Coletti

family, therefore, childbearing may not begin until the age of 30, 40, or even later. Conversely, data from 1985 indicates a rate of 71.1 pregnancies per 1000 girls aged 15 to 17 (U.S. Department of Health and Human Services, 1991).

As the range of active childbearing years broadens, so will the likelihood that nurses will meet women with addiction problems that affect not only her life, but her family's as well.

Factors Impacting Maternal–Child Nursing

An increasing number of births in the United States have greatly influenced maternal–child nursing. The demand for obstetricians, family practitioners, certified nurse midwives, and alternative birthing centers remain high due to the increasing population. Although federal funding has become available for the education of more family practice physicians as opposed to specialists, there will continue to be a shortage of health care providers especially in rural areas. Maternal–child nurse practitioners as well as nurse midwives will be asked to serve these underserved areas.

Another impacting factor is the recognition and acknowledgment of a woman's preference. Today's woman is more involved in the management of her pregnancy with regard to the setting and type of health care provider. Studies suggest nurse practitioners and nurse midwives are often preferred to their male counterparts due to the "female connection" as well as their ability to provide increased time, empathy, and gentleness with patients, expertise notwithstanding (Safriet, 1992; Hanson, Hodnicki, & Boyle, 1994).

Recognizing the trend of women's desire for more control, birthing rooms, which give an appearance of a "kinder and more gentle" birthing experience, are offered as alternatives to the traditional sterile delivery rooms. Birthing centers outside of hospitals also appear to be growing in popularity. These centers are often operated by nurse midwives who are trained specifically to empower and support women.

Health care reform also influences maternal–child nursing. As of publication date, no formal health care reform has been passed by Congress. However, there is a growing consensus that present day health care in the United States, while considered technologically the best in the world, is rapidly becoming unaffordable even for the "middle class." Therefore, it is expected that some type of health care reform is on the horizon. Some may view health care reform as already being here via managed care. Managed care is a gatekeeper approach to health care. Proponents believe managed care is the answer to improved access. However, critics believe overall quality of care will decline.

Due to future planning efforts such as Healthy People 2000 (U.S. Department of Health and Human Services, 1991), it is expected by many that preventive health care will become a major focus of health care reform. However, monies will need to accompany preventive health care to properly fund areas such as family planning, cancer screening, and well-baby care, just to name a few.

Perceived and actual barriers to access of prenatal health care influences maternal–child nursing. Factors such as transportation, child care, financial stress, insufficient time, and missed work are cited as examples (Johnson, Primas, & Coe, 1994). Declining rates in prenatal and postnatal attendance, in certain areas of the country, suggest that even when barriers have been eliminated there are still problems. Factors, such as cultural differences, locus of control, and fear of identification by the system, need to be researched as possible reasons for this drop in attendance. This is particularly true when women are perinatally addicted to drugs and alcohol. It is hypothesized that women fear detection by the authorities and do not want to lose their children. Nurses have great opportunities to educate families regarding benefits of prenatal care and well-baby care, as well as discuss dangers and risks of perinatal addiction.

Preventative Health Care

There are numerous areas of preventative health care that improve quality of life and lower health care costs. Preventative health care presents ongoing opportunities for nurses, particularly in the areas of family planning education, which includes preconceptual counseling and sexually transmitted disease prevention. Preconceptual counseling, which is supported by several perinatal groups, may become more available in the future because of the potential to reduce adverse pregnancy outcomes thus reducing medical care costs.

This type of counseling offers an excellent opportunity for maternal–child nurses to interact with women who are at high risk for becoming perinatally addicted and contracting the HIV virus. Components of preconception care include risk assessment, health promotion, and interventions.

Taking each of the three categories of risk assessment, health promotion, and interventions individually (as shown in Box 4-1), one can see how these guidelines could be used to intervene with women and children at risk. Furthermore, by offering interventions one does not just identify a potential problem, but provides solutions that can be implemented in a variety of settings.

Case Management

Case management and home visitation of perinatally addicted women and their families are seemingly the way of the future and offer an important means for nurses to truly support addicted women and their families. This type of health care has become more and more popular as the inpatient postdelivery time decreases from 2 to 4 days, to 12 to 24 hours. Due to this short time frame, it becomes even easier for addicted pregnant women to go undetected by hospital personnel.

This is evidenced by increased child abuse and neglect rates as well as increased incidence of children diagnosed with failure to thrive. The compilation of factors, such as undetected drug use prenatally and/or postnatally, shortened hospital postnatal stay, and reduction of attendance at postnatal appointments, sets up a potential life-threatening environment for the infant, one that seriously needs restructuring.

While preconceptual counseling and home visits are not total solutions, they will offer knowledge and support that troubled women need. In addition, case management is especially effective considering the fragmented and transient lives of many addicted women. Those who work in the field of perinatal addiction agree that these women tend to drift in and out of the system and that it is *not* uncommon for the same woman to have multiple substance-exposed infants.

With future emphasis and funding of preventative health care, nurses will find themselves more in the community and less in the hospital. Public health and community health nurses, as a result of their specific training, will greatly impact maternal–child health. Community outreach will become a primary avenue for nurses to offer health care to families in their own communities, thereby eliminating transportation barriers.

In summary, the area of maternal–child nursing with respect to perinatal addictions is greatly influenced by demographic trends, women's preferences, access to health care, and health care reform. The potential for nurses to meet a troubled pregnant or postpartum woman is increasing every day in a variety of settings. In communities, maternal–child

BOX 4-1. Components of Preconception Care

RISK ASSESSMENT

1. Individual and social conditions
2. Adverse health behaviors
3. Medical conditions
4. Psychological conditions
5. Environmental conditions
6. Barriers to family planning, prenatal care, and primary health care

HEALTH PROMOTION

1. Promotion of healthy behaviors
2. Social, financial, and vocational counseling
3. Family planning education
4. Identification of barriers to care and assistance

INTERVENTIONS

1. Treatment of medical conditions
2. Referral for treatment of adverse health behaviors (tobacco, alcohol, and illicit drug abuse)
3. Rubella and hepatitis immunization
4. Reduction of psychosocial risks (e.g., referral to spouse abuse shelters or assistance with housing)
5. Nutrition counseling
6. Home visitation
7. Family planning services
8. Case management services such as "Healthy Start" Coalitions in the state of Florida

Source: Jack, B.W. & Culpepper, L. (1990). Preconception care: Risk reduction and health promotion in preparation for pregnancy. *Journal of American Medical Association, 264*, 1147–1149.

nurses can serve perinatally addicted women by educating themselves regarding signs and symptoms of drug and other addictions, by becoming aware of referral sources to community addiction treatment programs, and by becoming aware of the benefits of preconceptual counseling to nonpregnant women.

Maternal–child nurses will care for women at risk for giving birth to one or more substance-exposed babies. Naturally, one would have wanted to prevent these occurrences, which adds to importance of early identification and treatment. As this is not always possible, it is extremely important to detect the woman whenever and wherever she presents herself in the health care system. Once identified, proper referrals, notification of social service, and follow-through with recommendations of drug treatment can commence. There are excellent protocols for the treatment of pregnant substance-using women and drug-exposed infants published by Center for Substance Abuse Treatment (1993a, 1993b). These publications are free and provide the most recent recommendations for management and treatment for women and infants addicted to drugs. Tables 4-1 and 4-2 provide a synopsis from this document in flowchart form, of how to manage these women if their point of entry into the health care system is drug treatment or if it is prenatal care. Readers are also referred to Redding and Selleck (1993) for strategies of assessing and managing perinatally addicted women and children. It is the experience of both authors that nurses can empower women not only by their knowledge but by their *real* and *nonjudgmental* concerns, which are key when working with perinatally addicted women.

The type of addiction may change, but it is unlikely that addictions will disappear in our lifetime. As perinatal addiction becomes even more complex due to increased incidence of heterosexual transmission of the HIV virus, it is imperative that nurses, regardless of their education or place of employment, remain informed on these issues of great importance.

MAGNITUDE OF THE PROBLEM

This section discusses the incidence and prevalence of alcohol, tobacco, and other drug addictions among clients cared for by nurses in the field of maternal–child nursing. Studies on women in the childbearing ages of 18 thorough 44, on fetal alcohol syndrome, on fetal alcohol effects, on cocaine, heroin, and tobacco effects on infants and children, as well as addictions afflicting adolescents are also reviewed in this section. Specific opportunities for nursing intervention are discussed. There is not adequate research to document true prevalence of the various addictions that afflict this population; however, the most recent findings of research will be offered.

Drug, Alcohol, and Tobacco Addictions

The May 13, 1994 issue of *Morbidity and Mortality Weekly Report* cited statistics from a recent Behavioral Risk Factor Surveillance System (BRFSS) survey on alcohol consumption among women of childbearing age. Of 26,615 women aged 18 to 44 years a total of 1067 women reported being pregnant at the time of the survey. Of these, 13.4% were light drinkers; 0.3% were heavy drinkers; 0.1% were moderate drinkers; and 1.3% were binge drinkers.   In addition, at the National Institute on Drug Abuse (NIDA) conference on Drug Addiction Research and the Health of Women held in Tyson's Corner, Virginia, in September 1994, the director of the Institute released the initial findings from the first nationally representative survey on the prevalence of drug abuse among women who gave birth in the United States (Leshner, 1994). These data, which are the findings from the National Pregnancy and Health Survey, represent actual estimates of both pregnant women who reported use of licit and illicit drugs during pregnancy and the number of infants born to them. Prior to this survey, true numbers of prevalence and incidence were speculative because of localized surveys and small studies.

According to the NIDA, the National Pregnancy and Health Survey is considered to reflect true incidence and prevalence of drug addiction in pregnant women. Data were collected from October 1992 through August 1993 from a national probability sample of 2613 women who delivered their babies in 52 metropolitan and nonmetropolitan area hospitals as well as federal hospitals. Estimates are based on self-reported use and include prenatal use of a number of illicit drugs, cigarettes, alcohol, and certain prescription medications. Drug use prevalence by type of drug, period of use, major race/ethnicity groups, age groups, and demographic variables, such as educational level and income were obtained.

TABLE 4-1   Pregnant, Substance-Abusing Women (Point of Entry: Drug Treatment)

Patients	Assessment ⟶ Detoxification and Treatment ⟶				

All Pregnant Substance-Using Women	Drug Use/Abuse
	• History
	  — Duration of use
	  — Past treatment
	  — Frequency of use
	  — Type of use
	  — Amount of use
	• Physical and laboratory work
	• Urine toxicology
	• Refer to prenatal care
		Alcohol
		• Setting
		  — Inpatient
		  — Under medical supervision
		
		▲ Monitor for S/S of AWS
		▲ Antabuse; contraindicated
		
		• Inpatient D/A treatment whenever possible
		• Outpatient D/A treatment with special focus on pregnancy issues and drug use
		• Urine toxicology monitoring
		• Encourage and monitor continued prenatal care
			Cocaine
			• Setting
			  — Inpatient most effective
			
			▲ Medication contraindicated except in cases of extreme agitation
			
			• Inpatient D/A treatment whenever possible
			• Outpatient D/A treatment if necessary, with emphasis on pregnancy and drugs
			• Random urine toxicology
			• Encourage and monitor continued prenatal care
				Opiates
				• Setting
				  — Outpatient or inpatient
				  — Dotox with methadone
				• Methadone maintenance with psychosocial counseling
				• Random urine toxicology
				• Clonidine detox not recommended
				• Encourage and monitor continued prenatal care
					Methadone
					• Detox from methadone not recommended
					• Random urine toxicology
					• Encourage and monitor continued prenatal care

	Psychosocial • Family history • Support system • Education • Employment • Abuse: physical, mental, sexual • Current crisis • Attitudes about pregnancy				
	Mental Health • Evaluation • Mental status • History of mental illness • Family history of mental illness • *DSM-III-R* diagnosis • Treatment recommendations				

Approximately 4 million women were estimated to have given birth in the United States in 1992 (the year of the study estimates). Preliminary results based on the probability sample indicated that an estimated 221,000 women (5.5%) used some illicit drug during pregnancy. The estimates show that at some time during pregnancy, 119,000 women (2.9%) reported use of marijuana and 45,000 women (1.1%) reported use of cocaine, the two most frequently used illicit drugs.

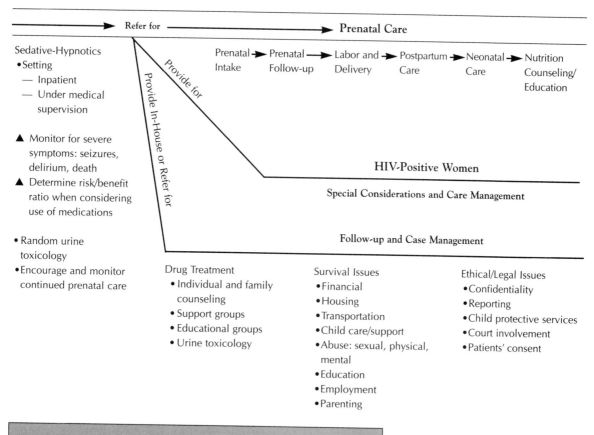

Refer for ——————————————————————→ Prenatal Care

Sedative-Hypnotics
• Setting
— Inpatient
— Under medical
supervision

▲ Monitor for severe
symptoms: seizures,
delirium, death
▲ Determine risk/benefit
ratio when considering
use of medications

• Random urine
toxicology
• Encourage and monitor
continued prenatal care

Provide for

Provide In-House or Refer for

Prenatal → Prenatal → Labor and → Postpartum → Neonatal → Nutrition
Intake   Follow-up   Delivery   Care   Care   Counseling/
                                                                                           Education

HIV-Positive Women

Special Considerations and Care Management

Follow-up and Case Management

Drug Treatment
• Individual and family
counseling
• Support groups
• Educational groups
• Urine toxicology

Survival Issues
• Financial
• Housing
• Transportation
• Child care/support
• Abuse: sexual, physical,
mental
• Education
• Employment
• Parenting

Ethical/Legal Issues
• Confidentiality
• Reporting
• Child protective services
• Court involvement
• Patients' consent

Legend	
▲	Medical caution
AWS	Alcohol withdrawal syndrome
D/A	Drug/alcohol
Substance-Abusing	Women at risk for problems because of their chemical dependency and use/abuse of drugs
Detox	Detoxification
S/S	Signs and symptoms

The survey also found that 757,000 women (18.8%) used alcohol and 820,000 women (20.4%) smoked cigarettes at some time during pregnancy. Thirty-two percent of those who reported use of one drug also smoked cigarettes and drank alcohol. Conversely, of those who reported no use of alcohol or cigarettes, only 0.2% used marijuana, and 0.1% used cocaine. Those who reported use of both alcohol and cigarettes, 20.4% also used marijuana, and 9.5% also used cocaine. Medical use and nonmedical use of any drugs including amphetamines,

TABLE 4-2 Pregnant, Substance-Abusing Women (Point of Entry: Prenatal Care)

Patients	Prenatal Intake →	Prenatal Follow-up →	Labor/Delivery With Prenatal Care →	Labor/Delivery With no Prenatal Care →	Postpartum →
All Pregnant Substance-Using* Women	• Complete health history • Psychosocial and drug use history • Physical examination • Family history • Health history of baby's father, if possible • Routine prenatal panel plus other laboratory tests, including urine toxicology • Tuberculin test and baseline sonogram ▲ Check for tracks, abscesses, poor general hygiene, poor dental hygiene • Refer to D/A treatment, social services, nutrition, counseling • Review sexual practices • Provide education regarding safer sex	• Identify medical and psychosocial problems • Provide health education opportunities • Random urine toxicology • Reinforce importance of D/A treatment • Reinforce importance of other service providers • Discuss reproductive options • Encourage involvement of father of baby or significant other • Reinforce importance of safer sex practices • Repeat laboratory tests as indicated	• Conduct complete history and physical • Query *recent* drug use • Repeat hepatitis B screen if previously negative • Urine toxicology ▲ Follow universal precautions ▲ Notify pediatric and social services	• Follow all guidelines in previous column, if possible, plus conducting — Sonogram — Complete baseline laboratory tests	• Encourage continued participation in D/A treatment • Encourage and educate about family planning • Permit breast feeding in methadone-maintained mothers • Review laboratory data, care plan, and education • Conduct postpartum physical • Encourage involvement of father of baby and of other family members (other children, significant other)
▲ Additions for HIV-Positive Women	• Refer to ID clinic for specific HIV medical treatment • Conduct extensive review of symptoms • Obtain CD$_4$ count	• Reinforce importance of attendance at ID clinic • Repeat CD$_4$ count in each trimester • Ensure special pediatric follow-up	• Provide special handling of cord, placenta, and neonate	• Follow previous guidelines	• Breast feeding contraindicated • Encourage continued participation with HIV specialist for medical follow-up for woman and infant • Educate woman regarding special needs of infant • Encourage and educate regarding family planning • Repeat CD$_4$ count

* Ensure special pediatric follow-up.

Neonatal →	Nutrition →	Refer for	Substance Abuse Treatment			

Neonatal →

- Obtain urine toxicology
- Monitor for effects of drugs on the infant
- Treat appropriately, depending on drug
- Review case with another and educate her regarding special care of infant
- Encourage involvement of father of baby or significant other
- Ensure special pediatric follow-up

Nutrition →

- Develop special care plans according to specific effects of each drug
  — Alcohol
  — Cigarettes
  — Marijuana
  — Heroin
  — Cocaine
  — Other
- Provide for
  — Prevention and intervention
  — Diet counseling
  — Multivitamin and mineral supplements

Provide In-House or Refer for / *Provide for*

Refer for

Assessment →
- Drug abuse
- Psychosocial
- Mental health

Detoxification →
- Alcohol
- Opiates
- Cocaine
- Methadone
- Sedatives/ hypnotics

Treatment →
- Methadone maintenance
- Inpatient
- Outpatient

Case Management
- Individual and family counseling
- Support groups
- Educational groups
- Urine toxicology

HIV-Positive Women

Special Considerations and Care Management

Aftercare Services

Social Services
- Housing
- Financial
- Transportation
- Children/support
- Parenting
- Education
- Employment

Mental Health
- Postpartum psychosis
- Abuse: physical, mental, sexual

Ethical/Legal Issues
- Confidentiality/ reporting issues
- Patients' consent
- Child protective issues
- Court involvement

Legend	
▲	Medical caution
D/A	Drug/alcohol
ID clinic	Infectious disease clinic
Substance-abusing	Women at risk for problems from their chemical dependency and use/abuse of drugs

sedatives, tranquilizers, and analgesics were reported as an overall estimate of 1.5% for non-medical use and 10.2% for medical use.

This research suggests that from a public health standpoint, more substance abuse during pregnancy stems from illicit drugs (5.5%) than nonmedical use of prescription drugs (1.5%). From a demographic standpoint, the survey found that in general, rates of any illicit drug use were higher in women who were not married, had less than 16 years of formal education, and relied on some public source of funding to pay for their hospital stay.

Another interesting finding was the type of drug use found among different ethnic groups. It was found that rates of cocaine use during pregnancy were higher among African-American women (4.5%) than for white women (0.4%) or Hispanic women (0.7%). Crack was the predominant form of cocaine used by African-American women, and accounted for the much higher rate of overall use of cocaine in this population. As for legal drugs, rates of alcohol use were highest among white women (22.7%) compared to African-American (5.8%) and Hispanic (8.7%) women. Whites had the highest rates of cigarette use as well, 24.4% compared with 19.8% for African-American and 5.8% for Hispanics.

Given the fact that there are clear ethnic distinctions in drug use patterns between African-Americans, whites, and Hispanics, it stands to reason other ethnicity's drug patterns differ. For example, it is unfortunate there are no national prevalence studies for ethnic/racial groups such as the Asian/Pacific Islander-American. This category comprises more than 60 separate ethnic/racial and subgroups. They are reportedly the fastest growing group identified by the U.S. Census Bureau, with 6.5 million, or 2.6% of the U.S. population (Kim, McLeod, & Shantiz, 1992). While no studies could be found addressing perinatal addiction within Asian/Pacific Islander-Americans, Trimble, Bolek, and Niemcryk (1992) do present current drug and alcohol research among American minorities including Asian Americans. Conditions of the perinatal period were identified as the sixth leading cause of death in Asian/Pacific Islander-American women in 1991 (National Center for Health Statistics, 1992).

There is a similar lack of nationally compiled statistics on drug and alcohol use among Native Americans. With the exception of fetal alcohol syndrome in the Native American population, no national surveys were found reporting drug and alcohol incidences of perinatally addicted Native American women. Streissguth (1990) reports that certain American Indian reservations have shown rates of fetal alcohol syndrome as high as 1 in 99 births and fetal alcohol effect at 1 in 49 births. Other research indicates an overall incidence rate of fetal alcohol syndrome in Southwest American Indians as 6.1 per 1000 with 25% of the mothers studied giving birth to more than one fetal alcohol-affected infant (Anderson & Novick, 1992).

Thus, the NIDA study, as well as the limited ethnic research, strongly suggests that drug use during pregnancy does appear to have cultural/ethnic differences with white women using more alcohol than African-Americans or Hispanics, and African-American women using more crack-cocaine. Caution, however, must be applied to these preliminary findings. For example, although there was an overall prevalence rate of illicit drug use during pregnancy of 5.5% in the NIDA study, there are smaller studies in which the rate has been documented as high as 31% (Khalsa & Gfroerer, 1991). Also, because it is known from abundant research studies that there are no absolutely *safe* drugs during pregnancy, it is important to think of any drug use during pregnancy as a risk versus benefit issue. Prescribed use of any medication during pregnancy carries risk. Thus, health providers who prescribe drugs are expected to determine whether it is worth the risk to obtain the benefit. In addition, even limited use of cigarettes or alcohol during pregnancy can be detrimental. Therefore, the authors believe it should be standard practice for health care providers to counsel women *not* to take any drugs, including alcohol or cigarettes without medical consent.

The fact that most drug users are not single-drug users but rather polydrug users offers another difficult challenge of determining synergistic effects as well as determining what drug causes what effect to the fetus. For a woman to give up all of her addictions (cigarettes, alcohol, and other drugs) simultaneously is very difficult. However, nurses must encourage pregnant women to do just that. It is interesting to note that federally funded treatment programs are now expected to offer smoking cessation treatment as part of their standard of care. In addition, there are prenatal stop smoking programs sponsored by the American Lung Association.

The effects of drug and alcohol use are totally preventable. However, early identification and treatment offer better outcomes to both mother and infant than if the problem is left undetected. Given that thousands of pregnant women are using licit/illicit, prescribed/nonprescribed drugs and alcohol, nurses must become aware of their increased probability of caring for women addicted and children exposed to illegal and legal substances.

Recent evidence suggests that the true picture of perinatal addiction is one of polysubstance use. However, most research continues to report the maternal and fetal effects of drugs and alcohol as though they were separate entities. The later studies on perinatal addictions address the fact that multiple attributable risk factors—including living environment, polysubstance use, as well as the woman's lifestyle—must be recognized. The polysubstance use factor as well as a mother's risky behavior lifestyle associated with drug and alcohol use are important to remember when reviewing the literature. Box 4-2 shows a compilation of complications and effects of maternal substance abuse based on research, as published by Center for Substance Abuse Treatment (1993a).

It should be noted that early research, particularly with cocaine-exposed infants, suggested long-term developmental and behavioral effects. More recent research has reported that developmental effects of prenatal drug exposure may be overcome by a fostering and nurturing postnatal environment (Mathias, 1992).

Since it has been documented women are more willing to change unhealthy behaviors during pregnancy, the perinatal period can be an ideal opportunity to promote healthy behaviors. The problem lies in the stigma attached to drug use during pregnancy as well as the perceived threat of criminal prosecution (Abma & Mott, 1991; Harrison, 1991; Smith, Dent, Coles, & Falek, 1992). However, as previously mentioned, studies such as those by Finnegan (1991) and Chang, Carroll, Behr, & Kosten (1992) indicate that mothers' and infants' health significantly improves with proper drug treatment and prenatal care.

Nurses must familiarize themselves with the effects of illicit drugs, alcohol, and tobacco on the mother as well as the fetus to properly educate women and their families. In addition, one can never have too many referral sources, particularly when budget cuts force nurses to act as the social worker, the counselor, and the care provider.

In spite of overwhelming evidence that purports that an addicted woman can be found in both private and public practice, there are those (including nurses) who still believe otherwise. A landmark study was conducted in Pinellas County, Florida, in 1990 in which Chasnoff, Landress, and Barrett (1990) sought the prevalence of illicit drug or alcohol use during pregnancy and discrepancies in mandatory reporting. Random urine drug screens were taken from five public health clinics and 12 private obstetrical offices in the county. Results indicated an overall positive result of 14.8%, with little difference in prevalence between public and private providers. African-American women had more frequent evidence of cocaine and white women had evidence of cannaboids (marijuana).

However, African-American women were reported to the authorities at a rate of 10 times more than white women. In addition, poor women were more likely than others to be reported.

This study had significant rebound effects regarding how health care providers view addicted women. Although the study pointed out distinct racial and economic biases in

MATERNAL COMPLICATIONS OF EXCESSIVE ALCOHOL CONSUMPTION

1. Nutritional deficiencies
2. Pancreatitis
3. Alcoholic ketoacidosis
4. Precipitate labor
5. Alcoholic hepatitis/cirrhosis
6. Deficient milk ejection

MATERNAL COMPLICATIONS OF OPIOID USE

1. Poor nourishment
2. Anemia
3. Medical complications from frequent use of dirty needles (abscesses, ulcers, thrombophlebitis, bacterial endocarditis, hepatitis)
4. Sexually transmitted diseases
5. Toxemia
6. Intrauterine growth retardation
7. Miscarriage
8. Premature rupture of membranes or premature labor

MATERNAL COMPLICATIONS OF COCAINE USE

1. Intrauterine growth retardation
2. Abruptio placentae
3. Premature labor
4. Spontaneous abortion

POSSIBLE FETAL/INFANT EFFECTS OF ALCOHOL EXPOSURE

FETAL ALCOHOL SYNDROME (FAS)

1. Prenatal/postnatal growth retardation
2. Central nervous system deficits, including developmental delay and neurological/intellectual impairments
3. Facial feature anomalies, including microcephaly

FETAL ALCOHOL EFFECTS (FAE)

1. Cardiac abnormalities
2. Neonatal irritability and hypotonia
3. Hyperactivity
4. Genitourinary abnormalities
5. Skeletal and muscular abnormalities
6. Ocular problems
7. Hemangiomas
8. No effect

BOX 4-2. (continued)

POSSIBLE FETAL/INFANT EFFECTS OF OPIOID EXPOSURE
1. Low birth weight
2. Prematurity
3. Neonatal abstinence syndrome
4. Stillbirth
5. Sudden infant death syndrome
6. No effect

POSSIBLE FETAL/INFANT EFFECTS OF COCAINE EXPOSURE
1. Increased congenital anomalies
2. Mild neurodysfunction
3. Transient electroencephalogram abnormalities
4. Cerebral infarction and seizures
5. Vascular disruption syndrome
6. Sudden infant death syndrome
7. Smaller head circumference
8. No effect

Adapted from U.S. Department of Health and Human Services. (1993a). Public Health Service; Substance Abuse and Mental Health Services Administration. Center for Substance Abuse Treatment, (CSAT). *Pregnant, Substance-Using Women; Treatment Improvement Protocol (TIP) Series.* (DHHS Publication No. SMA 93-1993). Rockville, MD: U.S. Department of Health and Human Services.

reporting of drug use, health care providers in general still see drug use as a poverty/African-American problem. Research such as Chasnoff et al.'s report otherwise. Studies by Mann, Battaglin, Cooper, and Mahan (1992), Schwarz (1993), Burke and Roth (1993), and Caulker-Burnett (1994) support Chasnoff's findings.

Bradley (1992) in her research reported that as many as 20% of patients seen in a primary care setting suffer from alcohol abuse and dependence. Tips on screening and diagnosis of alcoholism for family health care providers are offered. This is important because providers may encounter pregnant women in a primary care setting. Galanter, Egelko, DeLeon, Rohrs, and Franco (1992) emphasized the need to not only properly identify perinatally addicted women but also to assess the severity of addiction so that the proper treatment modality can be recommended.

Addictions Affecting Adolescents

Various addictions afflict the lives of adolescents. The Center for Substance Abuse Treatment (U.S. Department of Health and Human Services, 1993c, 1993d) offers excellent guidelines for screening, assessment, and treatment of alcohol and other drug-abusing adolescents. Standardized instruments are offered for screening and assessment. Once severity of addiction has been determined, guidelines are offered that suggest what type of treatment (e.g., intensive outpatient, day treatment, intensive inpatient, or residential) should be recommended.

An area interrelated to substance-abusing adolescents is that of pregnant adolescents. Both populations represent risk-taking and often intertwine. It has been reported that adolescents who smoke, use alcohol, or marijuana are more likely to be sexually active (American Society of Addiction Medicine, 1990). Huizinga, Loeber, and Thornberry (1993) reported results of a longitudinal study of delinquency, drug use, sexual activity, and pregnancy among children and youth in three cities. Most significant in this report of preliminary findings is the indication that high-risk behaviors "co-occur," suggesting a need for comprehensive intervention programs. In addition, there was a high rate of sexual activity and pregnancy, combined with alcohol and drug used, again suggesting a need to address this combination of behaviors.

Another national survey entitled "The National School-based 1991 Youth Risk Behavior Survey" (Kann, Warren, Collins, Ross, Collins, & Kolbe, 1993) asked 18,000 students, grades 9 through 12, about health risk behaviors related to unintentional and intentional injury; tobacco use; alcohol and other drug use; sexual behavior, dietary behavior, and physical activity. Results indicated that 70.1% had tried cigarette smoking and 27.5% were current smokers. Among all students, 81.6% had consumed alcohol and 50.8% did so during the past 30 days. Regarding sexual behaviors, 54.1% had participated in sexual intercourse and 81.8% had used a contraceptive method during their most recent sexual intercourse. Dietary intake was significantly high in fat content with physical activity decreasing with each grade level.

Findings from surveys such as these provide evidence that people establish risky behaviors at very early ages. One need only to look at "Joe Camel's" effect on youth smoking habits to know that the tobacco companies are well aware of what age to target billions of advertising dollars every year. The younger one becomes addicted to cigarettes the longer they will smoke.

Regarding tobacco, a report of the Surgeon General (U.S. Department of Health and Human Services, 1994) states that one in three adolescents in the United States uses tobacco by age 18. Not only do teens smoke tobacco but many start chewing or dipping tobacco as early as 10 years of age. The process of nicotine addiction ensures that many of today's adolescent tobacco users will continue use through adulthood.

The Center for Substance Abuse Prevention (CSAP) (formerly Office of Substance Abuse Prevention [OSAP]) is an excellent resource for learning about effective strategies for prevention of drugs and alcohol in adult and adolescent populations. Since that time, monographs offering prevention strategies have become available (U.S. Department of Health and Human Services, 1990). In addition, the National Clearinghouse for Alcohol and Drug Information (NCADI) offers many free publications. Strategies are offered that can be applied in everyone's community. Nurses must take responsibility for becoming "agents for change" in today's society. The more knowledge one has, the easier it is to become an effective change agent in your community.

In conclusion, it should be clear that infants, children, adolescents, and pregnant women in all walks of life may suffer from various addictions. With proper screening and assessment from nonjudgmental health care providers, families that are afflicted by addictions can receive needed treatment.

NURSING'S RESPONSE

Nurses are the largest group of health care professionals and they are usually the first points of contact for most people including addicted women and their children in clinics, health provider offices, hospitals, and community settings. As the recognition of perinatal addiction and its effects grows, so will the need for primary and secondary prevention efforts as well as access to treatment. It is apparent there is a deficiency in knowledge of addictive behaviors by entry level and advanced practice nurses. Hypotheses for this lack of knowledge include: stigmas attached to drug and alcohol addiction, scant addiction-focused curriculums in medical and nursing school, and lack of health promotion training.

While maternal–child nurses are not schooled to be experts in the field of addictions, it is still important to appreciate the value of addiction training in one's particular scope of practice. Since experts believe that there is great underreporting in the area of perinatal addiction, the ability to identify, treat, and refer is quite valuable. Nurses are trained to assess, counsel, teach, and effectively intervene in their particular area of practice. The added knowledge of perinatal addictions will allow the nurse to further enhance the role of health care provider.

Currently, there is a tremendous void in addiction education and training for nurses. However, there are gallant efforts underway.

Education Efforts

Sullivan and Handley (1993) cited numerous surveys indicating the amount of alcohol and drug abuse content in professional education. Studies consistently reported a minimal amount of content whether baccalaureate or master's degree nursing programs (less than five class hours). Associate degree programs had even less addiction content. The majority of psychiatric mental health nurse practitioner programs offer alcohol and drug abuse content. Some offer electives such as courses specifically dealing with drug and alcohol addiction across the life span (Dr. Ona Riggin, personal communication, October 1, 1994).

A major contribution toward faculty development and preparation for understanding drug and alcohol abuse was headed by the federal government in the late 1980s. Originally, intended for physicians, monies became available through federal grants to develop curriculum models for nurses (Redding, 1993). Currently, there are 11 schools of nursing who have received grants: Case Western Reserve University, Lehman College-CUNY, New York University, Ohio State University, University of Cincinnati, University of Connecticut, University of Illinois at Chicago, University of Kansas, University of South Florida, University of Texas at Houston, and University of Washington.

Master's programs with a major in addictions nursing are currently given at D'Youville College in Buffalo, New York, University of Maryland at Baltimore, and University of Texas in Houston. There may be other universities currently planning such a program. Information can be obtained through the American Nursing Association or the National League of Nursing. However, if one is not fortunate to have an addiction program nearby, information can be obtained from several sources that can be used to integrate addictions into the nursing curriculum. Sources include this book, attending conferences on addictions and nursing, or obtaining an addictions nurse expert as a consultant. Recent developments sponsored by the Center for Substance Abuse Prevention through the National Nurses Society on Addictions, are nationwide prevention training for nurses. These one-day training sessions focus on prevention of alcohol, tobacco, and other drug problems. Attitudes and values concerning cultural diversity are emphasized as well as learning local referral sources, networking, and coalition building (CSAP, 1994).

Research

Several outcomes besides needed education for nurses have emerged. There has been an increase in funded nursing research of that provides support for increased awareness and research-based knowledge and practice. Nurses in the substance abuse field have written outstanding articles offering specific intervention strategies and resources for maternal–child health addictions (Chisum, 1990; Janke, 1990; Kennard, 1990; Haller, 1991; Lindenberg & Keith, 1993; Redding & Selleck, 1993; Rassool, 1993; Sabella, 1993; Haack & Budetti, 1994) just to name a few. Selleck and Redding (1994) are currently conducting research to assess knowledge and attitudes of registered nurses toward perinatal substance abuse. Preliminary results indicate knowledge about perinatal abuse exposure, addiction, and its effects are limited. In addition, registered nurses tend to "hold punitive, negative attitudes toward the perinatal substance abuser." The preliminary data indicate stigmas still exist and knowledge deficits are present in the area of perinatal addictions. Therefore, it is extremely important to continue educating nurses, not only about drug and alcohol addictions, but also on compassion, understanding, and empathy. From personal experience, the authors for this chapter appreciate the value and success gained from treatment that is structured yet kind and nonjudgmental.

CONCLUSION

As Mayberry (1994) points out, nursing practice will continue to become more research-based, thus offering opportunities for nurses to conduct research in areas that are of personal interest. Parallel with nursing research is that of advanced nursing education, which will be necessary to conduct research-based clinical practice.

Some nurses propose Bachelor's degree in nursing as entry level. Regardless of the level of education nurses finally achieve, it is apparent that factors such as soaring health care costs and technology demand intensive programs to learn complex health care delivery systems (Oermann, 1994).

Nurses have much to offer in terms of knowledge, leadership, and compassion. In a predominately female occupation, nurses must not let go of their "female connection" particularly when working with perinatal addicted women and their children. "Ask any addicted person what it means to have a warm and consoling voice when they are desperately trying to find the road to recovery. Your compassion, understanding, and thoughtful nursing interventions will be repaid one thousand times" (Shirley D. Coletti, personal communication, November, 3, 1994).

REFERENCES

Abma, J.C., & Mott, F.L. (1991). Substance use and prenatal care during pregnancy among young women. *Family Planning Perspectives, 23*, 117–122.

Anderson, B., & Novick, E. (1992). *Fetal aAlcohol syndrome and pregnant women who abuse alcohol: An overview of the issue and the federal response.* Available from U.S. Department of Health and Human Services, Office of the Assistant Secretary for Planning and Evaluation, Office of Human Services Policy. Division of Children and Youth Policy. Washington, DC.

Bradley, K.A. (1992). Screening and diagnosis of alcoholism in the primary care setting. *Western Journal of Medicine, 156*, 166–171.

Burke, M.S., & Roth, D. (1993). Anonymous cocaine screening in a private obstetric population. *Obstetrics & Gynecology, 81*, 354–356.

Caulker-Burnett, I. (1994). Primary screening for substance abuse. *Nurse Practitioner, 19*, 43–48.

Centers for Disease Control. (1994). Alcohol Consumption Statistics among women of childbearing age. *Morbidity and Mortality Weekly Report*, May 13.

Center for Substance Abuse Prevention (CSAP). (1994, February). *Prevention works: Nurse training course: Prevention of alcohol, tobacco, and other drug problems.* (Available from Center for Substance Abuse Prevention, U.S. Department of Health and Human Services.

Chang, G., Carroll, K.M., Behr, H.M., & Kosten, T.R. (1992). Improving treatment outcome in pregnant opiate-dependent women. *Journal of Substance Abuse Treatment, 9*, 327–330.

Chasnoff, I.J. (1989). Drug use and women; establishing a standard of care. *Annual NY Academy of Science, 562*, 208–210.

Chasnoff, I.J., Landress, H.J., Barrett, M.E., (1990). The prevalence of illicit-drug or alcohol use during pregnancy and discrepancies in mandatory reporting in Pinellas County, Fl. *New England Journal of Medicine, 322*, 1201–1206.

Chisum, G. (1990). Nursing interventions with the antepartum substance abuser. *Journal of Perinatal Neonatal Nursing, 3*, 26–33.

Finnegan, L. (1991). Perinatal substance abuse: Comments and perspectives. *Seminars in Perinatology, 15*(4), 331–339.

Galanter, M., Egelko S., DeLeon, G., Rohrs, C., Franco, H. (1992). Crack/cocaine abusers in the general hospital: Assessment and initiation of care. *Addictions Nursing Network, 4*, 115–121.

Gomby, D., & Shiono, P. (1991). Estimating the number of substance-exposed infants. In R. Behrman (Ed.), *The future of children* (pp. 17–25). Los Altos, CA: Packard Foundation.

Haack, M.R., & Budetti, P.B. (1994). Perspectives: Part II—Center for Health Policy and Research: An analysis of resources to aid drug-exposed infants and their families. *Addictions Nursing, 6*(1), 2–12.

Haller, D. (1991). Recovery for two: Pregnancy and addiction.*Addiction & Recovery, July/Aug.*, 14–18.

Hanson, C.M., Hodnicki, D.R., Boyle, J.S. (1994). Nominations for excellence: Collegial advocacy for nurse practitioners. *Journal of the American Academy of Nurse Practitioners, 6*(10), 471–476.

Harrison, M. (1991). Drug addiction in pregnancy: The interface of science, emotion, and social policy. *Journal of Substance Abuse Treatment, 8*, 261–268.

Huizinga, D., Leober, R., Thornberry, T., (1993). Longitudinal study of delinquency, drug use, sexual activity, and pregnancy among children and youth in three cities. *Public Health Reports, 108*, 90–96.

Jack, B.W., & Culpepper, L. (1990). Preconception care: Risk reduction and health promotion in preparation for pregnancy. *Journal of American Medical Association, 264*, 1147–1149.

Janke, J.R. (1990). Prenatal cocaine use: Effects on perinatal outcome. *Journal of Nurse-Midwifery, 35*, 21–25.

Johnson, J.L., Primas, P.J., & Coe, M.K. (1994). Factors that prevent women of low socioeconomic status from seeking prenatal care. *Journal of the American Academy of Nurse Practitioners 6*(3), 105–110.

Kann, L., Warren, W., Collins, J.L., Ross, J., Collins, B., & Kolbe, L.J. (1993). Results from the national school-based 1991 Youth Risk Behavior survey and progress toward achieving related health objectives for the nation. *Public Health Reports, 108*, 47–55.

Kennard, M.J. (1990). Cocaine use during pregnancy: Fetal and neonatal effects. *Perinatal Neonatal Nursing, 3*(4), 53–63.

Khalsa, J.H. & Gfroerer, J. (1991). Epidemiology and health consequences of drug abuse among pregnant women. *Seminars in Perinatology, 15*(4), 265–270.

Kim, S., McLeod, J.H., & Shantiz, C. (1992). Cultural competence for evaluators working with Asian-American Communities: Some practical considerations. In *Cultural competence for evaluators: A guide for alcohol and other drug abuse prevention practitioners working with ethnic-racial communities* (pp. 203–260). Rockville, MD: U.S. Department of Health Human Services. Public Health Service. Alcohol, Drug Abuse, and Mental Health Administration.

Klerman, L.V. (1994). Perinatal health care policy: How it will affect the family in the 21st century. *Journal of Obstetric, Gynecologic and Neonatal Nursing, 23*, 124–128.

Leshner, A. (September 1994). *Drug addiction research and the health of women.* Paper presented at the meeting of National Institute on Drug Abuse; National Institute of Health, Tyson's Corner, VA.

Lindenberg, C.S., & Keith, A.B. (1993). Opiate abuse in pregnancy. In J.J. Fitzpatrick, & J.S. Stevenson (Eds.), *Annual review of nursing research: Vol. 11.* New York: Springer.

Mann, T., Battaglin, J., Cooper, S., & Mahan, C.S. (1992). Some of patients use drugs; Pregnancy/substance abuse and the physician. *Journal of Florida Medical Association, 79*, 41–45.

Mathias, R. (1992). Developmental effects of prenatal drug exposure may be overcome by postnatal environment. *NIDA Notes, January/February*, 14–16.

Mayberry, L. (1994). Intrapartal nursing care: Research into practice. *JOGGN, 23*(2), 170–174.

Moser, C. (1993). A response to Aviel Goodman's "Sexual addiction: Designation and treatment." *Journal of Sex and Marital Therapy, 19*(3), 220–224.

National Center for Health Statistics. (1992). *Health United States.* NCHS Publication No.(93-1232). Hyattsville, MD: National Center for Health Statistics.

Oermann, M.H. (1994). Professional nursing education in the future: Changes and challenges. *JOGGN, 23*(2), 153–159.

Rassool, G.H. (1993). Nursing and substance misuse:Responding to the challenge. *Journal of Advanced Nursing, 18*, 1401–1407.

Redding, B. (1993). Exploring substance abuse nursing. *Minority Nurse, Winter/Spring*, 12, 98.

Redding, B.A., & Selleck, C.S. (1993). Perinatal substance abuse: Assessment and management of the pregnant woman and her children. *Nurse Practitioner Forum 4*(4), 216–223.

Sabella, B. (1993). Identifying prenatal substance abuse: Improving your odds. *OB/GYN Nursing & Patient Counseling, Spring*, 14–18.

Safriet, B.J. (1992). Health care dollars and regulatory sense: The role of Advanced Practice Nursing. *Yale Journal on Regulation, 9*(2), 417–486.

Schwarz, R.H. (1993). Not in my practice. *Obstetrics & Gynecology, 82*, 603–604.

Selleck, C.S., & Redding, B.A. (1994). Poster presentation. CSAP conference. Resource Link III. Washington, DC. July 18–20, 1994. *Knowledge & attitudes of registered nurses towards perinatal substance abuse*. Unpublished.

Smith, I.E., Dent, D.Z., Coles, C.D., Falek, A. (1992). A comparison study of treated and untreated pregnant and postpartum cocaine-abusing women. *Journal of Substance Abuse Treatment, 9*, 343–348.

Streissguth, A.P. (1990). Fetal alcohol syndrome and the teratogenicity of alcohol: Policy implications. *King County Medical Society: The Bulletin, 69*, 32–39.

Sullivan, E.J., & Handley, S.M. (1993). Alcohol and drug abuse. In J.J. Fitzpatarick & J.S. Stevenson (Eds.), *Annual review of nursing research: Vol. 11*. New York: Springer.

Trimble, J.E., Boleck, C.S., & Neimcryk, S.J. (1992). *Ethnic and multicultural drug abuse:Perspectives on current research*. New York: Harrington Park.

U.S. Bureau of the Census. (1992). Population projections of the United States, by age, sex, race, and Hispanic origin: 1992 to 2050. *Current Publication Reports (P25-1092)*. Washington, D.C.: U.S. Department of Commerce.

U.S. Department of Health and Human Services. (1990). Public Health Service. Alcohol, Drug Abuse, and Mental Health Administration. *OSAP Prevention Monograph-1. Stopping aAlcohol and other drug use before it starts: The future of prevention*. Rockville, MD: U.S. Department of Health and Human Services.

U.S. Department of Health and Human Services. (1991). *Healthy People 2000*. Washington, D.C.: U.S. Government Printing Office.

U.S. Department of Health and Human Services. (1993a). Public Health Service; Substance Abuse and Mental Health Services Administration. Center for Substance Abuse Treatment, (CSAT). *Pregnant, substance-using women. Treatment Improvement Protocol (TIP) Series*. (DHHS Publication No. SMA 93-1998). Rockville, MD: U.S. Department of Health and Human Services.

U.S. Department of Health and Human Services. (1993b). Public Health Service; Substance Abuse and Mental Health Services Administration. Center for Substance Abuse Treatment, (CSAT). *Improving treatment for drug-exposed infants. Treatment Improvement Protocol (TIP) Series*. (DHHS Publication No. SMA 93-2011). Rockville, MD: U.S. Department of Health and Human Services.

U.S. Department of Health and Human Services. (1993c). Public Health Service. Substance Abuse and Mental Health Services Administration. Center for Substance Abuse Treatment, (CSAT). *Guidelines for the treatment of alcohol and other drug abusing adolescents. Treatment Improved Protocol (TIP) Series*. (DHHS Publication No. SMA 93-2010). Rockville, MD: U.S. Department of Health and Human Services.

U.S. Department of Health and Human Services. (1993d). Public Health Service. Substance Abuse and Mental Health Services Administration. Center for Substance Abuse Treatment, (CSAT). *Screening and assessment of alcohol and other drug abusing adolescents. Treatment Improvement Protocol (TIP) Series*. (DHHS Publication No. SMA 93-2009). Rockville, MD: U.S. Department of Health and Human Services.

U.S. Department of Health and Human Services. (1994). Public Health Service, Centers for Disease Control and Prevention, National Center for Chronic Disease Prevention and Health Promotion, Office on Smoking and Health. *Preventing tobacco use among young people: A report of the Surgeon General*. Atlanta, GA: U.S. Department of Health and Human Services.

Psychiatric Nursing

Karen M. Allen, PhD, RN, CARN
Laina M. Gerace, PhD, RN, CS

INTRODUCTION

The health care needs of clients who have a psychiatric disorder in combination with an alcohol and other drug (AOD) disorder differ significantly from the needs of clients with either an AOD use disorder or a psychiatric disorder by itself. As can be seen in Figure 5-1, having both disorders is intertwined with a number of social problems that result from the two disorders, or may contribute to the existence of the two disorders. Clients with this combination of disorders are referred to as being comorbid or dually diagnosed.

There are no "typical" dual-diagnosis clients (Fayne, 1993); and according to Kiesler, Simpkins, and Morton (1991) and Narrow, Regier, Rae, Manderscheid, and Locke (1993) they appear in all types of clinical settings. Other terms used for this problem are: dual-diagnosis disorders, mentally ill chemical abusers (MICA), comorbidity, mentally ill substance abusers (MISA), and substance abuse and mental illness (SAMI) (Substance Abuse and Mental Health Services Administration [SAMHSA], 1994).

The term dual-diagnosis is a common, broad term that indicates the simultaneous presence of two independent medical disorders. According to Miller (1993) and Raskin and Miller (1993), the dual disorders are always distinctly separate disorders presenting in the same individual. However, Zimberg (1993) identified three patterns of dual-diagnosis. Within two of these patterns, the AOD use disorder and the psychiatric disorder have a primary–secondary dimension; that is, one of the diseases is primary and the other is related to (or develops in response to) the first, and therefore, is viewed as secondary. These two patterns hold that the conditions are interactive with each other. The third pattern views each disorder as distinct or independent. For the purposes of this chapter, dual-diagnosis is the coexistence of an axis I or II psychiatric disorder along with an alcohol and other drug disorder, regardless of order of occurrence.

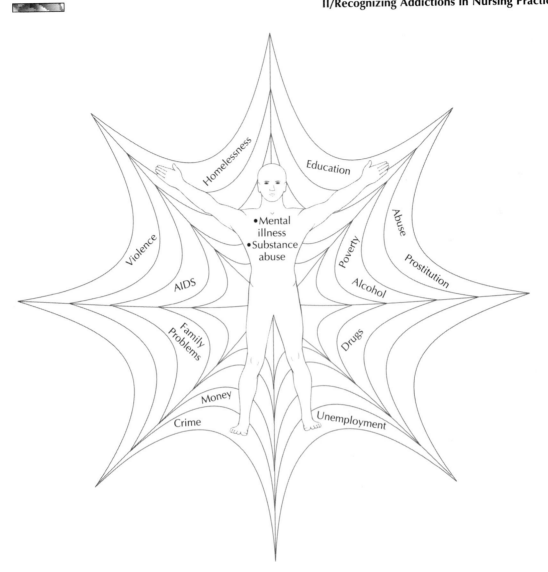

Figure 5-1.   Caught in web of social problems. (Source: Massaro, C., & Pepper, B. [1994]. The relationship of addiction to crime, health, and other social problems. In Substance Abuse and Mental Health Services Administration [Ed.], *Treatment for alcohol and other drug abuse: Opportunities for coordination* [pp. 11–23]. DHHS Publications No. [SMA] 94-2075. Rockville, MD: Department of Health and Human Services.)

While appearing in the literature since 1925 (Barbee, Clark, Crapanzano, Heintz, & Kehoe, 1989), the problem of addictions disorders existing as separate and distinct among persons with psychiatric disorders is just beginning to be acknowledged and studied. The purpose of this chapter is to present information pertinent to addressing the coexistence of an AOD disorder and a psychiatric disorder.

MAGNITUDE OF THE PROBLEM AND OPPORTUNITIES TO PROVIDE CARE

Prevalence rates for existence of AOD disorders along with psychiatric disorders differ depending on: 1) the population studied; 2) the perspective of the researcher; 3) the method of study; and 4) the length of follow-up. Clinical populations yield higher dual-diagnosis rates than the general population, and studies on psychiatric units yield higher rates than those conducted in addictions settings (Miller, 1993; Raskin & Miller, 1993).

The prevalence of dual-diagnosis among clients on an addictions unit have been noted in some studies to be 6% for phobias; 5% for major depression; 1.4% for obsessive-compulsive disorder; 1.1% for schizophrenia; 0.8% for bipolar disorder; 0.67% for panic disorder; 0.6% for antisocial personality disorders; and 0.1% for somatization disorder (Raskin & Miller, 1993). On the other hand, the prevalence of dual-diagnosis among clients in a psychiatric setting may be as high as 80% antisocial personality disorder; 50% schizophrenia; 50% bipolar disorder; 30% depressive disorder; 30% anxiety disorders; and 23% phobic disorder (Miller, 1993).

To determine the prevalence in the general population, the National Institute of Mental Health conducted the epidemiologic catchment area study. When arriving at a dual-diagnosis, special efforts were made to exclude transient mental disorder symptoms, such as may occur secondary to alcohol, tobacco, and other drug abuse. Results showed that among those with a psychiatric disorder, about 29% also had a drug or alcohol-related disorder. Among those with an alcohol disorder, 37% had a comorbid psychiatric disorder. The highest dual-diagnosis disorder rate was found for those with drug (other than alcohol) disorders, among whom more than half (53%) were found to have a psychiatric disorder. Among institutional settings, comorbidity of addictive and severe psychiatric disorders was highest in the prison population, specifically with antisocial personality, schizophrenia, and bipolar disorders (Regier, Farmer, Rae, Locke, Judd, & Goodwin, 1990).

Narrow, Regier, Rae, Manderscheid, and Locke (1993) described the utilization of health care services by persons with mental and substance abuse disorders. They reported that among those who used ambulatory mental health/addictive services, there were 1.9 million persons with comorbid mental and addictive disorders, with 35.1 million visits in a 1-year period. This seems like a lot; however, there were a significantly smaller proportion of visits to alcohol and other drug outpatient clinics and psychiatric hospital outpatient clinics than other health care and self-care settings.

The fact that a large number of persons with mental and addictive disorders (comorbidity or dual-diagnosis) are being seen in nonspecialty (substance abuse and psychiatric) health care settings underscores the importance of recognition and appropriate treatment of these disorders by *all professional providers* (Narrow et al., 1993). These findings emphasize the scope and seriousness of dual-diagnosis, and depict the need for identification and intervention of the dually diagnosed client.

THE RELATIONSHIP BETWEEN AOD USE AND PSYCHIATRIC SYMPTOMS AND DISORDERS

Although clients with psychiatric diagnoses often abuse and/or are addicted to the entire range of existing substances, according to Evans and Sullivan (1990) clients with certain major diagnoses show preferences for certain drugs as detailed in Table 5-1.

Evans and Sullivan (1990) also noted certain drug use and abuse preferences among their clients with certain axis II diagnoses—passive-aggressive, antisocial and borderline personality disorders—the ones who presented the greatest challenge because of their usage of "acting out"

TABLE 5-1 Mental Disorders and Drug Use Preferences

Mental Disorder	Drug Use
Schizophrenia	Polysubstance abuse and dependence; however, more use of alcohol and marijuana because of availability, less use of opiates and sedative-hypnotics
Mania	Polysubstance abuse and dependence; use of alcohol during highs and stimulants during highs and lows
Major depression	Polysubstance abuse and dependence; heavy use of alcohol and other depressant drugs
Anxiety disorders	Polysubstance abuse and dependence; some preference for alcohol and other sedative-hypnotics; may use cocaine in attempts to achieve euphoria
Organic mental disorder	Polysubstance abuse but generally with the more accessible drugs such as alcohol or marijuana; increased use of stimulants in attention-deficit disorder clients

as a defense mechanism. They defined acting out as behavioral patterns that 1) have an angry, hostile tone; 2) violate social conventions regarding appropriate ways to relate to others; and 3) result in negative consequences to self and others. They described their alcohol and other drug use as follows:

Mental Disorder	Drug Use
Passive-aggressive personality disorder	Alcohol and sedative-hypnotics (prescription medicines)
Antisocial personality disorder	Use of any and all substances
Borderline personality disorder	Episodic but intense use of a variety of drugs and alcohol with almost always some use of prescriptive medicines; dependency will most likely be on a tranquilizer, sedating antidepressant, or narcotic

According to SAMHSA (1994), there is great variability among dual-diagnosis disorders. However, some common patterns usually seen with dual-diagnosis include the combinations of 1) major depression with cocaine addiction; 2) panic disorder with alcohol addiction; 3) schizophrenia with alcoholism and polydrug addiction; and 4) borderline personality with episodic polydrug abuse. Furthermore, other relationships between AOD use and psychiatric symptoms or disorders include the following:

- AOD use can cause psychiatric symptoms and mimic psychiatric disorders; the type, duration, and severity of these symptoms are usually related to the type, dose, and chronicity of AOD use.

- Acute and chronic AOD use can prompt the development, provoke the reemergence, or worsen the severity of psychiatric disorders.
- AOD use can mask psychiatric symptoms and disorders.
- AOD withdrawal can cause psychiatric symptoms and mimic psychiatric syndromes.
- Psychiatric and AOD disorders can coexist independently.
- Psychiatric behaviors can mimic behaviors associated with AOD problems.

In addition, once it is ruled out that a medical condition—such as malnutrition, anemia, hyperthyroidism and hypothyroidism, dementia, brain disease, lupus, HIV/AIDS, postcardiac condition, stroke, and medication effects—did not precipitate or mimic the existing mood disorder, the following are examples of how drugs can mimic certain mood disorders. During intoxication, alcohol, benzodiazepines, opioids, barbiturates, cannabis, chronic steroid and stimulant use mimic depression and dysthymia. Use of stimulants, alcohol, hallucinogens, inhalants (organic solvents), and steroids (both chronic and acute) mimic mania and cyclothymia. During withdrawal, alcohol, benzodiazepines, barbiturates, opiates, chronic steroid and stimulant use mimic depression and dysthymia. Alcohol, benzodiazepines, barbiturates, opiates, and chronic steroid use mimic mania and cyclothymia (SAMHSA, 1994).

Clients with a coexisting AOD disorder and psychiatric disorder present a challenge when seeking health care. The nurse is faced with the difficulty of determining how best to care for a client exhibiting mania, depression, anxiety, paranoia, hallucinations, and incoherence, who is also abusing or addicted to drugs. Because of the ethical, medical, and financial challenge this client presents, it is important to have knowledge of existing similarities between the two disorders, and effective ways to complete an appropriate assessment that will lead to a differential diagnosis of the problem.

UNDERSTANDING PARALLEL ISSUES WITHIN DUAL-DIAGNOSIS

Parallel Issues

Although mental illness and addiction are distinct disorders, they have a great deal in common. Minkoff (1989) referred to these commonalities as "parallel concepts." For instance, each disorder has a biological and hereditary base that in some complex manner interacts with environmental components. Once present, they each need biological treatment to stabilize the symptoms, followed by ongoing education and rehabilitation. Shame, stigma, and guilt accompany each disorder. Furthermore, loss of control over behavior and often one's life characterizes both addiction and mental disorders. Last but not least, in both disorders, the family is seriously affected and participates in the denial system typically found in the earlier stages.

Evans and Sullivan (1990) provided other similarities: 1) a genetic/physiological component exists for each disorder; 2) both need care provided along a continuum; and 3) both need group, individual, and family therapy. Orlin and Davis (1993) discussed yet more similarities: 1) impairment in many or all areas of functioning (family relationships, school or job performance, financial stability, health, and ability to socialize); 2) chronicity and relapse; 3) denial as a primary defense; 4) social isolation; 5) inattention to health; and 6) extremes in behavior.

It takes the gathering of a careful history, testing, observation over time, and a good assessment to have sufficient data for a differential diagnosis of comorbidity (Greenman, 1994). These similarities among the disorders makes it easier to conceptualize them and assess for both disorders concurrently.

Assessments

DUAL-DIAGNOSIS

A number of ways have been suggested to assess the existence of a dual-diagnosis. Three methods that can be used in any clinical setting—because that is where dual-diagnosis clients can be found—will be presented.

Orlin and Davis (1993) also stated that time is the most reliable assessment tool for dual-diagnosis. However, they viewed taking a history that reflects the course of both disorders and their possible interactions as very important. Therefore, they recommended the use of a short form (see Box 5-1), which gathers data related to both the psychiatric and substance use/abuse disorders, from a historical perspective.

 Box 5-1: Dual-Diagnosis Assessment Form

HISTORY	PSYCHIATRIC	DRUG USE/ABUSE
1. Age of onset and circumstances		
2. Treatment history		
• hospitalizations		
• outpatient		
• medications		
3. Periods of remission		
• length of time and circumstances		
4. Triggers for return of symptoms/use of addicting substances		
5. Positive consequences of illness or illnesses		
6. Negative consequences of illness or illnesses		
7. Clients understanding of illness or illnesses; do they see connections?		
8. Family history of illness or illnesses		
9. Family responses to client's illness or illnesses		

Source: Orlin, L., & Davis, J. (1993). Assessment and intervention with drug and alcohol abusers in psychiatric settings. In S.L.A. Straussner (Ed.), *Clinical work with substance abusing clients*. New York: The Guilford Press. Reproduced with permission.

Gorski (1994) posited that differential assessment of the dual-diagnosed client is an evaluation that compares and classifies the symptoms of substance abuse/addiction, mental disorders, and personality disorders. Use of a clinical reasoning tool, such as the "biopsychosocial assessment grid" (see Table 5-2), helps to organize the data. Hence, it becomes easy to distinguish symptoms common to one or more of the disorders and requiring a general holistic treatment plan, from symptoms unique to only one disorder that require a disorder-specific treatment plan.

SAMHSA (1994) recommended that "irrespective of treatment or intervention setting—notwithstanding the crisis that may have initiated the contact made with the health care facility—all clients who may have a dual-diagnosis should receive a basic screening for the existence of both psychiatric and substance abuse/addictions disorders." Common screening tools for addiction are discussed in Chapter 10, and a simple screening tool for psychiatric status can be seen in Box 5-2. Then, the assessment should be completed and be sensitive to biological, psychological, and social issues. Box 5-3 provides a process that might be helpful (SAMHSA, 1994).

MEDICAL

In addition to a dual-diagnosis assessment, a current or recent comprehensive medical evaluation is important. Clinicians should become familiar with a client's medical history, specifically any possible relationship that may exist between a medical condition and the presenting symptoms. Generally, these clients have a high prevalence of medical problems—both acute and chronic—that are frequently untreated or undertreated.

Because the chances of these clients contracting tuberculosis, hepatitis, and HIV/AIDS are high, it is important that they have access to treatment for these medical conditions, which are so strongly associated with AOD use. These clients are also at high risk for diabetes, hypertension, cardiovascular, and respiratory and neurological disorders. Therefore, they should have easy access to basic medical care for these needs.

Frequently, psychoactive substances become replacements for adequate and nutritious food. Hence, a lack of regular meals and poor nutrition are common occurrences among clients

 TABLE 5-2 General Reasoning Structure for the Biopsychosocial Assessment Grid (BAG) for Dual-Diagnosis

	Substance Abuse/Addiction	Mental Disorder	Personality Style/Disorder
Physical symptoms	What are the physical symptoms of addiction?	What are the the physical symptoms of the primary mental disorder?	What are the physical symptoms of the primary personality style/disorder?
Psychological symptoms	What are the psychological symptoms of addiction?	What are the psychological symptoms of the primary mental disorder?	What are the psychological symptoms of the primary personality style/disorder?
Social symptoms	What are the social symptoms of the addiction?	What are the social symptoms of the primary mental disorder?	What are the social symptoms of the primary personality style/disorder?

Source: Gorski, T. (March/April, 1994). A suggestion for conceptualizing dual-diagnosis. *Behavioral Health Management*, 50–53. Reproduced with permission.

BOX 5-2. ABC Model for Psychiatric Screening

(A) APPEARANCE, ALERTNESS, AFFECT, AND ANXIETY

Appearance:	General appearance, hygiene, and dress
Alertness:	What is the level of consciousness?
Affect:	Elation or depression: gestures, facial expression, and speech
Anxiety:	Is the individual nervous, phobic, or panicky?

(B) BEHAVIOR

Movements:	Rate (hyperactive, hypoactive, abrupt, or constant
Organization:	Coherent and goal-oriented?
Purpose:	Bizarre, stereotypical, dangerous, or impulsive?
Speech:	Rate, organization, coherence, and content

(C) COGNITION

Orientation:	Person, place, time, and condition
Calculation:	Memory and simple tasks
Reasoning:	Insight, judgment, problem solving
Coherence:	Incoherent ideas, delusions, and hallucinations

with dual diagnoses; thus, access to regular meals should be assessed because nutritional impairment is associated with impaired cognition.

A proper assessment is most important with dually diagnosed clients. However, it is important to remember that 1) diagnoses of psychiatric disorders should be provisional and constantly reevaluated; and 2) treatment of AOD disorders along with an abstinence period of weeks or months may be required before a true definitive diagnosis of an independent psychiatric disorder can take place.

ISSUES RELATED TO CARE OF THE DUALLY DIAGNOSED CLIENT

Attitudes and Clinical Traditions

Nurses and other health care providers often have attitudes toward clients with dual-diagnosis disorders that are not optimistic, and resources for these clients are often inadequate or limited (Norris & Naegle, 1990). Psychiatric nurses consider addicted clients difficult to treat, and addictions nurses feel they are not prepared to work with psychiatric clients.

These attitudes have most likely evolved from the traditional division between fields of addictions and psychiatry. Each field has its own clinical experts and separate research institutes. Furthermore, each field has different ideas about causality and different theoretical foundations. For example, the currently held idea that alcoholism is a disease in and of itself evolved

BOX 5-3. Biopsychosocial Assessment: the AOD and Psychiatric Perspectives

	AOD	PSYCHIATRIC
Biological	Alcohol on breath Positive drug test Abnormal laboratory tests Injuries & trauma Toxicity & withdrawal Impaired cognition	Abnormal laboratory tests Neurological exams Use of psychotropic medications Use of other medications
Psychological	Intoxicated behavior Withdrawal symptoms Denial and manipulation Responses to AOD assessment AOD use history	Mental status examination (affect, mood, psychosis, etc.) Stress, situational factors Self-image, defenses, etc.

Social	Collateral information from
	   others
	Social interaction and lifestyle
	Involvement with other
	   AOD groups
	Family history of AOD use
	   disorders
	Housing and employment
	   history
		Support systems (family,
		   friends, others)
		Current psychiatric therapy
		Hospitalization
		Family history of psychiatric
		   disorders
		Housing and employment
		   history

in reaction to psychoanalytic notions that addicted clients had hidden emotional conflicts and excessive dependency needs. The self-help movement in addictions clearly separated addictions from psychiatry (Zimberg, 1993).

Clients with dual-diagnosis disorders bear the brunt of these turf issues. Often shunted from one system to the other, they are left without an integrated approach to care and treatment. Given the extent and complex nature of the problem, nurses specializing in addictions and those specializing in psychiatric nursing need to collaborate on behalf of the client.

Treatment Models

Screening, diagnostic, and assessment sessions can be the first intervention. The boundary between assessment and treatment is fluid. A diagnostic interview can be done during the course of several sessions.

Issues that have impacted the type of treatment dual-diagnosed clients have received include: 1) philosophical differences about the nature of dual disorders; 2) differing opinions regarding the best way to treat them; 3) limitations of available resources; and 4) differences in treatment responses for different types and severities of dual disorders. Consequently, treatment of clients with dual disorders have followed one of three models.

The first and historically most common model of dual-diagnosis is sequential treatment. In this model, the client participates in one system (mental health), then the other (addictions), or vice versa. The second model or approach is parallel treatment. In this model, the client participates in the two systems of mental health and addictions simultaneously. The third model, integrated treatment, combines elements of both mental health and addiction treatment into a unified and comprehensive program for these clients. Ideally, it involves clinicians being cross-trained in both mental health and addiction, as well as a unified case-management approach that allows for monitoring and treating clients through various psychiatric and AOD crises (SAMHSA, 1994).

Again, it is important to stress that differences in dual-disorder combinations, symptom severity, and degree of impairment impact on the appropriateness of a specific treatment model for a given client. For example, sequential and parallel treatment may be most appropriate for clients who have a very severe problem with one disorder, but a mild problem with the other. However, clients with dual disorders who obtain treatment from two separate systems frequently receive conflicting therapeutic messages. In addition, financial coverage and even confidentiality laws vary between the two systems.

Currently, clinicians are being advised to use an integrated system. It places the burden of treatment continuity on the health care provider who is expert in both psychiatric and AOD use disorders. In addition, it provides simultaneous treatment of both disorders in a setting designed to accommodate both problems. In situations where integrated treatment is not possible or available, the following method of decision making for client placement can be used (Greenman, 1994). It is known as "triage" or determination of the appropriate treatment setting (patient placement), and occurs initially at the time of admission.

- Dual-disordered clients with psychiatric instability who are more appropriate for the inpatient psychiatric unit include:
  1. Clients in danger of harming self or others while intoxicated or in drug withdrawal
  2. Clients with unstable or diagnostically unclear thinking or mood disorders requiring psychiatric evaluation or treatment
  3. Clients with an inability to function within a structured confrontive environment
  4. Clients with an axis I diagnosis with a history of repeated addictions treatment failures or drug abuse related to psychiatric symptoms

- Dual-disordered clients who are more appropriate for substance abuse treatment are those with stable axis I or only axis II diagnoses—
  1. Nonsuicidal, depressed clients will usually do better if first treated for their substance abuse
  2. Repeated psychiatric admissions while intoxicated (however, the person is stable while abstinent)
  3. Repeated substance abuse while in psychiatric treatment

Approaches to Providing Care

The following issues need to be considered by all nurses in all clinical settings who encounter dual-diagnosed clients.

- The initial focus of care should be on addressing the presenting symptoms—not on diagnosing one or the other disorder

- Acute crisis intervention and crisis management are the first order of business
- Acute, subacute, and long-term stabilization are the phases of treatment for these clients
- Multiple-contact longitudinal treatments are a major goal for these clients. Ongoing diagnostic efforts are important; there should be ongoing dual focus on both disorders
- For mild to moderate mental disordered symptoms, first try nonpharmacologic approaches; if these are unsuccessful and medications must be used, use those drugs that have a low abuse potential or that are nonpsychoactive. Finally, if necessary, use the psychoactive medications (SAMHSA, 1994).

In addition, four issues critical to treatment of clients with dual disorders are 1) engagement; 2) continuity and comprehensiveness; 3) treatment phases; and 4) continual reassessment and rediagnosis.

Nurses working in advanced practice as clinical nurse specialist in psychiatry or addictions and responsible for care on a long-term basis need to understand the processes of engagement and treatment continuity and comprehensiveness required for their clients, particularly if these nurses are in individual practice. Engagement begins with efforts designed to enlist individuals into treatment. This is a long-term process with the goals of keeping clients in treatment and helping them manage ongoing problems and crises. Essential to this process is a personalized relationship with the client, which takes place over an extended period of time, with the focus of the relationship being the stated needs of the client.

Treatment continuity and comprehensiveness for these clients should include an integrated dual-disorders case management program (a case manager trained to address addictions as well as mental health issues) that can be located within a mental health setting, an addictions treatment setting, or a collaborative program. Case management is important because it is critical to develop continuity between treatment programs and components, as well as treatment continuity over time.

Nurses are best prepared educationally within this capacity. Interventions or programs of care ranging from more to less intense—provided by clinical nurse specialists in mental health or addictions—should be available to accommodate various levels of severity and disability. Also, these programs should accommodate various levels of motivation and compliance, and accommodate clients in different phases of care. There should be access to abstinence-mandated programs, abstinence-oriented programs, as well as drug maintenance programs.

Phases of Care

Phases of treatment for the dual-diagnosed client are acute, subacute stabilization, and long-term stabilization.

ACUTE PHASE

The acute phase—phenomena that begin quickly and require rapid response— and stabilization—management of physical, psychiatric, or drug toxicity crises— includes injury, illness, AOD-induced toxic or withdrawal states, and behavior that is suicidal, violent, impulsive, or psychotic. Acute stabilization of psychiatric symptoms require acute psychiatric inpatient treatment and psychiatric medications for clients exhibiting severe symptoms such as psychotic, violent, suicidal, or impulsive behaviors. For clients with less severe symptoms, outpatient or day treatment settings may be sufficient. The acute stabilization of AOD-use disorders typically begins with detoxification (inpatient or outpatient) for clients in withdrawal.

It is important to note that there are certain risks associated with AOD use and withdrawal among clients who are also receiving medications to treat psychiatric disorders. Because of these risks, serious consideration should be given to inpatient treatment for withdrawal among dual-diagnosed clients. The risks include (SAMHSA, 1994):

- Alcohol and barbiturates can cause increased tolerance by increasing the amount of liver enzymes responsible for their metabolism. These same liver enzymes are also responsible to metabolize many antidepressant, anticonvulsant, and antipsychotic medications. Thus, serum levels of medications will be decreased, possibly to subtherapeutic levels. Without assessing for possible AOD use, some health care providers may mistakenly increase these medication doses.
- Alcohol interferes with the thermoregulatory center of the brain, as do antipsychotic drugs. Clients taking both drugs may be unable to adjust to their body temperature in response to extremes in the external environment.
- The interaction of stimulants in a person taking monoamine oxidase inhibitor antidepressants can lead to a life-threatening hypertensive crisis.
- Alcohol and cocaine enhance the respiratory depression effects of opioids and some neuroleptics such as the phenothiazines. This effect can increase vulnerability to overdose death.
- Marijuana has anticholinergic effects. In combination with the anticholinergic medications, such as cogentin, marijuana can lead to an anticholinergic (atropine) psychosis.
- Clients who are vulnerable to hallucinations, such as schizophrenics, are at high risk for having hallucinations during the withdrawal from alcohol and other sedative-hypnotics.
- Antipsychotics and antidepressants lower the seizure threshold and enhance seizure potential during withdrawal from sedative-hypnotics and alcohol.
- Alcohol intoxication and withdrawal disturbs the fluid electrolyte balance in the body, which can lead to lithium toxicity.

For other interactions between drugs of abuse and common psychiatric therapeutic agents see Gastfriend (1993).

Clinicians or health care settings providing an intervention of acute stabilization for dual-diagnosed clients should have the capability to:

- Identify medical, psychiatric, and AOD use disorders
- Treat a range of illness severity, through a range of intensities of service
- Provide drug detoxification, psychiatric medications, and other biopsychosocial levels of treatment
- Provide linkages to other necessary programs for ongoing care.

SUBACUTE STABILIZATION

The second phase is the subacute stabilization phase. In this phase nurses are dealing with a myriad of problems as the acute course of psychiatric or addictions illness begins to diminish, or symptoms emerge or reemerge, but are not severe enough to be described as acute. For example, a client could be dealing with symptoms related to postacute withdrawal, or to anxiety and insomnia as a prelude to relapse for depression. If these symptoms are ignored, rather than assessed and treated, symptom escalation, decompensation, and relapse of the psychiatric or addictions illness may result.

During the subacute stabilization phase nurses could be involved in educating clients about their disorders and symptomatology. Also, planning for long-term issues such as housing, long-term treatment, and financial stability should begin to be addressed.

LONG-TERM STABILIZATION

Long-term stabilization deals with treatment, rehabilitation, and recovery from dual-diagnosis in an outpatient, inpatient, or residential setting. Generally it is important to avoid premature, potent, and direct confrontation, as well as an insistence on abstinence. These approaches may prompt fragile clients to disengage from any interventions or treatment attempts.

The Role of Pharmacotherapy

Pharmacotherapy is a major component of care for persons with axis I psychiatric diagnoses, hence having a clear picture of what might be most effective is helpful. According to Gastfriend (1993) the following plans should be utilized.

SCHIZOPHRENIA

Schizophrenia is the most difficult comorbid condition to treat. Clearly, as in all dual-diagnosis disorders, the first priority is to achieve abstinence and then initiate antipsychotic pharmacotherapy. Inpatient hospitalization is usually essential to initiate treatment, and managed care approval may be more forthcoming in the dual-diagnosis state. Once hospitalized, if the diagnosis is at all uncertain, sparing use of antipsychotics just to manage behavior is preferable.

Although alcoholic hallucinosis may occur in 5% of alcoholics; stimulant or hallucinogen-induced psychosis—which is common—it resolves in hours to days. Therefore, prolonged antipsychotic administration may be unnecessary, and the frightening experience of side effects will only serve to alienate clients from providers. Neuroleptic drugs (antipsychotics) are not euphorigenic and do not cause acute mood or psychomotor alterations. They are most effective in suppressing the positive symptoms of psychosis such as hallucinations, delusions, and incoherence. They also help reduce disturbances of arousal, affect, psychomotor activity, thought content, and social adjustment (Africa & Schwartz, 1992). However, side effects are common.

The side effects of most of the antipsychotics is sedation, but an adaptation to the sedative effects develops within days or weeks. Other adverse effects include: dry mouth, constipation, blurred vision, and extrapyramidal symptoms, which are a frequent cause of medication noncompliance. Although antipsychotics are consistent with a psychoactive drug-free philosophy, they prompt clients to use AODs to self-medicate against the noxious symptoms (SAMHSA, 1994).

It is important to note that the combination of opiate dependence and chronic axis I disorders—especially psychosis—warrants serious consideration of methadone maintenance for initial treatment as opposed to detoxification and abstinence (Gastfriend, 1993).

AFFECTIVE DISORDERS

Gastfriend further stated that, in milder depressions, addicted clients do not benefit from pharmacotherapy, but rather require detoxification and abstinence. Therefore, clinicians need to offer vigorous education and support to help clients accept that these symptoms are to be expected, transient, and therefore, tolerable. On the other hand, in clearly diagnosed comorbid affective disorders, such as bipolar illness, standard pharmacotherapy serves multiple purposes: restoration of the euthymic state; treatment retention; and relapse prevention. Standard therapeutic levels for antidepressants and lithium, and adequate inhibition of platelet monoamine oxidase (MAO) activity, remain the pharmacologic objective.

Lithium is the standard first-line treatment for manic episodes, although 10 to 14 days may be required before full effect is achieved. The initial symptoms managed by lithium include increased psychomotor activity, pressured speech, and insomnia. Later, lithium diminishes the symptoms of expansive mood, grandiosity, and intrusiveness. Lithium does not cause acute mood alteration and is not psychoactive or mood altering. It is consistent with a psychoactive drug-free philosophy and does not compromise recovery from addiction, while it enhances recovery from bipolar disorder (SAMHSA, 1994).

Antidepressants include tricyclics, monoamine oxidase inhibitors, and other newer antidepressants such as trazodone (Desyrel), bupropion (Wellbutrin), sertraline (Zoloft), and fluoxetine (Prozac). They are effective for the treatment of depression and several are valuable for the treatment of anxiety disorders, including generalized anxiety disorder, phobias, and panic disorder. These antidepressants are not euphorigenic and do not cause acute mood alterations. Rather, they are mood regulators and diminish the severity and frequency of depressive episodes (SAMHSA, 1994).

Tricyclic antidepressants have side effects that may be unpleasant and often prompt the discontinuation of medication, which may provoke reemergence of the psychopathology. Tricyclics are quite toxic when combined with alcohol and other drugs of abuse. Therefore, their use in early recovery should be carefully monitored. The newer serotonin reuptake inhibitors are much safer to use in early recovery. Overall, the use of antidepressants is consistent with a psychoactive drug-free philosophy. It is believed by some to not compromise recovery from addiction and enhance recovery from depressive and panic disorders (SAMHSA, 1994).

ANXIETY DISORDERS

For clients who report anxiety symptoms, it is important to determine whether these represent a discrete anxiety disorder, because central nervous system depressant withdrawal often involves a protracted phase of 3 to 6 months, which can mimic generalized anxiety and agoraphobia. Stabilization of the anxiety disorder is expected after initial detoxification and the benefit of a period of drug-free observation. Buspirone is the drug of choice for use with anxiety disorders (Gastfriend, 1993). According to SAMHSA (1994), buspirone selectively diminishes multiple symptoms of anxiety without the acute mood alteration, sedation, or associated somatic side effects seen in sedative–hypnotics anxiolytics. It is useful for generalized anxiety disorder, chronic anxiety symptoms, anxiety with depressive features, and anxiety among elderly clients.

PERSONALITY DISORDERS

Personality disorders have the highest incidence of concurrent substance abuse diagnoses (especially antisocial, borderline, and passive–aggressive). The major problem in pharmacotherapy of dual-diagnosis with personality disorders may be that it leads to drug seeking in the client. These patients use psychotropic medications for concomitant problems such as depression. Addicted clients with impaired interpersonal relations cannot help but perceive that a drug offers them their most dependable relationship in life. On this basis, they may 1) suffer from intense fear of detoxification; 2) cultivate sociopathic behavior as a survival skill; and 3) usually have had multiple disastrous encounters with the health care system. In addition, many clients may have concurrent depressive symptoms from their addictive disorder and may present armed with a highly developed subjective sense of drug effects. Therefore, at best, medication is only a third-line intervention strategy after abstinence counseling and psychotherapy (Gastfriend, 1993). Gastfriend further discussed the fact that pharmacotherapy contracts should be established with dual-diagnosed clients and key components of a pharmacotherapy contract with dual-diagnosis clients should include the following:

- Medication is part of a rational psychosocial treatment "package," and will be discontinued if key psychosocial components are neglected.
- Urine or blood testing may be required at any time to provide an independent source of data about the course of the chemical dependence, or to determine whether prescribed medication is reaching adequate levels in the blood.
- Medication will be used only as prescribed. Any need for changes will first be discussed with the health care provider. A unilateral change in medication by the client often is an early sign of relapse.
- Changes in medication will be prescribed one at a time (i.e., two agents will not be initiated simultaneously).
- When used, the purpose of medication is to treat predetermined target symptoms. If the medication proves ineffective for these symptoms, it will be discontinued.
- Once target symptoms remit, a process of dose tapering may be initiated to determine the minimum dose necessary to maintain healthy function. Periodically, the medication strategy will include a period of discontinuation, or "drug holiday." Medication may not be necessary on a long-term basis.

NURSING'S RESPONSE

Historically, health care providers—of which nurses are the largest group—have been the largest single point of contact for clients seeking help with psychiatric and AOD-use disorders. Nurses are uniquely qualified to manage life-threatening crises and to treat medical problems related and unrelated to psychiatric and alcohol and other drug use disorders. Because nurses are in contact with such large numbers of clients, they have an exceptional opportunity to screen and identify clients with dual-diagnosis. Nurses can initiate prevention programs and persuasive educational programs for clients, other staff, and in community settings.

Greenman (1994) points out that a prime role for addictions nurse specialists or psychiatric nurse specialists exemplifies the contribution that they can make to comprehensive client care. They can perform clinical interventions ranging from triage to psychotherapy to case management.

As discussed earlier in this chapter, dual-diagnosis has been a problem for a number of years; however, it is only recently that it has come to the forefront of health care with psychiatric and addictions clients. What has nursing's response been, or what is nursing's current response? Are we engaging in research of nursing roles and actions that benefit these clients? Are we teaching in our schools and preparing our students to deal with clients in all clinical areas who may have the dual disorders of psychiatric and addictions problems? Are we advocating for better and more comprehensive and continuous dual-disordered care to be provided to these clients based on our experiences with them, as well as what we see happen to them? Professional psychiatric and addictions nursing organizations appear to be providing workshops and conferences related to caring for clients with dual disorders of psychiatric and addictions issues, but which audiences are they reaching and is it enough?

Dual-diagnosis is an issue in the forefront with health care providers, health care payors, and researchers. Is nursing anywhere in that picture?

REFERENCES

Africa, B., & Schwartz, S. (1992). Schizophrenic disorders. In H. Goldman (Ed.) *Review of general psychiatry* (3rd ed.). Norwalk, CT: Appleton & Lange.

Barbee, J., Clark, P., Crapanzano, M., Heintz, G., & Kehoe, C. (1989). Alcohol and substance abuse among schizophrenic patients presenting to an emergency psychiatric service. *The Journal of Nervous and Mental Disease, 177*(7), 400–407.

Evans, K., & Sullivan, J. (1990). *Dual-diagnosis: Counseling the mentally ill substance abuser.* New York: The Guilford Press.

Fayne, M. (1993). Recognizing dual-diagnosis patients in various clinical settings. In J. Solomon, S. Zimberg, & E. Shollar (Eds.) *Dual-diagnosis: Evaluation, treatment, training, and program development* (pp. 39–53). New York: Plenum Medical Book Company.

Gastfriend, D. (1993). Pharmacotherapy of psychiatric syndromes with comorbid chemical dependence. *Journal of Addictive Diseases, 12*(3), 155–170.

Gorski, T. (March/April, 1994). A suggestion for conceptualizing dual-diagnosis. *Behavioral Health Management,* 50–53.

Greenman, D. (1994). The role of the addictions nurse specialist in adult psychiatry. *Perspectives on Addictions Nursing, 5*(3), 3–4.

Kiesler, C., Simpkins, C., & Morton, T. (1991). Prevalence of dual diagnoses of mental and substance abuse disorders in general hospitals. *Hospital and Community Psychiatry, 42*(4), 400–405.

Massaro, C., & Pepper, B. (1994). The relationship of addiction to crime, health, and other social problems. In Substance Abuse and Mental Health Services Administration (Ed.) *Treatment for alcohol and other drug abuse: Opportunities for coordination* (pp.11–23). DHHS Publications No. (SMA) 94-2075. Rockville, MD: Department of Health and Human Services.

Miller, N. (1993). Comorbidity of psychiatric and alcohol/drug disorders: Interactions and independent status. *Journal of Addictive Diseases, 12*(3), 5–16.

Minkoff, K. (1989). An integrated treatment model for dual-diagnosis of psychosis and addiction. *Hospital and Community Psychiatry, 40*(10), 1031–1036.

Narrow, W., Regier, D., Rae, D., Manderscheid, R., & Locke, B. (1993). Use of services by persons with mental and addictive disorders. Findings from the National Institute of Mental Health Epidemiological Catchment Area Program. *Archives of General Psychiatry, 50*(2), 95–107.

Norris, E., & Naegle, M. (1990). The complexities of treating the dually diagnosed substance abuser. *Addictions Nursing Network, 2,* 4–7.

Orlin, L., & Davis, J. (1993). Assessment and intervention with drug and alcohol abusers in psychiatric settings. In S.L.A. Straussner (Ed.) *Clinical Work with substance abusing clients.* New York: The Guilford Press.

Raskin, V., & Miller, N. (1993). The epidemiology of the comorbidity of psychiatric and addictive disorders: A critical review. *Journal of Addictive Diseases, 12*(3), 45–57.

Regier, D., Farmer, M., Rae, D., Locke, B., Judd, L., & Goodwin, F. (1990). Comorbidity of mental disorders with alcohol and other drug abuse: Results from the epidemiologic catchment area (ECA) study. *Journal of the American Medical Association, 264*(19), 2511–2518.

Substance Abuse and Mental Health Services Administration. (1994). *Assessment and Treatment of patients with coexisting mental illness and alcohol and other drug abuse.* DHHS Publication No. (SMA) 94-2078. Rockville, MD: U.S. Department of Health and Human Services.

Zimberg, S. (1993). Introduction and general concepts of dual-diagnosis. In J. Solomon, S. Zimberg, & E. Shollar (Eds.) *Dual-diagnosis: Evaluation, treatment, training, and program development* (pp. 4–22). New York: Plenum Medical Book Company.

III

NURSING CARE OF ADDICTED CLIENTS

 INTRODUCTION: PREREQUISITES TO CARE

AN UNDERSTANDING OF MODELS FOR NURSING CARE

The Nurse Practice Act of each state delineates what health care activities are within nursing's jurisdiction to perform. There is a specific practice act for nurse generalists as well as for those who are appropriately prepared and certified to function as Advanced Practice nurses. Advance Practice nurses are allowed greater and more independent practice functions as well as responsibilities.

Fortunately for those clients addicted to alcohol and other drugs it is within the practice acts for both generalists and Advanced Practice nurses to participate in activities along the continuum of care for addicts. This continuum includes primary prevention, screening and detection, assessment and diagnosis, detoxification, interventions and treatment, and relapse prevention, otherwise known as sobriety-focused care.

Over the years, models that guided nursing practice have alternated and emerged in response to changes in the health care environment as well as within the profession. The current health care environment is heavily influenced by "managed care." The underlying focus in managed care is outcomes: What is expected to result from each intervention? What resources are necessary to achieve results? What is a reasonable time frame within which to expect these results? Was the provided service effective?

The core methods of managed care as it relates to behavioral problems, such as alcohol and other drug addiction, includes: 1) managing benefits; 2) managing care—the development and referral of the addicted client to a "complete" continuum of care that incorporates assessment and treatment; and 3) managing health—health promotion, disease prevention, and management of the disease state (Freeman & Trabin, 1994).

In response to the current environment, the nursing profession has developed and promoted nursing models within which nursing acts such as prevention, screening and detection, assessment and diagnosis, detoxification, and interventions and treatment are conducted. Two of the more common models currently being used are clinical pathways and case management.

A clinical pathway is a tool that identifies client outcomes, interventions to meet the outcomes, and the time frame in which they should occur. It is a map for use as a guide to care planned for a client with a particular diagnosis. Case management operationalizes the tenets of managed care by coordinating services across the continuum through referral and contract, in an attempt to link services with the client. It is concerned with all services within the continuum of care; it is not a new concept, it has been done for years by social work as well as community health nurses. Case management is being promoted as a model of care for other areas of nursing as well.

The current health care environment as it relates to cost and reimbursement, along with effective models of nursing practice, impacts on prognoses for addicted clients. However, what is going on inside the client as it relates to the change process associated with recovery, impacts as well.

UNDERSTANDING THE CLIENT IN RELATION TO NURSING CARE

More than a decade ago, the transtheoretical model of change in addictive behaviors was introduced. Prochaska and DiClemente posited that people who are trying to stop their addictive behaviors and take on new healthy behaviors, cycle through five stages of change in their process to recovery. These stages are: 1) precontemplation, 2) contemplation, 3) preparation, 4) action, and 5) maintenance (Prochaska & DiClemente, 1983; Prochaska, 1991; Prochaska, DiClemente, & Norcross, 1992).

During *precontemplation*, the first phase, persons deny that they have an alcohol or other drug addiction. One can expect to hear a client make statements along the lines: "As far as I am concerned, I do not have a problem that needs changing."

During *contemplation*, the second phase, persons acknowledge that there is a problem and recognize the need to change their behavior. Unfortunately, no attempts are made to change, although they are thinking about it. The client knows what needs to be done but is not quite ready yet. One can expect to hear a client make statements along the lines: "I have a problem and I really think I should work on it." Serious consideration is made, but no action taken. It is important to note that most people remain "stuck" in this phase for a long time during their process of change.

During the third phase, preparation, clients intend to take action within the next month. At this point some small steps toward change are taken. Previous action has been taken but proven to be unsuccessful. However, they prepare to take definite action in addressing their addiction. They report small behavioral changes or reductions in the behavior.

During the *action* phase, change is initiated involving actual, obvious change behaviors. Modification in behaviors, experiences, or environments take place in an attempt to overcome the problem. In this stage persons successfully alter their behavior for a period of 1 day to 6 months.

During the last phase, *maintenance*, there occurs a commitment for maintaining or continuing the changed behavior. Here the client is working to stabilize the changed behavior and prevent relapse.

Although a small number of persons progress through the stages in a linear fashion, most progress in a spiral fashion. And, because relapse is more the rule than the exception, nurses should expect clients to recycle through the stages.

When working with addicted clients, nurses frequently see clients only while they may be at the precontemplation or contemplation stage. The continued experience of only hearing clients deny their addiction to alcohol and other drugs, and/or acknowledge that a problem exists, but do nothing about it, may enhance a sense of frustration and futility. It is important for nurses to recognize the three remaining phases that an addicted client can cycle through toward recovery.

Clients do not have to remain at the precontemplation and contemplation phases until they move on their own accord. The nurse can increase their motivation to change. Prochaska (1994) stated that increasing the *pros* of changing by consciousness raising and self-reevaluation helps the client to become more aware of the benefits of stopping the behavior. This serves to assist the client in moving from the precontemplation to the contemplation stage. He further stated that decreasing the *cons* of changing by helping the client become aware of the multitude of consequences related to not quitting the behavior serves to assist the client in moving from the contemplation to the action phase. Both of these activities involves using effective confrontation.

Effective confrontation results from communicating with the client by 1) concreteness—asking what, how, who, when, and where questions; 2) genuineness—a match between the nurse's actions and words; 3) staying reality based—dealing only with the here and now; 4) showing empathy; and above all 5) treating the client with respect. In addition, it is important that the nurse not let common defense mechanisms (e.g., denial, minimization, rationalism, and projection) displayed by the addicted client interfere with attempts at effective confrontation and communication meant to motivate the client to the action phase of the change process.

Having a clear understanding of the current model of nursing practice as well as what stage of change and readiness for interventions and treatment a client may be at, gives the nurse insight into what point of care on the continuum a specific client needs. In addition, it will let the nurse know what type of motivation a client needs.

COMPONENTS OF COMPETENT ADDICTIONS NURSING CARE

Nurses need to be able to do primary prevention, screening and detection, assessment and diagnosis, detoxification, interventions and treatment, or sobriety-focused care often referred to as relapse prevention, with any of their clients who are addicted to alcohol and other drugs. In addition, it is imperative that nurses evaluate the effectiveness of the care they provide because, as discussed earlier, payors in the current health care environment want outcomes. They want to pay for care that has been effective in some way. Hence, nurses must understand how to determine the effectiveness of their care.

The following checklist allows nurses to evaluate whether they are currently up to par in the skills, knowledge, and competencies needed for care of addicted clients. It also allows current educators in schools of nursing to assess their curriculum as it now stands and determine whether the content for assuring appropriate care of addicted clients seen in all settings is included. The chapters in this section provide information specific to the knowledge, as well as the skills and competencies assessed in this checklist, and necessary for all nurses in all settings, because they all encounter addicted clients needing care.

INSTRUCTIONS: On a scale of 1–4 rate the amount of knowledge and skill you learned in your nursing education related to care of addicted clients. 1 = none; 2 = some—not enough to care for addicted clients; 3 = enough to provide some degree of care for addicted clients; and 4 = a lot—enough to provide good care to addicted clients.

A. Designing and conducting primary prevention programs for alcohol, tobacco and other drug (ATOD) addiction in various settings, based on prevention principles. ____

B. Conducting secondary prevention screening processes with appropriate tools, for detecting ATOD addiction. ____

C. Providing thorough assessments and DSM-IV diagnoses of ATOD addiction. ____

D. Providing appropriate detoxification for clients addicted to ATOD. ____

E. Referring clients to correct ATOD addiction intervention and treatment based on patient placement criteria. ____

F. Describing the types of interventions/treatment modalities and approaches available for ATOD addiction. ____

G. Recognizing relapse and engaging in prevention strategies with addicted clients. ____

H. Evaluating the effectiveness of ATOD prevention, intervention, and treatment programs. ____

A score below 24 indicates not enough knowledge and skills obtained to care for addicted clients.

REFERENCES

Freeman, M., & Trabin, T. (1994). *Managed behavioral health-care: History, Models, key issues and future course.* Paper prepared for the U.S. Center for Mental Health Services. Rockville, MD: Substance Abuse and Mental Health Services Administration.

Prochaska, J. (1991). Assessing how people change. *Cancer, 67*(3 Suppl.), 805–807.

Prochaska, J. (1994). Strong and weak principles for progressing from precontemplation to action on the basis of twelve problem behaviors. *Health Psychology, 13*(1), 47–51.

Prochaska, J., & DiClemente, C. (1983). Stages and processes of self-change of smoking: Toward and integrative model of change. *Journal of Consulting and Clinical Psychology, 51*(31), 390–395.

Prochaska, J., DiClemente, C., & Norcross, J. (1992). In search of how people change: Applications to addictive behaviors. *American Psychologist, 47*(9), 1102–1114.

6

Prevention

Karen M. Allen, PhD, RN, CARN

INTRODUCTION

Of the nine most prominent contributors to mortality rates in the United States in 1990, one-third were caused by tobacco, alcohol, and illicit use of drugs (McGinnis & Foege, 1993), and therefore, were preventable. According to the U.S. Preventive Task Force (1989) the majority of deaths experienced by Americans under the age of 65 are preventable.

"Prevention works" is a message being continuously promoted and, in terms of alcohol, tobacco, and other drug (ATOD) addiction, there are many examples of how the message works. There has been a reduction of the per capita consumption of alcohol; there has been a drop in costly hospitalizations for chronic liver disease by almost 40%; alcohol-related traffic fatalities have dropped by almost 30% within a 10-year period; and there is an increased public awareness of the effects of alcohol and tobacco on the fetus, as well as an awareness of effects of passive smoke (Center for Substance Abuse Prevention, 1994a).

It has been said that an "ounce of prevention is worth a pound of cure." This has clearly been proven, and according to Winslow (1992) prevention programs save $3.38 for every $1.00 spent. This is truly believed by the U.S. federal government. As seen in the introduction to section I, many different actions have been implemented toward preventing ATOD addiction. The most recent is the development of the Center for Substance Abuse Prevention (within the Substance Abuse and Mental Health Services Administration).

This organization has headed up tremendous efforts and successes toward preventing ATOD addiction. One is fostering the development of other ATOD prevention initiatives, such as the National Center on Prevention, and a comprehensive training of large groups in key positions to conduct primary prevention. These groups include: 1) health care delivery systems (hospitals, health management organizations [HMOs], preferred provider organizations [PPOs], and other managed care groups); 2) communities, by way of partnership programs; 3) volunteers; 4) state capacity building; 5) rehabilitation specialists; 6) community health and migrant centers; 7) physicians; 8) dentists; 9) mental health specialists; and 10) nurses. The information provided in this chapter largely comes from the work on prevention developed with the health care delivery systems and the nurses' programs.

It is important for nurses to understand that health care related to ATOD addiction occurs on a continuum of care and begins with primary prevention. Therefore, the purpose of this chapter is to provide: 1) an overall definition of prevention along with a description and specific working definitions for primary ATOD prevention; and 2) strategies for prevention.

DEFINITIONS

The most common prevention model used is the "Public Health Model" (discussed in Chapter 2), which posits that prevention occurs at three levels: primary, secondary, and tertiary. Primary prevention—the focus of this chapter—is the reduction or control of causative factors for a particular health problem or disease, and includes reducing risk factors, increasing protective factors, and participating in health service interventions (Teutsch, 1992).

According to the Center for Substance Abuse Prevention Training Systems (CSAP) of the Substance Abuse and Mental Health Services Administration (SAMHSA, 1994b), prevention is an anticipatory process that prepares and supports individuals and systems in the creation and reinforcement of healthy behaviors and lifestyles. Alcohol, tobacco, and other drug problem prevention focuses on risk and protective factors associated with the use of these substances, concentrating on areas in which research and experience suggest that success in reducing abuse and addiction is most likely. Furthermore, ATOD problem prevention makes use of such strategies as collaboration, cultural inclusion, advocacy, and networking, which have been proven by research to contribute to the effectiveness of primary prevention strategies.

PREVENTION STRATEGIES

The earliest prevention programs used information and scare tactics to influence behavioral change. However, studies found that for the most part, these techniques alone were not effective. Information alone is not enough to bring about changed behavior.

General Prevention Strategies

Currently, a more comprehensive, multisystemed approach is recommended, using the strategies described below (CSAP, 1994b,c):

- *Information dissemination*   This strategy provides awareness and knowledge of the nature and extent of ATOD use, abuse, and addiction and their effects on persons, families, and communities, as well as information to increase perceptions of risk. It also could include information about healthy lifestyles. It provides knowledge and awareness of prevention policies, programs services, and helps set and reinforce positive societal norms.
- *Development of life coping skills*   This strategy seeks to affect critical life and social skills. Examples are seen in Box 6-1.
- *Provision of alternatives*   This strategy provides for the participation of targeted populations in activities that exclude ATOD use. Displayed in Box 6-2 is what this prevention techniques tries to accomplish.
- *Community development*   This strategy aims to enhance the ability of the community to provide prevention and treatment services related to ATOD use disorders. Activi-

BOX 6-1. Life Coping Skills

1. Decision-making skills
2. Refusal skills
3. Critical analysis
4. Systematic and judgmental abilities
5. Communication techniques
6. Goal-setting skills
7. Values clarification skills
8. Problem-solving techniques
9. Self-responsibility/self-care
10. Responsible attitude toward alcohol/drugs
11. Stress management/relaxation techniques

BOX 6-2. Goals of the Provision of Alternative Prevention Strategies

1. Contribute to use of and growth in personal skills
2. Create a more positive self-image
3. Develop satisfaction and self-esteem
4. Develop respect for self and others
5. Create opportunity for positive interactions with others
6. Provide identification with appropriate role models
7. Alleviate boredom, unrest, and apathy

ties include organizing, planning, enhancing efficiency and effectiveness of services, implementation, interagency collaboration, coalition building, and networking. This strategy increases the ownership and participation of the community in problem solving. Nurses may facilitate this prevention process or participate as a member of a task force, forum, or in community-based activities.

- *Advocacy for a healthy environment* This strategy sets up or changes written and unwritten community standards, codes, and attitudes that influence incidence and prevalence of ATOD use problems in the general population. Included are laws to restrict availability and access, price increases, and community-wide actions. Displayed in Box 6-3 are the prevention activities a nurse could choose to do.
- *Problem identification* This strategy calls for identification, education, and counseling for those persons who have indulged in age-inappropriate use of ATOD. This includes screening for tendencies toward addiction and referral to brief interventions and/or treatment.

BOX 6-3. Methods for Healthy Environment Advocacy

1. Efforts to change policies, laws, and community norms
2. Support for social measures to limit the availability of alcohol, tobacco, and other drugs
3. Increasing access to health care and social agency assistance
4. Lobbying decision-makers
5. Activities to reduce discrimination
6. Participation in organizations with influence
7. Election to political office

To make a prevention program as effective as possible the following aspects should be considered at the planning stage. First, it needs to be comprehensive and address multiple systems (youth, families, schools, workplaces, community organizations, and media), using in combination a number of the strategies described above, which would lead to it being integrated into family, work, and community life. Any prevention effort needs to involve the entire community that is targeted, and focus on everyone rather than just those believed to be at high risk. It has been found that ATOD prevention programs that are part of a broader generic effort to promote health and reduce and eliminate risk, is more effective than if it stood alone (CSAP, 1994b). An example of a model of a multisystem, comprehensive prevention program is shown in Table 6-1.

Prevention programs should serve to build a supportive environment that enhances protective/resiliency factors, which mandates that they be culturally sensitive and specific. Furthermore, prevention programs can and should be made to focus across the lifespan—from prenatal to senior years—and last for some time, as opposed to being "one-shot" deals.

The definition of primary prevention in general and as it applies to ATOD use and abuse specifically identify the importance of risk factors and protective factors. As the nurse focuses the planned prevention programs for communities and individuals, as well as across the lifespan, knowledge of risk and protective factors that impact the use of ATOD at each level is necessary.

Risk Factors   A risk factor is an attitude, belief, behavior, situation, and/or action that may put a person, a group, an organization, or a community at risk for experiencing drug use, abuse, addiction, and its effects. However, it does not necessarily predict future drug use or addiction. Boxes 6-4 through 6-7 outline specific risk factors. This list is not exhaustive, other risk factors may come to mind while reading those outlined (CSAP, 1994b).

TABLE 6-1   A Comprehensive Model of Primary Prevention

	Target Groups				
Methods	**Individual** (across the life span)	**Family**	**Peers**	**School/Work**	**Community** (culture-specific)
Education/ information	Posters	Programs	Seminars	Teacher/ supervisor training	Brochure distribution
Personal development	Skill building	Parenting training	Work teams	Supportive environment	Wellness programs
Alternatives	After-school programs	Family night	Mentors	Company teams	Park facilities
Norms/ standards	ATOD use principles, beliefs, and behaviors	Health care coverage for treatment	Peer-support programs	SAP/EAP*	Money to agencies
Community mobilization	Clean-up projects	Family support	Alcohol-free events	Coalition building	Media Campaign

*SAP = student assistance programs; EAP = employee assistance programs.

BOX 6-4. Family Risk Factors

1. Lack of clear behavioral expectations
2. Lack of monitoring/supervision
3. Lack of caring
4. Inconsistent or excessively severe discipline
5. History of alcohol and other drug abuse
6. Positive parental attitudes toward alcohol and other drug abuse
7. Low expectations for children's success

Protective Factors   A protective factor is an attitude, belief, situation, and/or action that protects an individual, a group, an organization, or a community from the effects of drug use. However, it does not predict absence of future ATOD abuse or addiction. Some of the protective factors found to be effective in preventing ATOD addiction include: 1) a relationship with a caring adult role model; 2) having an opportunity to contribute and be seen as a resource; 3) effectiveness in work, play, and relationships; 4) healthy expectations and positive outlook; 5) self-esteem and internal locus of control; 6) self-discipline; 7) problem solving/critical thinking skills; 8) a sense of humor; and 9) strong identification with an ethnic or cultural group (CSAP, 1994b).

Individual Practice Strategies

Nurses can begin their quest to incorporate prevention into personal professional activities by first examining their own ATOD use and deciding whether or not it is consistent with personal professional responsibility. Then, they need to learn what they can do to contribute to ATOD prevention in general. Initially, give "brief advice" about the use and abuse of ATOD along with information on consequences of abuse and addiction to all clients. Next, become familiar with available resources in the area that clients can be referred to. Another strategy is to inform clients and their families about the side effects of combining alcohol and other drugs, and drug/drug interactions when prescribing or discussing medications.

Nurses can also work with their health care delivery system to institute primary ATOD prevention for their clients. The following strategies targeted at clients may include (CSAP, 1994c):

BOX 6-5. Individual and Peer Risk Factors

1. Early antisocial behavior
2. Alienation and rebelliousness
3. Later antisocial behavior
4. Favorable attitudes toward drug use
5. Susceptibility to peer influence
6. Friends who use tobacco, alcohol, and drugs

BOX 6-6. Community Risk Factors

1. Economic and social deprivation
2. Low neighborhood attachment
3. Community norms that facilitate drug use/abuse
4. Availability of tobacco, alcohol, and drugs

BOX 6-7. **Risk Factors According to Life Span**

CHILDHOOD

1. Fetal exposure to alcohol, tobacco, and other drugs (ATOD)
2. Children of addicts
3. Victims of physical, sexual, or psychological abuse
4. Economically disadvantaged youth
5. Delinquent youth
6. Youth with mental health problems such as depression and suicidal ideation
7. Disabled youth

ADOLESCENCE

1. ATOD drug use by parents
2. Low self-esteem
3. Depression
4. Psychological distress
5. Poor relationship with parents
6. Low sense of social responsibility
7. Lack of religious commitment
8. Low academic performance and motivation
9. Peer use of ATOD
10. Participation in deviant, aggressive behavior

YOUNG ADULTHOOD

1. Exposure to drug users in social and work environments
2. Marital and work instability
3. Unemployment
4. Divorce
5. Lack of social supports
6. Psychological or psychiatric difficulties

MIDDLE ADULTHOOD

1. Bereavement, especially from loss of spouse or significant other
2. Adverse work conditions or unemployment
3. Changes in health status or appearance
4. Socioeconomic stressors
5. Environmental changes or relocation
6. Divorce, separation, and/or remarriage
7. Difficulties with children or changes in childrearing responsibilities

OLDER ADULTHOOD

1. Retirement role status change
2. Loss of loved ones
3. Changes in health status and mobility
4. Increased sensitivity to effects of ATOD
5. Housing relocations
6. Affective changes (e.g., anxiety and depression)
7. History of previous misuse or abuse of ATOD
8. Solitary or social contexts fostering use of ATOD
9. Negative self-concept

- Information and education programs (lecture series, pamphlets, videos, etc.)
- Awareness events and seminars (lifestyle, early warning signs, etc.)
- General health risk appraisals, screenings, and follow-up for persons identified as potentially having an ATOD problem
- Early intervention and counseling related to health risk behaviors
- A workshop series for ATOD problem prevention including smoking cessation, lifestyle management, parenting
- Counter advertising (e.g., the benefits of not: smoking, drinking, misusing prescription medicines).

Strategies targeting the community and social policy that can be used by nurses include:

- School health education
- Server training
- Educating local and state legislators on topics such as limiting access to ATOD and creating appropriate tax incentives to reduce consumption
- Counteradvertising
- Seminars and materials targeting the corporate community
- Employee Assistance Programs for corporate clients
- Student Assistance Programs for schools
- Participation in post-traumatic event debriefings within workplaces, schools, and communities
- Collaboration with community-sponsored events that build prevention capacity and transfer prevention technology

With health care moving out into the community, nurses are finding that more and more they are being required to provide care to clients across the lifespan, as well as across settings. Hence, some helpful dos and don'ts follow (CSAP, 1994c).

COMMUNITY PREVENTION PROGRAMS

Nurses need to provide a comprehensive program to include all of the following: 1) current and accurate information; 2) education and life skills development; 3) training of leaders in the community; and 4) positive message and media campaigns. Community-based prevention programs need to be inclusive of and consistent with the values, beliefs, cultural norms, and needs of that community. It is critical that nurses not view prevention programs as "what worked for one community will work for all." In addition, the entire community should be involved in designing, planning, implementing, and evaluating prevention programs and strategies. This is a good time to cooperate and collaborate with other prevention and health promotion programs, organizations, and agencies.

WORKPLACE PREVENTION PROGRAMS

For nurses conducting prevention programs in the workplace, it is important to advocate for a clear communication of the policies about ATOD use, ATOD impairment during work hours, or use of illicit drugs on or off the job. In addition, employee education and awareness programs can include those that have clear ATOD "no use" messages. And last but not least, refer to and utilize employee assistance programs for impaired employees.

CHILDREN, ADOLESCENT, AND YOUNG ADULT PREVENTION PROGRAMS

Primary prevention programs centered on these groups should provide factual information, teach life skills, and address myths about ATOD. In addition, they should provide healthy, planned alternative activities with supervision. These programs should build individual resiliency focusing on protective factors (e.g., shared values and a sense of belonging; structure and consistent rules, availability of family and neighbors for emotional support). Nurses should view and treat this audience as a resource. It is recommended that presentations and materials related to previous use, which resulted in recovery, not be used with this group, because rather than hearing the "don't do as I did" message, they hear that the presenter used drugs and survived it O.K.

PARENT PREVENTION PROGRAMS

Suggestions for addressing prevention of ATOD with parents include: 1) providing opportunities and literature for parents to learn about the problem; 2) emphasizing to them the significance of listening to children and helping them succeed; 3) helping parents establish and consistently maintain clear family policies with consequences about ATOD use; and 4) pointing out the importance of knowing their children's friends and supervising their activities. This could take place within parenting classes.

EVALUATION

Research and evaluation has provided much insight into what works and does not work in programs geared toward ATOD prevention. Determining the effectiveness of a prevention program needs to be implemented by all persons, groups, organizations, or communities doing prevention. Often it is neglected because of time, confidence in ability to do it, money, and knowledge about the techniques of evaluation.

Evaluating the effectiveness of prevention strategies and programs can be done using debriefing sessions, observations, in-depth personal interviews, questionnaires, focus groups, or other methods. Teutsch (1992) recommended more formal approaches to evaluating the effectiveness of prevention programs. He stated that effectiveness of prevention strategies should include: 1) identifying whether or not it works; 2) determining the potential and practical consequences of the strategies (social, legal, ethical, economic, etc.); 3) determining which methods are best used when implementing which strategies; and 4) evaluating the impact of the program.

Impact evaluation asks the question "What effect did the prevention program have on the intended audience?" It is concerned with the outcomes, both positive and negative (CSAP, 1994d). Therefore, structured and well-planned evaluation efforts should be developed in conjunction with any prevention program. They need not be complicated and extensive. They can be as simple as giving a quiz on the effects of drugs on health before an education program, and giving it again afterward to assess any change in knowledge base. Another example is comparing statistics on before and after to determine the number of elderly who take time to find out about proper medication administration and not taking alcohol with certain drugs after listening to a prevention program disseminating this information. Another example is developing an after-hours community activity for young people as an alternative to hanging out in the streets, and assessing the impact it has on preventing gang, violence, or drug-related activities. More in-depth information required for use in evaluating the effectiveness of ATOD prevention programs is discussed in Chapter 12.

CONCLUSION

Nursing is a profession originally developed on a theory of prevention. Florence Nightingale's premise was that with more sanitation and less uncleanness patients would improve from their illness much quicker. Much of what happens that is *right* in the healing of illness and disease in medicine today is the result of prevention; however, it is not stated as such. Someone recovering from surgery or pneumonia is said to have done so because of the surgery itself or the use of antibiotics. Yet, the client was also kept clean; the health care staff used infection control or prevention procedures; maintenance staff also kept the floors clean, bathroom clean, etc, and other preventive actions were instituted. Nurses encouraged clients and worked with them on deep-breathing, ambulation, or repositioning them in bed to keep fluid from settling in the lungs. When clients are hospitalized for diabetes, nurses teach them the importance of exercise, proper diet, foot care, and medication management to prevent complications. Family members of persons in the intensive care units are given support as well as education about some of the lifestyle changes to be made for a client to prevent future heart attack or stroke. Nurses practice primary prevention automatically in a number of ways.

However, they need to embrace their responsibility to practice and promote primary prevention as it relates to ATOD use, abuse, and addiction. The nursing profession is the largest group of health care professionals in the United States, therefore, chances are that they are touched more by this problem than any other profession, whether it is through their own struggle with ATOD addiction, having a family member or significant other that is addicted, or encountering clients in their various work settings who are addicted.

The information provided in this chapter presents clear definitions and practical strategies that nurses can use to impact on and contribute to primary prevention of ATOD in their home, workplace, or community setting. Nursing care related to ATOD addiction begins at the tip of the continuum—with primary prevention. Although, nursing has been relegated to addressing the problem at the end—with tertiary prevention—while providing care for complications at the full-blown state of addictions, that has to change. The current health care plans—whether they be federal, state, or private payors—advocate prevention, improved lifestyles, and less money being spent on illness and disease states. Health care will not change in that respect without the profession of nursing. It will not change unless the focus of the largest group of health care providers changes from that of "cure" to one of "prevention," particularly for ATODs. Where to begin? With you. Adopt 1) a prevention strategy from those presented above or others known but not presented in this chapter; 2) a target group; 3) a setting; and go for it!

REFERENCES

Center for Substance Abuse Prevention. (1994a). *Invest in prevention: Prevention works in health care delivery systems. Pre-session materials*. Rockville, MD: U.S. Department of Health and Human Services Substance Abuse and Mental Health Services Administration.

Center for Substance Abuse Prevention. (1994b). *Nurse training course: Prevention of alcohol, tobacco and other drug problems*. Rockville, MD: U.S. Department of Health and Human Services Substance Abuse and Mental Health Services Administration.

Center for Substance Abuse Prevention. (1994c). *Invest in prevention: Prevention works in health care delivery systems*. Rockville, MD: U.S. Department of Health and Human Services Substance Abuse and Mental Health Services Administration.

Center for Substance Abuse Prevention. (1994d). *Prevention primer: An encyclopedia of alcohol, tobacco and other prevention terms*. DHHS Publication No. (SMA) 94-2060. Rockville, MD: Substance Abuse and Mental Health Services Administration.

McGinnis, J., & Foege, W. (1993). Actual Causes of Death in the United States. *Journal of the American Medical Association, 270*(18), 2207–2212.

Teutsch, S. (March 27, 1992). A framework for assessing the effectiveness of disease and injury prevention. *Morbidity and Mortality Weekly Report, 41*(RR-3), 1–12.

U.S. Preventive Services Task Force. (1989). *Guide to clinical preventive services: An assessment of the effectiveness of 169 interventions*. Baltimore, MD: Williams & Wilkins.

Winslow, R. (1992, May 1). Infant Health Problems Cost Business Billions. *Wall Street Journal*, p. B-1, B-12.

Screening and Detection

Christine Savage, MS, RN, CARN

INTRODUCTION

With the growing concern for health care reform, prevention has come to the forefront because reports are indicating of its effectiveness by savings $85 to $90 million each year in health care costs (Edleman, 1993; Rice, 1993). Prevention—as defined by the Public Health Model—incorporates three types: primary, secondary, and tertiary (Teutsch, 1992). Primary prevention was discussed in the previous chapter and has a goal of stopping the problem before it starts; secondary prevention's focus is on identification and detection of the problem early on, if it exists; and tertiary prevention deals with treating the problem to keep it from causing further damage. The purpose of this chapter is to discuss secondary prevention as it relates to alcohol and other drug (AOD) abuse/addiction.

Secondary prevention involves early detection of problems or disease in asymptomatic individuals. The importance of early detection of disease is based on the premise that treatment will retard or stop the progression of disease in cases where the disease is detected early (Morrison, 1992). Early detection is usually accomplished through a process known as screening.

Screening programs can be divided into two major types: 1) programs directed at asymptomatic persons such as those who seek medical care for specific problems unrelated to the disease needing to be screened for, or participate in random screening activities; and 2) programs directed toward identified individuals who *might* have the problem. Screening programs of the second type are accepted and well established with regard to AOD abuse and/or addiction. However, screening programs of the first type—screening asymptomatic persons in general populations—is less well established for this health problem (Stockwell and colleagues, 1994).

Models of secondary prevention programs—screening—can be found in other disease prevention programs. The use of regular mammography testing has been promoted to help identify women in the early stages of breast cancer. Blood pressure screening has been promoted to identify persons with hypertension in the general population. Glaucoma screening by ophthalmologists provides another example. These programs do not diagnose a disease, they assist in detecting which members of a given population probably have the disease or problem. Once individuals are identified as possibly having a given disease or problem, they are referred for assessment and diagnosis, then if necessary, treatment.

Nurses are in a unique position to impact AOD abuse/addiction by implementing screening in their clinical areas. Whether they are in a hospital setting, a health management organization (HMO) setting, an ambulatory care setting, a primary care setting, a community clinic setting, an occupational setting, a home health care setting, etc., they are on the front line with clients and better able to screen for problems. Notably, an important study conducted by Tolley and Rowland (1991) of 4898 clients over a 2-year period concluded that nurses were the preferred providers for developing and implementing AOD screening programs. Hence, it is important that this large group of health care providers have the necessary knowledge base. Therefore, the discussion in this chapter will include: 1) definitions of screening; 2) principles of the screening process; 3) a review of various screening mechanisms and instruments; 4) screening techniques; and 5) nursing interventions following the screening. In addition, identification and detection of drug seekers in primary care settings will be discussed.

DEFINITIONS OF SCREENING

Screening and detection reflect an attempt to identify unrecognized disease through the application of tests, examinations, or other procedures that can be applied within a reasonable amount of time. The purpose is to sort out well persons who probably have the disease from those who probably do not, so that effective intervention and/or treatment activities can take place (Mausner & Kramer, 1985; Teutsch, 1992).

The National Institute on Alcohol Abuse and Alcoholism (NIAAA) (1990) defined screening as a process that identifies people at risk for the disease. The two types of AOD screening methods most frequently used are: 1) self-report or interview-based questionnaires, and 2) clinical laboratory tests (Bush and colleagues, 1987).

Rahdert, Metzger, and Winters (1993) described AOD screening as being able to determine the presence or absence of a specific problem with AOD use. It should be differentiated from the assessment and diagnostic process that describes the problem in detail and results in a diagnosis indicative of the necessary care. According to the Substance Abuse and Mental Health Services Administration [SAMHSA] (1994a) screening refers to a brief procedure used to determine the presence of a problem, substantiate that there is reason for concern, or identify the need for further evaluation.

PRINCIPLES OF SCREENING

Rationale

Scientific evidence examined by the U.S. Preventive Services Task Force (1989) provided a rationale in support of routine screening for disease based on the following questions. Is the incidence high enough to justify the cost of a screening program for this problem? Does the problem have a significant effect on the quality or quantity of life? Is effective treatment available? Are screening tests available that meet the hallmarks for a screening program? Are there adverse effects from the screening, and if so, are these effects acceptable to clinicians and clients? Would early intervention and treatment reduce morbidity and mortality from this problem (U.S. Department of Health and Human Services, 1994). Because the answer is yes to the first four questions and no the last as it relates to AOD screening, it can be said that a rationale exists for the implementation of routine alcohol, tobacco, and other drug screening by nurses in their clinical areas of practice.

Critical Issues Impacting Screening Programs

With a rationale for screening programs clearly established, nurses should keep in mind five general issues that affect implementation of screening programs in health care settings. These issues are: 1) reimbursement; 2) professional education; 3) standards of care; 4) practice barriers; and 5) societal norms (U.S. Department of Health and Human Services, 1994).

Reimbursement for preventive services is a constant debate and to date it is not available; however, results can lead to the need for assessment and treatment, which are reimbursable. There must be a training or educational activity completed with health care providers to assure that appropriate knowledge and skills exist to implement the program. A number of efforts are contributing to this: 1) more schools are including this information in their curriculum; 2) the Center for Substance Abuse Treatment has funded 11 addictions training centers for existing health care professionals to learn required knowledge and skills; and 3) professional organizations, such as the National Nurses Society on Addictions, conduct training workshops for nurses to teach information related to screening.

Although there are no specific standards of care for screening and detection per se, there are standards of care specific to the addicted client, and initiating the process of providing care to addicted clients through screening meets those standards. Barriers to nurses implementing a screening program include: 1) attitude toward the AOD problem itself, not to mention the client; 2) lack of knowledge and skills; 3) resistance to participation from clients because of stigma attached to the diagnosis; and 4) time that the nurse may or may not have. Societal norms are impacted by whatever social, occupational, or familial settings the nurse and client come from, and has to be addressed at individual clinical settings. Once the above issues have been examined and addressed the screening process is ready to be initiated.

The Process

Screening procedures typically involve a single event. The hallmarks of a screening program are: 1) its ability to be administered rapidly—in about 10 to 15 minutes—and efficiently; 2) its broad applicability across diverse populations based on factors such as age, race and ethnicity, socioeconomic status, and literacy level; 3) its ability to be easily answered, scored, and interpreted (if using a written method); 4) the requirement of minimal training to prepare a nonprofessional to administer the tool; and 5) low cost of administering the screening (Rahdert et al., 1993; SAMHSA, 1994b).

Another important principle is to clearly state what is being screened. In a general population, screening for AOD abuse and dependence would reflect its presence or absence. Whereas in a population already identified as being at risk, the screening program may be looking for the presence or absence of severe addiction versus occasional AOD abuse. Unfortunately, studies relating to testing for AOD problems often fail to establish if the measures deal with severity as opposed to the mere presence or absence of the problem (Stockwell et al., 1994).

An effective screening program will also include a process for setting up further follow-up for those who have a positive screen, as shown in Figure 7-1. Once the screening procedure is administered and a positive result is found, the next step is to refer the client for a thorough assessment. If the assessment reveals information in support of diagnosed AOD

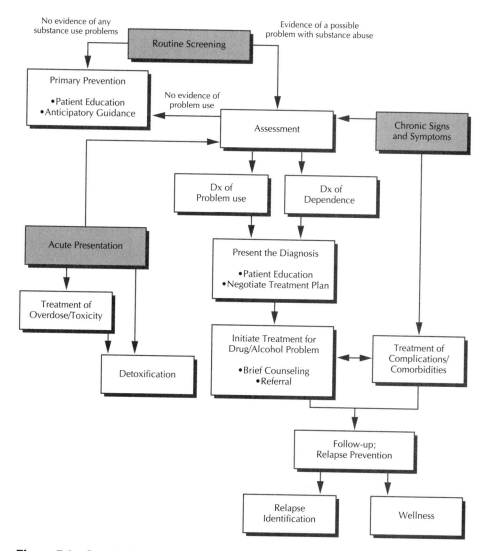

Figure 7-1. Screening process for substance abuse: The health care professional's role. (Source: Dube C, Goldstein MG, Lewis DC. [1989]. Project ADEPT Volume I: *Core modules.* Brown University, Providence, RI. Reproduced with permission.)

addiction, the appropriate level of intervention and/or treatment will be recommended to the client. The screening process is usually completed with tools such as written question- naires and/or laboratory tests. However, before using a tool for screening, it is essential to determine whether the tool will actually screen for the identified disease—in this case AOD problems. This can be done by examining its validity, reliability, and yield.

Validity, Reliability, and Yield

Validity, reliability, and yield are important characteristics of a screening tool (Mausner & Kramer, 1985). Validity refers to the determination of whether or not a tool is useful for the purpose for which it is intended; that is, if it measures what it purports to measure. Reliability refers to the consistency with which a device or method assigns scores to subjects (Waltz, Strickland, & Lenz, 1991). Yield also reflects the amount of disease detected in the population (Mausner & Kramer, 1985).

VALIDITY

The key to a screening tool is its ability to indicate which individuals in the given population actually have the disease and those who do not. In screening tools validity has two components: sensitivity and specificity.

Sensitivity reflects how well the tool measures members of the population who have the disease. Specificity relates to how well the tool identifies those without the disease (Mausner & Kramer, 1985). Sensitivity is equal to positive results. Its formula being [true positives + false negatives (i.e., all positives)]. While specificity is a measure of the likelihood that a positive test result is truly positive, specificity is equal to negative test results. Its formula being [true negatives + false positives (i.e., all negatives)] (SAMHSA, 1994b) (see Figure 7-2 for an example). Thus, tools with high sensitivity have less false negatives and those with high specificity have less false positives.

Therefore, if it is more important to identify as many potential positives as possible, then the chosen tool should be more heavily weighted on the sensitivity side. If it is more important to identify those without the disease, then the tool should be more heavily weighted on the specificity side.

As pointed out by Mausner and Kramer (1985), the predictive value of a screening tool remains dependent on the prevalence of the disease in the population. If screening for AOD abuse and addiction is being conducted in a general population with a low prevalence of the disease, a positive result is less likely to be predictive of disease. In a population where the prevalence is high, such as in the criminal population (Inciardi, 1994), a positive test is more likely to predict AOD dependence. The positive predictive value of a screening test reflects the proportion of true positives. Likewise, it is possible to calculate the negative predictive value of a screening tool that reflects the proportion of true negatives.

RELIABILITY

The reliability of a screening tool for AOD problems reflects the consistency of the results of the tool. Various factors can influence the reliability of the test. With laboratory tests used for screening AOD use, there has been a great debate over the variance between results from different laboratories (Holbrook & McCurdy, 1991). With questionnaire-style screening tools, issues such as imprecision of the measure itself, temporal factors, individual differences at measurement time, and/or imprecision in the administration or scoring of the measure can affect the reliability (Waltz, Strickland, & Lenz, 1991). In addition, due to the social undesirability of admitting to AOD use, the reliability of self-reported drug and alcohol use continues to be critiqued in the literature (Embree & Whitehead, 1991; Harris, Wilsnack, & Klassen, 1994).

Attempts have been made to standardize screening measures. A number of tools have been utilized over time with established validity and reliability that will be discussed later in the chapter. By definition, screening tools are designed to be easy to administer and require less expertise in interpretation. These factors help to increase the reliability of these measures.

	True Risk Drinking Status		
	Positive	Negative	Screening Test Totals
Results of Screening Test			
Positive	a (4)	b (10)	a + b (14)
Negative	c (1)	d (85)	c + d (86)
True Status Total	a + c (5)	b + d (95)	(100)

a = The number of women for whom the screening test for risk drinking is positive, and they actually are risk drinkers (true positive).

b = The number of women for whom the screening test for risk drinking is positive, but they are not risk drinkers (false positive).

c = The number of women for whom the screening test for risk drinking is negative, but they are risk drinkers (false negative).

d = The number of women for whom the screening test for risk drinking is negative, and they are not risk drinkers (true negative).

$$\text{Sensitivity}[1] = \frac{a}{a + c} = \frac{4}{5} = 80.0\%$$

$$\text{Specificity}[2] = \frac{d}{b + d} = \frac{85}{95} = 89.5\%$$

$$\text{Positive Predictive Value}[3] = \frac{a}{a + b} = \frac{4}{14} = 28.6\%$$

$$\text{Efficiency}[4] = \frac{a + d}{a + b + c + d} = \frac{89}{100} = 89.0\%$$

[1] The probability that a risk drinker is positive on the test.
[2] The probability that a nonrisk drinker is negative on the test.
[3] The probability that a woman with a positive screening score is a risk drinker.
[4] The overall percentage of women correctly identified.

Figure 7-2. Determining sensitivity and specificity (an example). (Source: Russell, M. [1994]. New assessment tools for risk drinking during pregnancy: T-ACE, TWEAK, and other. *Alcohol Health and Research World, 18*[1]; 55–61.)

YIELD

The yield of a screening program can be affected by the following factors: 1) sensitivity of the measure(s); 2) prevalence of unrecognized disease; 3) use of a multiphasic screening program; 4) identification of risk factors; and 5) participation in screening and follow-up (Mausner & Kramer, 1985). A test with high sensitivity will result in identification of more positive individuals providing a larger yield. If there is a high prevalence of undiagnosed disease in a certain population, a screening program should result in more positive results. For example, a screening program in an inner-city high school may have a higher yield than a similar program in a middle class suburban elementary school. One method of increasing participation in a screening program and producing a higher yield is the use of a multiphasic screening approach. In this approach more than one disease is screened for at the same time. An example may be a program that screens for high blood pressure and glaucoma. This approach could be useful in screening for AOD abuse and addiction. A screening program that wished to reach a larger general population might be effectively joined with larger screening programs that target more socially accepted diseases.

The screening of a general population with unknown prevalence of AOD abuse and dependence could be assisted by the identification of members of the population most at risk. A number of risk factors for AOD abuse and dependence have been described in the literature including family history, criminal behavior, lifestyle, trauma, or other medical disorders (Estes & Heinemann, 1986; Boyd, 1993; Caudill et al, 1994; Duncan, Duncan & Hops, 1994; Inciardi, 1994; Savage, 1994). Thus, if an emergency room staff wished to conduct an AOD screening program, they might first identify risk factors for the disease and then select clients for screening based on those factors.

Participation and follow-up are the final aspects of the yield of a screening program. It has been postulated that the low social desirability of the addiction as well as the high rates of denial, would most likely result in a low participation rate (Harris, Wilsnack, & Klassen, 1994). Currently, many screening programs are conducted with a population that must participate—such as employees prior to job assignment or following a work-related incident, or clients in health care settings. Hence, a fair to good yield is usually accomplished. However, these are captive populations. More work needs to be done to increase participation and follow-up among noncaptive populations.

OVERVIEW OF SCREENING TOOLS

A variety of screening tools are available for use. These include both questionnaires and laboratory tests. Some of the tools are specific to alcohol, some to drug use, and some to both.

Regarding the questionnaire-type tools, there are some that have been used for a period of time with established reliability and validity such as the CAGE and the DAST (the drug abuse screening test). However, new AOD screening questionnaires are being developed that attempt to answer the limitations of these more established tools. These include the T-ACE and the TWEAK. A number of laboratory tests are available to screen for alcohol use and drug use. However, urine screen remains the laboratory test of choice for other drug use. A brief description follows of the most commonly used screening questionnaires and laboratory tests, and their strengths and weaknesses. (See Appendixes for copies of these questionnaires.)

Questionnaires

The alcohol use disorder identification test (AUDIT) is a brief, two-part multicultural screening tool for the early identification of problem drinking (Babor & Grant, 1989). It was developed by a working group of the World Health Organization (WHO). This WHO working group selected questions that identified high-risk drinkers in a six-nation study (U.S. Department of Health and Human Services, 1994). It contains a series of 10 questions that include three items on alcohol use, four on dependence, and three about problems. These questions can be administered in an interview or as a paper-and-pencil questionnaire. Using a cut-off score of 8, the AUDIT displayed an overall sensitivity of 92% and a specificity of 93%. In addition, there is an updated version that has been revised to include drugs (Fleming & Barry, 1992).

The CAGE and CAGE-AID, which screen for problems with alcohol abuse and dependence, are the tests most widely used as standard screening in clinical practice (Mayfield, McLeod, & Hall 1974; Ewing, 1984; Buchsbaum, Buchanan, Centor, Schnoll, & Lawton, 1991).

It has a simple format that is easy to use. The title of the questionnaire was derived from the first letter of the key word in each sentence. The questions can be worked into a general conversation, thus placing the client at ease. The questionnaire consists of four questions: Have you ever felt the need to *Cut* down on your drinking? Do you feel *Annoyed* by people complaining about your drinking? Do you ever feel *Guilty* about your drinking? Do you ever need an *Eye* opener in the morning to relieve the shakes? A score of two yes answers or more is usually considered a positive screen. Studies using the CAGE questionnaire found that it correctly identified 75% of alcoholics (true positives) and accurately eliminated 96% of nonalcoholics (Inciardi, 1994).

Various studies have demonstrated the usefulness of the CAGE test. Bush et al. (1987) evaluated the ability of CAGE to detect alcohol abuse and dependence in a community hospital population. They found that CAGE had a sensitivity of 85% and a specificity of 89%. The positive predictive value of the CAGE test in this population was 62%. They compared these results with standard laboratory screening tests and found a much greater sensitivity, specificity, and positive predictive value for CAGE over all of the standard tests. For this study they considered one or more positive answers as a positive screen.

The CAGE test continues to be used in many settings. It has the advantage of being easy to administer. The questions can be included within a general interview of a client. It has well established reliability and validity and is easy to score. However, it has been utilized mainly on male populations who have already been identified as at risk for alcohol abuse or dependence. The CAGE-AID is the adapted version for inclusion of other drugs.

DAST was developed by Skinner (1982). It is composed of 28 questions that relate to problems associated with drug abuse. The stated reason for developing the tool was to provide a convenient instrument to assess the extent of problems related to drug use. The total score provided a quantitative index of problem severity. In practice it has been used as a screening tool. A DAST score greater than five is usually considered a positive score. An examination of studies using the DAST demonstrated that it has been primarily used with a population that has already been identified with a drug problem (Skinner, 1982; Nystrom, Perasalo, & Salaspuro, 1993).

Another screening tool used frequently to detect persons at risk for alcohol abuse or dependence is the MAST (Michigan alcohol screening test). It was developed in a self-report format; however, it can also be administered in a face-to-face interview. It consists of 24 questions that can be answered yes or no, and has established reliability and validity. This questionnaire has a number of shorter versions including the SMAST (short Michigan alcohol screening test) and the MM-MAST (Malmo Michigan alcohol screening test). In addition, there is a geriatric version—MAST-G— which has been developed and is being refined by Dr. F. Blow and colleagues at the University of Michigan (1992).

The MAST obtains information about difficulties with social relations, problems in employment, and difficulties in controlling the abuse of alcohol. The SMAST has 13 questions and the MM-MAST has 9 questions. A score on the MM-MAST of two or more is considered a positive screen. Nystrom, Perasalo, and Salaspuro (1993) demonstrated that the MM-MAST had a sensitivity of 66% for heavy drinking and 73% for alcoholism. Its specificity was 95% for both.

The problem-oriented screening instrument for teenagers (POSIT) test is a promising new tool developed by Tarter and an expert panel sponsored by the National Institute on Drug Abuse (McLellan & Dembo, 1992). It is a 139-item self-administered questionnaire designed for use with 12- to 19-year olds, which covers 10 problem areas including a 14-item subscale measuring alcohol and other drug use and abuse. One or more positive responses is considered a positive result. A number of studies are assessing the validity of the POSIT test in general population samples.

The Simple Screening Instrument for Alcohol and Other Drug Abuse was developed by a consensus panel of experts in AOD use, abuse, and dependence, as well as instrument development (SAMHSA, 1994b). The purpose of this instrument is to address a wide array of signs and symptoms, including AOD consumption, problem recognition, loss of control and recognition, adverse consequences, and physiological issues. It was developed to be used by all service agencies and service providers, and can be administered easily and quickly.

Although no reliability and validity testing has been reported on the instrument at this time, the majority of the items were adapted from existing tools found in published literature, with already established reliability and validity.

T-ACE and TWEAK are two instruments that have been adapted from the CAGE for use with pregnant women. They were tested on 4000 patients attending a prenatal clinic in Detroit, Michigan (Russell, Martier, Sokol, Jacobson, Jacobson, & Bottoms, 1991; Russell, 1994). The T-ACE developed by Sokol, Martier, and Ager (1989) substitutes a question on tolerance for one on guilt. The TWEAK is a similar modification that assesses *T*olerance; *W*orry—Have close friends or relatives worried or complained about your drinking?; *E*ye opener—Do you sometimes take a drink in the morning to wake up?; *A*mnesia—Has a friend or family member ever told you things you said or did while you were drinking that you could not remember?; and *K* (cut)—Do you sometimes feel the need to cut down on your drinking? TWEAK items are weighted, and a score of three is considered to be a positive test. In a sample of nonabstaining women attending an inner-city prenatal clinic, the TWEAK exceeded the T-ACE in predictive value relative to risk drinking during pregnancy.

The Trauma Scale Screening Tool was developed due to the possible correlation between trauma and the presence of alcohol abuse. It is a five-item tool and usually a score of two or more is considered a positive screen. Studies indicated that the results are similar to the CAGE and the MAST, although the sensitivity of the tool appears to be influenced by sociodemographic variables (Nystrom, Perasalo, & Salaspuro, 1993). See the Appendix for some of the screening tools.

SCREENING TECHNIQUES

There are a number of techniques that will increase the nurses screening results. These include the following steps: 1) start with general questions about use of prescribed drugs, over-the-counter drugs, and self-prescribed drugs; 2) ask about all alcohol, tobacco, and other drug use; 3) expect clients to use more than one substance; 4) use one of the above tools to determine whether the person is at risk for abusing or being addicted; 5) while asking the questions, address any avoidance or discrepancies in a nonjudgmental, nonattacking manner; 6) observe client behavior during the interview—in some cases, denial or false information may be indicated by uncomfortable posture, avoidance of eye contact, long pauses before answering, fidgety and restless movements, and hostile gestures; however, in some cases body language tells you nothing.

Laboratory Tests

A number of laboratory tests can be conducted that will screen for current AOD use. The popularity of these tests has grown with the need for compliance with the drug-free workplace legislation (Bush et al., 1993) and screening for possible driving while intoxicated (DWI) offenders (Hingson, 1993). Laboratory tests should be used with caution because they are not always indicative of AOD dependence. Bush et al. (1987) found that some of the laboratory tests used to screen for alcohol abuse had less sensitivity, specificity, and positive predictive value than the CAGE and the MAST.

BLOOD SCREENS

Testing for blood alcohol levels (BAL) can be accomplished through blood tests and breath analysis. In breath analysis a small sample of alveolar air is collected and analyzed for alcohol content. In blood tests, a sample of venous blood is drawn. The results are commonly expressed as a percentage of ethyl alcohol to blood volume (e.g., .10% BAL = 100 mg/ml). The results must be interpreted based on the time of the last drink and the ability of the subject to metabolize alcohol. In a healthy male client the rate of alcohol metabolism is approximately 25 mg per hour. Obtaining a BAL has use in detecting alcohol abuse in previously diagnosed alcohol abusers. However, it is less useful in undiagnosed clients (Foy, Cline, & Laasi, 1987); therefore, care should be taken in interpreting the results since they only reflect current drinking.

A BAL of .05% usually results in impaired vision and coordination. At a BAL of .05 to .10%, there is a removal of inhibitions and a sense of euphoria. From .1 to .2%, slurred speech, ataxia, poor judgment, and labile mood occur. At .25%, there is an inability to remain upright without support. At .3 to .4%, there is some degree of anesthesia and impending or actual coma. The anesthetic level of alcohol is close to the lethal dose. A blood alcohol level above .4% often results in respiratory failure and death.

It is important to note that when blood is used for the BAL level, the numbers might mean something different for women. Women have more fat tissue and less water than men, and they have less of the stomach enzyme that contributes to first-pass metabolism of alcohol; hence there is a higher content of alcohol in the bloodstream, even though they might have drank less than men. Therefore, if a woman has an inability to remain upright without support, do not be surprised if her BAL is different from a man exhibiting the same symptoms.

Another laboratory test frequently used to screen for alcohol use is the gamma-glutamyl transferase test. This laboratory tests screens for the presence of GTP (glutamyltranspeptidase), a liver enzyme that normally has low levels in the blood. It is a sensitive test of early liver dysfunction. Higher levels can be indicative of abusive drinking. Unlike the BAL it can indicate a longer time frame of alcohol use since it requires several weeks to return to normal. The results must be read with caution, since other disease processes can also effect the GGTP levels. Its usefulness usually depends on being combined with other screening tests.

Other tests used to screen for alcoholism include the mean corpuscular volume (MCV), serum aspartate transaminase (AST), total protein, alkaline phosphates, albumin and uric acid; the MCV and the AST tests are used most frequently. Elevated AST levels indicate possible damage to the liver, skeletal, and cardiac muscles. Elevated MCV reflects the effects of alcohol on the bone marrow or liver.

Estes and Heinemann (1986) suggested using the AST, GGTP, and MCV together to provide a middle of the road approach. Foy, Cline, and Laasi (1987) pointed out that the more laboratory tests used, the greater the sensitivity and specificity of the results. Unfortunately, the increased cost of this approach decreases its utility for screening purposes.

URINE SCREENS

The ideal urine drug screening program should be standardized, automated, easy to perform, and have minimal operator error (Holbrook & McCurdy, 1991). The results of these tests require a knowledge of the drug's half-life. As shown in Table 7-1, amphetamines can be detected in urine drug screens for 1 to 2 days after they were last used. Other drugs also have specific times in which they can be screened for.

The critical requirements for urine drug screens are 1) the reliability and accuracy of the test; 2) the ability to interpret drug test results; and 3) the applicability of the testing situation

TABLE 7-1   Drug Detectability in Urine Laboratory Screening Tests

Drug	Detection After Last Use (in days)
Amphetamines	1–2
Barbiturates	
Short-acting	3–5
Long-acting	10–14
Benzodiazepines	
Diazepam	2–4
Nordiazepam	7–9
Cocaine	
Cocaine proper	0.2–0.5
Benzoylecgonine (metabolite)	2–4
Methaqualone	7–14
Opiates	1–2
PCP	2–8
Cannabinoids (marijuana, THC)	14–42 (chronic use)
	2–8 (acute use)

(Bush et al. 1993). To assist with the first requirement, the National Laboratory Certification Program (NLCP) was established to assure that tests met specific criteria to insure higher reliability and accuracy. Training is necessary to meet the second requirement, and a careful examination of the purpose of the screening program is necessary to met the third requirement.

No studies were found that reviewed these screening tests in a general population. One factor may be the high costs involved in conducting these tests.

The initial phase of laboratory testing is the use of an immunoassay on the urine sample. A number of mechanisms for this exist. They include: 1) the enzyme immunoassay (EMIT), 2) the radioimmunoassy (RIAO), and 3) the fluorescence polarization immunoassay (FPIA). If the results of the immunoassay are negative, then the screening is concluded to be negative. If the results indicate a presumptive positive, then the specimen is tested using either a gas chromatography (GC) and/or a mass spectrometry (MS) test. These tests are able to separate a complex mixture of drugs and are often combined (GC/MS).

To insure that the urine specimen has not been altered and is truly the specimen of the desired subject, it is often obtained under observation, which reduces the possibility that people will volunteer to participate in such a screening program. In addition, a chain of security is developed and observed to ensure that no one has tampered with the sample.

NURSING INTERVENTIONS FOLLOWING SCREENING

Once the screening process has been completed—regardless of whether or not questionnaires or laboratory tests are used—the nurse needs to intervene. Although a determination will be made in concert with the flowchart of the screening process, there are specific activities that can be done.

If a client shows a low risk, based on screening results coming back negative, the nurse can: correct any misunderstandings by providing factual, valid information about AOD use through pamphlets or video; reinforce positive attitudes expressed by the client regarding problematic AOD use; and suggest strategies for avoiding problems with AOD use. If the client shows a high risk for problematic AOD use based on screening results coming back positive, the nurse can: express concern regarding the potential health effects of continued substance use; provide factual and valid information about AOD use and its effects; review risk factors for problematic use and addiction; and refer for an assessment.

Urine, blood, and questionnaires are all tools used for determining the presence of a possible problem with AOD. These tools can be used in institutional and community settings. However, in primary care settings an additional type of screening must take place: detecting whether a person presenting for care is there only to seek drugs and sell them on the street. Hence, the screening tool used is the professional's judgment based on the clues presented below.

SCREENING (DETECTION) IN PRIMARY CARE SITUATIONS

Drug-Seeking in Primary Care

Prescription drugs command a high price on the street because they are as powerful as many street drugs, yet are safer and more pure. Drugs can be diverted to the street at any point in the distribution system from manufacturer to pharmacy. However, health care providers are often the source of diverted drugs when they fall prey to schemes and scams (Goldman, 1993).

There are two types of clients seen in primary care settings: 1) legitimate and 2) drug-seeking. Legitimate clients include appropriate users of controlled substances, inappropriate users of controlled substances, and addicted clients. Drug-seeking clients include entrepreneurs and professional patients (Goldman, 1993).

Legitimate clients who are appropriate users of controlled substances have bona fide medical problems, and present seeking a diagnosis and treatment. They seek all drugs including controlled substances for the relief of their medical problem, are cooperative with the health care provider's duty to diagnose, are not rushed and do not place undue pressure on the health care provider to provide medication on demand.

Legitimate clients who are inappropriate users of controlled substances are those who take others medications without consulting a primary care provider. Also they tend to take medications for a certain condition around the clock to the point of tolerance, so that when the medication wears off, withdrawal symptoms occur. These clients can be recognized by taking an appropriate history.

Addicted clients seek drugs for their own use. They are most likely middle-aged and belong to the middle class. They are less likely to buy or sell prescription drugs on the street, but are likely to seek out substitute health care providers when their own stops prescribing for them. In addition, they seek the drugs that create psychological dependence: oral narcotics, analgesics, benzodiazepines, and barbiturates.

The key to recognizing and detecting these clients is awareness of the DSM-IV criteria for diagnosing abuse and dependence. Also, if they cannot obtain any drugs, they usually present with extreme anxiety, which may lead to verbal and sometimes physical demonstrations of anger. Emotional control is easily lost. These clients will need to be assessed over more than one visit, and corroborating information obtained from spouses or significant others (Goldman, 1993).

Drug seekers are persons who knowingly break the law by feigning illnesses, seeking controlled substances from multiple health care providers, forging prescriptions, and robbing pharmacies. The two types—entrepreneurial clients and professional clients—are different.

Entrepreneurial clients are con artists by definition. They make a living obtaining prescription drugs and selling to dealers on the street. They often visit several physicians per day in search of prescriptions for controlled drugs, and may travel from town to town.

Top selling drugs they seek include: opioid analgesics (including oxycodone-containing tablets), acetaminophen with codeine, hydrocodone, hydromorphone, morphine, and meperidine. Transdermal fentanyl patches are increasingly being sought by them, particularly if they operate on the West coast of the United States. Narcotics, cough syrups, and sedatives are frequently sought and diverted as well. Typically, this person is between the ages of 20 and 40, well-dressed, well-groomed, and behaves in an exuberant or inconspicuous manner.

Entrepreneurial clients seek out those health care providers who have a reputation for prescribing controlled substances on demand without taking a detailed history. New graduates are frequently viewed as "easy marks" (Goldman, 1993).

Professional clients are persons who use a genuine illness or obvious physical deformity as part of their pitch to obtain a prescription for controlled substances. Most work for a middle man and are paid a flat fee for every prescription they obtain. There are also groups that work for a "gang leader" who fills the prescriptions obtained by each professional client and sells the cache to local drug dealers. The final type are amateurs who hoard controlled substances prescribed to them, which they neither require nor take, but sell to drug dealers.

The main difference between professionals and amateurs is that amateurs do not stray away from their home town. Table 7-2 shows suspicious features to be observant for that will identify entrepreneurial clients (Goldman, 1993).

Steps for Detecting Drug Seekers

Goldman (1993) recommends these steps be taken to detect drug-seeking clients in primary care settings:

- Take a thorough history (including contacting the regular health care provider).
- Ask for ID from unfamiliar clients. When two or three pieces of identification are requested by the receptionist, drug seekers leave the primary care facility rather than provide ID.
- Take control of the encounter, make sure they answer direct questions.
- Take an independent history—ask detailed questions, appropriate clients will not become upset.
- Look for inconsistencies in the history provided, and ask about them.
- Identify previous physicians.
- Ask the question, "Have you seen a doctor in the last 48 hours?" The typical entrepreneur has seen 10 to 20 within that time period; if they name one, information can be obtained.
- Conduct a thorough physical examination, looking for evidence of addiction.

Steps for Managing Drug Seekers

The following steps are recommended for managing drug-seeking clients (Goldman, 1993):

- Identify unfamiliar clients.
- Develop a plan to deal with specific contingencies:
  — Out of town clients: prescribe only a 3-day supply of a controlled substance, using office samples and inform the client that these rules exist.

— Telephone clients: insist that all clients who telephone the office come in for reassessment and do not call in a replacement at the pharmacist.
- Present a strong, silent manner so that the person will not see you as afraid of confrontation.
- Do not assist drug seekers in telling their story; do not give names of medications, diagnostic tests, or consultants. This way they will get caught in their story much quicker.
- Avoid giving nonverbal signals; such signals tell whether the scam is working or not.
- Be familiar with "scams" (see Box 7-1).

In addition, if you have confirmed that this person is truly drug seeking: 1) take the client to a quiet room away from other clients; 2) if uncomfortable about confronting the client have a witness present as a show of force, and to validate by documentation that the health care provider remained professional; 3) inform the person of your suspicions; 4) maintain a calm, compassionate and sympathetic approach with the client, and do not get angry or lose control; 5) do not provide a small supply of drugs to get rid of a confirmed drug seeker; and 6)contact the police if threatened with violence. If suspicions are unconfirmed and one wants to give the client the benefit of the doubt, an alternative to the controlled substance can be prescribed (Goldman, 1993).

To prevent forgery 1) use numbered prescriptions so that stolen ones can be quickly identified; 2) use one prescription pad at a time; 3) never sign prescription blanks in advance; 4) choose an unusual dispensing number to make the prescription difficult to alter; 5) use preprinted colored scripts that display "void" when photocopied; 6) do not write your DEA number on the prescription unless required and previously arranged with the pharmacist; 7) establish a prearranged password with the pharmacist to verify identity over the telephone; 8) establish office policy regarding authorizations to call in or renew scripts; 9) report the theft of any prescriptions to local pharmacies, state board of pharmacy, and the police; and 10) be careful with faxed prescriptions (Goldman, 1993).

TABLE 7-2 Suspicious Features of Entrepreneurial Drug-Seeking Clients

- Refuses or is reluctant to present identification
- Out of town client
- History of substance abuse
- Allergy to codeine, nonsteroidal anti-inflammatory drugs (NSAIDs), or muscle relaxants
- Allergy to radiocontrast dye
- Urgently requires a controlled substance
- Appears to be in a hurry
- Presents at times when attending practitioner cannot be reached (evenings, night, weekends)
- Has not kept appointments for diagnostic tests and consultations
- Is conversant in street terminology
- Well versed in clinical terminology
- Is evasive; controls the interview
- Maintains constant eye contact with the physician
- Pays for the visit in cash
- Complicated history: a plethora of documentation or none at all

Source: Goldman, B. (1993). *Unmasking the illicit drug seeker.* Hagerman, ID: CME-TV. Reproduced with permission.

BOX 7-1.   Common Scams Used in Primary Care Settings to Obtain Drugs

1. The phony inspector
   The drug-seeker plays a law enforcement officer, telephones the primary care setting stating a known drug seeker is about to visit, urges the practitioner to give the person the medicine and he will be apprehended when leaving.

2. The Friday night special
   Three persons break into a physician's office on a Friday night. One pretends to be the secretary, one the patient, and one the physician. The pretending physician writes several prescriptions using the prescription pad, the pretending patient goes to several pharmacies and gets them filled, and the third person stays in the office to confirm prescriptions.

3. Family scams
   A. Grandma and Grandpa
      An elderly man or woman from out of town presents with a history of cancer—or some other major illness—and requests analgesics; a teenager usually appears as a grandchild. They usually request a large quantity (enough until we get home); and often the "grandchild" returns saying the prescription was lost and a replacement is needed.
   B. Mother and Daughter
      Parent seeks medication for self. He or she claims to have arrived in town to take child to the pediatric hospital and ran out of personal medication. Parent may also state that he or she is seeking medication for a child. Parents of children with "sickle cell anemia" encourage pretense of a crisis. Other examples include instructing children to behave as if they have attention deficit disorder to obtain methylphenidate.

4. Confessions of an addict
   In this scam the drug-seeker confesses to addiction and expresses desire to quit; then asks for an interim supply of drugs to ward off withdrawal symptoms.

5. The "inside" job
   In this scam, one of the employees may assist the drug-seeker and provide blank prescriptions, samples, and even client records. If they answer the telephone, they intercept calls from the pharmacist wishing to verify suspicious prescriptions.

Source: Goldman, B. (1993). *Unmasking the illicit drug seeker*. Hagerman, ID: CME-TV. Reproduced with permission.

CONCLUSION

Screening must be evaluated within the context of what it can accomplish as well as the purpose of the screening program. By definition it can only detect the presence or absence of disease. It should not be confused with an assessment for AOD abuse or dependence. It is not diagnostic. The utility of screening is linked to early intervention. It is hoped that persons with positive screens will seek further assessment and possible treatment. In this way effective secondary prevention can occur.

The choice of screening tool(s) should reflect both the purpose of the program and the population of interest. Currently, screening for AOD abuse and dependence is mainly conducted with populations who have been identified as high risk or who have entered a treatment facility for assessment. Frequently, the population is participating in the program due to legal or employment-related requirements.

Establishing effective screening programs for AOD that reach a population of asymptomatic individuals in a general public setting should be a goal for the near future. In addition, screening programs should be a primary goal in the public health arena, as well as all clinical settings in which nurses work, because the impact of addiction is of a serious nature, not only for the individuals who suffer with it, but for society as a whole.

Therefore, it becomes important to extend screening efforts to a type of detection not involving the standard questionnaires and blood and urine tests, but that of detecting drug seekers who come to primary care sites working schemes and scams to obtain prescription drugs to sell on the street. This, too, can be a point of major contribution to prevention of alcohol and other drug abuse in society.

REFERENCES

Babor, T., & Grant, M. (1989). From clinical research to secondary prevention: International collaboration in the development of the Alcohol Use Disorders Identification Test (AUDIT). *Alcohol Health and Research World* 13(4), 371–374.

Blow, F., Brower, J., Schulenberg, J., Demo-Dananberg, L., et al. (1992). The Michigan alcoholism screening test—geriatric version (MAST-G): A new elderly-specific screening instrument. Presented at the Research Society on Alcoholism Annual Meeting, June 1992. [abstract]. *Alcoholism: Clinical and Experimental Research,* 16(2), 372.

Boyd, C. (1993). The antecedents of women's crack cocaine abuse: Family substance abuse, sexual abuse, depression and illicit drug use. *Journal of Substance Abuse Treatment, 10,* 433–438.

Buchsbaum, D., Buchanan, R., Centor, R., Schnoll, S., & Lawton, M. (1991). Screening for alcohol abuse using CAGE scores and likelihood ratios. *Annals of Internal Medicine, 115* (10), 774–777.

Bush, B., Shaw, S., Cleary, P, et al. (1987). Screening for alcohol abuse using the CAGE questionnaire. *The American Journal of Medicine, 82*; 231–235.

Bush, D., Cone, E., Helshman, S., et al. (1993). Valid and reliable drug testing techniques. In *NIDA Second National Conference on Drug Abuse Research and Practice: An Alliance for the 21st Century* . Rockville, MD: U.S. Department of Health and Human Services.

Caudill, B., Hoffman, J., Hubbard, R., et al. (1994). Parental history of substance abuse as a risk factor in predicting crack smokers' substance abuse use, illegal activities, and psychiatric status. *American Journal of Drug and Alcohol Abuse, 20*(3), 341–354.

Duncan, T.E., Duncan, S.C., and Hops, H. (1994). The effects of family cohesiveness and peer encouragement on the development of adolescent alcohol use: A cohort-sequential approach to the analysis of longitudinal data. *Journal of Studies on Alcohol,* 588–599.

Edelman, P. (1993). Drug abuse and the public health. In *NIDA Second National Conference on Drug Abuse Research and Practice: An alliance for the 21st Century*. Rockville, MD: U.S. Department of Health and Human Services.

Embree, B.G., & Whitehead, P.C (1991). Validity and reliability of self-reported drinking behavior: Dealing with the problem of response bias. *Journal of Studies on Alcohol,* 334–344.

Estes, N.J., & Heinemann, M.E. (1986). *Alcoholism: Development, consequences and interventions* (3rd ed.). St Louis, MO: C.V. Mosby.

Ewing, J. (1984). Detecting alcoholism: The CAGE questionnaire. *Journal of the American Medical Association, 252*(14), 1905–1907.

Fleming, M., & Barry, K. (1992). *Addictive disorders.* St. Louis: C.V. Mosby.

Foy, D.W., Cline, K.A., & Laasi, N. (1987). Assessment of alcohol and drug abuse. In Nirenberg, T.D., & Maisto, S.A. (Eds.), *Developments in the Assessment and treatment of addictive behaviors.* Norwood, NJ: Ablex Publishing Corp.

Goldman, B. (1993). *Unmasking the illicit drug seeker.* Hagerman, ID: Greg Wokersien, publisher.

Harris, T.R., Wilsnack, R.W., & Klassen, A.D. (1994). Reliability of retrospective self-reports of alcohol consumption among women: Data from a U.S. sample. *Journal of Studies of Alcohol,* 309–314.

Hingson, R. (1993). Prevention of alcohol-impaired driving. *Alcohol Health and Research World, 17*(1), 28–34.

Holbrook, J.H., & McCurdy, H.H. (1991). Drug screening. In Bennett, G.& Wolf, D.S. (Eds.), *Substance abuse* (2nd ed.). Albany, NY: Delmar Publishers.

Inciardi, J.A. (1994). *Screening and assessment for alcohol and other drug abuse among adults in the criminal justice system*. Rockville, MD: U.S. Department of Health and Human Services.

Mausner, J.S., & Kramer, A. (1985). *Epidemiology: An introductory text*. Philadelphia: W.B. Saunders.

Mayfield, D., McLeod, G., & Hall, P. (1974). The CAGE questionnaire: Validation of a new alcoholism screening instrument. *American Journal of Psychiatry, 131*, 1121–1123.

McLellan, T., & Dembo, R. (1992). *Screening and assessment of alcohol and other drug (AOD) abusing adolescents (Treatment Improvement Protocol 3)*. Rockville, MD: Substance Abuse and Mental Health Services Administration.

Morrison, A.J. (1992) *Screening in chronic disease* (2nd ed.). New York: Oxford University Press.

National Institute on Alcohol Abuse and Alcoholism. (1990a). Screening for alcoholism. *Alcohol Alert, 8* (PH285), 1–4.

Nystrom, M.A., Perasalo, J., & Salaspuro, M. (1993). Screening for heavy drinking and alcohol-related problems in young university students: The CAGE, the Mm-Mast and the Trauma Score questionnaires. *Journal of Studies on Alcohol*, 528–533.

Rahdert, E., Metzger, D., & Winters, K. (1993). Adolescent diagnostic assessment. *NIDA Second National Conference on Drug Abuse Research and Practice: An Alliance for the 21st Century*. Rockville, MD: U.S. Department of Health and Human Services.

Rice, D.P. (1993). The economic cost of alcohol abuse and alcohol dependence: 1990. *Alcohol Health and Research World, 17*(1), 10–11.

Russell, M., Martier, S., Sokol, R., Jacobson, S., Jacobson, J., & Bottoms, S. (1991). Screening for pregnancy risk-drinking: TWEAKING the tests [Abstract]. *Alcoholism Clinical and Experimental Research, 15*(2), 368.

Russell, M. (1994). New assessment tools for risk drinking during pregnancy: T-ACE, TWEAK, and other. *Alcohol Health and Research, 18*(1); 55–61.

Savage, C.L. (1994). A model of risk for adverse neonatal outcomes in substance abusing women. Washington, D.C.: Proceedings of AMERSA Conference.

Skinner, H.A. (1982). The drug abuse screening test. *Addictive Behaviors, 7*, 363–371.

Sokol, R., Martier, S., & Ager, J. (1989). The T-ACE questions: Practical prenatal detection of risk-drinking. *American Journal of Obstetrics and Gynecology, 160*(4), 863–870.

Stockwell, T., Sitharthan, T., McGrath, D., et al. (1994). The measurement of alcohol dependence and impaired control in community samples. *Addiction, 89*, 167–174.

Substance Abuse and Mental Health Services Administration (SAMHSA), Center for Substance Abuse Treatment. (1994a). *Treatment for alcohol and other drug abuse: Opportunities for coordination*. DHHS Publication No. (SMA) 94-2075. Rockville, MD: Substance Abuse and Mental Health Services Administration.

Substance Abuse and Mental Health Services Administration (SAMHSA), Center for Substance Abuse Treatment. (1994b). *Simple screening instruments for outreach for alcohol and other drug (AOD) abuse and infectious disease*. DHHS Publication No. (SMA) 94-2094. Rockville, MD: Substance Abuse and Mental Health Services Administration.

Teutsch, S.M. (1992). A framework for assessing the effectiveness of disease and injury prevention. *Morbidity and Mortality Weekly Report, 41*(RR-3), 1–12.

Tolley, K., & Rowland, N. (1991). Identification of alcohol-related problems in a general hospital setting: A cost-effectiveness evaluation. *British Journal of Addictions, 86*(4), 429–438.

U.S. Department of Health and Human Services. (1994). Screening and brief intervention. In *Eighth Special Report to the U.S. Congress on Alcohol and Health*. NIH Publication No. 94-3699. Alexandria, VA: U.S. Department of Health and Human Services.

U.S. Preventive Services Task Force. (1989). Screening for alcohol and other drug abuse. In M. Fisher (Ed.) *Guide to clinical preventive services: An assessment of the effectiveness of 169 interventions*. Report of the U.S. Preventive Services Task Force (pp. 277–286). Baltimore, MD: Williams and Wilkins.

Waltz, C.F., Strickland, O.L., & Lenz, E.R. (1991). *Measurement in nursing research* (2nd ed.). Philadelphia: F.A. Davis & Co.

Assessment and Diagnosis

Sandra Jaffe-Johnson, *EdD, RN, CS, NPP, NCAC-II, CARN*

INTRODUCTION

Definitions and Conceptualization

Treatment for addiction in the 21st century dictates that there be effective and flexible assessment strategies that focus on all aspects of the levels of care. This is important because to design well-defined effective addiction treatment protocols for clients with heterogenous needs, accurate diagnoses based on a biopsychosocial assessment using data derived from interviews, laboratory tests, and diagnostic instruments, must occur.

Assessment is one of the five critical elements of effective treatment, and it is the first stage of the treatment process (Substance Abuse and Mental Health Services Administration, 1994). It is also the first stage of the nursing process and the most critical in terms of formulating client-oriented interventions and evaluation of treatment outcome.

Roget's International Thesaurus used verbs such as quantify, appraise, estimate, ask, and differentiate to describe components of the term assess (Chapman, 1992). The Institute of Medicine (1990) defined assessment as the systematic process of interaction with an individual to observe, elicit, and subsequently assemble the relevant information required to deal with his or her case, both immediately and for the foreseeable future. According to the Substance Abuse and Mental Health Services Administration (SAMHSA) (1994) assessment is a process that uses extensive procedures to determine the nature and complexity of the individual's problems. There are at least five objectives for conducting appropriate and comprehensive assessments of persons with substance abuse or addiction problems: 1) to identify those who are experiencing problems related to substance abuse and/or have progressed to the stage of addiction; 2) to assess the full spectrum of problems for which treatment may be needed; 3) to plan appropriate interventions; 4) to involve appropriate family members or significant others, as needed, in the individual's treatment; and 5) to evaluate the effectiveness of interventions implemented.

SAMHSA further states that the assessment process occurs over a period of time—rather than a moment in time as with screening—and involves three steps: 1) gathering of necessary information through interviews, laboratory testing, and diagnostic instruments; 2) analyzing that information and diagnosing the individual according to specific criteria; and 3) determining the appropriate level of intervention and/or treatment. The purpose of this chapter is to discuss these steps.

INFORMATION GATHERING

The Interview Process

The nurse's ability to conduct a comprehensive biopsychosocial interview is an essential first step in the assessment and treatment of clients. Each nurse needs to adopt an effective, flexible, and comfortable interview style that facilitates the gathering of data.

There are two interview styles used by mental health professionals: insight-oriented (psychodynamic) and symptom-oriented (descriptive) (Othmer & Othmer, 1994). An insight-oriented interview has the dual purpose of diagnosis and therapy. It includes such techniques as uncovering anxieties; confrontation of interpersonal behavior toward the nurse and others; and identification of defenses and analysis of the clients' resistance to the discussion of their conflicts (Othmer & Othmer, 1994, p. 2).

The method of interviewing that is most commonly used by nurses and other health professionals is symptom-oriented. This descriptive approach of interviewing derives from the concept that addictive disorders are manifested by a pattern of signs, symptoms, and behaviors; a predictable course characterized by continuous or periodic impaired control over the behavior; preoccupation with its effects and/or use; adverse consequences or impairments in the major functional areas; denial of these consequences; a somewhat specific treatment response; and often a familial occurrence (American Psychological Association (APA), 1994).

Sullivan (1954), Garrett (1982), and Hagerty (1984) described the interview as a goal-oriented interaction for both the nurse and the client. It is aimed at elucidating characteristic patterns of living of the client that are experienced as particularly troublesome or especially valuable, and the benefits the client expects to derive from the diagnostic interview.

Inherent in client expectation is their frame of reference. An example being the adult child of an alcoholic who did not have the opportunity to see either of the parents ever recover from active alcoholism; during the course of the interview it would be very important to present concrete information related to the client's specific needs that confronts this sense of hopelessness about recovery.

Previous attitudes, values, and beliefs related to those addicted to alcohol and other drugs often influence interactions with clients, colleagues, and significant others. Attitude surveys have indicated significant levels of anxiety, fear, and bias, which contribute to the professional avoidance of nurses willing to care for clients with self-destructive behaviors (Burkhalter, 1975; DiCicco & Unterberger, 1977; Jaffe, 1979). However, this need not be the case and seems to be improving, because more recent surveys such as the one conducted by Allen (1993) have found the attitudes of nurses toward addicted clients to be quite positive. The nurses' own patterns and amount of drinking may be similar to the clients and interfere with their willingness to identify the client as alcoholic (Tweed, 1989, p. 15). The misconceived belief that an addicted person has to be motivated before intervention is effective often perpetuates a pattern of reciprocal avoidance and further complicates the interview process.

Furthermore, using labels such as alcoholic, alcoholism, and addict, tend to have major stigma attached to them and may stop the interview before it gets started. Incorporating questions about alcohol use and associated problems into a standard part of any nursing history may help the nurse maintain a nonjudgmental approach and make denial or rationalization difficult for the client. It is also helpful to assess the client's level of knowledge about substance abuse and addiction and accompanying behaviors. Most often the definitions given by the client will exclude him or her from the classification. For example, a woman—shameful about her own alcoholism—described another female alcoholic as "a woman who neglected her children and her home," and "ran around with other men." Since her children got "a hot breakfast every morning before school," and "her kitchen sink and floors were immaculate," she could not be an alcoholic. By providing information about the problem of substance abuse and addiction in a factual manner, incongruence is created between fact and the client's own knowledge deficit.

When conducting the assessment interview, it is best to ask highly specific questions such as previous dates and reasons for other admissions to the hospital. Such questions may provide a clear pattern of admissions related to the sequelae of alcohol abuse. A careful chart review would also show a distinct progressive pattern of medically related admissions from which substance abuse would be recognized when using a focus-oriented approach.

Validity of an assessment depends on the degree of trust that the nurse interviewer is able to establish with the client (Senay, 1992, p. 419). Before conducting a focused interview, the following guidelines would be helpful in gaining the client's rapport in any setting where an interview is conducted.

- Put the client and self at ease. The client does not know what to expect and is unsure if the nurse will be able to help. The client is just another human being who wants to be understood.
- Questions that are of foremost concern to the client but are rarely verbalized to the nurse are often: "Will she or he be able to help me?" "Will she or he really understand what I'm telling her?" "Will she or he listen to me or think that I am crazy?"
- It is important that the nurse convey that she or he senses these doubts, respects the concerns, and is on the client's side.

At the onset of the interview nurses should introduce themselves and then ask what the clients would like to be called; how they pronounce their name; how they found their way to this facility or office; and why they are seeking help at this particular time. The latter question is a particularly important one since many clients tend to seek treatment during a period of introspection such as a birthday or anniversary of a significant event in their lives.

At the inception of an interview clients' mental state may be expressed by signs. They are territorial (locomotor), behavioral (psychomotor), emotional (expressive), and verbal (voice and mode of expression) (Othmer & Othmer, 1994).

It is very important to be able to read clients' signs accurately when initiating rapport. How a person moves into new territory for the first time gives clues related to the patient's boundaries. Are they timid and require a lot of space by taking a seat by the door, or are they intrusive and get too close by moving their seat close to the interviewer and using a loud voice so they can be heard by everyone in the facility.

Psychomotor behavior often is consistent with locomotor behavior. Shy clients may look down on their lap and avoid eye contact, while intrusive clients may attempt to make a phone call, turn on the computer, and rearrange the furniture.

Emotional or expressive signs are conveyed in facial expressions, eye contact, tone of voice, gestures, and posture. Clients may walk into the room with an indecisive gait, full of energy, stooped or slowed down. They may smile or look sad, tense, and tearful.

Clients may choose certain metaphors to describe the way they think and experience the world. They will give verbal signs about their mental state by the choice of words. Their problems may be represented in a visual way by saying "There is no light at the end of the tunnel" or "I can't see the way out—everything looks so bleak." The nurse may respond by saying "Since when did things look so dark?" (Othmer & Othmer, 1994, p. 17). It is helpful to respond with a metaphor to metaphorical language. Initially use the client's words instead of psychiatric, medical, or addiction terminology. For instance, when they talk about shakes, use that term. This will give them the feeling of being understood. Then ask them to describe what is meant by the word "shakes" to help in understanding what they mean.

These initial efforts will help put both the client and the nurse at ease and greatly facilitate the rapport necessary for a more specific addiction-focused interview. In addition to the above, the following are some interviewing guidelines that can be used in any setting when conducting a biopsychosocial assessment for the purpose of exploring a patient's addiction (see Box 8-1).

Important points to remember when interviewing are that 1) interviews should be adapted to the age and culture of the client; 2) cognitive abilities can affect the interview process, therefore, the interviewer must be aware of the client's cognitive ability level and try to structure the interview accordingly; and 3) if the person being assessed is not fluent in the same language as the interviewer, an experienced interpreter who is familiar with the client's culture and the interview questions, should be used (SAMHSA, 1994).

COLLATERAL INFORMATION FROM SIGNIFICANT OTHERS

Significant others of alcohol and drug-addicted individuals have more contacts with health care providers because of stress-related disorders such as migraine headaches, ulcer disease, hypertension, or simply somatic complaints without an organic basis (Kinney, 1991) Therefore, collaboration with significant others during this first level of contact can provide vital information related to the family sociocultural history of substance abuse or addiction, as well as level of support likely if treatment is provided (Sullivan, Handley, & Connors, 1994). Some questions that may be helpful when addressing the family would be the following:

Do you worry about this person's drinking or drug use?
Have you been embarrassed by it?
Are many of this person's friends heavy drinkers or drug users?
Are children afraid of this person while he or she is drinking or using drugs?
Are you afraid of physical or verbal attack?
How does the individual's alcohol or drug use affect you (e.g., by influencing the things that you now do or do not do)?
Has it created financial, legal, or social problems?

Once family members begin to acknowledge the impact of substance use on their lives, it is important to validate their concerns and problems. Referrals for counseling, Al-Anon or Alateen are potential resources. Explore with them the kind of interventions they would use if they were told their significant other had diabetes mellitus. The stigma of alcoholism and substance abuse must not stand in the way of getting the help that they need.

Areas of assessment needing to be addressed through client and collateral interviews include: drug history and current patterns of use; substance abuse treatment history; medical history and current status; mental health history and current status; personal status (critical life events, etc.); family history and current status of relationships; positive support systems; crime or delinquency; education; employment; readiness for treatment; and resources and responsibilities (SAMHSA, 1994).

BOX 8-1. Interviewing Guidelines: Biopsychosocial Assessment

1. Use an open-ended format so that it is difficult for client to be evasive and provide simple yes or no answers.
2. Be persistent in a low key nondemanding way. If the answer to a significant question is vague, ask again using different words or express lack of comprehension by saying "I really don't understand your response, could you please explain that again" (Kinney, 1991).
3. Be matter of fact, as one would be in assessing the client with diabetic or cardiovascular symptoms. If the client becomes antagonistic, recognize this as his or her chief characterological defense known as denial. It is unconscious and protects the person from feelings of inadequacy, vulnerability, and low self esteem. Fear underlies all denial. Fear may consist of the loss of control, the fear of rejection, and the fear of incurability.
4. Offer hope. Clients need to know that there is a way out. The future does not have to be like the present. Relief from bewilderment, shame, and remorse is possible.
5. Empathize. Show the ability to perceive and communicate having experienced some of the inner turmoil and confusion that the addict is feeling. It gives the individuals the impression that the nurse cares and it enhances your credibility. Empathy does not mean sympathy or supporting sick behavior.
6. Fight the disease, but support the client. There is a need to distinguish between an addict's sick behavior and the person suffering from addiction.
7. If the client talks about other individual's complaints about their substance use, ask "What is it like for you?"
8. Avoid discussion of rationalizations. This will divert the interview.
9. Avoid "Why" questions because individuals are most confused about what is happening to them and will only offer rationalizations for what they think may be the reason, which only reinforces the denial process because of their poor judgment. The strength of the denial system is directly related to both the duration and extent of harmful effects in the person's life (Tweed, 1989).
10. Recognize qualified answers. If the answer is "Practically never," the next statement might be "Tell me about the times when it does happen," or if the answer is "I wouldn't say so," the next question might be "Who would say so? Your wife? Your boss?"
11. Recognize any attempts to convince the interviewer that there is no problem. Clients will minimize effects by comparing companions whose substance use is heavier than theirs.
12. Clients may also use "euphoric recall" and remember only the positive fun times associated with their addiction. Create cognitive dissonance over what they say versus reality by presenting the harmful sequelae of their addiction.
13. Use other sources, such as the family, to obtain information related to the client's patterns of abuse and addiction, without violation of client rights or federal confidentiality regulations.
14. Finish the interview with less threatening material such as employment history.

The Biopsychosocial Data Base and Intake Form (Jaffe-Johnson & Johnson, 1993) found in Appendix 10 is an example of an initial assessment tool that has been used in addiction treatment facilities as well as a variety of clinical practice settings by nursing staff. It was developed to provide a systems based comprehensive determination of the patient's need for treatment. The tool provides the interdisciplinary treatment team with the opportunity to work collaboratively in the collection and evaluation of data. It includes as part of its assessment the following information:

a. Demographic data
b. Medical and psychiatric history
c. Sexual history
d. Patterns of alcohol, drug, and gambling behaviors; symptomatology; and treatment history
e. Family addiction history; patterns of abuse; and significant losses
f. Mental status and dimensions of cognitive, thought processes, and emotional response
g. Spirituality
h. DSM-IV (tentative diagnosis)
I. Treatment issues (nursing diagnosis)
j. Goals/interventions

Physical Assessment

Following interviews with the client and significant other, it is imperative that the nurse complete a physical assessment for clues that might be rendered in support of the diagnosis of substance abuse or addiction. The method used most frequently is the systems method of physical examination. Problems that the nurse will be looking for include:

- Debilitation: not related to medical problems
- Skin: abscesses, cellulitis, lymphedema, venous insufficiency, needle marks, scars, signs of ARC/AIDS, jaundice, burns, dehydration, bruises
- Head and neck: nasal septum abnormalities, dental caries, scleral icterus, retinal emboli and ischemia, inflamed throat, reddened eyes, hematomas
- Chest: right ventricular failure, dysrhythmias, palpitations, chest pains, myocardial ischemia, increase in heart rate and systolic blood pressure, chronic productive cough, respiratory difficulties, hypogonadism, pneumonia
- Abdomen: signs of hepatitis, splenomegaly, venereal disease, cervical cancer, blood in the stool, pain, nausea and vomiting, ascites
- Lymph nodes: adenopathy
- Nervous system: peripheral neuropathy, distal neuropathy, cerebellar ataxia, focal deficits, abnormal reflexes
- Extremities: arterial insufficiency, cyanosis (remember to include sternoclavicular and sacroiliac joints in the examination).

Other findings to look for include acute orthopedic injuries (point tenderness), hematuria, and amputees with stump infection.

The above findings are not all inclusive, nor do they give an exhaustive list of abnormal findings to look for when completing a physical assessment on a substance-abusing or addicted client. However, it provides some of the most frequent findings. In addition, those nurses working in clinical settings where persons treated for medical problems are not diagnosed as substance abusing or addicted, but rather as having medical diagnoses (i.e., alcoholic fatty liver, hepatitis, AIDS, cirrhosis, tuberculosis, pelvic inflammatory disease, malnutrition/ malabsorption, gastritis, esophagitis, ulcers, frequent unexplained nausea and vomiting, diarrhea, pancreatitis, uncontrolled diabetes, anemia, hypertension), completing a physical assessment will lead to some of the above findings, which will be major clues for completion of a comprehensive substance abuse and addiction assessment.

Laboratory Testing

Laboratory testing is the most accurate method of determining current or recent drug use. It can delineate the specific drugs being used and assist in the assessment process to diagnose the addictive disorder. Proper determination of the specific drugs being used is crucial to providing the appropriate level of treatment, as the abuse of differing substances often requires varied treatment approaches (SAMHSA, 1994).

Scientific methods of laboratory testing include:

- Breath analysis
- Saliva tests
- Urinalysis
- Blood analysis
- Hair analysis

Currently breath analysis, saliva tests, and urinalysis are the most practical, accurate, and cost-effective methods of testing available. Blood analysis is sometimes used in medical settings, but is much more costly. Breath analysis and saliva tests are used to detect alcohol consumption, while urinalysis is used to detect other drugs of abuse. Urinalysis cannot determine when the drugs were actually ingested, nor can the level of intoxication be identified, as it can be with breath analysis for alcohol (SAMHSA, 1994). However, urinalysis is the most commonly used method for laboratory assessment of drug use.

There are three methods to test for drug use. Thin layer chromatography (TLC) is the most inexpensive, relatively insensitive (may show negative results when some drugs or metabolites are actually in the sample), detects high level use of morphine, quinine (a diluent of heroin), methadone, codeine, dextromethorphan, propoxyphene, barbiturates, diphenyl hydantoin, phenothiazines, cocaine, amphetamine, or phenylpropanolamine; but it will not detect marijuana, PCP, LSD, MDA, MDMA, mescaline, and fentanyl. A positive result should be confirmed by another method. Enzyme immunoassay (EIA) is relatively inexpensive, extraction of drugs or metabolites is not required. It can detect alcohol, amphetamine, barbiturate, benozodiazepines, cocaine, methaqualone, opiates, methadone, PCP, propoxyphene (Darvon), and cannabinoids (THC metabolites, including marijuana). It can be done by the enzyme-multiplied immunoassay technique (EMIT), the radioimmunoassay (RIA), and the fluorescence polarization immunoassay (FPIA). With a single analysis the capillary gas–liquid chromatography (GLC) can identify 25 or more compounds. Its advantage is when there is no clue as to the identity of the abused or toxic substance in the sample. But it is time consuming, labor-intensive, and expensive, yet very sensitive and drug specific.

According to SAMHSA (1994) gas chromatography/mass spectrometry (GC/MS) is considered the gold standard in urinalysis. It is highly accurate and is the only method that reliably produces quantitative results. It is frequently used as a confirmation method if the initial immunoassay test produced positive results.

Blood tests for alcoholism include elevated plasma gamma-glutamyltransferase (GGT) and serum glutamic-oxaloacetic transaminase (SGOT), mean corpuscular volume (MCV), uric acid, and blood lipid measurements, as well as blood alcohol levels. Hand-held breathlyzers and urine dipstick testing are technologies that are inexpensive and correlate well with blood alcohol levels for measuring current alcohol use. The plasma GGT and MCV are the primary measures used when assessing for alcohol problems. The sensitivity of these tests varies from 20% to 60%, depending on the chronicity and severity of alcohol use (Perrson, Magnusson, & Borg, 1990). Analysis of plasma carbohydrate-deficient transferrin (CDT) has indications that it may be useful in the clinical evaluation of alcohol use disorders from total abstainers and from healthy normal drinkers. It has had a sensitivity of 91% and a specificity of 99%. CDT levels have also correlated with the amount of alcohol ingested in the previous month (Borg et al., 1992). Other tests that may be elevated include triglycerides, serum alkaline phosphatase, and serum bilirubin.

New developments in drug detection technologies are currently being researched. The National Institute of Corrections and the National Aeronautics and Space Administration have formed a partnership to explore ways in which space-age technology can benefit the process of laboratory analysis for drug abuse. The current project is the Visual Identification of Pupillary Eye Responses (VIPER), which is the development of an instrument called the optical funduscope that can evaluate the eye, pupil, and retina. It measures involuntary eye movements associated with drug-use impairment.

A second noninvasive method of testing for drug use is the telemetered drug use detection system, which evaluates the feasibility of a drug detection device worn on the wrist. Through analysis of perspiration, the device could detect drug use and send results to a central control station. This technology combines position identification (similar to electronic monitoring), chemical and biological processes, and microcommunications and signaling.

After information is gathered through the interview with the client and significant others, physical assessment and laboratory tests, the final methods for data gathering, are completed. Diagnostic assessment instruments are utilized.

Diagnostic Assessment Instruments

As important as laboratory testing is, it can only provide evidence of current or recent drug use. However, when establishing the presence of a substance abuse or addiction problem, it is necessary to show the development of the problem over a period of time. Therefore, in support of a history taken through the interview process, diagnostic assessment instruments are used to 1)characterize the severity of the patient's substance abuse or addiction; 2)determine the appropriate setting and intensity for treatment; 3)establish treatment goals and strategies appropriate to individual needs; and 4)facilitate outcome measurement. These instruments are more diagnostic and require complex responses from the client.

Brief information about several available assessment instruments is found in Appendix 11. These instruments do not represent an exhaustive list of what exists, nor do they represent an endorsement for use. Rather, they are offered as a compilation of what can be located through literature review. However, before selecting a diagnostic instrument to be used the following factors should be considered (SAMHSA, 1994):

- Ease of use
- Expertise and time required of staff to administer and score the test
- Training required and whether or not it is available
- Possibility of bias (cultural or in administration of the test)

- Validity (have studies proved that it accurately measures what it was intended to measure?)
- Reliability (have studies shown that if the tests were repeated, the same kind of results would be obtained?)
- Credibility of the test among members of the judiciary and treatment professionals
- Adaptation of the test to management information system input and retrieval
- Whether the test has been normed with the client group population and is culturally or ethnically relevant
- Availability of test in languages other than English
- Motivation level, verbal and reading skills required of persons to be assessed
- Propensity for test to be manipulated
- Most important—*whether or not the test provides a biopsychosocial diagnostic assessment.*

Confidentiality

During the process of data gathering, it is imperative that the nurse maintain confidentiality with information obtained from substance-abusing or addicted clients. A knowledge of the legal aspects of confidentiality is necessary for the nurse who works in either the field of alcoholism or drug abuse because the federal government has provided legal leverage to insure that this takes place—the *42 CFR Part 2 (Code of Federal Regulations Part 2).*

Two statutes were passed by Congress in the 1970s and amended in 1986 that narrowly define those circumstances in which information that would identify clients being treated for either alcoholism or drug abuse. These diseases, it was believed, possessed a stigma not known since the recognition of leprosy as a contagious disease. If, as it was hoped, individuals would seek treatment for these disorders, then it was believed their identities should be strenuously protected by the caregivers (Brooks, 1992). Following several more changes and amendments, on Tuesday, June 9, 1987, rules and regulations regarding what is known today as the "Confidentiality of Alcohol and Drug Abuse Patient Records" was published in the Federal Register vol. 52, No. 110, on behalf of the Department of Health and Human Services.

Although nurses are familiar with the need for confidentiality in the care of clients in either hospital or clinic settings, these regulations supersede any state or local law that may be less protective of the confidentiality of the clients' records. The regulations prohibit the disclosure of records or other information concerning any client in a federally assisted alcohol or drug abuse program. This prohibition on unauthorized disclosure applies whether or not the person seeking information already has the information, has other means of obtaining it, enjoys official status, has obtained a subpoena or warrant, or is authorized by state law. A program includes any person or organization that, in whole or in part, provides alcohol or drug abuse diagnosis, treatment, or referral for treatment.

Hospitals or other general medical care facilities are covered only if they have an "identified" alcohol or drug abuse unit or staff who specialize in substance abuse services (Brooks, 1992, p. 1050). Some drug or alcohol education programs are covered if they admit students on the basis of involvement or suspected involvement in substance abuse such as a drinking driving program (DDP). A program is federally assisted if it receives federal funds in any form, even if the funds do not directly pay for the alcohol or drug abuse services; is assisted by the Internal Revenue Service through grant of tax exempt status; and is authorized to conduct business with the federal government (e.g., licensed to provide methadone or chemotherapy; certified as a Medicare provider). A client is defined as any person who has applied for, participated in, or received an interview, counseling, or any other service by a federally assisted alcohol or drug abuse program, including someone who, after arrest on a criminal charge, is identified as a substance abuser during an evaluation of eligibility for treatment. Former clients as well as deceased clients are also protected.

Violations of these regulations by caregivers is punishable in the first offense by a fine of $500 and up to $5,000 for each subsequent offense. Also, governmental funding agencies usually require compliance with these regulations as a condition of such funding or grants; the violation of which may lead to termination of that funding.

DIAGNOSING BASED ON ANALYSIS OF DATA USING CRITERIA

Once information is gathered, it is interpreted for use in decision making. The severity and the contributing factors of the person's alcohol or drug problem are determined in this phase. Health care providers take all of the information gathered in the interviews, physical examination, laboratory tests, and diagnostic instruments, analyze it and apply it to established and standardized diagnostic criteria, and come up with a final diagnosis for use in determining appropriate intervention or treatment.

The Diagnostic and Statistical Manual of Mental Disorders (DSM-IV)

The official coding system in use in the United States is the International Classification of Diseases, Ninth Revision, Clinical Modification (ICD-9-CM). Most DSM-IV disorders have a numerical ICD-9-CM code. Nurses need to be familiar with the DSM-IV because the use of the diagnostic codes is essential for data collection and medical record keeping as well as for purposes of reimbursement (APA, 1994).

History

The *Diagnostic and Statistical Manual of Mental Disorders* was first published in 1952 to provide an official nomenclature of mental disorders that focused on clinical utility. When DSM-III was published in 1980, explicit diagnostic criteria, a multiaxial system, and a descriptive approach was used to present more empirical research data. Because of the substantial increase in the research on diagnosis, a number of inconsistencies in the system where the criteria was unclear initiated the publication of DSM-III-R in 1987.

The DSM-IV reflects extensive literature reviews and field trials by work groups sponsored by the National Institute of Mental Health (NIMH), the National Institute on Alcohol Abuse and Alcoholism (NIAAA), and the National Institute on Drug Abuse. The diverse sites for the field trials had representative groups of subjects from a range of sociocultural and ethnic backgrounds in an effort to ensure generalizability of the results in making more difficult differential diagnosis (APA, 1994, p. xix).

Syndromes and Criteria

A syndrome is a cluster of signs and symptoms that occur together and are characteristic for a specific disorder. Many psychiatric disorders include a core cluster of symptoms that are the prototype for the syndrome. For example, one common prototype for "Alcoholism" includes the following symptoms: tolerance, withdrawal, preoccupation, denial, impaired control, adverse physical health, recurrent use despite interpersonal, legal and work-related problems and unsuccessful efforts to decrease use.

Criteria are rules that describe or define a clinical disorder by specifying the type, intensity, duration, and effect of the various behaviors and symptoms required for the diagnosis. Many criteria also list the alternate disorders that must be excluded before a diagnosis can be made (Fauman, 1994).

The criteria used to describe "Alcohol Withdrawal" (291.8) is an example of a criteria-based diagnostic system. Criterion A would be the reduction or cessation of alcohol use that had been heavy and prolonged. In addition, two or more of criterion B would have had to develop within several hours to a few days after criterion A.

Criterion B consist of:

- Autonomic hyperactivity (e.g., sweating, or pulse rate greater than 100)
- Increased hand tremor
- Insomnia
- Nausea or vomiting
- Transient visual, tactile, or auditory hallucinations or illusions
- Psychomotor agitation
- Anxiety
- Grand mal seizures

Criterion C are when the symptoms in criterion B cause clinically significant distress or impairment in social, occupational, or other important areas of functioning.

Criterion D are when the symptoms are not due to a general medical condition and are not better accounted for by another mental disorder (APA, 1994, pp. 198–199).

The nurse is now able to specify whether there is perceptual "Disturbances." The specifier may be recorded when hallucinations with intact reality testing or auditory, visual, or tactile illusions occur in the absence of a delirium. Intact reality testing means that the person knows that the hallucinations are induced by the substance and do not represent external reality. This offers a significant relief to the patient who most often is very fearful of sharing this symptom with the team. When hallucinations occur in the absence of intact reality testing, a diagnosis of "Substance-Induced Psychotic Disorder, With Hallucinations," needs to be considered.

DSM-IV Axes

A multiaxial system involves an assessment on several axes, each of which refers to a different domain of information that may help the nurse plan treatment and predict process and outcome criteria for addictions nursing practice. There are five axes included in the DSM-IV multiaxial classification:

Axis I: Clinical Disorders
Axis II: Personality Disorders and Mental Retardation
Axis III: General Medical Conditions
Axis IV: Psychosocial and Environmental Problems
Axis V: Global Assessment of Functioning Disorders

Axis IV is for reporting psychosocial and environmental problems that may affect the diagnosis, treatment, and prognosis of mental disorders (Axes I and II). Nurses in all practice settings are usually the initial contact that the patient will have with the interdisciplinary team and is in an excellent position to conduct a complete biopsychosocial assessment to validate the stressors in the patient's life. The problems are grouped together in the following categories:

- Problems with primary support group (e.g., death of a family member; health problems; sexual or physical abuse; remarriage)
- Problems related to the social environment (e.g., death or loss of a friend; inadequate social support; difficulty with acculturation; adjustment to lives-cycle transition such as retirement)
- Educational problems (e.g., academic problems; discord with teachers or classmates; illiteracy)
- Occupational problems (e.g., unemployment; threat of job loss; job dissatisfaction; discord with boss or coworkers)
- Housing problems (e.g., homelessness; unsafe neighborhood; discord with neighbors or landlord)
- Economic problems (e.g., extreme poverty; inadequate finances; insufficient support)
- Problems with access to health care services (e.g., inadequate health care; inadequate health insurance; health care facilities unavailable)
- Problems related to interaction with the legal system/crime (e.g., arrest; litigation; victim of crime)
- Other psychosocial and environmental problems (e.g., exposure to disaster; war)

Axis V: Global Assessment of Functioning (GAF) is useful for the nurse to report the client's overall level of functioning at the time of the interview or current period so that treatment planning and evaluation of outcome criteria can be made more effectively. The GAF is to be used only to rate the client's psychological, social, and occupational functioning. The GAF scale ranges from 0 (inadequate information) to 100 (superior functioning).

The following are examples from the DSM-IV to show how one records the results of a DSM-IV multiaxial evaluation:

Example 1

Axis I	296.23	Major Depressive Disorder, Single Episode, Severe without psychotic features
	305.00	Alcohol Abuse
Axis II	301.6	Dependent Personality Disorder
Axis III		None
Axis IV		Threat of marital separation
Axis V		GAF = 45 (current)

Example 2

Axis I	300.4	Dysthymic Disorder
	312.31	Pathological Gambling
Axis II	V71.09	No Diagnosis on Axis II or
	799.9	Diagnosis Deferred on Axis II
Axis III	244.9	Hypothyroidism
Axis IV		Debt; litigation
Axis V		GAF = 60 (current)

There may be additional conditions that are a focus of clinical attention:

| V15.81 | Noncompliance with Treatment |

The reason may be discomfort resulting from the treatment (e.g., medication side effects), expense of treatment, decisions based on personal value judgments or religious or cultural beliefs about the advantages and disadvantages of a particular treatment (APA, 1994; p. 683).

V62.89	Religious or Spiritual Problem
V62.89	Phase of Life Problem (e.g., particular developmental phase such as entering college, starting a new career, retirement, separation or divorce)

Substance-Related Disorders

The core concept of the substance-related disorders group is the occurrence of adverse social, behavioral, psychological, and physiological effects caused by seeking or using (i.e., ingesting, injecting, or inhaling) one or more substances from the 13 classes of abused substances listed (Fauman, 1994):

Alcohol	Phencyclidine
Inhalants	Cocaine
Amphetamines	Sedatives
Nicotine	Hypnotics or Axiolytics
Caffeine	Hallucinogens
Opioids	Other or unknown substances
Cannabis	

Criteria Applicable to Multiple Disorders

Substance abuse, substance dependence, substance intoxication, and substance withdrawal are the four sets of general criteria that apply to multiple disorders in the substance-related disorders group.

CRITERIA FOR SUBSTANCE ABUSE

The criteria for substance abuse relate to the actual or potential consequences associated with the use of a substance. The criteria are identical for all 12 classes of substances and are as follows:

A. A maladaptive pattern of substance use leading to clinically significant impairment or distress, as manifested by one (or more) of the following, occurring within a 12-month period
  1. Recurrent substance use resulting in a failure to fulfill major role obligations at work, school, or home (e.g., repeated absences or poor work performance related to substance use; substance-related absences, suspensions, or expulsions from school; neglect of children or household)
  2. Recurrent substance use in situations in which it is physically hazardous (e.g., driving an automobile or operating a machine when impaired by substance use)
  3. Recurrent substance-related legal problems (e.g., arrests for substance-related disorderly conduct)
  4. Continued substance use despite having persistent or recurrent social or interpersonal problems caused or exacerbated by the effects of the substance (e.g., arguments with spouse about consequences of intoxication, physical fights)
B. The symptoms have never met the criteria for substance dependence for this class of substance (APA, 1994, pp. 182–183)(see Box 8-2)

BOX 8-2. Diagnostic Codes for Substance Abuse

Alcohol (305.00)   Cocaine (305.60)

Cannabis (305.20)   Amphetamines (305.70)

Hallucinogens (305.30)   Phencyclidine (305.90)

Sedatives, Hypnotics,   Inhalants (305.90)

   or Anxiolytics (305.40)   Polysubstance, Other

Opioids (305.50)   (or Unknown) (305.90)

Source: American Psychiatric Assocation (1994). *Diagnostic and statistical manual of mental disorders, (4th ed.).* Washington, DC: Author.

CRITERIA FOR SUBSTANCE DEPENDENCE

The essential feature is a cluster of cognitive, behavioral, and physiological symptoms indicating that the individual continues to use the substance despite significant substance-related problems. There is a pattern of repeated self-administration that usually results in tolerance, withdrawal, and compulsive drug-taking behavior.

A diagnosis of substance dependence can be applied to every class of substances except caffeine. The symptoms of dependence are similar across the various categories of substances. There needs to be a maladaptive pattern of substance use, as manifested by three (or more) symptoms from the categories discussed over a 12-month period. Craving, a strong subjective drive to use the substance, is not listed as a criterion item but is experienced by many patients during withdrawal and early recovery from the substance.

The criteria for substance dependence can be classified into two groups. The first group consists of the physiological signs and symptoms of tolerance and withdrawal. However, in certain classes such as hallucinogen dependence, withdrawal symptoms are not specified. Tolerance is defined by either of the following:

1. A need for markedly increased amounts of the substance to achieve intoxication or the desired physiological or psychological effect
2. A markedly diminished effect with continued use of the same amount of the substance

It is usually caused by the enhanced metabolism of the substance in the user's body. The degree to which tolerance develops varies greatly across substances. Individuals with heavy use of opiates and stimulants can develop substantial (e.g., tenfold) levels of tolerance, often to a dosage that would be lethal to a nonuser. Many cigarette smokers consume more than 20 cigarettes a day, an amount that would have produced symptoms of toxicity when they first started smoking. Tolerance to cannabis is very subtle and most individuals are not aware of being tolerant to the substance.

It may be difficult to determine tolerance by history alone when the substance is illegal because it may be mixed with various diluents. The nurse will also have to assess tolerance from individual variability in the initial sensitivity to the particular effects of substances such as alcohol. Some individuals report intoxication with three or four drinks in the early stages of their using alcohol, while others of similar weight and drinking histories have slurred speech and incoordination.

In addition to tolerance, symptoms associated with withdrawal are often specific to each general category of the substance. Those substances that have associated tolerance and withdrawal syndromes are opioids, alcohol, and cocaine. Some withdrawal syndromes appear within a few hours after cessation of the substance such as alcohol, whereas others appear in days or weeks.

The second group of criteria associated with diagnosis of substance dependence includes repeated behavior problems related to both obtaining the substance (frequently referred to as "drug-seeking behavior") and those behavioral problems associated with the pharmacologic effects of the substance after ingestion.

Compulsive use of a substance is another manifestation of substance dependence. Clients may spend a large amount of time trying to get the substance from physicians or other sources. They are frequently unable to control the amount of substance they use or the length of time it is used. This lack of control may be manifest by unsuccessful efforts to reduce or stop using the substance despite a persistent wish to do so. They may continue to use the substance, often in situations in which it is physically hazardous despite the awareness of persistent serious problems it causes.

A second group of problems may be related to the pharmacologic effects of the substance on the individual's ability to fulfill obligations associated with occupational, domestic, educational, and social activities. Recurrent legal or interpersonal problems may also develop with continued substance use.

The specifiers for the substance dependence diagnosis include:

With Physiological Dependence: Evidence of tolerance or withdrawal
Without Physiological Dependence: Evidence of no tolerance or withdrawal

Dependence is characterized by a pattern of compulsive use. The diagnosis of Substance Abuse and Substance Dependence is hierarchical: once patients meet the criteria for substance dependence, they can no longer qualify for a diagnosis of abuse for that substance. The course modifiers, as indicated below, can be applied to substance dependence but not substance abuse.

Early Full Remission: For at least 1 month but for less than 12 months, no criteria for dependence or abuse have been met
Early Partial Remission: For at least 1 month, but less than 12 months, one or more criteria (but not full criteria) for dependence or abuse have been met
Sustained Full Remission: No criteria for dependence or abuse have been met at any time for the last 12 months or longer
Sustained Partial Remission: At least one of the criteria for dependence or abuse has been met for 12 months or longer, but the full criteria have not been met
On Agonist Therapy: The patient is on a prescribed agonist medication and no criteria for dependence or abuse have been met for that class of medication for at least the past month (other than tolerance to, or withdrawal from the agonist)
In a Controlled Environment: The individual is in an environment where access to alcohol and controlled substances is restricted and no criteria for dependence or abuse have been met for at least the past month (APA, 1994) (see Box 8-3)

BOX 8-3. Diagnostic Codes for Substance Dependence

Alcohol (303.90)

Opioids (304.00)

Sedatives, Hypnotics,
    Anxiolytics (304.10)

Cocaine (304.20)

Cannabis (304.30)

Amphetamines (304.40)

Hallucinogens (304.50)

Inhalants (304.60)

Polysubstance (304.80)

Other (or Unknown) (304.90)

Phencyclidine (304.90)

Nicotine (305.10)

Source: American Psychiatric Assocation (1994). *Diagnostic and statistical manual of mental disorders,*
(4th ed.). Washington, DC: Author.

CRITERIA FOR SUBSTANCE INTOXICATION (292.89)

Each substance has unique and characteristic syndromes associated with specific behavioral, psychological, and physiological signs and symptoms. The generic criteria include the following:

1. The development of a reversible substance-specific syndrome due to recent ingestion of (or exposure to) a substance. Different substances may produce similar or identical syndromes.
2. Clinically significant maladaptive behavioral or psychological changes that are due to the effect of the substance on the central nervous system (e.g., belligerence, mood lability, cognitive impairment, impaired judgment, impaired social or occupational functioning) and develop shortly after use of the substance.
3. The symptoms are not due to a general medical condition and are not better accounted for by another mental disorder (see Box 8-4).

BOX 8-4. Diagnostic Codes for Substance Intoxication

Cannabis (292.89)

Sedatives, Hypnotives,
    Anxiolytics (282.89)

Inhalants (292.89)

Amphetamines (292.89)

Cocaine (292.89)

Opioids (292.89)

Hallucinogens (292.89)

Phencyclidine (292.89)

Alcohol (303.00)

Caffeine (305.90)

Source: American Psychiatric Assocation (1994). *Diagnostic and statistical manual of mental disorders, (4th ed.).*
Washington, DC: Author.

CRITERIA FOR SUBSTANCE WITHDRAWAL (292.0)

Most classes of substances have specific withdrawal syndromes consisting of behavioral, psychological, and physiological signs and syndromes that are discussed in Chapter 9 on detoxification. The generic criteria listed apply to all substance withdrawal diagnoses.

1. The development of a substance-specific syndrome due to the cessation of, or reduction in, substance use that has been heavy and prolonged.
2. The substance-specific syndromes cause clinically significant distress or impairment in social, occupational, or other important area of functioning.
3. The symptoms are not due to a general medical condition and are not better accounted for by another mental disorder (see Box 8-5).

DETERMINING APPROPRIATE INTERVENTION/TREATMENT

Once the assessment has been completed and all of the necessary data collected and compared to criteria resulting in a specific diagnosis, then the nurse determines the appropriate intervention or treatment based on the severity of illness—gleaned from the diagnosis after the assessment—and the intensity of services needed to address it. Severity of Illness and Intensity of Service are two parameters that are used to determine the medical necessity of specific treatment.

Severity of illness criteria refer to signs, symptoms, and functional impairments of such a nature and severity that they require treatment at a specified level at a given point in time. They address the question "How dysfunctional is the patient?"

Intensity of service criteria should match the patient's dysfunction. They represent modalities that, by virtue of their complexity or attendant risks, require a specified level of treatment for their safe, appropriate, and effective application. These criteria address the question: "Is the treatment medically necessary?" "Does the patient's signs and symptoms indicate the need for this level of service?" This is done best through the use of patient placement criteria.

Patient Placement Criteria

In June 1991, the American Society of Addiction Medicine published *Patient Placement Criteria for the Treatment of Psychoactive Substance Use Disorders* (Hoffmann, Halikas, Mee-Lee, & Weedman, 1991). This was a result of two years of work by this organization and the National Association of Addiction Treatment Providers.

BOX 8-5. Diagnostic Codes for Substance Withdrawal

Alcohol (291.8)   Amphetamine, Cocaine, Nicotine, Opioid, Sedatives, Hypnotives, & Anxiolytics (292.0)

Source: American Psychiatric Assocation (1994). *Diagnostic and statistical manual of mental disorders, (4th ed.).* Washington, DC: Author.

These criteria focus on six dimensions to define the severity of the addiction from a biopsychosocial perspective. The dimensions are: 1) acute intoxication and/or withdrawal potential; 2) biomedical conditions and complications; 3) emotional/ behavioral conditions or complications; 4) treatment acceptance/resistance; 5) relapse potential; and 6) recovery environment.

The criteria under these six dimensions are used to guide placement for admission, continued stay, and discharge of adult and adolescent clients in one of four levels of intervention or treatment. They include: Level I—outpatient; Level II—intensive outpatient/partial hospitalization; Level III—medically monitored intensive inpatient treatment; and Level IV—medically managed inpatient treatment.

LEVEL I—OUTPATIENT

This level of care is an organized nonresidential service of evaluation, care, and treatment with designated addictions professionals. It provides a structured program for clients that involves regular contact with the client according to a predetermined schedule of less than 6 hours per week, typically for up to 2 years (SAMHSA, 1995).

LEVEL II—INTENSIVE OUTPATIENT/PARTIAL HOSPITALIZATION

This level of care is an organized service of evaluation, care, and treatment with designated addictions professionals. It provides a structured program for clients and typically operates as integrated services of a minimum of 6 hours per week over a period of up to 12 weeks. Other Level II services operate as day treatment or partial hospitalization programs capable of treating clients within the limits of the criteria for Level II (SAMHSA, 1995).

LEVEL III—MEDICALLY MONITORED INTENSIVE INPATIENT TREATMENT
(RESIDENTIAL)

This level of care uses a multidisciplinary staff of designated addictions professionals to provide a planned regimen of 24-hour professionally directed evaluation, care, and treatment for addicted persons in an inpatient setting. Twenty-four-hour observation, monitoring, and treatment are available. Clients in Level III have a higher risk of withdrawal than those in Levels I and II, but do not necessitate hospitalization in a general hospital (SAMHSA, 1995).

LEVEL IV—MEDICALLY MANAGED INTENSIVE INPATIENT TREATMENT
(HOSPITAL-BASED)

This level of care is an organized service with designated addiction professionals that provides a planned regimen of 24-hour medically directed evaluation, care, and treatment for addicted persons in an inpatient setting. The full resources of a general hospital are available, allowing conjoint care for other physical illnesses as well as medically supervised withdrawal (SAMHSA, 1995).

Tables 8-1 and 8-2 provide an overview of specific biopsychosocial criteria dimensions and the fit within certain levels of care for adults and adolescents. They are summaries to illustrate the principal concepts and structure of the criteria.

Limitations of American Society of Addiction Medicine (ASAM) Patient Placement Criteria

Research is currently being completed by the National Institute on Drug Abuse to determine the reliability and validity of the dimensions and effectiveness of the criteria. However, ASAM has convened a National Advisory Panel of addictions experts who meet regularly to continue work and improvement on the patient placement criteria.

TABLE 8-1 Adult Patient Placement Criteria for the Treatment of Psychoactive Substance Use Disorders

Levels of Care	Level I Outpatient Treatment	Level II Intensive Outpatient Treatment	Level III Medically Monitored Intensive Inpatient Treatment	Level IV Medically Managed Intensive Inpatient Treatment
Criteria Dimensions				
1 Acute intoxication and/or withdrawal potential	No withdrawal risk	Minimal withdrawal risk	Severe withdrawal risk but manageable in Level III	Severe withdrawal risk
2 Biomedical conditions and complications	None or very stable	None or nondistracting from addiction treatment and manageable in Level II	Requires medical monitoring but not intensive treatment	Requires 24-hour medical, nursing care
3 Emotional/behavioral conditions and complications	None or very stable	Mild severity with potential to distract from recovery	Moderate severity needing a 24-hour structured setting	Severe problems requiring 24-hour psychiatric care with concomitant addiction treatment
4 Treatment acceptance/resistance	Willing to cooperate but needs motivating and monitoring strategies	Resistance high enough to require structured program, but not so high as to render outpatient treatment ineffective	Resistance high enough despite negative consequences and needs intensive motivating strategies in 24-hour structure	Problems in this dimension do not qualify patient for Level IV treatment
5 Relapse potential	Able to maintain abstinence and recovery goals with minimal support	Intensification of addiction symptoms and high likelihood of relapse without close monitoring and support	Unable to control use despite active participation in less intensive care and needs 24-hour structure	Problems in this dimension do not qualify patient for Level IV treatment
6 Recovery environment	Supportive recovery environment and/or patient has skills to cope	Environment unsupportive but with structure or support, the patient can cope	Environment dangerous for recovery necessitating removal from the environment; logistical impediments to outpatient treatment	Problems in this dimension do not qualify patient for Level IV treatment

NOTE: This overview of the Adult Admission Criteria is an approximate summary to illustrate the principal concepts and structure of the criteria.

Source: Hoffman, N., Halikas, J., Mee-Lee, D., & Weedman, R. (1991). *Patient placement criteria for the treatment of psychoactive substance use disorders.* Washington, D.C.: American Society of Addiction Medicine.

TABLE 8-2 Adolescent Patient Placement Criteria for the Treatment of Psychoactive Substance Use Disorders

Levels of Care Criteria Dimensions	Level I Outpatient Treatment	Level II Intensive Outpatient Treatment	Level III Medically Monitored Intensive Inpatient Treatment	Level IV Medically Managed Intensive Inpatient Treatment
1 Acute intoxication and/or withdrawal potential	No withdrawal risk	Manifests no overt symptoms of withdrawal risk.	Risk of withdrawal syndrome present, but manageable in Level III	Severe withdrawal risk
2 Biomedical conditions and complications	None or very stable	None or nondistracting from addiction treatment and manageable in Level II	Requires medical monitoring but not intensive treatment	Requires 24-hour medical, nursing care
3 Emotional/behavioral conditions and complications	None or very stable	Mild severity with potential to distract from recovery	Moderate severity needing a 24-hour structured setting	Severe problems requiring 24-hour psychiatric care with concomitant addiction treatment
4 Treatment acceptance/resistance	Willing to cooperate but needs motivating and monitoring strategies	Resistance high enough to require structured program, but not so high as to render outpatient treatment ineffective	Resistance high enough despite negative consequences and needs intensive motivating strategies in 24-hour structure	Problems in this dimension do not qualify patient for Level IV treatment
5 Relapse potential	Able to maintain abstinence and recovery goals with minimal support	Intensification of addiction symptoms and high likelihood of relapse without close monitoring and support	Unable to control use despite active participation in less intensive care and needs 24-hour structure	Problems in this dimension do not qualify patient for Level IV treatment
6 Recovery environment	Supportive recovery environment and/or patient has skills to cope	Environment unsupportive but with structure or support, the patient can cope	Environment dangerous for recovery necessitating removal from the environment; logistical impediments to outpatient treatment	Problems in this dimension do not qualify patient for Level IV treatment

NOTE: This overview of the Adolescent Admission Criteria is an approximate summary to illustrate the principal concepts and structure of the criteria.
Source: Hoffman, N., Halikas, J., Mee-Lee, D., & Weedman, R. (1991). *Patient placement criteria for the treatment of psychoactive substance use disorders.* Washington, D.C.: American Society of Addiction Medicine.

136

Meanwhile, because health care costs have been high in the addictions treatment field, many payors want clients assessed and placed in treatment based on some type of patient placement criteria. Therefore, a number of states as well as private insurance and managed care companies have designed their own patient placement criteria using ASAM's criteria as a guide or launching pad because of the rigor used in developing them.

The reason so many states and private companies are doing this is because the ASAM patient placement criteria as they currently stand are not all inclusive of situations needing to be addressed for treatment. For example, there are no levels for prevention, methadone maintenance, half-way house care, long-term residential care (therapeutic communities, TCs), or outpatient detoxification. Also, ASAM patient placement criteria seem to lack cultural relevance.

The use of patient placement criteria is a fairly new process in the addictions field but it is fast becoming a mandatory process. As stated before both public and private treatment systems are using and developing various types of criteria. In an effort to bring about some uniformity to the phenomenon, the Center for Substance Abuse Treatment has developed a treatment improvement protocol (TIP) that addresses the role and current status of patient placement criteria in the treatment of substance use disorders (SAMHSA, 1995). It is imperative that all nurses and other health care providers avail themselves of this document if they are assessing, diagnosing, and referring to interventions/treatment persons who are addicted.

This patient placement criteria TIP addresses the importance of realizing that this will be an ever-evolving process. The progress made with ASAM's criteria include the adoption by the State of Massachusetts of a methadone maintenance criteria and recognition of the need to modify the level of care determination based on intervening factors that exist within the client or treatment system (age, gender, culture/language/ethnicity, service availability/access, childcare, eldercare, client preference, etc.).

The TIP also discusses future directions of patient placement criteria. In particular, it stresses the fact that "level of care" needs to be reconceptualized as an umbrella system under which other more specific patient placement criteria and sublevels of criteria can be incorporated. In addition, a new level of prevention/pretreatment needs to be developed. Finally, experts developing this TIP unanimously agreed that future patient placement criteria would need to be far less categorical and allow treatment providers and purchasers to choose the most appropriate combination of setting, treatment, and intensity of services to meet most efficiently the client's individual needs. This is viewed as being less rigid and "unbundling" the services.

Why so much discussion on patient placement criteria? Because it is tied into assessment in that assessment is an ongoing, cumulative process that can provide certification to authorize certain levels of care, particularly if reimbursement is to come from a private entity. As a client moves from one level of care to another, one assessment builds on another, leading to a discharge plan (SAMHSA, 1995).

CONCLUSION

Assessment is a complex process involving an individualized, multidimensional approach for each client. It is ongoing, rather than static.

According to the Standards of Addictions Nursing Practice (American Nurses Association & the National Nurses Society on Addictions, 1988), Standard II states that assessment is continual and systematic. Data collection is the necessary first step in addressing the quality of the health of any client. The process must by continual, systematic, accurate, and comprehensive to enable health care providers to reach sound conclusions, plan, and implement interventions and treatment (p. 6).

Standard III promotes the idea that once data are collected through the assessment phase, the nurse is responsible for expressing conclusions in the form of a diagnosis supported by the data collected. Based on that diagnosis, Standard IV states that the nurse then establishes a plan of care to which the client is assigned (ANA & NNSA, 1988, pp. 7–8).

The discussion in this chapter has provided knowledge that will enable nurses in any clinical area who are faced with caring for addicted clients, to assess, diagnose, and assign a client to an area of care based on patient placement criteria. Hence, allowing them to meet Standards II, III, and IV of addictions nursing practice.

REFERENCES

Allen, K. (1993). Attitudes of registered nurses toward alcoholic patients in a general hospital population. *The International Journal of the Addictions, 28* (9), 923–930.

American Nurses Association & National Nurses Society on Addiction. (1988). *Standards of addictions nursing practice with selected diagnoses and criteria.* Kansas City: American Nurses Association.

American Psychological Association. (1994). *Diagnostic and statistical manual of mental disorders* (4th ed). Washington, D.C.: American Psychological Association.

Borg, S., Beck, O., Voltaire, A., et al. (1989). *Clinical characteristics and biochemical markers of alcohol consumption during long-term abstinence in relation to relapses: Results from a longitudinal study of alcohol-dependent male patients.* Presented at the 2nd Congress of the European Society for Biomedical Research on Alcoholism, Brussels.

Brooks, M. (1992). Ethical and legal aspects of confidentiality. In J.H. Lowinson, P. Ruiz, R. Milliman, & J. Langrod (Eds.), *Substance abuse: A comprehensive textbook.* Baltimore, MD: Williams & Wilkins.

Burkhalter, P. (1975). Alcoholism, drug abuse and addictions, a study of nursing education. *Journal of Nursing Education,* (14), 30–35.

Chapman, R. (1992). *Roget's International Thesaurus.* New York: HarperCollins.

DiCicco, L., & Unterberger, H. (Winter, 1977). Cultural and professional avoidance: A dilemma in alcoholism training. *Journal of Alcohol and Drug Education, 22,* 30–31.

Fauman, M. (1994). *Study guide to DSM-IV.* Washington, D.C.: American Psychological Association.

Garrett, A. (1982). *Interviewing.* New York: Family Service Association of America.

Hagerty, B. (1984). *Psychiatric-mental health assessment.* St. Louis: C.V. Mosby.

Hoffman, N., Halikas, J., Mee-Lee, D., & Weedman, R. (1991). *Patient placement criteria for the treatment of psychoactive substance use disorders.* Washington, D.C.: American Society of Addiction Medicine.

Institute of Medicine. (1990). *Broadening the base of treatment for alcohol problems* (pp. 242–302). Washington, D.C.: National Academy Press.

Jaffe, S. (Sept, 1979). Nurses need education in alcoholism. *NIAAA Information and Feature Service* (pp. 1–2). National Institute on Alcohol Abuse and Alcoholism (NIAAA).

Jaffe-Johnson, S., & Johnson, R. (1993). *Biopsychosocial data base and intake form.* Unpublished manuscript.

Kinney, J. (1991). *Clinical manual of substance abuse.* St. Louis: Mosby YearBook.

Othmer, E., & Othmer, S. (1994) *The clinical interview using DSM-IV.* Washington, D.C: American Psychiatric Press, Inc.

Persson, J., Magnusson, P., & Borg, S. (1990). Serum gamma-glutamyl transferase (GGT) in a group of organized teetotalers. *Alcohol, 7* (2), 87–89.

Senay, E. (1992). Diagnostic interview and mental status. In J.H. Lowinson., P. Ruiz., R. Millman, & J.Langrod. (Eds.) *Substance abuse: A comprehensive textbook.* Baltimore, MD: Williams & Wilkins.

Substance Abuse and Mental Health Services Administration. (1994). *Treatment for alcohol and other drug abuse: Opportunities for coordination* (pp. 47–66). DHHS Publication No. (SMA) 94-2075. Rockville, MD: Substance Abuse and Mental Health Services Administration.

Substance Abuse and Mental Health Services Administration. (1995). *Treatment Improvement Protocol (TIP): The role and current status of patient placement criteria in the treatment of substance use disorders.* DHHS Publication No. (SMA) 95-3021). Rockville, MD: Substance Abuse and Mental Health Services Administration.

Sullivan, H.S. (1954). *The psychiatric interview.* New York: W.W. Norton & Company.

Sullivan, E.S., Handley, S.M., & Connors, H. (1994). Role of nurses in managing alcohol-abusing clients. *Alcohol Health & Research World, 18,* 158–161.

Tweed, S. (March, 1989). Identifying the alcoholic. Nursing Interventions for Addicted Patients. *Nursing Clinics of North America, 24*(1), 13–29.

Detoxification

Janice Cooke Feigenbaum, PhD, RN
Karen M. Allen, PhD, RN, CARN

INTRODUCTION

Nurses in all clinical settings are caring for individuals who are withdrawing from a wide range of addictive substances, from nicotine to cocaine. Some of these substances, such as sedative-hypnotics and methadone, may have been taken for therapeutic reasons as prescribed by a physician. Others, such as alcohol, caffeine, or nicotine, may have been used legally, whereas others, such as cocaine, marijuana, or heroin, may have been taken illegally.

Regardless of the legal status of the addictive substances being used, the reality of what these individuals are experiencing must be acknowledged so that the detoxification process may proceed as safely as possible and persons are motivated to address the addiction problem. To accomplish this nurses must overcome their own denial regarding the existence of this type of health problem in a substantial number of their clients. Examples of the large numbers of people who experience withdrawal symptoms while being treated for other health problems can be seen with individuals who are dependent on caffeine or tobacco.

In contemporary North America, most hospitals are smoke-free zones. This fact means that patients cannot smoke once they are admitted to the institution. Yet, many of these individuals are addicted to nicotine. When they exhibit cues of being irritable, restless, and unable to sleep, most of the time the possibility of withdrawal from nicotine is overlooked as a cause of these responses.

Furthermore, people often have surgery that requires them to fast for varying amounts of time prior to the procedure. Then, they have the surgery and spend time recovering from the effects of the anesthetics they received. Afterward, they may be placed on a restricted diet for hours or a few days after the surgery, which means they will be unable to ingest any caffeine for at least 12 hours. However, many of these people are addicted to caffeine; yet when they begin to complain of having a severe headache, often this is not recognized as being a cue of withdrawing from the effects of caffeine.

To capitalize on the caring occasions presented during withdrawal, initially nurses must acknowledge that people are in fact experiencing withdrawal based on being addicted to alcohol and/or other substances. When this acknowledgment has been accomplished, nurses can move forward to properly plan and execute safe detoxification followed by necessary interventions such as screening, assessment, education, counseling, and consultation for individuals who are exhibiting signs of addiction. Therefore, the purpose of this chapter is to delineate the principles of detoxification by: 1) defining concepts related to detoxification; 2) discussing signs and symptoms of withdrawal from alcohol and other drugs; 3) providing objective measures for assessing intensity of withdrawal; 4) presenting appropriate methods for planning and implementing safe detoxification; and 5) describing indicators to be used as outcome measures for evaluating the effectiveness of detoxification interventions.

CONCEPTS RELATED TO DETOXIFICATION

Developing the ability to care for individuals who may be experiencing health problems related to withdrawing from the effects of alcohol and other addictive substances begins by understanding the concepts related to detoxification. These include: tolerance, dependence, withdrawal, kindling, and detoxification.

Tolerance

Tolerance is a phenomenon that results from the body's adaptation to the continual presence of the substance. Hanson and Venturelli (1995) define it as a reduced response over time to the same dosage. Therefore, one must increase the dose to elicit the same response.

Substances affect the body at the cell level—probably due to changes in the receptor sites of the neurotransmitters—which changes the neurochemical functioning of the body. Thus, the person adapts to having the substance within the system and requires higher doses of the substance to experience the effects that were previously experienced after consuming smaller amounts.

The extent of tolerance and the rate at which it is acquired depends on the drug, the person using it, and the dose and frequency of administration. There are four types: drug disposition, pharmacodynamic, reverse, and cross-tolerance (Hanson & Venturelli, 1995).

Drug disposition tolerance reflects the rate at which the body disposes of the drug, based on the body's production of metabolic enzymes—primarily in the liver—which deactivate the drugs. Because there is evidence that a considerable degree of central nervous system (CNS) tolerance to some drugs may develop independent of changes in rate of absorption, metabolism, or excretion, pharmacodynamic tolerance has been identified. This type of tolerance reflects the adaptation of nervous tissue or other target tissue (which may include changes in receptors) to the drug, so that effect of the same concentration of drug decreases (Hanson & Venturelli, 1995).

Reverse tolerance is the situation that exists when a response to a drug is elicited that is opposite to tolerance. This is also known as sensitization. When sensitized, drug users will have the same response to a lower dose of a drug that they did to the initial higher dose. It has been speculated that this heightened response may reflect changes in the receptors (site of drug action) or brain neurotransmitters to subsequent administration of these drugs (Hanson & Venturelli, 1995).

Cross-tolerance exists with certain drugs. It means that if persons develop a tolerance to one drug, they will also show tolerance to other related drugs. This effect may be due to altered metabolism resulting from chronic drug use. For example, a heavy drinker will usually exhibit tolerance to barbiturates, other depressants, and anesthetics because the alcohol has changed his or her liver and CNS metabolic enzymes (Hanson & Venturelli, 1995).

Dependence

Dependence is a phenomenon that is beginning to be understood more clearly as scientists are delineating the neurochemical influences of addictive substances on the human body (Blum & Payne, 1991). Until recently, the concept of dependence was categorized according to psychological or physical phenomena. Psychological dependence is defined as the individual experiencing a craving to use the substance to feel a sense of normal well being.

Physical (tissue) dependence is the biological adaptation of the body to long-term exposure to a drug. The first time the body is exposed to a drug it may have a strong reaction such as intoxication. But, after chronic consumption, the body physically adjusts, often stopping the production of natural neurochemicals that are similar to the drug of abuse. Therefore, the body begins to expect the presence of a chronically used drug (Landry, 1994).

The drugs that cause physical dependence also cause a condition known as the "rebound effect," which is seen during withdrawal. This is also known as the "paradoxical effect" because the symptoms at this stage are nearly opposite of the direct effects of the drugs. For example, a person taking barbiturates or benzodiazepines will be greatly depressed physically, but upon withdrawal will become extremely irritable, hyperexcited, nervous, and generally show symptoms of extreme stimulation of the nervous system. All these factors constitute the rebound effect (Hanson & Venturelli, 1995).

Dependence compels people to continue using a drug because they want to achieve a desired effect, or they fear an unpleasant reaction—withdrawal. Dependence has been associated with such benign over-the-counter drugs as nasal decongestant sprays and laxatives, as well as more potent drugs such as stimulants, narcotics, and alcohol (Witters, Venturelli, & Hanson, 1992). Tolerance and dependence are closely linked and related to withdrawal as shown in Figure 9-1.

Withdrawal

For the most part, the adaptations that cause the tolerance phenomenon are also associated with altered physical and psychological states that lead to dependence. These altered states reflect the efforts of the body and brain to reestablish a balance with the continual presence of a drug. Thus, when the drug is no longer taken, the systems of the body become overcompensated and unbalanced, causing unpleasant effects known as withdrawal (Hanson & Venturelli, 1995). In addition, for the most part withdrawal symptoms are opposite in nature to the direct effects of the drug that caused the dependence. Thus, dependence on CNS depressants tends to result in excitatory-type withdrawal symptoms during abstinence, and the opposite is true for CNS stimulant dependence (Goldstein, 1994).

According to the DSM-IV, withdrawal is the development of a substance-specific syndrome due to the cessation of, or reduction in, substance use that has been heavy and prolonged. In addition, the substance-specific syndrome causes clinically significant distress or impairment in physical, mental, social, occupational, or other important areas of functioning. Finally, it needs to be ruled out that the symptoms are not due to a general medical condition or mental disorder (American Psychiatric Association [APA], 1994).

Kindling

The kindling effect occurs with some substances, such as cocaine. This phenomenon refers to the individual who has been using a substance on a chronic basis, experiencing toxic effects by ingesting only small doses of the substance (Palfai & Jankiewicz, 1991, p. 305). The kindling effect suggests that individuals experiencing recurrent periods of withdrawal from certain drugs inevitably develop a seizure focus that then progresses to greater levels of severity with succeeding times of withdrawal (Morton, Laird, Crane, Partovi, & Frye, 1994).

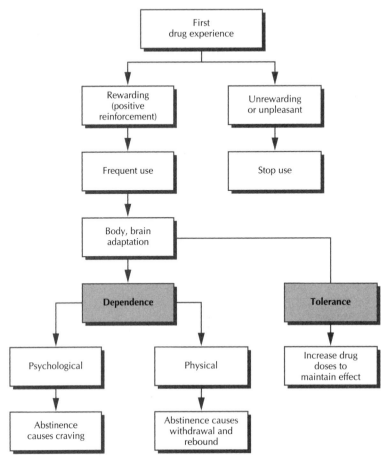

Figure 9-1. The relationship between tolerance, dependence, and withdrawal. (Source: Hanson, G., & Ventrelli, P. [1995]. *Drugs and society* [4th ed.] Boston: Jones and Bartlett.)

Detoxification

Detoxification involves the normalization of the person's body chemistry, primarily the neurochemistry, so that the individual is able to function in a manner similar to that experienced prior to the consumption of the substance (Daigle, Clark, & Landry, 1988, p. 291). Detoxification from a specific chemical agent takes a certain length of time, and this is based on the half-life of the drug, which is the amount of time required for the body to metabolize one half of the amount of the drug ingested.

This process includes two phases. The first is the process of clearing the body of the substance, and the second is the body's regaining a sense of balance or equilibrium. Thus, detoxification can be viewed as the systematic elimination of a toxic substance, as well as its effects. It is a process that requires careful monitoring because negative outcomes often result. This is evident when persons begin to inadvertently experience withdrawal from a substance because their addiction has not been identified, but they are seeking medical care for other illnesses.

All drugs in a given group have a common withdrawal syndrome that must be managed in detoxification; however, the intensity and time course of the withdrawal syndrome varies, depending on the specific agent, which impacts the intensity and time course of detoxification. Hence, the following section will discuss specific withdrawal symptoms for varying addicting drugs.

SYMPTOMS OF WITHDRAWAL

Four types of withdrawal symptoms are produced by substances that are addicting. These include: 1) restlessness, tremors, shakiness, and/or jitteriness; 2) anxiety, irritability, and/or tension; 3) sleep disturbances; and 4) gastrointestinal distress (Swanson, Lee, & Hopp, 1994). The specificity and severity of the symptoms, as well as the time of the onset of symptoms after the last dose of the substance, correlate with the substance ingested.

Table 9-1 highlights the time of onset of withdrawal symptoms after the last dose of the drug taken for the major addiction-producing drugs. An examination of withdrawal for each of the major categories of drugs follows.

Alcohol

The alcoholic person who is in fairly good physical condition can safely withdraw in an outpatient modality. However, the alcoholic person who is severely ill and experiencing health consequences because of the addiction needs to be medically monitored or managed.

When withdrawing from alcohol, as highlighted in Table 9-2, the person will experience symptoms of one of five stages, from tremulousness to the rum fits. The diagnostic criteria for alcohol withdrawal according to the DSM-IV include two or more of the following, which develops within several hours to a few days after cessation of, or reduction in, alcohol use that has been heavy and prolonged (APA, 1994):

- Autonomic hyperactivity (e.g., sweating or pulse rate greater than 100 beats/minute, elevated heart rate, increased blood pressure)
- Increased hand tremor
- Insomnia
- Nausea or vomiting
- Transient visual, tactile, or auditory hallucinations or illusions
- Psychomotor agitation
- Anxiety
- Grand mal seizures

Other symptoms include: restlessness, irritability, and agitation; anorexia; intense dreaming, nightmare; impaired concentration, memory, and judgment; increased sensitivity to sounds, alteration in tactile sensations; delirium (disorientation to time, place, situation); delusions (usually paranoid); and elevated temperature. Symptoms do not always progress from mild to severe in an orderly fashion; in some individuals a grand mal seizure may be the first manifestation of alcohol acute abstinence syndrome (withdrawal) (Substance Abuse and Mental Health Services Administration [SAMHSA], 1995).

The withdrawal symptoms typically begin when blood concentrations of alcohol decline sharply (i.e., within 4 to 12 hours) after alcohol use has been stopped or reduced. However, withdrawal symptoms can develop after longer periods of time—up to a few days. Because of the short half-life of alcohol, symptoms of alcohol withdrawal usually peak in intensity during the

TABLE 9-1 Half-Life and Peak Time for Onset of Withdrawal Symptoms From Addictive Drugs

Drug	Half-Life	Peak Time for Onset	Symptoms
Short-acting barbiturates	8–18 hr	12–24 hr	Seizures, restlessness, insomnia, nightmares, hallucination (tactile, visual), nausea/vomiting, abdominal cramps, tremors, diaphoresis, memory problems, delirium, hyperpyrexia, cardiovascular collapse
Long-acting barbiturates	60–100 hr	5–8 days	Same as for short-acting barbiturates
Short-acting benzodiazepines	8–18 hr	12–24 hr	Insomnia, nightmares, seizures, hyperpyrexia, tachycardia, palpitations, blurred vision, muscle spasms, confusion, anxiety, tremors, nausea/vomiting, increased sensitivity to light and sounds
Long-acting benzodiazepines	60–100 hr	5–8 days	Same as for short-acting benzodiazepines
Caffeine	3.5–5 hr	12–24 hr	Headache, (becomes more, severe with, movement), mild nausea, fatigue, lethargy, irritability, yawning, restlessness, rhinorrhea
Cocaine	?	12–96 hr	Lethargy, anhedonia, depression, constipation, irritability, loss of interests
Heroin	2.5–3 hr	10–12 hr	Abdominal cramps, nausea/vomiting, diarrhea, diaphoresis, hypertension, rhinorrhea, lacrimation, gooseflesh, yawning, mydriasis, backache, muscle aches, insomnia, anxiety, restlessness
Methadone	15–30 hr	24–96 hr	Same as for heroin
Marijuana (THC)	up to 45 days	7 days	Diarrhea, teeth chattering, wet dog shakes, salivation, ptosis, piloerection, yawning, restlessness, anxiety
Nicotine	20–30 minutes	24 hr	Irritability, anxiety, depression, drowsiness, fatigue, restlessness, short attention span, lightheadedness, tightness in chest, tingling in limbs, hunger, constipation, changes in electroencephalogram, sleep problems, diaphoresis, mouth ulcers, coughing

Data from Baltarovich, 1985 (p. 51); Greden & Walters, 1992 (pp. 362, 367); Gold, 1992 (p. 208); Jarvik & Schneider, 1992 (p. 342); Keltner & Folks, 1993 (p. 268); Wesson, Smith, & Seymour, 1992 (p. 276); Zweben & O'Connell, 1992 (p. 167).

TABLE 9-2 Stages of Alcohol Withdrawal

Stage	Peak Time of Onset After Last Drink	Symptoms	Potential Duration of Symptoms
1. Tremulousness	24 hr	At rest: slight tremors; during activities: gross and irregular tremors	7 days
		Diaphoresis	3–4 days
		Anorexia, nausea, and vomiting	3–4 days
		Increased vital signs	3–4 days
		Sense of agitation and inner shakiness	14 days
		Insomnia with nightmares of seemingly real events	14 days or longer
2. Tremors and transitory hallucinosis	24 hr	Above symptoms plus visual hallucinations of events (i.e., having an accident while drunk)	3 days
3. Auditory hallucinosis	24 hr	Cues of tremulousness state plus vivid persecutory and auditory hallucinations, agitation, increased suicide and preassaultive potential	3–14 days
4. Delirium tremens	24–48 hr	Cues of tremulousness delirium, grand mal seizures, disorientation for time and place, visual hallucinations, agitation, panic level of anxiety	3–5 days
5. Rum fits	24–48 hr	Two to six grand mal seizures; cues of delirium tremens	3–5 days

Adapted from Bittle, S., Feigenbaum, J.C., & Kneisl, C.R. (1986). Substance abuse. In C.R. Kneisl & S.W. Ames (Eds.), *Adult health nursing* (pp. 231–238). Menlo Park, CA: Addison-Wesley.

second day of abstinence and are likely to improve markedly by the fourth or fifth day. However, following acute withdrawal, symptoms of anxiety, insomnia, and autonomic dysfunction may persist for up to 3 to 6 months at lower levels of intensity (APA, 1994, p. 198).

Prior to the use of benzodiazepines, there was a mortality rate of approximately 30% associated with delirium tremens. This has now been reduced to 2 to 4% among individuals who are receiving expert, safe care (Worner, 1994, pp. 115–116). Controversy exists in the relationship between the type and severity of withdrawal experienced by an individual and the amount and duration of the person's alcohol intake (Daryanani, Santolaria, Reimers, Jorge, Lopez, Hernandez, Riera, & Rodriguez, 1994, p. 327).

Seizures occur most commonly among individuals who have: 1) previously had a convulsion while withdrawing from alcohol; 2) taken psychotropic agents, including antidepressants, benzodiazepines, sedative-hypnotics, and antipsychotics; 3) a history of suffering a head injury; 4) an absence of magnesium administration on admission; 5) a serum sodium level below 138 mEq during the initial 48 hours after the last dose of alcohol; or 6) a pulse rate over 93 beats/minute during the first 48 hours (Morton et al., 1994, p. 81). Experiencing withdrawal cues during the morning has also been suggested as being a feature of more severe withdrawal progression (Daryanani et al., 1994, p. 327).

Sedative-Hypnotic or Anxiolytic Agents

Barbiturates and benzodiazepines are two sedative-hypnotic agents that produce dependence. Suddenly stopping the ingestion of these drugs, even with long-term therapeutic low doses, can result in withdrawal symptoms (Hayner, Galloway, & Wiehl, 1993, p. 331). Withdrawing from the sedative-hypnotics and anxiolytics can be a dangerous, and a potentially fatal process. The seriousness of this syndrome must not be overlooked.

The withdrawal syndrome of this category of drugs is characterized by signs and symptoms generally the opposite of the acute effects likely to be observed in a first-time user of these drugs. The time course of the withdrawal syndrome is generally predicted by the half-life of the drug. The longer the drug has been taken and the higher the dosages used, the more likely the withdrawal will be severe. However, withdrawal has been reported with as little as 15 mg of diazepam when taken daily for several months (APA, 1994).

Since these drugs are CNS depressants, same as opioids and alcohol, their withdrawal symptoms are similar to all drugs in this classification. Barbiturates and benzodiazepines have wide ranges of action, from very short acting to long acting. Due to this, the onset of these symptoms will vary from 12 hours up to a week after the last dose of the drug. Other sedative-hypnotics, which are not barbiturates or benzodiazepines, have similar types of withdrawals. These drugs include meprobamate and methaqualone.

The general diagnostic criteria for sedative-hypnotic and anxiolytic withdrawal are identical to those of alcohol. This is to be expected since both categories of drugs are CNS depressants; however, some symptoms are specific to barbiturates and benzodiazepines and these are presented next.

BARBITURATES

Cues of barbiturate withdrawal include orthostatic hypotension; delirium, especially after bouts of insomnia; seizures; and high fever (Baltarovich, 1985, p. 51). The withdrawal cues from short-acting barbiturates, such as pentobarbital and secobarbital, begin 24 to 48 hours after the last dose, and peak in 12 to 72 hours (Wesson, Smith, & Seymour, 1992, p. 274). A long-acting barbiturate, phenobarbital, has a half-life of 100 hours, and the plasma levels of this drug decrease very slowly (Hayner, Galloway, & Wiehl, 1993, p. 333).

BENZODIAZEPINES

Cues of withdrawal from benzodiazepines may include blurred vision; confusion; muscle cramps and spasms; paresthesias and increased sensitivity to lights and sounds; as well as major motor seizures, psychotic reactions, and death due to cardiovascular collapse. The withdrawal cues from short-acting benzodiazepines, such as oxazepam, begin 12 to 24 hours after the last dose, and peak in 2 to 4 days. Meanwhile, the cues of withdrawal from long-acting benzodiazepines, such as diazepam and chlordiazepoxide, begin 3 to 8 days after the last dose, and peak on the fifth to eight day (Wesson, Smith, & Seymour, 1992, p. 274). Benzodiazepines are the pharmacological agents of choice in the medical treatment of anxiety disorders. Thus, it is important to acknowledge that when individuals are being treated with one of these medications for such an illness, they may demonstrate the symptoms of the illness as they withdraw from the chemical agent.

Opioids (Heroin and Methadone)

The withdrawal syndrome of this drug category can be precipitated by cessation of opioid use that has been heavy and prolonged. It can also be precipitated by the administration of an opioid antagonist (e.g., naloxone or naltrexone) after a period of opioid use (APA, 1994).

Opioid withdrawal is characterized by signs and symptoms that are opposite to the acute agonist effects. The initial symptoms are subjective and consists of 1) complaints of anxiety; restlessness and an "achy feeling" that is often located in the back and legs; a wish to obtain opioids ("craving") and drug-seeking behavior, along with irritability and increased sensitivity to pain. To diagnose opioid withdrawal, three of the following must be present within minutes to several days after cessation of use or administration of an opioid antagonist (APA, 1994):

- Dysphoric mood
- Nausea or vomiting
- Muscle aches
- Lacrimation or rhinorrhea
- Pupillary dilation, pilorection, or sweating
- Diarrhea
- Yawning
- Fever
- Insomnia

Opioids have a wide range of half-lives. Morphine, heroin, and hydromorphine (Dilaudid) have short half-lives. Symptoms of withdrawal from these drugs will develop within 8 to 12 hours after the last dose of the drug, reach their peak intensity level within 2 days, and gradually end within 5 to 7 days (Jaffe, 1992 p. 190). However, cues of withdrawal from drugs, such as methadone (opioids with half-lives of 16 to more than 60 hours), will develop within 36 to 48 hours after the last dose, reach their peak intensity level within the forth to the sixth day, and last for up to 2 weeks (Jaffe, 1992, p. 190).

Caffeine

As shown in Table 9-1, headache is the primary cue of withdrawal from caffeine, a CNS stimulant. The headaches typically occur 12 to 24 hours after the last ingestion of the substance (Swanson, Lee, & Hopp, 1994, p. 245). Cues of feeling sleepy and tired are also major symptoms of caffeine withdrawal, especially during the second and third day of the process (Swanson, Lee, & Hopp, pp. 246–247). The timing of the onset of these symptoms may be difficult to predict due to the many factors that influence the half-life of caffeine, which is lengthened by the use of alcohol and nicotine withdrawal (Swanson, Lee, & Hopp, 1994, p. 237) and tripled during pregnancy (Campinha-Bacote & Bragg, 1993, p. 24).

Cocaine

Much controversy exists regarding the process of withdrawing from the effects of cocaine, a CNS stimulant. This process, however, is not as medically dangerous as that of some of the other substances (Gold, 1992, p. 215). Three phases of this process seem to occur. The initial one is the crash, which occurs about 1 to 4 hours after a binge on cocaine. The cues of the crash include depression, anxiety, restlessness, and agitation. Then, within 12 to 96 hours after the crash, the symptoms of withdrawal from cocaine—which are relatively mild—are experienced (Gold, 1992, p. 215).

Table 9-1 highlights symptoms of cocaine withdrawal and these include: depression, irritability, anergia, anhedonia, and lack of interest in the environment and usual activities (Gawin & Ellinwood, 1988, p. 1176). Criteria for diagnosing cocaine withdrawal according to the DSM-IV include (APA, 1994):

- Cessation of or reduction in cocaine use that has been heavy and prolonged
- Dysphoric mood and two or more of the following physiological changes, developed within a few hours to several days after cessation of use:

  — Fatigue
  — Vivid, unpleasant dreams
  — Insomnia or hypersomnia
  — Increased appetite
  — Psychomotor retardation or agitation

Euphoric recall of the positive experiences associated with cocaine use also dominate the person's thoughts and dreams, leading to the desire to use the drug again. If abstinence from cocaine is maintained, the cues of withdrawal subside within 6 to 18 weeks (Gawin & Ellinwood, 1988, p. 1176).

 *phases of withdrawl*

Acute withdrawal symptoms (a crash) are often seen after periods of repetitive high-dose use ("runs" or "binges"). These periods are characterized by intense and unpleasant feelings of lassitude and depression, generally requiring days of rest and recuperation. In addition, depressive symptoms with suicidal ideation or behavior can occur and are generally the most serious problems seen during "crashing." It is important to note that a large number of persons addicted to cocaine have few or no clinically evident withdrawal symptoms on cessation of use (APA, 1994).

Extinction, the third phase of the process, continues for months or years after the last dose of cocaine. During this stage, cravings for cocaine occur.

Nicotine

Most, but not all persons who abstain from smoking for at least a few hours will experience symptoms of withdrawal. According to the DSM-IV, criteria for diagnosing nicotine withdrawal include (APA, 1994):

- The daily use of nicotine for at least several weeks
- Abrupt cessation of nicotine use, or reduction in the amount of nicotine use, followed within 24 hours by four or more of the following signs:

  — Dysphoric or depressed mood
  — Insomnia

— Irritability, frustration, or anger
— Anxiety
— Difficulty concentrating
— Restlessness
— Decreased heart rate
— Increased appetite or weight gain

Brunton (1991) stated that withdrawal-related changes in mood and performance may be seen within 2 hours after the last cigarette in many who smoke heavily. Mild withdrawal symptoms may occur in smokers who switch from high-tar/high-nicotine cigarettes to low-tar/low-nicotine brands. Withdrawal symptoms tend to be most intense within the first day or two after smoking cessation, declining gradually thereafter over a period of several days to several weeks. However, as pointed out by Jarvik and Schneider (1992), the onset and duration of the process of withdrawal from nicotine continues to be the focus of much controversy.

As highlighted in Table 9-1, anxiety, disturbances in sleeping, and constipation are also major cues of nicotine withdrawal. Depression may be significant for up to 3 weeks, before gradually receding (Swanson, Lee, & Hopp, 1994, p. 239). Irritability may last for 5 weeks, and a tendency to gain weight may persist for 10 weeks (Jarvik & Schneider, 1992, p. 343).

Marijuana

Tetrahydrocannabinol (THC) is the active ingredient of marijuana. The process of withdrawal from THC is still the focus of much controversy. Marijuana has a long half-life, possibly up to 45 days for some of its metabolites (Zweben & O'Connell, 1992, p. 166). The cues of withdrawal are not experienced until at least 1 week after the last dose of marijuana. As highlighted in Table 9-1 cues of withdrawal include diarrhea, teeth chattering, wet dog shakes, salivation, ptosis (drooping of the upper eyelid), piloerection, yawning, and restlessness. These symptoms mirror those experienced with a mild case of the flu, and are frequently not acknowledged to be due to an addiction (Grinspoon & Bakalar, 1992, p. 238; Zweben & O'Connell, 1992, p. 167).

Amphetamines

DSM-IV criteria for diagnosing amphetamine withdrawal include the cessation of or reduction in use that has been heavy and prolonged. In addition, the person has a dysphoric mood and two or more of the following physiological changes that develop within a few hours to several days after the cessation of use (APA, 1994):

- Fatigue
- Vivid, unpleasant dreams
- Insomnia or hypersomnia
- Marked increase appetite with rapid weight gain
- Psychomotor retardation or agitation

Goldstein (1995) states that, although claims have been made that amphetamines do not cause physical dependence, it is almost certain that the depression (sometimes suicidal), lethargy, and abnormal sleep patterns occurring after high chronic doses are part of withdrawal.

Although the nurse may have a history of the alcohol and other drug use from the client, it is difficult to determine whether or not withdrawal will occur, the degree to which it will occur, and at what point. Hence, it is imperative that accurate monitoring and assessment of clients who are expected to go into withdrawal or are showing cues of withdrawal takes place.

ASSESSMENT OF INDIVIDUALS WHO ARE WITHDRAWING

When beginning to care for a person, the nurse should anticipate that the individual may have problems related to an addiction. It is safer to assume this view to recognize the earliest cues of withdrawal and to prevent the dangerous complications that occur during detoxification. Thus, starting with the initial contact with each client, the nurse assesses vital signs, especially the pulse rate, and monitors for cues of withdrawal, especially diaphoresis and tremulousness. The nurse should remember that the pulse rate and temperature will rise prior to the onset of the more severe symptoms, including seizures and hallucinations.

To assess for withdrawal symptoms, some settings utilize subjective and objective tools. This helps to standardize the withdrawal symptoms and provides guidance with administering care or necessary treatments.

Box 9-1 shows the Addiction Research Foundation Clinical Institute Withdrawal Assessment for Alcohol (CIWA-Ar) [revised to include all sedative-hypnotics and anxiolytics] (Skinner & Horn, 1984; Sullivan, Sykora, Schneiderman, Naranjo, & Sellers, 1989; Alexander, Mello, & Gould, 1993). This tool consists of 10 items for assessing severity of the alcohol and other sedative-hypnotic withdrawal syndrome. A total score is obtained by summing the ratings from the 10 items. Its reliability and validity has been demonstrated, but mostly with alcoholic withdrawal (Rounsaville, Tims, Horton, & Sowder, 1993). Persons with a score of 20 or greater on the CIWA-Ar should be admitted to a hospital for detoxification. The maximum score that can be obtained is 67. It should be given at regular intervals. Increasing scores indicate the need for additional medication or a higher level treatment setting. Persons scoring less than 8 to 10 usually do not need additional medication for withdrawal.

Box 9-2 shows the Subjective Opiate Withdrawal Scale (SOWS), and Box 9-3 the Objective Opiate Withdrawal Scale (OOWS) was developed by Handelsman, Cochran, Aronson, Ness, Rubinstein, & Kanof (1987). Both scales are easily completed and both have demonstrated reliability and validity. The SOWS consists of 16 symptoms rated in intensity by patients on a five-point scale. The patients indicate the intensity of each symptom currently being experienced, and a total score ranging from 0 to 64 is obtained by summing the patient's ratings for each item. The OOWS would be completed by the nurse who rates the presence of 13 physically observable signs. In this case, a total score is obtained by summing the number of signs that were present during a brief (10-minute) observation period (Rounsaville et al., 1993).

Box 9-4 shows the stimulant withdrawal scale developed by Rounsaville, Tims, Horton, and Sowder (1993), which includes a set of signs and symptoms that can be scored from 0 to 2 based on presence and severity.

When assessing an individual for cues of withdrawal, the nurse must acknowledge the reality and significance of polydrug abuse, the concurrent abuse/misuse of several substances. This practice has become the norm for the majority of people who are dependent on substances. When individuals are dependent on more than a one substance, they will not follow the usual path of detoxification as expected from a single chemical agent. Instead, the process will be complicated and experienced over an extended period of time.

BOX 9-1. **Addiction Research Foundation Clinical Institute Withdrawal Assessment for Alcohol (CIWA-Ar)**

Patient _____ Date / / / / Time: ____:____
                     y d m   (24 hour clock: midnight = 00:00)

Pulse or heart rate, taken for one minute: _____ Blood pressure: _____ /_____

NAUSEA AND VOMITING
Ask "Do you feel sick to your stomach? Have you vomited?" Observation.
0   no nausea and no vomiting
1   mild nausea with no vomiting
2
3
4   intermittent nausea with dry heaves
5
6
7   constant nausea, frequent dry heaves and vomiting

TREMOR
Arms extended and fingers spread apart. Observation.
0   no tremor
1   not visible, but can be felt fingertip to fingertip
2
3
4   moderate, with patient's arms extended
5
6
7   severe, even with arms not extended

PAROXYSMAL SWEATS
Observation.
0   no sweat visible
1   barely perceptible sweating, palms moist
2
3
4   beads of sweat obvious on forehead
5
6
7   drenching sweats

ANXIETY
Ask, "Do you feel nervous?" Observation.
0   no anxiety, at ease
1   mildly anxious
2
3
4   moderately anxious, or guarded, so anxiety is inferred
5
6
7   equivalent to acute panic states as seen in severe delirium or acute
         schizophrenic reactions

BOX 9-1. (continued)

AGITATION
Observation.
0 normal activity
1 somewhat more than normal activity
2
3
4 moderately fidgety and restless
5
6
7 paces back and forth during most of the interview, or constantly thrashes about

TACTILE DISTURBANCES
Ask "Have you any itching, pins and needles sensations, any burning, any numbness, or do you feel bugs crawling on or under your skin?" Observation.
0 none
1 very mild itching, pins and needles, burning, or numbness
2 mild itching, pins and needles, burning, or numbness
3 moderate itching, pins and needles, burning, or numbness
4 moderately severe hallucinations
5 severe hallucinations
6 extremely severe hallucinations
7 continuous hallucinations

AUDITORY DISTURBANCES
Ask "Are you aware of sounds around you? Are they harsh? Do they frighten you? Are you hearing anything that is disturbing to you? Are you hearing things you know are not there?" Observation.
0 not present
1 very mild harshness or ability to frighten
2 mild harshness or ability to frighten
3 moderate harshness or ability to frighten
4 moderately severe hallucinations
5 severe hallucinations
6 extremely severe hallucinations
7 continuous hallucinations

VISUAL DISTURBANCES
Ask "Does the light appear to be too bright? Is its color different? Does it hurt your eyes? Are you seeing anything that is disturbing to you? Are you seeing things that you know are not there?" Observation.
0 not present
1 very mild sensitivity
2 mild sensitivity
3 moderate sensitivity
4 moderately severe hallucinations
5 severe hallucinations
6 extremely severe hallucinations
7 continuous hallucinations

BOX 9-1. (continued)

HEADACHE, FULLNESS IN HEAD

Ask "Does your head feel different? Does it feel like there is a band around your head?" Do not rate for dizziness or lightheadness; otherwise, rate severity.

0   not present
1   very mild
2   mild
3   moderate
4   moderately severe
5   severe
6   very severe
7   extremely severe

ORIENTATION AND CLOUDING OF SENSORIUM

Ask "What day is this? Where are you? Who am I?"

0   oriented and can do serial additions
1   cannot do serial additions or is uncertain about date
2   disoriented for date by no more than 2 calendar days
3   disoriented for date by more than 2 calendar days
4   disoriented for place and/or person

TOTAL CIWA-Ar Score   _____
Rater's Initials   _____
Maximum Possible Score: 67

Source: Rounsaville, B., Tims, F., Horton, A., & Sowder, B. (1993). *Diagnostic source book on drug abuse research and treatment.* NIH Publication No. 93-3508. Rockville, MD: National Institutes of Health.

The path of withdrawal that a specific person experiences is further determined by many other factors, such as age, gender, race, ethnicity, pregnancy, and concurrent illnesses. There is a need for nursing research that focuses on how individuals of various ages and cultural backgrounds proceed through the phases of withdrawal from various substances.

During the nursing history, each person should be questioned regarding the ingestion of alcohol and other substances. Priority questions should include "How often do you drink alcohol?" to assess the frequency of alcohol use; "When you do drink alcohol, how much do you usually drink?" to identify the magnitude of alcohol consumption; and "Under what circumstances and with whom do you usually drink?" to determine the environment surrounding the consumption of alcohol. To know when the earliest cues of alcohol withdrawal might arise, the person should also be asked, "When was your last drink of alcohol?"

Similar questions should also be asked regarding the person's ingestion of other drugs including nicotine and caffeine, as well as illicit drugs, such as cocaine and marijuana. The reason for focusing on these substances should be explained. For example, the nurse might state, "It is important for us to know what medications/drugs you have been taking so that we can be aware of the possible withdrawal symptoms you might experience if you stop taking them abruptly."

Even though the nurse explains the rationale for the staff needing to know this information, the person may tend to deny the use of illicit drugs due to concerns of legal actions. In light of this, the nurse must be alert to cues of withdrawal and acknowledge the reality that this phenomenon may be occurring. Observation of the person's response to anesthetics and medications administered during treatment are also important in recognizing individuals who are experiencing problems related to addictions. The nurse should focus on whether or not the person is experiencing the desired or expected effects from anesthetics, sedative-hypnotics, and/or analgesics. If the person is not experiencing the desired or expected effects, then the possibility of tolerance and cross-tolerance effects should be acknowledged. This will be demonstrated by the person having a less than desired response to the drugs. On the other hand, if the individual exhibits a greater than expected response, the possibility of the person taking drugs surreptitiously must be considered.

Other data, which will help in identifying the client who is dependent on various drugs, are the results of physical examination, diagnostic studies, along with toxicological screening of blood and urine. These findings are especially helpful when caring for individuals who have taken illicit substances, since they tend to be less than candid regarding their use when questioned.

 BOX 9-2. **Subjective Opiate Withdrawal Scale (SOWS)**

Instructions: Answer the following statements as accurately as you can. Circle the answer that best fits the way you feel now.

1 = Not at all
2 = A little
3 = Moderately
4 = Quite a bit
5 = Extremely

	Not at all	A Little	Moderately	Quite a bit	Extremely
1. I feel anxious.	1	2	3	4	5
2. I feel like yawning.	1	2	3	4	5
3. I'm perspiring.	1	2	3	4	5
4. My eyes are tearing.	1	2	3	4	5
5. My nose is running.	1	2	3	4	5
6. I have gooseflesh.	1	2	3	4	5
7. I am shaking.	1	2	3	4	5
8. I have hot flashes.	1	2	3	4	5
9. I have cold flashes.	1	2	3	4	5
10. My bones and muscles ache.	1	2	3	4	5
11. I feel restless.	1	2	3	4	5
12. I feel nauseous.	1	2	3	4	5
13. I feel like vomiting.	1	2	3	4	5
14. My muscles twitch.	1	2	3	4	5
15. I have cramps in my stomach.	1	2	3	4	5
16. I feel like shooting up now.	1	2	3	4	5

Source: Rounsaville, B., Tims, F., Horton, A., & Sowder, B. (1993). *Diagnostic source book on drug abuse research and treatment.* NIH Publication No. 93-3508. Rockville, MD: National Institutes of Health.

BOX 9-3. Objective Opiate Withdrawal Scale (OOWS)

Instructions: Rate the patient on the basis of what you observe during a timed 10-minute period.

ITEM	Score 1 point for Each item if:	Points
1. Yawning	present	_____
2. Rhinorrhea	3 or more	_____
3. Piloerection (observe client's arm or chest)	present	_____
4. Perspiration	present	_____
5. Lacrimation	present	_____
6. Mydriasis	present	_____
7. Tremors (hands)	present	_____
8. Hot and cold flashes (shivering or huddling for warmth)	present	_____
9. Restlessness (frequent shifts of position)	present	_____
10. Vomiting	present	_____
11. Muscle twitches	present	_____
12. Abdominal cramps (holding stomach)	present	_____
13. Anxiety (observable manifestations: finger tapping, fidgeting, agitation)	present	_____
Total OOWS Score (Sum Items 1–13):		_____

Source: Rounsaville, B., Tims, F., Horton, A., & Sowder, B. (1993). *Diagnostic source book on drug abuse research and treatment.* NIH Publication No. 93-3508. Rockville, MD: National Institutes of Health.

DETOXIFICATION

The immediate goals of detoxification are (SAMHSA, 1995): 1) to provide a safe withdrawal from the drug or drugs that the person is addicted to; 2) to provide withdrawal that is humane and protects the client's dignity, which includes a caring health care team attitude, a supportive environment, sensitivity to cultural issues, confidentiality, and the selection of appropriate detoxification medication (if needed); and 3) to prepare the client for ongoing treatment of his or her alcohol, tobacco, and other drug addiction.

Principles of detoxification to remember are (SAMHSA, 1995): 1) detoxification in and of itself is rarely adequate treatment for addiction to alcohol, tobacco, and other drugs; 2) when using medication regimens or other detoxification procedures, only protocols of established safety and efficacy should be used in routine clinical practice; 3) client's access to medication should be controlled to the greatest extent possible during detoxification, in that persons who are addicted generally cannot be relied on to take their medication as prescribed, therefore health care providers should administer these medications as much as possible; 4) initiation of withdrawal should be individualized; 5) whenever possible, a long-acting medication should be substituted for short-acting drugs of addiction; 6) the intensity of drug withdrawal cannot always

BOX 9-4.   Stimulant Withdrawal Scale

TIME: _____	LEVEL OF CONSCIOUSNESS*: _____

VITAL SIGNS:

SIGNS AND SYMPTOMS**:

Temperature (°C):   _____
Respirations (per min):   _____
Pulse (per min):   _____
Blood pressure (mmHg):   _____
Pupil size (mm):   _____
Weight (kg):   _____

Hyperactivity: _____
Tremor: _____
Diaphoresis: _____
Irritability: _____
Anorexia: _____
Apathy: _____
Psychomotor retardation: _____
Depression: _____
Insomnia: _____
Anxiety: _____
Labile mood: _____
Headache: _____
Nausea: _____
Hyperphagia: _____

*(alert wakeful, lethargic, obtunded, stuporous, or comatose).
**Graded: 0 = absent; 1 = mild; 2 = severe.

Source: Rounsaville, B., Tims, F., Horton, A., & Sowder, B. (1993). *Diagnostic source book on drug abuse research and treatment.* NIH Publication No. 93-3508. Rockville, MD: National Institutes of Health.

be accurately predicted; and 7) every means possible should be used to ameliorate the client's signs and symptoms of withdrawal. Medication should not be the only treatment; psychological support is extremely important in reducing client's distress during detoxification. Physical activity should be promoted among persons that are medically safe.

Watson (1989) identifies the "goal of nursing care as being to help persons gain a higher degree of harmony within the mind, body, and soul, which generates self-knowledge, self-reverence, self-healing, and self-care processes while allowing increasing diversity" (p. 226). Application of this definition to caring for a client going through detoxification means that, while caring for the person who is withdrawing from the effects of alcohol and/or other drugs, the nurse aims to help the individual discover his or her own inner power and ability to pursue the process of recovering. This care involves helping the individual proceed through the process of detoxification by relying on a minimum of medications.

Inherent within this care are the goals of preventing death and the serious problems related to withdrawal. Planning care to accomplish these goals emphasizes that people are responsible for making changes in their own life (Wing, 1991; Bohn, 1993; Brogdan, 1993). The nurse can help facilitate individuals in changing by helping them find their own healing potential and inner strength (Watson, 1989).

Planning Care Based on Implementing the Carative Factors

When caring for individuals, the nurse uses the carative factors as a basis for planning the care. These 10 factors form the structure for the care given, and each caring occasion between the client and the nurse (Watson, 1989, pp. 227–228). Table 9-3 highlights how the nurse may implement the factors when helping people find their own healing potential and inner strength while withdrawing from the effects of addictive substances.

Two of the carative factors, "provision for a supportive, protective, or corrective, mental, physical, sociocultural, and spiritual environment," and "assistance with gratification of human needs" (Watson, 1989, p. 228) will be the priority ones to implement during the period of detoxification. These factors will guide the nurse in providing safe care that prevents the severe complications of the withdrawal phenomenon from occurring.

The vital signs are the most dependable indication of the client's progression through the withdrawal process, since they will increase *prior* to the person experiencing the more critical symptoms, such as hallucinations, delirium, or seizures. When the person's vital signs are remaining fairly stable, the nurse should encourage the toleration of the milder withdrawal symptoms, such as tremors and inner restlessness. Enduring the milder symptoms of withdrawal is a necessary part of the person's overcoming the denial of the effects of the addiction on the body. Teaching that these cues are part of the withdrawal process and due to the effects of the substance on the body is important to help the person connect the reality of the addiction with what is happening. Empathy regarding how difficult it may be to tolerate this process, is imperative. An example of empathy would be the following statement: "It's difficult to go through this process."

Unfortunately, clients who are withdrawing from the effects of an addiction are frequently heavily sedated during the period of detoxification. This form of treatment tends to enable the person's addiction by preventing the individual from experiencing the effects of the addiction. Thus, helping the person through addiction is a challenging process as the health care team aims for the person to experience a midpoint between the dangerous withdrawal symptoms and oversedation (Bay, Goldman, & Flavin, 1992, p. 63).

Dall (1993) has shown that implementing therapeutic touch with clients withdrawing from alcohol helps them sleep longer and more peacefully. Nursing research is needed to determine what types of interventions are most effective in helping people proceed through detoxification with minimal complications.

When the client's vital signs increase or when the person begins to demonstrate a rise in the symptoms related to withdrawal from a specific substance, the nurse will need to consult with the physician to determine how to proceed. Medical care for individuals during detoxification tends to include one or more of the following approaches: slow decrease of the amount of the substance of choice being used; or replacing the substance of choice with a drug in the same classification (Sees, 1991, p. 373).

Clinical Detoxification Protocols

ALCOHOL

Benzodiazepines, such as Librium, Klonopin, Tranxene, and Valium, are currently the most commonly used drugs and are considered superior to all other agents in ameliorating signs and symptoms of alcohol withdrawal (Institute of Medicine, 1990). They effectively decrease the frequency of withdrawal seizures and delirium tremens (characteristic physiologic changes that set this syndrome apart from the other alcohol withdrawal states, and from other forms of delirium, as displayed in Figure 9-2). Librium is the most commonly administered

TABLE 9-3 Implementing the Carative Factors When Detoxifying Addicted Clients

Carative Factors	Application During Detoxification
Formation of a humanistic-altruistic system of values	Nurses must analyze their own feelings and thoughts regarding people who are withdrawing from the effects of alcohol and/or various substances. It is especially important to address their beliefs regarding detoxification: should individuals be heavily sedated throughout this process so they do not create problems and are easy to handle on the unit?
Nurturing of faith and hope	Show the person that the nurse has faith and hope that the person can abstain from the substance for the next hour, the next day. Emphasize that 1 hour of abstinence offers hope for the next hour
Cultivation of sensitivity sensitivity to one's self and others	Nurses capitalize on the sensitivity of their own feelings regarding addictions to focus on helping their clients increase their awareness to the effects of the addiction on their health and life
Development of a helping, trusting, human caring relationship	From the onset of each relationship, nurses show a high level of concern and care for the client as a unique human being. Using the times when monitoring vital signs to focus on the person's perspective of what is happening, which is important in building trust
Promotion and acceptance of the expression of positive and negative feelings	Acknowledging feelings that have been previously hidden by the effects of the addictive substance will arise during detoxification and encourage the person to express them when he or she experiences them
Promotion of transpersonal teaching–learning	Teach the person to recognize symptoms and when they should occur during detoxification
Use of creative problem-solving processes	Having knowledge of what to anticipate during detoxification will provide the opportunity to plan ahead on how the person will cope with the symptoms, including cravings
Provision for a supportive, protective, or corrective mental, physical, sociocultural, and spiritual environment	Careful monitoring of withdrawal symptoms and vital signs every 2 hours will provide a supportive approach as the early cues of withdrawal and protect the person from the severe symptoms by intervening to prevent them from developing
Assistance with gratification of human needs	Focus attention on the individual's problems related to eating, sleeping, and taking care of activities of daily living during the withdrawal period
Allowance for existential–phenomenological–spiritual forces	Help people understand and endure the milder symptoms of withdrawal to understand the effects of addiction on their health; Encourage people to pursue a process of recovering through a 12-step program that emphasizes relying on a power greater than oneself

Adapted from Watson, J. (1989). Watson's philosophy and theory of human caring in nursing. In J. Riehl-Sisca (Ed.), *Conceptual models for nursing practice* (pp. 219–236). Norwalk, CT: Appleton & Lange.

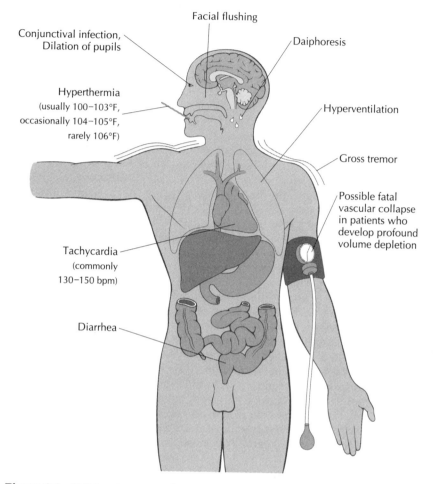

Facial flushing

Conjunctival infection, Dilation of pupils

Daiphoresis

Hyperthermia
(usually 100–103°F, occasionally 104–105°F, rarely 106°F)

Hyperventilation

Gross tremor

Possible fatal vascular collapse in patients who develop profound volume depletion

Tachycardia
(commonly 130–150 bpm)

Diarrhea

Figure 9-2 Delirium tremens—clinical picture. (Source: Compton, M. [1992]. Nursing care in withdrawal. In N. A. Nagle [Ed.], *Substance abuse education in nursing*, Vol. II. [pp. 409–462.] New York: National League for Nursing Press.)

medication for alcohol withdrawal in the United States (Saitz, Mayo-Smith, Roberts, Redmond, Benard, & Calkins, 1994). Serax or Ativan are sometimes used with persons who have severe liver disease because neither drug is metabolized by the liver.

Varying but acceptable medication regimens for treatment of alcohol withdrawal include (SAMHSA, 1995):

- *Gradual, Tapering Doses:* Oral benzodiazepines are administered on a predetermined dosing schedule for several days and gradually discontinued. This regimen is the one most commonly used (Saitz et al., 1994). Dosing protocols vary widely among treatment facilities. As an example, clients may be given 50 mg of Librium (or 10 mg of Valium) every 6 hours the first day and 25 mg (or 5 mg of Valium) every 6 hours the second and third days. Doses of withdrawal medication are usually omitted if the client is sleeping soundly or showing signs of oversedation.

- *Symptom-triggered Therapy:* Clients are carefully observed for signs and symptoms of alcohol withdrawal and only given a dose of benzodiazepine when signs and symptoms of alcohol withdrawal appear (Wartenberg, Nirenberg, Liepman, Silvia, Begin, & Monti, 1990; Saitz et al., 1994).
- *Loading Dose:* Clients are administered a slowly metabolized benzodiazepine for only the first day of treatment (Sellers, Naranjo, Harrison, Devenyi, Roach, & Sykora, 1983; Devenyi & Harrison, 1985). Clients in moderate-to-severe withdrawal are administered 20 mg of Valium (or 100 mg of Librium) every 1 to 2 hours until they show significant clinical improvement (such as a CIWA-Ar score of 10 or less) or become sedated.

When comparing regimens, a controlled study comparing fixed dose and symptom-triggered therapy found that clients treated with symptom-triggered therapy completed their treatment courses sooner and required less medication than clients treated using the standard-fixed schedule approach. Specifically, they received less Librium (100 mg versus 425 mg) and received treatment for a shorter period of time (9 hours versus 68 hours). This indicates that symptom-triggered therapy is an approach that could individualize and improve the management of alcohol withdrawal (Saitz et al., 1994, as cited in SAMHSA, 1995).

Tegretol, a medication used for treatment of seizures, has been reported effective in treatment of alcohol withdrawal. A controlled study found Tegretol (800 mg/day) and Serax (120 mg/day) used in the treatment of alcohol withdrawal resulted in equivalent scores on the CIWA scale (SAMHSA, 1995). It has also been suggested that Tegretol may prove more useful than benzodiazepines in the outpatient management of alcohol withdrawal states, because it is not a drug of abuse; however, this has not been tested in rigorous controlled clinical trials (Malcolm, Ballenger, Sturgis, & Anton, 1989).

Persons who develop delirium tremens with auditory, visual, or tactile hallucinations may need antipsychotic medications to ameliorate their hallucinations and decrease agitation. Haldol (0.5 to 2.0 mg every 4 hours by mouth or intramuscularly) generally provides control of symptoms. Phenothiazines, such as Thorazine, should not be used because of the increased risk of seizures. The client should also continue to receive benzodiazepines, because these drugs afford the best protection against alcohol withdrawal seizures (SAMHSA, 1995).

Phenobarbital can be used for alcohol detoxification when the client is physically dependent on both sedative-hypnotics and alcohol (SAMHSA, 1995). However, the therapeutic or prophylactic value of a routine prescription of Dilantin to prevent alcohol withdrawal seizures is not established (American Society of Addiction Medicine Committee on Practice Guidelines, 1994). Expert opinion is mixed as to whether Dilantin (or other anticonvulsants) should be used in addition to adequate sedative-hypnotic medication in clients with an increased risk of alcohol withdrawal seizures because of previous withdrawal seizures, head injury, meningitis, or other conditions. Intravenous Dilantin is not beneficial in clients with isolated acute alcohol withdrawal seizures, but may be indicated for clients who have multiple alcohol withdrawal seizures. In addition, metabolism of Dilantin is variable among clients. It should be administered orally or intravenously, as it is poorly absorbed after intramuscular administration (SAMHSA, 1995).

Also, the absorption of Valium or Librium after intramuscular administration is unpredictable. Intramuscular absorption of Ativan is more reliable than that of Valium or Librium. Ativan may be administered in doses of 2 mg every hour until signs and symptoms subside (SAMHSA, 1995).

The following medical complications could arise during alcohol withdrawal; if so, these recommendations should be kept in mind (SAMHSA, 1995).

Medical Complications of Alcohol Withdrawal:
- Fluid and electrolyte imbalances—Maintaining fluid and electrolyte balance is key during detoxification. Most clients can be managed with oral fluids. Those who are vomiting or having severe diarrhea should first be treated with sips of electrolyte-containing fluids. The amount can be increased to client tolerance. Intravenous fluids containing electrolytes—dextrose and thiamine (100 mg/bottle) should be administered to those who become dehydrated.

Clients withdrawing from alcohol are not always dehydrated, in fact, many are overhydrated and administration of parental fluid therapy can be harmful in these cases. Persons being detoxified from alcohol generally tolerate a mild degree of dehydration more than overhydration.

- *Hypoglycemia*—Hypoglycemia is a significant danger during detoxification. Oral fluids should contain carbohydrates; orange juice may be one choice. Parenteral fluids should contain 5% dextrose.
- *Fever*—Any elevation of temperature in a person in withdrawal should be vigorously investigated. If the elevated temperature is a result of drug withdrawal, there is a need for additional medication and reevaluation of the detoxification schedule. If a person has no other signs or symptoms of withdrawal, the elevated temperature is probably caused by an infection, and early, aggressive antibiotic treatment may be necessary.
- *Drug Interactions*—Certain drugs of abuse and certain medications used in detoxification may interact. It is important to be aware of other medications the client is taking and to consider potential drug interactions. For example, drugs that may interact include hypertensive medication and Clonidine; Dilantin and methadone; and Rifampin and methadone.

  Utilizing nutritional supplements has also been effective in helping people proceed safely through detoxification. One approach involves giving the person a high glucose supplement when the vital signs begin to rise. This supplement might be 6 to 8 ounces of Kool-Aid with 1 to 2 tablespoons of corn syrup (Karo syrup), or 4 to 6 ounces of apple juice with 1 to 2 tablespoons of sugar added. Thirty minutes after this supplement is ingested, the person's pulse should be checked again. If the pulse rate has dropped, then the nurse should encourage the person to continue tolerating the milder cues of withdrawal. If the pulse has continued to rise, then the nurse should administer a dose of a medication ordered as needed (PRN) by the physician.

OPIOIDS

Although all opioids have similar withdrawal signs and symptoms, the time and onset and duration of the abstinence syndrome vary. The severity of the withdrawal syndrome depends on many factors including the drug used, total daily dose, interval between doses, duration of use, and health and personality of the addict (SAMHSA, 1995).

Clonidine (Catapres), a medication marketed for hypertension, has been used for treatment of the symptoms of opiate withdrawal since 1978 (Gold, Redmond, & Kleber, 1978). Since then, addiction specialists have commonly used oral clonidine for this purpose. Although clonidine has not been approved by the Food and Drug Administration for treatment of opiate withdrawal, its use has become standard clinical practice (SAMHSA, 1995).

Advantages of clonidine over methadone for narcotic withdrawal include: 1) it is not a scheduled medication; 2) the use of opiates can be discontinued immediately in preparation for naltrexone induction or admission to a drug-free treatment program; and 3) clonidine does not produce opiate euphoria, therefore the client's "drug-seeking behavior" is reduced. Although clonidine alleviates some symptoms of opiate withdrawal, it is not effective for muscle aches, insomnia, or drug craving (SAMHSA, 1995).

An appropriate protocol for clonidine is 0.1 mg orally as a test dose (0.2 mg for persons weighing more than 200 lbs). If the client's symptoms are acute, the sublingual route of administration may be used. Blood pressure should be checked after 45 minutes. If diastolic blood pressure is normal and the client has no signs of orthostatic hypotension (a drop in systolic blood pressure of 10 mm Hg upon standing), then clonidine should be continued, 0.1 to 0.2 mg orally every 4 to 6 hours (SAMHSA, 1995).

The clonidine transdermal patch was approved for treatment of hypertension in the United States in 1986. However, safety of the patch for treatment of opiate withdrawal has not been sufficiently studied in controlled clinical trials; a problem being that if persons receive too much clonidine from the patch and become hypotensive, the effects are not rapidly reversed even if the patch is removed. The clonidine patch is 0.2 mm^2 and is applied in the same manner as a self-adhesive bandage. It is available in three sizes: 3.5, 7.0, and 10.5 cm. In a 24-hour period, these patches deliver an amount of clonidine equivalent to twice-daily dosing with the oral clonidine. Once the patch is placed on the epidermal surface, clonidine enters the circulatory system through the skin. A rate-limiting membrane within the patch governs the maximum amount absorbed. The patch supplies clonidine for up to 7 days, but in the treatment of opiate withdrawal, one application of the patch is sufficient (SAMHSA, 1995).

Advantages to using the clonidine patch for opiate withdrawal might include: 1) decrease in drug-seeking behavior; 2) clients receive continuous dosing; and 3) clients do not awake in the morning in the midst of withdrawal, because the patch continues to deliver during the night. However, more research is needed to document the clonidine patch's impact on opiate withdrawal.

Methadone is a method widely used for opiate withdrawal as well. However, it can only be dispensed under special licensure, with the exception of opiate addicts who are inpatients receiving care for a medical illness and needing to have withdrawal prevented because of potential complication to the medical illness.

It is important to note that federal regulations allow physicians to administer (but not prescribe) narcotic drugs for the purpose of relieving acute withdrawal symptoms when necessary, while arranging to refer the client to treatment. Not more than one day's medication may be administered to the person or for the person's use at one time. This emergency treatment may be carried out for not more than 3 days, and may not be renewed or extended (C.F.R. Part 1306.07). Hence, in states that allow the prescription of narcotics, a physician may administer methadone for 3 days without a special license under the Drug Enforcement Agency (DEA), if the client is undergoing acute withdrawal symptoms and cannot be referred for treatment immediately (SAMHSA, 1995).

Using methadone for detoxification of opiate-addicted persons takes place as inpatients as well as outpatients. According to SAMHSA (1995) withdrawal protocols using methadone vary—depending on the setting—but may be as follows:

- *Inpatient Health Care Facility Licensed for Methadone Detoxification:* A starting dose of 30 to 40 mg per day of methadone given orally is adequate to prevent severe withdrawal. The methadone should be administered four times daily, beginning with 10-mg doses. The client should be observed 2 hours after each dose, and if found to be sleepy, decrease the next dose to 5 mg. If objective signs of withdrawal are noted, the next dose is increased to 15 mg. After the first 24 hours, the methadone is withdrawn by 5 mg per day, resulting in most clients being withdrawn over a period of 8 days.
- *Outpatient Methadone Detoxification:* In an outpatient program the usual practice is to administer the dose no more than twice daily. Therefore, 20 mg of methadone given orally two times a day is a good starting point. To prevent an unacceptable level of withdrawal symptoms, some clients need up to 60 mg of methadone per day in divided doses. After the second day, the methadone is tapered by 2.5 mg per day.

- *Short-term Detoxification:* This can take place both as inpatient and outpatient, and is for a period of 30 days as allowed by federal regulations. This does not allow for take-home methadone, and a health care provider must monitor the client's progress toward the goal of detoxification and possible referral for treatment. A client must wait at least 7 days between concluding one short-term detoxification and beginning another. In addition, it must be documented by the physician that the client continues his or her physiological dependence to opiates.
- *Long-term Detoxification:* This can also happen as inpatient or outpatient, and extends for more than 30 days but not in excess of 180 days. For long-term detoxification, methadone must be administered by the program physician or an authorized health care provider who is supervised and under the order of the physician. It must be given on a regimen designed to become drug-free. Rules governing the allowance of long-term detoxification include:
  1. The client must be under observation while taking the methadone at least 6 days/week
  2. The program physician/authorized health care provider must document that short-term detoxification is not sufficiently long enough to provide the client with additional services necessary for rehabilitation
  3. An initial drug screen is required for each client; and at least one additional random urine screen obtained monthly
  4. An initial treatment plan and monthly treatment plan evaluation is required
  5. A person must wait at least 7 days between concluding one long-term detoxification attempt and starting another

To date, a 180-day detoxification program is still under investigation due to lack of controlled studies about its effectiveness, as well as the dosage that might be most effective with this method.

If clients on a methadone maintenance program wish to discontinue it, rapid discontinuance could lead to severe opiate withdrawal. Hence, clients should be tapered until they are receiving 30 to 40 mg a day. At this point, clonidine and other symptomatic medications may be used as previously described (SAMHSA, 1995). A number of clients addicted to opiates prefer methadone for withdrawal because of its mood-altering effects.

BENZODIAZEPINES AND OTHER SEDATIVE-HYPNOTICS

Use of benzodiazepines or sedative-hypnotics at above the therapeutic range for a month or more produces physical dependence. Without appropriate medical treatment, withdrawal from benzodiazepines or other sedative-hypnotics can be severe and life threatening.

There are three general medication strategies for withdrawing persons from sedative-hypnotics, including benzodiazepines: 1) use of decreasing doses of the particular addicted drug; 2) substitute phenobarbital or another long-acting barbiturate for the addicting drug and gradually withdraw the substitute medication; and 3) substitute a long-acting benzodiazepine, such as Librium, and taper it over 1 to 2 weeks. The method chosen depends on the particular benzodiazepine, the use of other addicting drugs, and the setting in which detoxification takes place (SAMHSA, 1995).

The first strategy—gradual reduction of the addicting drug—is used for managing clients who take long-acting medications, such as Librium or Valium, who are believed to be giving an accurate account of their use of medication, and who are not currently abusing alcohol or other drugs. The second strategy—phenobarbital substitution—is viewed by some as the most generally applicable method, because it is a long-acting medication in which there is little change in blood levels between doses, which allows the safe use of a progressively smaller daily dose, and is safer than the short-acting barbiturates (SAMHSA, 1995).

This second strategy is thought to be the best choice for persons who are polydrug addicted, or addicted to benzodiazepines. The first step in this protocol is to take the client's average daily sedative-hypnotic dose and convert it to phenobarbital equivalents; then this daily dose is divided into three doses. If the client is using a large amount of other CNS depressants (including alcohol), the amounts of all the drugs are then converted to phenobarbital equivalents and added (SAMHSA, 1995).

If the client is in acute withdrawal, and has had or is in danger of having withdrawal seizures, the initial dose of phenobarbital is given by intramuscular injection. Nystagmus or others signs related to intoxication may develop 1 to 2 hours after the intramuscular dose; however, the person is not in immediate danger from barbiturate withdrawal. Thus, clients are maintained on the initial dosing schedule of phenobarbital for 2 days, and if the client has no signs of withdrawal or phenobarbital toxicity (slurred speech, nystagmus, unsteady gait), phenobarbital withdrawal is begun (SAMHSA, 1995).

Unless the client exhibits signs and symptoms of phenobarbital toxicity or sedative-hypnotic withdrawal, phenobarbital is decreased by 30 mg per day. If signs of phenobarbital toxicity develops during withdrawal, the daily phenobarbital dose is decreased by 50%; and the 30-mg per day dose decrease is continued from the reduced dose. If the client shows objective signs of sedative-hypnotic withdrawal, the daily dose is increased by 50% and the client is restabilized before continuing the withdrawal (SAMHSA, 1995).

STIMULANTS

There is no specific detoxification protocol for stimulant withdrawal. Many health care practitioners medicate the symptoms of discomfort from the withdrawal with something for the inability to sleep, an antidepressant for the "crash," and/or a mild sedative for aggression.

POLYDRUG ADDICTION

Most persons addicted to alcohol, tobacco, or other drugs are addicted to more than one drug. As discussed earlier, this presents a complex situation for the nurse to handle. The combinations of drugs commonly used by addicted polydrug users and the recommended approach for handling detoxification are as follows (SAMHSA, 1995):

Polydrug Addiction	Recommended Detoxification Program
Alcohol and stimulant	Treat alcohol withdrawal
Alcohol and benzodiazepine	Detoxify with phenobarbital
Cocaine and benzodiazepine	Treat benzodiazepine withdrawal
Cocaine and opiate	Treat opiate withdrawal
Cocaine and amphetamine	No known detoxification protocol
Opiate and barbiturate	Gradually detoxify barbiturate first while giving methadone to prevent opiate withdrawal; when barbiturate free, withdraw methadone at a level of 5 mg/day
Opiate and benzodiazepine	Begin with partial reduction of benzodiazepine; while the person is still receiving a partial dosage of the sedative, the opiate is withdrawn; and finally, the benzodiazepine is totally withdrawn

Detoxification Settings

The choice of treating individuals withdrawing from the effects of alcohol and/or other drugs on an inpatient or outpatient basis depends on multiple factors, including the presence of other acute medical or psychiatric problems, types of available support, frequent relapses or inability to complete a previous treatment program, or polydrug abuse (Bay et al., 1992, p. 63). Currently detoxification can take place from a "medical" or "social" perspective.

MEDICAL DETOXIFICATION

Medical models of detoxification are usually under the direction of a physician; however, depending on a state's prescriptive authority, a nurse practitioner or clinical nurse specialist can direct medical detoxification. It can take place in inpatient, outpatient, community, or home-based locations. The client is usually under a medication protocol for withdrawal from an addicting drug.

SOCIAL DETOXIFICATION

Social models of detoxification focus on providing psychosocial services. Social workers and counselors may provide individual and family counseling while the client withdraws from an addicting drug without the benefit of a medication protocol, because in social detoxification the emphasis is on nonpharmacological management of withdrawal. For the most part, clients who end up needing medical care are referred to the nearest hospital emergency room for their crisis; although some social detoxification programs keep a physician or nurse practitioner on call to prescribe detoxification medications if necessary.

In some treatment programs, rather than using medical detoxification with appropriate nursing personnel, counselors assist clients in taking detoxification medications. The clients' medication supply must be in a container with their name and instructions for taking it on a label. Counselors can watch clients take the medication and keep a log. In addition, they need to monitor the clients' symptoms and call the physician or nurse practitioner if these persons become increasingly ill (SAMHSA, 1995).

Although this is a procedure that a number of facilities are attempting to use across the country—to avoid paying nurses—it results in poor detoxification as well as poor medical care. The problem with this method is that in some cases clients are just bringing in bags of medication and saying that they need them for detoxification, and no one checks to see if they do, or if the medications are what they say they are. In addition, counselors are not educated as to what withdrawal entails, and whether or not symptoms seen are related to withdrawal or other medical problems. The authors must support fully what SAMHSA (1995) posits: that it is of utmost importance that clients are properly evaluated medically when entering a social detoxification program. Currently, there is a move toward detoxifying clients in an outpatient setting.

OUTPATIENT DETOXIFICATION

Outpatient detoxification was initiated primarily for economic reasons; however, it is an approach that is being utilized by many and promoted among managed care companies. There has been some research pointing to some aspects as being effective.

Outpatient detoxification has three major advantages: 1) less expense; 2) less disruption of the client's life; and 3) the client remains in the same setting where he or she will function drug-free (SAMHSA, 1995). Outpatient detoxification can be offered in psychiatric clinics, community mental health centers, alcohol and other drug outpatient programs, alcohol and other drug clinics, private offices, and recent research has shown its effectiveness in the home setting.

The National Nurses Society on Addictions (1995) has published guidelines for nurses regarding outpatient detoxification and these guidelines include the following:

- Protocols for managing outpatient detoxification, specific for each substance of abuse, must be developed and followed. These are to include criteria for contacting the primary provider directing detoxification and provisions for client care.
- Protocols for management of emergencies, such as seizures, withdrawal delirium, and other psychiatric crises, must be developed.
- Guidelines and procedures for admission to inpatient detoxification, medical, or psychiatric units must be established and followed when necessary.
- Criteria for selecting clients for outpatient detoxification must include a competent support person who is available to stay with the client to assist in monitoring withdrawal, administer necessary medications, and communicate with the professional staff as needed.
- Nursing responsibilities/roles during outpatient detoxification include:
  — Data collection to determine appropriate selection of clients for treatment (includes laboratory tests, breathalyser, or other tests)
  — Assessment of the client including use of assessment instruments
  — Development of diagnoses and creation of treatment plans
  — Collaboration with the physician/health care provider to select protocols for medication management
  — Monitoring of client's symptoms through daily appointments, telephone communication, or when necessary, home visits
  — Utilization of brief intervention strategies
  — Client and family education regarding withdrawal signs and symptoms, expected response, and side effects of medication therapy as well as adverse responses that might occur, and the recovery process
  — Preparation of client and family for appropriate treatment program
  — Make referrals to more intensive education, therapy and self-help groups

Box 9-5 highlights the day-by-day progression of an outpatient detoxification program. Clients attend the program daily so that their withdrawal process can be monitored, and they can be given sufficient amounts of medication for the day. They need much support, encouragement, and education to maintain recovering throughout this period. Attending a minimum of one to two meetings of a 12-step program every day should also be required. It is of utmost importance that an outpatient detoxification program have established procedures for addressing client attrition.

Currently, nurses are in the position of being able to develop, implement, and direct detoxification care for persons addicted to alcohol, tobacco, and other drugs, whether they are inpatient or outpatient, community or home-based. Nurses can design the programs using the above discussed protocols, and nurse practitioners and clinical nurses specialists can prescribe appropriate detoxification medications. However, the job does not end there. Having a person engaged in a detoxification program of any type provides the nurse with an addicted person who is a "captive audience" so to speak. Hence, motivation for further treatment of some kind (inpatient, outpatient—traditional or intensive—, attendance at self-help meetings) should take place.

This program of motivation should not be intense or aggressively confrontational. Instead, it should include group sessions for peer support and feedback, and gentle con-

BOX 9-5. Schedule of Program for Outpatient Detoxification

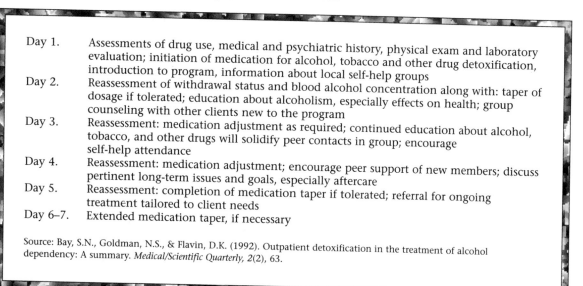

Day 1.   Assessments of drug use, medical and psychiatric history, physical exam and laboratory evaluation; initiation of medication for alcohol, tobacco and other drug detoxification, introduction to program, information about local self-help groups

Day 2.   Reassessment of withdrawal status and blood alcohol concentration along with: taper of dosage if tolerated; education about alcoholism, especially effects on health; group counseling with other clients new to the program

Day 3.   Reassessment: medication adjustment as required; continued education about alcohol, tobacco, and other drugs will solidify peer contacts in group; encourage self-help attendance

Day 4.   Reassessment: medication adjustment; encourage peer support of new members; discuss pertinent long-term issues and goals, especially aftercare

Day 5.   Reassessment: completion of medication taper if tolerated; referral for ongoing treatment tailored to client needs

Day 6–7.   Extended medication taper, if necessary

Source: Bay, S.N., Goldman, N.S., & Flavin, D.K. (1992). Outpatient detoxification in the treatment of alcohol dependency: A summary. *Medical/Scientific Quarterly, 2*(2), 63.

frontation through use of laboratory test results, videos, and discussion. This is just to keep clients aware of the consequences they are experiencing due to the alcohol, tobacco, or other drug addiction. This is not to get them to accept or admit vociferously to their addiction, or to have them be rehabed in 7 to 10 days. It is to have them begin the process of the stages of change so that they may make a decision for action.

Special Populations

THE INCARCERATED

Nurses need to be aware of detoxification issues specific to certain populations. For the most part, the large numbers of persons incarcerated are there because of drug addiction problems. However, when they are incarcerated they are in danger of severe withdrawal because often they are not observed, monitored, or managed with a detoxification protocol. Much of the time, they experience withdrawal without the aid of medications and the drugs most commonly being withdrawn are heroin and cocaine. It is important that prison, jail, and correctional facility nurses be trained and educated in alcohol, tobacco, and other drug addiction and appropriate withdrawal protocols.

WOMEN

Women need to be watched closely in detoxification because they do not metabolize alcohol the same way as men; their blood alcohol concentrations is higher while having drank the same amount of alcohol as a man. Most of the medication protocols have been validated on male addicts, whereas women may not need as much or they may need more medications. This is an area where nurses can really do research to determine the effectiveness of medication protocols for detoxification on women.

In addition, drugs such as barbiturates, benzodiazepines, and marijuana, all have an affinity for fat tissue, and is stored there for a long time. Because women have more fat tissue, their tolerance, tissue dependence, and withdrawal can appear different from men. Again, they may need to be withdrawn over a longer period of time, and may still feel the effects of the addicting drug for a longer time than men. In addition, according to Nixon (1994) women's brains and cognition are affected differently than men by alcohol and other drugs, impacting their ability to grasp concepts and perform certain mental and intellectual tasks. It is very important to *individualize detoxification*. If a client's response to a detoxification protocol does not fit the mold, consider the above mentioned specifics.

For women who are pregnant or nursing, the detoxification regimens need to be modified only if there is evidence that the detoxification medication crosses the placenta and therefore, can harm the baby, and enters the breast milk in amounts that could be harmful to the baby. It has been proven that benzodiazepines, antidepressants, and antipsychotics do cause harm to the fetus and breast-fed babies.

Opiate withdrawal can result in fetal distress resulting in miscarriage or premature labor. Hence, good prenatal care and an opiate substitute detoxification protocol contributes to a nonproblem delivery. According to Zweben and Payte (1990) these newborns have a lower birth weight and smaller head circumference than drug-free babies, but by age 6 months the developmental differences have disappeared.

ADOLESCENTS

For most adolescents, physical dependence and withdrawal is not as severe as for adults; thus, detoxification takes place more rapidly. However, there are some adolescents who have been alcoholic since 9 or 10 years of age, and will show the same withdrawal symptoms as adults do. Also, even though they are younger, for those adolescents addicted to benzodiazepines, withdrawal is just as dangerous as it is for the adult, depending on the amount, frequency, and duration of use (SAMHSA, 1995).

ELDERLY

The elderly truly present a very sensitive perspective to detoxification protocols. Alcohol and other drug-related disorders tend to be more severe than those in younger persons, and there is increased likelihood that other medical illnesses are present. In addition, elderly persons have a slowed metabolism of drugs and medications, and also take a number of different prescription and over-the-counter drugs, increasing their chances of drug interaction problems. Although the clinical detoxification protocols discussed above can be used with the elderly, the dosage will need to be reduced and monitoring for withdrawal symptoms for a longer time will need to take place. Also, increased severity of withdrawal symptoms will need to be addressed when providing symptomatic relief. Mudd, Boyd, Brower, Young, and Blow (1994) conducted research on detoxification among the elderly and found that as the age of the clients increased, their symptoms of withdrawal continued for a longer period of time.

HIV/AIDS

Increasingly, nurses will need to be instituting detoxification regimens on persons who are HIV/AIDS infected. One might wonder if the same protocols would be utilized or maybe something different. Although being infected with the HIV/AIDS virus does not change the indications for medication to treat the withdrawal a person is going through, nurses need to be aware if the client is receiving medication for the disease that could cause an interaction with the detoxification medications and render them less effective.

For those clients who have a psychiatric diagnosis as well as an addiction, and are experiencing withdrawal, it is important that they continue taking their psychiatric medication as prescribed. During detoxification some clients decompensate into psychosis, depression, or severe anxiety, and in such cases, careful evaluation of the withdrawal medication regimen is important. If the decompensation is secondary to inadequate dosing with the withdrawal medication, the appropriate response is to increase that medication. However, if it appears that the withdrawal medication is adequate, then other medications may be needed, after determining whether or not the response seen is related to side effects or drug interaction (SAMHSA, 1995).

A client who is psychotic may need neuroleptics. Medications that have a minimal effect on the seizure threshold are recommended, particularly if the client is being withdrawn from alcohol or sedative-hypnotic medication. Small, frequent doses of Haldol—1 mg every 2 hours—may be used until the psychosis responds. After detoxification is complete, the client's need for medication should be reassessed using a trial period with no medications (SAMHSA, 1995).

ETHNICITY

Although the above clinical detoxification protocols may be used effectively with persons from all races, cultures, and ethnicities, nurses need to be culturally sensitive and competent in understanding how alcohol, tobacco, and other drug addictions are viewed, and how best to approach for an effective detoxification. Behaviors, looks, language, and attitudes that are discriminatory or condescending will result in ineffective detoxification regimens.

It is important to remember that people of all ethnic groups vary by personality, geographic origin, socioeconomic class, religious upbringing, and so on. In addition, groups "lumped" together such as the Asian American/Pacific Islanders are in actuality very diverse. Nurses should be aware that cultural attitudes toward communication styles vary with regard to physical distance, physical contact, eye contact, and terminology of drugs used on the street.

In addition, responses toward authority may differ among cultures, and even among generations. This all impacts on whether or not clients are engaged in treatment and see themselves treated with humane respect and dignity. And last but not least, written materials should be provided to clients and their families that have been assessed for readability and cultural appropriateness.

EVALUATING THE EFFECTIVENESS OF DETOXIFICATION

Determining the effectiveness of a detoxification program should be based on established outcome indicators. The process for evaluating a program's effectiveness is discussed in detail in Chapter 11, therefore, only possible outcome indicators for detoxification interventions/programs will be presented.

If one uses the goals of detoxification (presented in the previous section) as a guideline, then outcome indicators for evaluating effectiveness of the interventions/program can flow from there. According to SAMHSA (1995):

Indicators for detoxification goal 1 (Safely manage withdrawal) include:

- Rate of completed detoxifications
- Incidence of adverse reactions because of a mistaken diagnosis, assessment, or detoxification protocol used
- Deviations from average length of stay for the program under study

- Rates and reasons for attrition from programs
- Numbers of incident reports

Indicators for detoxification goal 2 (Engage the client in the process of change for recovery) includes:

- Rate of client participation in various elements of detoxification interventions/program
- Percentage of clients for whom a discharge and continuing care plan was developed

Indicators for detoxification goal 3 (Treat clients with respect and dignity) includes:

- Number of incidents involving client rights
- Number of times client records were released without a properly signed consent or court order
- Number of times clients had complaints about staff attitudes or behavior toward them
- Number of times clients were deprived of rights that are generally given to participants in the detoxification intervention/program

Although this list is not exhaustive, it provides some suggestions for indicators to be evaluated in determining how effective detoxification interventions have been.

Thorough and effective detoxification is a result of inter- and intradisciplinary collaboration (discussed more in-depth in Chapter 18). A method in which this can take place is through the use of "critical/clinical pathways." Allen (1996) has developed the critical/clinical pathway for alcohol detoxification shown in Box 9-6 (based on information in the Section III introduction and this chapter) using the "CareMap" system outlined and trademarked by the Center for Case Management (1992), as an example.

"The CareMap system consists of: 1) the critical pathway with the x-axis representing the time line and the y-axis representing the multidisciplinary interventions incorporated into standard categories; 2) a client problem list; 3) intermediate goals that progress to clinical outcomes for each problem identified; and 4) a variance record designed to capture chronological deviations from the norm" (Center for Case Management, 1992; Hill, 1995, p. 175). Members of the health care team come together and decide who will be responsible for what interventions.

CONCLUSION

For all persons addicted to alcohol, tobacco, and other drugs, the road through the stages of change and up to recovery cannot begin unless the body has returned to some degree of tissue normalization. This process entails detoxifying clients as they withdraw in a safe manner with their dignity and respect intact and a desire for continued help verbalized.

Nurses in all settings, at all levels of practice are encountering clients addicted to one drug or another, most of the times more than one drug. With an appropriate understanding of the concepts related to detoxification such as tolerance, dependence, and withdrawal, as well as the most common clinical protocols used in detoxification, these nurses are poised to provide a service in demand.

Detoxification involves more than just the clinical protocols for safe withdrawal, it involves the caring role that nurses are known for. Watson's (1989) carative factors provide a theoretical framework that can be used by nurses in all settings as they administer to the needs of the detoxifying client.

(text continues on page 174)

BOX 9-6. CAREMAP®

CaseType: Detoxification
Expected L.O.S.: 3–10 days

DSM-IV Diagnosis: Alcohol Withdrawal (291.8)
Client Problem(s): 1) History of and potential for life-threatening withdrawal
2) Not involved in the process of recovery

HEALTH CARE TEAM: MD, RN, Social Worker, Addictions Expert, Case Manager (Clinical Nurse Specialist/Psychiatrist/Psychologist)

<u>Phase 1—Day(s) 1–3</u>

	CRITICAL/CLINICAL PATHWAY	VARIANCE AND ACTIONS
Assessment	❏ Complete H&P ❏ Nursing ❏ Mental status exam ❏ CIWA-Ar ❏ Vital signs and weight ❏ Review old records ❏ Psychosocial ❏ Dose, frequency, duration of use ❏ Level of detoxification based on patient placement criteria (PPC)	
Laboratory and Tests	❏ Order: ❏ SMA-20 ❏ UA ❏ BAL ❏ Toxicology ❏ RPR ❏ CBC ❏ Breathalyzer ❏ Chest X-ray ❏ Electrocardiogram ❏ Medication levels ❏ Other	
Therapeutic Interventions/ Treatment	❏ Team initiates interdisciplinary treatment plan ❏ Implement carative factors 6–9 ❏ Brief one-to-one as tolerated ❏ Determine level of treatment based on PPC	
Medication Interventions	❏ Order detoxification protocol ❏ Initiate detoxification protocol ❏ Continue standing medications used by client for medical conditions ❏ Order medication for newly diagnosed medical conditions ❏ Administer all medications ❏ Monitor for side effects or adverse effects ❏ Implement PRN medications	
Behavioral Interventions	❏ Evaluate need for observation for safety ❏ Evaluate need to restrain certain behaviors ❏ Identify specific limits to be set ❏ Provide daily schedule of expected activities	
Educational Interventions	❏ Orient to program and place of care ❏ Signs and symptoms of expected withdrawal ❏ Process of withdrawal	
Discharge Planning	❏ Identify degree of social supports for recovery: employment, housing, self-help groups, relationships ❏ Identify place for referral for next level of treatment	
Consults	❏ Psychiatric ❏ Psychological	
Legal Status	❏ Document legal status ❏ Review client's rights	
INTERMEDIATE **CLINICAL OUTCOME** *GOALS*	Client involved in the process of safe detoxification as evidenced by: ❏ Cooperation with detoxification protocol ❏ Stable vital signs ❏ Minimal withdrawal symptoms based on the CIWA-Ar	

Signature	Initials	Signature	Initials	Signature

BOX 9-6. (continued)

CaseType: Detoxification
Expected L.O.S.: 3–10 days

DSM-IV Diagnosis: Alcohol Withdrawal (291.8)
Client Problem(s): 1) History of and potential for life-threatening withdrawal
2) Not involved in the process of recovery

HEALTH CARE TEAM: MD, RN, Social Worker, Addictions Expert, Case Manager (Clinical Nurse Specialist/Psychiatrist/Psychologist)

Phase 2—Day(s) 4–6

	CRITICAL/CLINICAL PATHWAY	VARIANCE AND ACTIONS
Assessment	❑ Detoxification condition ❑ Changes in mental status ❑ Vital signs ❑ Status of medical conditions ❑ Psychiatric status ❑ Stage of change (pre-contemplation, contemplation, etc.)	
Laboratory and Tests	❑ Condition to review results of laboratory and other tests ❑ Discuss results of laboratory and other test with client ❑ Random toxicology and breathalyzer	
Therapeutic Interventions/Treatment	❑ Team review and update treatment plan ❑ Implement all 10 carative factors ❑ Individual counseling sessions ❑ Assign group sessions ❑ Assign self-help groups	
Medication Interventions	❑ Continue detoxification protocol ❑ Evaluate previous PRN orders ❑ Review medication history for medical purposes ❑ Continue medication for medical purposes problems	
Behavioral Interventions	❑ Reinforce limit setting as relates to aggressiveness, drug use, and nonparticipation in assigned activities	
Educational Interventions	❑ The process of addiction ❑ Consequences of addiction and benefits of nonuse ❑ Behaviors for an overall healthy lifestyle (exercise, nutrition, stress reduction)	
Discharge Planning	❑ Initiate contact with source of next level of care ❑ Begin to write the discharge plan ❑ Contact social supports pertinent to recovery (employment, significant others)	
Consults	❑ Review findings of psychiatric and psychological testing	
Legal Status	❑ Note changes in legal status ❑ Evaluate care provided for possible violation of patient rights	
INTERMEDIATE CLINICAL OUTCOME GOALS	Client continues in safe withdrawal and shows interest in recovery as evidenced by: ❑ Previous outcomes met ❑ Absence of withdrawal symptoms based on CIWA-Ar ❑ Maintains stable vital signs ❑ Attends all assigned activities and participates	

Signature	Initials	Signature	Initials	Signature

BOX 9-6. (continued)

CaseType: Detoxification
Expected L.O.S.: 3–10 days

DSM-IV Diagnosis: Alcohol Withdrawal (291.8)
Client Problem(s): 1) History of and potential for life-threatening withdrawal
2) Not involved in the process of recovery

HEALTH CARE TEAM: MD, RN, Social Worker, Addictions Expert, Case Manager (Clinical Nurse Specialist/Psychiatrist/Psychologist)

Phase 3—Day(s) 7–10

	CRITICAL/CLINICAL PATHWAY	VARIANCE AND ACTIONS
Assessment	❑ Absence of withdrawal symptoms ❑ Mental status ❑ Vital signs ❑ Status of medical conditions ❑ Discharge psychiatric status ❑ Progress through stages of change	
Laboratory and Tests	❑ Reorder abnormal laboratory tests and other tests to assess for return to normal levels	
Therapeutic Interventions/ Treatment	❑ Terminate counseling and group activities ❑ Continue to encourage self-help group attendance ❑ Write orders for discharge ❑ Discharge instruction form ❑ Make appointments for next level of medical and addictions treatment care	
Medication Interventions	❑ Discontinue detoxification protocol ❑ Terminate PRN orders ❑ Review medications for medical purposes ❑ Psychiatric medications ordered if necessary	
Behavioral Interventions	❑ None needed	
Educational Interventions	❑ The process of addiction	
Discharge Planning	❑ Complete discharge plan ❑ Counseling sessions with significant others and client to discuss role of social support in recovery	
Consults	❑ Recommendation regarding psychiatric follow-up	
Legal Status	❑ Note changes in legal status ❑ Evaluate care provided for possible violation of patient rights	
CLINICAL OUTCOMES	1) Client has safe, non-life-threatening withdrawal as evidenced by: ❑ Completion of ordered detoxification protocol and ❑ Absence of withdrawal symptoms on CIWA-Ar 2) Client is involved in the process of recovery as evidenced by: ❑ Attends all groups, educational sessions, and counseling sessions ❑ Makes contact with next level of treatment ❑ Progresses along the stages of change to at least "preparation and hopefully action."	

Signature	Initials	Signature	Initials	Signature

Health care reform has already begun with private payors and at some state levels. In demand is health care providers who can meet their goals of care in a cost-effective quality-focused way. Many outpatient detoxification programs are being established, and many home detoxification interventions are beginning to be implemented with reimbursement from private payors.

Whether working in the hospital setting, outpatient setting, community health setting, private clinic setting, or providing home care the principles provided in this chapter for detoxification are relevant and useful for all nurses. Detoxification is close to becoming about the only sure treatment clients addicted to alcohol, tobacco, and other drugs can receive. By having protocols and establishing outcome indicators to evaluate the effectiveness of interventions and programs developed, nurses can grab that corner of the market in addictions health care as well as improve the care provided in their current settings.

REFERENCES

Alexander, C., Mello, S., & Gould, J. (1993). Preventing severe alcohol withdrawal in the general acute care hospital inpatient. *Perspectives on Addictions Nursing*, 4(2), 3–6.

Allen, K. (1996). Clinical/critical pathway for alcohol withdrawal. Unpublished document.

American Psychiatric Association. (1994). *Diagnostic and Statistical Manual*, 4th ed. (DSM-IV). Washington, D.C.: American Psychiatric Association.

American Society of Addiction Medicine Committee of Practice Guidelines. (1994). *The role of phenytoin in the management of alcohol withdrawal syndrome*. Washington, D.C.: American Society of Addiction Medicine Committee of Practice Guidelines.

Baltarovich, L. (1985). Barbiturates. *Topics in Emergency Medicine*, 7(3), 46–54.

Bay, S.N., Goldman, N.S., & Flavin, D.K. (1992). Outpatient detoxification in the treatment of alcohol dependency: A summary. *Medical/Scientific Quarterly, 2*(2), 61–65.

Bittle, S., Feigenbaum, J.C., & Kneisl, C.R. (1986). Substance abuse. In C.R. Kneisl & S.W. Ames (Eds.) *Adult health nursing* (pp. 231–238). Menlo Park, CA: Addison-Wesley.

Blum, K., & Payne, J.E. (1991). *Alcohol and the addictive brain—New hope for alcoholics from biogenetic research*. New York: Free Press.

Bohn, M.J. (1993). Alcoholism. *Psychiatric Clinics of North America, 16*(4), 679–692.

Brogdan, K.E. (1993). Improving outcomes for patients experiencing alcohol withdrawal. *Journal of Nursing Care Quality, 7*(3), 61–70.

Brunton, S. (1991). *Nicotine addiction and smoking cessation*. New York, NY: Medical Informations Services, Inc.

Campinha-Bacote, J., & Bragg, E.J. (1993). Chemical assessment in maternity care. *Maternal Child Nursing, 18*(1), 24–28.

Center for Case Management. (1992). *Definitions*. South Natick, MA: Center for Case Management.

Daigle, R.D., Clark, H.W., & Landry, M.J. (1988). A primer on neurotransmitters and cocaine. *Journal of Psychoactive Drugs, 20*(3), 283–295.

Dall, J. (1993). Promoting sleep with therapeutic touch. *Addictions Nursing Network, 5*(1), 23–24.

Daryanani, H.E., Santolaria, F.J., Reimers, E.G., Jorge, J.A., Lopez, N.B., Hernandez, F.M., Riera, A.M., & Rodriguez, E.R. (1994). Alcohol withdrawal syndrome and seizures. *Alcohol & Alcoholism, 29*(3): 323–328.

Devenyi, P., & Harrison, M. (1985). Prevention of alcohol withdrawal seizures with oral diazepam loading. *Canadian Medical Association Journal, 132*, 798–800.

Gawin, F.H., & Ellinwood, Jr., E.H. (1988). Cocaine and other stimulants actions, abuse and treatment. *New England Journal of Medicine, 318*(18), 1173–1181.

Gold, M.S. (1992). Cocaine (and crack): Clinical aspects. In J.H. Lowinson, P. Ruiz, & R.B. Millman (Eds.) *Substance abuse—A comprehensive textbook, 2nd ed.* (pp. 205–221.) Baltimore: Williams & Wilkins.

Gold, M., Redmond, D., & Kleber, H. (1978). Clonidine blocks acute opiate withdrawal symptoms. *Lancet, 2*(8090), 599–602.

Goldstein, A. (1994). *Addiction from biology to drug policy*. New York: Freeman.Goldstein, F. (1995). Pharmacological aspects of substance abuse. In A.R. Genaro (Ed.) *Remington's pharmaceutical sciences, 19th ed.* Easton, PA: Mack.

Greden, J.F. & Walters, A. (1992). Caffeine. In J.H. Lowinson, P. Ruiz, & R.B. Millman (Eds.). *Substance abuse—A comprehensive textbook, 2nd ed.* (pp. 357–370.) Baltimore: Williams & Wilkins.

Grinspoon, L. & Bakalar, J.B. (1992). Marijuana. In J.H. Lowinson, P. Ruiz, & R.B. Millman (Eds.). *Substance abuse—A comprehensive textbook, 2nd ed.* (pp. 236–246.) Baltimore: Williams & Wilkins.

Handelsman, L., Cochran, K., Aronson, M., Ness, R., Rubinstein, K., & Kanof, P. (1987). Two new rating scales for opiate withdrawal. *American Journal of Drug and Alcohol Abuse, 13*, 293–308.

Hanson, G., & Venturelli, P. (1995). *Drugs and society, 4th ed.* Boston: Jones and Bartlett.

Hayner, G., Galloway, G., & Wiehl, W.O. (1993). Haight-Ashbury free clinics' drug detoxification protocols. Part 3: Benzodiazepines and other sedative-hypnotics. *Journal of Psychoactive Drugs, 25*(4), 331–335.

Institute of Medicine. (1990). *Broadening the base of treatment for alcohol problems.* Washington, D.C.: National Academy Press.

Jaffe, J.H. (1992). Opiates: Clinical aspects. In J.H. Lowinson, P. Ruiz, & R.B. Millman (Eds.), *Substance abuse—A comprehensive textbook, 2nd ed.* (pp. 186–194.) Baltimore: Williams & Wilkins.

Jarvik, M.E., & Schneider, N.G. (1992). Nicotine. In J.H. Lowinson, P. Ruiz, & R.B. Millman (Eds.), *Substance abuse—A comprehensive textbook, 2nd ed.* (pp. 334–356.) Baltimore: Williams & Wilkins.

Keltner, N.L., & Folks, D.G. (1993). *Psychotropic drugs* (pp. 120–121.) St. Louis: Mosby.

Landry, M. (1994). *Understanding drugs of abuse: The processes of addiction, treatment, and recovery.* Washington, D.C.: American Psychiatric Press.

Malcolm, R., Ballenger, J., Sturgis, E., & Anton, R. (1989). Double-blind controlled trial comparing carbamazepine to oxazepam treatment of alcohol withdrawal. *American Journal of Psychiatry, 146*(5), 617–621.

Morton, W.A., Laird, L.K., Crane, D.F., Partovi, N., & Frye, L.H. (1994). A Prediction model for identifying alcohol withdrawal seizures. *American Journal of Drug and Alcohol Abuse, 20*(1), 75–86.

Mudd, S., Boyd, C., Brower, K., Young, J., & Blow, F. (Oct. 1994). Alcohol withdrawal and related nursing care in older adults. *Journal of Gerontological Nursing, 17–26*.

National Nurses Society on Addictions (1995). Outpatient detoxification: Guidelines for nurses. *Perspectives on Addictions Nursing, 6*(2), 8–10.

Nixon, S. (1994). Cognitive deficits in alcoholic women. *Alcohol Health and Research World, 18*(3), 228–231.

Palfai, T., & Jankiewicz, H. (1991). *Drugs and human behavior.* Dubuque, IA: Wm. C. Brown Publishers.

Rounsaville, B., Tims, F., Horton, A., & Sowder, B. (1993). *Diagnostic source book on drug abuse research and treatment.* NIH Publication No. 93-3508. Rockville, MD: National Institutes of Health.

Saitz, R., Mayo-Smith, M., Roberts, M., Redmond, H., Benard, D., & Calkins, D. (1994). Individualized treatment for alcohol withdrawal: A randomized double-blind controlled trial. *Journal of the American Medical Association, 272*(7), 519–523.

Sees, K.L. (1991). Pharmacological adjuncts for the treatment of withdrawal syndromes. *Journal of Psychoactive Drugs, 23*(4), 371–385.

Sellers, E., Naranjo, C., Harrison, M., Devenyi, P., Roach, C., & Sykora, K. (1983). Diazepam loading: Simplified treatment of alcohol withdrawal. *Clinical and Pharmacological Therapy, 34*(6), 822–826.

Skinner, H.A., & Horn, J.L. (1984). *Alcohol dependence scale.* Toronto, Canada: Addiction Research Foundation.

Substance Abuse and Mental Health Services Administration's Center for Substance Abuse Treatment. (1995). *Detoxification from alcohol and other drugs.* Treatment Improvement Protocol Series.

Sullivan, J., Sykora, K., Schneiderman, J., Naranjo, C., & Sellers, E. (1989). Assessment of alcohol withdrawal: The revised clinical institute withdrawal assessment for alcohol scale (CIWA-Ar). *British Journal of Addiction, 84*, 1353–1357.

Swanson, J.A., Lee, J.W., & Hopp, J.W. (1994). Caffeine and nicotine: A review of their joint use and possible interactive effects in tobacco withdrawal. *Addictive Behaviors, 19*(3), 229–256.

Wartenberg, A., Nirenberg, T., Liepman, M., Silvia, L., Begin, A., and Monti, P. (1990). Detoxification of alcoholics: Improving care by symptom-triggered sedation. *Alcohol Clinical and Experimental Research, 13*, 71–75.

Watson, J. (1989). Watson's philosophy and theory of human caring in nursing. In J. Riehl-Sisca (Ed.), *Conceptual Models for nursing practice* (pp. 219–236.) Norwalk, CT: Appleton & Lange.

Wesson, D.R., Smith, D.E., & Seymour, R.B. (1992). Sedative-hypnotics and tricyclics. In J.H. Lowinson, P. Ruiz, & R.B. Millman (Eds.) *Substance abuse—A comprehensive textbook, 2nd ed.* (pp. 271–279.) Baltimore: Williams & Wilkins.

Wing, D.M. (1991). Goal setting and recovery from alcoholism. *Archives of Psychiatric Nursing, 3*, 178–184.

Witters, W., Venturelli, P., & Hanson, G. (1992). *Drugs and society, 3rd ed.* Boston, MA: Jones & Bartlett.

Worner, T.M. (1994). Propanolol versus diazepam in the management of the alcohol withdrawal syndrome: Double-blind controlled trial. *American Journal of Drug & Alcohol Abuse, 20*(1), 115–124.

Zweben, J.E., & O'Connell, K. (1992). Strategies for breaking marijuana dependence. *Journal of Psychoactive Drugs, 24*(2), 165–171.

Zweben, J., & Payte, J. (1990). Methadone maintenance in the treatment of opioid dependence: A current perspective. *Western Journal of Medicine, 152*(2), 588–589.

Interventions and Treatment

Marilyn Vranas, MS, RN, CS, CARN
Karen M. Allen, PhD, RN, CARN

INTRODUCTION

New information about the effectiveness and economic benefits of providing interventions and treatment for substance abuse/addictions is emerging rapidly. The Office of National Drug Control Policy (1990) has stated unequivocally that "we now know—based on more than two decades of research—that doing drug treatment can work" (p. 30). In 1994, news media around the country reported on the State of California's findings about the effectiveness of treatment. Based on interviews shortly after participants exited treatment and more than a year after treatment, it was found that: 1) while 73.6% of participants had been involved in criminal activity pretreatment, only 20.3% were involved in crime in the year following treatment; 2) for all types of drugs, use declined considerably in the post-treatment period as compared to the year before treatment (e.g., 40.4% used cocaine before treatment, but only 21.6% did so after treatment); 3) treatment *does not* do less for members of minority groups than for whites; and 4) savings to taxpayers—mostly from avoidance of crime-related costs— outpaced the public cost of treating addicts by a 7-to-1 margin (State of California, 1994).

There are three major categories of public health responses to alcohol and other drug use problems: 1) pretreatment (interventions); 2) outpatient treatment; and 3) inpatient treatment. Each category has several subsets but treatment is provided by two basic modalities: pharmacological, which affects biological processes, and behavioral, which influences behavior and/or learning processes. According to the National Institute on Drug Abuse (1991), these modalities are often combined to produce a greater effect.

Managed care and other health care payment systems, along with health care policy changes, are altering the approach to health care in general, and to addictions treatment in particular. Concurrent with the payor and health policy changes, approaches to treatment based on newly discovered information resulting from research are also changing. It is within this unpredictable climate that nurses in all settings are being confronted with the task of intervening with and treating addicted clients.

The purpose of this chapter is to provide information that will assist nurses in caring for addicted clients at varying levels and in diverse settings, in the midst of a transitioning and chaotic health care environment. This chapter will specifically present information on: 1) the history and trends of interventions and treatment of addictions; 2) current interventions and treatment for use with addicted clients; and 3) standards of care that influence approaches that nurses can use when intervening with and treating substance abusers or addicts.

HISTORICAL OVERVIEW

Alcohol Abuse

Before World War II, interventions and treatment of alcohol abuse and alcoholism, as we understand it today, did not exist. Individuals with alcohol abuse problems were sequestered from public view in back wards of institutions, with just a few clinics available. According to a well-known 1942 study conducted by Voegtlin and Lemere (as cited in Pattison, 1985) the rehabilitation rate in the 1940s was no more than 30%.

During this time a major self-help group, Alcoholics Anonymous (A.A.), which came into being in the mid-1930s while medicine and psychiatry were attempting to treat the disease of alcoholism more formally, began to have an increased impact on helping persons addicted to alcohol. This self-help, community-based organization offered social support and self-respect and contributed to the change in the image of alcoholics from moral degenerates to persons with a disease (Zinberg & Fraser, 1985).

Various theories about causes and subsequent models of treatment for alcoholism emerged, with the model of treatment following the current view of philosophical ideas of causation. By the mid-to-late 1970s, the moral, biological or disease, psychological, and sociological models concerning the nature of alcoholism were the more prominent. However, the theory that alcoholism has multiple causes was beginning to emerge and promoted the thought that diverse treatment approaches might be necessary to intervene with this problem (Tarter & Schneider, 1976). The accepted treatment approaches for alcohol abuse during the mid-1970s were psychotherapy (individual and group), behavioral and pharmacological methods, and the self-help group A.A. Fortunately, the notion of multiple etiology as it relates to alcohol abuse and alcoholism continues in current thinking today.

Drug Abuse

The medical–psychiatric hospital treatment setting was developed in the late 1920s along with the theory suggesting that drug addiction was essentially an illness/disease. Later, both alcoholism and drug abuse were officially defined as an illness/disease by the American Medical Association. However, prior to the mid-1960s, few individuals with drug abuse problems were placed in medical–psychiatric hospital treatment settings. Frequently, they were dealt with by the criminal justice system, in that individuals who possessed or used certain classifications of drugs were identified as criminal offenders and received punishment, rather than treatment. Then, in the mid-1930s the federal government in seeking an answer to this problem, opened the Lexington, Kentucky, and the Fort Worth, Texas, federal treatment programs for heroin addicts in the criminal justice system.

These medical–psychiatric hospitals, established for narcotic treatment and research provided: 1) detoxification; 2) attention to physical health; 3) a sheltered environment;

4) therapeutic relationships with psychiatrists and other health care professionals; and 5) some vocational rehabilitation. A small number of patients received "aftercare" following discharge and returned to the home environment. In numerous follow-up studies, both of these early approaches—the punitive–legal and the medical–psychiatric—generally failed to prevent the return to drugs (Adler, Moffett, Glaser, Ball, & Horvitz, 1974).

The early 1970s saw the federal government's war on drugs begin to take a strong prevention thrust. The Comprehensive Drug Abuse Prevention and Control Act was established to replace all other laws concerning narcotics and dangerous drugs; and the Drug Abuse Office and Treatment Act was established to make available $1.1 billion over 3 years to combat drug abuse and start treatment programs. This included research, education, training, rehabilitation, and treatment. A ninefold funding increase was seen from 1969 to 1974. This increase in resources begat an explosion in treatment facilities, including methadone maintenance facilities. In addition, a parallel growth of drug-free clinics and inpatient programs emerged (Musto, 1987; Witters, Venturelli, & Hanson, 1992).

According to Adler et al. (1974), the three categories and variants for drug abuse treatment during the 1970s included: 1) medical–psychiatric hospitals, 2) therapeutic communities, and 3) social action programs. The medical–psychiatric hospital model, which has since emerged, is now called the medical model of treatment. It includes detoxification, methadone maintenance, educational sessions, individual counseling, and group therapy.

The therapeutic community model includes residential and nonresidential therapeutic community, religious therapeutic community, and rap house. The social action model emphasizes societal rejuvenation and responsibility, community organization and community rehabilitation, rather than unilateral focus on the individual. Specific therapies include individual and group counseling, workshops, and community projects (Adler et al., 1974).

The 1970s were a time of roller-coaster drug politics, ranging from an easing in intolerance to hard ball opposition. It was a time of competition, conflict, and disagreement over treatment theories and goals. In later years, at the onset of and through the mid-1980s, funding for treatment and research did not increase (Musto, 1987).

EFFECT OF CURRENT HEALTH CARE ENVIRONMENT

Now, theories and approaches to treatment are becoming more eclectic, and more important, less territorial. The attitude of "our way is the only way" is ceasing to exist. A more prescriptive and systems-oriented thinking about treatment is emerging, which has the potential to work well within the developing health care system.

Without a doubt, the concepts of health care reform, managed care, and cost containment are activating both structural and process changes in how, where, when, and who treats addicted clients. Some of the general themes stimulating the overhauling of the general health care process and structure include: reinventing government; health care reform (streamlining, increasing accessibility, focusing on customer service); integration of services (health, housing, etc.); a targeting of underserved populations with interventions that are both appropriate and diverse; and emphasizing evaluation—increasingly practitioners are recognizing that having data is essential for strategic planning.

A message is contained in all this activity to the health care industry in general, to the field of addictions, and to nurses in general who provide care to addicted clients. The message is that considerable changes in payor and government policies reflect efforts to cope with and be responsive to trying circumstances in the economic, social, and health environment.

There are limited resources; therefore, the components of the health care industry faced with intervening and treating the substance abusing/addicted client must compete for those increasingly limited health care resources. Thus, it becomes imperative that the substance abuse/addictions discipline "get its collective act together" and systematically identify which interventions and treatments work, in what settings, and for whom. In addition, there must be an interdisciplinary and interagency approach taken to coordinate client care, and salvage the parts of the existing system that are effective so that clients can experience continuity of care, and survival of the changes can take place.

The magnitude of the window of opportunity in these changing times for the specialty of addictions nursing as well as nurses in other clinical specialties who encounter addicted clients, is immense. The message to nursing is clear: "let the creative juices flow, *make* the opportunities to participate in leadership decisions, as well as reimbursement allowed for interventions and treatments."

CURRENT INTERVENTIONS AND TREATMENT FOR ADDICTED CLIENTS

Theoretical Basis

In substance abuse/addictions treatment, as with other disciplines of health care, how one approaches practice flows from how one views the cause of the problem. Theory-based models guide interventions and treatment approaches and determines how, when, and where clinicians intervene (Shaffer, 1990).

There is support in the field that the theory of treatment must spring from, be integrated with, and accommodate the multiple nature of addictions within the complex mix of the client population. According to Lewis, McCusker, Hindin, Frost, and Garfield (1993), "while moral and medical models have dominated treatment and post-treatment environments, increasingly there has been an evolving biopsychosocial perspective of addictive behaviors that views addiction as a complex and progressive behavior pattern with component processes" (p. 46). According to the Substance Abuse and Mental Health Services Administration (SAMHSA) (1994a), an understanding of addiction has evolved and knowledge has been gained through research showing that the complexity of causes for, and persistence of substance abuse has been compounded. It now appears that a constellation of factors can be correlated with initiation and continuation of substance use and dependency. No single explanation appears adequate in most cases.

Biopsychosocial perspectives that can be used to guide interventions and treatment of addictions have been addressed in Chapter 2. They are important for nurses and other health care providers to use because "clinicians must develop the skills to organize individually tailored treatment strategies around the constellation of biological, psychological and social factors that shape each person's unique style of substance abuse/addiction and associate dysfunctions" (Milkman, 1991, p. xvii).

It is important to note here that in 1987 and 1988 the American Nurses Association (ANA) and the National Nurses Society on Addictions (NNSA) adopted the position that: "addiction represents a multi-determined and multidimensional disease process across all client populations, that requires intervention at all levels, and supports interdisciplinary cooperation." In essence everyone is saying the same thing—to intervene or treat, the approach must be comprehensive and all encompassing of biological, psychological, and social factors.

Interventions

Interventions are "brief therapies" so to speak, and suggest that not every client requires regular outpatient, intensive outpatient, inpatient, or residential treatment. Heather (1989) defined brief therapy as a *range* of intervention strategies rather than a specific approach. Minimal or brief interventions are time-limited, directed strategies that focus on reducing alcohol and other drug use in the nondependent substance abuser. Clinically based interventions include: assessment, brief counseling, follow-up procedures, and referral (U.S. Department of Health and Human Services, 1994).

Intervention strategies are important and workable for several reasons: 1) they are useful in early identification of problem substance abuse; 2) they may succeed in preventing a potentially more serious problem; and 3) they offer the promise that changing client substance abuse behavior early on may be more cost effective. Brief interventions are not intended for individuals with advanced, serious addictions, but are useful in assisting clients with a more serious problem to access appropriate treatment (Heather, 1989).

Brief intervention strategies include:

- One or two sessions of assessment followed by advice
- Referrals to more intensive treatment if the need is identified
- Distribution of self-help manuals and other pamphlets for home study for clients or significant others of addicted persons
- Educational sessions with large groups (i.e., communities, health professionals)
- Screening for early detection
- Brief counseling sessions to:
  1. Review findings with client and family
  2. Present evidence of physical, social, financial, spiritual, familial damage
  3. Negotiate and present diagnosis
  4. Establish drinking and drug use goals
  5. Review positive changes that occur
  6. Provide bibliotherapy
- Provide follow-up to:
  1. Review alcohol and other drug (AOD) use log daily
  2. Monitor physical indicators of AOD use
  3. Review progress on goals and contract
  4. Provide more intensive aftercare for those who are dependent and trying to continue abstinence

Brief intervention programs have many advantages in that they can be applied to communities and populations with minimal resources. Based on scientific evidence, the Institute of Medicine (1990) recommended that "clinicians should routinely ask all adults and adolescents to describe their use of alcohol and other drugs.... Certain questionnaires may be useful to clinicians in assessing important AOD use patterns.... All persons who use alcohol and other drugs should be informed of the health and injury risks associated with consumption and should be encouraged to limit consumption.... Many clients may benefit from referrals to appropriate consultants and community programs specializing in the treatment of AOD dependencies."

Brief intervention strategies have broad application within secondary and tertiary treatment settings, and they should be adapted by nurses to "seize the opportunity" to intervene.

They may be as limited or as extensive as indicated by both the client's needs and the nurse's level of practice. Detection and assessment, education, advice, referral, or intensive treatment are all options and opportunities for nursing intervention. One of the most promising delivery modes for brief interventions is to make it a part of health education and general community health promotion drives.

Nurses—being the largest group of health care providers in the country—are encountering the greatest number of clients in a wide array of settings such as schools, medical units in hospitals, employee health centers, home health care, physician's offices, and community clinics. They will repeatedly see individuals who are using substances in a harmful manner, because within the population seeking health care the rate of substance abuse is likely to be higher than in the general population due to the high rate of physical and mental problems associated with substance abuse. This front line arena is a natural opportunity and ripe turf for nurses to use the above strategies in the context of providing brief care for the purpose of intervening with the addicted clients they encounter.

Another method of intervention—although not viewed as being brief—is case management. According to Mejta, Monks, and Mickenberg (1993), case management emphasizes integration and coordination of several systems to address the multiple needs of clients. It is based on functions and is broadly defined as a system of locating, coordinating, and monitoring a group of services for a person. The models of case management may vary widely, but the model in concert with interventions is the "interventions case management" model. It provides the five basic functions of assessment, planning, linking, monitoring, and advocacy.

In this model, the case manager:

1. Conducts a comprehensive needs assessment identifying presenting problems
2. Develops an individualized case management plan including client goals and a plan to reach those goals
3. Links the client with various treatment providers
4. Monitors the treatment process and progress
5. Serves as client advocate when needed

Brief therapies and case management are two intervention areas that have potential for nurses in this evolving field of caring for addicted clients. Nurses matching their considerable expertise in multiple areas—at both the generalist and the advanced practice levels of care—with various levels of brief interventions and case management strategies, will thrive as well as survive in the existing, evolving health care environment.

For addictions nurse specialists, an *addiction intervention* is a structured, organized, professionally led process in which the objective facts of the addicted person's AOD-related behavior and consequences are presented in such a way that the defense mechanisms cannot reject the information (Landry, 1994). This intervention method was developed by Vernon Johnson and popularized by the Johnson Institute. The purpose of this type of intervention is to convince addicts that they have a problem, and help them recognize the need for treatment. This can take place with respect to family and friends or employment. This intervention involves a carefully rehearsed and controlled meeting with the client, significant others, and a professional in attendance most times.

It is important to note that this "addiction intervention" has specific characteristics that make it effective: 1) it needs to be loving as well as confrontational; 2) nonjudgmental; 3) humanistic; 4) educational; 5) organized and professional; and 6) seen as the starting point for addiction treatment. These type of interventions must be done by an "addictions nurse specialist" who has been trained in this procedure. Nurses who see the need to use this type of intervention should be mindful of this checklist recommended by Landry (1994):

Intervention Preparation:
- Find a professional intervention specialist
- Participate in Al-Anon, Nar-Anon, and Alateen immediately
- Assemble an intervention team as recommended by the specialist
- Learn about drugs of abuse, treatment, and recovery
- Review examples of addiction-related behavior
- Learn about local treatment resources
- Research insurance coverage of treatment
- Examine personal financial resources of client

Intervention Planning:
- Have statements written down and prepared
- Determine leverage to be used if client says "no" to treatment
- Select treatment programs to offer
- Verify that space is available
- Decide time and place of intervention
- Decide how the client will arrive at the intervention
- Decide how the individual will be taken to treatment
- Assist client in arranging time off from work for treatment, canceling appointments, handling obligations, and doing errands
- Review reasons for wanting to do the intervention
- Have a "walk-through" rehearsal to learn the format
- Have a "dress" rehearsal with someone playing the role of the addicted client
- Pack a suitcase

Treatment

According to Adler et al. (1974) treatment takes place based on a "centralized core and shell" premise. Central to this premise is that the client enters a *treatment system* rather than a *treatment program*. The system has available many modalities and approaches from which to select the one most appropriate for the unique set of difficulties of that client. The "core" and "shell" approach is fluidly interactive and provides a thorough assessment, diagnosis, and determination of the extent and breadth of the problem. This will facilitate the placement of the client in a treatment program match.

The system will accommodate monitoring of individual and collective client progress through central evaluation. And should a particular approach be found to not work for a particular client, the system accommodates reevaluation and programmatic change.

MAJOR TREATMENT MODALITIES AND CATEGORIES

As stated earlier, treatment is approached by two basic modalities: 1) *biologically based* pharmacotherapeutic treatment, acupuncture; and 2) *behaviorally based* influencing behavior and learning processes. These approaches to treatment take place with the following categories of care: *outpatient* methadone and nonmethadone treatment and *inpatient* treatment programs (i.e, residential, hospital-based, and therapeutic communities) (SAMHSA, 1994a).

Biologically based

Biologically based modalities (pharmacotherapeutic) have shown some favorable outcomes and include the use of approved medications with medical supervision. According to Lowinson, Marion, Joseph, and Dole (1992), the goals of pharmacotherapy include: 1) reduction in the use of illicit drugs or alcohol; 2) reduction in criminal behavior; and 3) improvement of social behavior and psychological well-being. A further goal is the urgent imperative to control and prevent the spread of substance abuse-related infectious diseases such as HIV/AIDS. Medications used include: agonists (methadone, clonidine, Levo-alpha-acetyl-methadol for use with heroin addicts), which are used to substitute for the drug of abuse and provide a more controllable form of addiction; antagonists (naltrexone, buprenorphine), which occupy the same receptor sites in the brain as specific drugs of abuse, but do not produce the same effects as the abused drug and are nonaddicting (opiate and alcohol addictions); antidipsotropics (antabuse for use with alcoholism), which interfere with the metabolism of alcohol, causing unpleasant side effects when alcohol is ingested; and psychotropics (antianxiety, antidepressants, antipsychotic), which control various symptoms associated with drug use and withdrawal.

Acupuncture applies a treatment method developed in China and other Far Eastern countries. Addiction represents an adaptation of the central nervous system's activity in response to chronic drug administration, resulting in withdrawal symptoms when drug use is discontinued. Acupuncture or transcutaneous electrical nerve stimulation can modulate central nervous system activity in those regions of the brain affected by substances of abuse.

Behavioral based

Behavioral-based modalities (behavior and/or learning focused) take place in inpatient and outpatient programs where the individual may or may not live in the facility while participating in treatment. Inpatient is most appropriate for individuals who have not been successful in outpatient settings, those needing concomitant medical or psychiatric care or observation, and those without a stable social support system in the community. Inpatient programs are the most restrictive, structured, and protective types of programs. Inpatient treatment provides comprehensive treatment services, constant support during the early stages of sobriety, and close supervision to prevent relapse and respond to medical emergencies.

Therapeutic communities are self-contained residential programs that emphasize self-help and rely heavily on ex-addicts as peer counselors, administrators, and role models. The goals of therapeutic communities include: habilitation or rehabilitation of the total individual; changing negative patterns of behavior, thinking, and feeling that predispose to drug use; and development of a drug-free lifestyle. Several adaptations of the therapeutic community model exists because of costs, availability, and insurance reimbursement.

Outpatient alcohol and other drug treatment can be defined as a system of providing help to substance abusers in a setting outside of an inpatient or residential program. Clients may remain at home or reside in a group home, a foster home, or a related setting. In addition, outpatient programs may take place in health care facilities, community health centers, private clinics, and private practices. Outpatient services may take place before, in place of, or following inpatient treatment (SAMHSA, 1993).

Outpatient nonmethadone programs involve trained professionals working with addicted persons to achieve and maintain abstinence while living in the community. Outpatient treatment programs offer a range of services and treatment modalities including: pharmacotherapy, individual counseling, group counseling, and family counseling.

Some treatment programs have been developed to capitalize on the advantages of both inpatient and outpatient treatment approaches, and maximize benefits while reducing costs. Two-by-four programs are two-phase approaches where the person is first hospitalized for a short time (usually 2 weeks) to ensure complete detoxification, then an outpatient treatment follows, with the option to return as an inpatient if the client is unable to function in the less restrictive environment. Day or partial hospitalization involves treatment in the program during normal working hours, but the person returns home in the evening. A prerequisite for this type of treatment is a supportive, stable family. Halfway houses provide an intermediate step between inpatient treatment and independent living. It is an alternative for persons who do not have a stable social support system.

MAJOR NONPHARMACOLOGICAL TREATMENT APPROACHES

According to SAMHSA (1994a) a variety of techniques are used as treatment modalities within the treatment categories. They include: self-help or 12-step approaches; individual, group, and/or family counseling; and behavioral modification.

Self-help or 12-step organizations involve mutual help among peers experiencing similar problems. The primary goals are to achieve total abstinence from alcohol or other drugs; effect changes in personal values and interpersonal behavior; and continue participation in the fellowship to both give and receive help from others with similar problems. Self-help groups may be the only intervention used by some persons to end substance abuse/addiction. However, they are often used in tandem with the above mentioned treatment modalities. Self-help groups include A.A., Narcotics Anonymous, and Cocaine Anonymous.

Individual counseling approaches assume a one-to-one encounter between a client and a counselor. Goals of individual counseling include: helping the person resolve to stop using psychoactive substances; teaching coping skills to help the person avoid relapse after achieving an initial period of abstinence; changing reinforcement contingencies; fostering management of painful feelings; and improving interpersonal functioning and enhancing social supports. Individual therapy provides privacy to those persons not willing to disclose their issues publicly. Much more time is spent on issues unique to the person involved. Studies show that no specific type of individual treatment approach is more effective than another.

Group therapy is often combined with other treatment modalities to provide a structured, comprehensive treatment program. Goals of group therapy include: establishing reduction in use or abstinence; integration of the individual into the group; stabilization of individual functioning; relapse prevention; and identifying and working through long-standing problems that have been obscured or exacerbated by substance abuse. Several types of group approaches used include: exploratory group, which explores and interprets members' feelings and helps them develop greater ability to tolerate distressing feelings without resorting to mood-altering substances; supportive group, which helps addicted members tolerate abstinence and assists them in remaining drug- or alcohol-free by enabling them to draw on their own resources; interactional group, which creates an environment of safety, cohesion, and trust, where members engage in in-depth self-disclosure and affective expression; interpersonal problem-solving group, which teaches an approach to solving interpersonal problems, including recognizing that a problem exists, defining the problem, generating possible solutions, and selecting the best alternative; educational group, which provides information on issues related to specific addictions, such as the natural course and medical consequences, implications of intravenous drug use, and availability of community resource (methods used include videotapes, audiotapes, lectures, and discussion); and activity group, which provides occupational and recreational means for socialization and self-expression.

CLIENT–TREATMENT MATCHING

Each client's personality, background, mental condition, and the duration, extent, and type of drug use must be considered when selecting a treatment program or approach. A comprehensive assessment and individualized, realistic, and goal-based treatment plan are the essential first steps for effective patient–treatment matching (SAMHSA, 1994a).

An analysis of program resources and characteristics are also important. Although various studies about client and program ingredients related to success of interventions and treatment have been conducted, there is still insufficient information. However, significant findings about selecting appropriate programs for clients with particular types of problems have evolved. For example, it is important to assess program proficiency and staff competency and attitudes; a comprehensive array of services is needed to meet a variety of client needs; and individual motivation, drug use patterns, psychological problems, and ethnic and gender variables are part of the equation for effective treatment matching leading to successful outcomes for treatment with the above modalities and approaches.

TREATMENT MODALITIES AND APPROACHES RECOMMENDED BY THE U.S. DEPARTMENT OF HEALTH AND HUMAN SERVICES

The field of substance abuse/addictions has had many isolated layers and levels of thinking on theory, and approaches to treatment that have hampered its movement in concert with the occurring health care system changes. However, a decision by the federal government, which has provided a vehicle to plan and change this, came about with the establishment of the U.S. Health and Human Services Substance Abuse and Mental Health Services Administration (SAMHSA).

SAMHSA was created in 1992. The legislation establishing it transferred the three research institutes of the Alcohol, Drug Abuse and Mental Health Administration (ADAMHA) into the National Institutes of Health. ADAMHA's service functions and programs were incorporated into SAMHSA, whose three centers are: 1) the Center for Substance Abuse Prevention (CSAP); 2) the Center for Substance Abuse Treatment (CSAT); and the Center for Mental Health Services (CMHS) (see Figure 10-1). In addition, the legislation created three units within SAMHSA that relate significantly to the substance abuse treatment program for women and children: the Office of the Associate Administrator for Alcohol Prevention and Treatment Policy, the Office of Applied Studies, and the Office of Women's Services.

With this organizational structure, SAMHSA's mission and program strategies are directed toward achieving three major objectives:

- To reduce the incidence and prevalence of substance abuse and mental disorders, and improve treatment outcomes for persons suffering from addictive and mental health problems and disorders
- To provide leadership to ensure the best use of knowledge based on science to prevent and treat mental and addictive disorders
- To improve access and reduce barriers to high quality, effective treatment programs, which means being committed to leading the nation in its efforts to ensure that prevention and treatment work for all those in need

The basic mission of CSAT is: "to empower the treatment and recovery infrastructure by working collaboratively with other government agencies." An overall specific goal is to provide a continuum of specific services, evaluate the effectiveness of the continuum, and utilize the evaluation results to reformulate approaches to care (U.S. Department of Health and Human Services, 1992); therefore, to develop acceptable standards of care for addicted persons.

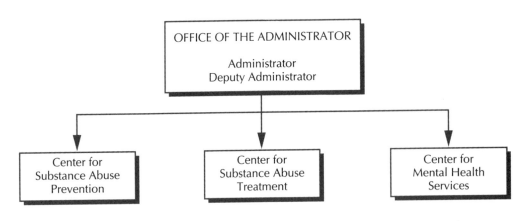

Figure 10-1.   Substance Abuse and Mental Health Services Administration.

The first step CSAT has taken to accomplish this is to develop and publish what is known as the *Guidelines and Models for Comprehensive Alcohol and Other Drug Abuse Treatment* (SAMHSA 1993, 1994a,b). Undergirding these guidelines and models of treatment is CSAT's belief that effective treatment contains five critical components as delineated by Messalle (1992): 1) Assessment. The clinician uses diagnostic instruments and processes to determine an individual's needs and problems. It is an essential first step in determining the possible causes of addiction for the person, as well as the most appropriate treatment modality for his or her needs. 2) Patient–Treatment Matching. The clinician ensures that an individual receives the type of treatment corresponding with his or her personality, background, mental condition, and the extent and duration of substance abuse/addiction determined by the assessment, and guided by patient placement criteria. 3) Comprehensive Services. Case management takes place to ensure that the range of services needed in addition to specific alcohol or drug treatment is included. The needs of addicted clients are often very complex, including health problems, financial and legal issues, and psychological problems. Effective treatment must help people access the full extent of additional services needed to make their lives whole. 4) Relapse Prevention. This is important because addiction is a chronic and relapsing disorder. Relapse prevention strategies are based on assessing an individual's "triggers"—those situations, events, people, places, thoughts, and activities—that rekindle the need for drugs. Strategies for coping with these when they occur are then developed by the clinician. 5) Accountability. This refers to the evaluation of treatment programs themselves, in that it is crucial for determining the effectiveness of specific modalities and approaches to insure quality on a continuous basis.

Model Treatment Programs

The standard of care for addicted clients incorporated in these model treatment programs as outlined by CSAT (SAMHSA, 1993, 1994a,b) is based on research and the core components for the three model programs follow.

MODEL FOR COMPREHENSIVE ALCOHOL AND OTHER DRUG ABUSE TREATMENT

- Assessment—to include a medical examination, drug use history, psychosocial evaluation, and where warranted, a psychiatric evaluation, as well as a review of socioeconomic factors and eligibility for public health, welfare, employment, and educational assistance programs
- Same Day Intake—to retain the client's involvement and interest in receiving care
- Documenting Findings and Treatment—to enhance clinical case supervision
- Preventive and Primary Medical Care—to be provided on site
- Testing for Infectious Diseases—to be done at intake and at intervals throughout treatment, for infectious diseases such as hepatitis, retrovirus, tuberculosis, HIV/AIDS, syphilis, gonorrhea, and other sexually transmitted diseases
- Weekly Random Drug Testing—to ensure abstinence and compliance with treatment
- Pharmacotherapeutic Interventions—to be done by qualified medical practitioners, as appropriate for those clients having mental health disorders, those addicted to heroin, and HIV-seropositive individuals
- Group Counseling Interventions—to address the unique emotional, physical, and social problems that arise, for example, with HIV/AIDS clients
- Basic Substance Abuse Counseling—to include psychological counseling, psychiatric counseling, and family or collateral counseling, provided by persons certified by state or other authorities. Staff training and education are integral to a successful treatment program.
- Dual Diagnosis Capabilities—comprehensive treatment to address addicted persons presenting with psychiatric disorders such as depression, bipolar disease, obsession, personality disorders. These disorders should be treated just as vigorously as the addictions disorders where applicable.
- Practical Life Skills Counseling—to include vocational and educational counseling and training, frequently available through linkages with specialized programs
- General Health Education—to include nutrition, sex and family planning, and HIV/AIDS counseling, with an emphasis on contraception counseling for adolescents and women
- Peer/Support Groups—to help particularly those who are HIV-positive or who have been victims of rape or sexual abuse

- Liaison Services—to help with immigration, legal aid, and criminal justice system authorities
- Social and Athletic Activities—to retrain clients' perceptions of social interaction
- Alternative Housing—to help homeless clients or those whose living situations are conducive to maintaining the addictive lifestyle
- Relapse Prevention—to combine aftercare and support programs such as A.A. and Narcotics Anonymous within an individualized plan to identify, stabilize, and control the stressors that trigger and bring about relapse to substance abuse
- Outcome Evaluation—to enable refinement and improvement of service delivery

MODEL FOR COMPREHENSIVE ALCOHOL AND OTHER
DRUG TREATMENT OF WOMEN AND CHILDREN

According to CSAT's Women and Children's Branch (1994b), a comprehensive model for treatment of alcohol and other drug problems among women should also include the following components:

Clinical Interventions and Comprehensive Health Assessment
- Intake screening and substance abuse, physical, and mental health, and social services assessments
- Gender-specific substance abuse counseling and psychological counseling to address such issues as relapse prevention, self-esteem, physical and sexual abuse-related trauma, and domestic violence
- Family counseling
- Medical and mental health interventions, including those for substance abuse, sexually transmitted diseases (STDs), hepatitis, tuberculosis, cancer, and malnutrition
- Counseling for HIV-positive/AIDS patients
- Health education and prevention activities (breast cancer, smoking and alcohol and other drug use during pregnancy)
- Discharge planning and continuing care (family needs, financial support)

Socioeconomic Services
- Life skills education
- Education and training services
- Parenting skills
- Job readiness and referral
- Transportation
- Housing (caregiver issues)
- Child care services
- Legal services for child care, custody, separation/divorce issues

MODEL OF CORE COMPONENTS FOR COMPREHENSIVE ALCOHOL AND
OTHER DRUG TREATMENT OF ADOLESCENTS

The following core components are specific to treatment for adolescents (SAMHSA, 1993):

Outpatient (in descending order of importance):
- Intake
- Screening
- Assessment

- Group therapy
- Family therapy
- Individual therapy
- Case management
- Drug testing
- Didactic groups
- Emergency services
- Recreational activities and peer socialization
- Other specialized groups
- Discharge, continuing care, and relapse prevention
- Multifamily groups
- Psychiatric interventions and services for dually diagnosed individuals
- Self-help
- Detoxification services
- Intervention
- Home-based services
- Educational services (applicable to partial hospitalization and other programs that preclude attendance in school)

Inpatient (in descending order of importance):
- Engaging the Adolescent in Care—getting the adolescent past resistance to treatment
- Assessment—must have medical and health history and assessment, biopsychosocial assessment, educational and vocational assessment, psychiatric consultation and assessment where applicable, cultural assessment, spirituality assessment
- Protocol for Progression—there should be a clear description of the progression and stages of treatment provided to the adolescent and the family; criteria for success in each phase must be defined
- Individualized Treatment Plan
- A Need for Structure—programs for adolescents must establish structure or reestablish missing structure in their lives. In general, adolescents thrive with structure and clear expectations
- Dual-Diagnosis Capabilities—must be able to address disorders such as depression, borderline personality, eating disorders, suicidal ideation and attempts, and self-mutilation along with the addiction
- Detoxification Services—although acute abstinence syndromes are not as common among adolescents, there must be adequate assessment capability to determine whether detoxification is needed; and if the program is unable to provide detox, arrangements must be made with a hospital or other medical setting where this can take place
- Pharmacologic Interventions
- Arrangements With Medical Care Facilities—for intense medical procedures and care that might be needed
- Role Modeling—those clients who are settled and working within the structure should be given a visible role so that new clients coming in will have positive peers, mentors, and advocates
- Client Participation in Therapeutic Milieu—clients should be allowed to help run and maintain the facility as well as be given a role in decision making
- Family Involvement Program—as much as possible, parents or guardians and siblings should participate in the required phases of the adolescents treatment, because it is the single best indicator for adolescent success in residential treatment; the program

would include orientation, group therapy, and didactic educational sessions (family boundaries, healthy families, sexual abuse education and prevention, adolescent sexuality, adolescent alcoholism and addiction, intergenerational nature of addiction, the role of parent (guardian) and siblings in clients' addiction, understanding self-help group importance for support, communication skills, co-dependency)

- Group Therapy—necessary to allow adolescents the opportunity to identify those feelings that may be contributing to AOD use behavior. It is important to use an eclectic approach including behavioral psychoanalytic, communication, and reality therapy; issues to focus on would include self-concept, AOD use and abuse, feelings, life traumas (i.e., abuse, violence, poverty, deaths, losses, family dysfunction)
- Didactic and Educational Groups—numerous topics might be addressed including the disease concept, medical aspects, progression of addiction, effects of intergenerational nature of addictions, effects on family, importance of self-help groups, relapse prevention in adolescence, co-dependency, stress management, basic human sexuality (in separate groups), contraception, physical and sexual abuse, HIV/AIDS and other STDs, values clarification, and positive peer relationships
- School Program—all adolescents need to continue school while in treatment. Most states mandate it and it should include traditional academic work, vocational training, affective education, special education. Adolescents often enter the educational experience with existing deficits that must be assessed and remedied
- Self-help Meetings
- Recreational Program
- Transition, Continuing Care, Follow-up—continuing care should be provided for orderly transition from residence to community
- Confidentiality, and Communication With Referring Agency or Individual—within the limits of confidentiality, there needs to be continued communication with referring agencies and individuals so that they are knowledgeable about the adolescent's progress
- Legal Services—in view of the laws related to illegal drugs and the amount of crime and drug dealing adolescents find themselves involved in, there could be a tremendous need for this service
- Monitoring of Client Progress—there needs to be continued assessment of the progress of the client as required to modify his or her treatment plan. Each client should be monitored in every phase of program activity

Agencies in place at the federal level to deal with substance abuse and addiction prevention, treatment, and research, such as the Substance Abuse and Mental Health Services Administration, the National Institute on Drug Abuse, and the National Institute on Alcohol Abuse and Alcoholism, exist under the control of the U.S. Congress. Therefore, it is highly likely that in the future they may experience changes in name, function, and funding. However, whatever is produced by these organizations at the time of their existence is done with thoroughness, rigor, and integrity and based on research, which is the purpose for including work developed by them in this chapter.

THE ROLE OF NURSING IN INTERVENING AND TREATING ADDICTION

The macroenvironment in which nurses practice is one of change, upheaval, increasing conflict, confusion, global stress, and cultural, racial, and ethnic diversity. The addictions treatment field itself is a veritable supermarket of settings and treatment modalities, with each treatment modality competing for the limited resources and projecting itself as the best product in the market. Each addicted client is a microcosm of the macroenvironment, with diverse backgrounds and individual problems and needs. There is certainly no lack of clients or treatment intervention selections from which nurses may choose.

Any intervention with addicted clients that nurses choose to use inculcates the understanding of the importance of: 1) intervention/treatment matching—fitting the treatment to the client—including the possibility that the client's treatment goals may differ from the program's treatment goals (i.e., abstinence versus maintenance); 2) the occurrence of a comprehensive assessment that is gender, age, and culturally relevant in fitting the client to treatment; 3) knowledge of existing intervention and/or treatment environments that foster cross-cultural communication; and 4) that positive regard, inherent respect, and a healing belief in the potential of the client—rather than failure—exists.

Nurses' roles in intervening and treating addicted clients may take place by incorporating the above mentioned modalities and approaches in an already existing clinical setting to address client-specific needs, in which case the nurse is providing care to addicted clients. Or, the nurse's role may be as an addictions nurse specialist working specifically with addicted clients. Regardless of which direction is chosen, the dimensions of care and the standards of criteria for nursing care of these clients in the above discussed modalities and approaches should be based on the existing standards of care as developed by the American Nurses Association in conjunction with the addictions nursing specialty organization, the National Nurses Society on Addictions, because both would be considered addictions nursing.

Addictions Nursing

Addictions nursing is the specialty practice concerned with care related to dysfunctional patterns of human response to actual or potential health problems related to abuse and addiction. The nursing process—assessment, diagnoses, intervention (including treatment), and evaluation—provides the framework for using nursing strategies with clients and families/significant others (ANA, Drug and Alcohol Nurses Association (DANA), & NNSA, 1987).

Professional Practice Standards

Standards of Addictions Nursing Practice (ANA & NNSA, 1988) puts forth twelve professional practice standards that cover the areas of theory, data collection, diagnosis, planning, intervention, evaluation, ethical care, quality assurance, continuing education, interdisciplinary collaboration, use of community health systems, and research. Each nurse engaged in care of the addicted client has a responsibility to incorporate these standards in his or her practice.

Standard V—Intervention

This standard is of particular value in that it identifies the parameters of intervention (i.e., the nurse may act independently and/or in collaboration in the areas of prevention, intervention, and rehabilitation phases of treatment of clients with patterns of abuse and addiction). It also presents the approaches of therapeutic alliance, education, self-help groups, pharmacological therapies, therapeutic environment, and counseling that nurses may be involved with.

Areas of Practice

Areas of practice include direct clinical nursing care, health teaching, and interpersonal support in schools, community agencies, home care, acute care general hospitals, specialty hospitals, health maintenance organizations, social settings, detoxification facilities, halfway houses, and occupational health settings. Categories of nurses who may practice various levels or intensity of addictions nursing are the registered nurses in any health care setting, the generalists in addictions nursing, and the specialists in addictions nursing.

Thus, the target audience of nurses for this chapter includes generalists, addictions nurse specialist, and advanced practice nurses, as well as other health care providers. In addition, nursing care of addicted clients is not limited to the above definition, because since that definition was developed the field of addictions and care of addicted clients has expanded in such a way that the National Nurses Society on Addictions is revising the above Standards of Practice in an effort to update them.

The 1990 NNSA publication, "Core Curriculum of Addictions Nursing" identifies that nursing care of the addicted client occurs in primary, secondary, and tertiary prevention settings. Wherever the setting, whatever the circumstances, the nurse may "seize the opportunity" to intervene. The degree and nature of the intervention will depend on the setting, the expertise of the nurse, available resources, and certainly the specific, individual needs of the client.

The specific modalities and approaches to treatment were presented to let nurses know of methods for seizing the opportunity and treating addicted clients that they encounter. With the proper knowledge base from education and training, nurses can complete any of these interventions, didactic educational sessions, group therapy sessions, and function as case managers. Unfortunately, nurses are not routinely educated with this information at the undergraduate or graduate level, but that will have to change in view of the numbers of addicted clients that they encounter and the amount of money available for their care.

CONCLUSION

Consistent themes among policy makers in the health care reform movement are that 1) reform must produce savings in the health care system; and 2) addictions treatment is a health care add-on (a service that uses resources, but does not deliver benefits or positive returns) (Lagenbucher, 1994). The multiple goals, or outcomes of treatment, desired by society in providing treatment to the drug-addicted population, which are identified in a 1990 Institute of Medicine (IOM) report, include: 1) reducing the overall demand for illicit drugs; 2) reducing street crime; 3) developing educational or vocational capabilities within the treatment framework; 4) restoring or increasing employment or productivity; 5) improving the overall health, psychological functioning, and family life of the client; and 6) reducing fetal exposure to drug dependence.

Just as the study conducted by Tolley and Rowland (1991) proved that nurses were the preferred providers for screening, nurses are also effective in these interventions and treatments. Whether it takes place in one of the many clinical settings in which nurses work or whether it takes place in an addictions-specific setting, nurses will be found to strongly impact the achievement of these goals of treatment as desired by society, and documented by IOM. Therefore, *"Nurses should seize the opportunity"*!

REFERENCES

Adler, F., Moffett, A.D., Glaser, F.B., Ball, J.C., & Horvitz, D. (1974). *A systems approach to drug treatment.* Philadelphia: The Medical College of Pennsylvania.

American Nurses' Association, Drug and Alcohol Nursing Association, and National Nurses Society on Addictions. (1987). *The care of clients with addictions: Dimensions of nursing practice.* Kansas City, MO: American Nurses' Association.

American Nurses' Association & National Nurses Society on Addictions. (1988). *Standards of addictions nursing practice with selected diagnoses and criteria.* Kansas City, MO: American Nurses' Association.

Heather, N. (1989). Brief intervention strategies. In R.K. Hester & W.R. Miller (Eds.), *Handbook of alcoholism treatment approaches, effective alternatives* (pp. 93–116). New York: Pergamon Press.

Institute of Medicine. (1990). *Broadening the base of treatment for alcohol problems.* Washington, D.C.: National Academy Press.

Landry, M. (1994). *Understanding drugs of abuse: The processes of addiction, treatment, and recovery.* Washington, D.C.: American Psychiatric Press, Inc.

Langenbucher, J. (1994). Offsets are not add-ons: The place of addictions treatment in American health care reform. *Journal of Substance Abuse, 6,* 117–122.

Lewis, B.F., McCusker, J., Hindin, R., Frost, R., & Garfield, F. (1993). Four residential drug treatment programs: Project IMPACT. In J.A. Inciardi, F.M. Times, & B.W. Fletcher (Eds.), *Innovative approaches in the treatment of drug abuse, program models and strategies* (pp. 45–60). Westport, CT: Greenwood Press.

Lowinson, J., Marion, I., Joseph, H., & Dole, V. (1992). Methadone maintenance. In J.H. Lowinson, P. Ruiz, R.B. Millman, & J.G. Langrod (Eds.) *Substance abuse: A comprehensive textbook* (2nd ed.). Baltimore, MD: Williams & Wilkens.

Mejta, C. Monks, R., & Mickenberg, J. (1993). A case management model for intravenous drug users. In J.A. Inciardi, F.M. Times, & B.W. Fletcher (Eds.), *Innovative approaches in the treatment of drug abuse, program models and strategies* (pp. 87–96). Westport, CT: Greenwood Press.

Messalle, R. (Nov. 15, 1992). *Meeting the challenge: A judicial perspective on substance abuse and the role of the courts.* Presentation at Oakland, CA.

Milkman, H.B. (1991). Introduction. In H.B. Milkman, & L.I. Sederer (Eds.), *Treatment choices for alcoholism and substance abuse* (pp. xix–xxxii). New York: Lexington Books.

Musto, D.F. (1987) *The American disease, origins of narcotic control* (Expanded ed.). New York: Oxford University Press.

National Institute on Drug Abuse. (1991). *Drug abuse and drug abuse research.* Rockville, MD: National Institute on Drug Abuse.

National Nurses Society on Addictions (1990). *The core curriculum of addictions nursing.* Skokie, IL: Midwest Education Association, Inc.

Office of National Drug Control Policy. (June, 1990). *Understanding drug treatment* (A White Paper). Washington, D.C.: Office of National Drug Control Policy.

Pattison, E.M. (1985). The selection of treatment modalities for the alcoholic patient. In J.H. Mendelson, & N.K. Mello (Eds.), *The diagnosis & treatment of alcoholism* (pp. 189–294). New York: McGraw-Hill Book Company.

Shaffer, H.J. (1990) Prologue. In H.B. Milkman, & L.I. Sederer (Eds.), *Treatment choices for alcoholism and substance abuse* (pp. 249–252). New York: Lexington Books.

State of California. (1994) *Evaluating recovery services; The California drug and alcohol treatment assessment (CALDATA).* Executive summary.

Substance Abuse and Mental Health Services Administration; Center for Substance Abuse Treatment Adolescent Treatment Branch. (1993). *Guidelines for the treatment of alcohol and other drug abusing adolescents.* DHHS Publication No. (SMA) 93-2010. Rockville, MD: Substance Abuse and Mental Health Services Administration.

Substance Abuse and Mental Health Services Administration; Center for Substance Abuse Treatment. (1994a). *Treatment for alcohol and other drug abuse: Opportunities for coordination.* DHHS Publication No. (SMA) 94-2075. Rockville, MD: Substance Abuse and Mental Health Services Administration.

Substance Abuse and Mental Health Services Administration; Center for Substance Abuse Treatment Women and Children's Branch. (1994b). *Practical approaches in the treatment of women who abuse alcohol and other drugs.* DHHS Publication No. (SMA) 93-3006. Rockville, MD: Substance Abuse and Mental Health Services Administration.

Tarter, R.E., & Schneider, D.U. (1976). Models and theories of alcoholism. In R.E. Tarter, & A.A. Sugerman (Eds.), *Alcoholism, interdisciplinary approaches to an enduring problem* (pp. 75–106). Reading, MA: Addison-Wesley Publishing Company.

Tolley, K., & Rowland, N. (1991). Identification of alcohol-related problems in a general hospital setting: A cost-effectiveness evaluation. *British Journal of Addiction, 86*(4), 429–438.

U.S. Department of Health and Human Services. (December, 1992). *SAMHSA News: ADAMHA Reorganization.* Rockville, MD: U.S. Department of Health and Human Services.U.S. Department of Health and Human Services. (1994). *Secretary of Health and Human Services eighth special report to the U.S. Congress on alcohol and health.* NIH Publication No. 94-3699. Rockville, MD: U.S. Department of Health and Human Services.

Witters, W., Venturelli, P., & Hanson, G. (1992). *Drugs and society* (3rd ed.). Boston: Jones and Bartlett Publishers, Inc.

Zinberg, N.E., & Fraser, K.M. (1985). The role of the social setting in the prevention and treatment of alcoholism. In J.H. Mendelson & N.K. Mello (Eds.) *The diagnosis and treatment of alcoholism* (pp. 457–483). New York: McGraw-Hill Book Company.

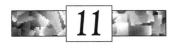

Sobriety-Focused Care

Karen M. Allen, PhD, RN, CARN

INTRODUCTION

"Addiction is a brain disease expressed in behavioral ways within a social context" (Leshner, 1994). Drug addiction and alcoholism are the result of complex interactions between biological, psychological, and sociocultural factors.

However, in spite of our increased understanding of addiction through modern scientific advances, there is still no simple answer for this problem, in that certain vulnerabilities in individuals who are biologically susceptible, perpetuate addictive disorders. Therefore, the goal of sobriety-focused care, as well as relapse prevention, should be to develop the resources necessary for an individual to manage or modify the vulnerabilities that perpetuate his or her addiction.

Studies of lifelong patterns of recovery and relapse indicate that approximately one third of clients achieve permanent abstinence through their first serious attempt at recovery. Another third have brief relapse episodes that eventually result in long-term abstinence. And an additional one-third have chronic relapses that result in eventual recovery from addiction (Gorski, Kelley, & Havens, 1993).

According to the Institute of Medicine (1990), cycling one or more times from recovery back through relapse to dependence or abuse is so common that it must be seen as an intrinsic feature of the natural history of individual drug behavior. Therefore, it is best to view clients as being either prone to recovery, briefly prone to relapse, or chronically prone to relapse. Furthermore, those who are relapse-prone can be divided into three subgroups (Substance Abuse and Mental Health Services Administration (SAMHSA), 1994):

- Transition clients—those who do not accept or recognize that they are suffering from addiction although it has created obvious adverse consequences; this usually is a result of the client's inability to perceive the reality of the problem due to denial.

- Unstabilized relapse-prone clients—those who have not been taught skills to identify their addiction; they have not been provided with the necessary skills to interrupt the process and therefore, are unable to adhere to a recovery program requiring either treatment, abstinence, and/or a lifestyle change.
- Stabilized clients—those who recognize and are aware of their addiction, know that an ongoing recovery program is required, and despite their efforts develop dysfunctional symptoms that ultimately lead them back to active alcohol or other drug (AOD) use.

Because relapse is a common occurrence during the process of addictions recovery, and a very relevant issue for sobriety-focused care, it is important that health care providers be informed about its relevant aspects. Therefore, the purpose of this chapter is to examine the biological, psychological, and sociocultural issues that impact on sobriety and contribute to relapse. In addition, the discussion in this chapter addresses pertinent issues related to the care of persons recovering from an addiction that health care providers need to be aware of to promote appropriate sobriety-focused care.

DEFINITIONS AND DESCRIPTION OF RELAPSE

The long-standing definition and description of relapse used most in the clinical setting is that posited about a decade ago by Gorski and Miller (1986). They provided an in-depth perspective on relapse when they stated it was "the sobriety-based disease" of addiction. The symptoms of the addiction do not stop with abstinence, they extend into sobriety and take a vicious toll while the person is attempting to recover. Gorski and Miller stated that this sobriety-based side of addiction is as powerful and destructive as the AOD use side.

Relapse is a term with many negative connotations. The derivation of the word is Latin, *relabi,* which means "to slip" or "to fall back." In medical language, relapse usually refers to a recurrence of the disease after a period of improvement (Marlatt, 1995).

Slips are sometimes referred to as "lapses" and denote an episode of using alcohol and other drugs during recovery. This is short in duration and may occur once or a few times. Whereas a full relapse is the return to a continued use of alcohol or other drugs during a time of recovery.

Neither a lapse nor a relapse takes place "suddenly," but happens after a return to two things: 1) relapse-prone thinking (reactivation of denial, isolation, impaired judgment and decision-making, and poor coping with periods of stress); and 2) placing oneself in high-risk situations.

Between a single lapse and a total relapse, a wide range of "in-between" responses or patterns have been identified, and not all lapses end in total relapse. There are some people who respond to a lapse as a warning signal or discriminative cue for renewed coping efforts, and thus, it is viewed as an error or mistake that calls for learning new coping strategies. However, for others abstinence is an all-or-none phenomenon, and, therefore, a lapse is the same as a relapse (Marlatt, 1995).

BIOPSYCHOSOCIAL ANTECEDENTS OF RELAPSE

Although many models for explaining the phenomenon of relapse exist, most tend to focus on "one" particular tenet that impacts on relapse.

In view of the fact that research has provided evidence of the combined biopsychosocial cause of addiction, it seems prudent to begin to view causes for relapse from that perspective as well. This would allow for a thorough approach to providing sobriety-focused care.

Biological Issues

Research shows that prolonged exposure to drugs leads to molecular adaptations in certain proteins found within neurons in the mesolimbic dopamine system—a brain pathway that is important for drug reward and craving. Long-term adaptations in these proteins caused by chronic drug use may contribute to such aspects of addiction as: 1) tolerance, 2) sensitization, 3) reinforcement, and 4) the compulsion to continue using a drug to achieve a desired effect (National Institute on Drug Abuse [NIDA], 1994). In addition, this research suggests that genetics contribute substantially to individual differences in vulnerability to drug addiction.

This is significant when providing care to an addicted client in the sobriety-focused phase. Along with biologically based postacute withdrawal symptoms that the client is experiencing (sleep disturbances, dizziness, trouble with balance, hand and eye coordination, slow reflexes, and accident proneness) (Gorski & Miller, 1986), there is now evidence that at the molecular level in the brain the compulsion to use AOD continues long-term during attempts at recovery and sobriety. Some specific examples include the findings that clear biochemical and functional changes occur in the brain of cocaine addicts, which may account for the compulsive, nonvolitional drug taking. Studies show that long-lasting decreases in the number of brain dopamine D2 receptors are associated with reduced brain activity in areas of the brain that control repetitive and impulsive behaviors (NIDA, 1994).

Biological forces exist that directly impact on an addict's ability to recover and maintain a program of sobriety. This is particularly pertinent when working with the "stabilized client" as described above, who does everything required and still relapses. Now it can be seen that the relapse may be due to an unaddressed biological phenomenon ongoing in the brain. In addition, psychological issues are influencing relapse.

Psychological Issues

According to Gorski (1990) the role of personal distress precipitated by distressing emotions, painful memories, irrational thoughts, serious life problems, chronic/daily stress and physical pain, without strong and consistently applied coping skills, will lead to emotional collapse. In turn, this results in use of AOD for relief.

On the other hand, addiction results in "emotional overreaction" that is very evident during recovery and work on sobriety. Researchers have documented that emotional symptoms when entering treatment for addictions were as high as levels of emotional symptomatology among newly diagnosed psychiatric clients, and these declined slowly, approaching normal levels after years of sobriety. The higher the level of emotional symptoms the rockier the recovery and the higher the level of relapse rate (Eells, 1991).

In the CATOR (Comprehensive Alcohol Treatment Outcomes Research) study, clients listed boredom, anger, loneliness and depression, relationship or family problems, and craving as most frequent antecedents of relapse. Other psychological influences on relapse include: physical or psychological reminders of past drug or alcohol use; desires to test personal control over drug or alcohol use; and recurrent thoughts or physical desires to use drugs or alcohol (Peters, 1993). In addition, Joe, Simpson, and Hubbard (1991) and McLellan, Grissom, Brill, Durell, Metzger, and O'Brien (1993) conducted research showing that comorbid psychiatric diagnoses contributed significantly to relapse rates.

Social Issues

Inadequate skills to deal with socioenvironmental pressure to use AODs, frequent exposure to high-risk situations that have led to use in the past, dysfunctional families, and lack of social support are a few of the many social aspects that influence relapse. Joe and colleagues (1991) also documented lack of family and other unmet social needs as contributing greatly to relapse.

Research shows that environmental stimuli may elicit "learned" drug withdrawal, craving and euphoria even in the absence of physiological addiction (Childress, McLellan, and O'Brien, 1986; O'Brien, Childress, McLellan, & Ehrman, 1990). Thus, learned responses contribute to continued drug use or to relapse.

In view of the biopsychosocial forces impinging on the recovery status of addicted persons, it is imperative that aftercare be provided to addicted clients. This would contribute to prevention of relapse so that sobriety would remain the focus of care rather than active addiction, and the client can continue progressing on the road to recovery.

PHASES OF RECOVERY

Recovery takes place in four phases (Landry, 1994). Phase one is biopsychosocial restabilization. Here the person begins to eat a healthy diet, sleeps more normally, exercises and increases physical activity, learns communication skills, learns problem-solving techniques, discusses the desire and craving for drugs, and learns stress reduction techniques.

Phase two is post-treatment restructuring. Here the person has external motivation for recovery: approval of others provides positive feedback central to self-esteem development.

Phase three is mature recovery. At this level there is an increasingly sobriety-centered lifestyle, along with a restructuring of one's personality. People begin to internalize certain values and guidelines they are exposed to in self-help groups, group therapy, and education during aftercare. Also during this time, people are making serious attempts to restore balance in their social and family relationships. Friendships with other recovering people become particularly important. In essence a new lifestyle is created.

Phase four is late recovery, which may begin a year or two after intervention or treatment. During this period a person experiences personality growth by resolving long-standing psychological issues. Earlier periods are concerned with behavioral changes and establishing healthy values, philosophies, and traits. Late recovery deals with self-esteem, intimacy, and other psychological problems. Landry (1994) further states that it is critical to understand that recovery from addiction is a process and not an event. This is why aftercare is of utmost importance. It provides sobriety-focused care to the client in a positive manner, rather than providing addiction-focused care, then leaving the client on his or her own to recover and be sober.

AFTERCARE

A system of comprehensive care includes a continuum of services that are available to clients and directed at their specific risk factors. Aftercare can be any service or services that follow and reinforce treatment and provide a continuum of care for clients as they return to family and community. Family involvement in the recovery process is often invaluable.

Education and involvement of the larger community can also be extremely valuable. To survive the pressures and stresses of life without drugs or alcohol, recovering addicts must learn to make sensible decisions, cope with stressors, resist peer pressure, and to quote an old 12-step adage, "live life on life's terms." These are skills many of us take for granted, skills most people do not even have to think about.

Because relapse occurs most frequently soon after treatment, many aftercare programs encourage early and frequent participation in self-help groups to help maintain abstinence, build a new lifestyle, and develop a social support group based on sobriety.

Many have criticized 12-step fellowships because they have received very little scientific evaluation. According to Kurtz (1993), although no major formal study has been conducted, various limited ones (mostly in dissertations) have been completed. As a result, only rudimentary data have been collected on these groups, because members guardedly follow a long-standing tradition of anonymity. However, if one were reminded of the important inroads made by science through qualitative methods, it would be clear that conducting content analysis of the comments made by speakers at open meetings or in discussions about their "stories" of success, would be acceptable research of the effectiveness of 12-step meetings.

Quantitative research has been hard to conduct mostly due to anonymity that is stressed as a requirement for this fellowship. However, anonymity has a number of useful features. Perhaps the most important feature is that it allows newcomers to the fellowship to feel safe from being ostracized or stigmatized by society, and therefore, less reluctant to participate. Furthermore, newcomers are generally in a state of denial and possibly resistant to help of any kind. They may not yet be fully cognizant of, or have admitted to, the depth and severity of their problems. Without the element of anonymity that 12-step participation provides, it would be extremely difficult, if not impossible, to persuade many of these individuals to participate at any level.

Alcoholics Anonymous (A.A.), Cocaine Anonymous (C.A.) and Narcotics Anonymous (N.A.) are fellowships of people who share their experience and derive strength and hope from each other so that they can help themselves and others recover from their addiction. During the 60 years since its founding in 1935, A.A. has been a mainstay of addiction recovery and relapse prevention.

These "Twelve-Step" fellowships hold an intuitive core belief that drug-addicted individuals are vulnerable to all drugs and not just the drug they are dependent on at the moment. Furthermore, members believe that an alcoholic or drug-addicted person is "always recovering and never recovered."

In 12-step fellowships, recovery is often described as a period of remission from disease. For those who view recovery in this light, complete addiction may return with any break in abstinence. Many individuals in recovery who are involved in 12-step programs, view themselves as having a temporary "reprieve" from the illness. This view necessitates an understanding that "controlled" drinking or drug use is not an option; there is no ability to control or gain control of substance use. Thus, a primary goal of this philosophy is abstinence.

It is important to note that some experts and lay persons do not believe that total abstinence is the goal for sobriety. Now some researchers are looking to see if some alcoholics can cut back on drinking without abstaining altogether, and if recovering alcoholics can safely go back to drinking at a moderate level. In response to this thought, the Center for Alcohol Studies at Rutgers University, NJ, recently established a treatment program to help alcohol abusers reduce their drinking through brief interventions (Contemporary Sexuality, 1995). Therefore, it is clear to see that use of relapse prevention techniques can also be helpful in meeting the goal of "cutting back" if the client does not wish to abstain.

The A.A., C.A., and N.A. meetings are not instructional in nature, nor does "therapy" take place. Participants speak about their own experience, strength, and hope and how they were able to overcome or learn to live with their problems. Each new participant chooses what to make of the information provided. Members tell their personal "stories," which include: what their lives were like before recovery, what happened to get them there, and what they are like today.

Social support and continued contact with a supportive environment such as aftercare programs, services and counseling, and/or participation in a 12-step fellowship, are critical components of sobriety-focused care. Their focus is how to support the client in a continued quest for recovery and sobriety. Unfortunately, the complexities of timing and conditions necessary for recovery often seem overwhelming to the addict. Furthermore, the social issues that they are faced with drain energy resources as well as desire necessary for recovery.

In general, relapse can best be understood as a progressive process, a transition between sobriety and active addiction. The continued use of drugs will lead to physical and/or psychological distress, which will lead the addicted person to health care providers.

Here it is crucial for the health care provider—particularly nurses—to understand that the relapse process can be interrupted. At that point, the health care provider must be available to these clients at the most vulnerable moments in their lives. Moments when they are open to change and self-evaluation. Hence, this is a window of opportunity that nurses in any clinical setting can use to provide an intervention to clients—prevention.

RELAPSE PREVENTION

Thoughts on Relapse Prevention

Relapse prevention teaches addicts new ways to identify and handle cravings and temptations, and how to make lifestyle changes that support drug-free living, because relapse is often the result of simply not knowing how to prevent it. In addition, relapse prevention emphasizes teaching recovering persons to recognize and manage relapse warning signs (Peters, 1993).

Relapse prevention approaches seek to maintain changes in attitudes and behavior that support recovery. Hopefully, these changes have altered the factors that reinforce or condition the abuse response. Other strategies seek to strengthen interpersonal and relationship skills that will help overcome family and social situations that may have contributed to the drug abuse in the first place.

Eliminating or decreasing drug use is only one indicator of potential long-term success. Improving physical and mental health status and addressing environmental factors and social problems will reduce the likelihood of relapse as well. Simply getting individuals off drugs will enhance their ability to take care of themselves, find a job, and will reduce medical and health problems associated with addiction. In addition, specific assistance concerning life skills and how to access resources and services, such as medical and mental health care, employment skills, educational and vocational training opportunities, and available social services, will enhance the ability of these persons to avoid relapse.

Relapse prevention strategies currently under investigation include community reinforcement, contingency management, motivational enhancement, operant behavioral research, and extinction training. Coupling certain behavioral treatments with traditional treatment methods may prove helpful in diminishing relapse rates.

It is important that an addict be motivated by internal factors to stay in recovery and learn relapse prevention skills. However, given client problems and resource limitations, even the most motivated client may be able to achieve only limited improvements, particularly if psychological impairment or severe emotional instability is present. Even when an optimal outcome is not achieved, incremental improvements may be extremely meaningful given individual and resource limitations.

On the other hand, many people have entered recovery because of entirely external motivations. The criminal justice system has forced many to seek help and, for some, this has been successful. The longer a person remains in a system of care, the greater the likelihood of long-term positive results.

Relapse prevention strategies, like treatment itself, are not uniformly effective for all people. Therefore, a couple of different types of intervention strategies will be discussed.

Gorski et al. (1993) stated that as the client's capacity to self-regulate thinking, feeling, memory, judgment, and behavior increases, the risk of relapse will decrease. Self-regulation can be achieved through stabilization, which may be: 1) detoxification from alcohol and other drugs; 2) recuperation from the effects of stress that preceded the alcohol and other drug use; 3) resolution of immediate interpersonal and situational crises that threaten sobriety or establishment of a daily structure including proper diet, exercise, stress management, and regular contact with both treatment personnel and self-help groups. During this period, the risk of relapse is highest.

Gorski and colleagues also stated that as understanding and acceptance increase, the risk of relapse will decrease. Therefore, the role of nurses in addressing relapse prevention is quite clear in that necessary relapse prevention strategies provide care during sobriety that helps clients maintain their recovery.

The beginning premise of relapse prevention is that, ultimately, the addicted person must sustain their own recovery. Thus, to be an appropriate candidate for an aftercare relapse prevention program clients should have achieved several objectives: 1) clients must have been stabilized physically as well as psychologically and achieved a period of abstinence or decreased use; 2) clients must acknowledge their chemical addiction to alcohol and other drugs, and clarify their goal of reduction in use or abstinence; 3) clients must be motivated to work on a long-term program of lifestyle change; and 4) clients must also have eliminated or reduced the most significant contributors to their recent drug use, such as psychological distress or physical pain (DeJong, 1994).

Relapse Prevention Strategies

It is important to remember that relapse is not only the actual return to the pattern of AOD use, it also is a process during which indicators appear prior to the client's resumption of alcohol and other drug use. Hence, one of the most important relapse prevention strategies for nurses and other health care providers is to be able to identify predisposing and precipitating factors and events of relapse that exist for their clients.

Predisposing factors for interruption of sobriety and recovery are relevant for adolescents and adults, and include (SAMHSA, 1994): 1) learning disabilities, 2) dual or multiple diagnoses, 3) high stress personalities, 4) inadequate coping skills, 5) lack of a support system, 6) dysfunctional families, and 7) lack of impulse control. Precipitating factors that interrupt an adolescent's ability to work through recovery and stay sober include (SAMHSA, 1994): 1) a disruption in the main caregivers (divorce, separation of parents); 2) moving away from old friends; 3) changing schools; 4) loss or death of family members; and 5) breakup of relationship with a boyfriend or girlfriend.

It is important to keep precipitating factors in perspective when dealing with varying socioeconomic and cultural groups. Thus, other real precipitating factors in the lives of some adolescents may include: 1) episodes of violence; 2) inability to secure a job that would contribute to increased self-esteem and lead to the ability to change a lifestyle and friends; 3) the jailing of a parent or custodian; and 4) severe losses of families and friends through AIDS and other drug-related illnesses. Precipitating factors for adults could be any myriad of events and vary for women and men.

On this basis, it becomes imperative that nurses assess on a continuous basis addicted clients to determine where they are on the continuum of recovery and relapse.

Gorski, Kelley, and Havens (1993) recommended the following relapse prevention approaches:

- Provide basic information including but not limited to:
  — Complicating factors in relapse
  — Identification of warning signs of relapse
  — Management strategies for the warning signs
  — How to develop an effective plan for recovery
- Self-knowledge related to identification of warning signs:
  — This intervention involves having clients identify the sequence of problems that has led from stable recovery to resumption of AOD use in the past, then having them synthesize those steps into future circumstances that could cause relapse
- Coping skills and warning sign management:
  — This intervention involves teaching clients how to manage or cope with warning signs as they occur using the clients' own coping skills and mechanisms, and if the clients have none, helping them obtain some
- Awareness and inventory training:
  — During this intervention, relapse-prone clients are taught to do daily inventories that monitor compliance with their plan for recovery, as well as check for developing relapse warning signs
- Significant other involvement:
  — During the process of recovery, support from others is important as well as necessary, clients should identify who their support system. It can include family, significant others, self-help group members, social services, parole officers, whoever gives the client positive support.
- Maintenance and relapse prevention plan updating:
  — This intervention involves a session wherein the client reviews the original warning sign list, management strategies, and recovery plan and the health care provider can update the relapse assessment by adding an addendum to any document that is significant to the client's progress or problems since the previous update. A revision of relapse warning signs to incorporate new warning signs that have developed since the previous update can take place. The development of management strategies for the newly identified warning signs can be discussed and a revision of the recovery program to add recovery activities that would address the new warning signs and eliminate activities that are no longer needed.

DeJong (1994) discussed relapse prevention strategies by the broad categories that they represent. Three major strategies that are common to current relapse prevention programs include: 1) cognitive-behavioral approaches (to avoid relapse when cravings occurs; and containing, interpreting, and learning from any lapses that do occur); 2) social support approaches (to explore the need for emotional support from family members and close friends); and 3) lifestyle change approaches (developing new social identities as drug-free individuals). These three strategies, as outlined by DeJong (1994) are presented below:

1. Cognitive-behavioral approaches
   - Identifying relapse cues by reviewing past relapses or recording when and under what circumstance drug urges are felt
   - Be alert to warning signs including: emotions (negative feelings, boredom), thoughts (negative self statements, preoccupation with using drugs, a belief that alcohol or

drugs are needed to have fun), and behaviors (erratic behavior, a return to behavior patterns that accompanied previous drug use
- Avoid high-risk situations (people, places and things that lead to relapse, including setting up "tests" of ability to resist temptation). It is important to note here that because of some peoples socioeconomic status, it is impossible for them to remove themselves from a drug-infested home environment, which makes it difficult to avoid people, places, and things that precipitate relapse. Therefore, it would be imperative for the health care provider to talk with the client about creative mechanisms for avoiding high-risk situations while remaining in the environment
- Coping with unavoidable high-risk situations: contact with drug-users and dealers, unstructured time, stressful work demands, throwing away drug paraphernalia, using relaxation skills, repeating motivational statements aloud, writing down thoughts and feelings in a journal, calling a sponsor. Clients need to understand that their cravings are not a sign of failure, but the result of automatic processes beyond their control; in addition if not followed by drug use, they will diminish over time
- Successfully manage lapses. This would involve the steps of: 1) first stopping drug use after the initial lapse, removing oneself from the situation, calling someone for support; and 2) analyze what happened and what they can learn from their experience. The health care providers' role is to teach the client how people normally react to a lapse, and how to view it as an isolated failure.

2. Social Support Approaches
- Encourage clients to take an active role in structuring beneficial social support. Of major importance here is establishing new relationships through a "buddy system" or self-help groups. Good social support provides: modeling desired behaviors, creating a supportive interpersonal environment, eliminating or helping the addict avoid or cope with sources of stress, praising and encouraging self-praise for continued progress. The health care provider can also do relapse prevention by teaching the addicts' significant others about the above supportive techniques. Also included in this aspect of relapse prevention is teaching the client social skills in avoiding drug use at social gatherings, interpersonal problem-solving, etc.

3. Lifestyle Change Approaches
- Extrication from a drug-using subculture and environment and accommodation to living in "conventional" society. This intervention calls for the health care provider connecting the client up with resources for remedial education, job training, vocational counseling, life skills training (budgeting, decision-making), etc. Also the client needs to be taught about developing rewarding alternatives to drug use: healthy recreational activities, relaxation strategies and others.

4. Other Strategies
- Cue extinction involves techniques of exposing the recovering person to alcohol and other drug-related stimuli, until the stimuli gradually lose the power to evoke the conditioned response. Examples include showing slides or videotapes of local "copping" sites and shooting galleries, drug paraphernalia, advertisements of alcohol, and audiotapes of other addicts talking about drugs. It is not recommended that this method be use by itself because of the craving it evokes.
- Pharmacotherapies are beginning to be used more frequently as an approach to relapse prevention. For years methadone has proven to be an effective strategy—in conjunction with individual and group therapy—for some heroin addicts in

maintaining their recovery program. Recently, research showed an increase in preventing relapse among alcoholics with the use of naltrexone and therefore, the Food and Drug Administration (FDA) approved it for use under the name Revia for that purpose. Researchers are now working to determine whether there is a drug that can be used to address cocaine addiction in the same manner as the above two drugs. Although abstinence is the important goal for sobriety, it is necessary to remember that antecedents for relapse occur within a "biochemical" realm as well as a psychosocial realm. Thus, pharmacotherapies that are nonaddicting that help with relapse prevention for a short period of time are useful to the clients' recovery.

- Dealing with postacute withdrawal. It has been well documented that postacute withdrawal symptoms persist for years into recovery. A very real intervention that needs to take place in relapse prevention—which the nurse is the key person for doing—is addressing postacute withdrawal with clients. Acknowledging that these symptoms exist, and that clients will indeed experience them helps relieve clients of the sense that something is wrong with them. It also helps them to understand what is going on, know what to expect, and look to the nurse to provide direction in ways to deal with these symptoms before they lead to relapse.

It is important to note that because addiction is a biopsychosocial process, relapse prevention needs to be addressed from that perspective as well. Therefore, while the above preventions strategies are all good, they are probably only effective in combination with each other. If one addresses relapse prevention from the cognitive perspective, regardless of the emotional or psychological issues going on, relapse is sure to occur. By the same token, if biological/biochemical factors that impact on relapse are ignored, relapse is sure to occur. If focus is placed on social support and lifestyle change, and physiological (biological) postacute withdrawal symptoms are allowed to escalate unaddressed, relapse is sure to occur.

As shown in the program developed by McAuliffe (1990) effectiveness of relapse prevention increases with the combination of strategies. Some strategies may be more effective than others with a particular person for a particular reason. For example, if a combination of strategies from all the above mentioned approaches is used, persons with cognitive deficits from their addiction will not experience frustration because the cognitive approach used alone did not work. It is important to keep in mind that certain strategies for relapse prevention might be more effective among certain ethnic groups. No studies have been done to date on which strategies work best among which ethnic groups. A good approach to take would be to determine as much from a cultural perspective from your clients. Get to know who clients and their backgrounds. They may not like to write, therefore, suggesting that they keep a journal of some sort is not going to be an effective relapse prevention strategy. If story telling, poetry, songs, dance, or art is a strong feature of your clients, use that as a vehicle for addressing the above relapse warning signs, needed coping mechanism, and recovery plans.

CONCLUSION

Relapse is the sobriety-based aspect of addiction. Therefore, nurses need to understand the importance of sobriety-focused care, rather than addressing active addiction only. Sobriety-focused care means working with the clients to continue their sobriety and recovery through active prevention of relapse.

Relapse prevention programs focus on developing new skills, handling high-risk situations, identifying warning signs, making positive lifestyle changes, increasing healthy activities, and developing cognitive and behavioral coping strategies to help prevent relapse. Relapse is a process as well as an event and involves risk factors that can be recognized early on in the process. Cravings and cues can often be avoided, and coping strategies can be learned to help individuals deal with cravings when avoidance is not possible. Understanding how to deal with social pressures and negative moods and emotions, and how to interrupt a relapse, are important tools for recovery. These skills appear to help prevent relapse as well as decrease the severity and duration of relapse when it occurs.

REFERENCES

Alcoholics Anonymous. *Grapevine*. New York, NY: The AA Grapevine, Inc.

Childress, A.R., McLellan, A.T., & O'Brien, C.P. (1986). Abstinent opiate abusers exhibit conditioned craving, conditioned withdrawal, and reductions in both through extinction. *British Journal of the Addictions 81*, 701–706.

DeJong, W. (1994). Relapse prevention: An emerging technology for promoting long-term drug abstinence. *The International Journal of the Addictions, 29*(6), 681–705.

Editorial Staff. (July, 1995). Studies in short: Moderate drinking suggested as a way to treat alcohol abuse. *Contemporary Sexuality, 29*(7), 6–7.

Eells, M.A. (1991). Strategies for promotion of avoiding harmful substances. *Nursing Clinics of North America, 26*(4), 915–927.

Gorski, T. (1990). The CENAPS model of relapse prevention: Basic principles and procedures. *Journal of Psychoactive Drugs, 22*, 125–133.

Gorski, T., Kelley, J., & Havens, L. (1993). An overview of addiction, relapse and relapse prevention. In *Relapse prevention and the substance-abusing criminal offender. An executive briefing*. (Technical Assistance Publication Series 8). Rockville, MD: Substance Abuse and Mental Health Services Administration, Center for Substance Abuse Treatment.

Gorski, T., & Miller, M. (1986). *Staying sober: A guide for relapse prevention*. Independence, MO: Herald House/Independence Press.

Hubbard, R.L., Marsden, M.E., & Rachal, J.V. (1989). *Drug abuse treatment: A national study of effectiveness*. Chapel Hill, NC: University of North Carolina Press, 1989.

Institute of Medicine. (1990). *Treating drug problems*. Volume 1. Washington, D.C.: National Academy Press.

Joe, G., Simpson, D., & Hubbard, R. (1991). Unmet service needs in methadone maintenance. *The International Journal of the Addictions, 26*(1), 1–22.

Kurtz, E. (1993). Research on Alcoholics Anonymous: The historical context. In B.S. McCrady, & W.R. Miller (Eds.), *Research on Alcoholics Anonymous: Opportunities and alternatives*. Brunswick, NJ: Publication Division, Rutgers Center of Alcohol Studies.

Landry, M. (1994). *Understanding drugs of abuse: The processes of addiction, treatment, and recovery*. Washington, D.C.: American Psychiatric Press, Inc.

Leshner, A. (1994). *Drug abuse and addiction research: Opportunities for progress in 1995*. Opening remarks, College on Problems of Drug Dependence.

Marlatt, G.A. (1995) Relapse: A cognitive-behavioral model. In K.D. Brownell and C.G. Fairburn (Eds.) *Eating disorders and obesity: A comprehensive handbook* (pp. 541–546). New York: The Guilford Press.

McAuliffe, W. (1990). A randomized controlled trial of recovery training and self-help opioid addicts in New England and Hong Kong. *Journal of Psychoactive Drugs, 22*, 197–209.

McLellan, T., Grissom, R., Brill, P., Durell, J., Metzger, D., & O'Brien, C. (1993). Private substance abuse treatments: Are some programs more effective than others? *Journal of Substance Abuse Treatment, 10*, 243–254.

National Institute on Drug Abuse. (Sept/Oct, 1994). *NIDA Notes*. Special Section: NIDA reflects on 20 years of neuroscience research. NIDA.

O'Brien, C.P., Childress, A.R., McLellan, T., & Ehrman, R. (1990). Integrating systematic cue exposure with standard treatment in recovering drug dependent patients. *Addictive Behaviors 15*, 355–365.

Peters, R. (1993). Relapse prevention approaches in the criminal justice system. In *Relapse prevention and the substance abusing criminal offender. An executive briefing*. Technical Assistance Publication Series 8. Rockville, MD: Substance Abuse and Mental Health Services Administration, Center for Substance Abuse Treatment.

Substance Abuse and Mental Health Services Administration, Center for Substance Abuse Treatment. (1994). Relapse Prevention. In *Treatment for alcohol and other drug abuse: Opportunities for coordination*. DHHS Publication No. (SMA) 94-2075. Rockville, MD: Substance Abuse and Mental Health Services Administration.

Evaluating the Effectiveness of Nursing Care

Mary Ann Eells, EdD, RN, CS
Elaine Feeney, BSN, RNC

INTRODUCTION

Evaluation that focuses on the effectiveness of interventions is known as assessment of treatment/intervention outcomes. Evaluation of intervention and treatment outcomes for care of addicted clients should be designed to answer six basic questions (National Institute on Alcohol Abuse and Alcoholism [NIAAA], 1992): Is treatment better than no treatment? Is treatment worse than no treatment? Is one treatment better than another? If treatment is effective, is a little just as good as a lot? Does quality of life change because substance abuse has changed? Are the benefits of treatment worth the cost? To answer these questions for nursing, every treatment intervention nurses render needs to be evaluated for effectiveness.

To date, however, there are no well-designed evaluation studies of the effectiveness of nursing care provided to addicted clients with regard to outcomes. Nursing is not alone in this regard. There has been a general failure to measure the effectiveness of any type of professional care provided to addicted clients. Until recently, "evaluation" consisted of a cursory assessment as to whether clients completing treatment programs had maintained abstinence for a month or so, postdischarge from 28-day inpatient treatment programs. How much longer abstinence lasted or what particular interventions worked, if any, remained unknown.

Not having interventions and treatment for addictions with known effectiveness has become intolerable in a climate of skyrocketing costs for all health care. As a result, drastic cost cutting has been imposed by managed care, and severe limits placed on the utilization of professional services for treating addictive disorders.

Driving forces for health care reform continue to transform health care delivery from an unfettered fee-for-service system to a heavily managed care system. As pressures to 1) cut cost, 2) decrease services utilized, and 3) provide interventions and treatment dictated by price have increased, concerns about intervention and treatment adequacy have emerged. Hence, professionals have responded by developing solutions such as placement criteria and treatment guidelines. Evaluation must respond to these changes and assess whether they have improved the quality and nature of expected outcomes, and consequently, effectiveness, because health care reform and its demands for accountability highlight the need for good evaluation in the field of addictions.

In the context of this current health care reality, nurses need a survival guide for evaluating the effectiveness of care provided to addicted clients. To that end, the intent of this chapter is to 1) clarify for the reader the emergent issues in evaluation, and 2) introduce a proactive approach useful for evaluating the effectiveness of nursing interventions and treatment with addicted clients.

WHAT IS EVALUATION?

Given the various types of evaluation that nurses encounter, there is a need for conceptual clarity on the basic definitions, purposes, and procedures for evaluation. The basic purpose of evaluation is to determine what works best. According to Rossi and Freeman (1993), evaluation research is an activity that includes the collection and analysis of information for the purpose of determining the need for interventions, their effectiveness, or their efficiency in accomplishing their purpose.

The Substance Abuse and Mental Health Services Administration (SAMHSA)(1994) authors, in agreement with Rossi and Freeman, view evaluation as a word having considerable variations in meaning—depending on the context in which it is applied. In its most general use, it includes gathering and analyzing information concerning an individual, program, group of programs, or other entities. It is useful in:

- Determining whether or not program objectives or individual intervention and treatment goals have been met
- Planning and making decisions about individuals or program elements based on appraisals of achievements compared to goals and objectives
- Monitoring standards of performance
- Generalizing the effectiveness of a program or program component to other populations
- Fostering program and individual accountability
- Promoting positive awareness of intervention and treatment effectiveness (Schinke, Botvin, & Orlandi, 1991).

Intervention and treatment outcome evaluations are conducted to inform practitioners, payors, and politicians about the efficacy of various treatment modalities and program components.

There are three levels of addictions intervention and treatment evaluations: 1) treatment outcome evaluation—which looks at information from many programs to determine the effectiveness of various treatment modalities; 2) program-level evaluation—which is essential for accountability, making informed decisions and modifying program elements; and 3) individual client progress evaluation—which assesses individual accountability and allows the client, direct treatment providers, and others to make decisions about the continuation of treatment based on feedback (SAMHSA, 1994).

Treatment outcome evaluation is also known as summative evaluation. It documents an intervention's effectiveness or ineffectiveness in reaching its intended goals, and measures such areas as changes in participant's attitudes and behaviors regarding addiction, changes in academic or work performance, or attendance (Schinke, Botvin, & Orlandi, 1991). Formative evaluation reviews program procedures and measures the integrity of an intervention, in that it is operating as planned. The results of this type of evaluation are used to improve program practices, which is why it is sometimes viewed as quality assurance.

All nurses are familiar with the type of evaluation required by accreditation bodies, such as the Joint Commission of the Accreditation of Health Care Organizations (JCAHO), which accredits health care facilities. It requires annual evaluations of client services and even provides manuals guiding the specifics of documentation necessary for evaluation (JCAHO, 1992).

It used to consist of answering questions about: program standards (in terms of hours of services), record keeping (extent to which program meets with those standards, timeliness (how long clients have to wait for the services), and regulatory issues (client rights to confidentiality). Such evaluation activities fall under the rubric of *process evaluation* (another name for formative evaluation) providing data about the extent to which the program is being implemented as originally planned. Its focus is primarily on the process or activities involved.

However, recently JCAHO has moved to a more outcomes-focused evaluation, which underscores the heightened demands for accountability related to client outcomes. Intervention and treatment designs include 1) client needs and characteristics, 2) components of the treatment program—including performance standards, and 3) the contribution of these components to treatment outcomes.

KEY COMPONENTS OF A GOOD EVALUATION

Even the best evaluative methods cannot override the impact of a poor program design. A poor intervention or treatment program design is more difficult and expensive to evaluate. Therefore, a key component necessary for effectiveness is a good program design congruent with the health care needs of the target population. Other key components for evaluating the effectiveness of an intervention or treatment program for addicted clients—according to the National Institute on Drug Abuse, 1993—are shown in Figure 12.1. Although a full elucidation of the dimensions of a good evaluation is beyond the scope of this chapter, key components can be briefly outlined.

The Evaluation Process

Based on the flowchart in Figure 12–1, it is clear that there are sequential, basic steps to the program evaluation process.

PROGRAM PLAN BASED ON COMMUNITY (CLIENT) NEEDS

Interventions and/or programs will be most relevant when based on relevant theory and empirical findings on the target population to be served. For example, the needs of a population with a known high prevalence of comorbid psychiatric disorders, in addition to substance abuse disorders, should be addressed in program planning, addressed in the intervention and/or treatment program, and included in program evaluation. The program plan sets the stage for the kinds of evaluation that will be needed.

RESOURCES

The resources include money from private or third-party payors; staff and their expertise or knowledge; the physical facilities; equipment, such as computers and software; community resources available, such as self-help groups; the clients to be treated, including their characteristics; and access to expert consultants, necessary to implement the evaluation process.

ACTIVITIES/STANDARDS (OBJECTIVES)

This category includes developed objectives and subobjectives for program interventions. Intervention and/or treatment guidelines and performance standards help reduce these

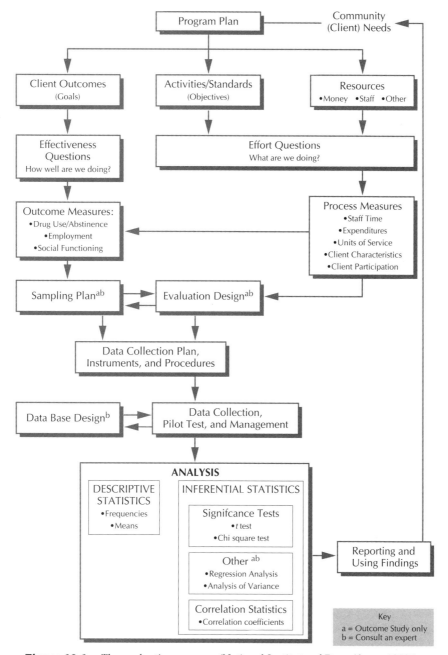

Figure 12-1. The evaluation process. (National Institute of Drug Abuse, 1993.)

objectives to a level needed for coding the role functions of the nurse. Examples of objectives include the completion of a differential diagnosis on individual clients according to a planned protocol such as the DSM-IV (American Psychiatric Association [APA], 1994), and performance standards for carrying out the protocol, as well as specifying the actual intervention.

CLIENT OUTCOMES (GOALS)

Measurable client outcomes are important. Examples of this could include: the maintenance of abstinence for 6 months or longer; change in a dysfunctional pattern of family relationships related to substance abuse; and interim outcomes such as by day 5 of treatment the client will have fully completed alcohol detoxification.

EFFORT QUESTIONS (PROCESS EVALUATION)

These questions measure the extent to which the program is doing what it set out to do. Questions may be framed in terms of who is doing what, when, and how is it being done, etc. One could measure the activity of differential diagnosis mentioned under "Activities" (above) in terms of how many clients are receiving the planned differential assessment.

EFFECTIVENESS QUESTIONS

Such questions measure how well the program is doing what it set out to do. For example, what percentage of clients receiving the identified intervention or treatment achieved the expected outcomes, compared with the percentage of clients who did not receive the identified intervention or treatment. This is the most important component that nurses providing care for addicted clients need to pay attention to. If smoking cessation advice has been given to clients on a general medical unit, have better health outcomes been achieved on another unit where clients did not receive the advice? Has screening for substance abuse in a community health center provided an increase in numbers of those referred to specific interventions and treatment for the problem? These are the kinds of questions that nurses need to ask and plan for to utilize the evaluation process and validate the effectiveness of the care they provide to addicted clients.

PROCESS MEASURES

Components may include examining staff time, expenditures, units of service, client characteristics, and client participation. An example could be units of group therapy delivered, staff time expended on each unit of therapy, its cost, and numbers of sessions in which clients participated. Although client characteristics are also stipulated for this category, according to the National Institute on Drug Abuse (NIDA) (1993), it may be better to specify these separately at the outset, as well as client needs. Client characteristics existing before treatment, such as unemployment and comorbid psychiatric diagnoses, may contribute directly to treatment outcomes. Decisions may be needed on whether to include at this point interim "client characteristics" that actually result from the unit of care being delivered or whether these should be accounted for in the above category of "Client Outcomes (Goals)."

OUTCOME MEASURES

Outcome measures include relevant postintervention or post-treatment discharge features of client behavior that may be the result of interventions delivered in the program. Drug use, decrease of use, and abstinence are always included here, as are aspects such as family/social functioning.

THE EVALUATION DESIGN

The evaluation design must take into account all the foregoing categories and provide an overall comprehensive scheme to guide evaluation activities. At this point all the categories of activity on the flowchart in Figure 12.1 should be addressed. Designs for outcome evaluations, more adequate to the demands of the managed care environment, are preferred. These require a "design that controls for factors that threaten your ability to claim responsibility for the improvements you see in your clients" (NIAAA, 1993, p. 13).

It is important at this step to specify unambiguously and operationally the questions to be answered targeted to intervention and/or treatment outcomes, the program elements to be included, and the client needs and characteristics. Operational definitions that are measurable and quantifiable must be developed for each variable. For example, client characteristics at admission may include several operational definitions for measurement including but not limited to demographic factors such as marital status, race, and employment status. Client needs requiring attention may be defined as family dysfunction, quantity and frequency of alcohol and other drug use, and presence of a comorbid mental disorder. Usually client needs include conditions that are addressed and presumably changed by means of interventions in the treatment program. It is also very important at this step to protect client rights, ensure confidentiality of client data, and seek review and approval by appropriate institutional bodies for the protection of human rights.

SAMPLING PLAN

The evaluation questions can be answered only with information obtained from an identified group of clients. The client group may be well defined in certain settings that appeal to a certain clientele or provide a specialized intervention or treatment. The client group may be homogeneous; for example, male white, blue-collar workers of similar educational background and income level who are involved in steel production. One could assume them to be similar demographically and, although these characteristics would be measured and accounted for, any differences in treatment outcome would probably not be attributable to these client characteristics. However, a subgroup entering the same treatment program may be female and gender characteristics may produce different treatment outcomes. In this case, both groups would need to be sampled and a plan produced to ensure this. Such clients could be selected randomly or the decision may be to sample 100 consecutive admissions of each group.

DATA COLLECTION PLAN, INSTRUMENTATION, AND PROCEDURES

An overall plan is produced at this step based on decisions as to what type of data is to be collected, the instrumentation to be used to tap into the data, and method by which data are to be obtained. Selection of instruments for measurement is based on satisfying the operational definitions developed above and the proven validity and reliability of instruments selected.

DATA COLLECTION, PILOT TEST, AND MANAGEMENT

A pilot test with a small sample of clients is an invaluable step for 1) highlighting potential problems in the evaluation design, 2) testing and validating the instruments selected, and 3) refining the methods of data collection. A refined final plan may then be developed so that final data collection may proceed. The utilization of existing sources of data—if these fit the evaluation questions and operational definitions—can greatly reduce the considerable workload this step entails.

Necessary elements to the plan include the training of data collectors to ensure that they collect and code data in the same way; pilot testing of data collection by the trained collectors of data; decisions as to how invalid data will be handled to ensure quality control; and editing and cleaning of the data set once collected.

DATA BASE DESIGN

It is essential to have devised in advance a plan for coding and managing the data set once it is collected. The data set can best be managed with a computerized data base, plans for which must be made at the outset.

DATA ANALYSIS

The statistical analyses should have been decided well in advance to fit the evaluation design. Analyses can be planned, for example, so as to test supposedly nonequivalent groups who either do or do not receive the intervention or treatment in addition to standard treatment. If statistical tests reveal that there is no significant difference between the two groups studied, more sophisticated analysis can be undertaken at this point.

REPORTING AND USING FINDINGS

Not only can results show effectiveness, they can be utilized to improve interventions and programs. For example, if relapse prevention was the intervention or treatment provided, and groups receiving relapse prevention by nurses did better on outcome measures, then an administrative decision can be made to include relapse prevention in the program delivered to clients with this need. One should also compare the evaluation findings to what is known in the literature to further refine program planning. Results may be reported at professional meetings and in journals and other publications.

Sources of Evaluation Invalidity

Numerous sources of bias exist that may invalidate an evaluation effort, some of which may be prevented with careful planning. Many result from poor intervention/program planning and design at the outset. The program may be so general that it is impossible to determine what worked or what caused it to fail.

Bias and faulty evaluation results may be due to: 1) an incomplete, unstandardized, or wrong intervention or treatment; 2) providing less or more treatment than what is needed to meet client needs; or 3) attempts to evaluate an evolving intervention or program before it is mature enough. This may lead to failure to make clear and specific the effective components of the intervention or treatment (Rossi & Freeman, 1993).

Other factors that may invalidate the evaluation process include: 1) an evaluation design that fails to account for certain factors impinging on treatment success, such as organization features, and patient demographics and needs; 2) evaluation methods may not have been tailored to the available resources; 3) failure to utilize multiple data sources and observers to document program elements; 4) failure to use methods interpretable by staff involved in the data documentation and collection; 5) faulty collaboration among evaluators and program personnel that results in poor data collection and possibly even poor evaluation design at the outset; and 6) the evaluation effort attempts to evaluate what cannot be evaluated.

Evaluation Methods

Various methods of evaluation are appropriate for different purposes. The three general evaluation designs are: 1) descriptive studies, 2) before and after studies, and 3) experimental studies (SAMHSA, 1994).

Descriptive studies are evaluations that do not provide explanations of results, explore causal factors, or make predictions. They merely describe a particular process or finding. Both quantitative and qualitative data may be used in descriptive studies. Quantitative data are obtained by counting categories, such as the number of persons entering treatment or participating in an intervention, the number of hours of service provided, or the number of lapses or relapses. Qualitative data can be collected through reviews of client records, interviews with staff or clients, and open-ended questions on surveys. However, typical ways of collecting data for descriptive studies include survey questionnaires, records reviews, meetings, observations, and structured interviews.

Before and after studies—sometimes referred to as pretest/posttest—attempt to show changes that have occurred as a result of an intervention or course of treatment. Data are collected before the program or a particular intervention is begun and at other intervals throughout the process, at its conclusion, and at intervals following discharge from the program or completion of the intervention, to provide a better picture of its effectiveness.

Experimental studies compare a group of persons receiving an intervention or treatment, to a control group that is similar in size and characteristics but does not receive the same treatment. These type of studies are much more expensive to conduct and are not practical for all agencies.

The above evaluation methods are by no means exhaustive. However, it is important when choosing a method to remember that the evaluation design must fit the reality of the program conditions, yet yield as few limitations as possible so as to provide valid and statistically defensible findings on intervention or treatment outcomes.

COST-BENEFIT, COST-EFFECTIVENESS, AND EVALUATION

Cost-benefit analysis is an "analytical procedure for determining the economic efficiency, expressed as the relationship between costs and outcomes, usually measured in monetary terms" (Rossi & Freeman, 1993, p. 362). Cost-effectiveness analysis—another method to assess economic efficiency—requires reducing the program costs to a dollar value, while its treatment benefits are expressed in outcome units. It may be a more fitting method than cost-benefit analysis for evaluation of addictions interventions. For example, the cost-effectiveness of a relapse prevention intervention can be expressed in terms of nurse-dollars spent to increase abstinence rates from 1 to 6 months on average.

Such cost-effectiveness studies of nursing functions have the potential of measuring the actual impact of competent nurse interventions. This is important because nursing practice is often narrowly viewed as cost inputs and too seldom codified as fully developed clinical practice protocols, with the potential of significantly impacting on client outcomes.

Standard VI of Nursing Practice With Addicted Clients (American Nurses Association & National Nurses Society on Addictions, 1988) posits the expectation that nurses will evaluate the responses of clients and revise interventions accordingly. Recommendations on how to structure such evaluations are also provided and include having a documented data base for the evaluation of therapeutic effectiveness.

Nurses must give careful attention to: 1) carving out the components of intervention and treatment for addicted clients that fall within the Nurse Practice Act; 2) developing clinical practice protocols or treatment guidelines; 3) installing professional performance standards; and 4) measuring the relative impact of such interventions on client outcomes. Otherwise, the evaluation of nursing effectiveness in the care of addicted clients will fall short of its potential.

NURSING INTERVENTIONS WITH ADDICTED CLIENTS THAT CAN BE EVALUATED FOR EFFECTIVENESS

In the past, nursing participation in the care of addicted clients was constrained by too narrow a role. It consisted of carrying out medical functions such as 1) admitting clients, 2) dispensing medications, 3) implementing doctors' orders, and 4) managing detoxification and other physical complications—activities not conducive to in-depth evaluation of nursing's real effectiveness.

Now, as various components of care with addicted clients are articulated and sets of functions are being identified, specific interventions—that favorably impact client outcomes and are implemented by nurses from any clinical specialty—can be subjected to measurement and therefore evaluated. Box 12–1 outlines those interventions that can be implemented and evaluated for effectiveness.

BOX 12-1.   Addictions Interventions Performed by Nurses That Can Be Evaluated for Effectiveness

PREVENTION
- Client education
- Family education
- Community education
- Screening for identification and risk
- Advocacy and actions to change policy and legislation

INTERVENTION
- Health, mental status, psychosocial, and addictions assessments
- DSM-IV diagnostic assessments
- Referring clients to treatment based on placement criteria
- Safe detoxification from alcohol and other drugs
- Physical examinations
- School-based interventions

TREATMENT
- Lecturing on various topics
- Individual counseling
- Group counseling
- Family counseling
- Case management
- Interruption of premature discharge

AFTERCARE
- Education about and provision of self-help group resources
- Relapse prevention education
- Follow-up

Other interventions, shown in Box 12–2, as presented by Greenman (1994), are related specifically to care provided to dually diagnosed clients. These too can be subjected to evaluation for effectiveness. However, it is important to note that to evaluate nurse effectiveness, the functions in Boxes 12–1 and 12–2 must be operationalized in measurable terms.

For example, a determination of safe detoxification from alcohol would include use of the Clinical Institute Withdrawal Assessment (CIWA) scale of alcohol to measure for absence of withdrawal symptoms after a client completes a specific protocol of withdrawal. Effectiveness is the percentage of clients who are detoxified without a life-threatening withdrawal experience.

Once functions are defined in measurable terms, they can be inserted in an evaluation model that incorporates client needs and client characteristics. Then they can be measured against client outcomes.

The role of the nurse case manager caring for addicted clients deserves separate attention as a broad organizing function that subsumes other elements, in that, if it is evaluated for effectiveness as related to client outcomes, it could yield valuable information on the effectiveness of nurses. This is critical because the current climate of health care—which is heavily influenced by managed care—is dominated by the concept of case management.

EVALUATING EFFECTIVENESS OF CASE MANAGING ADDICTED CLIENTS

Before managed care, the primary goal of conventional case management was not cost savings but the "management of case" (Woodward, 1992). Traditionally in nursing, the dimensions of case management included two major themes: 1) the direct delivery of care and 2) the coordination and continuity of the provision of services. Nursing further developed and emphasized another essential component, attention to the engagement and interaction with a client necessary to achieve these purposes and ensure optimal client outcomes.

BOX 12-2.   Addictions Interventions With Dual-Diagnosed Clients Performed by Nurses and Evaluable for Effectiveness

- Triage of clients to determine possible intervention or treatment setting
- Assessment of clients for differential diagnosis based on DSM-IV
- Integration and coordination of care for two primary illnesses
- Conducting dual-diagnosis lectures and groups
- Performance of case management to ensure treatment comprehensiveness and continuity
- Assessment of client's ability to benefit from support groups
- Engaging the client as discussed in Chapter 5
- Monitoring aftercare compliance for all diagnostic disorders
- Planning aftercare including appropriate options based on client needs

Exerpted from Greenman, D. (1994). The role of the addictions nurse specialist in adult psychiatry. *Perspectives on Addictions Nursing, 5* (3), 3–4.

Ridgely and Willenbring (1992) made an important differentiation between case management designed to *deliver* services and case management designed to *coordinate* the provision of those services. They reported that studies of case manager coordination of services showed mixed results on client outcomes. Furthermore, they suggested the following four activities necessary for evaluating the effectiveness of case management—designed to deliver services—as practiced with addicted clients: 1) a precise description of the intervention; 2) an analysis of actual implementation; 3) specification of the timetable for implementation; and 4) a description of the environment of the intervention program. If discernable, the particular conceptual framework on which the treatment program interventions are based may provide valuable clues to the evaluator as to not only the scope and nature of the program interventions but also client selection and desirable treatment outcomes.

The National Institute on Drug Abuse has sponsored some studies of case management, particularly the linkage function of the role (matching client needs to community resources) (Ashery, 1992). A review of these studies revealed the following: 1) a case management situation where there was a good fit between the case manager and the client led to a reduction in time to admission (Bokos, Mejta, Mickenberg, & Monks, 1992); 2) after case management was discontinued, attrition increased (Lidz, Bux, Platt, & Iguchi, 1992); 3) case management used in conjunction with centralized access to a range of services proved to be more effective (Schlenger, Kroutil, & Roland, 1992); and 4) structured case management that included screening, needs assessment, direct delivery, coordination of service, enforced rules, and graduated sanctions proved to be most effective with a difficult population—ex-offenders—it reduced their rearrest rates (Cook, 1992).

Although the various functions of the case manager role will continue to be studied, exciting factors that will impact on it in the future are new technologies and information systems, and having the potential of integrating case management across the continuum of care. Given the need to evaluate whether an intervention or treatment works, evaluation of case management needs to focus on what the intervention or treatment is (as part of the case management), and what the nurse does to render this intervention.

CONCLUSION

Evaluation is a purposeful activity undertaken to solve practical problems, one important one being the determination of effectiveness (Rossi & Freeman, 1993). The activities and results of good evaluation impact on organizational policy and the further development of treatment programs.

Nurses from all areas of health care provide care to addicted clients in a number of ways. The problem is that it is not documented and used to show impact on client outcomes as proof of effectiveness. This chapter has provided the necessary insight to correct this omission.

REFERENCES

American Nurses Association & National Nurses Society on Addiction (1988). *Standards of addictions nursing practice with selected diagnoses and criteria*. Kansas City, MO: American Nurses Association.

American Psychiatric Association (1994). *Diagnostic and statistical manual of mental disorders* (4th ed.). Washington, DC: American Psychiatric Association.

Ashery, R.S. (1992). *Progress and issues in case management. NIDA Research Monograph 127.* Rockville, MD: National Institute on Drug Abuse.

Bokos, P.J., Mejta, C.L., Mickenberg, J.H., & Monks, R.L. (1992). Case management: An alternative approach to working with intravenous drug users. In: R.S. Ashery (Ed.), *Progress and issues in case management, NIDA Research Monograph 127* (DHHS Publication No. [ADM]92-1946) (pp. 92–111). Rockville, MD: National Institute on Drug Abuse.

Cook, F. (1992). TASC: Case management models linking criminal justice and treatment. In: R.S. Ashery (Ed.), *Progress and issues in case management. NIDA Research Monograph 127* (DHHS Publication No. [ADM]92-1946) (pp. 368–382). Rockville, MD: National Institute on Drug Abuse.

Greenman, S. (1994). The role of the addictions nurse specialist in adult psychiatry. *Perspectives on Addictions Nursing, 5*(3), 3–4.

Joint Commission on Accreditation of Healthcare Organizations (1992). *Patient records in addictions treatment: Documenting the quality of care.* Oakbrook Terrace, IL: Joint Commission on Accreditation of Healthcare Organizations.

Lidz, V., Bux, D.A., Platt, J.J., & Iguchi, M.Y. (1992). Transitional case management: A service model for AIDS outreach projects. In: R.S. Ashery (Ed.), *Progress and issues in case management. NIDA Research Monograph 127* (DHHS Publication No. [ADM]92-1946) (pp. 112–144). Rockville, MD: National Institute on Drug Abuse.

National Institute on Alcohol Abuse and Alcoholism (1993). Treatment outcome research. *Alcohol Alert, 17* (PH322), July 1992, 1–3.

National Institute on Drug Abuse. (1993). *How good is your drug abuse treatment program? A guide to evaluation.* (NIH Publication No. 93-3609). Rockville, MD: National Institute on Drug Abuse.

Ridgely, M.S., & Willenbring, M.L. (1992). Application of case management to drug abuse treatment: Overview of models and research issues. In: R.S. Ashery (Ed.), *Progress and issues in case management. NIDA Research Monograph 127* (DHHS Publication No. [ADM]92-1946) (pp. 12–33). Rockville, MD: National Institute on Drug Abuse.

Rossi, P.H., & Freeman, H.E. (1993). *Evaluation: A systematic approach.* Newbury Park, CA: Sage Publications.

Schinke, S., Botvin, G., & Orlandi, M. (1991). *Substance abuse in children and adolescents: Evaluation and interventions.* Newbury Park, CA: Sage Publications.

Schlenger, W.E., Kroutil, L.A., & Roland, E.J. (1992). Case management as a mechanism for linking drug abuse treatment and primary care: Preliminary evidence from the ADAMHA/HRSA Linkage Demonstration. In: R.S. Ashery (Ed.), *Progress and issues in case management. NIDA Research Monograph 127* (DHHS Publication No. [ADM]92-1946) (pp. 316–330). Rockville, MD: National Institute on Drug Abuse.

Substance Abuse and Mental Health Services Administration (1994). *Treatment for alcohol and other drug abuse: Opportunities for coordination.* DHHS Publication No. (SMA) 94-2075. Rockville, MD: Department of Health and Human Services.

Woodward, A. (1992). Managed care and case management of substance abuse treatment. In: R.S. Ashery (Ed.), *Progress and issues in case management. NIDA Research Monograph 127* (DHHS Publication No. [ADM]92-1946) (pp. 34–53). Rockville, MD: National Institute on Drug Abuse.

ISSUES IMPACTING CARE OF ADDICTED CLIENTS

INTRODUCTION: COGNATE CONCERNS

More than 37 million citizens in the United States (15% of the population) have no health insurance. Also, an estimated 60 million have inadequate coverage even if they do have health insurance (U.S. Congress, 1992). This decrease in health insurance coverage is a result of: 1)higher unemployment; 2)employment with no benefits; and 3)increases in insurance premiums. This has a particularly harsh impact on persons from ethnic minority groups. The status of health care in America is a major issue that led to the federal focus of health care reform.

Although defeated and unresolved at the federal level, health care reform strategies continue to evolve and impact on care of addicted clients. Many states lead the movement by restructuring some of the ways that they address health care more in concert with "managed care" principles. All health care problems are affected by the turmoil in the present day environment; however, persons facing alcohol and other drug addictions are experiencing major problems with receiving appropriate care, from lack of access to ineffective interventions.

Health care services for addictive disorders to some extent mirror the public/private mix for the U.S. health care system as a whole. The federal government provides some type of services directly through the military, the Department of Veterans Affairs, the Indian Health Services, and the prison system. The federal government also finances addictive services through "block grants" to states (which in turn provide funding to the private sector for addiction services). These grants are operated by the Substance Abuse and Mental Health Services Administration—primarily through its Center for Substance Abuse Treatment.

The government also finances care through Medicare and Medicaid, which allows for limited benefits primarily for hospital-based care. And last but not least, services for alcohol and other drug addiction are provided through the private sector as well. In the private sector managed care companies have dominated care for addictions services.

Currently, most if not all benefit packages for addiction interventions and services are limited, consisting mainly of 3 to 7 days of detoxification and some outpatient services coverage. Most of the 28- to 30-day and longer residential/inpatient programs are financed by the Center for Substance Abuse Treatment, particularly for addicted pregnant women and their children. Some insurance companies and managed care companies provide residential/inpatient treatment for 14 to 21 days, but not many.

In an effort to control cost and yet promote quality care, managed care companies frown on "one-stop shopping" thinking that seemed to guide addictions services at one point in time. Now services are viewed as needing to be matched to the particular needs of the client and offered to health care providers who are qualified and show effective outcomes. This means that nurses can continue to intervene in some aspect of alcohol and other drug addiction and receive reimbursement for their services, whether it is as a generalists in conjunction with an outpatient, ambulatory care, community health service,or inpatient service, or whether it is independently as an advanced practice nurse.

Major decisions involving the care of these clients is related to cultural, ethical, and legal issues. Also, nurses need to be able to: 1) keep the client engaged in the intervention/treatment—thereby minimizing attrition; 2) maintain correct balance of intimacy in the therapeutic relationship; and 3) work within a collaborative practice framework.

According to Winegar (1995) managed care companies are utilizing nurses a lot. Clinical specialists are used extensively, advanced practice nurses with prescriptive authority, and nurses as case managers for providing direct treatment as well as crisis interventions. In addition, nurses are being utilized for consultation, wellness programs and more.

The fact that nurses are increasingly being utilized and relied on for client care in more of an independent role makes it imperative that they contribute to the inquiry of knowledge necessary to provide that care. Existence of the National Institute for Nursing Research within the National Institutes of Health confirms the fact that nurses are key players in the development of knowledge for health care.

There are a number of nurses conducting research on varying phenomenon related to alcohol and other drug addiction. Nurses are receiving funding from the National Institute on Drug Abuse and the National Institute on Alcohol Abuse and Alcoholism to research and reveal knowledge necessary for care of addicted clients. The National Nurses Society on Addictions has a research committee as well as a clinical practice committee in support of the important connection between the two.

To remain contenders for funding from those institutes, nurses must understand the process. Understanding also helps those who may not want to do research, but are interested in being able to apply it clinically.

The chapters in this section provide the reader with information on becoming culturally competent, ethically decisive, legally alert, appropriately therapeutic, obstructive with attrition, collaboratively focused, and aware of the importance of research as it impacts care.

REFERENCES

Congress of the United States. (1992). *Projections of national health expenditures* (p.38). Washington, D.C.: Congressional Budget Office.

Winegar, N. (1995). *The future of managed behavioral healthcare*. Conference Presentation: Prototypes for Managed Behavioral Healthcare—Mental Disorders and Addictions, Baltimore, MD.

13

Cultural Competence

Kem B. Louie, *PhD, RN, CS, FAAN*

INTRODUCTION

Nurses are in a key position to develop and maintain culturally competent health care. The literature in the last two decades has proliferated with articles and studies dealing with care for diverse groups whose cultural and ethnic backgrounds differ from the majority population. However, reservations are being expressed regarding whether or not culturally competent care is yet the norm in the United States. According to Andrews (1992), "A lack of sensitivity by health care providers: 1) wastes million of dollars annually; 2) alienates the very people whom nurses purport to help; and 3) results in misdiagnoses, often with tragic and dangerous consequences" (p. 7).

Whites comprise 70% of the population, African Americans comprise 12.1%, Hispanic/Latinos 9%, Asians and Pacific Islanders 2.9%, American Indians and Alaskan Natives 0.8%, and other groups 3.9% (U.S. Dept. of Commerce, 1990). These figures, when projected to the year 2000, show the ethnic minority population becoming increasingly diverse with new Asian and Pacific Islander and Hispanic/Latino groups growing rapidly across the country. The American population will grow by 6 million people through immigration, with the East and West coasts receiving the largest proportion of immigrants. Ethnic minorities constitute only a little more than one-third of the total nations population, but in some regions of the country, ethnic minorities constitute the majority (Trimble, 1995).

A summary of findings from ethnic minority drug abuse literature show that 1) ethnic minorities are overrepresented in drug abuse reporting systems; and 2) although regional and specific ethnic patterns may vary, drug abuse among ethnic minority groups is not declining (Trimble, 1995). Specific numbers often change, yet what seems to remain a constant is the level of prevalence of substance abuse among ethnic groups. Native Americans, followed by Hispanics, then African Americans, whites, and finally Asian and Pacific Islanders had the highest rates of substance abuse among a sample of incarcerated persons (Substance Abuse and Mental Health Services Administration (SAMHSA), 1994). While the picture may not be exactly the same for those ethnic persons not in prison, the proportion of addiction and resulting distress between whites and the ethnic groups are similar.

Nurses working in all areas of the health care system will come in contact with substance abusers who are from various ethnic minority groups (including those identified as "other" by the census), and will need to have culturally competent capabilities to provide effective health care to the client. Therefore, the purpose of this chapter is to present definitions, models, and methods for nurses to become culturally competent in dealing with the substance abusing ethnic minority client. The chapter will begin by providing a brief profile of the major minority groups—African-American/Caribbean Islanders, Hispanic/Latinos, Asian and Pacific Islanders, and American Indians and Alaska Natives.

PROFILE OF ETHNIC MINORITY POPULATIONS IN AMERICA

African-American/Caribbean Islanders

The story of how African-Americans came to be in the United States is well known. The phenomenon of "slavery" existed in this country for over 200 years (1600 to 1860) during which time Africans were taken from their homes and brought by ship to this country. This group of people suffered tremendous oppression and destruction. Unfortunately, over 130 years since the end of slavery, discrimination and oppression still exists.

This population was 400,000 at the end of slavery and just 1 million at the time of the first census in 1790. At the turn of the century it reached 10 million, and at the 1990 census it numbered 30 million. It is expanding at a much more rapid rate than the nation as a whole. In 1890 more than 90% of all African Americans lived in the rural south; most of the workers were farmers. Now, nearly 90% live in urban areas scattered throughout the nation (Billingsley, 1992).

The arrival of West Indians (Caribbean Islanders) in the early 1900s coincided with the mass migration of southern African- Americans to northern cities, which was a consequence of the mechanization of agriculture and the shortage of labor that existed in the industrialized northern states during World War I. West Indians began settling in Harlem along with African-Americans from the South to swell the small black population that already existed. However, the absolute numbers of Caribbean people were small due to the restrictions on immigration to the United States from this hemisphere, in favor of European populations (Billingsley, 1992).

After 1965, this changed with the passage of the Immigration and Naturalization Act. A shift in the U.S. immigration policy opened up admission from the Caribbean, as well as Latin America, Asia, and Africa. During the decade between 1966 and 1977 European immigration was held to 22.9%, whereas Caribbean Islanders and Latin Americans increased to 46.6%. As a result, English-speaking immigrant populations from the West Indies, the American Virgin Islands, Guyana, Haiti, and Panama have swelled to an estimated 1.7 million, constituting a significant segment of New York City's black population (Billingsley, 1992).

At the time of the 1980 census, 2.5 million of the 26 million blacks in the United States were of Caribbean origin. Caribbean blacks are much younger, with a median age of 39.6 years compared to a median age of 45.1 years for African-Americans. Although the myth prevails that Caribbean Islanders in this country do not experience the same amount of discrimination that African-Americans do, in some areas—employment, housing, and transportation—the Caribbean blacks experience greater levels of racial discrimination. In addition, they experience along with the African-American severe health problems due to poverty, addiction, lack of nutrition, and limited access to medical care (Billingsley, 1992).

Hispanics/Latinos

"Hispanic" is a term that made its first appearance in the late 1970s and then was used by the U.S. Bureau of the Census in 1980 to designate those individuals who reside in the United States and whose cultural origins are in Mexico, Puerto Rico, Cuba, Central America, and other Latin America countries. The majority (63%) are people of Mexican origin who reside primarily in the Southwest and West, followed by mainland Puerto Ricans (12%) located principally in the Northeast, and Cubans (5%) located primarily in the Southeast. Central and South Americans constitute 13% of the total Hispanic/Latino population (U.S. Department of Health and Human Services [USDHHS], 1992).

MEXICAN AMERICANS

The American Southwest and Far West were controlled by Mexico until 1848. Spanish was the primary language and Spanish-Indian culture flourished. During the first half of the 19th century, the United States instituted its policy of "Manifest Destiny," and this rationale for expansion into the Southwest gained momentum when the Santa Fe Trail was expanded through the territory in 1820. The U.S. drive for land led to war with Mexico in 1846. The war came to an end in 1848 when Mexico surrendered its northern territory, including the present-day states of New Mexico, Colorado, Utah, Nevada, Arizona, and California. Mexico's citizens in the territory were allowed to move south across the new border or to remain and became citizens of the United States (USDHHS, 1992).

The rights of those Mexicans who elected to remain in the United States were protected under the treaty of Guadalupe; however, no provisions were made in the treaty to integrate "native" people into the general mainstream of society. The Mexicans were granted cultural autonomy but were denied access to mainstream institutions. These Mexicans remained isolated until the period 1910 to 1920 when they were joined by Mexican emigrants fleeing the revolution in Mexico. These newcomers established colonies primarily in California and Texas (USDHHS, 1992).

Beginning with World War II, the United States found itself short of labor and it entered into an agreement with Mexico to obtain a steady supply of cheap laborers. In 1944 alone, a total of 110,000 Mexicans entered the country to work on railroads and in agriculture and manufacturing. Many of these workers eventually established roots in this country and remained. Older-generation Mexican Americans mix almost daily with Mexican immigrants. Despite the differences brought about by acculturation and adaptation to the United States, individuals of Mexican origin—regardless of their generation—share many communalities that bind them together as an identifiable ethnic community (USDHHS, 1992).

PUERTO RICANS

Current-day Puerto Rico was colonized by Spain in the 16th century. At that time the island was inhabited by Tainos Indians. However, the natives were outnumbered and largely eliminated by the Spaniards. Gradually Africans were transported against their will to work the land. Today, most Puerto Ricans claim both African-American and white origin. In 1898, at the end of the Spanish-American War, Spain ceded control of Puerto Rico to the United States. For a time, the island was assigned an ambiguous status that did not allow statehood because its citizens were considered "racially inferior" (USDHHS, 1992).

About 1900, Puerto Ricans began to move to New York City in search of employment. Later, they continued to settle in New York because of the ethnic social network already established there. With the Jones Act of 1917, Puerto Rico became a commonwealth territory of the United States. With commonwealth status, Puerto Ricans were granted U.S. citizenship and could move freely from the island to the continent without an immigration check. Puerto Ricans who migrate to the United States are of diverse socioeconomic backgrounds, and are just as likely to be members of all social classes. Second- and third-generation mainland Puerto Ricans can be found in all major northeastern urban areas. These later-generation Puerto Ricans share some cultural orientations with their island relatives, but at the same time they have developed a distinct Puerto Rican mainland culture (USDHHS, 1992).

CUBANS

Cuba was colonized by Spain. Slaves from Africa were brought into the country in the 1700s and mixing of slaves, Indians, and Spaniards began shortly thereafter. Cubans now contain the full range of genetic makeup from white to African American. With help from the United States in 1889, Cuba gained its independence from Spain and thereafter developed an agricultural and tourist economy that became highly dependent on American dollars. A small entrepreneurial class controlled most of the wealth (USDHHS, 1992).

Cuban immigration to the United States took place 1) when Castro seized power and 3000 members of the elite upper class came bringing their wealth with them; 2) in 1959 and 1960 when upper-class owners of farms, ranches, and businesses decided to leave; 3) at the end of 1960 when other middle-class Cubans (professionals, managers, technicians, etc.) came; 4) in 1961, 1962, 1965, and 1980 when approximately 125,000 Cubans left. That group was overwhelmingly working-class African-American, 70.9% blue-collar workers, and no more than 20% prison inmates or mental patients (USDHHS, 1992).

CENTRAL AMERICANS

Central Americans represent the most recent newcomers from Latin America to the United States. Many Central American immigrants relocated in the United States for a combination of reasons, including a desire to escape both the extreme economic hardship in their country and the political turmoil that threatened them. The majority come from Guatemala, El Salvador, and Nicaragua. Accurate data on the number of Central Americans living in the United States are not available. Few Central Americans are granted refugee status and possibly the majority are in the United States without legal documentation, and therefore, are subject to deportation if apprehended. However, more than 500,000 Central Americans have been reported in the Los Angeles metropolitan area alone (USDHHS, 1992).

Asians and Pacific Islanders

The term Asian/Pacific Islander comprises more than 60 separate ethnic/racial groups and subgroups. These groups are very heterogenous, differing in their histories experienced in the United States, languages and dialects, religions, cultures, immigration and generation histories, socioeconomic statuses, places of birth. Recently, Southeast Asian refugees, Filipinos, and Koreans have been the fastest growing groups within the Asian-American population. The Chinese (812,000), the Filipinos (782,000), and the Japanese (716, 000) constituted the largest groups among all Asian/Pacific Island-American groups identified. By the year 2000, it is estimated that the Filipinos will be the largest group, followed by the Chinese, Vietnamese, Koreans, Indians, and Japanese (USDHHS, 1992).

Many Chinese and Japanese families have been in the United States for three generations or more. Early immigration patterns more than 140 years ago tended to favor males for the labor market. As many as eight generations of Asian Pacific Islander families have lived in the United States. However, they faced anti-Asian laws that kept them from flourishing. Immigration of Asian women (particularly Chinese) was prohibited by law until 1943. These laws were designed to prevent the establishment of families and a second generation of U.S. citizens with Asian parentage. Chinese men arrived in the United States in the mid-1800s, recruited as laborers during the gold rush. They immigrated to the West coast to work in mines and railroads (Chen, 1995).

By and large, most Hawaiians, Samoans, Japanese, and Guamanians were born in the United States. The vast majority of Vietnamese, Koreans, Asian Indians, and Filipinos in the United States, however, were born overseas. There is also a great deal of variation in the degree to which particular communities maintain their cohesiveness in terms of traditional customs, values, languages, and ethnic organization. Thus, the tendency to group such diverse nationalities into a single Asian/Pacific Islander category will not allow health care providers to provide care from a culturally sensitive perspective in a culturally competent manner (USDHHS, 1992).

American Indians and Alaska Natives

During the time before contact with Europeans, it is estimated that there were about 2.5 million indigenous people representing over 300 distinct tribes in what would become the United States. Yet, by 1890, the year in which the Wounded Knee Massacre occurred, only 250,000 of this population remained. This 90% reduction in population resulted from several major factors, all of which were partially supported by federal policy concerning "the Indian problem": disease, malnutrition, and war and murder. Despite attempts to exterminate them or remove them from their traditional lands, relocation policies, extreme poverty, deployment of their young people to boarding schools, and the introduction of alcohol and other drugs, the American Indian population continues to exist (USDHHS, 1992).

At the turn of the last century, there were 220,000 American Indians and Alaska Natives in the United States; the 1980 census indicates that this population numbered approximately 1.5 million, nearly double the 1970 count. This exceptional increase is partially due to improved health care for all ages and to an accelerated birth rate. The current birth rate among Indians and Natives is twice as high as that of the country at large (USDHHS, 1992).

The diversity found in 512 federally recognized Native entities and in an additional 365 state-recognized Indian tribes defies distinct categorization. Each of these entities has had a unique set of social, religious, economic, and legal-political relationships with other tribes, other ethnic/racial groups, and Euro-American societies. Yet, as varied as Indian communities have been, they share the common experience of the almost wholesale suppression of the use of their language through policies and practices imposed by various government and educational systems (USDHHS, 1992).

As of the 1980 census, only seven states in the United States—Arizona, New Mexico, Oklahoma, California, North Carolina, Alaska, and Washington—had an Indian population of more than 50,000 persons. Over the past three decades, American Indians have become increasingly urbanized, thereby decreasing the population density that was at one time a hallmark of the rural reservation and Indian community system. Currently, more than half of the American Indian and Alaska Native population resides in suburban and urban area. Many thousands more may use the reservation as a principal residence but spend varying amounts of time away as they seek education, employment, or respite from stresses in their home communities (USDHHS, 1992).

As shown above, large numbers of differences exist among people in the United States, and while some changes and adaptations must occur to try and exist on a basic level, among ethnic minority groups, there is an increasing awareness, acceptance, and willingness to maintain and support their ethnic and cultural heritages. Biculturalism has been shown to be the norm for these groups where they are able to know and understand two different cultures (LaFromboise, Hardin, Coleman, & Gerton, 1993). Knowing this, it becomes imperative that health care providers seek to identify the knowledge base and methods of providing care in a culturally competent manner. And this is very important when working with addicted clients.

Based on a review of the literature, Lynam (1992) found that a range of approaches existed for facilitating cultural competence. A majority of the articles focus on the health beliefs, traditions, and practices of a particular cultural or ethnic group. Others examine the cultural concepts common to people in many cultures. Some researchers stress the need for nurses to develop skills to care for clients on a one-to-one basis and others stress skills needed to work within organizations and communities. Lynam points out that all these approaches are part of the multidimensional aspects of cultural competence. The remainder of this discussion will focus on definitions and varied approaches to increasing one's cultural competence.

DEFINITIONS

The United States is referred to as being culturally pluralistic. Cultural pluralism is defined as a state in which members of diverse ethnic, racial, religious, and social groups maintain autonomous participation in and development of their traditional culture. Cultural pluralism is a sociologic notion that advocates the recognition of cultural diversity and its acceptance and preservation (Katz and Taylor, 1989). Cultural pluralism provides challenges and opportunities for nurses in providing health care.

When caring for clients whose ethnic and/or cultural background is different from that of the nurse, various concepts must be examined. Nurses who are unfamiliar with these concepts may experience frustration and conflict when caring for clients from diverse cultures, which may result in reduced effectiveness and competence.

Culture

Common definitions of culture address the shared behaviors, ideas, and patterns of thought among different cultural groups (Shultz & Lavenda, 1990). According to Spradley (1990) culture is "acquired knowledge people use to interpret experience and generate behavior which may or may not be consciously recognized by the individual involved" (p. 25). More recently, others are subscribing to an ideational culture definition, which includes the shared *and learned* patterns of thought and values, attitudes, and beliefs (Peoples & Bailey, 1991). For example, the Center for Substance Abuse Prevention defined culture as the shared values, norms, traditions, customs, arts, history, folklore, and institutions of a group of people (USDHHS, 1992). Monroe, Goldman, and Dube (1994) defined culture as the learned and shared knowledge, beliefs, and rules that people use to interpret experience and to generate social behavior. It is the guiding force behind the behaviors and material products associated with a group of people.

Although the definitions of culture provide a framework for understanding cultural groups, there exists cultural variations in that there are cultural differences between groups and within groups. In addition, it is important to note, as does Carey (1993), that there is still considerable lack of consensus regarding the definition of culture.

Ethnic Identity (Ethnicity)

Ethnic identity refers to an individual's perspective of one's own heritage and a sense of belonging to an identifiable group. Ethnicity is a group identity based on culture, language, religion, or a common attachment to a place or kin ties; it is a relational concept (Monroe, Goldman, & Dube, 1994). When caring for ethnic persons of color, there is a tendency to be ethnocentric.

Ethnocentrism

Ethnocentrism is the interpretation of the behavior of others in terms of one's own cultural values and traditions (Monroe et al., 1994). It is perceiving that one's own way of knowing and norms are superior to those of others. This presents barriers in providing culture-specific care to clients because it overlooks the uniqueness of the individual and family.

A lack of knowledge of a cultural group's differences may contribute to a nurse's ethnocentrism. Everyone develops various degrees of ethnocentrism when growing up. This is taught and reinforced by families, in schools, and in society at large by reinforcing dominant Western knowledge and values. The recent term, Eurocentrism, refers to Western, white middle-class values, beliefs, and behaviors that predominate in many of our social and educational institutions. If nurses are to provide effective health care to clients they need *cultural relativism*, which means judging and interpreting the behavior and beliefs of others in terms of *their traditions and experiences*.

Stereotypes

Stereotypes are generalizations that are applied to all members of an ethnic or cultural group. Cultural stereotypes lead to misconceptions and misunderstandings. They tend to disguise important differences among individuals. Some stereotypes demean individuals and perpetrate unfavorable attitudes toward them. Negative stereotypes are harmful and violate an individual's dignity. Positive stereotypes can also distort the characteristics of groups. For example, Asians are referred to as "model minorities," referring to their ability to achieve opportunities in the United States. As a result, it is misperceived that all Asian Americans are self reliant and do not need special assistance or considerations. Individual differences exist within each group as well as among ethnic and cultural groups. The individual differences can be attributed to many factors (e.g., socioeconomic status, generational heritage of a family group, and reasons for being in this country). Both negative and positive stereotypes lead to *racism,* which is defined by Monroe et al. (1994) as the belief that some human population groups are inherently superior or inferior to others because of genetically transmitted characteristics.

In caring for culturally diverse clients, *cultural sensitivity* is a major goal. This refers to the nurse's ability to be aware of and respect the clients' values and lifestyles even when they differ from those of the nurse. The first step toward being culturally sensitive is to ask people from ethnic minority groups how they want to be referred to. For example, do not call everyone that appears to be Asian, Asian or Oriental. Ask if they want to referred to as Japanese, Chinese, Korean, Vietnamese, etc. Ask African-Americans if they want to be referred to as African-American or black. Caribbean Islanders do not want to be called African-Americans, they want to be called Caribbean Islanders with specific reference to their island of origin. American Indians do not wish to be called Native Americans, and Hispanic/Latinos prefer distinction and being referred to as Puerto Rican, or Mexican, or Cuban, etc.

Culture Shock

Culture shock is a phenomenon that also can affect cultural and ethnic groups. Brink (1976) described it as a person's responses when placed in an unfamiliar environment, in that previous coping abilities are ineffective in the new situation. Monroe et al. (1994) refer to the person's responses as "a form of anxiety that results from an inability to predict the behavior of others, or act appropriately in a cross-cultural situation."

Culture shock is viewed within the context of the stress syndrome. There are four phases of culture shock. Phase one is the "honeymoon phase" where there is excitement and a desire to learn about the people and their customs. Phase two is referred to as the "disenchantment phase" when there is more time spent in the new situation. There is beginning awareness that activities of daily living are time consuming and done differently. Various feelings and behaviors are exhibited during this phase: frustration, anxiety, loneliness, depression, withdrawal, and anger. Phase three is the "beginning resolution phase" where the person seeks new ways and patterns of behavior appropriate to the culture. Phase four is the "effective function phase" where the person feels more comfortable in the new surroundings. Some view this as the beginnings of acculturation (Brink, 1976).

Acculturation

Acculturation is the process that takes place when contact between two societies is so prolonged that one or both cultures change substantially. With regard to immigrant groups, acculturation is the process of incorporating values, beliefs, and behaviors from the host culture into the immigrants' cultural world view (Monroe et al., 1994). It refers to the change process of a cultural group or member when in contact with another culture (Lipson & Meleis, 1985). Acculturation is the process of learning or adapting to behaviors, attitudes, and beliefs of another cultural group. This is often defined in terms of such observable characteristics as dress, food, language, and values. A person who is acculturated may no longer always wear traditional dress or only eat foods traditionally associated with his or her culture. There are varying degrees of acculturation among members of a given cultural group. Acculturation does not mean that one gives up their basic ethnic/cultural beliefs and values (Louie, 1992).

The term *culturally competent care* is preferred to the use of culturally sensitive care. Sensitivity to cultures is only one aspect of competence in providing care that is congruent with diverse heritage traditions, beliefs, values, and norms preferences. Cultural sensitivity is seen as one important dimension of the continuum of cultural competence.

MODELS OF CULTURAL COMPETENCE

Culturally competent care is directed toward broadly defined groups such as ethnic minority populations (African Americans and Caribbean Islanders, Hispanics/Latinos, Asian/Pacific Islanders, and American Indians) as well as other groups that have received little attention. Other groups that are now being included are: gay and lesbian populations, old immigrants (from South America and Middle East among others); new immigrants (from Haiti, Cuba, Russia, and Afghanistan, among others); and a certain economic sector of immigrants differentiated by low-income, no personal income, or unemployed. However, as stated before, the first step in becoming culturally competent is becoming culturally sensitive.

Figure 13-1 shows the continuum of individual intercultural sensitivity. This can be used as a method for self-assessment and growth in this area. At one extreme of the continuum is ethnocentric stages where the health care provider is in denial that other cultures even exist, let alone matter. The continuum shows behaviors seen in persons who are at certain places on the continuum, with the goal of achieving ethnorelativism. Here, the health care providers integrate knowledge of other cultures in policy and practice, and exhibit in their behavior an appreciation for different cultures. Once this point is achieved, cultural sensitivity is achieved. At this point, one begins to examine where they stand in terms of cultural competence.

The attainment of cultural competence is a developmental process and is defined as a set of congruent behaviors, attitudes, and policies that come together in a system, agency, or among professionals that enables them to work effectively in diverse cultural situations. There will always be the need for individuals or organizations to assess their progress in developing a culturally competent system of care (Cross, Bazron, Dennis, & Isaac, 1989).

The continuum method serves as a means of measuring and guiding interpersonal responsiveness to the needs of members of diverse cultural groups as well as organizations, and provides a logical and manageable progression toward higher levels of cultural competence. The "cultural competence continuum" (Cross, Bazron, Dennis, & Isaac, 1989) ranges along six points from cultural destructiveness to cultural proficiency (see Figure 13-2).

Cultural Destructiveness

Culturally destructive behaviors and attitudes have the effect of actually damaging or destroying another culture or its people. Some examples of cultural destructiveness include: slavery of the African people here in America and Exclusion Laws of 1885–1965, which prohibited Asians from bringing spouses to the United States and thereby created generations of single males.

Figure 13-1. Continuum of individual intercultural sensitivity.

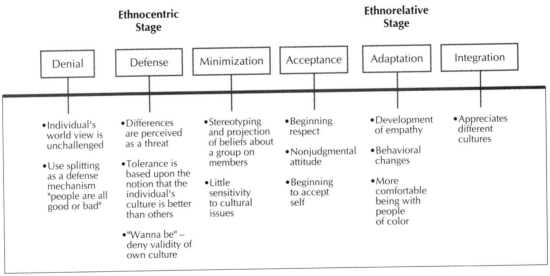

Cultural Incapacity

Cultural incapacity refers to behaviors or policies that may not be intentionally destructive but rather lacks responsiveness to groups. There is a basic assumption of superiority of the dominant culture. For example, persons falling into this category may disproportionately apply resources, have discriminatory hiring practices, lowered expectations of people of color, maintain and reinforce stereotypes, and give subtle messages that people of color are not welcomed or valued.

Cultural Blindness

Cultural blindness involves treating all people in the same manner thereby assuming that there are no differences among cultural groups. Their philosophy is "we are all equal." They propose to be totally unbiased. The difficulty with this view is the assumption that all strategies (in this instance health care strategies) applicable to the dominant culture are effective with all people.

Cultural Precompetence

Cultural precompetence is recognition of the inability to provide appropriate services to clients of a different culture within current structure. Therefore, there is an attempt to improve some aspect of service. At this point on the continuum there is evidence of a desire to deliver quality service, even though there is a lack of information to perform effectively. This can be seen in activities such as hiring people of color, providing cultural training to staff from the dominant culture, and searching strategies and methods thought to be effective with minority cultures.

Cultural Competence

Persons and organizations viewed as being culturally competent have respect for differences among cultural groups, participate in continuous self-assessment on this issue, expand their cultural knowledge, and give attention to the dynamics of difference. They provide support for all their staff to continually upgrade skills and abilities to work cross-culturally and seek advice from the minority community regarding service delivery. Most important, they understand the relationship between the sociopolitical factors affecting people of color.

 Figure 13-2. Cultural competence continuum.

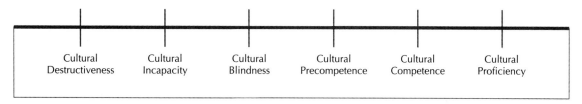

Cultural Proficiency

Cultural proficiency involves the incorporation of the concepts of cultural competency in policy, practice, and attitudes by adding to the knowledge base through research and teaching these concepts to others.

No one is expected to go from cultural destructiveness to cultural competence overnight. There are too many years of negative input from society, family, and media regarding ethnic minorities. The culturally competent continuum allows one to assess where they are and what they need to do to become more culturally competent, and ultimately, culturally proficient.

Based on the definition that cultural competence is "a set of academic and interpersonal skills that allow individuals to increase their understanding within, among, and between groups; which requires a willingness and ability to draw on community based values, traditions, and customs and to work with knowledgeable persons from the community in developing focused interventions, communications, and other supports" (p. vi), Orlandi (1992) developed a schematic representation and organizing framework to assess cultural competence.

Orlandi suggests that cultural competence is multidimensional, involving aspects of knowledge (cognitive dimension), attitude (affective dimension), and skill development (skills dimension). His "Cultural Sophistication Framework" (Table 13-1)—which describes the multidimensional aspects of cultural competence—is an approach that allows for individual assessment along a continuum of cultural incompetence, cultural sensitivity, and cultural competence. Therefore, an individual could be highly knowledgeable and fully committed to change but completely lacking in the requisite skills. It shows individuals where they need to be to be culturally competent.

Campinha-Bacote (1994) proposed the culturally competent model of care. This model is viewed as dynamic and an on-going process of cultural awareness, cultural knowledge, and cultural encounter. Cultural awareness involves the process of becoming sensitive to members from different backgrounds. Cultural knowledge includes the ability to conduct a culturiological assessment as well as gain information from the cultural group. Cultural encounter addresses the interaction of the nurse and client in cross-cultural situations.

 TABLE 13-1 Cultural Sophistication Framework

	Culturally Incompetent	Culturally Sensitive	Culturally Competent
Cognitive dimension	Oblivious	Aware	Knowledgeable
Affective dimension	Apathetic	Sympathetic	Committed to change
Skills dimension	Unskilled	Lacking some skills	Highly skilled
Overall effect	Destructive	Neutral	Constructive

Source: Orlandi, M. (1992). Cultural sophistication framework. In M. Orlandi, R. Weston, & L. Epstein, *Cultural competence for evaluators* (OSAP Cultural Competence Series). DHHS Publication (ADM) 92-1884. Washington, DC: , U.S. Government Printing Office.

STRATEGIES FOR INCORPORATION OF CULTURAL COMPETENCE

Nurses are in a central position to provide culturally competent care. Nurses in advanced practice are characterized by their in-depth knowledge and specialization that are applied within a broad range of client populations in a variety of health settings (American Association of Colleges of Nurses [AACN], 1994). These advanced practice nurses are prepared at the graduate level either as a clinical specialist, nurse anesthetist, nurse midwife, or nurse practitioner.

The role of the advanced practice nurse in caring for and providing programs of health care to clients from diverse cultures gives rise to challenges and opportunities to incorporate cultural competence. However, before incorporating cultural competence, individual nurses need to recognize one's own cultural perspective. The attitudes and values we hold affect our behavior, especially toward people who are perceived as different. These attitudes and values are often unconscious unless they have been examined. Therefore, it is important to examine how we perceive our own culture and ethnic identity.

Cultural Competence in Practice

As practitioners, there are skills that are critical when interacting with clients from different cultural backgrounds. These skills involve knowing how and when to apply the cultural concepts in practice situations within the context of the nurse–client relationship. Effective communication is most important; it involves knowing how to interview and gather assessment data. Several points must be kept in mind when interviewing clients:

- Know that clients expect a period of "small talk" before the formal interview
- Be aware of cultural differences in the connotative and denotative meanings of words and phases
- Realize that clients will exhibit cultural variations in their expression of emotions and feelings
- Be conscious of time orientation—knowing that the tempo or speed of conversation often varies among cultural groups
- Be aware that nonverbal facial and body gestures, expressions, and social distance are interpreted culturally
- Understand the need for a translator or interpreter with non-English-speaking clients (Louie, 1984).

Cultural Patterns Affecting Communication

According to Monroe et al. (1994) differing cultural patterns that can affect the clinical encounter include the following:

Nonverbal Communication
- *Silence* This may be valued and used by clients to formulate complete, thoughtful responses to questions. Silence may or may not signify a client's disinterest in the topic being discussed; learn whether it is appropriate to speak before the client has finished talking.
- *Facial Expression* Smiling, frowning, or flat affect may be used to mask other emotions. It is useful to describe the perceived emotion displayed by the client, or ask the client how he or she feels to facilitate understanding.

- *Emotional Expressiveness*   This varies significantly from one culture to another; some cultures value expressions of joy, pain, sorrow, fright, or anxiety, whereas others value maintenance of stoic demeanor or flat affect.
- *Sense of Appropriate Personal Space*   Members of some cultural groups prefer greater distances between people (at least an arm's length); others prefer less space between client and provider (a client can be given the option of sitting in any chair in the room in which he or she would be most comfortable).
- *Eye Contact*   Some cultures encourage members to look at other people "in the eye" to communicate respect and honesty; others consider direct eye contact to be a sign of hostility, impoliteness, or disrespect. Direct eye contact between a man and a woman may be interpreted as an invitation.
- *Body Movements*   This can mean different things in different cultural contexts (e.g., finger pointing, toe pointing, crossing legs, vigorous handshaking, touching, head patting, waving arms) and as a result may be perceived by the client as insulting or rude; observation of a client interacting with others can suggest which body gestures are acceptable and which are not.

Verbal Communication

- *Names*   Avoid using a client's first name prior to being given permission to do so, or prior to asking the client by which name he or she prefers to be called.
- *Languages*   Ask the client about languages spoken and his or her comfort in using English.
- *Word Choice*   Avoid the use of idioms, nonliteral expressions, or medical jargon because their use can contribute to misunderstandings.
- *Privacy*   Some cultural groups discourage disclosure of personal information to persons outside the family or community, other groups have a cultural tendency toward openness and verbal disclosure. Rapport and trust need to be developed before certain information about family problems and conflicts may be disclosed.
- *Communication Style*   A passive (nonconfrontational) rather than an aggressive (confrontational) style of communication may be culturally appropriate. Some cultural groups value harmony and respect more than speaking a truth that may be associated with hurtful consequences; some groups perceive that it is improper to judge, comment on, or try to direct the behavior of others.
- *Yes Does Not Always Mean Yes*   A client's responses suggesting understanding (head nodding or smiling) of information provided or agreement with treatment plans may reflect the client's attempt to maintain dignity or self-esteem, or this may be a culturally appropriate verbal behavior toward symbols of power, authority, knowledge.

In addition, it is imperative that during the assessment process information be obtained from the client and significant others on family patterns and structure, social organization, religious beliefs, and beliefs about health, illness and healing.

STRATEGIES THAT CAN ENHANCE DELIVERY OF CULTURALLY COMPETENT CARE

The American Academy of Nurses Expert Panel (1992) has identified a number of useful and effective strategies that have been used in nursing to enhance cultural sensitivity and the delivery of cultural competent care. The panel members provide some general principles for the design and implementation of culturally competent care. Culturally competent care strategies include:

1. Acknowledging the client's situation and being sensitive for the need to have cultural-specific content
2. Respecting cultural norms, values, and communication/time patterns
3. Providing support for the cultural group/members to implement (if possible) their own solutions to their health care needs
4. Interpersonal competence and sensitivity on the part of the nurse

Determining mutually set goals with clients is another skill needed by nurses. Knafl, Cavallari, and Dixon (1988) noted that effectiveness of care had been shown to be improved when the nurse took the client's perspective into account when developing a plan of care. This is especially important when caring for clients from different cultural backgrounds. This approach is referred to as the client–practitioner model.

The client–practitioner model of care involves the following steps:

1. Creating a dialogue with clients on care-related issues
2. Establishing mutual understanding with clients
3. Identifying a common goal in care
4. Establishing a plan to work toward the common goal

Nurses also need to develop skills in the identification of cultural bias, recognizing that the development of culturally sensitive health care is not simply one person or institution's problems. Cultural bias results from the interaction of multiple factors. Two questions asked in assessing cultural bias are, "What policy has guided the development of the service or program? and "What was the process involved in identifying groups to benefit from the program?" Issues of cultural bias may include discrimination, social isolation, access to health care system, regional disparities, and the lack of use of interpreters (Lynam, 1992).

Cultural Competence in Education

There is considerable variation in the way nurses are educated to deal with cultural diversity. It is not possible for nurses to be familiar with all of the groups they may encounter in practice but they have a responsibility to develop knowledge about groups with whom they most often work with.

Basic exposure to cultural content is very helpful; however, the practice arena cannot depend totally on the educational system to prepare nurses to practice with a specific group. Collaboration between practice and education provides the best model. The nurse needs to learn and understand the balance of knowledge that is culture specific, and the concepts or processes that are useful in understanding people across cultures.

Several principles needed when planning education of nurses on cultural competence include:

1. Learning to appreciate intergroup and intragroup cultural diversity and commonalities in racial/ethnic minority populations
2. Understanding how social structural factors shape health-related behaviors and practices in racial/ethnic minorities to foster nurses avoiding a blaming and victim ideology
3. Understanding the dynamics and challenges inherent in biculturalism and bilingualism where groups may live and function in two cultures
4. Confronting their own ethnocentrism and racism
5. Rehearsing, practicing, and evaluating services provided to ethnic/minority populations

Research

Porter and Villarruel (1993) have suggested guidelines in developing and critiquing research of ethnic populations. They assert that models should include theoretical and methodological designs congruent with the realities of racial and ethnic populations. These guidelines examine various components of the research process such as the framework, sample, measurement, investigator, analysis, and discussion for cultural relevancy. The guidelines are posed in question format, for example, "Is there evidence that the conceptual framework or concepts are relevant to the populations?"; "Is the instrument reliable and valid for racial and ethnic populations?"; and "Is the race or ethnicity of the research team included and specified?" (p. 60). These guidelines are helpful for nurses conducting research.

CONCLUSION

There are many issues that exist surrounding cultural competence in the United States. Consensus has not been reached on terms. For example, the general population can no longer be dichotomized as "minority" and "nonminority" because some ethnic/culture groups consider this inappropriate and offensive. Experts are continuing to strive for consensus in terms because the four broad ethnic/cultural categories used in the beginning of this chapter mask important differences between subgroups as stated earlier.

In 1985, the Secretary of Health and Human Services published the landmark document on the health status of ethnic/minority groups—African-American, Hispanic, Asian/Pacific Islander, and American Indian—in the United States. The consensus was that there was greater rate of mortality in these groups and the leading causes of death of among them all were the same: diabetes, cardiovascular disease, stroke, cirrhosis, and cancer. However, what needs to be emphasized is that the leading cause of death was alcohol and other drug abuse.

The number one public health issue in this country needs to be recognized as alcohol, tobacco, and other drug problems. And nurses are going to continue to see clients from these ethnic/minority groups with failing health as a result of these addictions. Therefore, it is imperative that nurses be culturally competent in the care they provide. Ensuring culturally competent care means:

1. Utilizing a theory and research knowledge base in providing care to diverse populations
2. Identifying culture-specific knowledge as it pertains to specific cultural groups
3. Applying culturally related processes (i.e., cultural shock) to diverse cultural groups
4. Maintaining respect for members of ethnic and cultural groups and examining one's own assumptions
5. Utilizing the client-negotiation model in practice
6. Teaching nurses and other health care providers application of culturally competent principles and skills
7. Participating and initiating research that would provide models of culturally competent care
8. Examining cultural bias within programs, services, and institutions that provide care to ethnic communities
9. Building alliances and collaborating with ethnic communities and leaders.

REFERENCES

American Association of Colleges of Nurses (1994). *Certification and regulation of advanced practice nurses: Position statement.* Washington DC: American Association of Colleges of Nurses.

American Association of Nurses Expert Panel Report (1992). Culturally competent health care. *Nursing Outlook, 40*(6), 277–283.

Andrews, M.M. (1992). Cultural perspectives on nursing in the 21st century. *Journal of Professional Nursing, 8*(1), 7–15.

Billingsley, A. (1992). *Climbing Jacob's ladder: The enduring legacy of African-American families.* New York: Simon & Schuster.

Brink, P. (1976). Cultural shock: Theoretical and applied. In P.J. Brink & J.M. Saunders (Eds.) *Transcultural nursing: A book of readings.* Englewood Cliff, NJ: Prentice Hall.

Campinha-Bacote, J. (1994). *The process of cultural competence: A culturally competent model of care* (2nd. ed). Ohio: Transcultural CARE Associates Press.

Carey, J.W. (1993). Linking qualitative and quantitative methods: Integrating culture factors into public health. *Qualitative Health Research, 3*(3), 298–318.

Chen, V. (1995). Asian-American and Pacific Islander women. In K. Allen & J. Phillips (Eds.) *Women's health across the lifespan: A comprehensive perspective.* Philadelphia: J.B. Lippincott (in press).

Cross, T., Bazron, B., Dennis, K., & Issac, M. (1989). *Toward a culturally competent system of care.* Monograph produced by CASSAP. Technical Assistance Center, Georgetown University Child Development Center.

Katz, P., & Taylor, D. (Eds.). (1989). *Eliminating racism: Profiles in controversy.* New York: Plenum Press.

Knafl, K. Cavallari, K., & Dixon, D. (1988). *Pediatric hospitalization: Family and nurse perspectives.* Boston: Scott Foresman.

LaFrombosie, T., Hardin, L., Coleman, K., & Gerton, J. (1993). Psychological impact of biculturalism: Evidence & theory. *Psychological Bulletin, 114*(3), 395–412.

Lipson, J.G., & Meleis, A. I. (1985). Culturally appropriate care: The case of immigrants. *Topics in Clinical Nursing, 7*(3) 48–56.

Louie, K.B. (1992). Spanning cultural differences. Addictions *Nursing Network, 4*(2), 48–52.

Louie, K.B. (1984) Cultural issues in psychiatric nursing. In S. Lego (Ed.) *American handbook of psychiatric nursing* (pp. 608–614.). Philadelphia: J.B. Lippincott.

Lynam, M.J. (1992). Towards the goal of providing culturally sensitive care: Principles upon which to build nursing curricula. *Journal of Advanced Nursing, 17,* 149–157.

Monroe, A., Goldman, R., & Dube, C. (1994). *Race, culture and ethnicity in primary care: Addressing alcohol and other drug problems.* Instructor's Guide. Project ADEPT, Vol. 5. Providence, RI: Brown University.

Orlandi, M. (1992). Defining cultural competence: Organizing framework. In Orlandi, M., Weston R., & Epstein L. *Cultural competence for evaluators.* DHHS Publication No. (ADM)92-1884, Rockville, MD: Office for Substance Abuse Prevention.

Peoples, J., & Bailey G. (1991) *Humanity: An introduction into cultural anthropology* (2nd ed.) St. Paul, MN: West.

Porter, C.P., & Villarruel, A.M. (1993). Nursing research with African Americans and Hispanic people: Guidelines for action. *Nursing Outlook, 41*(2), 59–66.

Schultz, E., & Lavenda R. (1990) *Cultural anthropology: A perspective on the human condition* (2nd ed.) St. Paul, MN: West.

Spadley, J. (1990). Ethnography and culture. In Spadley, J., & McCurdy, D. (Eds.). (1990). *Conformity and conflict: Reading in cultural anthropology* (pp. 12–29.). Glenview, IL: Scott Foresman.

Substance Abuse and Mental Health Services Administration; Center for Substance Abuse Treatment. (1994). *Treatment for alcohol and other drug abuse: Opportunities for coordination.* DHHS Publication No. (SMA) 94-2075. Rockville, MD: Substance Abuse and Mental Health Services Administration.

Trimble, J. (1995). *Historical overview of minority alcohol and other drug abuse, and related research.* Presentation at the National Institute on Drug Abuse Minorities in Drug Abuse Research Workshop. Bethesda, MD: National Institute on Drug Abuse.

U.S. Department of Commerce. Bureau of the Census. (1990). *1990 Census of population.* Washington, DC. U.S. Government Printing Office.

U.S. Department of Health and Human Services. (1992). *Cultural competence for evaluators.* DHHS Publication No. (ADM) 92-1884. Rockville, MD: U.S. Department of Health and Human Services.

14

Ethical Issues in the Care of Addicted Clients

Karen M. Allen, PhD, RN, CARN
Lotty Inselberg, PhD, RN, CARN
Faith Hawley Howarth, EdM, BSN, RN, CMC

INTRODUCTION

> Virtue, morality, and ethics—as applied to our working lives—are not words or notions
> we spend a lot of time defining, debating, or carving in stone. (Harwood, 1994)

Changes in health care along with changes in level of autonomy, accountability, and responsibility, contribute to creating ethical issues and dilemmas in nursing practice. Nurses are educated to make decisions related to the care of clients, and therefore, receive ample learning experiences to achieve this goal. However, they are rarely given the same learning opportunities and practical experience to prepare for dealing with ethical issues that interface with their work.

Hence, except for religious training, nurses have few resources with which to examine the ethical components of life. Ethical decisions made in their personal lives are based on convictions from family and culture, formulated over time. However, ethical dilemmas in providing care to clients are complex. Therefore, nurses must look beyond family, culture, religious training, and personal belief of right and wrong for help in making ethical decisions in the workplace (Chinn, 1986). Ethical decision making must be based on an ethical analysis of problems.

Research on ethical issues and decision making in nursing practice has tended to focus on some areas of nursing more than others. Studies have been conducted on the ethical issues and decision making in care of clients with medical illnesses (Keller, 1985; Holly, 1986); care of the critically ill client (Otto, 1986; Cooper, 1991; Holly & Lyons, 1992); care of the client in the community (Aroskar, 1989; Lanik & Webb, 1989); care of clients in long-term settings (Norberg, Backstrom, Athlin, & Norberg, 1988; Lever, 1992); and care of the neonatal client (Elizonda, 1991).

However, ethical situations and decision-making experiences in providing care to addicted clients has not been researched. In addition, it has not been addressed in many articles and books. Therefore, the purpose of this chapter is to: 1) provide definitions, theoretical perspectives, and principles on ethics; 2) suggest decision-making methods for solving ethical issues and dilemmas that arise with clients; and 3) give examples of ethical issues surrounding care of the addicted client.

DEFINITIONS, THEORIES, AND PRINCIPLES

Definition

It was Winston Churchill who stated that ethics is the rational assessment of behavior that can be taken in relation to ethical principles, rules, or codes. However, in addition, ethics is a scientific and philosophic study of human conduct that concentrates on morality, moral problems, and moral judgments. It is concerned with questions of right and wrong, duty and obligation, and moral responsibility for the patient/client.

For most, ethics specifically relates to a particular code one follows in conduct. However, one needs to be mindful of Tunna and Conner's (1993) comment that "A degree of misdirection exists in contemporary nursing ethics. The focus is almost exclusively on what nurses *ought to do,* with little emphasis on how nurses themselves should be. Consequently, practitioners may believe that character is not the issue and that doing the right thing [according to predetermined rules] is what matters" (pp. 25–26).

Theories

Most ethical theories utilized in the Western world are either consequential or nonconsequential. Consequential theories measure the worth of actions by their consequence, whereas nonconsequential theories do not. Utilitarianism is the most widely accepted consequence theory, and deontology—humanity's oldest theory—is nonconsequential.

Utilitarianism promotes the concept that rightness and wrongness of actions are based solely on the consequences produced, for the best long-term interests of everyone concerned. Therefore, one should act as to promote the greatest happiness (pleasure) for the greatest number of people (Husted & Husted, 1995).

Deontology promotes the concept that some actions are by themselves intrinsically good or evil (i.e., truth-telling or killing). Ethicists from this perspective are only concerned with how a person recognizes and performs his or her duty (Husted & Husted, 1995).

Presently there is no universal ethical theory agreed upon that is best for guiding the resolution of ethical dilemmas in nursing. And as can be seen, these theories do not focus on who one is or what one's values are, but on action—what one ought to do—when faced with ethical dilemmas. Therefore, it is recommended that an eclectic approach be taken, with the goal to balance a consideration for good consequences to as many parties as possible. One's duty is to carry out certain ethical principles, particularly as they pertain to health care.

Three types of ethics exist: 1) principle based, 2) care based, and 3) normative ethics.

Ethical Principles and Components

PRINCIPLE-BASED ETHICS

This type of ethical reasoning or decision making is guided by the following bioethical principles. Traditional ethical principles include: autonomy, beneficence, nonmalfecience, and justice. However, contemporary nursing ethicists view the important bioethical principles as being autonomy, beneficence, fidelity, veracity, freedom, and privacy. Both traditional and contemporary principles will be described.

AUTONOMY   Persons have the right to make decisions affecting their own lives (Keffer, 1992). This involves, but is not limited to, the right of a person (client, patient) to take individual actions with individual actions being directed toward goals that are exclusively the individual's own (Husted & Husted, 1995). The principle of autonomy is concerned with the nurse respecting the autonomy of others (clients, patients) including their value judgments, attitudes, and actions, even when they may involve serious risk to that person.

There are limits on the principle of autonomy. An autonomous person has the ability to plan, choose, and act on his or her own course of deliberations. However, autonomy can be diminished due to psychological or physical limitations or impairment. Hence, this would lead to increased dependence on others for their well-being.

NONMALEFICENCE   This principle asserts an obligation not to inflict harm intentionally (Beauchamp & Childress, 1994). It requires that the nurse act carefully toward others so as not to knowingly inflict harm. The duty not to injure others is separate and more stringent than the duty to help others. Both intentional harm and risk of harm are encompassed under this principle. Negligence would be considered an act of nonmaleficence. Omitting to do a procedure, health education, or screening could be considered an act of negligence, if the omission resulted in harm such as the progression of an illness.

Health professionals have certain legal and moral standards for providing due care that include minimum standards of knowledge, skills, and diligence. Nurses should keep abreast of current and new knowledge pertinent to the care of the patients in their charge. They also should not act or assume responsibility beyond their education and experience, as to do so may inflict harm.

BENEFICENCE   This principle demands more than the principle of nonmaleficence because agents must take positive steps to help others, rather than merely refrain from harmful acts (Beauchamp & Childress, 1994). Beneficence is a "quality of actions." It characterizes actions that are motivated by benevolence—a consistent attitude of good will (Husted & Husted, 1995). This principle infers that one has a duty to help others further their legitimate interests when it is possible to do so, with minimal personal risk. Yet, if this conflicts with the person's autonomous decision to not cooperate with the treatment regime, an ethical dilemma may arise.

JUSTICE   This principle states that there is a moral requirement that people be treated fairly, that they get what is due or owed based on what they deserve or can legitimately claim. This fair opportunity principle states that any differences between persons can be made relevant only if those persons can be held responsible for the differences. The American Nurses Association Code of Ethics—based on this principle as well as others—makes it clear that nursing practice cannot be influenced by age, sex, race, personality, personal attributes, individual differences in customs, beliefs, attitudes, or disease (American Nurses Association, 1985).

FIDELITY   Otherwise known as promise keeping, this principle means that the nurse will remain faithful to the commitment made to care for the client. This is a fundamental principle of nursing and ensures that the client will be supported through all stages of the illness (including relapse). It is rooted in the assurance that the nurse will remain faithful to the client even when disagreeing with his or her choices (Fleming, 1992).

VERACITY   This principle requires that a nurse accept the truth concerning the unique nature of the client. In addition, all communication and interaction between nurse and client require truth telling (Husted & Husted, 1995).

FREEDOM   This is the doctrine that nothing should be done to a client without consent. Under this principle, a nurse may not interfere with a client's purpose. Clients are viewed as having the power to pursue goals peculiar to their own unique desires, as long as the action taken is reasoned and practical (Husted & Husted, 1995).

PRIVACY In the health care setting, this is the right of a client to be protected against any form of intrusive contact from others. Furthermore, protecting the privacy of a client is precisely a recognition of his or her worth and dignity (Husted & Husted, 1995).

CARE-BASED ETHICS

Ethics based on caring is not based on fixed rules, principles, or theories, but rather on regard for the client (Hays & Gallo, 1992). Because there is one who is caring (the nurse) and another who is cared for (the client), caring is relational. The ethic of caring is used as a framework, hence citing either the principle of autonomy or beneficence as a rationale would be inappropriate within this context. The action is judged by the following criteria:

- Whether the specific actions brings about a favorable outcome for the client (or seems reasonably likely to do so)
- Whether the nurse displays a characteristic variability in action (i.e., acts on behalf of the client in a non-rule-bound fashion) (Hays & Gallo, 1992).

NORMATIVE ETHICS

Normative ethics take a moral position. They examine what ought to be and presupposes what ought to be in accordance with certain moral principles, whether or not such behavior promotes one's own interests (Inselberg, 1991).

Using the existing ethical theories and bioethical principles, "Codes of Ethics" have been developed by many professional disciplines to use in guiding care provided to clients. One such example is the American Nurses Association's (ANA) Code for Nurses, which was last revised in 1985, and is based on the traditional bioethical principles of autonomy, beneficence, nonmaleficence, and justice. Nurses are expected to resolve ethical issues and situations that arise using this code as a guide. However, the fact that contemporary principles have evolved and are not a part of this code needs to be kept in mind.

DECISION MAKING IN ETHICAL DILEMMAS

Before discussing methods for resolving ethical dilemmas, it is necessary to distinguish between practice dilemmas and ethical dilemmas. Care and treatment dilemmas involve confusion over what treatment is medically appropriate, whereas ethical dilemmas involve a tension that exists between two obvious moral principles either with no clear solution or all alternatives result in harm (Beauchamp & Childress, 1989). Thus, any nurse who is in a position where ethical action needs to be taken should clearly delineate the following: 1) the nature of the situation—that it indeed calls for an ethical decision; 2) underlying forces or issues within the situation that serve to make it an ethical problem; 3) the current condition of persons involved in the situation; 4) what everyone involved in the situation wants; and 5) what factor might be helpful or hindering in the nurse's efforts to achieve his or her purposes.

Next, it is important for nurses to be aware of the resources and tools available for assistance in decision making. Some use the traditional and contemporary bioethical principles outlined above as a guide in examining the situation and determining if a violation or conflict is occurring. While some use an ethical decision making model. Two examples are discussed.

A model for ethical decision making recommended for advance practice nurses and based on the nursing process involves the following steps (Furlow & Estes, 1995):

- Identify the problem
- State your values and ethical position as related to the case or situation. Explore the client's (colleague's) values in regard to the ethical question
- Generate alternatives for resolving the dilemma
- Examine and categorize the alternatives
- Predict the possible consequences of the acceptable alternatives
- Prioritize the acceptable alternatives
- Develop a plan of action
- Implement the plan
- Evaluate the action taken

Another model is Husted & Husted's (1995) bioethical decision-making model I (shown in Figure 14-1), which is predicated on the nurse/client agreement. According to these experts if a nurse performs well within the context of the nurse/client agreement (nurse and client are acting together by agreement, and the terms of the action are understood by both parties, neither is forced and neither is deceived), then the nurse should be ethically effective. In addition, the bioethical standards are used as a guide, otherwise the nurse/client agreement is undermined.

The Husted & Husted model is derived from the nurse/client agreement and based on the six contemporary bioethical standards: autonomy, freedom, veracity, privacy, beneficence, and fidelity. This model is to be used as a contextual application of the bioethical standards. It is to help nurses make appropriate (justifiable) ethical decisions based on the context of the situation.

- *Autonomy* The nurse must realize that every client is a unique person, therefore, for any action of the nurse to be justifiable it must directly or indirectly be an action toward or for the client. Failure to do this is failure to honor the nurse/client agreement.
- *Freedom* The nurse must respect the client's freedom in any action taken. Failing to respect that freedom means the nurse is not interacting with the client and does not honor the agreement.
- *Veracity* The nurse must engage in communication and action with the client based on objective truth so as not to violate the agreement.
- *Privacy* This refers to self-ownership and the fact that any interaction is based on agreement. If a situation is coerced on a client, self-ownership no longer exists, privacy is violated and so is the nurse/client agreement.
- *Beneficence* Every agreement by nature calls for a beneficent action. A nurse not acting for the good of the client is not beneficent and violates the agreement.
- *Fidelity* This deals with honor toward the client and the agreement made to the care.

All these considerations surround the ethical circumstances within which the interaction between the nurse and the client takes place. The nurse's ethical decision should be based on the context of the ethical dilemma and needs to include a wide context of knowledge on the part of the nurse (Husted & Husted, 1995).

Other investigators choose to analyze an ethical dilemma using the Code of Ethics for Nurses, which is based on bioethical standards and principles as well. Box 14-1 shows the tenets of the American Nurses Association *Code of Ethics* based on the traditional bioethical principles.

A method of ethical decision making not based on rules and principles (caring rather than bioethical standards) involves the following steps (Hays & Gallo, 1992):

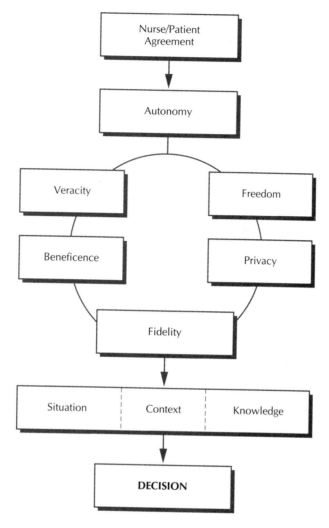

Nurse/Patient
Agreement

Autonomy

Veracity

Freedom

Beneficence

Privacy

Fidelity

| Situation | Context | Knowledge |

DECISION

Figure 14-1. Husted's bioethical decision-making model I. (Source: Husted, G., & Husted, J. [1995]. *Ethical decision-making in nursing* [2nd ed.]. St. Louis, MO: Mosby Yearbook, Inc. Reproduced with permission.)

- First, the nurse would work to gain a clear understanding of the client's concerns and beliefs, abilities and preferences, as well as the basis for them
- Next, the nurse would impart information, clearly communicated, that his or her role in the ethical situation is primarily to assist the client (and significant others) in clarifying beliefs and options
- Ethical resolution has occurred when the nurse outlines and stresses the entire context of the client's situation. Regardless of whether the nurse chooses to act using principle-based, care-based, or normative ethics, the nurse's obligation to the client must come first.

(text continues on page 246)

BOX 14-1. An Expansion on the ANA Code of Ethics

ANA CODE OF ETHICS	CODE OF ETHICS FOR CARE OF ADDICTED CLIENTS
1. The nurse provides services with respect for human dignity and the uniqueness of the client, unrestricted by considerations of social or economic status, personal attributes, or the nature of health problems.	1. The nurse provides services with respect for human dignity and uniqueness of the client, unrestricted by considerations of social or economic status, personal attributes, or nature of health problems.
2. The nurse safeguards the client's right to privacy by judiciously protecting information of a confidential nature.	2. The nurse adheres to Federal Confidentiality Regulations (42 CFR, Part 2) "Confidentiality of alcohol and drug abuse patient records" to safeguard the client's right to privacy, by protecting information provided in conversation as well as records.
3. The nurse acts to safeguard the client and the public when health care and safety are affected by incompetent, unethical, or illegal practice of any person.	3. The nurse acts to safeguard the client and the public from incompetent, unethical, or illegal practice, by: 1) continued assessment of self and peers for personal use of Alcohol and other drugs that might interfere with practice; 2) avoiding inappropriately intimate and sexual relationships with clients; and 3) advocating for the rehabilitation of identified addicted peers;
4. The nurse assumes responsibility and accountability for individual nursing judgments and actions.	4. The nurse assumes responsibility and accountability for individual nursing judgments and actions.
5. The nurse maintains competence in nursing.	5. The nurse increases her competence in caring for addicted clients by increasing knowledge and skills specific to their care; and makes sure that thorough, accurate procedures are performed as necessary.

Expanded with permission of the American Nurses Association.

BOX 14-1. (continued)

ANA CODE OF ETHICS

6. The nurse exercises informed judgment and uses individual competence and qualifications as criteria in seeking consultation, accepting responsibilities, and delegating nursing activities to others.

7. The nurse participates in activities that contribute to the ongoing development of the profession's body of knowledge.

8. The nurse participates in the profession's efforts to implement and improve standards of nursing.

9. The nurse participates in the profession's efforts to establish and maintain conditions of employment conducive to high nursing care.

10. The nurse participates in the profession's effort to protect the public from misinformation and misrepresentation and to maintain the integrity of nursing.

11. The nurse collaborates with members of the health professions and other citizens in promoting community and national efforts to meet the health needs of the public.

CODE OF ETHICS FOR CARE OF ADDICTED CLIENTS

6. The nurse practices intra- and inter-disciplinary collegiality and collaboration, using other health care members to approach care of the client in a team format, and insure that all client needs are met.

7. The nurse utilizes research-based care with addicted clients, and participates in research activities given the opportunity, in order to foster ongoing development of addictions knowledge.

8. The nurse familiarizes herself with standards of care for addicted clients that are available from the JCAHO and, ANA/NNSA organizations for use as a guide in providing nursing care to addicted clients.

9. The nurse participates in the profession's efforts to establish and maintain conditions of employment conducive to high quality quality nursing care.

10. The nurse makes a commitment to practice nursing with addicted clients in such as way that the integrity of nursing and persons suffering with addictions are protected from myths and misrepresentation.

11. The nurse uses opportunities on the job, in the home, and in the community to work to destigmatize the problem of addiction and facilitate better attitudes for meeting the demands and challenges the problem currently presents in the health care arena.

The function of nursing ethics is to avoid harm and guide nursing practice in behalf of good. Avoiding the difficult patient's needs would be an example of harm, while the act of caring would be an example of doing good. The central question of nursing ethics is "What are the morally justifiable reasons for my nursing actions" (Bandman & Bandman, 1990). The following are examples of ethical issues, situations and/or dilemmas that arise surrounding care of addicted clients.

ETHICAL DILEMMAS WITH ADDICTED CLIENTS

Although nurses are continuously faced with issues that arise in the midst of caring for addicted clients, the ethical issue that seems to receive a great deal of attention from nursing is that of the addicted colleague and concerns of how that might affect clients. The main ethical dilemma is whether to report the person and how that would impact on loss of licensure.

The focus of this section is to give examples of ethical issues arising among addicted clients who are not health professionals. However, the authors do recognize that addicted nurses fall within this category, and hence recommend that the above-mentioned models for solving ethical dilemmas be used when faced with addressing the addicted nurse as well.

Managed Care

Many ethical issues faced by many providing care to addicted clients are by-products of managed care. Decreases in coverage for alcohol and other drug addiction, and methods utilized by payors to be "cost-effective" in managing health care for this problem causes many dilemmas. For one, many managed care and health maintenance organizations reward health care providers for keeping clients out of hospitals, treatment, or other types of "costly" care. Therefore, someone really needing long-term treatment is only given approval for a certain number of outpatient days or certain types of services.

One example involves a client who came to a treatment program for admission and was determined to be in withdrawal based on a thorough nursing assessment. Upon calling his insurance provider and reporting the results of the assessment, and the diagnosis—that the client needed detoxification—the request for coverage was denied because the client's withdrawal symptoms were declared to be "not wacky enough" by the managed care company's physician. Here the nurse is faced with an ethical dilemma.

Another scenario involves the fact that some managed care companies, responsible for covering mental health and substance abuse problems, refuse to pay for addictions problems but will pay for psychiatric diagnoses. In an effort to help the client receive treatment for alcohol and other drug addiction, many health care providers give a client a psychiatric diagnosis and inform the staff to make all notations in the chart concerning this client relate to that psychiatric diagnosis, when the problem really is alcohol, tobacco, and other drug addiction. How much does the nurse emphasize to this client that he or she has a psychiatric diagnosis that is needed for admission, and to follow those treatments rather than those for addiction in and of itself. An ethical dilemma exists.

Another example is with an addicted client who is diagnosed in a general primary care setting. This primary care setting refers the client to a treatment program for the alcohol and other drug problem that has a good reputation, and good reported outcomes. However, the managed care company handling his health care benefits has an agreement with another program with not such a good reputation, that the client has gone to already and does not think will be helpful. The nurse is 1) this client's case manager, 2) responsible for advocating for the appropriate care for this client, and 3) facing an ethical situation.

Treatment matching is a state-of-the-art aspect of care for addicted clients. A nurse that has been case manager for a family discovers that the teenage girl who is alcoholic has relapsed. Based on patient placement criteria following an assessment, it is determined that the client be admitted into an adolescent residential treatment. The managed care company handling the family's benefits only approves a few outpatient days, although her last attempt at recovery was in outpatient treatment. The teenage girl begs the nurse to get her into an inpatient program because she wants the support and protection, and needs the structure, but the nurse has to do what the health care payor directs.

These are all examples of ethical situations that continue to arise currently when dealing with addicted clients and trying to follow-up appropriately on screenings, assessments, and brief interventions, but having to deal with managed care companies. What follows are a few examples of ethical situations that nurses are likely to encounter in specific clinical practice settings.

Maternal/Child Health

Several ethical dilemmas arise within the maternal/child health clinical setting. One includes having a pregnant woman come for prenatal care and discovering that she is an intravenous drug abuser. Ethical questions arise related to: 1) whether or not the nurse addresses the mother's addiction from a health perspective or a criminal perspective (child abuse to the fetus)? Should she be referred for treatment or threatened to be reported to social services for child abuse, or in some cases, face losing the child? 2) Research has shown that AZT during pregnancy reduces the transmission of HIV to the fetus. Should pregnant HIV-positive addicted women who decline AZT be forced to take the drug as a benefit to the child? 3) While visiting a pregnant mom in the community to follow-up on a drug-exposed infant, the nurse discovers that the mother is still an active addict, and the husband deals drugs, but the child is progressing well and very healthy. An ethical dilemma exists. Nurses in these situations are frequently faced with the question of which client to consider most important or which one to consider as the prime client—the mother or the fetus (or baby).

Primary Care Settings

In primary care settings health care providers are faced with clients presenting themselves as being addicted and requesting the provider to sign papers validating this diagnosis for the purposes of receiving "disability" benefits from the state. Because providers are not astute in assessing alcohol and other drug addiction, they see a client who could or could not be addicted but clearly wants to receive benefits. Is the nurse making a correct ethical decision in assuming that the client is telling the truth, and therefore, it is O.K. to sign the form?

The nurse practitioner has made a decision to conduct alcohol, tobacco, and other drug screenings of all adult clients seen in the clinic. After clients are screened the entire process is followed and referral for assessments, brief interventions, and treatment—if appropriate—are made. Screening all adult clients has resulted in spending more time with clients and seeing fewer than the expected quota. Management of the clinic that the nurse practitioner works for has presented the nurse with the edict that the screenings are not justified, and are slowing up the goal of the clinic—to provide *necessary* health care to as many persons as possible—therefore the screenings must stop. The nurse practitioner knows that having instituted this secondary prevention procedure has resulted in her identifying eight alcohol and other drug addicted clients in a 3-week period and that if she/he stops, a number of other persons will go undetected. The nurse has encountered an ethical dilemma.

Community Health

In one city jail, the nurse responsible for health care knows that 80% of the inmates come in addicted to alcohol and other drugs, mostly heroin, or methadone for those on a maintenance program. However, no detoxification procedure is even considered, much less instituted and as a result, a number of them go through withdrawal without any detoxification support (including monitoring of vital signs, medications, nutrition, vitamins, and emotional support). A new inmate presents to the nurse requesting to be formally detoxed from an addiction to alcohol, heroin, and cocaine. The nurse knows that prudent and competent care requires at least taking and monitoring vital signs; however, the usual standard of practice in the prison has been not to provide detoxification. The jail wants to reserve all health care resources for "real medical situations."

Hospital Care

Many ethical dilemmas arise in caring for addicted clients in the hospital setting. Among these include confidentiality issues, informed consent, advocacy, responsibilities regarding restraints, and rights and accountability. Nurses should be familiar with how to access hospital ethics committees who will provide consultations for troublesome situations that arise.

CONCLUSION

The ethical dilemmas discussed above are by no means exhaustive in number. They serve to provide an idea of the types of concerns faced by health care providers caring for addicted clients. The demands and pressures of current day nursing practice are as intense, chaotic, and unnerving as the current health care environment in which nurses practice. Anticipating this situation, the American Nurses Association in conjunction with the National Nurses Society on Addictions (1988) outlined in Standard XII of the Standards of Nursing Practice with Addicted Clients that nurses' decisions and activities on behalf of clients be in keeping with personal and professional codes of ethics.

Today, nurses have found themselves in the midst of numerous situations involving addicted clients that call for choices that are not black and white. Therefore, they will need to make decisions and resolve dilemmas using the models of ethical decision making discussed in this chapter. It is also important that nurses begin inquiry into ethical issues encountered by nurses caring for addicted clients and decision-making processes that have proven most effective.

An expansion of the American Nurses Association Code of Ethics for Nurses specific to care of addicted clients is outlined in Box 14-1 alongside the American Nurses Association's Code of Ethics and can be used as a guide in caring for these clients. It is believed that use of this expanded Code of Ethics will assist in interactions necessary while in the midst of ethical situations and dilemmas with addicted clients.

REFERENCES

American Nurses Association. (1985). *Code for nurses with interpretive statements.* Kansas City, MO: American Nurses Association.

Aroskar, M. (1989). Community health nurses: Their most significant ethical decision-making problems. *Nursing Clinics of North America, 24*(4), 967–975.

Bandman, E., & Bandman, B. (1990). *Nursing Ethics through the life span* (2nd ed.). Norwalk, CT: Appleton & Lange.

Beauchamp, T., & Childress, J. (1989). *Principles of biomedical ethics* (3rd ed.). New York: Oxford University Press.

Beauchamp, T., & Childress, J. (1994). *Principles of biomedical ethics* (4th ed.). New York: Oxford University Press.

Chin, Pegg L. (1986). *Ethical Issues in nursing*. Rockville, MD: Aspen Systems Corporation.

Cooper, M. (1991). Principle-oriented ethics and the ethic of care: A creative tension. *Advances in Nursing Science, 14*(2), 22–31.

Elizondo, A. (1991). Nurse participation in ethical decision-making in the neonatal intensive care unit. *Neonatal Network: Journal of Neonatal Nursing, 10*(2), 55–59.

Fleming, C. (1992). The patient who refused to be fed. In G. White (Ed.) *Ethical dilemmas in contemporary nursing practice* (pp. 1–12). Washington, D.C.: American Nurses Publishing.

Furlow, L., & Estes, J. (1995, Fall/Winter). Ethical dilemmas: When a clearly right answer is unavailable. *Advanced Practice Nurse*, 4–5.

Harwood. (Nov. 21, 1994). Ethics in the workplace. *The Washington Post.*

Hays, B., & Gallo, B. (1992). Ethical considerations in the delivery of home health care. In G. White (Ed.) *Ethical dilemmas in contemporary nursing practice* (pp. 71–87). Washington, D.C.: American Nurses Publishing.

Holly, C. (1986). Staff nurses' participation in ethical decision-making: A descriptive study of selected situational variables. *Dissertation Abstract International, 47,* 2372B.

Holly, C., & Lyons, M. (1992). Ethical practice in acute care nursing: Are we there yet? *Journal of Community Health Nursing, 6*(2), 103–112.

Husted, G., & Husted, J. (1995). *Ethical decision-making in nursing* (2nd ed.). St. Louis, MO: Mosby Yearbook, Inc.

Inselberg, L. (1991). An ethical analysis of the detection, discipline and treatment of the alcoholically impaired nurse in practice. *Addictions Nursing Network, 3*(1), 20–23.

Keffer, J. (1992). A postsurgical patient and the Do-Not-Resuscitate decision. In G. White (Ed.) *Ethical Dilemmas in contemporary nursing practice* (pp. 31–44). Washington, D.C.: American Nurses Publishing.

Keller, M. (1985). Nurses' responses to moral dilemmas. *Dissertation Abstracts International, 46,* 1870B.

Lanik, G., & Webb, A. (1989). Ethical decision-making for community health nurses. *Journal of Community Health Nursing, 6*(2), 95–102.

Lever, J. (1992). Variability in nurses' decisions about the care of chronically ill elderly patients: An international study. *Humane Medicine, 8*(2), 138–144.

Norberg, A., Backstrom, A., Athlin, E., & Norberg, B. (1988). Food refusal amongst nursing home patients as conceptualized by nurses aides and enrolled nurses: An interview study. *Journal of Advanced Nursing, 13*(4), 478–483.

Otto, B. (1986). An ethical problem facing nurses: The support of patient autonomy in the Do-Not-Resuscitate decision. *Dissertation Abstracts International, 47,* 1930B.

Tunna, K., & Conner, M. (1993). You are your ethics. *The Canadian Nurse, 89,* 25–26.

Legal Issues in the Care of Addicted Clients

Ann B. Mech, *JD, RN*
Carolyn Buppert, *JD, RN, CRNP*

INTRODUCTION

Every professional has ideas about what is ethical, what is moral, and what is valuable. But if one presents a case with ethical dilemmas to a group of ten professionals, certainly there will be more than one idea about what is "right."

In some areas of medical practice, laws have been written to provide strong guidance for professionals and to relieve them of the burden of choosing the correct path from a variety of possibilities. Addictions is one of the areas of medical practice where "the law" affects everyday practice.

Caring for an addicted client calls for the same legal considerations as does caring for any other client. Like other professionals, those health care providers caring for addicted clients must: 1) be licensed to practice, 2) provide an acceptable level of care, and 3) respect the rights of clients. All clients receiving health care are entitled to confidentiality and privacy; however, because of the stigma and legal issues associated with the addiction, issues of confidentiality and privacy for the addicted person are larger than for the average client. As a result, specific laws are in place that health providers must be aware of when caring for addicted clients.

Therefore, the purpose of this chapter is to 1) discuss basic law surrounding this area of practice, and 2) provide examples as well as guidance for avoiding legal pitfalls with the addicted client.

TYPES OF LAW

There are three types of law: common, statutory, and regulatory.

Common Law

The common law of the United States is made up of all of the decisions made by U.S. judges since 1776, and by the King's Court (England) before that. Today when a judge makes a decision, the legal tradition is to follow the precedent set by judges in previous generations. Common law is also referred to as "Tort" law. Tort is a legal term for having grounds for legal action based on one person's noncriminal harm to another.

Statutory Law

Statutory law is the law made by the U.S. Congress or by a state's legislature. Statutes may be found in volumes in law libraries (see the U.S. Code Annotated [U.S.C.A.] or the Annotated Code of any state).

Regulatory Law

Regulatory law is written by governmental agencies and is based on the statutory law, but covers more specific situations and includes more detail than the law made by legislators. The authority by which governmental agencies have to write this law is based on the U.S. Constitution.

PATIENT RIGHT TO PRIVACY

Special laws relating to mental health care, in general, and addictions, in particular, protect clients from public scrutiny of their life. These legal protections encourage individuals to seek treatment, because they can trust that appropriate confidentiality and privacy will be given to their issues.

Breach of privacy is an intentional tort and can be the basis for a lawsuit by a patient. Breach of privacy can also be: 1) malpractice, 2) the basis for disciplinary action by a state's Board of Nursing, and 3) a violation of federal and state law.

The federal government has seen fit to give special protection to persons receiving interventions or treatment for substance abuse/addiction. The special protection is meant to further the general public good by encouraging addicted individuals to seek treatment. Under Title 42, U.S. Code of Federal Regulations (regulatory law), a client must give written consent before a hospital, agency, or clinic's staff may send a client's records to another site. The law applies even when records are being sent to another health clinic, health care provider, or hospital. The law applies to individuals being treated in programs that receive federal assistance. In addition, many states have laws resembling the federal law.

A health care provider who breaches client privacy will find that clients do not tolerate it. Clients not only will leave the care of the provider (that is, fire the provider), but will tell their friends what happened, leaving the provider with a reputation for not protecting confidences. Therefore, when meeting a new client suffering with an addictive disorder, a health care provider's first job is to explain to the client his or her right to confidentiality. There are exceptions to the general right to privacy and the client should understand those exceptions.

Complying With Federal Law

The federal law applies to any agency, whether private or public, that is regulated by, assisted by, or receives funds from the federal government. Even if a provider's agency is not federally assisted, state law may require similar safeguards for patient confidentiality. Even if no federal or state law applies to an agency, it is good practice to comply with the federal requirements.

Records of client identity, diagnosis, prognosis, and treatment are covered by the federal law. Therefore, providers should follow these basic steps to comply with the federal regulations:

1. Inform the client that it will be necessary, at times, for the provider to share information about the client with other providers, or to ask other providers for information about them.
2. When the time comes that a provider needs to *obtain* information about a client, the provider should then explain the need for the information, and should ask the client to sign an authorization approving release of specific information by a specific third party. A sample consent form is provided in Box 15-1.
3. When a provider wants to *share* information about the client with a third party, the provider should discuss the need with the client, and ask for the client's written permission to share specific information with a specific third party. Each disclosure must include the "prohibition on redisclosure" provided in Box 15-2. The written authorization, including the prohibition on redisclosure, may be mailed or faxed to the third party. Providers often receive inquiries from third parties for information about a

BOX 15-1. Sample Consent Form

1. I (name of client) ___ Request ___ Authorize
2. (name or general designation of program that is to make the disclosure)
3. To disclose: (kind and amount of information to be disclosed)
4. To: (name or title of the person or organization to which disclosure is to be made)
5. For (purpose of the disclosure)
6. Date (on which this consent is signed)
7. Signature of client
8. Signature of parent or guardian (where required)
9. Signature of person authorized to sign in lieu of the patient (where required)
10. This consent is subject to revocation at any time except to the extent that the program which is to make the disclosure has already taken action in reliance on it. If not previously revoked, this consent will terminate on: (specific date, event, or condition)

This form complies with 42 CFR Ch.1 (10-1-93 edition), but other elements may be added.

client. Before responding to each inquiry, the provider must obtain written authorization from the client.

4. When a client ceases to be a client of the agency, the prohibitions on release of information continue to apply.

5. Keep client's charts and other written records containing patient identifying information in a secure room, locked file cabinet, safe, or other similar container when not in use. Adopt procedures for controlling access to the storage areas.

6. Clients may have access to their own records without written consent.

PRIVILEGED COMMUNICATION

The law has recognized a tradition of confidential disclosures made in trusting, fiduciary, and/or private relationships, and has taken steps, either through legislation or court decisions, to protect such disclosures from public exposure. Examples of trusting relationships receiving privacy protection are husband/wife, priest/penitent, attorney/client, and doctor/patient. It is easy to see that these relationships are often therapeutic or helpful. Frank communication and open dialogue are necessary if such relationships are to prove beneficial to one or both parties. Obviously, the parties to these relationships would not speak candidly to one another if they thought what they said might be subject to publication. Protection from forced public disclosure is part of the doctrine of "privileged communication."

Disclosures considered privileged communication cannot ordinarily be made public, even in a court of law, without the consent of the individual holding the privilege (client, patient, penitent, or spouse). The person to whom the disclosure was made (lawyer, doctor, priest, or other spouse) must not make public the communication unless directed to do so by the person holding the privilege or by a court of law under special circumstances. Health care providers, often the recipients of highly sensitive information from their clients who are substance abusers/addicts, may wonder if their clients can hold communication between them as privileged, preventing disclosure even in court. Health care providers may also be

---

BOX 15-2. Notice on Prohibition on Redisclosure

Each disclosure made with the client's written consent must be accompanied by the following written statement:

"This information has been disclosed to you from records protected by federal confidentiality rules (42 CFR, part 2). The federal rules prohibit you from making any further disclosure of this information unless further disclosure is expressly permitted by the written consent of the person to whom it pertains or as otherwise permitted by 42 CFR, part 2. A general authorization for the release of medical or other information is NOT sufficient for this purpose. The federal rules restrict any use of the information to criminally investigate or prosecute any alcohol or drug abuse client."

concerned that a court may, under certain circumstances, override the client's privilege, and force the health care provider to disclose information that may be detrimental to the client's legal status or well being.

Privileged communication between client and health care provider *is not* automatic in each jurisdiction in the United States. The District of Columbia, a majority of the 50 states, and the U.S. Virgin Islands have statutes addressing the issue of privileged communication between client and health care provider. Table 15-1 charts the privileged communication status of statements made to four categories of health care providers who may be involved in *counseling* substance abusers: physician–psychiatrist, nurse–psychotherapist, psychologist, and social worker. It is evident that not all substance abusers being counseled by health care providers have the privacy protection privileged communication affords.

Most jurisdictions grant privileged status to disclosures made in the physician/patient relationship. Disclosures made by clients to psychologists are also frequently protected, although not to the same extent as confidences entrusted to physicians. Information revealed by clients to nurses and social workers is *infrequently* protected by statute as privileged communication, unless the professionals are engaged in the psychotherapeutic counseling of patients. It should be noted that several states, such as California, Florida, and Oklahoma, grant the protection of privilege to disclosures made to psychotherapists, which could include nurses or social workers counseling substance abusers. Also, statutes in Louisiana grant privilege to clients of health care providers, whereas legislation in Nevada addresses the doctor/patient privilege and Michigan speaks of privilege for mental health practitioners. These categories may be broadly defined to include nurses and social workers, as well as a host of other practitioners who may counsel substance abusers. In jurisdictions where statutes have not been enacted granting privileged status to disclosures made to specific health care providers, case law may serve to clarify which health care providers may carry privilege in the context of their professional relationships.[1]

As statutes may protect confidential disclosures between client and health care provider, they may also dictate certain circumstances when disclosure is mandated. The most frequently occurring reason for compelled disclosure is in cases of child abuse. Health care providers may be required to report child abuse under both privileged communication and professional licensure laws. Some states, such as Arizona, require the reporting of abuse of adults as well.[2] Many state laws make an exception to the doctrine of privileged communication when they require mental health practitioners to warn third parties of possible harm. Health care providers would do well to keep abreast of laws governing privileged communication in the jurisdictions where they live and work. Practitioners should also be cognizant of reporting requirements found in professional licensing laws.

Thus, in some situations a provider *is obligated* to breach patient confidentiality. Again, if a provider suspects that the client is abusing children, the provider is required by law[3] to notify the appropriate authority, which, in most areas, is the county's Department of Social Services. Likewise, if a client tells a provider of a plan to kill the President or Vice President of the United States, the provider must notify the U.S. Secret Service.

If a provider learns that a client intends to harm a third party, in most states, the provider is required to warn the intended victim.[4] Finally, if ordered by a court of law to reveal sensitive information about a client, a provider should do so.[5]

Possible Exceptions

In some specific situations a provider *may* breach patient confidentiality. The wise health care provider will go over these possibilities at the first meeting with the client.

TABLE 15-1 Statutory Privilege For Patient–Provider Communications

STATE	PSYCHOLOGIST	NURSE–THERAPIST	PHYSICIAN–PSYCHIATRIST	SOCIAL WORKER
Alabama	X		X	
Alaska			X	
Arizona	X		X	
Arkansas			X	
California	X	X	X	X
Colorado	X		X	
Connecticut	X			
Delaware			X	
District of Columbia	X		X	
Florida	X		X	
Georgia	X			
Hawaii			X	
Idaho				
Illinois	X			
Indiana	X		X	
Iowa	X			
Kansas	X		X	X
Kentucky				
Louisiana	X	X	X	X
Maine			X	
Maryland	X	X	X	X
Massachusetts				X
Michigan	X		X	
Minnesota				X
Mississippi	X		X	
Missouri	X		X	
Montana	X		X	
Nebraska			X	
Nevada	X		X	X
New Hampshire	X		X	
New Jersey	X			
New Mexico			X	
New York	X	X	X	X
North Carolina	X			
North Dakota				
Ohio				
Oklahoma	X		X	X
Oregon			X	X
Pennsylvania	X			
Rhode Island				
South Carolina				

(continued)

TABLE 15-1 (continued)

STATE	PSYCHOLOGIST	NURSE–THERAPIST	PHYSICIAN–PSYCHIATRIST	SOCIAL WORKER
South Dakota			X	X
Tennessee	X			
Texas	X		X	
Utah				
Vermont		X	X	
Virginia			X	
Virgin Islands			X	
Washington	X	X	X	
West Virginia			X	
Wisconsin	X	X	X	X
Wyoming	X			

EMERGENCY TREATMENT

When a client's life is in danger and it is, in the opinion of the care provider, medically necessary to breach confidentiality, the provider may breach confidentiality to the extent needed medically.

INSURANCE INFORMATION

Most insurers require a diagnosis, at minimum, before the company will reimburse the health care provider. A provider who is doing client intake must discuss this predicament with each client. It is the client's choice whether to pay the treatment fee out-of-pocket, thereby avoiding the necessity for the agency to report the diagnosis to the client's insurance company, or to authorize the reporting of the client's diagnosis to the insurance company.

THREAT OF SUICIDE

There is no law requiring a health care provider to notify a client's friends, family, or other health care providers when a client threatens suicide. However, it is appropriate for a provider to tell new clients that the provider intends to notify appropriate parties if the client threatens suicide.

CLIENTS WHO ARE MINORS

When clients are less than 18 years of age,[6] there are additional considerations. States differ on the issue of parental notification and consent for treatment of minors. Providers seeing children must first determine whether parental consent for treatment or parental notification of treatment is needed in their state. Then, the provider should discuss with the minor client the need for parental consent if needed. No matter what the state requires regarding parental consent for treatment, providers with children as clients should tell the client that the provider will notify the child's parents if the child threatens suicide. And, of course, the provider should follow through and notify the child's parents if a child–client threatens suicide.

MATERNAL SUBSTANCE ABUSE

When a mother is a substance abuser, there will undoubtedly be consequences for her children, born or unborn. In the case of a fetus, a mother's use of alcohol, tobacco, and various drugs can lead to both physical and mental problems in the unborn child. Maternal substance abuse may also lead to mistreatment or neglect of children already born. As previously discussed, if a health care provider is aware that the client is abusing children, then that person is required by law to notify the appropriate authority. What, then, should a health care provider do when continued substance abuse seems likely to harm the client's unborn child?

According to Merrick (1993), several states, including Florida, Massachusetts, and Minnesota, now require certain health care providers to report a newborn's positive drug screen as evidence of prenatal child abuse or neglect. Reporting is done, however, after the fact, when the child is born and definite evidence of exposure to maternal substance abuse exists in the newborn child. Such concrete evidence of drug transmission to a fetus in utero may not exist. The purpose of these state reporting requirements is to notify local social service agencies to investigate and refer mothers for treatment of substance abuse/addiction. Such reporting laws do not provide criminal penalties for giving birth to an infant exposed to illegal drugs in utero (Merrick, 1993).

There have been several attempts to criminally prosecute mothers for child abuse for delivering drugs to their fetuses in utero. The Florida case of Jennifer Johnson serves as an example.[7] When Ms. Johnson gave birth to a daughter in 1989, she told hospital personnel that she was addicted to cocaine. Both she and her newborn tested positive for cocaine. Ms. Johnson was later charged with child abuse and with illegally delivering a controlled substance to her daughter. She was acquitted on the child abuse charge due to lack of evidence. Her daughter had not shown symptoms of drug addiction at birth, nor did she appear to be disabled. Ms. Johnson was, however, convicted on the charge of illegally delivering a controlled substance to her daughter. The focus of the charge did not relate to the delivery of illegal drugs to the fetus in utero. The conviction was based on the theory that Ms. Johnson delivered cocaine to her daughter through the umbilical cord immediately after birth before the umbilical cord was cut. This conviction was later overturned by Florida's Supreme Court on two grounds. The Supreme Court found insufficient evidence to support the finding that cocaine was actually delivered to the newborn during the birth process. The Court also reasoned that public policy demanded drug-dependent mothers be treated, not punished. Threat of criminal punishment would only deter pregnant women from seeking the help they needed to overcome their substance abuse and prevent harm to their unborn children.[8] Other courts have reached similar conclusions. Current policy is against criminal convictions for the mother for delivering illegal drugs or other harmful substances to a child in utero or during the birth process.

Criminal child abuse statutes have often been construed by the courts to apply only to neglect or abuse of children already born, not to fetuses in utero. The statutes themselves are not specific on how the term "child" is defined. Rather, courts have looked to the legislative history of child abuse laws and concluded that the statutes were not intended to be used to prosecute pregnant women for harm to their unborn children, which is often difficult to prove. However, all health care providers should follow their states' child abuse and neglect laws to see if the definition of "child" is amended to include fetuses. If state legislatures include fetuses in the scope of child abuse laws, health care providers operating under mandatory reporting statutes would be required to report cases of maternal substance abuse where harm to the fetus is suspected.

RESEARCH PROJECTS AND PROGRAM EVALUATION

Researchers, managers, financial auditors, and program evaluators may have access to data on clients and their treatments. However, no reports may identify, either directly or indirectly, any individuals. In addition, they are bound by confidentiality law not to discuss clients' names or any information about them with persons not related to the research or involved in the evaluation.

PUBLICITY ABOUT THE AGENCY

When journalists want to write about an agency or when internal public relations staff want to publicize a program, extreme care should be taken to guard the identity of clients. It is not easy to write about a program and not give examples of client stories or show photographs. However, an agency is risking its reputation with clients, and possible lawsuits, if the agency allows information or photographs of clients to be publicly disseminated.[9] A principle of public policy is: Vulnerable populations need to be protected (see Box 15-3).

DRUG TESTING IN THE WORKPLACE

In recent years drug testing in the workplace, especially pre-employment drug testing, has become more commonplace. There is some dispute as to the cost-effectiveness of drug-testing programs. However, a large and well-designed study reported by Normand, Salyards, and Mahoney (1990) concluded that positive drug test results were significantly related to absenteeism and involuntary turnover of employees. The use of alcohol, cocaine, and other drugs impairs employee performance, leads to injury and property damage, and contributes to increases in the cost of health and worker's compensation insurance. Drug abuse in the workplace is a serious enough problem that certain federal agencies (the Departments of Transportation and Defense) require outside contractors' employees to be subject to random substance abuse testing.

BOX 15-3. Indicators for Privacy

Consider need for privacy when:
- ❐ Discussing clients with other providers
- ❐ Friends or family call to ask about a client
- ❐ Sending out or asking for medical records from other sites
- ❐ Responding to requests for information from agencies, businesses regarding client
- ❐ Doing research
- ❐ Arranging for or allowing publicity about an agency
- ❐ Talking with reporters regarding the clinic/clients
- ❐ Doing documentation (charts left out on desks, papers thrown in trash cans)

Health care providers attempting to assist their clients in achieving the goals of maintenance or return to productive employment while overcoming substance abuse are faced with questions about how to advise clients concerning the consequences of drug testing in the workplace. There may be confusion concerning how much statutory protection substance abusers have in various stages of their rehabilitation.

Two recently enacted federal laws have provided guidance on the subject of drug testing in the workplace. The Civil Rights Act of 1991 prohibits employment testing that has little validity in predicting future success on the job and that has the effect of discrimination based on race, gender, or ethnic origin. The Civil Rights Act does not protect an employee who currently uses drugs illegally against the consequences of drug testing, unless such testing is applied with the intent to discriminate (Harris, 1993).

The Americans with Disabilities Act of 1990 (ADA) has expanded the protection given recovering substance abusers to private sector employees (U.S. Equal Employment Opportunity Commission [EEOC], 1992). Employees undergoing rehabilitation for substance abuse are afforded the protection against discrimination other disabled workers are given under the Act. However, no protection is given to employees who continue to abuse drugs or alcohol in violation of employment policy. In fact, the U.S. Equal Employment Opportunity Commission stated in 1992 that "ADA does not prevent efforts to combat the use of drugs or alcohol in the workplace." Furthermore, tests to determine illegal drug use are not considered medical examinations under ADA and therefore, are not restricted to the post-offer phase of pre-employment screening.

An employer may test current employees when there is reasonable suspicion that an employee has violated the employer's substance abuse policy or after an accident in the workplace. Drug testing may be part of a periodic physical examination. Random testing, perhaps most likely to uncover substance abuse, is probably the most controversial approach. Employees should be informed in advance about the employer's drug testing policies, and efforts to guard an employee's privacy must be maintained. Testing must be done by a reputable laboratory—state law may dictate specific certification requirements. Finally, an employer cannot use drug testing to discriminate against members of groups protected by equal employment opportunity law (race, religion, gender, age, national origin). For employers with unionized employees, federal labor law requires the institution of a drug testing policy be the subject of collective bargaining negotiations for current employees. Unionized employers are able, however, to implement a policy to test job applicants for substance abuse without the prior approval of the union (Kellner & Warbasse, 1994).

Health care providers would do well to advise their clients there is scant legal protection in the workplace for the employee who continues to abuse drugs or alcohol on the job. However, once a client is in rehabilitation and remains drug free, both the Civil Rights Act of 1991 and the 1990 ADA will protect that employee from various attempts to discriminate.

Health care providers and counselors in Employee Assistance Programs (EAP), while on the payroll of the employer, are subject to the same rules protecting patient privacy and confidentiality of information as outside persons. Disclosure to third parties, including the employer, are governed by federal and state laws protecting client privacy in a therapeutic relationship. Exceptions to these privacy protections, found in state mandatory reporting laws, are the same for all health care providers, whether or not they are part of an EAP. EAPs must be certain the employer is aware of confidentiality requirements for information gained as part of the client/therapist relationship. The employer cannot have automatic access to counseling records the way an employer would have ready access to the standard employment files.

MALPRACTICE

Malpractice or negligence is a legal action in which a client who has suffered some injury sues the professional who caused the injury. The only relief a court can offer an injured client is monetary damages.

To win a malpractice case, a client's attorney must convince a jury that the facts of the case satisfy five elements: 1) there was a professional–client relationship between the parties, 2) the professional breached the standard of care, 3) the injury to the client was caused by the substandard care, 4) the harm was foreseeable, and 5) the injury was real.

Duty

A client suing for malpractice must prove that a client–professional relationship existed and therefore, that the provider has a duty to provide standard care to the patient. A relationship may be established when a client arrives at a clinic and is seen by a health care provider. Less obvious ways in which a provider might establish a client–professional relationship include telephone conversations, giving professional advice at a social gathering, writing a prescription for a friend, or supervising treatment given by another professional.

Breach of Standard of Care

To prove malpractice, the injured party must prove that the care given was substandard. The standard of care is measured by asking: What would a reasonably diligent practitioner of comparable education and training have done? When malpractice cases go to court, the jury decides whether the care given in the case at hand was substandard. The jury bases its decision on testimony of expert witnesses provided by both the plaintiff (the injured party) and the defendant (the professional).

Practicing professionals learn what other "reasonably diligent" practitioners consider to be the standard of care by reading current professional journals, consulting textbooks or nationally recognized guidelines, following the protocols of the clinic, and consulting with colleagues.

Proximal Cause

A causal link must exist between the care given and the injury. In a court of law, a jury would decide whether there was a link between what the practitioner did or did not do and the client's injury, and whether that link was foreseeable. The jury will base its decision on the testimony of expert witnesses, and perhaps a little common sense.

Consider this example: A client takes methadone and has a reaction to the drug causing a permanent loss of function. The client learns that the nurse at the clinic dispensed the wrong dose. The client sues the methadone clinic claiming malpractice. The case goes to court. The client establishes that he was a patient at the clinic and that the nurse employed by the clinic gave him an incorrect dose. The client provides the jury with an expert witness who testifies that the incorrect dose caused the injury. On the other hand, the clinic's attorney provides an expert witness who testifies that the incorrect dose would not be likely to have caused the client's injury and that some other factor—for example, drinking excessive alcohol along with taking the methadone—caused the client's injury. If the jury believes the testimony of the defendant's expert and finds no connection between the incorrect dose and the injury (i.e., no proximal cause), then there is no malpractice.

Injury

Finally, a client suing for malpractice must prove the presence of an injury. If a client proves that the care given was substandard, but fails to prove the injury, the client will lose the case.

Common Mistakes Leading to Malpractice Lawsuits

According to Calfee (1992) mental health professionals, addictions counselors, and nurses working with addicted clients are sued very infrequently. And of the lawsuits that have been reported, the most frequent complaints are sexual misconduct with a patient or inappropriate mandatory hospitalization.

A provider who is sued will derive little comfort from the fact that such lawsuits are rare. Therefore, it is wise to examine the mistakes of others as carefully as possible so that they may be avoided in the future.

Other bases of lawsuits for malpractice have included:

- Abandonment of the client
- Failure to provide a substitute therapist during vacation times
- Failure to follow a client who has been hospitalized
- Inability to reach a mental health professional between appointments
- Failure to respond to requests for emergency treatment
- Promising cures
- Marked departure from established therapy methods
- Failure to obtain informed consent
- Failure to monitor[10]
- Unhealthy transference relationships
- Inappropriate treatment of severely depressed patients
- Interruptions in treatment
- Practicing beyond the scope of competency
- Misdiagnosis
- Harm caused by use of psychotropic medication
- Failure to control a dangerous client

CONCLUSION

The prudent health care practitioner will do his or her best to keep current on the standards of care for addicted clients, and follow them. They should not, however, let the fear of being sued intimidate them or stand in the way of taking care of addicted clients.

Issues such as: 1) privacy in relation to confidentiality of records and clinician–client trust, 2) coercion of treatment, 3) reporting drug metabolites in newborns to child protective services, 4) workplace drug testing, and 5) refusal of managed care companies to pay for treatment provided because of not meeting a particular criteria, are among many legal concerns facing nurses as well as other health care providers who encounter the addicted client. The above information provides the necessary knowledge that will help decrease potential anxiety surrounding many issues that arise, and provide protection for legal pitfalls made in ignorance when caring for addicted clients.

ENDNOTES

[1] Statutes granting privileged status to communications between patient and health care provider can often be found in state rules of evidence and civil and criminal procedure. Examples noted are: *Annotated Code of California*, Evidence, Division 8 Privilege; *Florida Statutes Annotated*, Title VII, Evidence, Chapter 90; *Louisiana Annotated Code*, Evidence, Chapter 5; *Michigan Compiled Laws Annotated*, Mental Health Code, Chapter 9; *Nevada Revised Statutes*, Title 4 Witnesses and Evidence, Chapter 49; *Oklahoma Statutes Annotated*, Title 12 Civil Procedure, Chapter 40.

[2] *Arizona Revised Statutes Annotated*, Title 46, Chapter 4 Adult Protection Services.

[3] All states have laws requiring that health care providers report suspected child abuse. These laws immunize health care workers from suits for defamation by the suspected child abuser. Many states require health professionals to report suspected abuse of elders as well.

[4] See Tarasoff *v.* Regents of the University of California, 529 P.2d 553 (Cal. 1974). The court held that a physician has a duty to use reasonable care to warn persons threatened by a patient. On the other hand, some states have laws that hold a therapist harmless for failing to warn a potential victim.

[5] Counselors should follow *court orders*. A subpoena is not a court order. A counselor receiving a subpoena should consult the client, the client's attorney, and the counselor's attorney before responding.

[6] In some states the age of majority is 17 years.

[7] Florida *v.* Johnson, No. E89-890-CFA (Seminole City, Fla. Circuit Court July 13, 1989).

[8] Johnson *v.* State, 602 So. 2d 1288 (Fla. 1992).

[9] See Anderson *v.* Strong Memorial Hospital, 531 NYS 2d 735 (NY 1988).

[10] Woman admitted for drug detoxification. Died of overdose on third day in hospital. Harrington *v.* Rush Presbyterian-St. Lukes Hospital, 569 N.E.2d 15 (Ill. 1990).

REFERENCES

Calfee, B. (1992). *Lawsuit prevention techniques for mental health professionals, chemical dependency specialists and clergy.* Cleveland, OH: ARC Publishing Company.

Harris, M. (1993). Drugs in the workplace: Setting the record straight. *The Journal of Drug Issues, 23*(4), 727–732.

Kellner, R., & Warbasse, B. (1994). Testing for drugs and alcohol in the workplace. *Maryland Bar Journal, 27*(6), 21–25.

Merrick, J. (1993). Maternal substance abuse during pregnancy. *The Journal of Legal Medicine, 14*, 57–71.

Normand, J., Salyards, S., & Mahoney, J. (1990). An evaluation of preemployment drug testing. *Journal of Applied Psychology, 75*(6), 629–239.

U.S. Equal Employment Opportunity Commission. (1992). *A technical assistance manual on the employment provisions (Title I) of the Americans with Disabilities Act.* Washington, D.C.: U.S. Equal Employment Opportunity Commission.

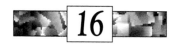

Intimate Behavior of Clients, Nurses, and Family Members During Treatment and Recovery

Susan E. Hetherington, DrPH, CNM, CS-P

INTRODUCTION

While providing health care—whether addressing emotional, psychological, spiritual, or physical distress— intimacy always becomes a part of the equation to some degree. Sometimes it is a cause of, or a contributing factor to, the illness or distress being treated, and sometimes it arises as an issue of the provider–client relationship. Ultimately it ends up needing to be addressed before progress toward health and recovery can occur.

Throughout the addictions phenomenon there are intimacy issues that range from personal intimacy dysfunction, to problems between the addict and his or her significant other, to drug-related physiological problems, to addict-to-addict issues, to nurse–client relationship issues. This chapter will explore the intimacy issues facing addicted individuals, their significant others, and clinicians involved in their care, which impact on their treatment and recovery. Case examples will illustrate inappropriate intimacy and sexuality between clients, between clients and nurse-clinicians, and between clients and significant others during treatment and recovery. Methods for maintaining secure boundaries to ensure appropriate intimate behaviors, and methods for addressing issues related to intimacy and sexuality problems will be presented.

THE CONCEPT OF INTIMACY

Intimacy and sexuality can be conceptualized as comprising four core dimensions: cognitive, emotional, physical, and spiritual (Figure 16-1). Although these four interrelated and dynamic dimensions are of equal importance, at times, one may be more frequently embraced than the others. None should be emphasized to the exclusion of others and all should be included.

Intimacy between people is characterized by very close association, contact, or familiarity. Although one's primary association with intimacy may be the physical act of sexual contact,

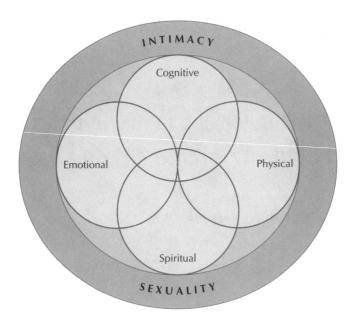

Figure 16-1. Intimacy and sexuality.

other verbal and nonverbal means of demonstrating intimacy are through the purposeful giv-ing and receiving of information about personal thoughts, feelings, emotions, and experiences. Manley (1991) defines healthy sexuality as "the experience of feeling whole and worthy as a sexual person, willing and able to consent to ... an established committed primary sexual rela-tionship, in which expression of sexual behavior is by personal choice and is consistent with one's value system ... and further that one is connected in all parts of one's sexuality to one's spiritual core" (p. 33).

All four dimensions of intimate and sexual behavior are impacted by an addiction. For example, the *cognitive* area relates to the addict's perceptiveness, communication skills, intel-lectual level, and decision-making style. The *emotional* component includes feelings and emotions such as satisfaction with self, desire for others, self esteem, trust, love, and anger. In the *physical* realm, intimacy and sex are played out through activities such as touch, mas-sage, masturbation, and intercourse. Finally, *spirituality* within intimacy includes love and faith in self as well as belief in a power greater than one's self. Clearly, intimacy, sexuality, and addictions influence every aspect of our personhood.

INTIMACY ISSUES DURING TREATMENT FOR ADDICTIONS: THE IMPORTANCE OF BOUNDARIES

During the initial phases of treatment for addictions, the client is highly vulnerable. Along with possible physical illnesses, the addict suffers from low self-esteem, guilt and shame, lack of trust, spiritual bankruptcy, possible history of abuse, and multiple economic, social, and psychological problems. Many addicts and their partners spent their childhoods with addicted parents, assuming dysfunctional roles and rarely experiencing healthy functional interper-sonal relationships (Hetherington, 1988a). For these reasons, treatment approaches must include provision of a safe, secure, and structured haven where appropriate boundaries are demonstrated, taught, and incorporated into the daily lives of the clients.

Boundary systems—as conceptualized by Pia Mellody (1989), based on her extensive clinical experiences—have been used successfully by hundreds of clinicians nationwide. According to Mellody, boundaries are "invisible and symbolic 'fences' that have three purposes: 1) to keep people from coming into our space and abusing us, 2) to keep us from going into the space of others and abusing them, and 3) to give each of us a way to embody our sense of 'who we are.' Boundary systems have two parts: external and internal" (p. 11).

The external boundary provides a means to protect one's physical dimension by allowing individuals to chose their distance from other people and enabling them to give or refuse permission for others to touch them. External boundaries also keep one's body from offending someone else's body. When external boundaries are intact, one knows to ask permission to touch another, and not to stand too close to others for their comfort. This boundary protects one's physical and sexual self from unwanted or intrusive touch.

The internal boundary protects one's cognitive, emotional, and spiritual dimensions. People with intact internal boundaries take responsibility for their thoughts, emotions, and actions and keep them separate from those of others. People learn to stop blaming others for what they think, feel, and do. With intact internal boundaries, individuals also stop taking responsibility for the thoughts, feeling, and behaviors of others as well as manipulating and controlling those around them.

Nurses intervening with and treating addicted persons must be aware of the importance of boundaries and model appropriate boundaries to their clients. One important method for creating an awareness of boundaries is through visualization. According to Mellody (1989), some find it helpful to visualize their external boundary as a bell-shaped jar that surrounds their body making it impenetrable and thus, protective from the intrusion of others. The internal boundary can be visualized as a bullet-proof vest protecting against the onslaught of any abusive statements, behaviors, or feelings of others.

Persons abusing or addicted to alcohol or other drugs have impaired or nonexistent boundaries. Whether or not this is a result of childhood family dysfunction or erosion due to the addiction problem, the result is the same—these persons have little or no sensitivity to themselves or to others. Not only have they offended against others with physical, verbal, emotional, or sexual abuse, they have also experienced offensive abuses from others. Therefore, they need to learn that with intact, flexible, external and internal boundaries they can have intimacy in their lives and still be protected against being abused physically, cognitively, emotionally, and spiritually.

Major boundary offenses, such as verbal and sexual abuse, are usually easily recognized. More subtle intrusiveness may be more difficult to recognize by individuals who have never experienced intact boundaries. For example, being hugged or touched by someone who has not asked permission is an intrusion into one's external boundary. This boundary intrusion is commonly committed during interventions and treatment for addictions by health care providers as well as clients. Offensive acts that indicate a lack of internal boundaries include blaming others for what we feel, think, or do, and using anger or sarcasm to hurt and belittle another person.

Developing an intact boundary system is a lengthy process and requires guidance, counseling, and many gentle reminders to accomplish. As clients learn to recognize their right to have boundaries, they learn to set limits with their thoughts, feelings, and behaviors as well as the thoughts, feelings, and behaviors of others. For example, all people have the right to be spoken to calmly and directly and without hostility, sarcasm, put-downs, and loudness. For many clients and families in recovery, communicating in this manner is a major departure from their dysfunctional patterns. Because the best education about appropriate boundaries and limit setting occurs through role modeling, nurses caring for addicted clients must be aware of how boundary systems function and must strive to keep their clients' as well as their own boundaries intact to avoid destructive consequences.

Consequences of Dysfunctional Boundaries

Dysfunctional boundaries allow inappropriate intrusions into one's intimate being, eventually disrupting one's state of equilibrium. According to Mellody (1989, p. 13), "four basic kinds of (boundary) dysfunction are: 1) having no boundaries; 2) having damaged boundaries; 3) having walls instead of boundaries; and 4) moving back and forth from walls to no boundaries." People with nonexistent boundaries have no sense of being abused or of being abusive. With damaged boundary systems, people fluctuate between appropriate and inappropriate setting of limits and boundaries. People with walls instead of boundaries keep others out because of deep-seated feelings of anger or fear.

Unfortunately, intrusions into the internal and external boundaries of clients and staff frequently occur during the processes of intervention and treatment, which results in disrupting the equilibrium of very vulnerable persons, thereby compromising their recovery. Examples of inappropriate intimate behavior between clients, staff and clients, and clients and their family or significant others will be illustrated with case examples.

CASE EXAMPLE # 1:

INAPPROPRIATE INTIMACY BETWEEN CLIENTS

Jane and Bob met in the 28-day inpatient treatment facility where both are beginning the recovery process from their cocaine addiction. Jane has a history of sex work to support her habit and a history of sexual abuse by her stepfather between 9 and 11 years of age. Psychological assessment reveals low self-esteem, a poor sense of her femininity, and confusion about her sexual orientation. Jane has relied on her sexuality to define herself and to cope with loneliness. She has rarely had "sober sex," that is, sex without using substances, and is fearful of intimacy. Jane's clothing is form-fitting and provocative. She is observed using flirtatious behavior and excessive hugging with Bob.

DISCUSSION

In the case of Jane and Bob, it is clear to see that problems from her family of origin resulted in her lack of boundaries and being unable to see and respect the boundaries of others. Bob, having had an erosion of his boundaries due to the addiction and being in a state of impulsivity for instant gratification, becomes a willing participant. However, interruption of progress in treatment, possible transmission of sexually transmitted diseases (STDs), further damage to self-esteem, and increased intimacy dysfunction for both persons will be the end result if this behavior is not intervened on and addressed.

CASE EXAMPLE # 2:

INAPPROPRIATE INTIMACY BETWEEN HEALTH CARE PRACTITIONER AND CLIENTS

Sarah, the evening nurse in the outpatient addictions program, has been sober and in recovery for the past 2 years. Lately, she and her husband have been having a series of disagreements about money, discipline of the children, and delegation of household duties. Sarah has

been struggling with low self-esteem and feelings of depression that she formerly medicated with alcohol. She finds herself drawn to an alcoholic patient, Jim, who seems to be dealing with similar issues in his homelife. During their evening chats, each perceives to "understand" what the other is going through. To stay in touch with Jim, Sarah offers to go to some 12-step meetings with Jim when he leaves treatment. Sarah rationalizes her behavior with the thought that she will be supporting Jim's recovery by making sure he gets to his meetings.

DISCUSSION

The case of Sarah and Jim illustrates the classic psychiatric concept of countertransference. Wilson and Kneisl (1992) define this as irrational attitudes taken by a therapist toward a client. Countertransference affects the clinician's (therapist) ability to set reasonable limits on their clients, and reasonable expectations for themselves (Vannicelli, 1991). With countertransference role reversal occurs when Sarah shares confidences with Jim. As a result, judgement becomes cloudy and the level of emotional involvement reaches another level. This is unfair to the client who is very vulnerable and, to some degree, under the control of the therapist. The therapist has intruded on the external and particularly the internal boundaries of the client. According to Rohrer, Thomas, and Yasenchak (1992), along with interfering in the progress of Jim's treatment, the feelings of partiality and favoritism shown toward this client is observed by the other clients and the morale of these other clients becomes adversely affected. Eventually a double bind will occur where one or both parties will compromise the relationship under the threat of exposure. Early intervention from professional supervision can lead to self assessment and resolution of most countertransference problems (Wilson & Kneisl, 1992).

CASE EXAMPLE # 3:

INAPPROPRIATE INTIMACY BETWEEN HEALTH CARE PRACTITIONER AND CLIENTS

Ben is responsible for group sessions with addicted clients and family group with their significant others. One of the topics for both sessions is intimacy and sexuality issues as impacted by substance abuse/addictions. Ed, the nurse, is the co-therapist with Ben in the groups and notices that a number of times the discussions become very explicit regarding sexual specifics in relationships. The nurse is uncomfortable but has had no formal training in this area, so he is unsure about how to address the issue. A few weeks later, two addicted clients have emotional breakdowns and share with the program director that Ben has been approaching them for sex. In addition, a family member admits to having sex with Ben during their professional relationship. Ed is confronted by administration regarding anything he might have seen or heard, and his rationale for responding or not responding.

DISCUSSION

The case of Ben illustrates major boundary dysfunction in that he has nonexistent boundaries. He has used the position he is in to gain the trust of vulnerable families and clients, and intruded into their internal and external boundaries by proceeding—without any sensitivity to them—to offend against them with a form of emotional and sexual abuse. Although the clients and the family members have dysfunctional intimacy due to the impact of the addiction, they recognize the inappropriate behavior and approach someone in authority. Ed as a co-therapist has the responsibility to act as an advocate for these clients. He realizes something inappropriate might be happening; however, because he is unaware of boundaries he is unable to intervene in the situation.

CASE EXAMPLE # 4:

INAPPROPRIATE INTIMACY BETWEEN CLIENT AND FAMILY/ SIGNIFICANT OTHER

Ted has been abstinent from alcohol, marijuana, and gambling for 6 weeks while he has been attending the hospital outpatient treatment program. Ted was sent to treatment by his employer because of poor work performance and frequent absences. As Ted's body has detoxified from these substances, his interest in sex has returned. He has made a number of sexual advances to his wife who has refused to engage in sex because of unresolved anger about his substance abuse and frequent gambling excursions. Ted is now demanding sex from his wife and is engaging in angry and abusive verbal assaults on her and the children.

DISCUSSION

Ted is exhibiting what is referred to as "codependent" behavior—preoccupation and dependency on another person. He is letting his wife's behavior affect him, in that he has become focused on controlling some aspect of his wife's behavior. As a result, his anxiety level has increased and he is experiencing boundary distortions around intimacy and separation.

Codependent Behavior

The term "codependency" derived from the experience of a number of therapists working in the addictions field in the 1980s. It is viewed from three perspectives: 1) as a psychological concept, 2) as a disease entity, and 3) as a didactic tool (Cermak, 1986; Morgan, 1991).

One of the first definitions of codependency was proposed by Subby in 1984 and is as follows: codependency is an emotional, psychological, and behavioral condition that develops as a result of an individual's prolonged exposure to, and practice of a set of rules that prevent the open expressions of feelings as well as the direct discussion of personal and interpersonal problems. Then in 1985, Wegsheider-Cruse described codependency as a specific condition that is characterized by preoccupation and extreme dependency (emotionally, socially, and sometimes physically) on a person or object. Eventually, this dependence on another person becomes a pathological condition that affects the person in all of his or her relationships.

A codependent is viewed as someone who lets another person's behavior affect him or her, and who then becomes obsessed with controlling that person's behavior (Beattie, 1987). Whitfield (1989) stated that the codependent is a person suffering from a dysfunction associated with the needs and behaviors of others.

Although this concept has not been empirically tested and proven based on statistical significance, it has been proven to exist based on the clinical experiences of a number of experts in the addictions field, and therefore, has enormous clinical significance. In the codependent person, some of each one of the above definitions can be observed. Hence Cermak (1991) proposed that codependency be viewed as a personality disorder based on the presence of: 1) investment of self-esteem in the ability to control one's self or others; 2) assumption of responsibility for meeting others' needs to the exclusion of one's own needs; and 3) anxiety and boundary distortion around intimacy and separation. On this basis, the connection between boundary and intimacy issues and codependency can be clearly seen.

For addicted persons, their significant others, and some health care providers who are caught up in the whirlwind of addiction and codependency, the inability to appropriately deal with feelings, along with having low self-esteem and self-hate, renders them incapable of examining their own behavior. The end result is a focus on and intrusion into the boundaries of others, which can happen before treatment, during treatment, and after treatment in recovery.

INTIMACY ISSUES DURING RECOVERY

It has been said that "recovery is a process, not an event." For addicts and their families and/or significant others, recovery is a lifelong process that begins when an intervention and/or treatment process begins. For many, recovery is associated with that time after the intervention and/or treatment process ceases and the client begins aftercare by attending self-help programs, such as Alcoholics Anonymous (A.A.), Narcotics Anonymous (NA), Cocaine Anonymous (CA), Al-Anon, Adult Children of Alcoholics (ACOA), Codependents Anonymous (CoDA), Gamblers Anonymous (GA), Sexaholics Anonymous (SA), Food Addicts Anonymous (FAA), or continued outpatient therapy for various issues. During the recovery process, numerous opportunities for inappropriate intimacy and boundary invasions may appear as illustrated by the following case examples.

CASE EXAMPLE # 5:

INAPPROPRIATE INTIMACY BETWEEN CLIENTS

Mike has been attending A.A. for 6 months during which time his wife and child moved out. He has maintained his sobriety; however, he feels tense, anxious, and confused about himself and his future. Although he has heard about the dangers of "13th stepping"—a term that refers to a recovering person seeking out a self-help program newcomer for dating and sexual gratification—he rationalizes that Kim, the attractive woman who just began attending meetings will be greatly pleased with and benefited by his support and guidance. He approaches her after the meeting and invites her to have coffee with him at a nearby restaurant.

DISCUSSION

In the case of Mike and Kim, becoming overly dependent on recovering persons both in or out of 12-step meetings is a common occurrence. To escape feelings of anxiety, fear, depression, and loneliness that frequently occur after program discharge, addicted persons may share confidences with the intent to 1) become overly close; 2) seek affection from another recovering person; and/or 3) manipulate. These boundary invasions hurt both parties. Mike will fail to make progress in his recovery if he remains "other" focused in dealing with his pain and anxiety. He must, with the help of his counselor, begin the long, often difficult process of self-examination and behavior change. If Kim's fear and vulnerability allow her to become intimately or sexually involved with Mike, her external boundaries will have been invaded, eventually leading to feelings of powerlessness, shame, and despair. For Kim, this invasion may be reminiscent of other self-destructive relationships fostered by her dependency on men.

CASE EXAMPLE # 6:

INAPPROPRIATE INTIMACY BETWEEN HEALTH CARE
PRACTITIONER AND CLIENTS

Before Joe completed treatment, he told his nurse Betty that he had a TV repair shop and would be happy to repair her TV at no charge for his labor. Because of Joe's constant need for others' approval to feel good about himself, he frequently offers his services to friends for little or no charge. Betty is very tempted to take Joe up on his offer as expenses have been heavy this month and her children have been pestering her to get the TV fixed. She also reasons that letting Joe fix her TV will boost his self-esteem.

DISCUSSION

In the trust-based relationship between Betty and Joe, Betty is considering a serious boundary invasion by entering into an inappropriate business transaction with her client. Joe, who is trying to be a "nice guy," does not know enough about boundaries to realize that his offer is inappropriate. His need for approval overshadows his need to operate his business in a professional manner. It is Betty's responsibility to foster Joe's independence, help him appreciate his professional skills, and recognize that he deserves to be paid for his endeavors. She needs to abide by the dictates of an ethical, professional relationship in which she, as the powerful helper, must not take advantage of her vulnerable, dependent client (Plaut, 1993). It is her responsibility to control the necessary boundary between herself and Joe to ensure that their relationship is confined to therapeutic sessions only.

Case Example # 7:

INAPPROPRIATE INTIMACY BETWEEN FAMILY/SIGNIFICANT OTHER

Geena has been attending the 12-step meetings of Overeaters Anonymous at least four times a week since completing the intensive outpatient program 6 months ago. Although she has two small children, 2 and 4 years of age, her boyfriend Marty was willing to care for them during her absences to support her recovery. Now, however, Geena has been going out for coffee with other recovering persons after the meetings and has been getting home late. Although Marty is used to assuming the codependent role in dysfunctional family situations, he is beginning to get in touch with his feelings of being left out and abused by Geena's prolonged absences from the family. He now wonders how his life has improved since she began recovery from her eating disorder. He realizes that he is still the primary caretaker for the children and has little or no intimate connection with his girlfriend. And yet, he is fearful of asserting his own needs, believing that such a confrontation might upset her and cause her to start binge eating again.

DISCUSSION

In the case of Geena and Marty, inappropriate intimacy can include distancing from loved ones, as well as overcloseness to them. For some, boundaries become walls that are impenetrable. Geena is terrified of closeness and has little confidence in her ability to parent. She never learned to share her feelings, trust her caretakers, or identify her feelings of anger, rage, and sadness. Distancing from the family helps to temporarily control her anxieties. Although she wants to be close to her boyfriend and children, she is afraid of being hurt or rejected by them. She was attracted to Marty because he was easily manipulated and made few demands on her physically or emotionally.

BOUNDARY MAINTENANCE: A LEARNED SKILL

At birth, babies are vulnerable and without boundaries. The ending of the symbiotic relationship with one's mother teaches that each person is separate and distinct. However, there is still the need to learn that internal and external boundaries exist to protect from unwanted physical, sexual, and psychological affronts. There are actions that can be taken to protect from intrusions into one's private spaces.

Few children growing up in dysfunctional homes learn these lessons. In fact, they come to accept abnormal, abusive behaviors as the norm (Cork, 1969; Black, 1981; Wegscheider, 1981;

Woititz, 1983, Starling & Martin, 1990, Domenico & Windle, 1993). Treatment and recovery programs must begin with an educational process that empowers clients to assertively protect their boundaries and say "no" to inappropriate requests or demands without shame or guilt.

With reinforcement and encouragement from clinicians, initially clients will develop their awareness of boundaries, but it will require much time and practice for behavioral adjustments to occur. These adjustments will be small and inconsistent at first and many lapses into old behaviors will occur. Acceptance of these frequent "emotional slips" is an essential aspect of recovery.

As shown previously in Figure 16-1, strategies for boundary maintenance must encompass the four dimensions of one's personhood: the cognitive, emotional, physical, and spiritual. However, before utilizing these strategies to support the development of healthy boundaries, an assessment to determine concerns and needs within the four dimensions as well as education on pertinent intimacy and sexual issues, must occur with the client.

ASSESSMENT OF INTIMACY AND SEXUAL CONCERNS

The following questions and issues need to be addressed in the assessment. Cognitively, what is the client's level of knowledge about human sexuality, reproduction, anatomy and physiology, and the sexual response cycle? How aware is the patient of the impact of addiction on one's physiology and sexuality? Assessments must also be made about the patient's comfort level with discussions about sexual and intimate topics, perceptions about sex and intimate relationships, and decision-making styles related to sexual encounters.

In the physical realm, the nurse needs to assess any disorders, limitations, or dysfunctions that have developed subsequent to addictive behaviors such as AIDS, herpes, and other sexually acquired diseases. Does the patient have concerns about sexual desire, responsiveness and performance, including erectile functioning, orgasms, and dyspareunia related to inadequate vaginal lubrication? Are any of these concerns related to a history of sexual or physical abuse?

Assessment of the emotional dimension helps to identify problems with intimacy that are commonly experienced by addicted persons and to determine the existence of anger, resentment, anxiety, fear, and mistrust that can adversely affect one's relationships with self and significant others. How satisfactory is the sexual relationship? Were substances used to deal with anxiety about intimacy or to avoid sexual contact? What is the person's sense of personal worthiness and wholeness?

Finally, the spiritual dimension includes the ability and willingness to love and forgive oneself, and to enter into an intimate relationship with one's "higher power." Once the assessment is complete, the nurse needs to acknowledge that the client's belief system has an impact on intimacy and sexuality.

BELIEF SYSTEMS THAT IMPACT ON INTIMACY AND SEXUALITY

Addicts have incorporated many dysfunctional social and sexual patterns and beliefs that must be addressed. These beliefs are perpetuated by the media, which depicts smoking, drinking alcohol, eating, gambling, and sexiness as sophisticated, stimulating, and essential aspects of social situations in general, and of intimate relationships in particular. Fear of intimacy is common in many of us and often something such as alcohol, tobacco, and other drugs replaces the risk of learning how to interact with others on a genuine and intimate level.

Alcohol and drugs are also used to reduce inhibitions. This is especially damaging for adolescents who in their formative years may develop a pattern of dependence on alcohol, cigarettes, and other drugs to negotiate intimate and sexual situations. Substances create an illusion of being powerful and comfortable with sexual behaviors, which may lead to sexual abuse. In fact, addicts feel self-conscious, shameful, and inadequate and bury these feelings with their drug of choice. As sex is a barter commodity in the marketplace for drugs, substances are frequently linked with irresponsible sexual behavior, unwanted pregnancies, and sexually transmitted diseases. These practices are life-threatening in this era of AIDS.

Many addicts believe that alcohol and other drugs enhance their sexual performance. Mood-altering drugs, such as marijuana, LSD, and cocaine, are often reported to enhance sexual experiences (Pinhas, 1988), although the placebo effect—the drug's perceived effect being generated by the user's expectations—may play a major role (Kelly, 1990). Anxiety and fears about sexual performance can contribute to a man's dependence on the depressive effects of alcohol or cocaine to "numb out" the penis to delay ejaculation during sexual intercourse (Dudek & Turner, 1982; Fewell, 1985; Pinhas, 1988a). However, in larger amounts, substances will eventually cause secondary impotence, that is, the inability to have an erection, when that function had been previously possible (Metcalfe & Fischman (Hetherington), 1985; Stotland, 1989). In their classic work on human sexuality, Masters and Johnson (1970) determined that secondary impotence in 40- to 50-year-old men has a higher incidence or direct association with excessive alcohol consumption than with any other single factor. Alcohol impairs spinal reflexes that control erection and ejaculation, thus decreasing sensations and enervation for erection (Buffum, 1982; Fogel & Lauver, 1990; Frank & Lang, 1990; Schiavi, 1990). Women who use substances experience difficulties in arousal and may have a reduction in frequency or intensity of orgasm (Kolodney, Masters, & Johnson, 1979; Fewell, 1985; Fogel & Lauver, 1990; Frank & Lang, 1990). Vaginal vasocongestion is also decreased resulting in decreased vaginal lubrication and painful intercourse (Dudek & Turner, 1982; Metcalfe & Fischman (Hetherington), 1985; Pinhas, 1988b).

INTIMACY AND SEXUALITY ISSUES TO ADDRESS DURING TREATMENT AND RECOVERY

Issues to Address During Treatment

Although frequently overlooked, all treatment programs—inpatient or outpatient—should begin to address sexual concerns within the first week. Although coeducational groups can be very beneficial by enabling each sex to hear the viewpoints, beliefs, and biases of the opposite sex, separate groups also allow for more open discussions on sensitive topics such as sexual abuse, sex work, and homosexual practices, and the guilt, shame, anger, and fear associated with these experiences. These discussions may arouse uncomfortable memories and provoke severe reactions, necessitating supportive counseling from the nursing staff who must be well informed about sexual issues and also comfortable with their own sexuality.

To recover, addicts need to learn new social and sexual values and skills to cope with "sober sex." Many will have a confused sexual identity and may exhibit values and behaviors that are consistent with the age at which their addictive behaviors began, as opposed to their current chronological age. When active substance use begins, the emotional development of the misuser is adversely affected as drugs impair interpersonal exchanges and lead to social isolation (Teichman, Teichman, Converse, & Foa, 1992). Thus, adults may exhibit adolescent sexual behaviors, if that is when their addiction began. Some will reach for sex, as they have reached in the past for drugs, to cover their feelings of inadequacy.

Others, especially women with sexual abuse histories, may experience a repugnance toward sex, which they had previously covered up with their substance use.

Educational sessions should begin with a basic sex education course to give patients an understanding of their bodies and how they function. Responsible sexual practices and the use of condoms in all sexual encounters must be stressed and patients should be apprised where free condom distribution centers are located. The proper application of a condom should be demonstrated and reasons for nonuse of condoms should be explored. Women should be empowered to carry condoms, demand their usage, and learn techniques to avoid dangerous sexual encounters. Addicts need to be confronted with the fact that substances have made their sex lives unmanageable and that drugs have had a negative impact on responsible sexual decision making.

Single people who have a fragile sense of their sexual selves have great difficulty resuming their sexual lives without their substances. Addicts who have combined sex with cocaine use find that a sexual encounter triggers a craving for cocaine and vice versa (Gorski, 1989; Braithwaite & Hendrickson, 1992). This reciprocal relapse pattern also applies to other addictive behaviors such as compulsive drinking and gambling or binge eating and using drugs (Washton & Stone-Washton, 1990). Single people are often advised to refrain from sexual involvement for several months to a year to avoid potential relapses from such triggers. Patients should be given permission to use masturbation for relief of sexual tensions and the many myths surrounding this practice should be discussed. For example, some men believe that self-pleasuring is a sign of homosexuality, or that this practice will deplete one's supply of sperm. Because some religions proscribe masturbation, the guilt and shame that often exist in individuals should be acknowledged. However, nurses should present information about human growth and development that clearly reveals that masturbation is considered normal sexual behavior that, for many, begins in infancy and continues throughout one's lifetime (Fogel & Lauver, 1990; Kelly, 1990).

Couples also need guidance in reestablishing intimacy and affection and determining what is a healthy and permissible level of sexual activity (Manley, 1991). Again, it might be beneficial to postpone sexual activity until both partners are established in their recovery programs. Both the addicted person and the codependent partner need to become acutely aware of their previous dysfunctional roles before beginning the long process of change. Couples need to discuss what their sexual practice patterns were during the active addictive phase and examine whether sexual boundaries had been invaded with, for example, manipulative, abusive, or intrusive practices (Mellody, 1989). During the recovery phase, the non-addicted partner may harbor feelings of anger and repugnance toward the patient and express unwillingness to resume sexual activities (Pinhas, 1988a,b). The recovering partner may experience guilt about past sexual behaviors or fears about the ability to perform sexually without substances. These feelings and reactions must be acknowledged and strategies outlined during treatment to help the couple heal long-term resentments and blame. Only with the permission of both partners should sexual activity be slowly reintroduced into the relationship. Nurses caring for addicted clients and their partners need to help them understand how their inappropriate behaviors were related to substance use. Increasing *awareness* of their destructive beliefs and behaviors will facilitate *acceptance* of their shortcomings and "slips." The gradual long-term *adjustments* take considerably more time to integrate into one's life.

Couples should be helped to process their thoughts and feelings as they continue to examine their values, attitudes, and beliefs about intimate activities. Developing comfortable sexual attitudes and behaviors to manifest a satisfying intimate relationship is a long-term learning process and most couples need at least 6 months of sobriety before beginning this process. People must be warned to be patient and gentle with themselves as they experience the pain, fear, and anxieties associated with the delicate task of reestablishing, or perhaps establishing for the first time, an intimate relationship.

Issues to Address During Recovery

Supportive counseling after completing treatment of any kind allows for continued exploration of new values and behaviors as well as a forum to process the ongoing experiences, upsets, and dilemmas that are part of everyone's life. Although the 12-step groups of A.A., N.A., Co.D.A., G.A., O.A., S.A., Nar-Anon, and Al-Anon should be part of the recovery program for the addict and family members/significant others, issues of sex and intimacy are rarely mentioned in meetings. Other sources of support and information for these areas are individual, family, and group therapy, aftercare programs, half-way houses, and abstinent social support groups. Recovering people need to learn to have nonsexual relationships and friendships with both sexes, and to learn to use these friends when they are feeling vulnerable, lonely, and needy. Recovering people need to be reminded again and again not to abuse someone else's sobriety, and if selecting a partner from the recovering community, to associate with one who has the same length of sobriety to ensure a commonality in their experiences with abstinence and recovery. Recovering people are urged to find a sponsor from one of the 12-step meetings. A sponsor should be one who has been in the meeting rooms for a number of years, is solidly sober, expresses the wisdom of the program, and can provide support and guidance when the recovering person is scared, confused, and fearful. Sponsors should always be of the same gender (unless the recovering person is homosexual) to avoid possible boundary intrusions in the relationship or other distractions from recovery.

When recovering people attend A.A., N.A., or other 12-step recovery groups, they learn that the concept of a higher power as a source of strength and guidance is derived from a spiritual focus, not religious (Alcoholics Anonymous, 1976, Berenson, 1987). Furthermore, they learn that each person's spiritual boundaries are strongly supported without intrusion or judgement from others. Members are encouraged to define and conceptualize a higher power in their own way. Those who have difficulty forming a relationship with their higher power are advised to live with their ambiguity, confusions, or anger at formalized religions and "fake it till you make it." The spiritual focus will help addicts develop a loving, nurturing, and intimate relationship with themselves as well as their higher power in which self-love and self-forgiveness are the cornerstones of continuous recovery. Addicts need to be reminded on a daily basis to be gentle with themselves. Gradually, they will learn to give up trying to control all that is happening in their lives as well as the lives of others and instead, "let go and let God."

Relapse Issues

The most difficult aspect of abstaining from drugs, alcohol, sex, gambling, and other addictive behaviors is dealing with emotions and feelings that have been buried for many years (Murphy, 1993). After 6 months of solid recovery, a few individuals may be coping well with both intimacy and recovery. Old patterns, however, are hard to change, causing the majority to experience significant sexual and relationship dysfunctioning. This may precipitate a relapse that is a reversion to old patterns of thinking, believing, and behaving (Gorski, 1989). Relapse is a return to the former (pretreatment) pattern of use after a period of stable abstinence, which completely derails and destroys the client's recovery plan (Washton & Stone-Washton, 1990).

Many concerns about intimacy and sex can lead to relapse. Some alcoholics believe that they cannot meet their social needs without the bar setting, and yet they feel uncomfortable and vulnerable in such places. Many addicted people have never been clean or sober in social situations and may feel overwhelmed with this new experience (Dudek & Turner, 1982). Furthermore, they must discontinue association with most of the people, places, and things that were part of their lives before sobriety, such as other addicts, nonrecovering family members, bars, and use of sex to obtain drugs or money.

If a substance or behavior was needed to make one feel sexually comfortable and socially competent, internal pressure to engage in the behavior will increase to regain those feelings (Gorski, 1989). Some believe that initiating a sexual encounter and being rejected is not a survivable experience and that they cannot cope without their chemical safety net. Without their drugs, they do not know how to handle the strong emotions of guilt, fear, hurt, and shame that may be triggered by memories of past experiences, behaviors, and patterns. The fear of rejection by former drinking or drugging buddies or pressure from them to use again can be very powerful. For some men, drinking and wild sex is a sign of manhood, which has now been taken away. Others may find that they now have to confront their erectile difficulties as they no longer have the excuse of being drunk. And those who could only maintain an erection while experiencing the anesthetic effect of alcohol or drugs might chose to be a potent user rather than an impotent abstainer.

Individuals struggling with questions about their sexual orientation may have previously covered up their homosexual feelings with substance abuse. They may have rationalized their homosexual activities as a consequence, rather than a cause, of their drinking or drugging. In sobriety, sexual identity confusion must be dealt with. This may be as difficult and painful as recovering from an addiction (Dudek & Turner, 1982). For such people, referral to a gay counselor who has struggled with similar issues can be very helpful.

Women may experience relapse when they confront their sexuality without substances and discover that they dislike sex, or that they cannot experience orgasm without being high, or that painful memories about previous sexual abuses come flooding in. Without therapeutic insights, they may continue to choose abusive and inconsiderate sexual partners who are reminiscent of earlier men in their lives. Some may continue to use sex to make money or to escape loneliness, only to find their guilt and shame reinforced. Counseling is needed to help women reduce these negative emotions and feel that they have control over their sexual activities (Pinhas, 1988b).

Infidelity may also lead to relapse. Often, recovering people are sexually attracted to other addicted persons whom they encounter in the meeting rooms. The commonality of their problems and the sharing of their stories may offer the illusion that this new relationship will provide a safe harbor from the stresses common to married couples. In truth, an affair is a relationship built on a foundation of dishonesty and will probably lead to relapse. In these situations, the program reminder, "You're as sick as your secrets," can be very helpful.

Even in the healthiest of relationships, issues surrounding intimacy and sexuality can be problematic for two people with different desire levels, schedules, beliefs, values, and attitudes. Thus, it is not surprising that these issues are even more difficult to negotiate when recovering from an addiction. One must always remember that abstinence from substance use takes priority and that couples should be comfortable with being substance-free before tackling their intimate relationship issues. If the codependent's anger toward the recovering addict is not acknowledged, the addict's recovery can be easily sabotaged with comments such as, "At least when you were drunk we had sex once in a while." Conversely, if the spouse is not interested in sex, the partner's relapse may be subtly encouraged so as to have an excuse to refuse to engage in intimate behavior.

Repairing the damage to one's intimate and sexual life is a long-term process, as is recovery from an addiction. The pitfalls, crises, and challenges along the path are many. Motivation must be sustained through many difficult and painful times as one begins to examine and reexamine every belief, value, and attitude previously held. When one realizes the enormity of the task, it is not surprising that "slips" back into substance use are common. The addict must be provided with anticipatory guidance about the potential problems ahead and supported through the turmoil and confusion. Gradually, as addicts experience longer and longer periods of being clean and sober, as their bodies become free of toxicity, as their thinking and decision making become clearer, the desire to remain free of their addiction will override their desire to use again.

Referrals for Sex Therapy

Many couples require professional assistance to deal with their psychiatric and marital issues as well as sexual dysfunctions. Annon (1976a,b) developed the PLISSIT model, an acronym for four levels of sexual counseling that uses the first initial of each word. Nurses working with addicted clients in treatment and recovery programs should have the required knowledge to adequately function in the first three levels of the PLISSIT model and should only have to refer clients to certified sex therapists when intensive therapy is required. Competency in the field of addictions should also be required of the sex therapist.

The PLISSIT model includes the following:

1. *Permission.* The nurse allows clients to talk about sex in their own terms and provides reassurance that they are normal. Sexual thoughts, fantasies, and behaviors that occur between informed, consenting adults are sanctioned. History taking provides a good opportunity for the nurse to give permission for discussion of sexual issues. As victimization and abuse commonly coexist with addictions, the permission to verbalize and release suppressed material can be very cathartic.
2. *Limited Information.* The nurse provides explanations about such areas as anatomy and physiology, sexual response cycle, reproduction, birth control, condom usage, sexually transmitted diseases, and ranges of sexual behavior. Addicted persons need to be apprised of how drugs have impacted their physiological state and how they affect sexual response.
3. *Specific Suggestions.* The nurse provides ideas and suggestions for self-help such as sensate focus exercises (see Box 16-1), relaxation techniques, and self-pleasuring, all important ingredients in initiating and maintaining an addict's recovery.
4. *Intensive Therapy.* When highly individualized or couple therapy is indicated, referral to a sex therapist/addiction specialist is advisable. Many recovering individuals and couples need the ongoing, intensive support and guidance of a professional therapist.

It may be useful for the therapist or counselor to assess the physical, cognitive, and emotional changes that have occurred in the intimate relationships of addicts and their partners since the cessation of substance misuse. This can be easily accomplished with the Intimate Relationship Scale, a 12-item, Likert-type tool developed by Hetherington (Fischman (Hetherington), Rankin, Soeken, & Lenz, 1986; Hetherington & Soeken, 1990) (Box 16-2), which has been used successfully to measure changes in intimacy and sexuality in a variety of populations (Hetherington, 1988b; Higgins, 1988). With this tool, recovering couples will become aware of areas in their intimate and sexual lives where they have made improvements and what troublesome aspects may require additional focus.

BOX 16-1. Sensate Focus Exercise Instructions

These exercises are designed to help you maintain your intimate relationship and feelings for one another. To achieve this goal, you must achieve three basic states on a cognitive, emotional, and physical level: 1) a willingness to be intimate with each other; 2) relaxation during love making; 3) and the ability to concentrate on sensation. These three basic ingredients will foster greater intimate and sexual pleasure in your lives and an enhanced sense of connection as a couple.

When people make love, their behavior includes both giving and receiving pleasure. At times, the partners take turns giving and receiving; at times these behaviors occur simultaneously. Both activities are important because they make each partner feel competent, powerful, and valued. Remember, kissing, touching, and massaging are intimate and sexual activities important onto themselves; they are not merely a warm-up for intercourse.

I would like you to do the following exercises exactly according to the instructions at least once a week.

1. Plan two sessions of approximately 1 hour in length each over the next week.
2. There is to be only nondemanding, pleasure giving touching during this exercise, no sexual intercourse.
3. Each of you is to take 30 minutes to give pleasure and 30 minutes to receive pleasure. Preferably you should both be unclothed, in a comfortable bed, with some light in the heated room.
4. As the giver, you are to use your hands, lips, and tongue to kiss and caress your partner's whole body, front and back, top to bottom, with the exception of the breast and genital areas. Spend 15 minutes on each side of the body. Your responsibility is to provide your partner with pleasant sensations. Experiment: touch firmly, massage, touch lightly. Do not tickle. Touch parts of the body you usually bypass: buttocks, armpits, feet, between fingers. Watch your partner's responses: facial expressions, breathing—and do more of what seems enjoyable.

As the receiver, you should relax and feel what is happening to you. Your concentration should be at the skin level when your partner is touching you. Make your partner aware of what is pleasurable, through words, sounds, smiles, movements. Do not touch your partner during this experience. Just relax and receive the sensations. When this task is over switch roles. If you prefer, wait until the next day to exchange roles. Be sure to schedule sufficient time each week for both of you to give and receive this exercise.

Source: Kolodny, R.C., Masters, W.H., & Johnson, V.E. (1979). *Textbook of sexual medicine.* Boston: Little, Brown and Company.

CONCLUSION

The major aspects to be considered in the reestablishment of intimate relationships subsequent to recovery from addictions are summarized using the four dimensions of the conceptual framework. The cornerstone of treatment and recovery programs is *cognitive* development through education. Boundary maintenance requires skills in communication, negotiation, confrontation, and assertiveness. Those skills must be taught as part of the

BOX 16-2. Intimate Relationship Scale

Name
or Number_____

Please circle
Client or Partner

Date_____

Many couples experience changes in their patterns of lovemaking <u>from the time substance use was occurring to after becoming clean and sober.</u> We would appreciate it very much if you would share with us some of the ways these changes may or may not have occurred to you.

Please <u>underline the phrase that most accurately completes each statement,</u> and give as honest an account of your own feelings and beliefs at this time as possible. Feel free to add additional comments in the space provided.

Your answers will be held in strictest confidence.

If you have not resumed sex, please indicate why, and then return this form without filling out the attached questions. Otherwise, please complete the following questions. Thank you.

1. Since substance use has stopped, the frequency that my partner and I are having sex is:
   (1) much less; (2) less; (3) unchanged; (4) more; (5) much more
   Comments:

2. Since substance use has stopped, my feelings of fatigue interfere with our making love:
   (1) much more; (2) more; (3) unchanged; (4) less; (5) much less
   Comments:

3. Since substance use has stopped, my partner and I find time for quiet conversations:
   (1) much less; (2) less; (3) unchanged; (4) more; (5) much more
   Comments:

4. Since substance use has stopped, I derive satisfaction from our sexual activities:
   (1) much less; (2) less; (3) unchanged; (4) more; (5) much more
   Comments:

5. Since substance use has stopped, my desire to touch and hold is being satisfied:
   (1) much less; (2) less; (3) unchanged; (4) more; (5) much more
   Comments:

6. Since substance use has stopped, my partner initiates sexual activity which leads to intercourse:
   (1) much less; (2) less; (3) unchanged; (4) more; (5) much more
   Comments:

7. Since substance use has stopped, my feelings of sexual fulfillment are:
   (1) much less; (2) less; (3) unchanged; (4) more; (5) much more
   Comments:

8. Since substance use has stopped, my feelings of closeness to my partner are:
   (1) much less; (2) less; (3) unchanged; (4) more; (5) much more
   Comments:

9. Since substance use has stopped, my desire to be held, touched, and stroked by my partner is:
   (1) much less; (2) less; (3) unchanged; (4) more; (5) much more
   Comments:

BOX 16-2. (continued)

10. Since substance use has stopped, my desire for sexual intercourse is:
    (1) much less; (2) less; (3) unchanged; (4) more; (5) much more
    Comments:

11. Since substance use has stopped, my comfort in talking with my partner about sex is:
    (1) much less; (2) less; (3) unchanged; (4) more; (5) much more
    Comments:

12. Since substance use has stopped, I initiate sexual activity which leads to intercourse:
    (1) much less; (2) less; (3) unchanged; (4) more; (5) much more
    Comments:

Please add any additional comments: THANK YOU.

This tool was developed by: Dr. Susan E. Hetherington, Professor, Department of Psychiatric Nursing, University of Maryland School of Nursing, 655 West Lombard Street, Baltimore, MD 21201.

recovery process with opportunities provided for practice. Treatment opportunities—whether they are inpatient, outpatient, in community health centers, private practices or clinics—must be safe places where issues can be discussed and inappropriate behaviors addressed immediately and made part of the learning process. Clients should understand that their dysfunctional behaviors may be the result of inappropriate and deficient role modeling from caretakers, who themselves had never adequately learned the techniques of parenting or developing and maintaining healthy interpersonal relationships.

Education must also address the intimate and sexual needs and concerns of clients and their families/significant others. Once again, clients will need guidance in identifying those behaviors that are appropriate, positive, and supportive. Health care practitioners must be comfortable with their own sexuality if they are to be understanding and permission-giving while discussing intimate and sexual topics with clients and their families/significant others. A group format is an ideal setting for these discussions. Those less comfortable with the topics under discussion can submit anonymous, written questions. Topics to discuss include initiating relationships, appropriate social and sexual behaviors, and setting limits with self and others. As group members feel increasingly comfortable and begin to share their own experiences, other members can provide useful and supportive feedback. Group facilitators need to role-model the provision of beneficial feedback offered in the spirit of support, care, and concern for others.

Sexuality, the *physical* aspect of intimacy, will undergo major changes in recovery. Sexual relationships formed too early into recovery can cause emotional upset, divert attention away from self, and allow oneself to be manipulated or to manipulate others. For these reasons, recovering people who are not in a committed relationship are advised to avoid sexual liaisons during the first year of sobriety. Recovering people need to understand that a year without a sexual relationship provides them the opportunity to concentrate on developing friendships with potential partners, a step in the courtship process that had been frequently overlooked. Free of sexual involvements, people can practice their communication skills, learn to express anger appropriately, and experience what it means to be able to talk, feel, and trust in a relationship.

All recovering addicts need constant *emotional* support as they return to a life without substances. They soon learn that getting sober is the easiest part of recovery; the hard work of making amends and of reconnecting with loved ones begins when self-medication is no longer used to escape anxieties, problems, and emotional baggage that accumulated from years of substance misuse. The maintenance of contact with 12-step recovery groups and a program sponsor are important factors in the development of supportive and intimate networks. If needed, a therapist knowledgeable in addictions and sexuality is strongly recommended. All of these strategies are vital in times of stress, anxiety, fear, and depression, times when recovering persons need to be continually reminded to be accepting, gentle, and patient with their recovery status.

Finally, the *spiritual* focus must be ever-present, reminding the addict that one cannot do the business of recovery alone. Developing and nurturing a relationship with a power greater than oneself provides the freedom to love and accept family and friends without judging, criticizing, and trespassing into their external and internal boundaries. Acceptance of a higher power or other spiritual symbol opens the doorway to self-forgiveness and self-love, essential concepts after years of suffering from guilt and shame.

The addict and program staff must always be mindful that recovery from addictive diseases and the reformation of vital, loving relationships is a lifelong process. The cognitive, emotional, physical, and spiritual dimensions must be interwoven into their fabric of support. Continuous vigilance in these four areas will serve to foster a dependable and secure recovery as well as a loving and intimate relationship with self and others.

REFERENCES

Alcoholics Anonymous World Services. (1976). *Alcoholics anonymous* (3rd ed.). New York: Alcoholics Anonymous World Services.

Annon, J. (1976a). *Behavioral treatment of sexual problems, vol 1: Brief therapy.* Hagerstown: Harper & Row.

Annon, J. (1976b). The PLISSIT model: A proposed conceptual scheme for the behavioral treatment of sexual problems. *Journal of Sex Education and Therapy, Spring-Summer,* 1–14.

Baudhain, J. (1985). *Now about sex.* Center City, MN: Hazelden Foundation.

Beattie, M. (1987). *Codependent no more.* Center City, MN: Hazelden Foundation.

Berenson, D. (1987). Alcoholics anonymous: From surrender to transformation. *Networker 11*(4), 25–31.

Black, C. (1981). *It will never happen to me.* Denver, CO: MAC Printing and Publications Division.

Braithwaite, H.S. & Hendrickson, C. (1992). Crack cocaine addiction: Behavior patterns of homeless African-American males. In *Today's agenda for a better tomorrow* (pp. 5–12). Atlanta, GA: Southern Council on Collegiate Education for Nursing.

Buffum, J. (1982). Pharmacosexology: the effects of drugs on sexual function—A review. *Journal of Psychoactive Drugs 14*(1-2), 5–41.

Cermak, T.L. (1991). Co-Addiction as a disease. *Psychiatric Annals, 21*(5), 266–272.

Cermak, T.L. (1986). *Diagnosing and treating co-dependence.* Minneapolis, MN: Johnson Institute Books.

Cork, M. (1969). *The forgotten children: A study of children with alcoholic parents.* Don Mills, Ontario: General Publishing.

Domenico, D. & Windle, M. (1993). Intrapersonal and interpersonal functioning among middle-aged female adult children of alcoholics. *Journal of Consulting and Clinical Psychology, 61*(4), 659–666.

Dudek, F.A., & Turner, D.S. (1982). Alcoholism and sexual functioning. *Journal of Psychoactive Drugs, 14*(1-2), 47–54.

Fewell, C.H. (1985). The integration of sexuality into alcoholism treatment. *Alcoholism Treatment Quarterly, 2*(1), 47–60.

Fischman (Hetherington), S., Rankin, E., Soeken, K., & Lenz, E. (1986). Changes in sexual relationships in postpartum couples. *JOGN Nursing, 15*(1), 58–63.

Fogel, C.I., & Lauver, D. (1990). *Sexual health promotion.* Philadelphia: W.B. Saunders.

Frank, D.I., & Lang, A.R. (1990). Alcohol use and sexual arousal research: Application of the health belief model. *Nurse Practitioner, 15*(5), 32–35.

Gorski, T. (1989). Cocaine craving and relapse: A new ballgame for counselors. *Professional Counselor, 3*(4), 42–44, 79–80.

Hetherington, S.E., & Soeken, K. (1990). Measuring changes in sexuality and intimacy: A self-administered scale. *Journal of Sex Education & Therapy, 16*(3), 155–163.

Hetherington, S.E. (1988a). Children of alcoholics: An emerging mental health issue. *Archives of Psychiatric Nursing, 11*(4), 251–255.

Hetherington, S.E. (1988b). Common postpartum sexual problems: A management guide. *The Female Patient, 13*(4), 43–53.

Higgins, P.G. (1988). Changes in intimacy behaviors in antepartum couples. *Journal of Nursing Science and Practice, 1*(4), 17–21.

Kelly, G.F. (1990). *Sexuality today: The human perspective* (2nd ed.). Guilford, CT: Dushkin Publishing Group, Inc.

Kolodny, R.C., Masters, W.H., & Johnson, V.E. (1979). *Textbook of sexual medicine.* Boston: Little, Brown and Company.

Manley, G. (1991). Sexual health recovery in sex addiction: Implications for sex therapists. *American Journal of Preventive Psychiatry & Neurology, 3*(1), 33–39.

Masters, W.H., & Johnson, V.E. (1970). *Human sexual response.* Boston: Little Brown and Company.

Mellody, P., & Miller, A.W. (1989). *Breaking free: A workbook for facing codependence.* San Francisco, CA: Harper San Francisco.

Mellody, P., Miller, A.W., & Miller, J.K. (1989). *Facing codependence.* San Francisco: Harper Collins Publishers.

Metcalfe, M.C., & Fischman (Hetherington) S. (1985). Factors affecting the sexuality of patients with head and neck cancer. *Oncology Nursing Forum, 12*(2), 21–25.

Morgan, J.P. Jr. (1991). What is codependency? *Journal of Clinical Psychology, 47*(5), 720–729.

Murphy, S.A. (1993). Coping strategies of abstainers from alcohol up to three years post-treatment. *Image Journal of Nursing Scholarship, 25*(1), 29–35.

Pinhas, V. (1988a). Sexuality counseling of people with chemical dependency. In E. Weinstein & E. Rosen (Eds.), *Sexuality counseling: Issues and implications* (pp. 224–242). Pacific Grove, CA: Brooks/Cole Publishing Co.

Pinhas, V. (1988b). Sexuality counseling of people with alcohol problems. In E. Weinstein & E. Rosen (Eds.), *Sexuality counseling: Issues and implications* (pp. 243–259). Pacific Grove, CA: Brooks/Cole Publishing Co.

Plaut, M.S. (1993). Boundary issues in teacher-student relationships. *Journal of Sex & Marital Therapy, 19*(3), 210–219.

Rohrer, G.E., Thomas, M., & Yasenchak, A.B. (1992). Client perceptions of the ideal addictions counselor. *The International Journal of the Addictions, 27*(6), 727–733.

Schiavi, R.C. (1990). Chronic alcoholism and male sexual dysfunction. *Journal of Sex & Marital Therapy, 16*(1), 23–33.

Starling, B.P., & Martin, A.C. (1990). Adult survivors of parental alcoholism: Implications for primary care. *Nurse Practitioner, 15*(7), 16–24.

Stotland, N.L. (1989). Alcohol and sex. *Medical Aspects of Human Sexuality, 23*(8), 42–49.

Subby, R. (1984). Inside the chemically dependent marriage: Denial and manipulation. In *Co-dependency: An emerging issue* (pp. 25–29). Pompano Beach, FL: Health Communications, Inc.

Subby, R., & Friel, J. (1984). *Co-dependency & family rules.* Deerfield Beach, FL: Health Communications, Inc.

Teichman, M., Teichman, Y., Converse, J. Jr., & Foa, U.G. (1992). Interpersonal needs of drug addicts: Are they similar across cultures? *The International Journal of the Addictions, 27*(3), 281–288.

Vannicelli, M. (1991). Dilemmas and countertransference considerations in group psychotherapy with adult children of alcoholics. *International Journal of Group Psychotherapy, 41*(3), 295–312.

Washton, A.M., & Stone-Washton, N. (1990). Abstinence and relapse in outpatient cocaine addicts. *Journal of Psychoactive Drugs, 22*(2), 135–147.

Wegscheider, S. (1981). *Another chance.* Palo Alto, CA: Science & Behavior Books.

Wegscheider-Cruse, S. (1985). *Choicemaking.* Pompano Beach, FL: Health Communications.

Whitfield, C.L. (1989). Co-dependence: Our most common addiction—Some physical, mental, emotional, and spiritual perspectives. *Alcoholism Treatment Quarterly, 6*, 19–36.

Wilson, H.S., & Kneisl, C.R. (1992). *Psychiatric nursing* (4th ed.). Redwood City, CA: Addison-Wesley Nursing.

Woititz, J. (1983). *Adult children of alcoholics.* Hollywood, FL: Health Communications, Inc.

17

Attrition

Judith Sutherland, *PhD, RN, CS, LCDC*

INTRODUCTION

Client dropout is a major issue when caring for addicted persons because the odds of anyone maintaining sobriety decreases once this occurs. In addition, premature termination of care represents no return on investments of effort, cost, energy, resources, and time to health care providers and programs. Therefore, it becomes imperative that health care providers understand 1) that the phenomenon of attrition exists, 2) what it means, 3) that it has been and still is being researched, and 4) how to address it.

Attrition research for the general psychiatric population has been conducted since the late 1950s. The aggregate of these studies indicate that psychiatric clients fail to return to outpatient treatment after the first visit at a rate of 20% to 57%, and 32% to 79% of the inpatients leave against medical advice (Baekeland & Lundwall, 1975; Pekarik, 1983; Good & Hendrickson, 1986; Sledge, Moras, Hartley, & Levine, 1990).

Paralleling attrition rates of the psychiatric population, substance abusers terminate outpatient treatment at a frequency ranging from 15% for those who failed to keep their first appointment to 89% for those who received only 1 month of service (Verinis, 1986; Agosti, Nunes, Stewart, & Quitkin, 1991; Mammo & Weinbaum, 1991; Schilling & Sachs, 1993). Inpatient termination rates do not appear much better for substance abusers, demonstrating a range between 13.7% and 39.5% usually within the first month of treatment (Baekeland & Lundwall, 1975; Siddall & Conway, 1988; Brewer, Zawadski, & Lincoln, 1990).

Although attrition rates of substance abusers do not differ significantly from those of general psychiatric clients, the consequences of terminating treatment are much more detrimental. While 75% of the psychiatric dropouts expressed no further need of treatment and were satisfied with the services they received after three or more sessions, outcomes were more negative for substance abusers.

Baekeland and Lundwall (1975) found that terminators from inpatient or outpatient substance abuse programs had worse abstinence outcomes than program completers. Also, alcoholics who dropped out of treatment before 6 months of sobriety were not likely to maintain it. Similarly, O'Leary, Rohsenow, and Chaney (1979) identified a positive relationship between duration of alcoholism treatment aftercare and employment, time lapsed to the first drinking episode, and number of drinking days at 6-month follow-up. Walker, Donovan, Kivlahan, and O'Leary (1983) discovered that 70.2% of the alcoholics who completed treatment and aftercare programs were abstinent at a 9-month follow-up examination compared to only 23.4% of those who dropped out of aftercare. Finally, Mammo and Weinbaum (1991), in their study with a sample of 12,697 patients, found that of the 49.5% of men who completed treatment, 67% of them had stopped drinking and 25% had decreased their drinking. Conversely, of the dropouts only 35.5% abstained and 7.8% decreased their drinking. In addition, Mammo and Weinbaum found that other treatment outcome factors, such as family situation; job, financial, and legal status; as well as physical, emotional, and psychological health state were advantageous for those who completed, but absent for those who did not.

Few researchers who discuss addictions treatment attrition rates cite the long-term recovery process required of substance abusers. A study conducted by DeSoto, O'Donnell, Alfred, and Lopes (1985), found high levels of deleterious symptomatology that only progressively decreased with prolonged abstinence, achieving normal levels in subjects who were abstinent 10 years or more. At all stages of recovery, for both men and women, symptomatology remained highest on depression, interpersonal sensitivity, obsessive–compulsive behaviors, and guilt. These findings support the need for extending the parameters of time when treating substance abusers, since remission of symptoms is not achieved for many years after abstinence.

In view of recovery longevity, the incidence of attrition must be examined from multiple perspectives. Complicating the understanding of treatment terminations are such issues as the disease and recovery process itself, attributes of the abuser, type and number of chemicals used, varying expectations of treatment length, and the treatment program itself. For the purpose of this chapter, these critical elements are incorporated into an examination of the following areas related to substance abuse treatment attrition: 1) prevalence of client dropout by program type, 2) definitions of attrition, (3) theoretical perspectives on attrition, and (4) methods for attrition prevention and reduction based on current research.

PREVALENCE RATES BY PROGRAM

General prevalence percentages have already been cited. It is important, however, to examine attrition rates by program as these statistics reflect elements of the disease process that are crucial to prevention and intervention. Prevalence rates by alcohol and drug abuse treatment are displayed in Table 17-1 and Table 17-2, respectively. The studies cited in these tables were derived from the author's literature review. Cursory perusal of the two tables supports the enormous body of research on program attrition that indicates a larger percentage of dropout from outpatient treatment than from inpatient. Though more outpatient data are displayed in the tables than inpatient, the results are consistent with the recent and extensive review of the literature on program attrition conducted by Stark (1992). Both Stark's summary on attrition and Baekeland and Lundwall's (1975) earlier critical review of empirical studies indicate a substantial difference between outpatient and inpatient attrition.

Inpatient dropout occurs at a rate of 13.7% to 39.5%, whereas outpatient dropout ranges from 15% to as high as 89%. Certainly, lower dropout rates would be expected in an inpatient treatment program for three reasons: 1) the treatment structure itself is more staff-contact intensive and certainly should, if it is working appropriately, reduce terminations; 2) leaving against medical advice is a more complicated process in the inpatient setting than

TABLE 17-1 Prevalence of Alcoholism Program Attrition

Authors	Patients	Findings
Brewer, Zawadski, & Lincoln (1990)	803 inpatients in 28-day program for alcohol dependence & codependency	14% female termination; 25% male termination
Makela (1994)	4478 men and women attending A.A.	50% of men and women drop out in the first year of sobriety
Mammo & Weinbaum (1991)	10,027 men and 2670 women in outpatient treatment	38% of men dropped out; 48.8% of women dropped out
Rees (1986)	92 male and 25 female admissions to an alcoholism clinic	35% dropped out after the initial visit; 18% dropped out in 1 month
Schilling & Sachs (1993)	16 women and 87 men in an evening outpatient program	62% of the women and 76% of the men dropped out before completing the 25-week program
Verinis (1986)	123 men in outpatient VA program	38% never returned after initial screening; 64% dropped out after 1–9 sessions; 74% dropped out after 10 or more sessions

simply not returning for a session. Such action involves many levels of staff notification, which may result in interventions to prevent the premature termination; and 3) outpatient treatment requires a great deal of client motivation to attend treatment at a time when the person is feeling exhausted and confused.

Inpatient programs externally evoke compliance until the patient is able to develop intrinsic motivation. Even with these factors operating, inpatient dropout is relatively high and usually occurs very early in the hospitalization. Siddall and Conway (1988) noted that the largest number of inpatient treatment terminations (29%) occurred within the first 23 days of admission. These findings are consistent with an earlier study performed by DeLeon and Schwartz (1984) who reported rates comparable to Siddall and Conway's, but found that attrition occurred much sooner, actually within the first 14 days of treatment.

Close scrutiny of attrition percentages indicates an unusually high occurrence early in the disease state for both inpatient and outpatient treatment or therapy. Clients in these groups may actually be in the active, intoxicated disease state or experiencing the preliminary stages of withdrawal. However, none of the articles reviewed for this chapter, including the two articles that reported a comprehensive literature review of attrition studies (Baekeland & Lundwall, 1975; Stark, 1992), identified biochemical disease status as a significant attribution factor. After delineating the definition of attrition, theoretical perspectives related to this phenomenon will be discussed with a specific focus on including the influence of biochemical status.

DEFINITION OF ATTRITION

Definitions of attrition vary considerably but can be categorized into five generally prescribed groups. These groups incorporate the client who: 1) fails to keep the first scheduled appointment, 2) fails to return, 3) refuses to return, 4) leaves against medical advise, and 5) is expelled from treatment due to lack of compliance or poor response to treatment protocols. The research literature indicates that these five types of clients—who drop out for varying reasons and at different times, with the exception of the first group—are a heterogenous group.

Although most of the current thrust of attrition investigations has been directed at identifying and categorizing patient attributes with the goal of developing predictive and interventive strategies, information related to program attributes would provide helpful data for addressing attrition. Identification of client attributes may ultimately be useful as generic predictors; in that, regardless of program type, clients with these certain characteristics might tend to drop out at a much higher rate. In addition, examining characteristics and components of programs may actually reveal more about the disease and recovery process related to patient attributes than about the appropriateness of the program itself.

Few inpatient or outpatient studies report treatment dropout with the inclusion of termination rates prior to the first scheduled appointment. This seems to be a critical factor since engagement with program staff is vital to retention. When clients drop out prior to this engagement it would be useful to know the significance and nature of the problem so appropriate strategies to intervene could be instituted.

Some attrition studies of outpatient programs have defined dropout by the number of treatment sessions attended—this includes persons providing therapy within private practice—while other studies define dropout by length of time in program such as 2 weeks,

TABLE 17-2 Prevalence of Drug Program Attrition

Authors	Patients	Findings
Agosti, Nunes, Stewart, & Quitkin (1991)	39 men and 21 women admitted to cocaine outpatient research clinic	66% of the men and 34% of the women dropped out before completing the 4-week program
Chan, Wingert, Wachsman, Schuetz, & Rogers (1986)	299 mothers enrolled in a pediatric clinic for drug abusing mothers	34% dropped out in the first year
Siddall & Conway (1988)	100 drug-abusing residential program patients	34% dropped out of treatment prior to completion of Level I; largest terminations occurred within the first 23 days
Stark & Campbell (1988)	100 consecutive admissions to outpatient drug counseling	26% remained active after 1 month
Stark, Campbell, & Brinkerhoff (1990)	117 consecutive callers making an initial appointment for drug abuse counseling.	50% picked up the forms; 11% continued in treatment after 1 month

1 month, or 2 months, rather than by treatment sessions. Inpatient programs define it this way as well. Categorizing client dropout by program length of stay is critical to understanding the phenomenon. For example, those who leave prior to the completion of detoxification reflect different attributes and aspects of the disease itself than do those who terminate at 6 months from a therapeutic community–residential program.

In summary, patients tend to fall into the five general attrition categories previously identified. However, discussions of the number of sessions and expected program length of stay are also critical to the analysis of premature termination of treatment by clients. In addition, information about factors that contribute to attrition augments the development of generic predictors that may lead to research on preventive and interventive strategies to reduce these terminations. Ultimately, such research will provide more data about the disease and recovery process.

THEORETICAL PERSPECTIVES ON ATTRITION

Most attrition research has examined causation by focusing on a wide variety of client demographic variables and incidence of psychopathology. Therefore, considerable data exist on client attributes and attrition rates, although some of the results are conflicting. However, factors that affect commitment to treatment also involve the disease itself. Despite the fact that the disease model of addiction has been broadly embraced by the addictions discipline, the biochemical disease state has not been studied in relation to attrition. None of the articles reviewed for attrition factors identified attributes of the disease process itself related to patient dropout, even though attrition is highest during the earliest and most toxic stage of the illness. Therefore, the two theoretical perspectives on attrition discussed below will be attribution theory and biochemical state.

Attribution Theory

Critical factors related to patient attributes and treatment terminations have emerged from the research literature. Stark (1992) conducted an extensive analysis of substance abuse attrition attributes in an attempt to determine appropriate therapeutic interventions. His examination of such variables as socioeconomic status, gender, race, prior treatment history, and psychopathology did not produce consistent results for determining risk factors related to attrition, which refuted commonly held views based on findings from single studies or clinical lore. For example, such components of socioeconomic status as income, education, and occupation were actually explained by a "resources for treatment" variable. That is, patients with high socioeconomic status ratings had greater resources (insurance, transportation, child care, etc.) that supported retention. Another example is conflicting results produced by numerous studies aimed at gender as a contributing variable in attrition. Higher dropout rates overall have been assumed for women, and related to the premise of greater social stigma attached to female substance abuse; however, a comprehensive review of the research literature does not support this view. Any differences in dropout rate between men and women identified in specific studies may actually be due to the resources for treatment variable again rather than gender-driven differences. Similarly, race has produced mixed results in the literature with the interaction of client–therapist race being more influential on retention than race as a single element, underscoring the importance of absence or presence of ethnic sensitivity of the therapist in the interracial dyad. Although commonly held as absolute indicators for high attrition risk, neither previous substance abuse treatment histories nor psychopathology have shown consistent predictive capabilities.

Client attributes that *have* demonstrated a positive impact on attrition and retention from both Stark's 1992 review and the author's analysis of even more recent studies are: 1) supportive significant others (negative significant others have a decidedly deleterious impact on treatment retention); 2) number of chemicals abused (clients who are polydrug abusers demonstrate higher attrition rates); 3) court-mandated treatment up to the first 30 days in program; 4) ethnic sensitivity expressed in the interracial therapist–patient dyad; 5) clients' belief that their substance abuse problem is severe combined with them having high expectations of improvement through treatment compliance; and 6) attributes of the therapist and treatment program itself.

Biochemical Disease State

In general, the preferred psychological defense structure of the abuser, along with brain dysfunction due to chemical abuse, are believed to be primary factors complicating treatment of substance abusers (Chernus, 1985; DeSoto et al., 1985; Committee on Alcoholism and Addictions, 1991; Kelley, 1991). The preferred defense structure is comprised of such defense mechanisms as denial, projection, rationalization, and obsessional focusing. Utilization of these mechanisms protects the abuser from facing the reality of chemical dependence and distorts responses to treatment.

Though it is unknown in what way brain dysfunction contributes to the development of such defenses, Kelley (1991) identified the post acute withdrawal (PAW) phase of substance abuse as lingering brain dysfunction due to the toxic effects of the chemical even after the acute detoxification phase has passed. As many as 70% to 90% of recovering persons experience long-term organic deficits. According to Kelley (1991, p. 42), these deficits typically fall into six categories:

1. *Cognitive Functioning.* The clients experience difficulty concentrating, thinking logically, and understanding cause and effect.
2. *Affective Functioning.* The clients have wide mood swings and emotional numbness. They experience "artifact emotions" that are not connected to the present or past situations but are a response to brain dysfunction. Such emotions can include anger, depression, and anxiety.
3. *Memory Deficits.* Short-term memory and memory of major adult and childhood events are often problematic for the client.
4. *Sleep Deprivation.* Inability to get to sleep, lack of rest obtained from sleep, over sleeping, sleeping at inappropriate times, and nightmares are common complaints.
5. *Psychomotor Dysfunction.* The clients stumble, experience dizziness, eye–hand coordination problems, and general clumsiness.
6. *Stress.* The clients lack the ability to recognize minor signs of stress until the stress becomes overwhelming.

In a previous study, DeSoto et al. (1985) found that both male and female alcoholics demonstrated significant symptomatology over a period of abstinence ranging from 3 months to 10 years. At all stages, symptoms remained highest on depression, interpersonal sensitivity, and obsessive compulsiveness, with guilt being a pervasive symptom.

Any or all of these factors can seriously impair a client's commitment and motivation while in treatment. In addition, the ability to cognate issues critical to abstinence and recovery may be distorted or delayed.

Given this body of information, it seems imperative that researchers examine attrition rates in conjunction with the biochemical disease state as well as client attributes. It is also imperative that persons providing care to addicted clients increase their knowledge of methods for prevention and intervention with client dropout.

METHODS FOR ATTRITION PREVENTION AND INTERVENTION

Although most methods for addressing attrition can be useful across all addictions programs, outpatient and inpatient programs differ in service delivery structure and attrition percentages. Therefore, preventive and interventive strategies will be discussed by program type after some general recommendations are given.

General recommendations, based on research found to be effective for preventing client attrition include: 1) decreasing the time between the client's request for treatment and the initial appointment; 2) welcoming clients with respect and interest; 3) assisting clients in resolving concrete obstacles to treatment; 4) reducing waiting times and increasing client–staff contact hours; 5) instituting home visits and phone calls to establish client status; and 6) demonstrating attitudinal flexibility and sensitivity to ethnic differences and issues (Baekeland & Lundwall, 1975; Bauman, Nieporent, Klein, Dunne, & Rudolte, 1988; Stark, Campbell, & Brinkerhoff, 1990; Agosti et al., 1991).

Methods for Detoxification

Detoxification is a critical time period for dropping out, evidenced by the finding that 30% or more inpatient dropouts occur during the first 3 to 14 days of abstinence. According to Allen (1990), a program should be developed for the period of acute detoxification to provide activity for these clients and increase their motivation for treatment, ultimately leading to engagement and retention in treatment. The program should be light and nonconfrontive, and include group sharing, meditation, short films, or talks. In addition, Allen recommended that the client be assigned a "buddy" (someone who is working a good program and is graduating from the program in a few days) to provide support and ease anxiety and fear. If the client is in active withdrawal and must be restricted to bed or room, that buddy should be allowed to make frequent visits to see the client.

Given the acute nature of detoxification and the long withdrawal process inherent to recovery from alcohol and drugs, it is imperative that the client be assessed and monitored closely throughout the continuum of treatment. This monitoring implies regular evaluations and consistent contact with health care provider or team.

There are a great many outpatient detoxification programs being implemented now. Most experience great attrition rates which points to the need for developed attrition prevention aspects to these programs. As talked about in the next section, methods of engaging these clients even while they are away from the facility at home is very important considering the physical and psychological distress they are experiencing during their detoxification.

Methods for Outpatient Treatment

Outpatient treatment should incorporate numerous treatment approaches, a range of ancillary services and individualized treatment plans. Outpatient service delivery for substance abusers has typically followed the pattern of psychiatric outpatient services by utilizing a high rate of individual therapy. However, due to the complex nature of the problem involving physical, psychological, emotional, and social elements, it is no surprise that this method of service delivery has resulted in a high level of client attrition.

Most of the recommendations for reducing outpatient attrition could be subsumed under the general category "client attendance and engagement." All efforts should be directed at optimizing the client's engagement with the health care provider and the treatment program. According to the U.S. Substance Abuse and Mental Health Services Administration (1994), engagement begins with efforts that are designed to enlist people into treatment, but it is a long-term process with goals of keeping clients in treatment and helping them manage ongoing problems and crises. Essential to the engagement process is: 1) a personalized relationship with clients; 2) the existence of the relationship over an extended period of time; and 3) focus on clients' needs. In addition, for clients with dual diagnosis, engagement is most essential. The techniques used will depend on the nature, severity, and disability caused by the individual's dual diagnosis. With respect to severe conditions such as psychosis and violent behaviors, therapeutic engagement techniques may need to be coercive and include involuntary detoxification, psychiatric treatment, or court-mandated acute treatment.

Methods for Inpatient Treatment

Inpatient programs have the decided advantage of the therapeutic milieu for enhancing retention rates. Since a critical factor in retention is related to the treatment environment, it is logical that the treatment milieu should be structured with a high level of client-to-staff contact. In addition, because PAW exists—making recovery fragile and tenuous—it is imperative that this high level of contact occur to address the problems that are inevitable to living without chemicals.

When the milieu is functioning at its best, issues related to attrition should be addressed immediately by a multidisciplinary team available 24 hours a day. It is an inherent function of these professionals—who constitute a major element in the milieu—to address emerging issues related to the psychological defense structure, abstinence syndrome, and biochemical status.

Inpatient programs for substance abusers are usually intensive with an average of 50 to 70 hours of active programming weekly. The dynamism created by such a structure elicits attendance, and for the most part, ultimately engagement. The peer group exposure created by active programming adds a crucial element to the milieu, the influence on addictive behaviors by the recovering peer (social) network. One critical factor of the disease process in substance abusers is the social isolation through development of a primary relationship with chemicals. Resocialization is an important function of the milieu and contributes to the power of the peer (social) network in influencing change of addictive behaviors such as attrition.

Sidall and Conway (1988) recommended that specialized treatment interventions be utilized to prevent attrition. Therefore, in 1991, Sutherland developed an Against Medical Advice (AMA) Prevention and Intervention Policy and Procedure with the Siddall and Conway recommendations in mind.

The purpose of the policy is to identify clients at high risk for premature termination of treatment and describe methods for intervening in impending dropouts. It was developed after analyzing 100 dropout cases, with procedures designed to reflect current research and actual attributes of terminators discovered in the analyzed cases. The Policy and Procedures are as follows:

EXAMPLE OF AMA PREVENTION AND INTERVENTION POLICY AND PROCEDURE

Each client's potential for AMA is assessed at admission and continuously throughout treatment with the goal of preventing termination of treatment by AMA. Welfare of the client is the primary motivation for implementing this procedure.

Admission Prevention Procedure

Assess clients for their AMA risk potential using the following checklist of risk factors. Document risk indicators in the admission assessment and mark the patient's chart with a red label indicating high risk for AMA. Include indicators in the client's treatment plan and develop interventions for each of the indicators.

Checklist of factors associated with high AMA risk:

1. Previous treatment failure. The client left another treatment program AMA or was administratively discharged.
2. Polysubstance abuse. The use of any combination of alcohol, drug, or food abuse.
3. Dual diagnosis. The presence of a psychiatric illness accompanying the addictive illness.
4. Nonsupportive significant others. Family members who are abusers themselves and those constantly attempting to undermine treatment through a variety of methods.
5. Two or more relapses within the last 2 years requiring treatment.
6. Negative attitude toward health care providers.
7. Previous negative treatment experience.
8. History of physical and/or sexual abuse.

Document information about the client's commitment to treatment in the admission assessment, along with information about leverages that might be used to keep the client in treatment (i.e., job demands he or she be there, family demands he or she be there, physical illnesses, threatened loss of financial support, court-mandated treatment). Assess and document family and significant other's support of the client's treatment. Make every attempt to integrate the family/significant other into a treatment alliance with the staff.

Intervention Procedure During the Program

A. Monitor clients closely for significant behavior changes that may indicate AMA potential and use the following Checklist of Behavioral Indicators of Impending AMA.

Checklist of Behavioral Indicators of Impending AMA

1. Focusing on Issues External to Treatment. Client demonstrates obsessive preoccupation with issues external to treatment such as employment, finances, family, and friends. The concerns may be real or imagined. The client may request release time to perform work-related activities (brings a briefcase full of work to do while hospitalized and/or seeks special telephone privileges such as being called out of group to receive calls). The person may be overly concerned about visitation, restrict family involvement in treatment, ask for special privileges such as passes or express anxiety about financial deadlines that must be met.
2. Responds to Negative External Influences. Client has friends or family members who do not support the person's treatment program. There is constant pressure to leave treatment that may be initiated by family members. Family or friends interfere with treatment by such aggressive acts as bringing drugs or alcohol into the hospital or visiting the client while intoxicated.
3. Exhibits Attitude of Narcissism. Client expresses attitudes of being unique or special and not belonging in the treatment program. He or she may be: too different, too well educated, not sophisticated enough, too young or too old, not like those "drug addicts" or "alcoholics," not as severe, or not accustomed to this kind of environment or treatment.
4. Attempts to Dictate Treatment. Client argues with the staff about assignments, refuses treatment activities, demands medication, complains about the food and the lodging, requests changes of therapist or primary nurse, and delivers frequent ultimatums about what he or she will and will not do. Frequent power struggles are set up by the client with the staff around rules or unit guidelines.

5. Exhibits Manipulative Behavior. Client attempts to undermine the milieu by initiating splitting among the staff and between staff and clients. Through enactment of the roles of victim, persecutor, or rescuer (or all three), the person attempts to manipulate the staff and other clients. Passive–aggressive behavior expressed in sarcasm, covert aggressive acts, and games indicates the severity of the client's defenses.

6. Somatizing. The client focuses his or her attention on medical or psychiatric problems rather than the issue of addiction. Demands for attention to the real problem, such as a physical or "nervous" condition, and shifts the focus away from the substance abuse issue. Physical complaints are numerous and may even progress to the hysterical. Demands for medical attention are frequent and often threaten dire consequences if not attended to by staff.

B. Be aware that detoxification is a critical time period for AMAs. Thirty percent or more inpatient AMAs occur during the first 3 to 14 days of treatment.

C. At admission, assign a "buddy" to each new patient from the client community. The buddy system facilitates integration into the treatment community. Select a buddy who has participated in the recovery program and is not at high risk for AMA.

D. Form peer group of clients to work specifically with patients who are at risk for leaving AMA.

E. Implement the following immediately if the client demonstrates behavioral signs indicating impending AMA:

1. Engage the person in a dialogue about his or her concerns over leaving the program. Do not argue, but listen and assess the problems.

2. Attempt to problem solve the issues with the client.

3. Find the area of ambivalence related to treatment and focus on the positive points.

4. Ask the client peer group to work with the high-risk client around the issues identified.

5. Inform the physician, primary nurse, primary therapist, director of nursing and program administrator of the probable AMA.

6. Document all interventions in the client's chart.

F. If the AMA risk potential continues to escalate:

1. Arrange an in-house intervention with the client's significant other, physician, nurse, and therapist. Include friends or the employer, if appropriate.

2. If an in-house intervention with significant others is not possible, consider implementing the following:
   a. Have the person discuss AMA intentions in group therapy.
   b. Arrange a special meeting with the entire treatment team.
   c. Arrange a special counseling session with the client's physician or therapist.

3. Call a special community meeting of clients and staff to address the AMA potential and its consequences.

G. If the patient elects to terminate treatment:

1. Isolate the person as much as possible from other clients.

2. Provide the client with the option to return to treatment at another time.

3. Offer community resources to the client for support after leaving.

4. Document the AMA in the client's chart.

5. After the person has left AMA call a community meeting with all of the remaining clients to process the event.

CONCLUSION

Substance abuse/addiction is a complex phenomenon comprised of physical, psychological, emotional, and social attributes. Biochemical factors inherent to the disease process can have a greater systemic, negative impact and impair the substance abuser for a longer period of time than has been previously believed. What seems to be clear from the literature is that attrition rates are high and the outcomes from treatment dropout are decidedly negative for the client.

Factors that appear to enhance retention are 1) supportive significant others; 2) absence of polydrug abuse; 3) court-mandated treatment up to the first 30 days in program; 4) ethnic sensitivity expressed in the interracial therapist–patient dyad; 5) the clients' belief that their substance abuse/addiction problem is severe combined with their high expectations of improvement through treatment compliance; 6) greater structure applied to outpatient services; 7) warmth, interest, and attendance from treatment staff; and 8) policies and procedures designed to intercede in impending dropout.

In addition, detoxification is a critical period for clients. Therefore, as much supportive activity as possible should be instituted to initiate engagement and motivation for the next level of care. Continuous assessment of the client and active engagement of client with the program as well as health care providers are vital to prevention and intervention in premature terminations. Given the fatal and progressive nature of addiction, it is crucial that the patient proceed from the phase of abstinence through the recovery and rehabilitative phases of treatment.

Future areas of research need to focus on the relationship of biochemical alterations to abstinence behaviors and the incidence of attrition; tabulation of attrition rates occurring before the first outpatient appointment or inpatient admission appointment and factors associated with these rates; program adaptations needed to fully meet ethnic needs; reasons for relapse; and, finally, the relationship of treatment structure and intensity to reduction in program termination and relapse rates.

REFERENCES

Agosti, V., Nunes, E., Stewart, J., & Quitkin, E. (1991). Patient factors related to early attrition from an outpatient cocaine research clinic: A preliminary report. *The International Journal of Addictions, 26*(3), 327–334.

Allen, K. (Summer, 1990). Nursing methods for dealing with patient attrition from addictions treatment. *Addictions Nursing Network, 2*(2), 4–7.

Baekeland, F., & Lundwall, L. (1975). Dropping out of treatment: A critical review. *Psychological Bulletin, 82*(5), 738–783.

Bauman, L., Nieporent, J., Klein, J. Dunne, G., & Rudolte, C. (1988). Demystifying the patient dropout: A study of 122 brief-stay day treatment center admissions. *International Journal of Partial Hospitalization, 5*(3), 215–224.

Brewer, L., Zawadski, M., & Lincoln, R. (1990). Characteristics of alcoholics and codependents who did and did not complete treatment. *The International Journal of Addictions, 25*(6), 653–663.

Chan, L., Wingert, W., Wachsman, L., Shuetz, S., & Rogers, C. (1986). Differences between dropouts and active participants in a pediatric clinic for substance abuse mothers. *American Journal of Drug and Alcohol Abuse, 12*(1,2), 89–99.

Chernus, L. (1985). Clinical issues in alcoholism treatment. *Journal of Contemporary Social Work, 2,* 67–75.

Committee on Alcoholism and Addictions. (1991). Substance disorders: A psychiatric priority. *American Journal of Psychiatry, 148*(10), 1297.

DeLeon, G., & Schwartz, S. (1984). Therapeutic communities: What are the retention rates? *American Journal of Drug and Alcohol Abuse, 10,* 267–284.

DeSoto, C., O'Donnell, W., Alfred, M., & Lopes, C. (1985). Symptomatology in alcoholics at various stages of abstinence. *Alcoholism: Clinical and Experimental Research, 9*(6), 505–511.

Doweiko, H. (1989). The Sladen and Mozdzierz AMA Scale: A failed replication attempt. *The International Journal of the Addictions, 24*(5), 397–404.

Good, M.I., & Hendrickson, P.A. (1986). A study of post evaluation change in clinician and treatment dropout rates. *Hospital and Community Psychiatry, 37,* 76–77.

Kelley, J. (1991). Extended stabilization: The future of inpatient treatment. *Addiction Recovery, 11*(3), 40–43.

Makela, K. (1994). Rates of attrition among membership of Alcoholics Anonymous in Finland. *Journal of Studies on Alcohol, 55*(1), 91–95.

Mammo, A., & Weinbaum, D. (1991). Some factors that influence dropping out from outpatient alcoholism treatment facilities. *Journal of Studies on Alcohol, 54*(1), 93–10 O'Leary, M.R., Rohsenow, D.J., & Chaney, E.F. (1979). The use of multivariate personality strategies in predicting attrition from alcoholism treatment. *Journal of Clinical Psychiatry, 40,* 190–193.

Pekarik, G. (1983). Follow-up adjustment of outpatient dropouts. *American Journal of Orthopsychiatry, 55,* 501–511.

Rees, D.W. (1986). Changing patients' health beliefs to improve compliance with alcoholism treatment: A controlled trial. *Journal of Studies on Alcohol, 47,* 436–439.

Schilling, R., & Sachs, C. (1993). Attrition from an evening alcohol rehabilitation program. *American Journal of Alcohol Abuse, 19*(2), 239–248.

Sidall, J., & Conway, G. (1988). Interactional variables associated with retention and success in residential drug treatment. *International Journal of Addictions, 23*(2), 1241–1254.

Sledge, W., Moras, K., Hartley, D., & Levine, M. (1990). Effect of time-limited psychotherapy on patient drop out rates. *American Journal of Psychiatry, 47*(10), 1341–1347.

Stark, M. (1992). Dropping out of substance abuse treatment: A clinically oriented review. *Clinical Psychology Review, 12,* 93–116.

Stark, M.J., & Campbell, B.K. (1988). Personality, drug use and early attrition from substance abuse treatment. *American Journal of Drug and Alcohol Abuse, 14,* 475–487.

Stark, M. Campbell, B., & Brinkerhoff, C. (1990). Hello, may we help you? A study of attrition prevention at the time of the first phone contact with substance abusing clients. *American Journal of Drug and Alcohol Abuse, 16*(1,2), 67–76.

Substance Abuse and Mental Health Services Administration. (1994). Mental health and addiction treatment systems: Philosophical and treatment approach issues. In *Assessment and treatment of patients with coexisting mental illness and alcohol and other drugs abuse: Treatment Improvement Protocol Series.* DHHS Publication No. (SMA) 94-2078. Rockville, MD: U.S. Department of Health and Human Services Substance Abuse and Mental Health Services Administration Center for Substance Abuse Treatment.

Sutherland, J. (1991)). Intervening in premature termination of treatment in substance abuse programs. *Addictions Nursing Network, 3*(4), 108–114.

Verinis, J.S. (1986). Characteristics of patients who continue with alcohol outpatient treatment. *International Journal of Addictions, 21*(1), 25–31.

Walker, R.D., Donovan, D.M., Kivlahan, D.R., & O'Leary, M.R. (1983). Length of stay, neuropsychological performance and aftercare: Influences on alcohol treatment outcome. *Journal of Counseling and Clinical Psychology, 51,* 900–911.

18

Interdisciplinary Collegiality

Bettye J. Beatty Wilson, MEd, RN, CS, CNA
Kathleen A. S. Cannella, PhD, MS, MN, RN, CS
Keith Plowden, MS, RN, CCRN

INTRODUCTION

> While some of our mutual concerns are matters of resources and techniques, a more urgent concern is of human organization and relationships. The focal human problem that we have not yet solved is how best to employ particular skills of each of the health professions synergistically to the benefit of the patient. (Pellegrino, 1966, p. 78)

Despite efforts of the American Medical Association and the American Nurses Association to foster interdisciplinary collaborative practice, leaders continue to call for the development of a cooperative rather than a competitive agenda to benefit patient care (Prescott & Bowen, 1985). In other words, we still have not achieved the goal of working together. However, this is not a problem that exists just between nursing and other disciplines, it is also a problem intraprofessionally as nursing begins to expand its list of advanced practices.

Decreasing sources for reimbursement available to care for clients is promoting a sense of "turfism" and "jack of all trades" rather than respect for knowledge and competence of others and a sense of "collaboration." In their standards of care with addicted clients, both the American Nurses Association (ANA) and the National Nurses Society on Addictions (NNSA) (1988) recommended that nurses collaborate with an interdisciplinary team and consult with other health care providers in planning, implementing, and evaluating interventions and/or treatments for these clients.

As nurses and professionals in other disciplines become more aware of the complexities involved in caring for addicted clients and of the importance of comprehensive assessment and treatment, the goal for collaborative practice, research, and education in a collegial manner will emerge as being primary. Current methods of practice, such as case management, critical pathways, and partnerships, are forcing nursing to think and practice within an intra- and interdisciplinary collaborative mode. Hence, the purpose of this chapter is to provide: 1) definitions; 2) necessary components; and 3) methods for intra- and interdisciplinary collaborative practice with addicted clients.

DEFINITIONS

Collegiality and collaboration, what are they? They come from a collection of words with the prefix *co*. In relationship to joint working environments, this prefix connotes sharing of information, responsibility, and authority.

Collegiality is the actual sharing of one's innermost identity with one's colleagues. This sharing has been heralded as a way of finding both common ground and solutions to problems among multiple parties (Coeling & Wilcox, 1994). The nature of collegial environments is embodied in respect for ideas and persons (Copp, 1994). There is a search for understanding, interest-based bargaining, and face-to-face discussion. It is critical to recognize this relationship as a form of communication between two parties. This communication cannot occur unless both parties are actively involved in the process. This communication is similar to a rowing team—at its best when all participants have a common goal and work together to accomplish that goal. There is a bonding with other disciplines through social contact, professional thought, and conscience (Styles, 1982). A bond is developed with associates. As a result of this bond, a professional relationship is developed and sharing takes place. With collegiality, there is a bonding of individuals who share common causes, convictions, and identity. The sharing involved in collegiality has become a reality in all segments of society. Like romances, a relationship is built on hopes and dreams—What might happen if this bond is developed? (Kanter, 1994).

Collaboration involves working together toward a common goal. In collaborative efforts, people are actively involved in joint planning, problem solving, decision making, and accountability (Baggs & Schmitt, 1988). In the health care arena, collaboration is the sharing of professional knowledge and skills in working together to achieve high quality outcomes, whether these outcomes are related to practice, education, or research. The interpersonal relationships occurring in collaborative efforts may or may not be collegial. However, successful collaboration occurs in a collegial manner, with ideas, efforts, and roles moving back and forth in a fluid manner.

Interdisciplinary collegiality and collaboration occur *between individuals of different disciplines*, and intradisciplinary collegiality and collaboration occur *between individuals of different expertise within the same discipline.* Although most information in this chapter is discussed from an interdisciplinary perspective, it applies to intradisciplinary collegiality and collaboration as well.

Frequently, responsibility for direct client care and the methodology used for delivery of that care overlap within and among disciplines (Patton, 1992). "Interdisciplinarity should capitalize on the unique as well as the overlapping" (Mariano, 1989a, p. 286).

An early definition of interdisciplinarity by Mariano (1989a) stated: "professionals interacting and working in collegial and collaborative ways value each other and their work together, believing that together they will be more productive and achieve more effective outcomes than they could working alone. These professionals have moved beyond the barriers often created by different perspectives and uses of language, in order to work together effectively. It is the sharing of ideas and work which make such efforts interdisciplinary, rather than multidisciplinary. An interdisciplinary team 'is a group of highly diverse and skilled people, within the healthcare setting, who join their talents and competencies'" (Mariano, 1989a, p. 286).

Mariano (1992) later defined an interdisciplinary team as being more than a collection of people. She stated that they are an entity that has a structure, a definition, a direction, an identification, and group energy or "synergy."

According to Purtilo (1994) interdisciplinary teams are a group of two or more professionals of different disciplines who apply their complementary professional knowledge and skills to direct client care, with the primary goal of providing competent and coordinated care. That definition can be expanded to include an intradisciplinary team viewed as two or more professionals of different expertise within the same discipline who apply their complementary professional knowledge and skills to educate and provide client care; and to direct the inquiry of knowledge (research) that impacts client care.

COMPONENTS OF INTERDISCIPLINARY COLLABORATION

The following components of interdisciplinary collaboration apply across practice, education, and research realms. And this must be embraced before true interdisciplinarity can occur.

Mariano (1989a) has studied interdisciplinary and interprofessional collaboration from a qualitative perspective. She stressed that the human service professions are facing problems so complex that interdisciplinary and comprehensive approaches are needed for their resolution. She focused on interdisciplinarity from three perspectives: 1) theoretical, 2) interpersonal team issues, and 3) institutional variables.

Theoretical Understanding

The theoretical perspective posits that for a group of people to function as an interdisciplinary team, they need to have a clear, understood and mutually accepted definition of interdisciplinarity. This shared understanding enables them to move in the same direction, strive to achieve common objectives, and focus on integrated outcomes. Without it, confusion, fragmentation, and isolation abound.

Interpersonal Team Issues

Three factors facilitate or hinder activities of interdisciplinary teams: 1) goal and role conflict, 2) decision making, and 3) interpersonal communication. Specifics related to these factors are discussed (Mariano, 1990).

Reduced goal and role conflict promotes team functioning (Mariano, 1989a). Without the identification of clearly specified goals, sharing of members' perceptions of goals, attainment of consensus regarding priorities and actions, and a focus on outcomes, goal conflict may arise. Differences in members' values or value operationalization may also engender goal conflict. Role conflict may arise from 1) role ambiguity; 2) professionals' perceptions of their own roles; 3) professionals perceptions—often stereotypic—of the roles of professionals in other disciplines; and 4) overlapping competencies and responsibilities.

The effectiveness of any interdisciplinary approach depends primarily on a thorough knowledge of one's own discipline and an understanding of how that discipline contributes to the whole (Mariano, 1989a). Mariano asserted that, "Team members who feel secure and competent professionally can communicate their discipline's strengths, limitations, and contributions.... Security in one's own discipline allows each member the freedom to be truly interdisciplinary."

Effective decision making by interdisciplinary teams involves clear understanding of members' roles and involvement in the decision-making process, as well as effective use of the problem-solving process. This decision-making process is enhanced by a climate of respect for all members' contributions and expertise, encouragement of constructive feedback, and shared responsibility for outcomes of this process (Mariano, 1989a).

Effective interdisciplinary communication occurs in a climate of trust, openness, and respect, where team members feel free to express their feelings and opinions without fear of reprisal (Mariano, 1989a). Furthermore, as feelings and opinions are shared, constructive, issue-oriented feedback and thoughtful consideration of differences improve interdisciplinary functioning.

Institutional Variables

The functioning of interdisciplinary teams is also significantly affected by organizational variables. Mariano emphasized that interdisciplinary teams need institutional commitment. This commitment is operationalized in the form of time, room, support, relevance, legitimation, positive motivation, and reward. Unfortunately, the traditional bureaucratic methods of institutional functioning often hinder the development and maintenance of interdisciplinary teams (Mariano, 1989a).

However, in view of the fact that more and more health care is moving outside of institutions into the community, legitimation, motivation, reward, relevance, support, and time are provided by reimbursement. Payors are increasingly looking for and promoting and rewarding collaborative practice in the care of addicted clients. It is easy to see the support for outpatient treatment as opposed to inpatient treatment. According to the Substance Abuse and Mental Health Services Administration's Center for Substance Abuse Treatment (1995) patient placement criteria are being reexamined with a view of "unbundling services." Rather than addicted clients receiving all care in one place or with one provider, managed care companies are paying for different services to be provided by professionals with varying areas of expertise on an outpatient basis.

Care such as detoxification, screening, assessment, brief intervention, and counseling is now even being provided in some homes. Working intra- and interdisciplinarily is mandatory to provide addicted clients with comprehensive, unfragmented care.

Other Components for Interdisciplinary Collaboration

Allen (1995) delineates the importance of interpersonal communication in collaborative practice by identifying the need to "speak the same language." He asserts that professionals vary their use of language, often unknowingly, in accordance with the different purposes and/or different audiences they are dealing with at the time. They may use the same language differently or use a different language.

Allen uses map making as a metaphor for how language is used differently. Similarities and distinctions are identified for a particular purpose; if the map is too simple or too complex for the identified need, it is not used. Therefore, there is no one true map. He further points out that the boundaries between disciplines vary with who is drawing them. While these boundaries become very distinct when the map is drawn by insiders, reducing the boundaries by limiting the definitions of disciplines to only those areas where no overlap occurs is usually not accepted by the professionals involved. "Difference" map makers are those who focus on differences between disciplines, whereas "pragmatic" map makers focus on solutions to problems. Allen (1995) posits that much of the conflict that arises in intra- and interdisciplinary work results from this mapping problem.

Focusing on interdisciplinary collaboration in research activities, Cannella, Roman, & York (1995) identified three ingredients basic to successful endeavors: 1) interpersonal relationships characterized by genuineness, respect, and trust between team members from different disciplines; 2) clear and open communication; and 3) flexibility in expectations and roles. Interdisciplinary collegiality and collaboration enabled this research team to take advantage of individual expertise in different areas, enhancing decision making and yielding stronger research design, protocol, and findings.

Kanter (1994) viewed collaboration as "intercompany relationships" and conducted international research over a number of years related to this issue. Components of successful intra- and interdisciplinary collaboration based on this research are described by Kanter as characteristics. These characteristics are "EIGHT I's THAT CREATE SUCCESSFUL WE's." Kanter considered these eight I's as essential components of effective collaboration. As shown in Box 18-1, they include: 1) individual excellence, 2) interdependence, 3) investment, 4) information, 5) integration, 6) institutionalization, 7) integrity, and 8) importance. As can be seen, these components are similar to others identified as important for collaboration. If members of different expertise within a profession as well as members of other disciplines use these components and principles in dealing with each other, more effective team work can take place.

METHODS FOR INTRA- AND INTERDISCIPLINARITY WITH ADDICTED CLIENTS

There are a number of ways to promote and enhance collegial collaboration. Specific methods for intra- and interdisciplinarity with addicted clients are important in education, practice, and research.

BOX 18-1. Identification and Description of Kanter's Eight I's

Individual Excellence. All members of the teams have values that contribute to the relationship. They all possess a skill or body of knowledge to accomplish the ultimate goal of the group. Their motives are positive and not negative.

Interdependence. The members need each other. They complement each other's skills and body of knowledge. The goals cannot be accomplished without the contributions of others.

Investment. The members invest in each other. They all contribute something to the accomplishment of the goal.

Information. Communication is a large segment of the team. Members share information required to make the relationship work, including their objectives and goals, technical assistance, and knowledge.

Integration. A linkage is developed among the members and a shared way of operating. A broad connection is developed between all members.

Institutionalization. A relationship is given a formal status with clear responsibility and decision processes. It extends beyond the particular people who formed it and cannot be broken on a whim.

Integrity. The members behave toward each other in an honorable way that justifies and enhances mutual trust. They do not abuse the information they gain, nor do they undermine each other.

Importance. The relationship fits major strategic objectives of the members to achieve the identified goals. Members have long-term goals in which the relationship plays an important role.

Source: Kanter, R.M. (1994, July-August). Collaborative advantage. *Harvard Business Review*, 96–108.

Education

An old psychiatric axiom is "to begin at the level of least anxiety." This would be education—it is paramount. In academic settings, classes on addiction should be taught from an interdisciplinary perspective, with a member from each discipline teaching some aspect of the class, and students from each discipline enrolled in the class.

This provides not only the knowledge related to the focus of care from each discipline, but also the opportunity to give feedback and determine how to plan care intra- and interdisciplinarily. Furthermore, continued education in the form of workshops, training, conferences, and seminars on addiction can be presented to interdisciplinary audiences from an interdisciplinary perspective.

Currently, The U.S. Public Health Service's Substance Abuse and Mental Health Services Administration's Center for Substance Abuse Treatment has funded 11 "addictions training centers" across the country. These are for the sole purpose of training and educating counselors, nurses, social workers, physicians, psychologists, and therapists, interdisciplinarily about addiction. They specifically are focusing on persons already in practice, who see addicted clients but are not trained in the area. In addition, colleges and universities have specifically developed addictions courses that emphasize interdisciplinary learning.

Practice

Several methods for interdisciplinary practice when caring for addicted clients will be discussed. These methods are applicable to inpatient, outpatient, community, and home-based care.

MULTIDISCIPLINARY CASE CONFERENCES

Two major specialty areas exist when working with addicted clients: medical and therapeutic. In the medical realm there are nurses and physicians of various skills (addictionologist, internist, psychiatrist, family practitioner, etc). While the therapeutic realm consists of counselors, psychologists, social workers, and therapists. In the initial years of caring for addicted clients, each would provide care only in concert with their specific realm.

However, changes in expectations and requirements in both professional and regulatory realms impacted this method of interacting, which led to more multidisciplinary efforts. The Joint Commission on Accreditation of Healthcare Organizations, as well as state and professional accrediting bodies, demanded evidence of "team" meetings among all disciplines. Also, treatment for addictions became more accepted, which caused an increase in therapy caseloads. As a result, the therapeutic realm requested assistance from nurses from the medical realm, which fostered more "talking together." The demand for team meetings led to the implementation of "multidisciplinary case conferences."

This step toward interdisciplinary practice involves bringing all staff together who are involved in care of the addicted client. It can take place either daily, weekly, biweekly, or monthly, depending on the program, and is attended by physicians, psychologists, nurses, therapists, social workers, recreationists, and administrators. Sometimes clients are included as well, but this needs to be all the time. According to Mariano (1989b), it is imperative to include the client as an integral member of the team—particularly in the case of alcohol, tobacco, and other drug addiction, because empowering the client through the ability to contribute to his or her treatment goals and evaluation cannot be underestimated as a therapeutic value.

During this process professionals from each discipline present problems, goals, and solutions for the client, progress made or not made, and provide feedback and input to other discipline. This is a good example of collaboration; however, it is not interdisciplinary, in that everyone works from a set of problems as identified in each discipline. To make the case conferences more interdisciplinary they should work from one treatment plan, and have persons who present the client cases rotate among disciplines.

The myth that there is no "discipline-specific" activity in team performance should be debunked. Mariano (1989b) documented experts who noted that individual activities (data collection, data interpretation, reporting, and specific intervention assignments) do exist, but must complement team endeavors (diagnosis, problem identification, goal setting, development, and coordination of plan of care for the addicted client, and evaluation of outcomes). The team is a vehicle for coordinating and integrating the activities of various disciplines and experts; however, it does not eliminate discipline-specific functions.

CLINICAL EVALUATION TEAMS

A true design of interdisciplinary care of addicted clients starts that way from the very first contact with the client. This can best be achieved through clinical evaluation teams for intake and assessment. All disciplines would interview the addicted client and gather data, then together they would meet and come up with medically and DSM-IV–appropriate diagnoses and problems or issues. The natural process to follow would then be to develop the treatment plan as a team, identifying problems, goals, and solutions.

Based on this team work, treatment plan issues can be consistently worked on and addressed with the client in group sessions, in individual sessions, on the milieu (if inpatient), at home visits, etc. This way the team is treating the client together, all saying the same thing to the client, and decreasing the likelihood of fragmentation or of the client falling through the cracks.

Treatment plans become the blueprint that guides all members of the team in working collaboratively with the client. In the end, this will have helped the client to construct a firm foundation for recovery.

CARE MAPS, CLINICAL PATHWAYS, CASE MANAGEMENT

Methods for intra- and interdisciplinary collaboration currently being utilized in hospital, outpatient, community, and home-based settings are care maps, critical/clinical pathways, and case management. According to Tonges (1995) the care map is a system that identifies expected client/family and staff behaviors against a timeline for a certain defined homogeneous population. Integrated clinical pathways are used in a care map system.

Integrated clinical pathways (ICP) are an interdisciplinary treatment plan used to manage addicted clients through their illness. It is a tool used to care-manage clients based on their diagnoses. It maps out or outlines the care (interventions) on a timeline, which can be visits (for outpatient, ambulatory, and home-based settings), day-by-day, steps or stages, presenting signs and symptoms, etc. Of the four goals listed for use of this method, promoting interdisciplinary collaboration was among them (Koerner, Bunkers, Gibson, Jones, Nelson, & Santema, 1995). According to Hill (1995), key elements necessary for inclusion in a care map system are:

- The clinical pathway with the x-axis representing the timeline and the y-axis representing multidisciplinary interventions incorporated into standards categories
- A client problem or issues list
- Intermediate goals that progress to clinical outcomes for each problem or issue identified
- A variance record designed to capture chronological deviations from the norm

With this method, Interdisciplinary progress notes based on an interdisciplinary addictions treatment plan would be established, accessible to all disciplines. The plan of care would be the pathway, which would address medical, nursing, social work, addiction therapist, and psychologist interventions.

When examining the case manager role, it is clear to see that it actually cannot be done without interdisciplinary collaboration. Because the role involves assessing, monitoring, planning, brokering, coordinating health care services, and at times providing treatment services, the nurse must work with professionals from other disciplines to ensure comprehensive care of the client.

Based on Bower (1992) and Quinn (1992), Hill (1995) clearly outlined a number of specific functions for the case manager role. Two very important functions are to:

- Develop, coordinate, implement, monitor, and modify a plan of care with the health care team, client, caregivers, individuals providing custodial services, and payors; and
- Develop collaborative relationships with an interdisciplinary team representing the continuum of care and create a cooperative relationship with a network of quality service providers.

One working definition of case management is "an integrated health management network in which care is coordinated over the continuum for individuals or groups" (Koerner et al., 1995). Optimal case management with addicted clients includes facilitating access to services and delivering services (therapy, interventions). And the continuum of care for the client addicted to alcohol, tobacco and other drugs includes prevention, assessment, detoxification, interventions, and treatment, as well as acute care and relapse prevention.

Case management can also be done from an interdisciplinary team perspective with alcohol, tobacco, and other drug addiction, and is referred to as "full team" case management. The team authors the care map, and as a collaborative group manages the delivery of the clients' treatment.

An example of "full team" case management is the Program for Assertive Community Treatment (PACT). Multidisciplinary professionals come together and, as an interdisciplinary team, incorporate components of case management to deliver care for alcohol, tobacco, and other drug addiction. They are the treatment services system. They do the assessment together and meet as a team regularly to develop diagnoses, a team treatment plan, and then deliver the services. This program has been very successful in the community and home settings (Ridgely, 1995). This is a system that was developed in Madison, Wisconsin, and is being used as a prototype across the country to provide interdisciplinary care to addicted clients.

PROCESS IMPROVEMENT TEAMS

This is a continuous quality improvement activity from an interdisciplinary perspective. Members of the team—representative of all disciplines—examine existing treatment plans and other aspects of care in an effort to identify opportunities for improvement. When a problem is identified, the team brainstorms and arrives at solutions to the problem to enhance the treatment process. Problems interfering with the treatment process may be client centered, provider related, or systems related.

Other interdisciplinary activities include teams for health education endeavors (i.e., alcohol, tobacco, and other drug prevention education in schools, correctional settings), as well as staff retreats to work out problems and clarify evidence of the components of interdisciplinary collaboration as discussed above.

Research

Interdisciplinary pursuits in research are happening consistently. The National Institute on Alcohol Abuse and Alcoholism along with the National Institute on Drug Abuse are encouraging experts from various disciplines to come together and address treatment outcomes, clinical protocols, and other issues, so that more comprehensive studies and results can produce information important to all disciplines in the care of addicted clients.

Physicians, nurses, social workers, therapists, psychologists, and so on are uniting to examine major issues that impact on addiction, particularly AIDS. What has helped this to work is use of the components of interdisciplinarity discussed above.

CONCLUSION

Addicted clients do not get better alone, and they do not get better based on care provided by one discipline. Unfortunately, what does happen is that care is fragmented, clients can fall through the cracks, and never improve because of egos, role conflicts, inability to communicate, and nonacceptance of competence among other disciplines.

With an understanding of how intra- and interdisciplinary collaboration is defined and what components are necessary to make it successful, when methods for intra- and interdisciplinary collaboration are implemented problems can be minimized. Interdisciplinary collegial collaboration is being called for by all disciplines. Some years ago that was not the case; but now the time is right and the opportunity is ripe. Nurses caring for addicted clients need to realize that unless this care is provided from an interdisciplinary perspective it will not be effective. Therefore, it is important that they have a clear understanding of the concepts related in this chapter as well as the methods that will enhance this approach.

REFERENCES

Allen, D.G. (1995, April 7). *Identity and coalition: Nursing and interdisciplinary research collaboration.* Keynote address presented at the 7th Annual Emory Nursing Research Conference: Interdisciplinary Collaboration, Atlanta, GA.

American Nurses Association & National Nurses Society on Addictions. (1988). *Standards of addictions nursing practice with selected diagnoses and criteria.* Kansas City, MO: American Nurses Association.

Baggs, J., & Schmitt, M. (1988). Collaboration between nurses and physicians. *Image: Journal of Nursing Scholarship, 20*(3), 145–149.

Bower, K. (1992). *Case management by nurses.* Washington, D.C.: American Nurses Publishing.

Cannella, K.A.S., Roman, J., & York, T.A. (April, 1995). *The comparative effectiveness of metered dose inhalers (MDI) with spacers and small volume nebulizers in delivering albuterol to hospitalized patients with obstructive lung disease.* Paper presented at the 7th Annual Emory Nursing Research Conference: Interdisciplinary Collaboration, Atlanta, GA.

Coeling, H.V., & Wilcox, J.R. (1994). Steps to collaboration. *Nursing Administration Quarterly, 18*(4), 44–45.

Copp, L. (1994). Faculty behavior: Collegiality or conflict? *Journal of Professional Nursing, 10*(4), 195–196.

Hill, M. (1995). Care map and case management systems: Evolving models designed to enhance direct patient care. In D.L. Flarey (Ed.), *Redesigning nursing care delivery: Transforming our future* (pp. 173–185). Philadelphia, PA: J.B. Lippincott Company.

Kanter, R.M. (1994, July-August). Collaborative advantage. *Harvard Business Review,* 96–108.

Koerner, J., Bunkers, L., Gibson, S., Jones, R., Nelson, B., & Santema, K. (1995). Differentiated practice: The evolution of a professional practice model for integrated client care services. In D.L. Flarey (Eds.), *Redesigning nursing care delivery: Transforming our future* (pp. 109–127). Philadelphia, PA: J.B. Lippincott Company.

Mariano, C. (1989a, November/December). The case for interdisciplinary collaboration. *Nursing Outlook,* 285–288.

Mariano, C. (1989b). Interdisciplinary collaboration in the treatment of addictions. *Addictions Nursing Network, 1*(4), 7–9.

Mariano, C. (Sept., 1990). Qualitative research: Instructional strategies and curricular considerations. *Nursing and Healthcare, 11*(7), 354–359.

Mariano, C. (1992). Interdisciplinary collaboration, a practice imperative. *Health Care Trends and Transition, 3*(5), 10–25.

Patton, D.L. (1992). Addictions head nurse competencies: Directions for the 1990's. *Perspectives on Addictions Nursing, 3*(1), 3–6.

Pellegrino, E.D. (1966). What's wrong with the nurse–physician relationship in today's hospitals? A physician's view. *Hospitals, 40*(24), 70–80.

Prescott, P., & Bowen, S. (1985). Physician–nurse relationships. *Annals of Internal Medicine, 103*(4), 127–133.

Purtilo, R. (1994). Interdisciplinary health care teams and health care reform. *The Journal of Law, Medicine, and Ethics, 22*(2), 121–126.

Ridgely, M.S. (June, 1995). *Case management: Lessons from research.* Paper presented at the 1st Annual Prototypes for Managed Behavioral Healthcare Conference, Baltimore, MD.

Quinn, J. (1992). *Successful case management in long-term care.* New York: Springer.

Styles, M.M. (1982). *On nursing: Towards a new endowment.* St. Louis: C.V. Mosby Company.

Substance Abuse and Mental Health Services Administration, Center for Substance Abuse Treatment. (1995). *The Role and current status of patient placement criteria in the treatment of substance use disorders.* DHHS Publication No. (SMA) 95-3021. Rockville, MD: U.S. Dept. of Health and Human Services.

Tonges, M.C. (June, 1995). *Critical path/care map and case management systems: Managing quality and cost across the continuum.* Paper presented at the 1st Annual Prototypes for Managed Behavioral Healthcare Conference, Baltimore, MD.

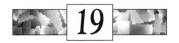

19

Research in Addictions Nursing

Margaret Compton, RN, PhD

INTRODUCTION

In a recent editorial, Parse (1994) explored the meaning of scholarship within the context of developing and nurturing nursing scholars. She defined scholarship as, "a reflection of beliefs and values honored through concentrated attention to a pattern of study of phenomena for the purpose of expanding the knowledge base of a discipline" (p. 143). Parse characterizes the scholar as having a perpetual curiosity about the nature of the world around us, a focused commitment to describe in a rigorous way the characteristics and likely outcomes of a phenomenon of interest, and a willingness to risk challenge from others when presenting new conceptualizations of, or findings on, these phenomena. The requisite process of scholarship is the research process, and each of these scholarly characteristics are essential for the addictions nurse who aspires to be a nurse researcher.

In the mid-1990s, research in addictions nursing is no small or unsophisticated exercise. The nurse investigator serious about embarking on a career of empirical study of an aspect of addiction central to his or her practice must be willing to undertake serious training and skill development not typically within the scope of nursing practice. No matter how significant his or her research question or potential contributions to the field, if the nurse investigator cannot compete in the increasingly complex, multidisciplinary addiction research arena, study findings may never be appreciated and the research itself may never occur. This chapter on research nursing in the addictions field is written for nurse investigators who recognize the necessity for doctoral and post-doctoral training and grant writing skills to fully participate in, and make meaningful contributions to, the field of addiction. Following a general discussion of the definitions and significance of nursing research, the process of research in addictions nursing will be presented with special emphasis on the methodological and human subjects issues that uniquely face addictions researchers. The chapter is completed with an overview of grant writing and the federal funding mechanisms available for addictions nurse investigators.

ADDICTIONS NURSING RESEARCH

Research is a systematic, logical process, the goal of which is to provide or improve knowledge about an event or phenomenon important for practice. It adheres to a set of well-established rules designed to maximize the reliability and trustworthiness of its findings. In essence, the researcher seeks to uncover and identify the regularities or patterns that exist in the world; with knowledge of how the world works, prediction and determination of outcomes becomes more likely. An intervention that has been demonstrated in several research studies to result in a specific patient outcome in a specific proportion of patients can be implemented with a certain degree of confidence by the health care provider to achieve desired health-related goals.

The phenomena with which addictions nurses are concerned (i.e., abstinence, withdrawal, relapse) are referred to by researchers as concepts or variables. These terms connote their broad and somewhat intangible nature, and their ability to vary or appear differently in different situations. Research is always aimed at gaining a better understanding or description of these variables, either in isolation, or through their relationships with associated phenomena or events.

Significance of Nursing Research

Although not always obvious, the relationship between addictions nursing research and addictions nursing practice is integral. Practice not based on the findings of scientific research is doomed to be haphazard, inappropriate, and unsuccessful in meeting goals. Conversely, it is from clinical problems or unexpected patient responses encountered in practice that research questions arise. Addictions nursing practice and research are closely interrelated; neither can evolve without the other.

Directing and improving addictions nursing practice is perhaps the most straightforward reason for trained addictions nurses to engage in research, but its significance to the nursing discipline extends beyond this. The ultimate goal of research is to develop theories that predictably guide practice, describe and explain human responses, and assist the addictions nurse to predict and influence health outcomes. Theories become refined or refuted on the basis of how well they describe and predict reality, and are formally created and tested through the research process. To develop a theoretical basis for addictions nursing practice, research is necessary (ANA and NNSA, 1988).

Participation in the research process also provides the nursing discipline credibility within the sciences as a distinct and important profession. A discipline participating in research, and learned within a unique body of knowledge, attains professional status. In that research can demonstrate the effectiveness or significance of addictions nursing interventions, it makes explicit the value of nursing practice. According to Standard XII of addictions nursing practice, nursing should contribute to the nursing care of clients with addictions and to the addictions area of practice through participation in research.

Definitions of Nursing Research

Certainly, not all research in which the addictions nurse participates would be considered *nursing* research in the strictest sense of the term. The question frequently arises, and graduate nursing school courses spend semesters attempting to delineate, what constitutes nursing research. Just because a nurse is involved in the research process does not make the research *nursing* research. It is not uncommon for addictions nurses to collect data for medical or psychiatric research, or for nurses to study topics (i.e., staff nurses, nursing students) that are the content of central interest to other professionals (i.e., administrators, educators).

Ensuring that addictions nurses engage in nursing research is not straightforward, as imprecision exists about what nursing research is. Certain nursing scholars take a broad perspective, calling all research that may indirectly influence nursing practice (e.g., looking at stress responses in rats), nursing research. Others take a much narrower view, believing that unless an extant theory of nursing is being tested or explored (i.e., Orem's Self-Care Theory of Nursing, Rogers' Theory of Unitary Human Beings), nursing is not being researched. A compromise between these extreme views is probably best; nurses are concerned with achieving maximally positive human responses to health changes, and any research that attempts to explain or promote such responses can safely be considered within the domain of nursing research.

Nursing research has been defined by the federal nursing research funding agency, the National Institute of Nursing Research (NINR), as:

> Research directed to understanding the nursing care of individuals and groups and the biological, physiological, social, behavioral, and environmental mechanisms influencing health and disease that are relevant to nursing care. It includes basic and clinical studies associated with the diagnosis and treatment of human responses to actual and potential health problems.
>
> The objective of nursing research is to develop clinical interventions and systems of care at the individual, family, community or institutional level in order to prevent or treat disease and disability and enhance independence and optimal functioning. Like medical research, the field of study is broad, with the ultimate goal of providing basic and clinical information that can be used to improve the quality of nursing practice. (NINR, 1994, p. 3)

The NINR defines the nurse scientist (also referred to in this chapter as nurse researcher or nurse investigator) as a doctorally prepared registered nurse who conducts basic or clinical research in areas relevant to nursing practice and patient care (NINR, 1994, p. 3). Although these nurses are not referred to as nurse scientists, those who are prepared with a Master's of Science in nursing frequently participate in research activities as well, because of the research-specific education and training they received in acquiring their degree.

Research in addictions nursing is, in several ways, unlike any other type of nursing research. Addiction, to a greater degree than almost any other health problem nurses confront, involves the biological, psychological, and social aspects of the patient, such that successful treatment of addiction must simultaneously address all three domains. The multiple types of interventions substance abusers require is evident in the wide range of professionals who consider addiction within their realm of expertise (i.e, pharmacologists, epidemiologists, psychologists, criminologists, public health specialists, social workers).

Unlike other health problems, physicians (including psychiatrists) have not historically played a dominant role in the research and treatment of addiction until recently with the growth of organizations such as the American Society of Addiction Medicine (ASAM) and the American Academy of Psychiatrists in Alcoholism and Addictions. Clearly, during this period of health care reform, reimbursement issues are driving many professional groups to stake a formal claim in the treatment of addictive disorders, which are so widespread and costly to society.

Thus, addictions nursing research finds itself in a uniquely multidisciplinary context. A new nursing journal strictly devoted to addictions-focused scholarly work and research has evolved. It is called *Journal of Addictions Nursing* and will replace *Addictions Nursing Network* and

Perspectives on Addictions Nursing. This will provide a venue for addiction nursing research, which is necessary because few mainstream nursing journals do. However, most journals specifically devoted to the publication of research in the addictions have a clearly multidisciplinary focus and readership (see Box 19-1). Therefore, a thorough review of the literature on a specific addiction treatment intervention cannot be limited to what exists in the nursing literature.

Research Questions in Addictions Nursing

Nursing research always begins with a clinical problem, and the extant addictions nursing literature reflects three broad categories of research questions: 1) those exploring substance abuse patterns in specific populations (i.e., youth, women, ethnic minorities, health care professionals); 2) those aimed at improved management of health problems suffered by substance abusers; and 3) those evaluating the effectiveness of independent nursing interventions with substance abusing patients.

These categories reflect the multiplicity of clinical contexts within which nurses are likely to encounter and treat drug- or alcohol-addicted patients. Psychiatric mental health nurses may be involved directly in the management or treatment of addictive behaviors or responses, and may want to evaluate the effectiveness of a particular detoxification strategy, a modified relapse prevention protocol with female cocaine addicts, or a 12-step group with patients who require psychopharmacotherapy for depression. Public health nurses are more interested in health problems that occur in substance-addicted persons, and may evaluate the use of a needle exchange program in a certain community, the relationship between maternal substance abuse and the quality of parenting skills, or the success of implementing 12-step programs in a local battered women's shelter. Relevant to their clinical experiences, nurses working in acute care settings may want to develop protocols for managing

BOX 19-1.   Addiction-Related Journals Indexed in Index Medicus 1994

Addiction	*Drug and Alcohol Dependence*
Addictive Behaviors	*International Journal of the Addictions*
Alcohol	*Journal of Addictive Diseases*
Alcohol and Alcoholism	*Journal of Drug Education*
Alcoholism, Clinical and Experimental Research	*Journal of Psychoactive Drugs*
	Journal of Studies on Alcohol
American Journal of Drug and Alcohol Abuse	*Journal of Substance Abuse*
	Journal of Substance Abuse Treatment
American Journal on Addiction	*Recent Developments in Alcoholism*
Bulletin on Narcotics	

cocaine overdose in the emergency room, adapting acute HIV care protocols for gay men and opiate-abusing populations, or identifying alternatives to the use of restraints in persons suffering from delirium tremens.

Across disciplines, current trends in the study of drug and alcohol problems and their treatment provide nursing research questions. In the basic sciences, a molecular neurochemistry focus is evident, with investigators exploring neurophysiological responses to psychoactive drugs. Increasingly described are the molecular sites and mechanisms of different drug actions, such as the "rush," the "high," withdrawal, craving, and tolerance. Acute neurotransmitter and receptor level changes, specifically within dopaminergic, serotonergic, and endogenous opiate systems, associated with drug ingestion have been described. Furthermore, the neuroadaptive changes that co-occur within these and other (i.e, NMDA) neurotransmitter systems with chronic drug use are being explored with respect to their relationship to such phenomena as tolerance and relapse. Ongoing clinical trials are aimed at establishing the efficacy of different medications in treating drug dependence based on accumulating knowledge about the neurochemical changes that accompany acute and chronic drug ingestion.

Biomedical research has several identified foci. Concurrent with the cataloging of the human genome, there is noted interest in the role of genetic markers that predispose, or in some way make individuals vulnerable, to substance dependence. Extant studies have explored heritable differences in individuals' central nervous system responsivity to psychoactive drugs (most notably alcohol), genetic predisposition for psychological or psychiatric problems that tend to co-occur with substance dependence, and heritable differences in drug metabolism. The medical consequences of drug abuse are also a focus of biomedical researchers. Of current concern are the effects of substance dependence on immune system function and HIV disease progression, as well as the effects of the same on the fetus in drug- and alcohol-abusing women.

Psychological and psychiatric researchers are evaluating the role of preexisting personality or psychological characteristics, such as poor self-image/self-esteem, depression, antisocial personality disorder, or other psychopathology, in predisposing individuals for substance dependence. Learned or conditioned aspects of intoxication, craving and withdrawal, and the influence of social setting on drug use and drug effects reflect current psychosocial research interests. High-risk family systems, as well as societal and cultural influences in drug-taking behaviors are also the subject of empirical description.

Epidemiological research has as its goal measurement of the prevalence and health consequences of substance abuse within certain populations. It reflects current definitions (a disease) and patterns (a syndrome) of substance abuse, thus provides a temporal context to who is identified as a drug or alcohol abuser (Peele, 1990).

The research interests of addictions nurses are usually clinical in nature, thus nursing studies tend to be designed with prevention or treatment outcomes in mind. Current trends in prevention research include evaluation of interventions such as traditional school-based drug education, those targeting high-risk groups, those teaching adolescents how to "say no" and self-esteem enhancing exercises, those designed to be appropriate to the developmental stage of the learner, those providing alternative social/recreational activities, and those related to the implementation of social and legal controls on substance abuse. Recent treatment research has evaluated the efficacy of psychopharmacologic medications, behavioral and relapse prevention strategies, "matching" subjects with different types of intervention strategies, alternate health-enhancing strategies (i.e., acupuncture, nutrition, exercise), and managing concurrent psychopathology.

Methodological Issues in Addictions Research

The addictions nurse scientist encounters multiple methodological issues that are relatively unique to addictions research, and must be considered when designing addictions studies. Limitations are inherent in many of the commonly used addictions research designs. For example, although drug effects are increasingly believed to be evident in neurophysiological changes or adaptations, demonstrating these changes is complicated. Plasticity of the brain is difficult to measure, and the complex interrelated nature of multiple neurotransmitter and neuromodulator systems in the human brain obscure full description of neurobiological responses to drug abuse. Furthermore, extrapolating neurochemical changes to complex human responses, such as craving, or behaviors, such as relapse, is currently impossible.

Many basic scientists study addiction, drug abuse liability, tolerance, and withdrawal in animal models that produce data difficult to generalize to human beings. Animals tend to reside in artificial, asocial environments, in which addiction often has to be induced (i.e., does not develop spontaneously). Inferring that certain animal behaviors are analogous to drug-induced euphoria, craving, or withdrawal in humans is problematic (Iwamoto & Martin, 1988). Animals provide less than perfect models to study aspects of psychoactive drug use, which may be uniquely human.

Furthermore, it is well-accepted that the substance abuse syndrome develops over time, yet its time course and development have been described primarily through retrospective designs. Few good prospective studies exist looking at the development of substance dependence in at-risk or normative populations. Data on risk factors for drug and alcohol abuse are primarily correlational and drawn from samples already drug or alcohol dependent; descriptions of causal relationships and identification of protective (rather than risk) factors are lacking (Hubbard, Marsden, Rachal, Harwood, Cavanaugh, & Ginzberg, 1989; Shiffman, 1991).

Multiple sampling issues surround addiction research. Most samples utilized are either treatment-seeking addicts or nonaddicted, recreational drug- or alcohol-using students. These individuals tend to represent the extreme ends of drug-abusing populations; the great majority of recreational users never become addicted, and those seeking treatment are heavily addicted. Thus, knowledge about interventions for drug or alcohol abusers who fall between these categories is lacking (Herrero & Baca, 1990; Cunningham, Sobell, Sobell, Agrawal, & Toneatto, 1993; Sobell, Sobell, Toneatto, & Leo, 1993; Blaine, Ling, Kosten, O'Brien, & Chiarello, 1994). Also, definitions of who constitutes a substance abuser change over time; thus, issues of identifying and labeling persons as belonging to the substance-dependent population changes over time (Lesch, Kefer, Lentner, Mader, Marx, Musalek, Nimmerrichter, Preinsberger, Puchinger, & Rustembegovic, 1990). However, the *Alcohol and Other Drug Thesaurus* (NIAAA and CSAP, 1993), which provides definitions and was developed by the federal government, along with DSM-IV criteria for substance abuse or dependence, serves as the gold standard diagnostic in medical and psychiatric literature, even though disciplinary biases may be reflected.

In designs evaluating the effectiveness of treatment interventions, multiple threats to the internal validity of the study exist. Characteristics of the counselors or research staff can have a confounding influence on outcome (Blaine et al., 1994), as can the demonstrated effects of maturation on drug and alcohol use over time (Anglin, Brecht, Woodward & Bonett, 1986; National Institute on Drug Abuse, 1993). Subjects tend to self-select certain types of treatment research. Those for whom behavioral techniques are more acceptable than pharmacological interventions tend to choose and do relatively well in studies evaluating behavioral techniques (Office of Technology Assessment, 1990). Existing social, legal, and supply and demand factors in the community strongly influence illicit drug use, in some cases to a greater degree than any specific treatment intervention. Polysubstance abuse is increasingly the norm in most substance-abusing samples, and the effect of one drug on the use of another must be considered. There are also difficulties in establishing valid control groups, in that true non-drug-using controls are difficult to define (i.e., must they be caffeine- and nicotine-free?), and ethical issues exist around true placebo groups (groups receiving no or sham interventions)(Blaine et al., 1994). Furthermore, subject compliance with treatment interventions is difficult to establish unless studies are tightly controlled, as in costly inpatient designs. The validity of outpatient research trials hinges on subjects actually showing up and participating in treatment.

There also exist difficulties in operationalizing and measuring independent and dependent addiction variables. Self-reports of drug use and drug history tend to be suspect measures as the outcomes or goals of prevention or treatment research (Sitharthan, McGrath, Sitharthan, & Saunders, 1992); thus, alternate objective (i.e., breathalyzer, urine toxicology) methods must be employed. High rates of attrition are the norm in drug and alcohol treatment studies. It is difficult to maintain sample sizes providing adequate statistical power. Across treatment studies, retention is always a strong predictor of success in treatment (Pickens & Fletcher, 1991). Yet, subjects who are retained in treatment tend to be those for whom the treatment is successful, therefore, tending to inflate an intervention's effectiveness. Relapse is a common outcome of treatment, and the effectiveness of treatment interventions must include follow-up measures and account for expected relapse behaviors (Pickens & Fletcher, 1991; McLellan, 1992). Furthermore, few standardized treatment evaluation or outcome measurement tools exist for drug abuse specifically (Rounsaville, Tims, Horton, & Sowder, 1993).

Confidentiality Issues in Substance-Abusing Samples

Conducting research with drug- and alcohol-abusing patients carries with it unique human subjects concerns. Specifically, the subjects of addictions nursing research may engage in illegal drug-taking activities, or may be patients in a drug or alcohol treatment program, disclosure of which information could put them in jeopardy with law enforcement, employment, or insurance agencies. Specific safeguards must be built into the research protocol to protect subject confidentiality, as well as assure treatment programs, funding institutions, and/or investigational review boards (IRB) that the researcher will protect and treat human subjects ethically.

Providing such assurance is simplified if subject data are obtained from a treatment program in such a way that no patient-identifying information is disclosed. Therefore, information that does not identify an individual as an alcohol or drug abuser, or that does not verify anyone else's identification of the patient as an alcohol or drug abuser, may be released. Aggregate data that provide an overview of patients served in a program is one such type of information. For example, if the nurse scientist is interested in how many Latina women remained in a city's seven methadone maintenance programs for at least 6 months, these data could easily be released to the investigator without concern for human subject protection. Also, if a program or hospital provides medical services for a wide range of health problems, including drug and alcohol services, patient-specific data may be disclosed as long as the subject is not identified as an alcohol or drug abuser. For example, the names of persons with positive tuberculosis tine tests may be identified for follow-up nursing intervention, although the fact that the tuberculosis screening test was administered during heroin detoxification treatment cannot be disclosed. This second type of data cannot be released from a program or hospital that only provides drug treatment services, since the subject will automatically be identified as a drug or alcohol abuser.

In most cases the data of interest to the nurse scientist must contain some sort of patient identifying information, to enable linkage of patient-specific independent and dependent variables by case. Although the subject should be identified only by a study-specific code number in the raw data, at some point the investigator must record patient-identifying information (i.e., name, social security number, clinic patient identification number) that corresponds to the study code number. Federal regulations stipulate that, whether for treatment or research purposes, patient-identifying information must be kept in a secure room, locked file cabinet, safe, or other similar container. If more than one researcher will have access to the records, written procedures must exist to regulate access and use of these records. Usually the principal investigator alone has access to these files; therefore, unauthorized persons, as well as general research or office staff who may have access to the coded data, cannot identify who is a drug- or alcohol-abusing person. Coded data may be and are usually best organized and stored electronically; patient-identifying information should never be entered into a computer file, unless access to that file is limited by a foolproof password program.

Researchers are prohibited from identifying an individual patient in any research report, presentation, or publication, or from otherwise disclosing any subject identities (Brooks, 1992). An exception is if the researcher is reporting back to the program from which the subject was identified as a patient, although the circumstances under which such disclosure occurs must be negotiated with the treatment program before the research begins. If, for example, over the course of data collection, the researcher learns something about a subject that would result in expulsion from the treatment program (i.e., the subject continues to generate income by selling drugs), the researcher may want to protect the subject, and encourage truthful responses and study participation, so will negotiate up-front not to disclose this information back to the treatment program. On the other hand, the researcher may find through data collection that the subject meets diagnostic criteria for depression and will want to alert the treatment counselor so appropriate assessment and intervention can occur. In designing the study protocol, the nurse must consider what may be learned about the subject through data collection, and what portion of this information can be disclosed to the treatment program without penalizing the subject for participating in the study.

If the nurse investigator is concerned about the effectiveness of a certain intervention or treatment, it is increasingly recognized that follow-up data (data collected months or years after completing the study) are necessary to evaluate the duration of treatment effects. Human subject protection is especially important when attempting to make follow-up contact, as it must be done without disclosing to others the subject's connection to a drug treatment program or intervention (Brooks, 1992). If follow-up contact is attempted by telephone, the caller must make sure he or she is talking to the subject before identifying himself or herself, or mentioning a connection to the drug study or research program. If the follow-up is done by mail, the return address should not disclose information that could lead someone seeing the envelope to conclude that the addressee has been in treatment. In any case, it is desirable that subjects know that the investigator will be attempting to contact them at some specified timepoint(s) in the future, so that a call or letter is not unexpected, and subjects can be prepared to explain these to others unaware of study involvement.

A major exception to protecting subject confidentiality, with which nurse clinicians are familiar, is when there is reasonable cause to believe or suspect child abuse or neglect. All 50 states have statutes requiring reporting, although the specific rules differ from state to state on the kinds of conditions that must be reported, who must report them and, when and how reports must be made. It is expected that the nurse investigator be familiar with his or her state statutes. Most states require an immediate oral report, and many have toll-free numbers to facilitate reporting. All states extend immunity from prosecution to persons reporting and provide for penalties for failure to report child abuse and neglect. This exception to the general rule prohibiting disclosure of any information about a drug or alcohol abuser applies only to initial reports of child abuse or neglect; without patient consent, the researcher may not respond to follow-up requests for information, even if the records are sought for use in legal proceedings (Brooks, 1992).

There are several strategies the addictions nurse investigator employs to ensure adequate protection of human subjects. First, many researchers obtain a Certificate of Confidentiality from the Secretary of the Department of Health and Human Services. This certificate protects the investigator involved in a specific research project from having to reveal the identity of research subjects in any federal, state, or local court or legal proceedings (Public Health Service, 1993).

Second, and most important, the nurse scientist must devise an informed consent form that not only describes the particulars of the research design, risks, and benefits to subject's participation, but clearly outlines how the subject's confidentiality will be protected if he or she chooses to participate (see Box 19-2). In the consent form itself, subjects should be assured of how patient-identifying information will be secured, how their identity will never be revealed in reports or publications generated from the research, and which types of information will and will not be shared with a related treatment program. If a Certificate of Confidentiality is on file, the subject should be informed of this and what it provides. If follow-up or home contact is likely to be made in the course of the research, the subject should be aware

BOX 19-2.   Sample Confidentiality Section of an Informed Consent Form

CONFIDENTIALITY
In all records of this study you will be identified by a code number; your name will be known only to the study investigator(s) and will be kept in a locked file. Any presentation of publication of the results from this study will not refer individually to you or in any way identify you.

A Certificate of Confidentiality has been filed with the Department of Health and Human Services. This certificate protects the investigator(s) from being forced to release any research data in which you are identified, even under a court order or subpoena. This protection, however, is not absolute. It does not, for instance, apply to any state requirement to report certain communicable diseases or to the disclosure of any medical information in cases of medical necessity. In addition, the investigator(s) may choose to voluntarily report certain cases of child abuse and/or domestic violence, to the appropriate authorities.

Throughout the duration of the study, your participation will involve permitting a representative of the research team to contact the following family members or acquaintances in the event of a missed research session, medical emergency, or to schedule you for your one- and three-month follow-up visits in the event that we cannot reach you directly. If we speak with any one other than yourself, we will identify ourselves as identified as doing a health survey and ask them to have you contact us.

of when and under what conditions it will occur. Often, the potential subject will be asked to list personal contacts the researcher may call in attempts to locate the subject, and should be informed of how the researcher will identify him or herself to those contacts. The consent should also inform the subject about the exception for suspected child abuse or neglect. Overall, subjects must be made aware of how their confidentiality will be protected, and not protected, before agreeing to participate in the study.

Finally, the study protocol and informed consent form must be approved by the IRB of the agency or institution in which the research will take place. In addition to assessing the safety and potential risks of study participation, this group of researchers, legal experts, ethicists, and lay persons aims to ensure that the subject's confidentiality is protected; breech of confidentiality is considered a specific type of risk to study participation for alcohol- and drug-abusing subjects. Members of the IRB are experienced in looking for ways that a protocol does not protect subject anonymity. Recommendations of an IRB incorporated into a protocol provide further assurance that the researcher has taken all possible steps to protect subject confidentiality.

GRANT WRITING AND RESEARCH FUNDING

As has been noted throughout this chapter, the ability to write good quality grant applications and receive funding to support research is an increasingly necessary skill for addictions nurse scientists. Nursing grantsmanship must be especially well-developed as the nurse investigator is often competing for funds within a multidisciplinary context, and contending with researchers who have better established funding histories and more sophisticated grant-writing skills. Also, addictions nurses are entering the grant-writing arena at a time when research dollars are relatively scarce and competition is especially high.

Funding Agencies

This discussion will focus primarily on applying for federal research dollars from three divisions of the National Institutes of Health (NIH) that are the likely or possible sources of funding for addictions nurse investigators: the National Institute on Drug Abuse (NIDA), the National Institute on Alcohol Abuse and Alcoholism (NIAAA), and the National Institute on Nursing Research (NINR). Within each of the institutes, there exist divisions or branches, which further define the scope of their research programs (see Box 19-3).

This chapter's focus on these three federal institutes is not intended to rule out other funding sources, such as government agencies, nursing organizations (i.e., Sigma Theta Tau, the Honor Society of Nursing, the American Nurses' Foundation) or private foundations; in fact, with many of these sources, the novice nurse scientist can begin to build a funding history or seek funding to help support doctoral or post-doctoral training. The grant-writing principles reviewed in this chapter are applicable across all funding sources.

NINR, NIDA, and NIAAA are three of 21 NIH funding institutes (see Box 19-4), which comprise the principal biomedical research organization of the U.S. Department of Health and Human Services; thus, it is the branch of the federal government that supports biomedical research. Funding for NIH research consists of taxpayer dollars that Congress appropriates to the NIH institutes on an annual basis. Different amounts of money are appropriated to different institutes (see Table 19-1), based on their size, the budgets they submit and various political factors, which ultimately determine how many and the types of research projects an institute will fund during a given time period.

BOX 19-3. Branches or Divisions of the National Institute on Drug Abuse (NIDA), the National Institute on Alcohol Abuse and Alcoholism (NIAAA), and the National Institute on Nursing Research (NINR)

EXTRAMURAL BRANCHES OF NINR
Acute and Chronic Illness Branch
Health Promotion and Disease Prevention Branch
Nursing Systems Branch

DIVISIONS OF NIDA
Division of Clinical Research
Division of Epidemiology and Prevention Research
Addiction Research Center (Intramural)
Division of Basic Research
Medications Development Division
Division of Community Research

DIVISIONS OF NIAAA
Division of Basic Research
Division of Biometry and Epidemiology
Clinical and Prevention Division

Through these institutes, the NIH funds clinical and basic research related to a broad spectrum of diseases and health problems, both at its own research facilities (so-called intramural research) and at other research organizations and educational institutions around the country (extramural research). As can be noted in Table 19-1, different institutes allocate different percentages of their total budget to intramural work, which is typically done at the NIH clinical center and campus in Bethesda, Maryland, by salaried NIH scientists. Unlike extramural researchers, these scientists do not have to compete, or prepare grants, to fund their work. The remaining research dollars go toward funding extramural projects as well as providing for training of extramural research investigators. Thus, the amount of money an institute puts toward intramural research affects how much is available to extramural researchers, and inconsistencies among institutes in how budgets are split is under current NIH review. The goal is to enhance consistency in intramural funding across institutes to approximately 11% of the total budget (Marshall, 1994a).

TABLE 19-1 Budget and Intramural Percent of Total by Institute

NIH Institute	1993 Budget (in millions of dollars)	Percent Allocated to Intramural Spending
National Institute on Drug Abuse	404	12.0
National Institute on Alcohol and Alcoholism	176	5.9
National Institute of Nursing Research	48	2.1

BOX 19-4. National Institutes of Health Institutes

National Institute on Aging (NIA)
National Institute on Alcohol Abuse and Alcoholism (NIAAA)*
National Institute of Allergy and Infectious Diseases (NIAID)
National Institute of Arthritis and Musculoskeletal and Skin Diseases (NIAMS)
National Cancer Institute (NCI)
National Institute of Child Health and Human Development (NICHD)
National Institute of Deafness and other Communication Disorders (NIDCD)
National Institute of Dental Research (NIDR)
National Institute of Diabetes and Digestive and Kidney Diseases (NIDDK)
National Institute on Drug Abuse (NIDA*)
National Institute of Environmental Health Sciences (NIEHS)
National Eye Institute (NEI)
National Institute of General Medical Sciences (NIGMS)
National Heart, Lung, and Blood Institute (NHLBI)
National Institute of Mental Health (NIMH)
National Institute of Neurological Disorders and Stroke (NINDS)
National Institute of Nursing Research (NINR)*
National Library of Medicine
National Center for Human Genome Research
National Center for Research Resources
Fogarty International Center

*Possible funding sources for addictions nursing research.

Although the content areas addressed by NIDA and NIAAA are congruent with those of addictions nurse scientists, the number of grant recipients from these institutes who are nurses is actually quite low. In 1992, funding for nursing research was only 0.5% of total funding from NIDA and 0.1% from NIAAA. Yet, these represent improvements over recent previous years, and reflect the recommendations of the 1989 NIH Task Force Report on Nursing Research. The task force aimed to foster awareness of nursing research as an area of inquiry at NIH, and increase the number of nurse reviewers and advisors on other than NINR review groups and advisory councils. Between 1989 and 1992, three nurse scientists served on NIAAA advisory groups and six on NIDA advisory groups. Other efforts of the NINR to increase the visibility of nursing research at NIH include increasing nursing participation in NIH consensus development conferences, providing a roster of nurse scientists to other institutes for filling openings on review committees, and cosponsoring grants with other institutes. Thus far, no NINR cosponsored programs has been developed with either NIDA or NIAAA (NINR, 1994).

The addictions nurse investigator must carefully consider which institute to approach for funding. Although, NINR may be more sympathetic to, or familiar with, the skills of nurse scientists, addiction is not a NINR priority, and proposals may be rejected on the grounds that there is money for these projects elsewhere (i.e., NIDA, NIAAA). In the addiction-relevant institutes, the content area is congruent, but reviewers tend to be unclear or uninformed on the

BOX 19-5. National Institutes of Health Research Grants

Research Project Grants (RO1)	Awarded to an eligible institution on behalf of a principal investigator for a discrete project related to the investigators' expertise and experience. Basic research project grant. Available to scientists at all levels of research experience. Awarded up to 5 years.
Program Project Grants	Awarded to an eligible institution on behalf of a principle investigator for the support of a broadly based, often multidisciplinary program of research projects related to an overall program objective.
First Independent Research Support and Transition (FIRST) Awards (R29)	Awarded to an eligible institution to support the first independent investigative efforts of an individual to assist with the transition toward regular (i.e., RO1) types of research sponsorship. Funds up to $350,000 are provided for project periods up to 5 years.
Small Business Innovation Research (SBIR) Grants	Awarded to for-profit institutions on behalf of a principal investigator to develop research technologies which result in commercial products or services.
Method to Extend Research in Time (MERIT) Awards	Awarded to eligible institutions to provide long-term support to distinctly superior (and usually senior) researchers, who are identified by NIH program staff (the individual investigator does not apply).
Center Grants	Awarded to eligible institutions on behalf of a program director and a group of collaborating investigators to support multidisciplinary long-term research programs of research and development. Differ from Program Project Grants in that a center tends to have a clinical focus and is developed in response to a specific institute announcement.
Research Career Program Awards Scientist Development and Research Awards (Scientist Awards at NIAAA and NIDA)	Comprised of several different types of awards for eligible institutions on behalf of scientists with clear research potential.
Academic Investigator and Clinical Awards (Investigator Awards at NINR) (K20, K21)	Referred to collectively as the "K Awards."
Small Grant Awards (RO3)	Awarded to eligible institutions on behalf of principal investigator, specifically limited in time and budget for pilot projects, testing of new techniques or feasibility studies on new or high-risk techniques, which would provide a basis for more extended research.
Academic Research Enhancement Award (AREA) (NINR only)	Awarded to eligible colleges and universities that are not research intensive on behalf of a principal investigator for small-scale or development-type discrete research projects, to provide these scientists and universities the opportunity to participate in the nations biomedical research effort.
Faculty Education Grants (NIDA and NIAAA only)	Awarded to eligible schools of medicine, nursing, social work and clinical psychology to support career development programs in alcohol and other drug abuse for academic faculty.

role of nursing in addictions research. Applications to these non-nursing institutions must provide education and promote consciousness raising about key role of addictions nurse experts in preventing and treating addiction.

Funding Mechanisms

NIH institutes have a number of different types of extramural funding mechanisms for a variety of research projects, research career development, and the training of new and established scientists. These can be divided into two major award classes of interest to nurse scientists: research grants and training awards. Research grants (see Box 19-5) make up the largest category of extramural funding and are awarded to nonprofit organizations and institutions, governments and government agencies, individuals, and for-profit organizations to support research in health and biomedicine. They provide for salaries, equipment, supplies, travel to conferences or research sites, and other direct costs of doing the research. Also provided are the indirect costs, which are the costs charged by the organization or institution in which the research will occur for administering, or the overhead associated with, the grant. These indirect charges can vary considerably depending on where the research is completed. Large universities may charge 30% to 50% of the total grant budget for such services as provision and maintenance of the space in which the research takes place, salary and benefits for support staff, and the accounting costs associated with managing the grant money (Division of Research Grants [DRG], 1993).

Training awards provide NIH institute support for the research training of scientists in the behavioral and biomedical sciences, which may be made on behalf of an individual for training or an institution to provide training. The majority of these awards are classified as National Research Service Awards (NRSA) of which there are several different types (see Box 19-6). The stated objectives of the NRSA awards are 1) to increase the number of individuals trained for research and teaching in specifically designated biomedical areas, and 2) to improve the environment within which biomedical training is provided (DRG, 1993).

When considering what type of award to apply for, it is imperative that nurse investigators speak with support staff at the potential funding institute to ensure that their application for funding will receive an appropriate review. In the NIH institutes (as with all large organizations), there exist unwritten priorities or agendas that the nurse scientist cannot perceive or appreciate from his or her office in Madison, Wisconsin or Los Angeles, California (Marshall, 1994c). Such undisclosed information becomes evident in conversations with institute personnel.

Two important and unwritten considerations in the selection of a funding mechanism are the 1) stage of career of the applicant and the 2) interest area or research focus of the application. Many awards are more appropriate for new or previously unfunded nurse scientists (i.e., NRSA Post-doctoral Fellowship Awards, Research Career Program (K) Awards, FIRST Awards, Small Grant Awards), who, despite submitting a high quality application with a well-designed research plan with noted significance, would never be funded within mechanisms (i.e., RO1) that are intended for those investigators with significant research experience and an established funding history.

Funding Priorities

The other important goal of conversation with institute support staff involves the content area of the proposal. The nurse scientist must determine how his or her proposed research project fits within the funding priorities of the institute. For example, a proposal examining

BOX 19-6. NIH NRSA Training Awards

Short-term Research Training Grants (F31, F32)	Provide pre- and post-doctoral students in the health professions with research experience during off-semester or summer periods to encourage them into clinical investigation careers.
Institutional Awards	Awarded to eligible institutions with the appropriate facilities and faculty to provide research training programs in scientific specialties. Awards cover personnel, supplies, and trainee stipends.
Individual Pre-doctoral Fellowship Awards	Awarded to eligible institutions for the graduate training of individuals in the biomedical and behavioral fields important to the specific institutes.
Individual Post-doctoral Fellowship Awards	Awarded to eligible institutions for qualified individuals holding a doctoral or equivalent degree to support full-time research training in designated biomedical science areas.
Senior Fellowships	Awarded to investigators with at least 7 years of relevant research or professional experience to support major changes in the direction of their research careers or to increase their capabilities for engaging in health-related research.
Minority Access to Research Careers Program (MARC)	Awarded to eligible minority institutions for the purpose of providing advanced training in research areas of interest to NIDA and NIAAA.
Minority Institutions Research and Development Program (MIRDP)	Awarded to institutions with a substantial minority enrollment for the support of research or advanced training of faculty.
Supplements for Underrepresented Minorities in Biomedical and Behavioral Research	Research and salary support available to underrepresented minority undergraduate students, graduate research assistants, and minority investigators. The proposed research must be an integral part of the approved ongoing research grant.

a specific nursing intervention to minimize relapse to heroin may have little relevance to the research agenda set forth by NINR, although application of the same treatment within a prenatal care context to decrease the rate of low birthweight infants to drug-dependent women may have a much better chance of being funded by the same institute (see Box 19-7, priority 1). Addiction is a broad content area, and since there are many aspects of addiction a nurse investigator may choose to focus on, it is important that if he or she desires federal funding, the research application be devised to match the funding priorities of an NIH institute.

Funding priorities of an institute may be published and available as such, or may be gleaned from program announcements (PA) or requests for applications (RFA) put forth by the institute. PAs and RFAs are developed as the result of a perceived need within the institute in an effort to encourage research on a specific topic. Although it may appear to the nurse scientist that a proposal addresses an identified institute funding priority, it is still necessary to discuss with institute personnel the details of the proposal, to learn how current or pressing the priority is, and how well the application specifically fits with their funding agenda. Funding priorities of NINR, NIDA, and NIAAA are listed in Boxes 19-7 through 19-9.

Thus, it behooves the nurse investigator who wishes to receive federal research funds to become informed about the type or content of projects that relevant organizations or agencies fund, and to tailor his or her research question as much as possible to the needs or priorities of the funding agency. This is especially important early in the nurse investigator's research career, when he or she needs to establish a funding history to compete for future funding. Responding to the needs of a funding agency utilizing existing clinical resources, although not specifically addressing the nurse's primary research interest, provides a way for the nurse investigator to "break into" the funding arena. Once a funding history and credibility with funding agencies are established, the nurse investigator can begin to seek funding for his or her own particular research interest, and may even be eligible to participate in the process of developing funding priorities for the agency. Seasoned clinical investigators frequently will use the funding obtained for a project not only to complete the identified project, but also to collect pilot data to support the application for another project in which they are particularly interested. Nurse investigators must become comfortable adopting this model as one method of establishing a research career.

Priorities for funding in all NIH Institutes are shaped by three major sources; the federal government, experts from the scientific community, and the American citizenry, as shown in Figure 19-1. Federal government priorities are set by the Congress, who determines

BOX 19-7. Funding Priorities at NINR

PRIORITIES FOR FISCAL YEARS 1989–1994
1. Low birthweight—mothers and infants
2. HIV infection—prevention and care
3. Long-term care for older adults
4. Symptom management—pain
5. Nursing informatics—support for patient care
6. Health promotion of children and adolescents

PRIORITIES FOR FISCAL YEARS 1995–1999
7. Technology dependency across the life span
8. Community-based nursing models
9. Health promoting behaviors and HIV/AIDS
10. Remediation of cognitive impairment
11. Living with chronic illness
12. Biobehavioral factors related to immunocompetence

**BOX 19-8. Selected NIDA Program Announcements (PA)
July 1990–June 1994**

PA #	PROGRAM ANNOUNCEMENT
PA-90-19	Research on the Prevalence and Impact of Drug Use in the Workplace
PA-94-054	Strategies to Reduce HIV Sexual Risk Practices in Drug Users
PA-94-023	HIV-Related Therapies in Drug Users
PA-94-010	Research on Needle Hygiene and Needle Exchange Programs
PA-93-110	Health Care Services for Persons With HIV Infection
PA-93-098	Drug Abuse Aspects of AIDS
PA-93-080	Determinants of Effective HIV Counseling
PA-93-44	The Spread of TB Among Drug Users
PA-94-006	Inhalant Abuse Research
PA-93-060	Biomedical Factors in Drug Abuse Etiology and Consequences
PA-93-059	Etiology, Consequences, and Behavioral Pharmacology of Female Drug Abuse
PA-92-80	Research on Anabolic Steroid Use
PA-91-33	Vulnerability to Drug Abuse
PA-94-056	Comprehensive Prevention Research in Drug Abuse
PA-94-007	Survey Research on Drug Use and Associated Behaviors
PA-94-047	Dug Abuse Health Services Research
PA-93-12	Novel Drug Delivery Systems Treatment of Drug Abuse
PA-93-106	Drug Abuse Treatment for Women of Childbearing Age and Their Children
PA-93-100	Research Program to Improve Drug Abuse Treatment
PA-93-27	Psychotherapy, Behavior Therapy, and Counseling in Drug Dependence Treatment
PA-93-21	Drug Abuse Treatment of Criminal Justice Involved Populations
PA-92-110	Development of Theoretically Based Psychosocial Therapies for Drug Dependence
PA-93-46	Drug Use and Abuse in Minority and Underserved Populations
PA-92-16	Studies on the Medical and Health Consequences of Drug Abuse

the budget for each institute and thereby, decides what activities will and will not be funded. The current administration also determines agenda by the philosophical tone it sets in how it tends to view drug and alcohol abuse (i.e., a crime versus a disease versus a social problem), and therefore, how abusers should be handled (i.e, tougher laws and more jails, more treatment slots or more social programs) (Office of National Drug Control Policy, 1994). Finally, other government agencies, such as the Department of Justice or the Department of Defense, may influence institute decisions, either by making their priorities salient in Congress, in the administration, or in the institute itself (Kleber, 1992).

The scientific community also sets priorities through their understanding of the accumulating body of knowledge about addiction, addiction prevention, and addiction treatment. Scientists argue for projects, especially basic science projects, that may not appear to the general public as having much relevance for addressing addiction, but are deemed critical to the field based on the experts' in-depth understanding of the problem and literature. Because

BOX 19-9. Selected NIAAA Program Announcements (PA) August 1990–September 1994

PA #	PROGRAM ANNOUNCEMENT
PA-94-077	Neurobiology of Ethanol-Related Behaviors
PA-93-095	Research on Relationships Between Alcohol and Violence
PA-93-086	Genetic Studies in Alcohol Research
PA-93-47	Preventing Alcohol-Related Problems Among Ethnic Minorities
PA-92-101	Research on Economic and Socioeconomic Aspects of Alcohol Abuse
PA-92-75	Research on Alcoholism Patient–Treatment Matching
PA-92-74	Research on Children of Alcoholics
PA-92-70	Research on the Homeless With Alcohol Problems
PA-92-46	Research on the Prevention of Alcohol Abuse Among Youth
PA-92-12	Alcohol and Immunology Including AIDS
PA-91-75	Research on Relationships Between Alcohol Use and Sexual Behaviors Associated With HIV Transmission
PA-90-27	Applied Research into the Process of Alcoholism Treatment
PA-90-26	Alcohol-Related Trauma: Research on Referral and Treatment

these scientists also tend to be those who make up the review committees and directors of institute programs, they have a strong voice in determining what will and will not be funded. In fact, the 1990s marks the end of an era during which the scientific community had almost unchallenged authority to set research priorities. Congress and the federal administration are now starting to hold institutes accountable for the scientific progress made relative to the amount of taxpayer dollars spent (Cohen, 1993b).

Citizen groups and voluntary organizations are becoming increasingly vocal and influential in setting the spending agendas of the NIH institutes (Cohen, 1993b). This trend was recently evident in the cases of AIDS activists and the National Breast Cancer Coalition, which, by flooding Congress and the White House with letters and demonstrations, restructured how health care research dollars were distributed and budgeted within NIH institutes.

The Federal Grant Review Process

As can be seen in Figure 19-2, once the nurse scientist has completed the grant application for federal funding, it is sent to the NIH Division of Research Grants (DRG), which is the central receipt point for all applications. It is anticipated that by 1997 much of the preparation and submission of grant applications will be electronic, obviating the need for multiple photocopies and overnight delivery services. Currently, many software packages are available within which the necessary application forms preceding and following the text of the application can be generated and completed on screen.

Within 2 to 3 weeks of receipt, the principal investigator will receive a copy of the "green sheet," which contains important information on the status of the application (see Figure 19-3). In the DRG, each application is assigned to 1) an appropriate scientific review committee (SRC), or study section, for scientific merit review, and 2) an appropriate institute (i.e., NINR,

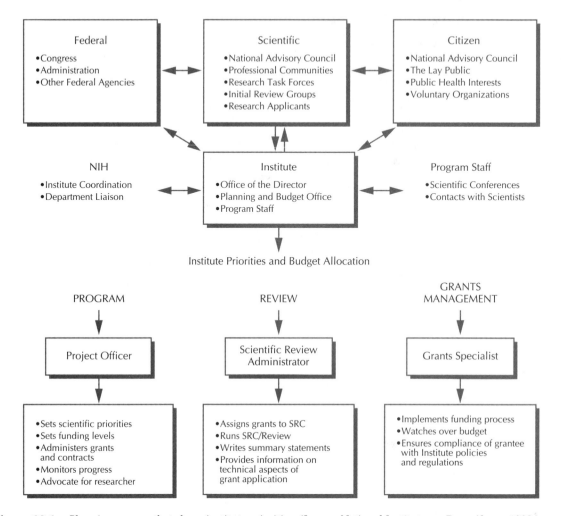

Figure 19-1. Planning sources that shape institute priorities. (Source: National Institute on Drug Abuse, 1993.)

NIDA, NIAAA) for a second level review by its advisory council or board. At both levels, the NIH uses peer review procedures, in which scientists actually engaged in relevant research are invited to assist in the selection of projects that are of high quality and worthy of funding. Due to the amount of time necessary to participate in grant reviews, these scientists are not always the most well-known or productive in the field. The two review levels are sequential and are referred to as the "dual review system" (DRG, 1993).

The first level of review is referred to as a scientific review committee (SRC). Each SRC has a scientific review administrator (SRA) who is the contact person for the principal investigator. The SRC is composed of a panel of experts established generally according to scientific disciplines or organ or disease areas, who review the scientific and technical merit of a research grant application. Thus, this is the group that evaluates the design, measurement, sample, feasibility, and protection of human rights of a project. Based on this first level review, each application is judged as approved or disapproved for the review process. If disapproved no review takes place and no priority score is given. If approved it goes through the review process and receives a priority score. Priority scores range from 1.0 to 5.0, with lower scores indicating a better application. Generally an application with a priority score less than 1.2 has a high probability of being funded; scores ranging from 1.5 to 3.0 indicate that the proposal will likely not be funded, but the principal investigator should consider revising the application according to the SRC's feedback and resubmit it at the next deadline. Higher priority scores indicate that even with significant revision, the application is unlikely to be funded and, as with applications judged as disapproved and not reviewed, the principal investigator should view this as an opportunity to rework the research project, taking into account the feedback of the group, and develop an essentially new application. This may actually work to the principal investigator's advantage, in that the new application may be assigned to a different review group better able than the original assignment to evaluate the application.

The second level of review is a national advisory board or council within the assigned institute. These councils/boards are comprised of both scientific and lay representatives who have a demonstrated interest in health areas relevant to the particular institute. For example, NIDA has advisory committees devoted to drug abuse and AIDS research, drug abuse biomedical research, and drug abuse epidemiology and prevention research, among others.

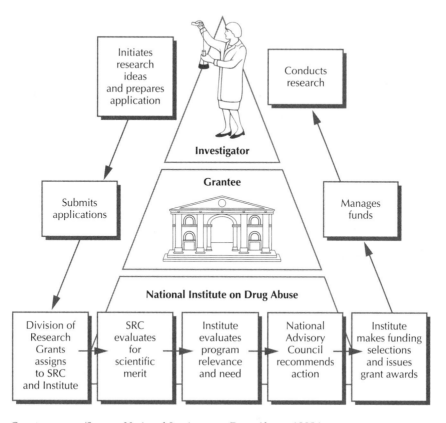

Figure 19-2. Grant process. (Source: National Institute on Drug Abuse, 1993.)

These groups assess the quality of, and rely heavily on, the SRC review of grant applications and priority scores. They also take into account the relevance of each application to the institute priorities and goals, and based on these, make recommendations for funding. Thus, an excellent priority score from the SRC does not ensure funding; if the project is not relevant to the priorities of the institute, funding will not occur. Funding also depends on the amount of money an institute has available to award; a low priority score does not ensure funding if available dollars within the institute are limited.

Thus, the dual review system permits the separation of the assessment of scientific and technical merit from subsequent policy decisions, resulting in a more objective evaluation than that which may occur with a single level review. Overall the steps to the review process once an application arrives at NIH are summarized in Box 19-10.

As noted, the decision of whether a particular grant application is sent to NIAAA, NIDA, or NINR for consideration is made at the level of the DRG. The DRG makes assignments for hundreds of grant applications at a time, usually based only on information culled from the title and abstract of the application. Therefore, it is imperative that both clearly reflect the content and disciplinary focus of the application, as the success of an application depends heavily on being assigned to an appropriate and knowledgeable IRG and NIH institute. For example, if an application is prepared with a focus on a nursing clinical problem, reflecting an NINR priority, and using a nursing outcome as a dependent measure, yet the grant title and abstract result in a NIDA assignment, it is unlikely to be funded, despite its scientific merit, as the NIDA advisory board will not appreciate or value its nursing focus. Another problem with a poorly assigned application is that even if the principal investigator makes changes in the application and resubmits it to the DRG, it will be assigned to the same IRG and institute for review. Only rarely, and with much effort, will the DRG make a new assignment for a previously submitted grant; thus, once "misassigned," the application is doomed to be reviewed by a group that may never be able to appropriately evaluate its merit. The only exception to the DRG assignment is if the grant is written in response to a specific institute RFA or PA (see Boxes 19-8 and 19-9); in these cases the PA or RFA number is listed on the application cover page, and it is automatically assigned to that institute.

In addition to devising an unambiguous title and abstract, another strategy the nurse scientist can employ to help assure a proposal is assigned to an appropriate review group and institute is through the cover letter sent in with the application. Although the principal investigator cannot demand a certain type of assignment, he or she can guide the assignment by summarizing the content area or disciplinary focus of the application and making sugges-

BOX 19-10. Federal Grant Review Process After Submission

1. Division of Research Grants (DRG) assigns to scientific review committee (SRC) and Institute.
2. SRC evaluates for scientific merit and assigns priority score.
3. Institute evaluates program relevance and need.
4. National Advisory Council recommends action.
5. Institute makes funding selections and issues grant awards.

tions about the type of expertise required to best evaluate the application. The intent is to assist the DRG in making an appropriate assignment while acknowledging the difficulty inherent in assigning a large number of grants to appropriate review groups and institutes. Institute support staff contacted prior to the submission can be helpful in describing how the cover letter should be worded, or providing key words it should contain, to maximize the chance of an appropriate assignment.

Finally, the "green sheet" provides information the principal investigator can use to probe a perceived poor assignment. Telephone numbers for both the DRG referral office and the SRA (see Figure 19-3) are provided to which the principal investigator can voice assignment concerns. Although reassignments remain rare, at least the SRA is aware and can inform the SRC of a less than ideal assignment, which can be taken into account during scientific merit evaluation.

It is important that the nurse scientist not become discouraged if an application receives a poor score or is not recommended for review. Current NIH estimates indicate that less than 15% of all unsolicited grant applications actually receive funding. Seasoned researchers expect poor success rates, especially on the first submission of a new application. It is not

SRC: NAME OF REVIEW GROUP
DR. SUSAN SMITH, SRA
DRG/NATIONAL INSTITUTES OF HEALTH
RM 352   5333 WESTBARD AVENUE
BETHESDA, MD 20892 (301) 594-7080

Your grant application has been received by NIH and assigned to a scientific review committee (SRC) for scientific merit evaluation and to an Institute for funding consideration. The initial Peer Review should be completed by 11/95 and a funding decision made shortly after the appropriate National Advisory Group meets in 01/96. For questions about the assignment, contact the Referral Office (301) 594- 7250. For questions prior to the review, contact the SRC Scientific Review Administrator (SRA) named above. For questions after the review, contact the Institute listed below.

PRINCIPAL INVESTIGATOR: SALLY NURSE-SCIENTIST, RN, PhD   COUNCIL: 01-96
TITLE: MATERNAL METHADONE BLOOD LEVEL, HIV STATUS AND FETAL OUTCOME
ASSIGNMENT NUMBER: 1R43DA08653-01   SRC: NSRC

NATL INST ON DRUG ABUSE
EXTRAMURAL ACTIVITIES   PK 10-25
5600 FISHER LANE
ROCKVILLE, MD 20857   (301) 443-6710

SALLY NURSE-SCIENTIST, RN, PhD
STEPHENS COLLEGE
DIVISION OF NURSING
150 EAST MAIN STREET
OAKLAND, CA 97654

Figure 19-3. Sample "green sheet."

uncommon for active research groups to submit at least one new application and one resubmission each funding cycle, simply to improve their chances of being funded. Although funding for the first few projects is difficult and time consuming to achieve, it is well worth the scientific credibility and professional advancement, as well as contributions to nursing knowledge that federal funding provides.

Grant-Writing Helpful Hints

Because nurses have less collective expertise in grant writing than do other professionals or PhD's seeking funding, and because reviewers outside the NINR are likely to be relatively unfamiliar with nursing research and nursing concerns, the grant applications nurse scientists submit have to be of top quality to compete. There are specific steps the nurse scientist can take to maximize the chance of an application receiving a favorable review.

First and perhaps most important, the application must be complete, well-written, and well-organized. The primary reviewer of the grant has more than one grant to critically review and, in reality, is probably reviewing your application as he or she travels to Bethesda for the meeting. For this reason, writing cannot be cryptic or stylistic, but must be straightforward and in the somewhat dry form of a research report. Do not assume the reviewer will intuit what you mean, and avoid nursing jargon (i.e., self-care, nursing diagnosis) in applications going to institutes outside NINR. Review and re-review the application instructions over the course of the application preparation to ensure that critical elements (inclusion of women and minorities, human subject considerations, power analysis, etc.) are not only addressed, but highlighted, in the text so that reviewers can easily locate these.

Furthermore, page, font size, and density of type limitations must be adhered to strictly. The last thing you want to leave with the primary reviewer is eyestrain. Take the same care in the development of your ideas and presentation of the product as you would in preparing a manuscript for a referred journal. A sloppy application with grammatical and spelling errors communicates to the reviewer that you do not care about the quality of the work you produce, which presumably generalizes to the research for which you are requesting funds. Keep in mind that you are representing nurse scholars to the reviewers; the careful job you do will translate into more positive attitudes in general about the quality of nurse applications and applicants.

Whenever possible include pilot data for the proposed project. In describing these data make it clear to reviewers that they support the proposed research and provide evidence that you have experience in its collection, and the resources available to do so. Include well-designed tables and figures to present these data, and demonstrate to the reviewers how the proposed protocol was informed by the pilot experience (Tornquist & Funk, 1990).

If the nurse scientist is relatively unseasoned or an unknown entity to the applicant institution (which is almost a certainty with NIDA and NIAAA), it is critical that key co-investigators or collaborators be identified, especially those with a successful funding history at NIH. In many cases this will require collaboration with non-nursing professionals who have identified expertise in a content area relevant to the proposal. For example, input and agreed on collaboration or letters of support from experts in the fields of relapse prevention and HIV disease would greatly strengthen the application of a nurse scientist evaluating the effectiveness of relapse prevention skills with needle-sharing component. As a rule, grant reviewers tend to be suspicious of any clinician applicant's ability to analyze data. Even if the nurse investigator feels confident in his or her ability to analyze study findings, it is wise to name and include a letter of support from a consultant or collaborator with statistical expertise and published experience in analyzing the type of data generated by the chosen study design.

Ensure that the budget is well-prepared, well-justified, and clearly presented for the reviewer. In requesting money for supplies or equipment, provide catalog or model numbers to demonstrate that you have priced these items. If you are not spreadsheet proficient, utilize the skills of someone who is. In applications with larger budgets (i.e., anything over $50,000/year) and/or budgets spanning over multiple years, include spreadsheet pages of the budget as application continuation pages.

For revised applications that are resubmitted, ensure that changes made in response to IRG review are significant and clearly identified (Oetting, 1986). Provide sound rationale for IRG recommendations not incorporated in the resubmission.

Box 19-11 lists the 10 most common reasons for grant application disapproval presented at a 1994 NIDA-sponsored grant-writing workshop.

Current Trends Conducive to Federal Nursing Funding

Although the past funding history of nurses at NIH has been less than optimal, current trends at the agencies bode well for nurse scientists. In 1993, when NIH presented Congress with its 1994 budget, Congress sent it back, asking the agency for an in-depth self-assessment before resubmitting the budget (Marshall, 1994a). This self-evaluation resulted in several findings that should impact positively on the chances of nurse scientists being funded. First, inequalities in the ways in which female investigators' proposals were scored and funded were made evident. At the National Cancer Institute, for example, it was found that during 1992, female researchers on average received less than two-thirds the budget, 63% of personnel, and 200 square feet less of laboratory space than those allocated to male counterparts at same level of seniority (Seachrist, 1994). A recently released report from the General Accounting Office of the Congress found that scores awarded grant proposals were related to gender, with those written by women receiving poorer scores (Marshall, 1994c). Increased sensitivity to gender bias than has occurred in the past is likely, ultimately benefiting the majority of nurse scientists who are female.

BOX 19-11.   Most Common Reasons for Proposal Disapproval at NIDA, 1994

1. Lack of new or original ideas
2. Diffuse, superficial, or unfocused research plan
3. Lack of knowledge of published relevant work
4. Lack of experience in the essential methodology
5. Uncertainty concerning the future directions or implications
6. Questionable reasoning in experimental approach
7. Absence of an acceptable scientific rationale
8. Unrealistically large amount of work
9. Lack of sufficient experimental detail
10. Uncritical approach

Another trend at NIH beneficial to nursing research is an increased emphasis on clinical work. Across institutes, clinical researchers have complained that the agency has de-emphasized patient-oriented research in favor of molecular and basic work. A 1994 Institute of Medicine survey found that only 15% to 17% of 14,535 NIH grants awarded in 1990-1991 were for human research, broadly defined as those utilizing human subjects, and only 4.5% could be classified as clinical human research (Marshall, 1994b). This lack of clinical focus has been related to the number of basic scientists and nonclinical experts who sit on the SRCs, as well as the better-developed grant-writing skills of these individuals. As NIH attempts to address the concerns of clinicians and turns more favorable eye on clinical research, nursing research projects with clinical foci or implications are likely to receive favorable reviews.

All extramural investigators will benefit from the NIH self-evaluation focus on the relative efficacy and accountability of the intramural versus extramural research programs (Cohen, 1993a,b; Marshall, 1994a). There has been concern within the agency that intramural projects receive proportionately bigger budgets, personnel support, and laboratory space than extramural projects, to the point where Congress has asked for evaluation of the intramural programs and what they are specifically supposed to provide in contrast with the extramural programs. Efforts to equalize the distribution of resources between extramural and intramural projects should benefit nurse scientists applying for extramural funds.

Across institutes, trends toward content areas conceptually and historically within nursing's domain are evident. Specifically, there is an emphasis on the merits of preventative health care, which have been strongly espoused by the current administration (Marshall, 1993). This emphasis goes hand in hand with efforts to reform health care and seek less costly or at least more cost-effective methods of delivering care (Anderson, 1993). In both these areas, nurse investigators can claim advantages. Nurses have always valued prevention and many have well-defined expertise in preventative care. Nurses are also involved in less costly models of care, from their work as nurse practitioners and midwives, to utilizing interventions that are less technology oriented, more behaviorally oriented, and ultimately less costly. Nursing expertise is closely in line with current administration priorities; thus, the likelihood of a favorable review of applications reflective of these is increased.

CONCLUSION

Research in addictions nursing is critical to the development of effective nursing interventions, the generation of nursing theory, and the elevation of nursing's professional status within the scientific disciplines. To make meaningful research-based contributions to addictions, nurse scientists must ensure that their work clearly addresses nursing concerns and they must engage in extensive doctoral and postdoctoral training.

The process of addictions nursing research involves specific methodological and humans subjects concerns, which the nurse scientist must address in study design. Research questions nurses devise tend to be clinical in nature and reflect current knowledge in addiction across disciplines.

In an effort to find solutions to the nation's health problems, the U.S. government sets aside large amounts of taxpayer dollars each year to fund relevant research. Clearly, addictions nurse scientists have the scholarly qualities to provide some of the solutions. As nurse scientists gain the specialized knowledge to apply for and receive these research funds, and attain a prominent role in the federal funding arena, society, the nursing profession, and, most important, the alcohol- and drug-abusing persons will mutually benefit.

REFERENCES

ANA/National Nurses Society on Addictions. (1988). *Standards of addictions nursing practice with selected diagnoses and criteria*. Kansas City, MO: American Nurses' Association.

Anderson, C. (1993). Research and health care costs. *Science, 261*, 416–418.

Anglin, M.D., Brecht, M.L., Woodward, J.A., & Bonett, D.G. (1986). An empirical study of maturing out: Conditional factors. *International Journal of the Addictions, 21*, 233–246.

Blaine, J.D., Ling, W., Kosten, T.R., O'Brien, C.P., & Chiarello, R.J. (1994). Establishing efficacy and safety of medications for the treatment of drug dependence and abuse: Methodologic issues. In R.F Prien & D.S. Robinson (Eds.). *Clinical evaluation of psychotropic drugs: Principles and guidelines* (pp. 593–623). New York, NY: Raven Press, Ltd.

Brooks, M.K. (1992). Ethical and legal aspects of confidentiality. In J.H. Lowinson, P. Ruiz, & R.B. Millman (Eds.). *Substance abuse: A comprehensive textbook* (2nd. ed.) (pp. 1049–1066). Baltimore: Williams & Wilkins.

Cohen, J. (1993a). Is NIH's crown jewel losing luster? *Science, 261*, 1120–1127.

Cohen, J. (1993b). Conflicting agendas shape NIH. *Science, 261*, 1674–1679.

Cunningham, J.A., Sobell, L.C., Sobell, M.B., Agrawal, S., & Toneatto, T. (1993). Barriers to treatment: Why alcohol and drug abusers delay or never seek treatment. *Addictive Behaviors, 18*, 347–353.

Division of Research Grants. (1993). *Grants and awards: Funding mechanisms*. Bethesda, MD: National Institutes of Health.

Herrero, M.E., & Baca, E. (1990). Specific treatment demand as a definitory trait of typology in heroin addicts. *International Journal of the Addictions, 25*, 65–79.

Hubbard, R.L., Marsden, M.E., Rachal, J.V., Harwood, H.J., Cavanaugh, E.R., & Ginzberg, H.M. (1989). *Drug abuse treatment: A national study of effectiveness*. Chapel Hill: The University of North Carolina Press.

Iwamoto, E., & Martin, W. (1988). A critique of drug self-administration as a method for predicting abuse potential of drugs. In L.S. Harris (Ed.), *Problems of drug dependence, 1987* (NIDA Research Monograph Series, No. 81, pp. 457–465). Rockville, MD: National Institute on Drug Abuse.

Kleber, H.D. (1992). Federal role in substance abuse policy. In J.H. Lowinson, P. Ruiz & R.B. Millman (Eds.). *Substance abuse: A comprehensive textbook* (2nd. ed.) (pp. 32–38). Baltimore: Williams & Wilkins.

Lesch, O.M., Kefer, J., Lentner, S., Mader, R., Marx, B., Musalek, M., Nimmerrichter, A., Preinsberger, H., Puchinger H., & Rustembegovic, A. (1990). Diagnosis of chronic alcoholism—Classificatory problems. *Psychopathology, 23*, 88–96.

Marshall, E (1993). Prevention research: A new growth area of NIH? *Science, 262*, 1508–1509.

Marshall, E. (1994a). Strong Medicine for NIH. *Science, 264*, 896–898.

Marshall, E. (1994b). Does NIH shortchange clinicians? *Science, 265*, 20–21.

Marshall, E. (1994c). Congress finds little bias in system. *Science, 265*, 863.

McLellan, A.T. (1992). Measurement issues in the evaluation of experimental treatment interventions. In M.M. Kilbey & K. Asghar (Eds.). *Methodological issues in epidemiological, prevention and treatment research on drug-exposed women and their children* (NIDA Research Monograph Series, No. 117, pp. 18–30). Rockville, MD: National Institute on Drug Abuse.

National Institute on Alcohol and Alcoholism and Center for Sustance Abuse Prevention. (1993.) *The alcohol and other drug thesaurus*. Washington, DC: U.S. Department of Health and Human Services.

National Institute on Drug Abuse. (1993). *How good is your drug abuse program? A guide to evaluation*. Rockville, MD: U.S. Department of Health and Human Services.

National Institute of Nursing Research. (1994). *Nursing research at the National Institutes of Health*. Bethesda, MD: U.S. Department of Health and Human Services.

Nieswiadomy, R.M. (1993). *Foundations of nursing research* (2nd. ed.). Norwalk, CT: Appleton & Lange.

Oetting, E.R. (1986). Ten fatal mistakes in grant writing. *Professional Psychology: Research and Practice, 17*, 570–573.

Office of National Drug Control Policy. (1994). *National drug control strategy: Reclaiming our communities from drugs and violence*. Washington, DC: Office of National Drug Control Policy.

Office of Technology Assessment. (1990). *Effectiveness of drug abuse treatment. Implications for controlling AIDS/HIV infection*. Washington, DC: Government Printing Office.

Parse, R.R. (1994). Scholarship: Three essential processes (editorial). *Nursing Science Quarterly, 7*, 143.

Peele, S. (1990). Why and by whom the American alcoholism treatment industry is under siege. *Journal of Psychoactive Drugs, 22*, 1–13.

Pickens, R.W., & Fletcher, B.W. (1991). Overview of treatment issues. In R. W. Pickens, C.G. Leukefeld, & C.R. Schuster (Eds.), *Improving drug abuse treatment* (NIDA Research Monograph Series, No. 106, pp. 1–19). Rockville, MD: National Institute on Drug Abuse.

Polit, D.F., & Hungler, B.P. (1993). *Essentials of nursing research. Methods, appraisal and utilization* (3rd ed.). Philadelphia: J.B. Lippincott.

Public Health Service. (1993). Confidentiality of alcohol and drug abuse patient records. In M.W. Parrino (Ed.), *State methadone treatment guidelines* (Treatment Improvement Protocol Series No. 1, pp. 189–211). Rockville, MD: Center for Substance Abuse Treatment.

Rounsaville, B.J., Tims, F.M., Horton, A.M., & Sowder, B.J. (Eds.). (1993). *Diagnostic source book on drug abuse research and treatment.* Rockville, MD: National Institute on Drug Abuse.

Seachrist, L. (1994). Disparities detailed in NCI division. *Science, 264,* 340.

Shiffman, S. (1991). Refining models of dependence: Variations across persons and situations. *British Journal of Addiction, 86,* 611–615.

Sitharthan, T., McGrath, D., Sitharthan, G., & Saunders, J.B. (1992). Meaning of craving in research on addiction. *Psychological Reports, 71,* 823–826.

Sobell, L.C., Sobell, M.B., Toneatto, T., & Leo, G.I. (1993). What triggers the resolution of alcohol problems without treatment. *Alcoholism, Clinical and Experimental Research, 17,* 217–224.

Tornquist, E.M., & Funk, S.G. (1990). How to write a research proposal. *IMAGE: Journal of Nursing Scholarship, 22,* 44–51.

SUGGESTED READINGS ON FUNDING SOURCES

The Annual Register of Grant Support. A Directory of Funding Sources. 27th ed., 1994. (1993). New Providence, NJ: R.R. Bowker.

Bauer, D.G. (1988). *The Complete Grants Sourcebook for Nursing and Health.* New York, NY: MacMillan Publishing Company.

Executive Office of the President. (1994). *Catalog of Federal Domestic Assistance 1994.* Washington DC: Government Printing Office.

The Foundation Center. (1988). *AIDS Funding. A Guide to Giving by Foundations and Charitable Organizations.* New York, NY: The Foundation Center.

The Foundation Center. (1994). *The Foundation Directory 1994 Edition.* New York, NY: The Foundation Center.

Institute of Medicine. (1991). *AIDS Research Program of the NIH.* Washington, DC: National Academy Press.

National Institute of Health. (1994). *1994 Research Grants.* Volume 1. NIH pub. # 92-1042. Bethesda, MD: NIH Division of Research Grants.

Olson, S., & Kovacs, R. (Eds.). (1993). *National Guide to Funding in Health* (3rd. ed.). New York, NY: The Foundation Center.

The Robert Wood Johnson Foundation. (1992). *Annual Report: Substance Abuse.* Princeton, NJ: The Robert Wood Johnson Foundation.

Schwartz, S.M., & Friedman, M.E. (1992). *A Guide to NIH Grant Programs.* New York, NY: Oxford University Press.

U.S. Conference of Mayors. (1991). *Directory of Federal Grants for HIV/AIDS Prevention and Services. Fiscal Year 90.* Washington, DC: U.S. Conference of Mayors.

APPENDIX 1: Alcohol Use Disorders Identification Test (AUDIT) (Revised to Include Drugs)*

This questionnaire asks you some questions about your use of alcohol and drugs during the past year. Alcoholic beverages include beer, wine, and liquor (vodka, whiskey, brandy, etc.). Drugs include cocaine, marijuana, narcotics, and tranquilizers.

1. How often do you have a drink containing alcohol or use other drugs (e.g., marijuana, cocaine, narcotics)?

    ❑   Never   (0)   [   ]
    ❑   Less than monthly   (1)
If *more* than once a month:

Alcohol	❑ Monthly	(2)	[ ]
	❑ Weekly	(3)	
	❑ Daily or almost daily	(4)	
Cocaine	❑ Monthly	(2)	[ ]
	❑ Weekly	(3)	
	❑ Daily or almost daily	(4)	
Marijuana	❑ Monthly	(2)	[ ]
	❑ Weekly	(3)	
	❑ Daily or almost daily	(4)	
Tranquilizers	❑ Monthly	(2)	[ ]
	❑ Weekly	(3)	
	❑ Daily or almost daily	(4)	
Other _____	❑ Monthly	(2)	[ ]
	❑ Weekly	(3)	
	❑ Daily or almost daily	(4)	

2. On a day when you drink alcohol or use other drugs, how many drinks (alcohol), lines (cocaine), joints (marijuana), or tranquilizer pills do you use?

Alcohol	❑ None	(0)	[ ]
	❑ 1 or 2	(1)	
	❑ 3 or 4	(2)	
	❑ 5 or 6	(3)	
	❑ 7 to 9	(4)	
	❑ 10 or more	(5)	
Cocaine	❑ None	(0)	[ ]
	❑ 1 or 2	(1)	
	❑ 3 or 4	(2)	
	❑ 5 or 6	(3)	
	❑ 7 to 9	(4)	
	❑ 10 or more	(5)	
Tranquilizers	❑ None	(0)	[ ]
	❑ 1 or 2	(1)	
	❑ 3 or 4	(2)	
	❑ 5 or 6	(3)	
	❑ 7 to 9	(4)	
	❑ 10 or more	(5)	

Other

- ❑ None   (0)   [   ]
- ❑ 1 or 2   (1)
- ❑ 3 or 4   (2)
- ❑ 5 or 6   (3)
- ❑ 7 to 9   (4)
- ❑ 10 or more   (5)

3. How often do you have 6 or more drinks, 1 or more joints, 10 or more lines, or 3 or more tranquilizer pills on one occasion?

Alcohol   Other drugs

- ❑ Never   (0)   [   ]   ❑ Never   (0)   [   ]
- ❑ Less than monthly   (1)   ❑ Less than monthly   (1)
- ❑ Monthly   (2)   ❑ Monthly   (2)
- ❑ Weekly   (3)   ❑ Weekly   (3)
- ❑ Daily or almost daily   (4)   ❑ Daily or almost daily   (4)

4. How often during the last year have you found that you were unable to stop drinking or using other drugs once you had started?

Alcohol   Other drugs

- ❑ Never   (0)   [   ]   ❑ Never   (0)   [   ]
- ❑ Less than monthly   (1)   ❑ Less than monthly   (1)
- ❑ Monthly   (2)   ❑ Monthly   (2)
- ❑ Weekly   (3)   ❑ Weekly   (3)
- ❑ Daily or almost daily   (4)   ❑ Daily or almost daily   (4)

5. How often during the last year have you failed to do what was normally expected from you because of drinking or using other drugs?

Alcohol   Other drugs

- ❑ Never   (0)   [   ]   ❑ Never   (0)   [   ]
- ❑ Less than monthly   (1)   ❑ Less than monthly   (1)
- ❑ Monthly   (2)   ❑ Monthly   (2)
- ❑ Weekly   (3)   ❑ Weekly   (3)
- ❑ Daily or almost daily   (4)   ❑ Daily or almost daily   (4)

6. How often during the last year have you needed a drink or drug in the morning to get yourself going after a heavy drinking or drug-using session?

Alcohol   Other drugs

- ❑ Never   (0)   [   ]   ❑ Never   (0)   [   ]
- ❑ Less than monthly   (1)   ❑ Less than monthly   (1)
- ❑ Monthly   (2)   ❑ Monthly   (2)
- ❑ Weekly   (3)   ❑ Weekly   (3)
- ❑ Daily or almost daily   (4)   ❑ Daily or almost daily   (4)

7. How often during the last year have you had a feeling of guilt or remorse after drinking or using other drugs?

Alcohol   Other drugs

- ❑ Never   (0)   [   ]   ❑ Never   (0)   [   ]
- ❑ Less than monthly   (1)   ❑ Less than monthly   (1)
- ❑ Monthly   (2)   ❑ Monthly   (2)
- ❑ Weekly   (3)   ❑ Weekly   (3)
- ❑ Daily or almost daily   (4)   ❑ Daily or almost daily   (4)

8. How often during the last year have you been unable to remember what happened the night before because you had been drinking or using other drugs?

Alcohol

❑ Never	(0)	[ ]
❑ Less than monthly	(1)	
❑ Monthly	(2)	
❑ Weekly	(3)	
❑ Daily or almost daily	(4)	

Other drugs

❑ Never	(0)	[ ]
❑ Less than monthly	(1)	
❑ Monthly	(2)	
❑ Weekly	(3)	
❑ Daily or almost daily	(4)	

9. Have you or someone else been injured as a result of your drinking or drug use?

Alcohol

❑ Never	(0)	[ ]
❑ Less than monthly	(1)	
❑ Monthly	(2)	
❑ Weekly	(3)	
❑ Daily or almost daily	(4)	

Other drugs

❑ Never	(0)	[ ]
❑ Less than monthly	(1)	
❑ Monthly	(2)	
❑ Weekly	(3)	
❑ Daily or almost daily	(4)	

10. Has a relative, friend, or a doctor or other health worker been concerned about your drinking or drug use or suggested you cut down?

Alcohol

❑ Never	(0)	[ ]
❑ Less than monthly	(1)	
❑ Monthly	(2)	
❑ Weekly	(3)	
❑ Daily or almost daily	(4)	

Other drugs

❑ Never	(0)	[ ]
❑ Less than monthly	(1)	
❑ Monthly	(2)	
❑ Weekly	(3)	
❑ Daily or almost daily	(4)	

Record the total of the specific items. In a general population, a score of 11 or greater may indicate the need for a more in-depth assessment.

*Developed by the World Health Organization, AMETHYST project, 1987. Modified by Fleming and Barry, 1990.
Source: Fleming, M. F., & Barry, K. L. (1992). *Addictive disorders*. St. Louis: Mosby, with permission.

APPENDIX 2: The CAGE and CAGE-AID Questions
(CAGE Adapted to Include Drugs)

1. In the last three months, have you felt you should cut down or stop drinking *or using drugs?*
   ❑ Yes   ❑ No
2. In the last three months, has anyone annoyed you or gotten on your nerves by telling you to cut down or stop drinking *or using drugs?*
   ❑ Yes   ❑ No
3. In the last three months, have you felt guilty or bad about how much you drink *or use?*
   ❑ Yes   ❑ No
4. In the last three months, have you been waking up wanting to have an alcoholic drink *or use drugs?*
   ❑ Yes   ❑ No

Each affirmative response earns one point. One point indicates a possible problem. Two points indicates a probable problem.

The original CAGE questions appear in plain type. The CAGE questions Adapted to Include Drugs are the original CAGE questions *modified by the italicized text.*

Source: Ewing, J. (1984). Detecting alcoholism: The CAGE questionnaire. *Journal of the American Medical Association, 252*(14), 1905–1907, with permission (original CAGE questions) and Dube, C., Goldstein, M.G., & Lewis, D.C. 1989. Project ADEPT Volume I: Core Modules. Brown University, Providence, RI, with permission.

APPENDIX 3: DAST—Drug Abuse Screening Test

 1. Have you used drugs other than those required for medical reasons?
 2. Have you abused prescription drugs?
 3. Do you abuse more than one drug at a time?
*4. Can you get through the week without using drugs (other than those required for medical reasons)?
*5. Are you always able to stop using drugs when you want to?
 6. Do you abuse drugs on a continuous basis?
*7. Do you try to limit your drug use to certain situations?
 8. Have you had "blackouts" or "flashbacks" as a result of drug use?
 9. Do you ever feel bad about your drug use?
10. Does your spouse (or parents) ever complain about your involvement with drugs?
11. Do your friends or relatives know or suspect you abuse drugs?
12. Has drug abuse ever created problems between you and your spouse?
13. Has any family member ever sought help for problems related to your drug use?
14. Have you ever lost friends because of your use of drugs?
15. Have you ever neglected your family or missed work because of your use of drugs?
16. Have you ever been in trouble at work because of drug use?
17. Have you ever lost a job because of drug abuse?
18. Have you gotten into fights when under the influence of drugs?
19. Have you ever been arrested because of unusual behavior while under the influence of drugs?
20. Have you ever been arrested while driving under the influence of drugs?
21. Have you engaged in illegal activities in order to obtain drugs?
22. Have you ever been arrested for possession of illegal drugs?
23. Have you ever experienced withdrawal symptoms as a result of heavy drug intake?
24. Have you had medical problems as a result of your drug use (e.g., memory loss, hepatitis, convulsions, bleeding, etc.)?
25. Have you ever been in a hospital for medical problems related to your drug use?
26. Have you ever gone to anyone for help for a drug problem?
27. Have you ever been involved in a treatment program specifically related to drug use?
28. Have you been treated as an outpatient for problems related to drug abuse?

Rating Scale: Each question carries either a scale of 0 for a *no* or 1 point for a *yes* answer (*except questions 4, 5, and 7, which carry 1 point for a no and 0 for a yes). Therefore, a person's individual score can range from 0 to 28. The higher the score, the more likely the person may have a potential drug problem.

Source: Skinner, HA. (1982). The drug abuse screening test. *Addictive Behaviors, 7*(4), 363. Copyright 1982. Pergamon Press. Reprinted with permission

APPENDIX 4: MAST—Michigan Alcohol Screening Test

	Yes	No
0. Do you enjoy a drink now and then?	Yes (0)	No (0)
1. Do you feel you are a normal drinker? (Normal means you drink less or no more than other people)	Yes (0)	No (2)
2. Have you ever wakened in the morning after drinking the night before and found you could not remember part of the evening?	Yes (2)	No (0)
3. Does your spouse, parent, or other close person ever complain or worry about your drinking?	Yes (1)	No (0)
4. Can you stop drinking without a struggle after one or two drinks?	Yes (0)	No (2)
5. Do you ever feel guilty about your drinking?	Yes (2)	No (0)
6. Do friends or relatives think you are a normal drinker?	Yes (0)	No (2)
7. Are you able to stop drinking when you want to?	Yes (0)	No (2)
8. Have you ever attended a meeting of AA (Alcoholics Anonymous)?	Yes (5)	No (0)
9. Have you gotten into physical fights when drinking?	Yes (1)	No (0)
10. Has your drinking ever created problems with your spouse, a parent, or other close relative(s) or person(s)?	Yes (2)	No (0)
11. Has your spouse or any family member ever sought help from anyone about your drinking?	Yes (2)	No (0)
12. Have you ever lost friends because of your drinking?	Yes (2)	No (0)
13. Have you ever gotten in trouble at work or school because of your drinking?	Yes (2)	No (0)
14. Have you ever lost a job because of drinking?	Yes (2)	No (0)
15. Have you ever neglected obligations, family, or work for two or more days in a row because of drinking?	Yes (2)	No (0)
16. Do you drink before noon fairly often?	Yes (2)	No (0)
17. Have you ever been told you have liver trouble (cirrhosis)?	Yes (2)	No (0)
18. After heavy drinking, have you ever had delirium tremens, the "shakes," seen or heard things that weren't really there?	Yes (2)	No (0)
19. Have you ever gone to anyone for help about your drinking?	Yes (5)	No (0)
20. Have you ever been in a hospital because of drinking?	Yes (5)	No (0)
21. Have you ever been in a psychiatric hospital or psychiatric unit of a general hospital where drinking was part of the reason for hospitalization?	Yes (2)	No (0)
22. Have you ever been seen at a psychiatric or mental health clinic or gone to any doctor, social worker, or counselor for help with an emotional problem where drinking was involved?	Yes (2)	No (0)
23. Have you ever been arrested for drunk driving, driving while intoxicated, or driving under the influence of alcoholic beverages? If yes, how many times?	Yes (2)	No (0)
24. Have you ever been arrested or taken into custody, even for a few hours, because of drunken behavior of any kind? If yes, how many times?	Yes (2)	No (0)

Total   _____ + _____ = _____

A score of 5–6 points is suggestive of alcoholism (except for a positive response to questions 8, 19, or 20, which are diagnostic). A score of 7 or more points indicates alcoholism.

If given in written form omit the numbers (in parentheses on the right), so as not to influence the responses.

The Michigan Alcoholism Screening Test (MAST): The quest for a new diagnostic instrument, 176–181, Copyright 1971, the American Psychiatric Association. Reprinted by permission,

APPENDIX 5: Brief MAST—
Short Michigan Alcohol Screening Test

Questions	Response Score Yes	No
1. Do you feel you are a normal drinker?	0	2
2. Do friends or relatives think you are a normal drinker?	0	2
3. Have you ever attended a meeting of Alcoholics Anonymous?	5	0
4. Have you ever lost friends or girlfriends/boyfriends because of drinking?	2	0
5. Have you ever gotten into trouble at work because of drinking?	2	0
6. Have you ever neglected your obligations, your family, or your work for two or more days in a row because you were drinking?	2	0
7. Have you ever had delirium tremens (DTs), severe shaking, heard voices, or seen things that weren't there after heavy drinking?	2	0
8. Have you ever gone to anyone for help about your drinking?	5	0
9. Have you ever been in a hospital because of drinking?	5	0
10. Have you ever been arrested for drunk driving or driving after drinking?	2	0

Total   _____ + ____ = _____

Score of 6 or more indicates possible diagnosis of alcoholism, except for questions 3, 8, or 9, which are diagnostic.

Source: Pokovny, A. D., Miller, B. A., & Kaplan H. B. (1972). The Brief MAST: A shortened version of the Michigan Alcohol Screening Test. *American Journal of Psychology, 129*, 342–345.

APPENDIX 6: Simple Screening Instrument for Alcohol and Other Drug Abuse

Note: Bold-faced questions constitute a short version of the screening instrument that can be administered in situations that are not conducive to administering the entire test. Such situations may occur because of time limitations or other conditions.

I am going to ask you a few questions about your use of alcohol and other drugs during the past six months.

1. **Have you ever used alcohol or other drugs? (Such as wine, beer, hard liquor, pot, coke, uppers, downers, or hallucinogens)**
2. **Have you felt that you use too much alcohol or other drugs?**
3. **Have you tried to cut down or quit drinking or using drugs?**
4. Have you gone to anyone for help because of your drinking or drug use? (These may include Alcoholics Anonymous, Narcotics Anonymous, Cocaine Anonymous, counselors, or a treatment program.)
5. Have you had any of the following health problems? For example, have you ever:
   - ❑ Had blackouts or other periods of memory loss?
   - ❑ Injured your head?
   - ❑ Had convulsions, delirium tremens ("DTs")?
   - ❑ Had hepatitis or other liver problems?
   - ❑ Felt sick, shaky, or depressed when you stopped?
   - ❑ Felt "coke bugs" or a crawling feeling under the skin?
   - ❑ Been injured after drinking or using?
   - ❑ Used needles to shoot drugs?
6. Has drinking or other drug use ever caused problems between you and your family or friends?
7. Has your drinking or other drug use ever caused problems at school or at work?
8. Have you been arrested or had other legal problems? (Such as bouncing bad checks, driving while intoxicated, theft, or drug possession)
9. Do you sometimes lose your temper or get into arguments or fights while drinking or using other drugs?
10. Are you needing to drink or use drugs more and more to get the effect you want?
11. Do you spend a lot of time thinking about or trying to get alcohol or other drugs?
12. Does your drinking or drug use make you do something you wouldn't normally do, such as breaking rules, breaking the law, selling things that are important to you, or having sex with someone?
13. Do you ever feel bad or guilty about your drinking or drug use?
14. Have you ever had a drinking or other drug problem?
15. Do any of your family members have a drinking or drug problem?
16. **a. Do you feel that you have a problem now?**
    b. Is there something I can do to help you?

- Thanks for taking this questionnaire.
- Do you have any questions for me?

Observation Checklist

Observation of the following may indicate an AOD abuse problem?

- ❏ Needle track marks
- ❏ Skin abscesses, cigarette burns, or nicotine stains
- ❏ Tremors (shaking and twitching of hands and eyelids)
- ❏ Unclear speech; slurred, incoherent, or too rapid
- ❏ Unsteady gait; staggering, off balance
- ❏ Dilated or constricted pupils
- ❏ Scratching
- ❏ Swollen hands or feet
- ❏ Smell of alcohol or marijuana on breath
- ❏ Drug paraphernalia such as pipes, paper, needles or roach clips
- ❏ "Nodding out" (dozing or falling asleep)
- ❏ Agitation
- ❏ Inability to focus

Interpreting Responses to Treatment

Score	Degree of Problems Related to AOD Abuse	Suggested Action
0	None reported	None at this time
1–2	Low level	Monitor, reassess later
3+	Moderate to severe	Refer for comprehensive assessment

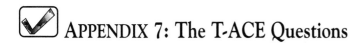

APPENDIX 7: The T-ACE Questions

1. How may drinks does it take to make you feel high (TOLERANCE)?
2. Have people ANNOYED you by criticizing your drinking?
3. Have you felt you ought to CUT DOWN on your drinking?
4. Have you ever had a drink first thing in the morning to steady your nerves or get rid of a hangover (EYE-OPENER)?

Scoring: A response of 3 or more drinks is considered a positive score on question 1. Persons who have 2 or more positive responses on these 4 questions are considered at risk for problematic alcohol use.

Source: Sokol, R., Martier, S., & Ager, J. (1989). The T-ACE questions: Practical prenatal detection of risk-drinking. *American Journal of Obstetrics and Gynecology, 160*(4), 863–870, with permission.

☑️ APPENDIX 8: TWEAK Test

The TWEAK test is a screening tool for identifying women who are risk drinkers. It combines questions from the MAST, CAGE, and T-ACE tests that have been found most effective in identifying these women drinkers.

T   **Tolerance:** How many drinks can you hold?
W   Have close friends or relatives **Worried** or complained about your drinking in the past year?
E   **Eye-Opener:** Do you sometimes take a drink in the morning when you first get up?
A   **Amnesia:** Has a friend or family member ever told you about things you said or did while you were drinking that you could not remember?
K(C)   Do you sometimes feel the need to **Cut Down** on your drinking?

A 7-point scale is used to score the test: The Tolerance question scores 2 points if a woman reports that she can hold more than five drinks without falling asleep or passing out. A positive response to the Worry question scores 2 points, and a positive response to the last three questions scores 1 point each. A total score of 2 or more points indicates the woman is likely to be a risk drinker.

Source: Russel, M., & Bigler. (1979). Screening for alcohol-related problems in an outpatient obstetric-gynecologic clinic. The TWEAK questionnaire. *American Journal of Obstetrics and Gynecology, 412,* with permission.

 APPENDIX 9: Trauma Scale Screening Tool

Five questions about history of trauma since 18th birthday

1. Have you had any fractures or dislocations of your bones or joints?
2. Have you ever been injured in a traffic accident?
3. Have you ever injured your head?
4. Have you ever been in an assault or fight (excluding sports)?
5. Have you ever been injured while drinking?

More than one positive response would indicate a probable drinking problem.

Skinner, H. A., Holt, S., Schuller, R., Roy, J., & Israel, Y. (1984). Identification of alcohol abuse using laboratory tests and a history of trauma. *Annals of Internal Medicine, 101,* 847–851.

APPENDIX 10: Biopsychosocial Data Base and Intake Form©

CONFIDENTIAL

Interview Date: _____ Staff Name: _____

DOB _____ Title: _____

This form asks questions which will be used to determine the most suitable treatment for you. Please answer every question and be as honest as you can. Your answers will be kept strictly CONFIDENTIAL. Circle any question you are unable to answer.

1. SEX/Age

❑ Male ❑ Female Age:

2. REFERRAL SOURCE:

❑ Self ❑ Physician ❑ CPL ❑ TASC
❑ Family ❑ Psychiatrist ❑ Inpatient
❑ Friend ❑ Employer ❑ Outpatient
❑ Clergy ❑ Police ❑ D.M.V.
❑ E.A.P. ❑ Probation ❑ Other

3. CURRENTLY RESIDE:	**4. TYPE OF RESIDENCE:**	**5. ETHNICITY:**
❑ Alone	❑ House	❑ White
❑ Parent	❑ Apartment	❑ Black
❑ Spouse	❑ Group home	❑ Hispanic
❑ Friend	❑ Furnished room	❑ Oriental
❑ Supervised living setting	❑ Nursing home	❑ Native American
❑ Other	❑ Homeless	❑ Other
	❑ Other	

Is your ethnicity important to you? ❑ Yes
❑ No

5. PRESCRIPTION OR OVER-THE-COUNTER MEDICATIONS:

NAME	DOSE	FREQUENCY

What allergies do you have to foods, medications, or other causes:
Describe reaction:

Have you been taking your medications daily? ❑ Yes ❑ No

When was the last time you took your medication?

6. HEALTH PATTERNS:

Do you consider your health
❑ Good
❑ Fair
❑ Poor

Do you have a history of
❑ Anorexia
❑ Bulimia
❑ Overeating ❑ None

Do you follow a regular exercise routine
❑ Yes
❑ No

7. DO YOU HAVE A HISTORY OF:

- ❑ Syphilis
- ❑ Gonorrhea
- ❑ Other venereal disease
- ❑ None
- ❑ Treated
- ❑ Untreated

8. MEDICAL HISTORY:

	YES	NO	COMMENTS
Head injury			
Recent falls			
Periods of unconsciousness			
Seizure disorder			
Stroke			
Esophageal varices			
Cirrhosis of the liver			
Hepatitis			
Pancreatitis			
High blood pressure			
Heart attack/heart disease			
Diabetes			
Cancer			
Lung/breathing problems			
Tuberculosis			
Stomach/digestive problems			
Orthopedic problems			
Arthritis			
Significant surgery			
Surgical implants			
Vein disorders			
Rectal bleeding			
Body rashes or sores			
Penile/Vaginal discharges			
Mouth sores			
Urinary/bowel problems			
Recent loss or gain in weight			
Loss of sensation in extremities			
Muscular weakness			
Muscle rigidity			
Impaired vision			
Impaired speech			
Impaired hearing			
Immunodeficiency			

Date of your last physical exam   By whom?

Date of last laboratory work

Any other tests?

9. SPIRITUALITY

❑ Roman Catholic ❑ Protestant ❑ Jewish
❑ Moslem ❑ Atheist ❑ Other
❑ None

| Is your spirituality important to you? | ❑ Yes | ❑ No |
| Do you presently maintain an affiliation with a recognized religious group? | ❑ Yes | ❑ No |

10. SEXUAL HISTORY:

| What is your sexual preference? | ❑ Heterosexual | ❑ Homosexual |
| | ❑ Bisexual | ❑ Celibate |

Do you, at times, have concerns about your sexual identity?
❑ Yes
❑ No
❑ Maybe

During periods of alcohol or other drug abuse have you ever participated in sexual behavior which you were ashamed of?
❑ Yes
❑ No
❑ Maybe

Have you experienced reduced sexual drive?
❑ Yes
❑ No
❑ Maybe

Do you use safer sex practice (condoms)?
❑ Yes
❑ No
❑ Maybe

How old were you when you first had sex?

11. RECENT ALCOHOL/DRUG USE:

Beer, ale
❑ Never ❑ Weekly 1–5 times a wk.
❑ Rarely ❑ Daily
❑ Monthly 1–3 times a mo. Amount

Wine, wine coolers, champagne
❑ Never ❑ Weekly 1–5 times a wk.
❑ Rarely ❑ Daily
❑ Monthly 1–3 times a mo. Amount

Brandy, cordials, liqueurs
❑ Never ❑ Weekly 1–5 times a wk.
❑ Rarely ❑ Daily
❑ Monthly 1–3 times a mo. Amount

Vodka, gin, whiskey, etc.
❑ Never ❑ Weekly 1–5 times a wk.
❑ Rarely ❑ Daily
❑ Monthly 1–3 times a mo. Amount

Marijuana, hashish
❑ Never ❑ Weekly 1–5 times a wk.
❑ Rarely ❑ Daily
❑ Monthly 1–3 times a mo. Amount

Cocaine, How? (   )
❑ Never ❑ Weekly 1–5 times a wk.
❑ Rarely ❑ Daily
❑ Monthly 1–3 times a mo. Amount

Crack
❑ Never ❑ Weekly 1–5 times a wk.
❑ Rarely ❑ Daily
❑ Monthly 1–3 times a mo. Amount

Heroin	❑ Never ❑ Rarely ❑ Monthly 1–3 times a mo.	❑ Weekly 1–5 times a wk. ❑ Daily Amount
Pills, type? ( )	❑ Never ❑ Rarely ❑ Monthly 1–3 times a mo.	❑ Weekly 1–5 times a wk. ❑ Daily Amount
LSD (Acid)	❑ Never ❑ Rarely ❑ Monthly 1–3 times a mo.	❑ Weekly 1–5 times a wk. ❑ Daily Amount
Hallucinogens ( )	❑ Never ❑ Rarely ❑ Monthly 1–3 times a mo.	❑ Weekly 1–5 times a wk. ❑ Daily Amount
Other drugs ( )	❑ Never ❑ Rarely ❑ Monthly 1–3 times a mo.	❑ Weekly 1–5 times a wk. ❑ Daily Amount

12. SYMPTOMOLOGY:

Shakes	❑ Yes	❑ No
Nausea or vomiting	❑ Yes	❑ No
Excessive perspiration	❑ Yes	❑ No
Heart palpitations	❑ Yes	❑ No
Depressed mood	❑ Yes	❑ No
Irritability	❑ Yes	❑ No
Anxiety or fear	❑ Yes	❑ No
Insomnia	❑ Yes	❑ No
Muscle cramps	❑ Yes	❑ No
Hallucinations	❑ Yes	❑ No
Seizures	❑ Yes	❑ No
Delusions	❑ Yes	❑ No
Blackouts (amnesia)	❑ Yes	❑ No
Unconsciousness	❑ Yes	❑ No
Morning drinking	❑ Yes	❑ No

13. RECENT ALCOHOL/DRUG HISTORY:

How much do you spend each week on alcohol and/or other drugs?

Date of last drink:

Date of last drug use:

Describe the pattern of your most recent alcohol or other drug use:

Have you found that lately you need more alcohol or other drugs to get the desired effect? ❑ Yes ❑ No ❑ Not sure

Are you becoming intoxicated faster with less alcohol or other drugs? ❑ Yes ❑ No ❑ Not sure

Your age when you first used alcohol:

Your age when you first used other drugs: _____

Your age when you first got "drunk" or "high": _____

Your age when either alcohol or drug use became a problem: _____

14.   PREVIOUS ADDICTION TREATMENT:

List below any and all treatment you received for alcoholism, other drugs, gambling or eating disorders. include rehabilitation units, alternative sentencing, drinking driver programs, detoxes and emergency room visits.

Dates	Facility	Type of Program	Completed Program	
			❏ Yes	❏ No
			❏ Yes	❏ No
			❏ Yes	❏ No
			❏ Yes	❏ No
			❏ Yes	❏ No
			❏ Yes	❏ No

Have you ever been a member of, or attended meetings of any Twelve-Step Programs? If you have, which one(s)?

❏ Yes   ❏ No

If you were a member of a Twelve-Step Program, did you have a sponsor?   ❏ Yes   ❏ No

What is the name of your Home Group (if any) and where does it meet?

_____

Has your use of alcohol or other drugs affected your:

Physical health	❏ Yes	❏ No	❏ Don't know
Work performance	❏ Yes	❏ No	❏ Don't know
Mental health	❏ Yes	❏ No	❏ Don't know
Relationships with friends	❏ Yes	❏ No	❏ Don't know

Describe:

_____

15.   GAMBLING HISTORY

Do you enjoy gambling for money?	❏ Yes	❏ No	❏ Sometimes
Do you ever gamble until you lose all your money at one event, in one game or one episode (day, evening, weekend, etc.)?	❏ Yes	❏ No	❏ Sometimes
Do you sometimes borrow money to gamble?	❏ Yes	❏ No	❏ Sometimes
Has your gambling ever caused disharmony between yourself and a significant person in your life?	❏ Yes	❏ No	❏ Sometimes

Do you gamble more, less or not at all when you are drinking or using other drugs? Explain:

_____

16. EDUCATION

Indicate the last year of school you completed. _____

List any degrees you have earned: _____

Did you ever complete any specialized vocational or professional training? Explain: _____

Did your alcohol or other drug use interfere with the attainment of your educational goals?	❏ Yes	❏ No	
Do you have any problems or difficulties in reading or writing?	❏ Yes	❏ No	

17. LEGAL HISTORY: Include DWI's, DWAI's, Orders of protection, etc.

Charge	Date	Disposition	Alcohol/Drug related
			❏ Yes ❏ No
			❏ Yes ❏ No
			❏ Yes ❏ No
			❏ Yes ❏ No
			❏ Yes ❏ No

Are you currently admitted under CPL status? ❏ Yes ❏ No

18. SIGNIFICANT LOSSES:

Have you experienced the death of a close friend or family member during the past twelve months?
❏ Yes ❏ No

If yes, who: _____ Cause of death: _____

Any of the following losses during the same period?

❏ Home ❏ Property ❏ Auto
❏ Employment ❏ Relationship (who) ❏ Money

19. FAMILY OF ORIGIN HISTORY:

Your father's name:
First

Is your father living? ❏ Yes Age _____
❏ No
❏ Don't know

If deceased state the cause of death:

Your mother's name:
First

Is your mother living? ❏ Yes Age _____
❏ No
❏ Don't know

If deceased state the cause of death:

Are you adopted? ❏ Yes ❏ No

As a child, were you subjected to physical, emotional or sexual abuse? ❏ Yes ❏ No

If yes, describe:

List below your brothers and sisters. Include half, step and adopted brothers and sisters.

First Name	Age	Alcohol/Drug use?
		❏ Yes ❏ No
		❏ Yes ❏ No
		❏ Yes ❏ No
		❏ Yes ❏ No
		❏ Yes ❏ No
		❏ Yes ❏ No

Describe any history of alcoholism, heavy drinking or other drug use in your family of origin. Include parents, aunts, uncles, cousins and grandparents as well:

_____

Describe any history of other problems such as eating disorders, compulsive gambling or spending in your family of origin. Include parents, aunts, uncles, cousins and grandparents as well:

_____

20. MARITAL BACKGROUND

❑ Never married   ❑ Married
❑ Separated   ❑ Unmarried couple
❑ Divorced   ❑ Widowed

How many times have you been married?			
How long in your present status?			
Does your spouse drink or use drugs?	❑ Yes	❑ No	
Do you have minor children (under 18 years of age)?	❑ Yes	❑ No	

Indicate minor children by name   Age   Sex

_____	❑ Male	❑ Female
_____	❑ Male	❑ Female
_____	❑ Male	❑ Female
_____	❑ Male	❑ Female

Do you have custody of them?	❑ Yes	❑ No
Do you have adult children (over 18 years old)?	❑ Yes	❑ No

Indicate adult children by name   Age   Sex

_____	❑ Male	❑ Female
_____	❑ Male	❑ Female
_____	❑ Male	❑ Female
_____	❑ Male	❑ Female

Are there any particular circumstances or conditions regarding your children that cause you distress, i.e., learning disabled, handicapped, behavioral problems, in foster care etc.?   ❑ Yes   ❑ No
Explain:

_____

Do any of your children drink or use drugs?   ❑ Yes   ❑ No
Explain:

_____

Has your alcohol or drug use affected your relationship with your children?   ❑ Yes   ❑ No
Explain:

_____

21. PSYCHIATRIC INFORMATION

Describe any history of psychiatric treatment or hospitalization you may have had for conditions such as schizophrenia, bipolar disorder, depression, anxiety or suicide attempts, etc.

When	Where	Diagnosis	Why	Improvement noted
				❏ Yes ❏ No
				❏ Yes ❏ No
				❏ Yes ❏ No
				❏ Yes ❏ No

Have you ever been treated, or are you presently being treated with medicine for any psychiatric condition?

Medicine	Dosage	Frequency	Last use	Reason prescribed	Prescribed by

Describe any side effects that you experience from your medications:

Do you take medication while using drugs or alcohol?	❏ Yes ❏ No

22. PSYCHIATRIC SYMPTOMOLOGY

❏ Alert	❏ Suicidal	❏ Assaultive	❏ Delusions
❏ Lethargic	❏ Elated/euphoric	❏ Homicidal	❏ Disorientation
❏ Depressed	❏ Restlessness	❏ Hallucinations	❏ Withdrawn
❏ Self-abusive	❏ Agitation	❏ Paranoid ideas	

Do you have any present suicide thoughts?	❏ Yes ❏ No
Have you ever made a suicide attempt?	❏ Yes ❏ No

Describe such attempts:

23. EMPLOYMENT HISTORY

Are you presently employed?   ❏ Yes ❏ No   If no, when did you work last?

Answer the following questions about your present (or last) employer:

Company Name:

Location:

Dates of employment: From   To

Job Title:

Duties:

Salary: Reason for leaving:

24. INTERVIEWER'S IMPRESSIONS

Appearance:	Insight:
Behavior:	Judgment:
Quality of Verbalization:	Thought Organization:
Motivation for Treatment:	Orientation:
Defense utilization:	Hallucinations:

Tentative diagnosis: DSM-III-R

Axis I

Axis II

Axis III

Axis IV (Severity of stress 0–6)

Axis V (GAF—a global assessment of functions, 1–90)

25. TREATMENT ISSUES (Nursing diagnoses)

Biological:

Psychosocial:

Cognitive:

Spiritual:

Marital/Family:

Vocational/Educational:

Cultural/Ethnic/Racial:

Goals/Interventions

Short-term objectives:

Long-term objectives:

Staff Signature/Date

APPENDIX 11: Substance Abuse Assessment Instruments

Instrument Name	Description	Contact/Source
Addiction Severity Index (ASI)	Most widely accepted and used assessment instrument in the addictions field. It is for use in face-to-face interview and collects information in seven problem areas of the client's life to yield a score of severity of addiction (Soucy, Kelly, & Cardenas, 1994).	National Institute on Drug Abuse 1-800-729-6686
Adolescent Drinking Index	A 24-item self-report rating scale. Measures severity of drinking problems (Hoshino, 1992).	Psychological Assessment Resources, Inc. 1-800-331-TEST
Alcohol Dependence Scale (ADS)	A 25-item questionnaire to assess the alcohol dependence syndrome. It yields an index of severity of alcohol dependence (Crist & Milby, 1990; NIAAAA, 1990).	Addiction Research Foundation 1-800-661-1111
Assessment of Chemical Health Inventory (ACHI)	A 128-item self-administered tool that assesses the nature and extent of substance abuse and associated psychosocial problems, and facilitates communication between treatment providers (McClellan & Dembo, 1992).	Recovery Software, Inc. 612-831-5835
Chemical Dependency Assessment Profile (CDAP)	A 235-item self-administered instrument that assesses alcohol and other drug use and chemical dependency problems (McClellan & Dembo, 1992).	Multi-Health Systems 1-800-456-3003
Chemical Use, Abuse, and Dependence Scale (CUAD)	An 80-item brief semistructured interview designed to assess problems with all drugs of abuse. It is based on DSM-III-R diagnostic criteria and gleans information about current use (McGovern & Morrison, 1992).	McGovern & Morrison

Instrument Name	Description	Contact/Source
Comprehensive Addiction Severity Index for Adolescents (CASI-A)	A structured interview designed to assess drug and alcohol use and psychosocial severity in adolescents in a variety of settings (Shaefer, 1992).	Center for Studies of Addiction 215-823-5809
Personal Experience Inventory (PEI)	A two-part instrument designed to assess the extent of psychological and behavioral issues with alcohol and drug problems as well as psychosocial risk factors associated with teenage substance involvement, etc. (McClellan & Dembo, 1992; Shaefer, 1992).	Western Psychological Services 310-478-2061

Source: Substance Abuse and Mental Health Services Administration (Center for Substance Abuse Treatment). (1994). *Treatment for alcohol and other drug abuse: Opportunities for coordination.* DHHS No. (SMA) 94-2075. Rockville, MD: Substance Abuse and Mental Health Administration.

INDEX